To the Student: A Study Guide for this textbook is available through your college bookstore under the title *Student Study Guide to Accompany Modern Auditing* by Walter G. Kell, William C. Boynton, and Richard E. Ziegler. The Study Guide can help you with course material by acting as a tutorial, review, and study aid. If the Study Guide is not in stock, ask the bookstore manager to order a copy for you.

Modern Auditing

Accounting Textbooks from John Wiley and Sons

Arpan and Radebaugh: INTERNATIONAL ACCOUNTING AND
  MULTINATIONAL ENTERPRISES

Bedford, Perry and Wyatt: ADVANCED ACCOUNTING, 4th

Buckley, Buckley and Plank: SEC ACCOUNTING

Burch and Sardinas: COMPUTER CONTROL AND AUDIT

Burch, Strater, and Grudnitski: INFORMATION SYSTEMS: THEORY AND
  PRACTICE, 3rd

Copeland and Dascher: FINANCIAL ACCOUNTING

Copeland and Dascher: MANAGERIAL ACCOUNTING, 2nd

DeCoster, Ramanathan, and Sundem: ACCOUNTING FOR MANAGERIAL
  DECISION MAKING, 2nd

DeCoster and Schafer: MANAGEMENT ACCOUNTING: A DECISION
  EMPHASIS, 3rd

Delaney and Gleim: CPA EXAMINATION REVIEW—AUDITING

Delaney and Gleim: CPA EXAMINATION REVIEW—BUSINESS LAW

Delaney and Gleim: CPA EXAMINATION REVIEW—THEORY AND PRACTICE

Delaney and Gleim: CPA EXAMINATION SOLUTIONS (Semi-annually May and
  November)

Gleim and Delaney: CPA EXAMINATION REVIEW Volume I OUTLINES AND
  STUDY GUIDE

Gleim and Delaney: CPA EXAMINATION REVIEW Volume II PROBLEMS AND
  SOLUTIONS

Gross and Jablonsky: PRINCIPLES OF ACCOUNTING AND FINANCIAL
  REPORTING FOR NONPROFIT ORGANIZATIONS

Guy: STATISTICAL SAMPLING IN AUDITING

Haried, Imdieke and Smith: ADVANCED ACCOUNTING, 2nd

Helmkamp, Imdieke and Smith: PRINCIPLES OF ACCOUNTING

Kell and Ziegler: MODERN AUDITING, 2nd

Kieso and Weygandt: INTERMEDIATE ACCOUNTING, 4th

Loeb: ETHICS IN THE ACCOUNTING PROFESSION

McCullers and Schroeder: ACCOUNTING THEORY, 2nd

Mock and Grove: MEASUREMENT, ACCOUNTING, AND ORGANIZATIONAL
  INFORMATION

Moscove and Simkin: ACCOUNTING INFORMATION SYSTEMS

Ramanathan: MANAGEMENT CONTROL IN NONPROFIT ORGANIZATIONS,
  TEXT AND CASES

Ramanathan and Hegstad: READINGS IN MANAGEMENT CONTROL IN
  NONPROFIT ORGANIZATIONS

Sardinas, Burch and Asebrook: EDP AUDITING: A PRIMER

Stenzel: APPROACHING THE CPA EXAMINATION: a Personal Guide to
  Examination Preparation

Taylor and Glezen: AUDITING—INTEGRATED CONCEPTS AND
  PROCEDURES, 2nd

Taylor and Glezen: CASE STUDY IN AUDITING, 2nd

Wilkinson: ACCOUNTING AND INFORMATION SYSTEMS

Modern Auditing

Second Edition

Walter G. Kell, Ph.D., CPA
University of Michigan

Richard E. Ziegler, Ph.D., CPA
University of Illinois

Consulting Editor:
William C. Boynton, Ph.D.
University of Virginia

John Wiley & Sons
New York   Chichester   Brisbane   Toronto   Singapore

Cover Art and Design by Joan A. Willens

Library of Congress Cataloging in Publication Data

Kell, Walter Gerry, 1921-
    Modern auditing.

    Includes index.
    1. Auditing. I. Ziegler, Richard E. II. Title.
HF5667.K39 1983   657′.45   82-24735
ISBN 0-471-87749-2   .

Printed in the United States of America

10 9 8 7 6 5 4 3 2 1

About the Authors

WALTER G. KELL (Ph.D., University of Illinois at Urbana—Champaign) is Professor of Accounting at the University of Michigan, where he has served as Chairman of the Department of Accounting. A certified public accountant, he has had professional experience with several accounting firms, including Arthur Andersen & Co., Touche Ross & Co., and Arthur Young & Company. He has been an active member of the American Institute of Certified Public Accountants and has served on its Committee on Auditing Procedure (predecessor to the Auditing Standards Board) and Auditing Standards Advisory Council. He is a past president of the American Accounting Association and has been a consulting editor to the *Accountants' Handbook*. He is currently a member of the Board of Directors of the Michigan Association of Certified Public Accountants.

RICHARD E. ZIEGLER (Ph.D., University of North Carolina at Chapel Hill) is Associate Professor and Assistant Head of the Department of Accountancy at the University of Illinois in Urbana—Champaign. A certified public accountant, he served for five years as an audit senior on the staff of Price Waterhouse & Co. In addition to authoring several articles on accounting, he completed a research study for the Cohen Commission on Auditors' Responsibilities concerning users' interpretations of the standard audit report.

Preface

MODERN AUDITING offers a unique blend of the contemporary and traditional approaches to the study of auditing. It recognizes the importance of transaction cycles in the study and evaluation of internal control while retaining the time-honored balance sheet approach in the verification of transaction cycle balances.

The textbook is designed primarily for the first course in auditing either at the undergraduate or graduate level. Throughout the book, every effort has been made to integrate auditing concepts with auditing methodology and auditing theory with auditing practice. In addition, emphasis is given to the professional responsibilities of the independent auditor.

ORGANIZATION

As in the first edition, the book is divided into four parts:

Part	Subject	Chapters
I	Fundamental Relationships	1–3
II	Study and Evaluation of Internal Control	4–10
III	Verification of Account Balances	11–15
IV	Reporting and Other Responsibilities	16–20

This arrangement reflects both sound pedagogy and current auditing practices within the public accounting profession. Part I establishes basic auditing concepts and relationships, Part II describes interim field work, Part III explains year-end work, and Part IV emphasizes the auditor's reporting and professional responsibilities.

Chapter 1 distinguishes among independent, internal, and governmental audits and auditors, illustrates the standard audit report, and describes the organization of the public accounting profession. Chapter 2 includes the standards that relate to quality control in an audit engagement, an overview of the auditing process, and audit planning. Chapter 3 combines a conceptual explanation of audit evidence and auditing procedures with a practical discussion of the nature and importance of audit working papers.

Part II deals with internal control systems and the auditor's study and evaluation of internal control. Internal control principles and review concepts are explained in Chapter 4. These basic relationships are then applied to electronic data processing systems in Chapter 5. Chapter 6 explains the role of audit sampling in the study and evaluation of internal control, and a case study is used to demonstrate a statistical sampling application. Chapters 7 to 10 discuss internal control principles and the auditor's methodology for reviewing and testing internal controls for significant classes of transactions within three transaction cycles. These chapters also contain case studies of statistical sampling and electronic data processing applications.

There are five chapters in Part III. Chapter 11 explains the role of audit sampling in the verification of account balances and contains case study applications of both probability-proportional-to-size and classical variables sampling. Chapters 12 and 13 contain audit programs for verifying the principal account balances resulting from the transaction cycles described in Part II. Chapter 14 relates primarily to the verification of investing and financing cycle balances. The concluding chapter (Chapter 15) considers the verification of income statement balances and the steps in completing the audit.

Part IV deals with the independent auditor's reporting and professional responsibilities. Chapter 16 explains the four reporting standards, and actual audit reports are used to illustrate departures from the standard report. Chapter 17 describes and illustrates additional reports that may be issued in an audit engagement and the reporting standards in review and accounting service engagements. Chapter 18 focuses primarily on the AICPA Code of Professional Ethics, but also considers the Institute of Internal Auditor's Code of Ethics. Chapter 19 describes the auditor's potential legal liability under both common and statutory law. Ethics and legal liability are presented in Chapters 18 and 19 because we believe that students can obtain a much greater understanding of the CPA's responsibilities in these two areas at the end of the course rather than at the beginning. These are freestanding chapters, however, and may be assigned earlier by the instructor. The concluding chapter of this textbook (Chapter 20) provides in-depth coverage of the independent accountant's responsibilities relating to the filing of reports with the Securities and Exchange Commission.

SPECIAL FEATURES

The following are among the special features of this book:

- Learning objectives for each chapter.
- Identification of functions, common documents, accounting records, and data files for transaction cycles.
- Extensive coverage of the prevention and detection of errors and irregularities.
- Manual and electronic data processing flowcharts for significant classes of transactions within transaction cycles.
- Statistical sampling case studies for tests of transactions and tests of balances.
- Electronic data processing case studies for transaction cycles and computer-assisted techniques in the verification of account balances.

- Integration of authoritative auditing and professional literature throughout the text.
- Full chapter coverage of SEC accounting and reporting requirements.
- Appendixes on flowcharting and significant legal cases.

NEW FEATURES

This edition contains several new features. They include updated or expanded coverage of the following topics.

- Operational, internal, and governmental auditing (Chapter 1).
- The auditor's study and evaluation of internal control (Chapter 4).
- Statistical and nonstatistical sampling (Chapter 6).
- Online realtime EDP systems applications (Chapters 8 to 10).
- Probability-proportional-to-size and difference and ratio estimation in the verification of account balances (Chapter 11).
- Identifying and examining related party transactions (Chapter 15).
- Reporting on required supplementary information, condensed financial statements, and selected financial data (Chapter 16).
- The Institute of Internal Auditor's Code of Ethics, and practice standards for management advisory services and tax services (Chapter 18).
- Securities and Exchange Commission's "Integrated Disclosure" Rules (Chapter 20).
- Content specifications for the Uniform CPA Examination in Auditing (Appendix X).

This edition, of course, includes the most recent Statements on Auditing Standards and other authoritative professional pronouncements that are relevant in performing auditing services for clients.

END-OF-CHAPTER MATERIALS

This book contains an abundance of end-of-chapter materials that have been carefully integrated with the chapter content. Each chapter contains 20 review questions and 10 to 15 comprehensive questions. In addition, 16 of the chapters contain case studies drawn from actual practice. The comprehensive questions include questions and problems from uniform examinations given by professional organizations. In total, there are more than 700 questions and cases, which have been carefully edited and adapted to the book.

SUPPLEMENTARY MATERIALS

The supplements to this edition consist of (1) an Instructor's Manual and (2) a Student Study Guide.

The instructor's manual has been significantly expanded. In addition to answers to all end-of-chapter questions and cases, the manual also contains (1) suggested course outlines for both a one semester and a one quarter course, (2) selected exhibits for use as transparencies, and (3) comprehensive interim and final examinations for the course.

As in the first edition, the study guide is co-authored with William C. Boynton of the University of Virginia. For each chapter of the text, the study guide contains chapter highlights, true or false statements, completion statements, and multiple choice questions taken primarily from the AICPA examination. Solutions to the statements and questions are included at the end of the study guide.

ACKNOWLEDGMENTS

We take this opportunity to thank the individuals who have made significant contributions to this edition.

William C. Boynton in his capacity as Consulting Editor provided excellent editorial assistance throughout the book, and played a leading role in the updating of the chapters on audit sampling.

Again, as in the first edition, David B. Pearson of Arthur Young & Company made myriad important suggestions on many of the updated chapters.

We were fortunate in this edition to have three comprehensive critiques of the first edition. These were made by Joe R. Fritzemeyer, Arizona State University, Alan P. Johnson, California State University, Hayward, and Robert W. Vanasse, California State University, Fullerton.

The following people made helpful suggestions on selected chapters: Richard W. Andrews, The University of Michigan, George R. Bruha, Arthur Andersen & Co., Timothy R. Cash, Ernst & Whinney, Mary Finan, Arthur Young & Company, Robert W. Scharff, Peat, Marwick, Mitchell & Co., and George Siedel, The University of Michigan.

Special thanks are extended to the many adopters of the first edition for their acceptance, compliments, and helpful suggestions.

We wish to express our appreciation to our editors, Cynthia Hausdorff of Warren, Gorham & Lamont and Lucille Sutton of John Wiley & Sons, and to our senior production supervisor Elizabeth Doble at Wiley. Without their help, this edition would not have been possible.

January, 1983

Walter G. Kell
Richard E. Ziegler

Contents

BALANCES. Clerical Accuracy. Existence or Occurrence, Rights
and Obligations, and Valuation or Allocation. Completeness.
Statement Presentation and Disclosure. TESTS OF RECEIVABLES
BALANCES. Clerical Accuracy. Existence or Occurrence and
Rights and Obligations. Completeness. Valuation or Allocation.
Statement Presentation and Disclosure. Statistical Sampling of
Receivables Balances. Computer-Assisted Tests of Accounts
Receivable Balances.

TESTS OF INVENTORY BALANCES. Clerical Accuracy. Existence
or Occurrence. Completeness. Rights and Obligations.
Valuation or Allocation. Statement Presentation and Disclosure.
Statistical Sampling of Inventory Balances. Computer-Assisted
Tests of Inventory Balances. TESTS OF PLANT ASSET BALANCES.
Comparison with Audit of Current Assets. Initial Audit
Engagement. Recurring Audit Engagement. Clerical Accuracy.
Existence or Occurrence. Completeness. Rights and
Obligations. Valuation or Allocation. Statement Presentation and
Disclosure. TESTS OF CURRENT LIABILITY BALANCES.
Comparison with Tests of Asset Balances. Audit Program.
Clerical Accuracy. Existence or Occurrence, Completeness, and
Rights and Obligations. Valuation or Allocation. Statement
Presentation and Disclosure.

THE INVESTING CYCLE. Basic Considerations. Materiality and
Risk. Internal Accounting Control Objectives. Study and
Evaluation of Internal Control. Substantive Tests of Investment
Balances. THE FINANCING CYCLE. Basic Considerations.
Materiality and Risk. Internal Accounting Control Objectives.
Study and Evaluation of Internal Control. Substantive Tests of
Long-Term Debt Balances. Substantive Tests of Stockholders'
Equity Balances.

SUBSTANTIVE TESTS OF REVENUE AND EXPENSE BALANCES.
Materiality and Risk. Approach to Verification of Income
Statement Balances. Direct Tests of Income Statement Balances.
COMPLETING THE AUDIT. Make Subsequent Events Review.
Make Inquiry of Client's Lawyer. Identify and Examine Related
Party Transactions. Obtain Client Representation Letter. Make
Overall Analytical Review. Make General Review of Statement of
Changes in Financial Position. Formulate an Opinion on Financial

Statements.   Complete Review of Working Papers.   Make
Technical Review of Financial Statements.   Make Independent
In-House Review of Working Papers.   Make Required
Communication of Material Weaknesses in Internal Accounting
Control.   Prepare and Issue Management Letters.   POSTAUDIT
RESPONSIBILITIES.   Responsibility for Subsequent Events Occurring
After Completion of Field Work but Before Issuance of Report.
Responsibility for Postaudit Discovery of Facts Existing at Date of
Audit Report.

Modern Auditing

I | Fundamental Relationships

In auditing, as in other fields of knowledge, there are fundamental relationships that are essential to a comprehensive understanding of the subject. The basic relationships of auditing are discussed in the three chapters that comprise Part I of this book.

Chapter 1 describes the function of auditing in society, the auditor's standard report, and the nature of the public accounting profession.

In Chapter 2 consideration is given to quality control, the audit process, and audit planning.

Chapter 3 explains the types of audit evidence that may be obtained by the auditor in an audit engagement and the importance of documenting the auditor's work and findings in audit working papers.

1 Auditing and the Public Accounting Profession

STUDY OBJECTIVES

The study objectives of this chapter are to acquire an understanding of the nature of auditing, the auditor's standard report, and the public accounting profession. To achieve these objectives, it is necessary for the reader to

- Know the meaning of the term *auditing.*
- Comprehend the reasons for financial statement audits.
- Realize the responsibilities, functions, and relationships of the independent auditor in performing financial statement audits.
- Understand the meaning of the term *generally accepted auditing standards.*
- Know the form and content of the auditor's standard report.
- Understand the organization of the public accounting profession.

In a lifetime, an individual makes thousands of representations, claims, or assertions. For example, a student represents that he has knowledge of a subject by completing a homework assignment; a job applicant claims that he is qualified and in good health; and a taxpayer asserts to a revenue agent that his tax return is correct. In some instances, the recipient of the communication may be willing to accept the representation at face value. In other cases, however, an investigation is made to determine the validity of the assertion. The teacher can grade the homework paper. The personnel manager can interview the applicant, obtain letters of recommendation from previous employers, and require the applicant to have a physical examination by a licensed physician. And the revenue agent can examine (or audit) the tax return. These examples indicate the wide range of reasons for investigating assertions and the variety of subject matter that may be the basis for the examination.

Auditing Defined

Auditing may be defined as

> a systematic process of objectively obtaining and evaluating evidence regarding assertions about economic actions and events to ascertain the degree of correspondence between those assertions and established criteria and communicating the results to interested users.[1]

Several parts of this definition merit special comment:

- A *systematic process* connotes a logical, structured, and organized series of steps or procedures.
- *Objectively obtaining and evaluating evidence* means examining the bases for the assertions (representations) and judiciously evaluating the results without bias or prejudice either for or against the individual (or entity) making the representations.
- *Assertions about economic actions and events* are the representations made by the individual or entity. They comprise the subject matter of auditing. Assertions include information contained in financial statements, internal operating reports, and tax returns.
- *Degree of correspondence* refers to the closeness with which the assertions can be identified with established criteria. The expression of correspondence may be quantified, such as the amount of a shortage in a petty cash fund, or it may be qualitative, such as the fairness (or reasonableness) of financial statements.
- *Established criteria* are the standards against which the assertions or representations are judged. Criteria may be specific rules prescribed by a legislative body, budgets and other measures of performance set by manage-

---

[1] Auditing Concepts Committee, "Report of the Committee on Basic Auditing Concepts," *The Accounting Review,* Vol. 47 Supp. 1972, p. 18.

ment, or generally accepted accounting principles (GAAP) established by the Financial Accounting Standards Board (FASB) and other authoritative bodies.

- *Communicating the results* is often referred to as attestation. By attesting to the degree of correspondence with established criteria, the investigator enhances (or weakens) the credibility of the representations or claims that have been made by another party. The communication of findings is achieved through a written report.
- *Interested users* are all individuals who use (rely on) the auditor's findings. In a business environment, this includes stockholders, management, creditors, governmental agencies, and the public.

Types of Audits

Audits are generally classified into three categories: financial statement, compliance, or operational.

Financial Statement Audit

A financial statement audit involves an examination of the statements for the purpose of expressing an opinion on whether the statements are presented fairly in conformity with established criteria—usually GAAP. It is customary to have annual audits of financial statements. The results of financial statement audits are distributed to a wide spectrum of users such as stockholders, creditors, regulatory agencies, and the general public. Extensive consideration will be given to this type of audit in this text. The relationship between the definition of auditing and a financial statement audit is shown in Figure 1–1.

Compliance Audit

A compliance audit is made to determine whether the auditee is conforming with specified conditions, rules, or regulations. The established criteria in a compliance audit may come from a variety of sources. Management, for example, may prescribe certain operating procedures such as no overtime work. Bondholders may specify the maintenance of a minimum current ratio during the term of a bond issue. Probably the widest application of this type of auditing relates to government regulations. Business enterprises, not-for-profit organizations, governmental bodies, and individuals are required to prove compliance with myriad regulations. The audit of an individual's tax return is a prime example. The results of a compliance audit are generally reported to the authority that established the criteria.

Operational Audit

An operational audit involves a systematic review of an organization's activities, or of a stipulated segment of them, in relation to specified objec-

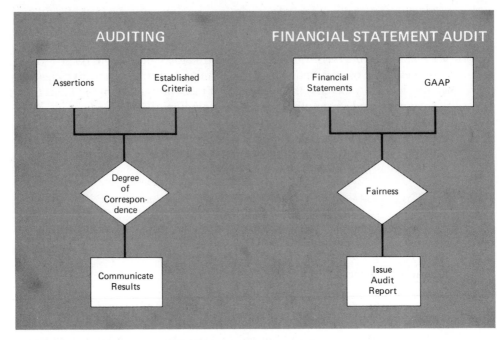

FIGURE 1–1. Auditing and the Financial Statement Audit

tives.[2] In an operational audit, the auditor is expected to make an objective observation and comprehensive analysis of the operation(s) in question. While the scope of the audit may be the entire organization, it is common to limit the audit to segments such as a division, department, or governmental agency. The objectives of the audit may range from a major problem that requires corrective action, such as excessive absenteeism or spoiled work in a production department, to improving overall operating efficiency. The established criteria may be more subjective in an operational audit than in other types of audits.

The purposes of an operational audit are to (1) assess performance, (2) identify opportunities for improvement, and (3) develop recommendations for improvement or further action.

Operational audits may be requested by management or by a third party, such as a regulatory body. Generally the results of the audit are distributed by the auditor only to the party who requested it. Appendix 1A at the end of this chapter contains a summary of an operational audit engagement.

Types of Auditors

Individuals who are engaged to audit economic actions and events for individuals and legal entities are generally classified into three groups: (1)

[2] Report of the Special Committee on Operational and Management Auditing, *Operational Audit Engagements,* (New York: American Institute of Certified Public Accountants, 1982), p. 2.

independent auditors, (2) internal auditors, and (3) government auditors. A brief description of each group and the type of auditing done by each are explained below.

Independent Auditors

Independent auditors are either sole practitioners or members of public accounting firms who render professional auditing services to clients. By virtue of their education, training, and experience, independent auditors are qualified to perform each of the types of audits described above. The clients of independent auditors may include profit-making business enterprises, not-for-profit organizations, governmental agencies, and individuals.

Like members of the medical and legal professions, independent auditors work on a fee basis. There are similarities between the role of an independent auditor in a public accounting firm and an attorney who is a member of a law firm. However, there is also a major difference: The auditor is expected to be *independent* of the client in making an audit and in reporting the results, whereas the attorney is expected to be an *advocate* for the client in rendering legal services.

Audit independence involves both conceptual and technical considerations. It is enough to say at this point that to be independent, an auditor should be without bias with respect to the client under audit and should appear to be objective to those relying on the results of the audit. More attention will be given to independence in later chapters.

Most independent auditors are licensed to practice as certified public accountants (CPAs). In general, licensing involves passing a uniform CPA examination, and obtaining practical experience in auditing. The national association of CPAs which prepares the CPA examination and establishes the rules regarding independence and standards of practice for its members is the American Institute of Certified Public Accountants (AICPA).

Internal Auditors

Internal auditors are employees who function in a staff, rather than a line, capacity within an entity. This type of auditor is involved in an independent appraisal activity, called *internal auditing*, within an organization as a service to the organization. The objective of internal auditing is to assist the management of the organization in the effective discharge of its responsibilities.

The attainment of this overall objective involves such activities as:

- Reviewing and appraising the soundness, adequacy, and application of accounting, financial, and other operating controls, and promoting effective control at reasonable cost.
- Ascertaining the extent of compliance with established policies, plans, and procedures.

- Ascertaining the extent to which company assets are accounted for and safeguarded from losses of all kinds.
- Ascertaining the reliability of management data developed within the organization.
- Appraising the quality of performance in carrying out assigned responsibilities.
- Recommending operating improvements.[3]

The scope of the internal audit function extends to all phases of an organization's activities. Internal auditors are primarily involved with compliance and operational audits. However, as is explained later, the work of internal auditors may supplement the work of independent auditors in financial statement audits.

Many internal auditors are certified (CIAs) and some are also CPAs. The international association of internal auditors is the Institute of Internal Auditors (IIA). In addition to establishing certification criteria, the IIA administers the certified internal auditing examination, and it has established a code of ethics and practice standards. The standards are summarized in Appendix 1B at the end of this chapter.

Internal auditors are expected to be objective in the performance of their work and in reporting their findings. In many companies they now report, or have direct access, to the board of directors. The role and stature of internal auditors have expanded significantly in the past decade.

Government Auditors

Government auditors are employed by various local, state, and federal governmental agencies. The two primary agencies are the U.S. General Accounting Office (GAO) and the Internal Revenue Service (IRS).

The GAO is a nonpartisan federal agency responsible for conducting the audit function for Congress. The term *audit* is used by the GAO to describe work done in examining (1) financial reports, (2) compliance with applicable laws and regulations, (3) efficiency and economy of operations, and (4) effectiveness in achieving program results.[4] This definition includes financial, compliance, and operational audits. Practice standards, classified as general, examination and evaluation, and reporting, are prescribed by the GAO. These standards are conceptually similar to the generally accepted auditing standards for independent auditors that are explained later in this chapter. The findings of GAO auditors are reported to Congress and are available to the public.

The IRS is an agency of the Treasury Department that is responsible for

---

[3] *Statement of Responsibilities of Internal Auditors* (Altamonte Springs, Fla.: Institute of Internal Auditors, 1978), pp. 3-4.

[4] Comptroller General of the United States, *Standards for Audit of Governmental Organizations, Programs, Activities and Functions* (Washington, D.C.: U.S. General Accounting Office, 1972).

administering the federal tax laws. IRS auditors (or agents) audit the returns of taxpayers for compliance with applicable tax laws. Their findings are generally restricted to the agency and the taxpayer.

The national association for government accountants is the Association of Government Accountants (AGA). The AGA has not yet developed a certification program for government accountants. However, some government auditors hold CPA and/or CIA certificates.

Need for Financial Statement Audits

Financial reporting involves the communication of economic information about an entity (individual, company, or governmental unit) by management to interested users. A common medium for the communication of financial statements is the entity's published annual report, which includes an independent auditor's opinion on the financial statements.

Financial statement audits are by far the most common and most important type of examination made by independent auditors. The need for independently audited financial statements is attributed to four conditions: (1) conflict of interest, (2) consequence, (3) complexity, and (4) remoteness.[5]

Conflict of Interest

Users of financial statements may have diverse interests in the reporting entity, and their interests may not coincide with the interests of those who have prepared the data. Many users are particularly concerned about an actual or potential conflict of interest between themselves and the management of the entity.

This apprehension extends to the fear that the financial statements and accompanying data which management is providing may be intentionally or unintentionally biased by the provider. Thus, users seek assurance from outside independent experts that the data are free from the perceived conflict of interest.

Consequence

Published annual reports represent the *primary*—and, in many cases, the *only*—basis for decision making by users. In making significant investment, lending, and other decisions, users want the financial statements to be free from bias and they also seek assurance that the financial statements are prepared in conformity with GAAP, including all disclosures that are necessary for a reasonably knowledgeable user.

Complexity

Both the subject matter of accounting and the process of preparing financial statements are becoming more and more complex. The accounting and

[5] Auditing Concepts Committee, *op. cit.*, p. 25.

reporting of earnings per share, leases, and pensions are but a few of many examples of this fact.

As the subject matter becomes more complicated, there is a greater risk of misinterpretation and a greater possibility of unintentional error. Users therefore are finding it more difficult or even impossible to evaluate the quality of the statements. Accordingly, they look to the report on the statements by the independent auditor for assurance as to the quality of the information being received.

Remoteness

Few users have direct access to the accounting records from which financial statements are prepared. Furthermore, in instances where records are available for scrutiny, time and cost constraints normally prevent users from making a meaningful examination. Remoteness prevents users from directly assessing the completeness of the statements. Under such circumstances, users have two alternatives: (1) accept the quality of the financial data on faith or (2) rely on the attestation of a third party. In terms of financial statements that are included in published annual reports, users clearly prefer the second alternative.

Responsibilities of the Independent Auditor in Financial Statement Audits

The objective of the ordinary examination of financial statements by the independent auditor is the expression of an opinion as to whether the financial statements, taken as a whole, present fairly the financial position, results of operations, and changes in financial position in conformity with GAAP. Henceforth, the term *auditor(s)* used without a modifying adjective will refer to the independent auditor(s).

The auditor's responsibilities in a financial statement audit are to

- Make an examination of the statements in accordance with professional standards, and
- Communicate the findings through the issuance of an audit report.

The auditor's function is to lend credibility to the financial statements. This function is often misunderstood by users of the auditor's report. Many believe, for example, that an audit can always be relied on to detect errors (unintentional mistakes) and irregularities (deliberate distortions and misrepresentations, commonly referred to as *fraud*). In a financial statement audit, the auditor has a responsibility to search for errors and irregularities that may have a material effect on the financial statements and discovery of such items should result. However, when employees and/or management deliberately withhold information from the auditor, the discovery of material irregularities may be a difficult, if not impossible, task.

Other users presume that a financial statement audit will always uncover illegal acts committed by management. The auditor is expected to be alert to the possibility of such acts during an audit and the discovery of an improper political contribution or a bribe of a foreign official may result. However, the determination of an illegal act is a matter of law, and the auditor is not expected to be a legal expert.

Management Responsibility for Financial Statements

Whereas the auditor is responsible for examining financial statements before he expresses an opinion as to their fairness, the preparation of the financial statements is the responsibility of management. This division of responsibility is well established in accounting and auditing literature, in legal decisions, and in actions by regulatory agencies, as illustrated by the following quotations:

> Management has the responsibility for adopting sound accounting policies . . . that will help assure the production of proper financial statements. . . . [T]he fairness of the representations made through financial statements is an implicit and integral part of management's responsibility.[6]

> The fundamental and primary responsibility for the accuracy of information filed with the Commission and disseminated among the investors rests upon management. Management does not discharge its obligations in this respect by employment of independent public accountants, however reputable . . . . [An auditor's opinion is] required not as a substitute for management's accounting of its stewardship, but as a check upon that accounting.[7]

Both statements recognize that management is accountable to shareholders and creditors. Moreover, there is implicit acknowledgment that the auditor can audit but not originate the financial information.

Management's responsibility for the statements has not been sufficiently understood by many statement users. As a result, a large number of companies are now including a report on management's responsibilities for the financial statements in their annual reports. In the report management also acknowledges its responsibility for maintaining a system of internal control to safeguard assets and enhance the reliability of the accounting records.

The auditor may assist in the preparation of financial statements. For example, he may counsel management as to the applicability of a new accounting principle, and, during the course of the audit, he may propose adjustments to the client's statements. However, acceptance of this advice and the inclusion of the suggested adjustments in the financial statements do not alter the basic separation of responsibility. Ultimately, management is responsible for all decisions concerning the form and content of the statements.

---

[6] Auditing Standards Board, *Codification of Statements on Auditing Standards* (New York: American Institute of Certified Public Accountants, 1983), Auditing Section 110.02 (hereinafter referred to and cited as AU §).

[7] *In re* Interstate Hosiery Mills, Inc., 4 S.E.C. 706, 721 (1930).

Verifiability of Financial Statement Data

Auditing is based on the assumption that financial data are verifiable. Data are verifiable when two or more qualified individuals, working independently of one another, reach essentially similar conclusions from an examination of the data. *Verifiability* is primarily concerned with the availability of evidence attesting to the validity of the data being considered.[8] The importance of this attribute of accounting information is closely related to the existence of potential conflicts of interest in the communication of accounting information and to the fact that many users of financial statements have neither access to the underlying records nor the competence to audit them.

In some disciplines, data are considered verifiable only if the examiners can prove beyond all doubt that the data are either true or false, or right or wrong, but this is not the case in accounting and auditing. The auditor seeks a reasonable basis for the expression of an opinion on the financial statements, and his opinion is an assertion as to the fairness of the statements. In making his examination, he obtains evidence in order to ascertain the validity and propriety of the accounting treatment of transactions and balances. In this context, *validity* means *sound* or *well-grounded,* and *propriety* means *conforming to established accounting rules and customs.*

Financial statements contain many specific assertions about individual items. With respect to inventories, for example, management asserts that inventory is on hand, owned, and properly stated at cost (or market). In examining the statements, the auditor believes the individual assertions are verifiable (or auditable) and that it is possible to reach a conclusion as to the fairness of the statements taken as a whole by verifying the elements that comprise the statements. The use and importance of audited financial statements provide proof that the assumption of verifiability is well founded.

Auditor Relationships in Financial Statement Audits

The auditor is the intermediary in the communication of accounting data. In the discharge of his responsibilities, the auditor must be independent of both the preparers and the users of the financial statements that represent summaries of such data. In an audit engagement, the auditor maintains professional relationships with three important groups: (1) management, (2) the board of directors, and (3) stockholders.

Management

The term *management* refers collectively to individuals who actively plan, coordinate, and control the operations and transactions of the client. In an auditing context, management refers to the company officers, controller, and key supervisory personnel.

---

[8] Committee to Prepare a Statement of Basic Accounting Theory, *A Statement of Basic Accounting Theory* (Sarasota: American Accounting Association, 1966), p. 1.

During the course of an audit, there is extensive interaction between the auditor and management. To obtain the evidence needed in an audit, the auditor often requires confidential data about the entity. It is imperative therefore to have a relationship based on mutual trust and respect. An adversary relationship will not work.

The auditor should have an interest in the well-being and future of his client. However, this concern should be tempered by a posture of professional skepticism about management's assertions. Moreover, the auditor must be prepared to evaluate critically the fairness of management's financial statement representations.

Board of Directors

The board of directors of a corporation is responsible for seeing that the corporation is operated in the best interests of the stockholders. The auditor's relationship with the directors depends largely on the composition of the board. When the board consists primarily of company officers, the auditor's relationship with the board may be the same as with management.

However, when the board has a number of outside members, a different relationship is possible. Outside members are not officers or employees of the company. In such case, the board or a designated audit committee composed primarily of outside members of the board can serve as an intermediary between the auditor and management. In the past decade, there has been a marked increase in the use of audit committees as a means of strengthening the independence of auditors. Further consideration is given to audit committees in Chapter 2.

Stockholders

Stockholders rely on audited financial statements for assurance that management has properly discharged its stewardship responsibility. The auditor therefore has a direct responsibility to stockholders as the primary users of his report.

In reporting to stockholders, the auditor must be aware of possible conflicts of interest between existing stockholders and other statement users, such as bondholders, potential investors, and regulatory agencies. The auditor's primary duty is to the group that has an ownership interest. During the course of an engagement, the auditor is not likely to have direct personal contact with stockholders who are not officers or key employees of the client.

Relationship Between Accounting and Auditing

There are significant differences in both methodology and objectives between the accounting process by which the financial statements are prepared and the audit of the statements.

Accounting methodology involves the identification of events and transactions that affect the entity. Once identified, these items are measured, recorded, classified, and summarized in the accounting records. The result of this process is the preparation and distribution of accounting reports and statements.

Conceptually, it is accurate to say that the ultimate objective of accounting is the communication of relevant financial data in a form that will be useful for decision-making. In this sense, accounting is clearly a creative process. The individuals directly involved in the company's accounting are generally employed as company accountants.

Auditing methodology in a financial statement audit includes a review of the client's system of internal control and the gathering and evaluating of evidence about management's financial statement assertions. Auditing culminates in the expression of an opinion on the financial statements produced by the accounting process. Rather than creating new information, auditing enhances the value of accounting reports. In a literary sense, accounting is writing, and auditing is editing. Independent auditors are not company employees.

The relationship between accounting and auditing in the preparation and audit of financial statements is depicted graphically in Figure 1-2.

Generally Accepted Auditing Standards

The AICPA has promulgated auditing standards for its members. The standards, which have been adopted and approved by the members, are referred to as generally accepted auditing standards (GAAS). There are ten standards which are classified into three categories as follows:[9]

General standards

Competency
- The examination is to be performed by a person or persons having adequate technical training and proficiency as an auditor.

Independence
- In all matters relating to the assignment, an independence in mental attitude is to be maintained by the auditor or auditors.

Due Care
- Due professional care is to be exercised in the performance of the examination and the preparation of the report.

Standards of field work

Planning
- The work is to be adequately planned and assistants, if any, are to be properly supervised.

Evaluating
- There is to be a proper study and evaluation of the existing internal control as a basis for reliance thereon and for the determination of the resultant extent of the tests to which auditing procedures are to be restricted.

Evidence
- Sufficient competent evidential matter is to be obtained through inspection, observation, inquiries, and confirmations to afford a reasonable basis for an opinion regarding the financial statements under examination.

[9] Auditing Standards Board, *op. cit.*, AU § 150.02.

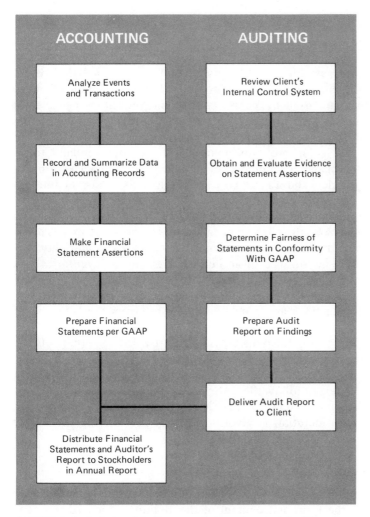

FIGURE 1–2. Relationship Between Accounting and Auditing

Standards of reporting

G AAP
- The report shall state whether the financial statements are presented in accordance with generally accepted accounting principles.

Consistency
- The report shall state whether such principles have been consistently observed in the current period in relation to the preceding period.

Reasonability
- Informative disclosures in the financial statements are to be regarded as reasonably adequate unless otherwise stated in the report.

Opinion
- The report shall contain either an expression of opinion regarding the financial statements, taken as a whole, or an assertion to the effect that an opinion cannot be expressed. When an overall opinion cannot be expressed, the reasons therefor should be stated. In all cases where an auditor's name is associated with financial statements, the report should

contain a clear-cut indication of the character of the auditor's examination, if any, and the degree of responsibility he is taking.

These standards establish the quality of performance and the overall objectives to be achieved by the auditor in a financial statement audit. Accordingly, they are used by peers, courts, and regulatory agencies in evaluating the auditor's performance. GAAS are applicable regardless of the size of the client, the form of business organization, the type of industry, or whether the entity is for profit or nonprofit. They apply equally to an examination of the financial statements of an unincorporated corner grocery store, a school district, and a large corporation such as Exxon or International Business Machines Corporation.

The auditing standards are interrelated and interdependent. The elements of *materiality* and *risk* affect the application of all the standards. This is particularly true of the field work and reporting standards. Materiality pertains to the relative importance of an item. For example, inventories in a manufacturing company are more important to the auditor than prepaid insurance. Risk relates to the likelihood that an item is incorrect. For example, cash transactions are more susceptible to errors than plant asset transactions.

Specific guidelines for meeting GAAS are provided by other AICPA publications. The most authoritative source is *Statements on Auditing Standards (SASs),* which are recognized as interpretations of GAAS. Members of the AICPA who do not follow the SASs must either justify their actions or face possible disciplinary action under the AICPA's Code of Professional Ethics. Further consideration is given to each of the ten GAAS in later chapters.

Auditor's Standard Report

Because of its importance in the attestation of financial statements, a basic understanding of the form and content of the auditor's standard report is essential. This report constitutes the auditor's only formal means of communication with interested users.

In the early days of public accounting in the United States, audit reports were descriptive, and the auditor had considerable latitude in their wording. Since 1948, however, the auditor's standard report has consisted of two paragraphs and standardized language, as illustrated in Figure 1-3.

The first paragraph of the report describes the nature of the auditor's examination and is referred to as the *scope paragraph*. The second paragraph contains the auditor's findings and is referred to as the *opinion paragraph*. Any substantive change in wording is considered to be a departure from the auditor's standard report.

In published annual reports, the three most common designations for the auditor's report are independent accountant's report, auditor's report, and accountant's report. It may be noted that this report is addressed to the company or its board of directors or its stockholders, and that it is signed in

REPORT OF INDEPENDENT ACCOUNTANTS
The Coca-Cola Company and Subsidiaries

Board of Directors and Stockholders
The Coca-Cola Company
Atlanta, Georgia

We have examined the consolidated balance sheets of The Coca-Cola Company and subsidiaries as of December 31, 1981 and 1980, and the related consolidated statements of income, retained earnings and changes in financial position for each of the three years in the period ended December 31, 1981. Our examinations were made in accordance with generally accepted auditing standards and, accordingly, included such tests of the accounting records and such other auditing procedures as we considered necessary in the circumstances.

In our opinion, the financial statements referred to above present fairly the consolidated financial position of The Coca-Cola Company and subsidiaries at December 31, 1981 and 1980, and the consolidated results of their operations and the changes in their financial position for each of the three years in the period ended December 31, 1981, in conformity with generally accepted accounting principles applied on a consistent basis.

Atlanta, Georgia
February 25, 1982

Ernst & Whinney

FIGURE 1–3. Auditor's Standard Report

the name of the auditing firm rather than in the name of the individual auditor(s) that made the examination. The standard report contains three representations:

- An examination was made of specified financial statements.
- The examination was made in accordance with *generally accepted auditing standards (GAAS)*.
- The financial statements (in the auditor's opinion) *present fairly* the financial position, results of operations, and changes in financial position in conformity with *GAAP* applied on a consistent basis.

The significant aspects of the auditor's standard report are considered below.

We have examined the . . . Balance Sheets . . . for the years then ended. The scope paragraph begins with a representation that the auditor has made an examination of certain specified statements of a designated company. This sentence implies, but does not explicitly state, that the financial statements examined by the auditor were prepared by management and that the statements are management's responsibility.

Each of the financial statements examined by the auditor is identified in the first sentence of the auditor's standard report, together with the dates appropriate to each statement.

Our examinations were made in accordance with generally accepted auditing standards. . . . These words acknowledge the existence of professional standards for the examinations. In addition, the auditor states that he has met these standards (GAAS) in making his examinations of the specified financial statements.

. . . such tests of the accounting records and such other auditing procedures as we considered necessary in the circumstances. This clause further explains the nature of the auditor's examination. The word *tests* is used to imply that less than a 100 percent examination was made of the transactions and events that are summarized in the financial statements. In testing the accounting records that support the financial statements being examined, the auditor focuses primarily on material items and may use sampling techniques in gathering and evaluating evidence.

The methods used and the acts performed by the auditor during his examinations are referred to as *auditing procedures*. Auditing procedures include such steps as counting petty cash, reviewing a client-prepared bank reconciliation, observing an inventory count, and examining legal title to a motor vehicle purchased by a company.

The specific procedures used by the auditor are not disclosed in the auditor's report. In contrast to auditing standards which are applicable in every financial statement audit, auditing procedures may vary from client to client. For example, an auditor will usually perform more auditing procedures or apply the same procedure more extensively for clients with poor internal control than for clients with good internal control.

The concluding phrase, *as we considered necessary in the circumstances,* indicates that the auditor used professional judgment in deciding what tests to make and what auditing procedures to apply. It further infers that decisions pertaining to this aspect of the examination were made independently of management. Stated conversely, this phrase says that the auditor's examination was not circumscribed by any management-imposed limitations on the scope of the work.

In our opinion, these financial statements. . . . In interpreting the meaning and significance of this clause, it is proper to conclude that the opinion is being expressed by a *professional, experienced,* and *expert* person or persons. Alternatively, the word *judgment* could be substituted for *opinion.* It is incorrect, however, to conclude that this phrase says, *We certify, We guarantee,* or *We are certain (or positive).*

The second part of this clause makes reference to the financial statements identified in the scope paragraph; the titles of the individual statements are not repeated.

The opinion expressed in the auditor's standard report is an *unqualified opinion.* Such an opinion is justified when (1) the examination has been made in accordance with GAAS, (2) the financial statements satisfy the first three reporting standards, and (3) the statements are not affected by a major uncertainty (such as a lawsuit) whose outcome depends on a future event. When these conditions are not present, other types of opinions may be appropriate, as follows:

- *Qualified opinion or disclaimer of opinion* (no opinion) when there is
    A significant limitation on the scope of the auditor's examination
    The existence of a major uncertainty.
- *Qualified opinion or adverse opinion* when there is
    Lack of conformity with GAAP.
    Inadequate disclosure of essential information.
- *Qualified opinion* when there is inconsistency in applying GAAP.

The auditor's decision as to whether to render a qualified opinion or to disclaim an opinion in the first category above and a qualified opinion or an adverse opinion in the second is determined on the basis of materiality (i.e., the importance of the matter to the financial statements).

. . . present fairly . . . in conformity with generally accepted accounting principles. . . . The auditor's opinion is expressed in terms of present fairly. The intended connotation of present fairly is *reasonably* or, in a slightly more technical sense, *in all material (or important) respects*. It may also be construed to mean that the statements are free of material misstatements and/or omissions, and are not misleading. Such terms as *accurately, truly, factually, correctly,* or *exactly* are not used because of the existence of estimates in the financial statements and the nature of the examination.

The auditor's opinion on fairness (reasonableness) pertains to each financial statement taken as a whole. It does not apply to the accuracy or correctness of individual accounts or components of each financial statement. An unqualified opinion expresses the auditor's belief that the financial statements accomplish their stated purpose by fairly presenting financial position (balance sheet), the results of operations (income statement and retained earnings statement), and changes in financial position (statement of changes in financial position).

The term *generally accepted accounting principles* provides the criteria for the auditor's judgment as to the fairness of the financial statements. Statements of the FASB, for example, are recognized as GAAP.

GAAP includes adequate disclosure.[10] Moreover, the third standard of reporting provides that disclosures in the statements are reasonably adequate unless otherwise stated in the auditor's report. Thus, the auditor's standard report does not contain an explicit assertion as to the adequacy of management's financial statement disclosures.

. . . applied on a consistent basis. The concluding words of the opinion paragraph incorporate the second standard of reporting into the standard

---

[10] Auditing Standards Board, *op. cit.,* AU § 411.04.

audit report. They assure interested users of the statements that comparability between the statements of the two or more years being reported on has not been affected by changes in accounting principles. This acknowledgment is not a guarantee that the statements are comparable. Other changes that may affect comparability, such as the purchase of a business, discontinuance of a product line, or adoption of a pension plan, are not included in the auditor's opinion on consistency. However, if the effects of such changes are material, they may require disclosure in the financial statements.

Public Accounting as a Profession

A *profession* is a field of practice with the following characteristics:

- A specialized body of technical knowledge.
- Admission standards.
- Self-regulation.
- Community sanction.

Specialized Body of Technical Knowledge

Many occupations require specialized training and skill. Trades, such as electrical work, plumbing, and bricklaying, meet these criteria. However, these and similar trades have not been given professional recognition because formal academic training is not required.

The knowledge required for a profession is generally associated with postbaccalaureate college education in separate professional schools, such as the schools of law and medicine. However, the structure in which the knowledge is obtained is viewed by many individuals as secondary to the substance of the knowledge. These individuals argue that the primary test should be whether there is a common body of knowledge required for entry into the professional field.

Public accounting has a common body of knowledge, and both professional academic programs and professional schools of accounting exist.

Admission Standards

Every profession has standards that must be met before an individual can become licensed to practice as a professional. In accounting, one admission standard is a uniform professional examination, which is a rigorous, extensive test of the body of knowledge considered to be necessary for professional practice.

The uniform CPA examination is prepared and graded by the Board of Examiners of the AICPA. It is administered and given biannually (May and November) by state boards of accountancy. The examination tests a candidate's knowledge in four subjects: accounting practice, accounting theory, auditing, and business law. Content specification outlines have been issued for each subject. The specifications for auditing are reproduced in Appendix

X, at the end of the text. Further information about this examination is available in an AICPA publication, *Information for CPA Candidates*.

A second admission requirement in most jurisdictions is practical experience in auditing. On satisfactory completion of the CPA examination and fulfillment of the experience requirement, the individual receives a license to practice as a certified public accountant. The licensing of the CPA is controlled by state boards of accountancy.

Self-Regulation

A hallmark of a profession is the right, ability, and willingness to regulate itself in the public interest, beyond the strict letter of the law, into areas of moral and ethical conduct. In the United States, accounting's self-regulating agencies are state and national accounting organizations of CPAs.

Each of these organizations, for example, has codes of professional ethics pertaining to the practice of public accounting. There are also requirements pertaining to the continuing professional education of CPAs, quality control standards for public accounting firms, and peer reviews of public accounting firms.

Community Sanction

In recognition of its status, a profession is given certain rights and privileges by the community or public it serves. Two such rights, the ability to control entry into the profession and self-regulation, have already been discussed. Community sanction also pertains to the right to practice as a professional, to be free from interference in the formulation of professional standards, and to have privileged communication rights in legal cases.

The public accounting profession has experienced relatively little interference from state and federal governments in the formulation of auditing standards and accounting principles. However, in the late 1970s, the public accounting profession was subjected to scrutiny by two congressional subcommittees. Both subcommittees recommended more stringent self-regulation by the profession.

The right of privileged communication is the right to withhold disclosure of confidential client information in legal suits. In this respect, accounting has still not been granted this status of a profession in some states. Whereas practically all states have given this privilege to medicine and law, less than half have extended it to CPAs.

Organization of the Profession

As illustrated in Figure 1-4, the public accounting profession consists of organizations and practice units. A brief explanation of each component is given below.

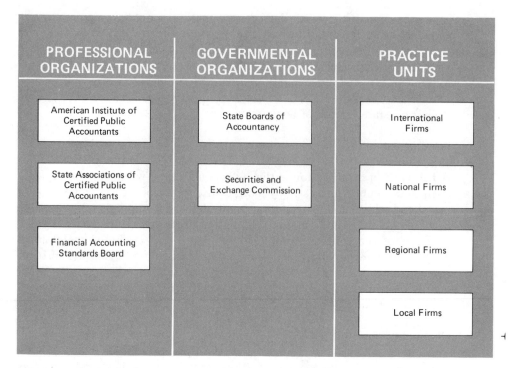

PROFESSIONAL ORGANIZATIONS	GOVERNMENTAL ORGANIZATIONS	PRACTICE UNITS
American Institute of Certified Public Accountants	State Boards of Accountancy	International Firms
State Associations of Certified Public Accountants	Securities and Exchange Commission	National Firms
Financial Accounting Standards Board		Regional Firms
		Local Firms

FIGURE 1–4. Organization of the Public Accounting Profession

AICPA

The public accounting profession's national professional organization is the AICPA. Membership in the AICPA is voluntary. Currently, there are approximately 225,000 CPAs in the United States, of whom 180,000 are members of the AICPA. One of the AICPA's major objectives is to promote and maintain high professional standards within the profession. Since its formation in 1887, the AICPA has been very influential.

The AICPA operates through a number of divisions. Those that pertain most directly to the audit function are (1) Auditing Standards, (2) Division for CPA Firms, (3) Quality Control Review, and (4) Professional Ethics. The Auditing Standards Division is briefly explained below; the other divisions are described in later chapters.

The *Auditing Standards Division* is headed by a vice-president of auditing. It consists of the Auditing Standards Board (ASB), an advisory council, subcommittees, task forces, a director of auditing research, and a small staff.

The ASB currently consists of 15 CPAs. It is the senior technical body designated to issue pronouncements on auditing matters. The board makes its pronouncements through Statements on Auditing Standards (SASs). Before issuance, each statement is widely circulated for public comment. The advisory council monitors the activities of the ASB. Its membership is drawn from business, practicing CPAs, government, the legal profession, and academia.

Other AICPA publications of interest to auditors are (1) auditing interpretations, (2) audit guides, and (3) audit and accounting guides. These publications are not as authoritative as SASs.

State Associations (Societies) of Certified Public Accountants

CPAs within each state have formed a state society or association of CPAs. Like the national organization, membership in a state society is voluntary. Many CPAs are members of both the AICPA and a state society. State societies function through small full-time staffs and committees composed of their members. State associations have their own codes of professional ethics that closely parallel the AICPA Code of Ethics. Although they are autonomous, state societies usually cooperate with both each other and the AICPA in areas of mutual interest, such as continuing professional education and ethics.

Financial Accounting Standards Board

The FASB is an independent private body whose primary function is the development of GAAP. Statements and interpretations issued by this Board have been officially recognized by the AICPA as constituting GAAP. The Board consists of seven full-time members who are assisted by a large research staff and an advisory council. Before most *FASB Statements of Financial Accounting Standards* are issued, there are both extensive public exposure and public hearings.

State Boards of Accountancy

There are 54 boards of accountancy: one in each state, one in the District of Columbia, and one in each U.S. territory. State boards usually consist of five to seven CPAs and at least one public member who are generally appointed by the governor. A full-time executive secretary and a small (three- to five-member) administrative staff are common. Each board administers its state accountancy laws, which set forth the conditions for licensing of CPAs, codes of professional ethics, and in some cases mandatory continuing professional education requirements. State boards are also becoming more active in positive enforcement programs aimed at maintaining the quality of audit practice. The primary functions of the boards are issuing licenses to practice as a CPA, renewing licenses, and suspending or revoking licenses to practice. State boards work independently of the AICPA and state societies.

Securities and Exchange Commission

The Securities and Exchange Commission (SEC) is a federal government agency that was created under the 1934 Securities Exchange Act to regulate the distribution and trading of securities offered for public sale and subsequent trading of securities on stock exchanges and over-the-counter markets. Under the provisions of this Act, the SEC has the authority to establish GAAP for companies under its jurisdiction. Throughout its history, the SEC has, with few exceptions, delegated this authority to the private sector, and it currently recognizes the pronouncements of the FASB as constituting GAAP in the filing of financial statements with the agency. In some instances, however, the SEC's disclosure requirements exceed GAAP.

The SEC also exerts considerable influence over auditing and the public accounting profession. Its regulations contain qualifications for determining the independence of the accountant, as well as standards of reporting. These requirements are basically the same as the standards prescribed by the AICPA. Further consideration is given to the SEC in Chapter 20.

Practice Units

A CPA may practice as a sole practitioner or as a member of a firm. A CPA firm may be organized as a proprietorship, a partnership, or a professional corporation. There are approximately 30,000 practice units (CPA firms) in the United States. These firms are generally classified into four groups: (1) international, (2) national, (3) regional, and (4) local.

International firms have offices in the principal cities of the United States and major cities throughout the world. The eight largest firms in this group are referred to as the "Big Eight."[11] Over 90 percent of the "Fortune 500" companies and thousands of smaller clients are served by the Big Eight. In its largest office, a Big Eight firm may have more than a thousand professionals.

National firms have offices in the major cities in the United States. These firms serve some SEC clients and thousands of medium and small clients. National firms compete with international firms for domestic clients.

Regional firms have offices in a limited geographical area such as the East or Midwest. These firms usually serve smaller clients than international and national firms.

Local firms may have one office or several offices within a state or county. The local firm is by far the most common form of practice unit. Local firms serve small entities and individual clients.

Other Types of Services by CPA Firms

Through their professional staffs, CPA firms are qualified to render a variety of services in addition to auditing. The principal types of nonauditing services are tax, management advisory, and accounting and review services.

---

[11] The Big Eight are Arthur Andersen & Co.; Coopers & Lybrand; Deloitte Haskins & Sells; Ernst & Whinney; Peat, Marwick, Mitchell & Co.; Price Waterhouse; Touche Ross & Co.; and Arthur Young & Company.

Tax Services

Individuals and business enterprises are required to file and pay a variety of taxes. CPAs who specialize in taxation are thoroughly knowledgeable about the intricacies of the tax laws.

Most CPA firms have tax specialists and many have separate tax departments. Tax services include assistance in filing tax returns, tax planning, estate planning, and representation of clients before governmental agencies in tax matters. Tax services constitute a very significant part of the practice of individual practioners and small (local) CPA firms.

The AICPA, through its senior tax committee, issues *Statements on Responsibilities in Tax Practice*. These statements will be considered in Chapter 18.

Management Advisory Services

Management advisory services (MAS) are defined as "the management consulting function of providing advice and technical assistance where the primary purpose is to help the client improve the use of its capabilities and resources to achieve its objectives.[12] There are two categories of MAS practice for a CPA firm: (1) *engagements* which involve applying an analytical approach and process in a study or project for an extended time period such as the installation of an EDP system, and (2) *consultations* that consist of informal advice during a short time frame such as a recommendation to use a collection agency to collect past due receivable. MAS include

- Counseling management in its analysis, planning, organizing, operating, and controlling functions.
- Conducting special studies, preparing recommendations, proposing plans and programs, and providing advice and technical assistance in their implementation.
- Reviewing and suggesting improvement of policies, procedures, systems, methods, and organization relationships.
- Introducing new ideas, concepts, and methods to management.

The AICPA, through its MAS Executive Committee, issues a *Statement on Standards for Management Advisory Services*. These standards will be considered in Chapter 18.

When rendering management advisory services, the CPA is acting as an outside, expert business consultant. In this capacity, the CPA should not be making management decisions. Many of the larger firms have separate management services departments. Today, it represents a significant proportion of the total billings of many CPA firms.

[12] Management Advisory Services Executive Committee, *Statement on Standards for Management Advisory Services, No. 1,* Definitions and Standards for MAS Practice, (New York: American Institute of Certified Public Accountants, December 1981), p. 2.

Accounting and Review Services

A CPA firm may be engaged by a client to perform a variety of accounting services. These services include doing manual or automated bookkeeping, journalizing and posting adjusting entries, and preparing (or compiling) financial statements. In performing an accounting service, the firm serves as a substitute for or a supplement to the accounting personnel of the client. Accounting services are a major activity for some individual practitioners and local firms.

A review service consists primarily of inquiries of management and comparative analyses of financial information. The purpose of a review is to give limited assurance that no material modifications are necessary for the financial statements to be in conformity with GAAP. The scope of a review is significantly less than the scope of an audit. Reviews are rendered by all types of CPA firms in accordance with standards established by the AICPA. Further consideration is given to accounting and review services in Chapter 17.

CONCLUDING COMMENTS

This chapter has provided a basic introduction to the nature and importance of auditing, the auditor's standard report, and the organization of the public accounting profession. Independent audits of financial statements serve a vital need in our society for meaningful and reliable financial data. Auditing is neither a sedate nor a sterile process. To fulfill its role in society, auditing must be responsive to contemporary business developments and to the changing expectations of users of financial information.

APPENDIX 1A

Illustrative Operational Audit Engagement Summary[13]

Organization Audited	Data processing department.
Type of Organization	Financial institution.
Background of Operational Audit	The senior management of the organization was concerned that the data processing department was not operating effectively.
Principal Recipients of Operational Audit Report	President, executive vice president, and vice president of data processing.
Purpose(s)	To assess performance, identify opportunities for improvement, and outline recommendations for improvement.
Objective	To assess the adequacy of data processing operations in meeting the needs of the organization.
Scope	The review included administration, organization, user evaluation, planning and operations, hardware utilization, data communication, and information resource management.
General Procedures/ Approach to Conducting Engagement	Key users in the organization were interviewed. Major documents were reviewed, including plans, budgets, employee training records. Actual operations were observed over a period on a random basis. Hardware records on usage were analyzed.
Measurement Criteria	The areas contained in the AICPA publication, *Operational Reviews of the Electronic Data Processing Function.*
Specific Findings and Recommendations	Findings and recommendations were presented in six major categories: Administration, Organization, Planning, Hardware, Utilization, and Information Resources.
Special Comments and Limitations	None.

---

[13] Report of the Special Committee on Operational and Management Auditing, *op. cit.*, p. 19.

APPENDIX 1B

Summary of General and Specific Standards for the Professional Practice of Internal Auditing[14]

100   INDEPENDENCE. Internal auditors should be independent of the activities they audit.

>   110   **Organizational Status.** The organizational status of the internal auditing department should be sufficient to permit the accomplishment of its audit responsibilities.
>   120   **Objectivity.** Internal auditors should be objective in performing audits.

200   PROFESSIONAL PROFICIENCY. Internal audits should be performed with proficiency and due professional care.

THE INTERNAL AUDITING DEPARTMENT

>   210   **Staffing.** The internal auditing department should provide assurance that the technical proficiency and educational background of internal auditors are appropriate for the audits to be performed.
>   220   **Knowledge, Skills, and Disciplines.** The internal auditing department should possess or should obtain the knowledge, skills, and disciplines needed to carry out its audit responsibilities.
>   230   **Supervision.** The internal auditing department should provide assurance that internal audits are properly supervised.

THE INTERNAL AUDITOR

>   240   **Compliance with Standards of Conduct.** Internal auditors should comply with professional standards of conduct.
>   250   **Knowledge, Skills, and Disciplines.** Internal auditors should possess the knowledge, skills, and disciplines essential to the performance of internal audits.
>   260   **Human Relations and Communications.** Internal auditors should be skilled in dealing with people and in communicating effectively.
>   270   **Continuing Education.** Internal auditors should maintain their technical competence through continuing education.
>   280   **Due Professional Care.** Internal auditors should exercise due professional care in performing internal audits.

300   SCOPE OF WORK. The scope of the internal audit should encompass the examination and evaluation of the adequacy and effectiveness of the organization's system of internal control and the quality of performance in carrying out assigned responsibilities.

>   310   **Reliability and Integrity of Information.** Internal auditors should review the reliability and integrity of financial and operating information and the means used to identify, measure, classify, and report such information.
>   320   **Compliance with Policies, Plans, Procedures, Laws, and Regulations.** Internal auditors should review the systems established to ensure compliance with those policies, plans, procedures, laws, and regulations which could have a significant impact on operations and reports and should determine whether the organization is in compliance.
>   330   **Safeguarding of Assets.** Internal auditors should review the means of safeguarding assets and, as appropriate, verify the existence of such assets.

---

[14] *Standards for the Professional Practice of Internal Auditing,* (Altamonte Springs, Fla.: Institute of Internal Auditing, 1980), pp. 3-4.

340 **Economical and Efficient Use of Resources.** Internal auditors should appraise the economy and efficiency with which resources are employed.

350 **Accomplishment of Established Objectives and Goals for Operations or Programs.** Internal auditors should review operations or programs to ascertain whether results are consistent with established objectives and goals and whether the operations or programs are being carried out as planned.

400 **PERFORMANCE OF AUDIT WORK.** Audit work should include planning the audit, examining and evaluating information, communicating results, and following up.

410 **Planning the Audit.** Internal auditors should plan each audit.

420 **Examining and Evaluating Information.** Internal auditors should collect, analyze, interpret, and document information to support audit results.

430 **Communicating Results.** Internal auditors should report the results of their audit work.

440 **Following Up.** Internal auditors should follow up to ascertain that appropriate action is taken on reported audit findings.

500 **MANAGEMENT OF THE INTERNAL AUDITING DEPARTMENT.** The director of internal auditing should properly manage the internal auditing department.

510 **Purpose, Authority, and Responsibility.** The director of internal auditing should have a statement of purpose, authority, and responsibility for the internal auditing department.

520 **Planning.** The director of internal auditing should establish plans to carry out the responsibilities of the internal auditing department.

530 **Policies and Procedures.** The director of internal auditing should provide written policies and procedures to guide the audit staff.

540 **Personnel Management and Development.** The director of internal auditing should establish a program for selecting and developing the human resources of the internal auditing department.

550 **External Auditors.** The director of internal auditing should coordinate internal and external audit efforts.

560 **Quality Assurance.** The director of internal auditing should establish and maintain a quality assurance program to evaluate the operations of the internal auditing department.

REVIEW QUESTIONS

1–1. Identify the essential parts of the definition of auditing.

1–2. Describe the principal types of audits and indicate the primary purpose of each.

1–3. Contrast the activities of independent, internal, and governmental auditors.

1–4. Why do financial statements need to be audited?

1–5. What are the auditor's responsibilities and functions in a financial statement audit?

1–6. Some people claim there is no basic difference between the responsibility of management and the responsibility of the auditor for financial statements. Do you agree? Why or why not?

1–7. What is meant by the verifiability of data in auditing?

1–8. How does the auditor's relationship with management differ, if at all, from his relationship with the board of directors and stockholders?

1–9. Contrast accounting and auditing as to (a) methodology and (b) purpose.

1–10. a. Describe the nature and importance of generally accepted auditing standards.
   b. Identify the three categories of GAAS.

1–11. a. What are the AICPA's most authoritative pronouncements in auditing?
   b. What is the relationship between the pronouncements and GAAS.
   c. What authority is attached to these pronouncements?

1–12. a. What representations are made by the auditor in the auditor's standard report?
   b. What circumstances justify the issuance of an unqualified opinion?

1–13. Identify the three types of opinions that may appear in a nonstandard audit report and indicate the circumstances when each opinion is appropriate.

1–14. Explain both the meaning and misconceptions of "present fairly" as used in the auditor's report.

1–15. Explain the meaning of the following phrases in the scope paragraph of the auditors report (1) tests of the accounting records and (2) auditing procedures we considered necessary in the circumstances.

1–16. a. What are the essential characteristics of a profession?
   b. Give two examples of each characteristic that enables public accounting to be a profession.

1–17. a. Identify the three types of organizations that comprise the public accounting profession.
   b. What are the major objectives of the (1) AICPA, (2) state boards of accountancy, and (3) SEC?

1–18. a. Describe the composition of the Auditing Standards Division of the AICPA.
   b. Why is the Auditing Standards Board (ASB) important? What form do its pronouncements take?
   c. Identify other AICPA publications that may be of interest to auditors.

1–19. a. Identify the categories of CPA practice units in the public accounting profession.
   b. What types of services, other than auditing, are CPA firms qualified to render?

1–20.* a. Identify the five categories of general standards for the practice of internal auditing established by the Institute of Internal Auditors (IIA).
   b. Compare the categories of auditing standards established by (1) the IIA and (2) the Government Accounting Office (GAO) with the categories established by the AICPA.

COMPREHENSIVE QUESTIONS

1–21. After performing an audit, the auditor determines that

1. The financial statements of a corporation are presented fairly.
2. A company's receiving department is inefficient.
3. A company's tax return does not conform with IRS regulations.
4. A government supply depot is not meeting planned program objectives.

* This question relates to Appendix material.

5. The financial statements of a physician are properly prepared on a cash basis.
6. A foreman is not carrying out his assigned responsibilities.
7. The IRS is in violation of an established government employment practice.
8. A company is meeting the terms of a government contract.
9. A municipality's financial statements correctly show actual cash receipts and disbursements.
10. The postal service in midtown is inefficient.
11. A company is meeting the terms of a bond contract.
12. A department is not meeting the company's prescribed policies concerning overtime work.

Required
a. Indicate the type of audit that is involved: (1) financial, (2) compliance, or (3) operational.
b. Identify the type of auditor that is involved: (1) independent, (2) internal, (3) government-GAO, or (4) government-IRS.
c. Identify the primary recipient(s) of the audit report: stockholders, management, Congress, etc.
d. Use the following format for your answers:

Type of Audit	Type of Auditor(s)	Primary Recipient(s)

1–22. The president of your company (a multidivision company) has been discussing his company's internal operations with several colleagues in the business community. He has discovered that most of them have an internal audit staff.

Required
He has asked you to describe for him the meaning of the terms (a) financial audits, (b) compliance audits, and (c) operational audits.

CMA (adapted)

1–23. G. Johnson, a local real estate broker, is a member of the board of directors of Pennset Corporation. At a recent board meeting, called to discuss financial plans, Mr. Johnson discovered two planned expenditures for auditing. In the Controller's Department budget, he found an estimate for internal audit activity and in the Treasurer's budget he found an estimate for the annual audit by a CPA firm.

Mr. Johnson could not understand the need for two different expenditures for auditing. Since the CPA fee for the annual audit was less than the cost of the internal audit activity he proposed eliminating the internal audit function.

Required
a. Explain to Mr. Johnson the different purposes served by the two audit activities.
b. What benefits does the CPA firm performing an audit derive from the existence of an internal audit function?

CMA

1–24. The following two statements are representative of attitudes and opinions sometimes encountered by CPAs in their professional practices:
1. Today's audit consists of test checking. This is dangerous because test checking depends upon the auditor's judgment, which may be defective. An audit can be relied upon only if every transaction is verified.

2. An audit by a CPA is essentially negative and contributes to neither the gross national product nor the general well-being of society. The auditor does not create; he merely checks what someone else has done.

Required
Evaluate each of the above statements and indicate
a. Areas of agreement with the statement, if any.
b. Areas of misconception, incompleteness or fallacious reasoning included in the statement, if any.
Complete your discussion of each statement (both parts a and b) before going on to the next statement.

AICPA (adapted)

1–25. Listed below in alphabetical order are the steps that are included in preparing, auditing, and distributing financial statements:

Acc.   ① 1. Analyze events and transactions.
Aud.   ⑨ 2. Deliver audit report to client.
Aud   ⑧3. Determine fairness of statements in conformity with GAAP.
Acc   ⑩ 4. Distribute audited financial statements and audit report to interested users.
Acc   ② 5. Make financial statement assertions.
Aud   ⑥6. Obtain and evaluate evidence on statement assertions.
Aud   ⑦7. Prepare audit report on findings.
Acc   ③8. Prepare financial statements in conformity with GAAP.
Acc   ②9. Record and summarize data in accounting records.
Aud   ⑤10. Review client's internal control system.

Required
a. Prepare a diagram of the relationship between (1) accounting and (2) auditing in the preparation and audit of financial statements. Show each of the steps in the proper sequence.
b. Management and the independent auditor share the responsibility for the assertions contained in financial statements. Evaluate and discuss the accuracy of this contention.

1–26. The auditor's standard report contains the words *generally accepted auditing standards, auditing procedures,* and *generally accepted accounting principles.*

Required
a. Indicate the paragraphs of the standard report in which each term appears.
b. Distinguish between the three terms.
c. Why is it important that the auditor state that the audited financial statements are in conformity with GAAP?
d. What is the relationship, if any, between Statements on Auditing Standards and GAAS?

1–27. An auditor may issue four types of opinions: (1) unqualified, (2) qualified, (3) adverse, and (4) disclaimer (no opinion). Listed below are unrelated circumstances pertaining to different types of opinions. Assume in each case that the auditor would issue an unqualified opinion except for the identified circumstance.
1. The financial statements are not in conformity with GAAP.
2. A major uncertainty exists at the balance sheet date that will not be resolved until next year.
3. The auditor is unable to perform all auditing procedures deemed to be necessary in the circumstances.
4. Accounting principles are not applied on a consistent basis.

5. There is inadequate disclosure of essential suplemental information in the financial statements.

Required
a. Identify the conditions that must exist to justify the issuance of an unqualified opinion.
b. Indicate the opinion(s) that an auditor may render for each of the above circumstances.

1-28. The auditor's standard report contains standardized wording. Listed below are a number of incorrect sentences, clauses, and phrases pertaining to the standard report. Assume that the report pertains to the balance sheets at December 31, 19X1 and 19X0, and the related statements of income, retained earnings, and changes in financial position of the X Company for each of the three years ended December 31, 19X1.

1. In our opinion, the aforementioned statements present accurately. . . .
2. Our examinations were made in accordance with auditing standards promulgated by the AICPA. . . .
3. We have examined the balance sheets at December 31, 19X1 and 19X0 and the accompanying statements for the years then ended.
4. Our examinations . . . accordingly included such tests of the financial statements. . . .
5. . . . on a basis consistent. . . .
6. . . . in conformity with promulgated accounting principles. . . .
7. . . . present fairly the balance sheet of X Company at December 31, 19X1 and 19X0. . . .
8. Our examinations . . . and such other auditing principles as we considered necessary. . . .
9. . . . present fairly the financial position and results of its operations for each of the three years then ended. . . .
10. We have reviewed . . . and the related statements of income, retained earnings, and changes in working capital for each of the three years. . . .

Required
a. Rewrite the portions of the above items that are incorrect using standard report language. You may assume that the portions of sentences identified as . . . are correct.
b. Following each revision, indicate whether the item will appear in (1) the scope paragraph or (2) the opinion paragraph of the auditor's standard report.

1-29. There are ten GAAS. Listed below are statements that relate to these standards:

1. The auditor is careful in doing the audit and in writing the audit report.
2. A more experienced auditor supervises the work of an inexperienced auditor.
3. The auditor investigates and reaches conclusions about the client's internal controls.
4. A predesigned schedule is followed during the examination.
5. The auditor is an accounting graduate with several years of experience in auditing.
6. In the auditor's judgment, the financial statements conform to all FASB statements.
7. The auditor is objective and unbiased in performing the examination.
8. The client used the same accounting principles this year as last year.
9. The examination produced all the evidence needed to reach a conclusion about the client's financial statements.
10. The client's notes to the financial statement contain all essential data.
11. The auditor expresses an opinion on the financial statements.

Required

a. Identify by category and by number within each category the GAAS to which each statement relates (i.e., general standard No. 1, field work standard No. 2, etc.).

b. For each answer in (a) above provide the full statement of the standard. Use the following format for your answers:

Identification of Standard	*Statement of Standard*

1–30. Public accounting is generally recognized as a profession. In response to a homework assignment on the characteristics of public accounting that make it a profession, a student gave the following answer:

1. Specialized knowledge
    a. Bachelor of science programs in accounting.
    b. Separate professional schools of accounting.
2. Uniform entrance requirements
    a. Licensing of a CPA by state associations of CPAs.
    b. Uniform CPA examination administered by the AICPA.
3. Self-policing
    a. The SEC.
    b. State boards of accountancy.
4. Community acceptance
    a. Freedom from state government interference.
    b. Code of Professional Ethics.

Required

Indicate the proper identification of the four characteristics of a profession and identify at least two reasons per characteristic that are properly applicable to public accounting.

1–31. The public accounting profession consists of five professional and governmental organizations: (1) the AICPA, (2) state associations of CPAs, (3) the FASB, (4) state boards of accountancy, and (5) the SEC. The following are activities that are associated with the public accounting profession:

1. Licensing individuals to practice as CPAs.
2. Promulgating GAAP.
3. Issuing Statements on Auditing Standards.
4. Regulating the distribution and trading of securities offered for public sale.
5. Establishing its own code of professional ethics.
6. Issuing Statements on Financial Accounting Standards.
7. Imposing mandatory continuing education as a requirement for renewal of license to practice as a CPA.
8. Issuing disclosure requirements for companies under its jurisdiction that may exceed GAAP.
9. Issuing auditing interpretations.
10. Cooperating with the AICPA in areas of mutual interest such as continuing professional education and ethics enforcement.

Required

a. Indicate the organization(s) associated with each activity.
b. Identify the divisions of the AICPA that directly affect the independent auditor.

1-32. The following audit report was issued at the turn of this century[15]:

New York
March 12, 1903

To the Stockholders of the United States Steel Corporation:

We have examined the books of the U.S. Steel Corporation and its Subsidiary Companies for the year ending December 31, 1902, and certify that the Balance Sheet at that date and the Relative Income Account are correctly prepared therefrom.

We have satisfied ourselves that during the year only actual additions and extensions have been charged to Property Account; that ample provision has been made for Depreciation and Extinguishment, and that the item of "Deferred Charges" represents expenditures reasonably and properly carried forward to operations of subsequent years.

We are satisfied that the valuations of the inventories of stocks on hand as certified by the responsible officials have been carefully and accurately made at approximate cost; also that the cost of material and labor on contracts in progress has been carefully ascertained, and that the profit taken on these contracts is fair and reasonable.

Full provision has been made for bad and doubtful accounts receivable and for all ascertainable liabilities.

We have verified the cash and securities by actual inspection or by certificates from the Depositories, and are of opinion that the Stocks and Bonds are fully worth the value at which they are stated in the Balance Sheet.

And we certify that in our opinion the Balance Sheet is properly drawn up so as to show the true financial position of the Corporation and its Subsidiary Companies, and that the Relative Income Account is a fair and correct statement of the net earnings for the fiscal year ending at that date.

PRICE, WATERHOUSE & CO.

Required
a. Contrast the scope of the examination in this report with the scope of the examination in the auditor's standard report.
b. Contrast the manner in which the nature of the examination is indicated in this report with the manner of explaining the nature of the examination in the standard report.
c. Compare the last paragraph of the above report with the opinion paragraph of the auditor's standard report.

1-33. On completion of all field work on September 23, 19X1, the following report was rendered by Timothy Ross to the directors of The Rancho Corporation:

To the Directors of The Rancho Corporation:

We have examined the balance sheet, the related statement of income and retained earnings of The Rancho Corporation and the statement of changes in financial position as of July 31, 19X1 and 19X0. Our examinations were made in accordance with the standards of the profession and included all tests of the statements that you considered appropriate in the circumstances.

In our opinion, with the exception of some minor errors that are considered immaterial, the aforementioned financial statements present fairly the financial position of The Rancho Corporation at July 31, 19X1 and 19X0, and the results of its operations

---

[15] The Commission on Auditors' Responsibilities, *Report, Conclusions, and Recommendations* (New York: American Institute of Certified Public Accountants, 1978), p. 2.

for the years then ended, in conformity with pronouncements of the Financial Accounting Standards Board applied consistently throughout the period.

Timothy Ross, CPA
September 23, 19X1

Required
a. List and explain deficiencies and omissions in the auditor's report.
b. Organize your answer sheet by paragraph (scope and opinion) of the auditor's report.

AICPA (adapted)

CASE STUDY

1–34.   Ray, the owner of a small company, asked Holmes, CPA, to conduct an audit of the company's records. Ray told Holmes that an audit is to be completed in time to submit audited financial statements to a bank as part of a loan application. Holmes immediately accepted the engagement and agreed to provide an auditor's report within three weeks. Ray agreed to pay Holmes a fixed fee plus a bonus if the loan was granted.

Holmes hired two accounting students to conduct the audit and spent several hours telling them exactly what to do. Holmes told the students not to spend time reviewing the controls but instead to concentrate on proving the mathematical accuracy of the ledger accounts, and summarizing the data in the accounting records that support Ray's financial statements. The students followed Holmes' instructions and after two weeks gave Holmes the financial statements which did not include footnotes. Holmes reviewed the statements and prepared an unqualified auditor's report. The report, however, did not refer to generally accepted accounting principles nor to the year-to-year application of such principles.

Required
Briefly describe each of the generally accepted auditing standards and indicate how the action(s) of Holmes resulted in a failure to comply with *each* standard.

Organize your answer as follows:

Brief Description of Generally Accepted Auditing Standards	*Holmes' Actions Resulting in Failure to Comply with Generally Accepted Auditing Standards*

AICPA

2

Quality Control and the Audit Process

STUDY OBJECTIVES

The study objectives of this chapter are to acquire an understanding of quality control in auditing, the audit process, and audit planning. To achieve these objectives, it is necessary for the reader to

- Understand the applicability of generally accepted auditing standards (GAAS) to quality control.
- Appreciate the nature and importance of the first four GAAS.
- Recognize the responsibilities of the accounting firm for quality control.
- Comprehend the nature and role of peer reviews.
- Know the three principal parts of the audit process.
- Realize the essential considerations involved in audit planning.

Quality control applies to every phase of the auditor's examination and to the writing of the auditor's report. This chapter is divided into three sections: (1) quality control, (2) overview of the audit process, and (3) audit planning. The scope of the chapter extends to four generally accepted auditing standards (GAAS): the three general standards and the first standard of field work.

QUALITY CONTROL

Every profession emphasizes the quality of the services it renders, and the public accounting profession is no exception. The quality of audit services rests on two sets of standards: GAAS that relate to the conduct of individual audit engagements, and *quality control standards* that pertain to the conduct of an accounting firm's audit practice as a whole. These standards are closely related since a firm also must comply with GAAS in its audit engagements. Thus, quality control in auditing is the responsibility of the individual auditor and the accounting firm, as shown in Figure 2-1.

Nature of the General Standards

The three general standards relate to the character and conduct of the auditor and the quality of his work. Thus, they are personal standards that apply equally to all phases of field work and reporting. Each of the general standards is explained below.

Technical Training and Proficiency

In every profession, there is a premium on technical competence. Consider, for example, the training and proficiency required to be a physician, attorney, or dentist. Similar demands for competence are made on members of the public accounting profession. Because of the need for accountability in all segments of society, auditors are expected to be expert in both accounting and auditing and to render service to their clients with a high degree of professionalism.

The first general standard states:

> The examination is to be performed by a person or persons having adequate technical training and proficiency as an auditor.

The competency of the auditor is determined not only by education and practical experience but also by his skill and efficiency in doing his work. Accordingly, this standard refers to (1) education for entry into the profession, (2) practical training and experience in auditing, and (3) continuing professional education.

Currently, an individual can enter the accounting profession with either a baccalaureate or a master's degree. However, there are indications that both

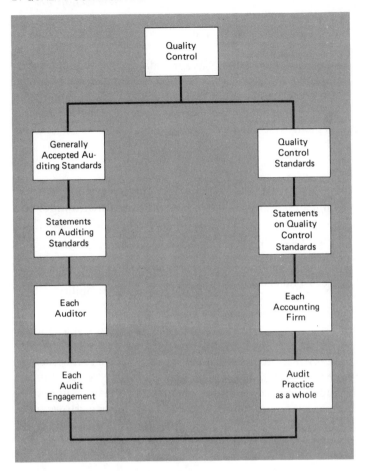

FIGURE 2–1. Quality Control Relationships in Auditing

the quantity and quality of academic preparation may be changing. The American Institute of Certified Public Accountants (AICPA) and the National Association of State Boards of Accountancy (NASBA), for example, have recommended a five-year professional academic program, and state boards of accountancy are raising academic requirements for admission to the uniform certified public accountant (CPA) examination. In addition, the American Assembly of Collegiate Schools of Business (AACSB), a private sector organization which accredits business schools, has (with the full cooperation of the accounting profession) recently established standards for accreditation of accounting programs. The first programs were accredited in 1982.

Training and experience in auditing are indispensable if an individual is to acquire proficiency as an auditor. All international and national accounting firms and some regional and local firms have their own formal staff training programs. Others may send new employees to training programs offered by the AICPA, state societies, and other professional groups. Practical experience is acquired by doing auditing work under the supervision of an experienced auditor.

More than three-fourths of the states have mandatory continuing professional education requirements for CPAs in their accountancy laws, and many others encourage such education. Typically, the CPA is required to complete 120 hours of such education over a three-year period with a minimum of 20 hours in any one year as a prerequisite for the renewal of his license.

Independence

Competency and technical training alone are not sufficient for an auditor. An auditor must also be free of client influence in performing his work. Thus, the second general standard stipulates:

> In all matters relating to the assignment, an independence in mental attitude is to be maintained by the auditor or auditors.

This standard likens the auditor's role to that of an umpire in a baseball game, an arbitrator in labor disputes, or a one-man grand jury in a criminal indictment.

Two factors are critical to independence, and neither is precisely measurable. One is the individual's character; the other is the public's acceptance of that individual. For example, an arbitrator may be intellectually honest and completely neutral on the issue he is arbitrating. However, if one side or the other regards him as pro-labor or pro-management, the arbitrator's effectiveness is correspondingly reduced. Thus, the auditor must not only be independent in fact but also be *recognized or accepted* by the public as being independent.

Independence in fact is a state of mind. This aspect of independence is determined by personal attributes and integrity, and cannot be judged by tangible criteria. Independent auditors should maintain an attitude of judicial impartiality or objectivity, recognizing an obligation for fairness not only to management but to all interested users of their reports.

To maintain public confidence and acceptance, independent auditors must avoid situations that might cause reasonably informed individuals to believe that their independence might be impaired. An auditor could perform an unbiased audit of a company of which he is a principal stockholder or director, but the public would likely believe that a conflict of interest exists that impairs the objectivity of the examination and the audit report.

The requirements for independence extend beyond GAAS. The Code of Professional Ethics of the AICPA and the regulations of the Securities and Exchange Commission (SEC) both have specific rules pertaining to independence, as is discussed in later chapters.

Two contemporary developments pertaining to independence merit comment: (1) the use of audit committees and (2) the rendering of management advisory services to audit clients.

Audit committees. As indicated in Chapter 1, many corporations now have audit committees composed of outside members of the board of directors. The independence of the auditor is believed to be strengthened by an audit committee. The functions of an audit committee that impact most directly on the auditor are:

- Nominating the public accounting firm to conduct the annual audit.
- Discussing with the auditor the scope of his examination.
- Inviting direct auditor communication on material problems encountered during the course of the audit.
- Reviewing the financial statements and the auditor's report with the auditor on completion of the engagement.

An audit committee serves as an important intermediary between management and the auditor. Consequently, it provides greater confidence to stockholders and others that every effort is being made to have an independent examination of management's financial statements.

Audit committees have been endorsed by the AICPA, the American Stock Exchange, and the SEC, and they are required by the New York Stock Exchange. In the past decade, the proportion of publicly held companies with audit committees has increased significantly.

Management advisory services. Concern has been expressed in some segments of the government and academic communities that the rendering of management advisory services (MAS) to an audit client by an auditor impairs the auditor's independence. This position is based on the belief that the auditor would be reviewing his own work and might not be unbiased in doing so.

The AICPA has consistently maintained that MAS are entirely compatible with independence as long as the CPA serves only as an adviser to management in making the management services decision. If the auditor is the decision-maker, audit independence is impaired. To date, there have been no known instances where management advisory services have compromised independence.[1] However, a CPA firm that is a member of the SEC Practice Section, which is described on page 47, is required to refrain from performing the following MAS for its SEC audit clients:[2]

- Psychological testing.
- Public opinion polls.
- Merger and acquisition assistance for a finder's fee.
- Executive recruitment.
- Actuarial services to insurance companies.

[1] Commission on Auditors' Responsibilities, *Report, Conclusions, and Recommendations* (New York: American Institute of Certified Public Accountants, 1978), p. 102.

[2] SEC Practice Section, Division for CPA Firms, *Peer Review Manual,* Revised Edition (New York: American Institute of Certified Public Accountants, 1981), pp. 1-9.

Due Professional Care

Just as the patient expects the physician to follow professional standards of care in performing a physical examination and rendering a diagnosis, so the client and the general public expect the auditor to exercise due care throughout the auditing process.

The third general standard states:

> Due professional care is to be exercised in the performance of the examination and the preparation of the report.

Note that this standard involves both the standards of field work and the standards of reporting.

Criteria for judging the care exercised by a professional are based primarily on custom, convention, and judgment in the light of the attendant circumstances rather than on a list of universally accepted steps or procedures. For example, the surgeon is expected to be qualified to perform the operation, have qualified nurses and assistants on hand, and order blood transfusions if needed. Similarly, an auditor is expected to be competent, have sufficient help to complete the examination, and modify his audit plan, if necessary, as the audit progresses.

An auditor who accepts glib answers from management on important questions, overlooks the obvious, or fails to complete major portions of the audit examination is not exercising due care. Nor is the auditor whose report has findings that are not supported by the evidence obtained during his examination or whose report omits relevant data known to him. Due care has been an issue in many legal suits brought against auditors, as is explained in Chapter 19.

The standard of due care requires critical review of both the work done and the judgment exercised by those assisting in the examination. This standard has been associated with the image of a prudent, reasonably competent practitioner whose degree of skill is taken as the standard of measurement whenever the quality of performance of a fellow practitioner is questioned.[3] In acting as a prudent practitioner, an auditor should

- Take steps to obtain any knowledge readily available that will enable him to foresee unreasonable risk and to identify material items.
- Consider any unusual circumstances or relationships in planning and performing his examination.
- Take all appropriate steps to remove from his own mind any doubtful impressions or unanswered questions considered material to expression of an opinion.
- Keep abreast of developments in the field of auditing and accounting.
- Recognize the necessity for both the supervision and review of the work of his assistants.

[3] Robert K. Mautz and Hussein A. Sharaf, *The Philosophy of Auditing* (Sarasota: American Accounting Association, 1961), p. 132.

AICPA Quality Control Review Division

This Division was established in 1978. Through its senior technical committee, the Quality Control Standards Committee, the Division is responsible for

- Developing quality control standards for auditing and accounting and review services of CPA firms.
- Issuing statements on quality control standards.
- Administering the AICPA's voluntary peer review program.

In addition, the Division works closely with the peer review committees of the SEC and Private Companies Practice Sections of the AICPA Division for CPA Firms, described later in this chapter.

Quality Control Considerations for a CPA Firm

A CPA firm should establish quality control policies and procedures to provide it with reasonable assurance of conforming with GAAS in its audit engagements.[4] A firm's system of quality control also extends to the conduct of its audit practice as a whole. Guidance for appropriate quality controls is provided by the Quality Control Standards Committee. The initial pronouncement of this committee contains nine elements of quality control for a CPA firm:[5]

- Independence.
- Assigning personnel to engagements.
- Consultation.
- Supervision.
- Hiring.
- Professional development.
- Advancement.
- Acceptance and continuance of clients.
- Inspection.

These elements apply to all firms. However, the measures taken by a firm to meet the guidelines may vary because of its size, organizational structure, and operating philosophy. While the elements are discussed separately below, the reader should realize that they are interrelated.

---

[4] Auditing Standards Board, *Codification of Statements on Auditing Standards* (New York: American Institute of Certified Public Accountants, 1983). Auditing Section 161.02 (hereinafter referred to and cited as AU §).

[5] Quality Control Standards Committee, *Statement on Quality Control Standards No. 1* (New York: American Institute of Certified Public Accountants, November 1979), p. 3.

Independence

The importance of independence in auditing has already been stressed. This element of control is designed to assure that persons at all organizational levels within the firm be independent both in fact and in appearance.

To meet this quality control objective, a CPA firm may keep records of professional staff previously employed by clients or who have relatives in key client positions. In addition, audit personnel should be notified as to the names of audit clients having publicly held securities, and there should be periodic confirmation with personnel that financial interests do not exist. The firm should also continuously emphasize the importance of independence of mental attitude in training programs, in the performance of the work, and in the writing of the audit report. The rotation of audit staff and audit partners for a given client also enhances independence.

Assigning Personnel to Engagements

This element is designed to assure that audit work will be performed by persons having the degree of technical training and proficiency required by the engagement.

The steps that a firm may take to meet this objective are: (1) annual planning for the total professional staff needs of all the firm's audit engagements, (2) timely identification of staffing requirements on specific engagements, and (3) use of time budgets in determining manpower requirements and in scheduling the audit work.

Consultation

The objective of this quality control element is to provide assurance that the auditor will seek assistance on accounting and auditing questions, when necessary, from persons having appropriate expertise, judgment, and authority. The need for consultation will vary with the complexity of the audit engagement and the competence of the auditor. Consultation may occur both inside and outside the firm.

Within a firm, individuals who possess the training and experience may be designated as an SEC or industry expert or be recognized as the senior technical partner in accounting or auditing. A firm should also maintain a technical reference library, and, where resources permit, a research staff. Outside the firm, assistance may be obtained from the AICPA's Technical Information Service and similar services provided by some state CPA societies.

Supervision

There should be supervision at all organizational levels within a firm to assure that the work performed meets the firm's standards of quality. In this context, supervision refers to the procedures adopted by a firm in reviewing the work done on audit engagements. This responsibility is distinct from the first standard of field work, which requires an experienced auditor to supervise the work of assistants during the course of a particular engagement. This standard will be discussed later in the chapter.

In meeting this objective, the procedures usually apply both before and after the fact. The former may include direction as to the form and content of working papers and the use of audit programs, checklists, and questionnaires. The latter may consist of the review of working papers by supervisory personnel, and the review of the auditor's report and the client's financial statements by a partner who did not participate directly in the audit engagement.

Hiring

The quality of audit work is directly affected by the integrity, competence, and motivation of audit personnel. The objective of this element is to assure that the firm hires personnel who possess the characteristics that enable them to perform competently. A firm's recruiting policies and procedures are vital in meeting this objective.

Hiring may occur at both beginning and advanced levels. At the entry level, a firm should establish standards of academic preparation and accomplishment; at a higher level, minimum standards of experience should be set. A firm should also have established personal standards of integrity for new employees. When new personnel are acquired through merger with another firm, there should be indoctrination programs on the firm's practices and procedures.

Professional Development

A firm has the responsibility to see that personnel have the knowledge required to enable them to fulfill assigned responsibilities. This element of quality control relates directly to the first GAAS. The emphasis here, however, is on postdegree or continuing professional education designed to keep personnel abreast of contemporary accounting and auditing issues.

The policies and procedures may include instruction during the performance of engagements, requiring personnel to attend seminars, and distribution of technical information on current developments in accounting and auditing within the firm.

Advancement

A firm's policies and procedures for advancing audit personnel should provide assurance that the individuals have the qualifications necessary to fulfill the greater responsibilities they will be called upon to assume. Advancement is important in motivating personnel. The criteria for promotion and the review procedures pertaining thereto should be clearly established and carefully followed.

In pursuing this quality control objective, a firm may require supervisory personnel to furnish periodic appraisals of assistants, increase assigned responsibilities gradually, and appoint partner review committees to decide on the qualifications of individuals being considered for promotion.

Acceptance and Continuance of Clients

This element focuses on the quality of a firm's clients. A firm should establish practices for deciding whether to accept a new client or to continue an existing client in order to minimize the likelihood of association with a client whose management lacks integrity.

For a new client, a firm's procedures should include: (1) reviewing the financial statements of the potential client, (2) inquiring of bankers and lawyers in the community as to the reputation of the proposed client, and (3) communicating with the predecessor auditor. For continuance of a professional relationship with an existing client, there should be procedures for periodically evaluating the integrity and reliability of the client.

In deciding whether to accept or to continue a client, a firm should also consider whether its professional staff has the training and proficiency to properly service the client (the first GAAS), and whether it is independent with respect to the client (the second GAAS).

Within the profession, there is some turnover of auditors. The reasons for auditor changes include

- The desire of the client for a broader range of professional services (especially management advisory expertise).
- Regular rotation policies adopted by a client.
- The desire to reduce the audit fee.
- The desire to be associated with a more prestigious firm.
- Disagreements between the client and the auditor.

In recent years, four of the largest U.S. corporations—Minnesota Mining and Manufacturing (3M), Gulf Oil, Hewlett-Packard, and RCA—have changed auditors.

Communication with predecessor auditor. The knowledge of the client acquired by the previous (or predecessor) auditor is a valuable source of information for a new auditor. Before accepting an engagement with a client that has been previously audited, the successor auditor should take the initiative to communicate with the predecessor auditor.

In the communication, the successor auditor should make specific and reasonable inquiries about matters relevant to the audit, such as the integrity of management and disagreements with management on accounting principles and auditing procedures.[6] The predecessor auditor, in turn, is expected to respond promptly and fully, assuming the client gives consent.

Information obtained in an audit is confidential, and professional ethics forbid its disclosure without the consent of the client. If the successor fails to receive a response or receives a limited response from the predecessor, he should consider the implications in deciding whether to accept the engagement.

Engagement letter. When a decision has been made to accept an initial or continuing audit engagement with a client, it is good professional practice to confirm the agreement by an engagement letter. An engagement letter is shown in Figure 2-2.

Of paramount importance in an engagement letter is a clear statement of the nature of the auditor's examination and the responsibility assumed by the auditor. In addition, the letter should include such matters as any limitations on the scope of the audit and the basis for determining the audit fee. Observe that the letter shown in Figure 2-2 also includes a commitment by the auditor to review tax returns and be available for consultation on the tax effects of transactions.

An engagement letter should contain space for the client's acceptance. It should be sent to the client in duplicate, with one copy to be signed and returned to the auditor. An engagement letter constitutes a legal contract between the auditor and the client. The engagement letter should be renewed each year because both client and accounting firm personnel may change.

Inspection

A firm should have established inspection or review practices to determine whether the policies and the procedures adopted are being effectively applied. This element can be viewed as a firm's own internal audit, or *in-house* review of its quality control procedures.

Procedures for inspection usually include designating individuals or review teams to make periodic and/or unannounced inspections of quality control practices in one or more offices within a firm. Established procedures extend to providing for appropriate follow-up of recommendations made by reviewers. The use of standardized checklists or evaluation forms facilitates the inspection.

AICPA Division for CPA Firms

In 1977, the Council of the AICPA provided for a Division for CPA Firms with two sections: the SEC Practice Section and the Private Companies Practice Section. The Division for Firms provides an organizational structure for more self-regulation within the profession. Membership in either or both sections is voluntary. Virtually all entities subject to SEC jurisdiction

---

[6] Auditing Standards Board, *op. cit.,* AU § 315.06.

REDDY & ABEL   Certified Public Accountants

March 15, 19X1

Mr. Thomas Thorp, President
Melville Co., Inc.
Route 32
Midtown, New York 11746

Dear Mr. Thorp:

This will confirm our understanding of the arrangements for our examination of the financial statements of Melville Co., Inc., for the year ending December 31, 19X1.

We will examine the Company's balance sheet at December 31, 19X1, and the related statements of income, retained earnings, and changes in financial position for the year then ended, for the purpose of expressing an opinion on them. Our examination will be in accordance with generally accepted auditing standards and will include such auditing procedures as we consider necessary to accomplish this purpose.

These procedures will include tests (by statistical sampling, if feasible) of documentary evidence supporting the transactions recorded in the accounts, tests of the physical existence of inventories, and direct confirmation of receivables and certain other assets and liabilities by correspondence with selected customers, creditors, legal counsel, and banks.

Although defalcations and similar irregularities may occasionally be disclosed by this type of examination, it is not designed for this purpose and should not be relied on to disclose fraud, should any exist. We will, of course, report to you anything that appears to us during our examination to be unusual or abnormal.

We will review the Company's Federal and State [identify states] income tax returns for the year ended December 31, 19X1. These returns, we understand, will be prepared by you. Further, we will be available during the year to consult with you on the tax effects of transactions or contemplated changes in business policies.

Our fee for this examination will be at our regular per diem rates, plus travel and other costs. Invoices will be rendered every two weeks and are payable on presentation.

We are pleased to have this opportunity to serve you. If this letter correctly expresses your understanding, please sign the enclosed copy and return it to us.

Very truly yours,

REDDY & ABEL

Ivan M. Reddy

Partner

APPROVED:

By: _____
Date: _____

FIGURE 2–2. Engagement Letter

are audited by firms that are members of the SEC Practice Section. In contrast, less than 10 percent of the practice units have elected to become members of the Private Companies Practice Section.

Each section has its own objectives, membership and peer review requirements, and governing body (executive committee). In general, the objectives and requirements of the SEC Section are more extensive than those of the Private Section. In addition, the effectiveness of the SEC Section's regulatory system is monitored and evaluated by an independent public oversight board. The objectives and membership requirements common to both sections are as follows:

Objectives
- Improve the quality of service (or practice) by CPA firms through the establishment of practice requirements for member firms.
- Establish and maintain an effective system of self-regulation of member firms by means of mandatory peer reviews, required maintenance of appropriate quality controls, and the imposition of sanctions for failure to meet membership requirements.

Membership requirements
- Adhere to quality control standards established by the AICPA Quality Control Standards Committee.
- Submit to peer reviews of the firm's accounting and audit practice every three years or at such additional times as designated by the executive committee, the reviews to be conducted in accordance with review standards established by the section's peer review committee.
- Ensure that all professionals in the firm resident in the United States, including CPAs and non-CPAs, participate in at least twenty hours of continuing professional education every year and in at least one hundred twenty hours every three years.

Independent Peer Review

One of the most significant recent developments in the public accounting profession has been the emergence of independent peer review of a firm's quality control procedures by other CPAs or other CPA firms. Peer review did not exist in the profession a decade ago, but today it affects directly or indirectly virtually every firm within the profession.

Mandatory Peer Review

As indicated previously, peer review is mandatory for SEC and Private Companies Practice Section member firms. The peer review objectives common to both sections are to determine that

- Member firms, as distinguished from individuals, are maintaining and applying quality controls in accordance with standards established by the

AICPA Quality Control Standards Committee. Reviews for this purpose include a review of working papers.
- Member firms are meeting membership requirements.

The quality control standards for peer reviews are based on the nine elements of quality control discussed earlier in the chapter. Mandatory peer review extends to a firm's accounting and auditing services but not to tax and management advisory services.

Peer reviews are conducted by review teams (1) appointed or authorized by the peer review committee of the section, (2) formed by a member firm engaged by the firm under review (currently, for example, every Big Eight firm is reviewed by another Big Eight firm), or (3) formed by an authorized entity engaged by the firm under review such as a state CPA society or an association of CPA firms. Each review team is required to report on its findings, and these reports are included in the public files of the Section. The evaluation of a firm's quality control policies and procedures is accomplished by:

- Study and evaluation of a reviewed firm's quality control system.
- Review for compliance with a reviewed firm's quality control policies and procedures by
  - Review of each organizational or functional level within the firm.
  - Review of selected engagement working paper files and reports.
- Review for compliance with membership requirements of the section.[7]

Sanctions may be imposed on firms that do not meet the quality control standards. On recommendation of the Peer Review Committee, the Executive Committee of the section has the authority to impose such sanctions as: (1) corrective measures by the firm, (2) additional continuing professional education requirements, (3) accelerated or special peer review, (4) admonishments, censures, or reprimands, (5) monetary fines, (6) suspension from membership, and (7) expulsion from membership.

Voluntary Peer Review

The AICPA has a voluntary quality control review program, whose requirements are set forth in *A Guide to Implement the Voluntary Control Review Program for CPA Firms.*

This program is available to firms that do not elect to join either the SEC or Private Companies Practice Sections. Since the establishment of the Division for Firms, no reviews have been made under this program.

---

[7] SEC Practice Section, Division for CPA Firms, *Peer Review Manual,* Revised Edition (New York: American Institute of Certified Public Accountants, 1981), pp. 2-7.

OVERVIEW OF THE AUDIT PROCESS

The audit of a small company may involve only one or a few auditors, less than 100 hours of work, and an audit fee of less than $1,000. In contrast, for a *Fortune* 500 corporation, the audit process may require scores of auditors, many thousands of hours of work, and an audit fee of several million dollars. Three separate and distinct phases can be identified in the audit process: (1) planning the audit, (2) performing the field work, and (3) reporting the findings.

Planning the Audit

Each audit should be tailored to the unique characteristics of the client. Thus, an essential starting point in the audit process is to obtain an understanding of the client's business, the industry in which it operates, and its accounting policies and procedures. In an initial audit of a client, considerable effort may be necessary to obtain this knowledge; in a recurring audit engagement, only inquiries about current year changes may be needed.

The second step in this phase of the audit process is to design detailed audit programs for the specific engagement. The programs identify the individual tasks (technically called *tests or auditing procedures*) to be performed during the examination. Next, the timing or scheduling of the work must be determined. In the typical engagement, work will be done before, at, and after the balance sheet date. The final step in planning is to assign qualified auditors to the engagement. Comprehensive consideration is given to this part of the audit process later in this chapter.

Performing the Field Work

This phase of the audit process consists primarily of executing the audit programs. Field work involves two major activities: (1) making a study and evaluation of the client's system of internal control, and (2) verifying financial statement account balances. The former is done during the year; the latter is done at or near the balance sheet date. The final step in this phase of the audit process is to evaluate the evidence obtained to determine whether there is a reasonable basis for the expression of an opinion on the financial statements under examination. The field work phase of the audit process is extensively discussed and illustrated in Chapters 4-15.

Reporting the Findings

In the final phase of the audit process, the auditor either expresses an opinion or indicates that an opinion cannot be given. If there is a reasonable basis for an opinion the auditor is required to express an opinion on the fairness of the financial statements, using generally accepted accounting principles (GAAP) as the established criteria. The auditor reports his findings through the writing and issuing of an audit report. This phase of audit is discussed and illustrated in Chapter 16.

The three phases and principal steps of the audit process in a recurring audit engagement are diagrammed in Figure 2-3.

AUDIT PLANNING

It is now appropriate to explain in some detail the major considerations involved in audit planning. The first standard of field work states:

> The work is to be adequately planned and assistants, if any, are to be properly supervised.

Audit planning involves the development of an overall strategy (or game plan) for the expected conduct and scope of the examination.

Essential Planning Information

In order to adequately plan an audit engagement, the auditor should consider

- Matters relating to the entity's business and the industry in which it operates.
- The entity's accounting policies and procedures.
- Anticipated reliance on internal controls.
- Preliminary estimates of materiality levels for audit purposes.
- Financial statement items likely to require adjustment.
- Conditions that may require extension or modification of audit tests, such as the possibility of material errors or irregularities.
- The nature of reports expected to be rendered (e.g., a report on consolidated or consolidating financial statements, reports on financial statements filed with the SEC, or special reports such as those on compliance with contractual provisions.[8]

A variety of techniques are used by an auditor to acquire the essential data. Those with the widest application are discussed below.

Communicating with the Audit Committee

One of the primary functions of an audit committee is to discuss the scope of the examination with the auditor. The communication is a two-way street. On the one hand, the audit committee seeks information as to the auditor's plans for the audit, including critical dates, scheduling, and staffing of the engagement. On the other hand, the auditor desires information from the committee about special areas of concern. For example, the audit committee may wish to have selected plants, divisions, or types of transactions included in the audit program because of possible weaknesses in internal

---

[8] Auditing Standards Board, *op. cit.,* AU § 311.03 (adapted).

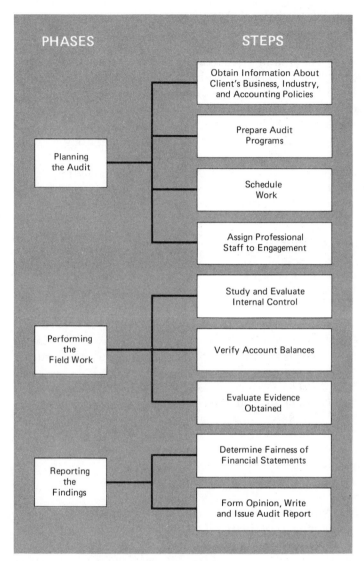

FIGURE 2–3. Diagram of Audit Process

control. Similarly, the committee may request expanded audit coverage of recently acquired subsidiaries and new EDP systems applications.

The audit committee may also ask the auditor to perform services that are not part of a financial statement audit. These may involve (1) reviews of compliance with specific company policies and (2) efficiency studies of selected activities. Ordinarily, these additional services are considered in planning the regular audit to achieve maximum efficiency in the overall engagement.

Communicating with the Predecessor Auditor

As indicated earlier in this chapter, the successor auditor should communicate with the predecessor auditor prior to accepting the engagement. Information obtained in this manner may also be helpful in planning the initial audit. In addition, the successor auditor's examination may be facilitated by (1) making specific inquiries of the former auditor regarding matters that the successor believes may be relevant to the initial examination and (2) reviewing the predecessor's working papers.[9] The successor should ask the client to authorize the predecessor to give the successor access to the predecessor's working papers. The review of working papers is normally limited to matters of continuing accounting significance such as analyses of balance sheet accounts and schedules pertaining to contingencies.

Reviewing Industry and Business Data

Information about the industry in which the client operates may be obtained from industry data accumulated by the auditing firm, industry audit guides prepared by the AICPA, industry publications, and discussions with designated industry specialists within the firm. The AICPA, for example, has published audit guides on approximately twenty industries, such as banks, investment companies, colleges and universities, and construction contractors.

The auditor should also be familiar with the client's business, its organization, its operating characteristics, and the economic environment in which it operates. To obtain this knowledge, it may be necessary to

- Review the articles of incorporation and bylaws.
- Read the minutes of directors' and stockholders' meetings.
- Analyze recent financial statements, tax returns, and reports to regulatory agencies.
- Determine which governmental regulations are applicable.
- Report important continuing contracts.

The information obtained should be documented by the auditor and retained in a file for use in subsequent examinations.

Touring Client Operations

A tour of the operating facilities and offices is a significant help to an auditor in obtaining knowledge about a new client's business. From a tour of the plant, an auditor should become familiar with the layout of the plant, the operating (manufacturing) process, storage facilities, and potential trouble

---

[9] Auditing Standards Board, *op. cit.,* AU § 315.08.

spots, such as unlocked storerooms, obsolete materials, and excessive scrap.

During a tour of the office, an auditor should become knowledgeable about the types and locations of the accounting records and EDP facilities, and the work habits of personnel. An important by-product of both tours is the opportunity to meet personnel who occupy key positions within the client's organization. The auditor should document the information obtained from plant and office tours.

Reviewing the Client's Accounting Policies and Procedures

A company's accounting policies and procedures are often summarized in an accounting manual. From a study of the manual, the auditor can obtain an understanding of the client's accounting system and gain some insights into its system of internal control. In addition, the auditor may be able to identify accounting policies that are unique to the company or the industry in which the client operates. During this review, the auditor should also consider the applicable effects of accounting pronouncements on the client's financial statements. In a repeat engagement, a review of last year's audit should be helpful.

Performing an Analytical Review

Analytical review procedures involve a study and comparison of relationships among financial statement data. Methods used may range from ratio to regression analysis. The purpose of analytical review procedures is to determine the reasonableness of the financial statement relationships and identify significant fluctuations in such data. When used in planning, these procedures enable the auditor to make a preliminary assessment of financial statement items and relationships that may require either greater or less consideration during the examination. For example, an abnormal fluctuation in the gross profit rate might suggest the need for extended audit procedures for sales and inventories.

In the planning phase of the audit, comparisons of financial data may be made with corresponding budget data, data of one or more preceding years, and relevant industry data. The uses of analytical review procedures in other phases of the audit are explained in later chapters.

Making Inquiries of Management

Discussions with management may reveal current business developments affecting the entity that may have audit significance. Moreover, areas of particular interest to management may be discussed.

The discussions with management should also determine whether client personnel may be able to prepare schedules and analyses for the auditor. The following are illustrative of the tasks assignable to client personnel:

- Preparing a trial balance of the general ledger.
- Reconciling control and subsidiary accounts.
- Aging accounts receivable (i.e., current, thirty days past due, etc.).
- Preparing schedules of insurance policies in force, notes receivable, and plant assets.

Material prepared by the client must be so identified (usually by the letters PBC to signify "Prepared by Client") and must be reviewed and tested for accuracy and completeness by the auditor.

In audit planning, the auditor also considers the effect of an internal auditing function on the examination. In some cases, the work of internal auditors can be used to supplement the work of the independent auditor.

Audit Programs

An important part of planning is the writing of audit programs. Audit programs are listings of the auditing procedures to be performed during field work. Different audit programs are required in the study and evaluation of internal control than in the verification of account balances. The procedures to be performed should be set forth in reasonable detail. A partial audit program for the verification of cash is illustrated in Figure 2-4.

Audit programs serve a number of purposes in an examination. They provide

- An outline of the work to be done and instructions as to how it is to be accomplished.
- A basis for coordinating, supervising, and controlling the audit.
- A record of the work done.

ABC COMPANY

CASH

Working Paper Reference	Audit Procedures	Done by	
		Staff	Date
	1. Obtain or prepare summary of cash balances. 2. Count cash on hand. 3. Verify client prepared reconciliation of bank balance. 4. Confirm bank balances. 5. Obtain and use bank cutoff statement.		

FIGURE 2–4. Partial Audit Program

Audit programs should be tailored to meet the particular needs of each engagement. Their basic design is determined during the planning of the examination, but programs should be modified throughout the examination as conditions warrant. Audit programs should not be viewed as unalterable flight plans or inflexible blueprints. Modification of original programs may be necessary to assure that the examination is made in accordance with GAAS.

Audit Programs in Initial Engagements

The design of audit programs for new clients is complicated by uncertainties that are not present in a recurring engagement. For example, the auditor may not be able to obtain a good understanding of the strengths and weaknesses of the company's internal controls, the actual complexity of the client's transactions, or the number of problem areas. The design of the audit program in such cases may be done in stages, beginning with a list of procedures to be followed to study and evaluate the client's internal control system. When this phase of the examination is completed, the program for the remainder of the audit can be developed.

In initial engagements, two additional audit concerns must be recognized in designing programs: (1) determining the propriety of the account balances at the beginning of the period being examined and (2) ascertaining the accounting principles used in the preceding period as a basis for determining the consistency of application of such principles in the current year.

Audit Programs in Recurring Examinations

In a repeat engagement, the auditor has access to audit programs used in the preceding year(s) and the working papers pertaining to those programs. From a review of such data and his experience and knowledge of the client, the auditor should have sufficient information to design both the interim and the year-end audit programs for the current year prior to performing any field work. For example, he should be aware of troublesome areas and unusual items in the past, and be able to anticipate the likelihood of similar problems recurring in the current year.

When the year-end audit program is prepared prior to field work, certain assumptions are made about the strengths and weaknesses of the client's internal controls. If audit tests of internal controls substantiate these assumptions, the program can remain unchanged. However, if the assumptions prove to be incorrect, modifications of the program will be necessary.

Scheduling the Work

Early appointment of the auditor facilitates the planning of the work and is beneficial to both the auditor and the client. Early planning results in better scheduling of the audit work, expedites the execution of the audit program, and permits the rendering of the audit report at an earlier date. Scheduling includes the timing of the audit work.

Audit tests may be performed at almost any time during the year. It is customary to classify the time frames of an audit into two categories: (1) interim work and (2) year-end work. The former is usually associated with work done two to six months before the end of the client's fiscal year. The latter refers to work done at or near the balance sheet date. Much of the year-end work is, in fact, done after the balance sheet date.

Interim work is primarily (but not exclusively) concerned with audit tests that pertain to the study and evaluation of internal control. A substantial part of the auditor's examination may be done at interim dates. Year-end work is primarily (but not exclusively) concerned with the verification of financial statement balances.

The time dimensions of an audit engagement are graphically portrayed in Figure 2-5. The time frames are intended to suggest that the related activity would be done during that period of time rather than the length of time that should be allocated to the given activity.

The February 15 date in this example is of considerable importance. It marks the end of the auditor's basic responsibilities under GAAS. The time period from this date to the issuance of the report relates to the preparation and processing of the audit report. In the audit of RCA Corporation, which has a December 31 closing, audit planning is done in April and May, internal control work is performed from July through September, verification of balances occurs primarily from November through early February, and the audit report is generally issued in late February.

The timing of audit work also involves other considerations. In some

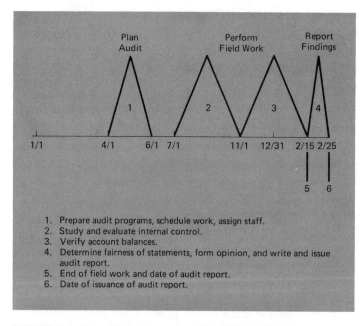

1. Prepare audit programs, schedule work, assign staff.
2. Study and evaluate internal control.
3. Verify account balances.
4. Determine fairness of statements, form opinion, and write and issue audit report.
5. End of field work and date of audit report.
6. Date of issuance of audit report.

FIGURE 2–5. Time Dimensions of an Audit Engagement

instances, there is a need for simultaneous examination of related items. For example in a count of cash, both cash and negotiable instruments must be controlled by the auditor until all items have been counted. In other cases, an unannounced performance of an auditing procedure may be appropriate. Thus, the audit program may call for a surprise count of cash on hand. Alternatively, the timeliness of the procedure may be important. A count of securities on hand ten days after the balance sheet date does not establish the securities on hand at the statement date unless measures are taken to prevent substitutions in the intervening period.

While early appointment is preferable, it is permissible for the auditor to accept an engagement late in the year or even after the year-end date. Late appointment, however, may preclude the performance of some tests and adversely affect the nature and timing of other tests.

Assignment of Professional Staff

From knowledge of the client's business and the planned audit program, the auditor is in a position to determine the professional staff needs for the engagement. In making staff assignments, consideration should be given to the composition of the audit team in terms of overall responsibility, supervision, and technical expertise. Staff assignments should also be coordinated with the nature and timing of the audit tests to be performed.

A typical audit team consists of

- A partner who has both overall and final responsibility for the engagement.
- One or more managers who coordinate and supervise the execution of the audit program.
- One of more seniors who may have responsibility for parts of the audit program and who supervise and review the work of staff assistants.
- Staff assistants who perform most of the required procedures.

The audit team ordinarily has backup resource staff in the accounting firm, as needed, such as an EDP expert, a tax specialist, and an industry expert.

Audit Supervision

Planning and supervision are closely related. Both planning and supervision continue throughout the engagement, and they frequently overlap. Supervision involves directing the work of less experienced auditors while the audit engagement is in progress. It includes: (1) instructing assistants as to the objectives of the procedures they are to perform, (2) keeping informed of significant problems encountered in performing the procedures, (3) reviewing the work done, and (4) dealing with differences of opinion among members of the audit staff.[10] This requirement applies to every level of supervision.

[10] Auditing Standards Board, *op. cit.*, AU § 311.09.

This standard is not satisfied by just reviewing working papers and other "after the fact" discussions and evaluations of the work done by assistants. Supervision requires the supervisor to watch, analyze, witness, and question the work of assistants as it is being done. Such factors as the complexity of the engagement and the technical training and experience of the assistants will influence the nature and extent of the supervision appropriate in a given instance.

CONCLUDING COMMENTS

Quality control is essential if users of audited financial statements are to continue to have confidence in the audit function. Through GAAS and peer reviews, the public accounting profession is earnestly striving to maintain high standards of quality in the performance of an audit.

Both the individual auditor and the accounting firm have a vital role in quality control. However, in the final analysis, the primary responsibility rests with the individual auditor. The concept of a prudent practitioner is indispensable. Those who aspire to careers in public accounting should be fully aware that they will be held to high standards of performance. Some guidance in properly planning an audit has been given in this chapter. Our concern with the audit process continues in the next chapter, with a consideration of audit evidence.

REVIEW QUESTIONS

2–1.   a. Identify the two sets of standards that pertain to quality control.
　　　　b. Explain the relationship between the standards in an audit engagement.
2–2.   a. Explain the nature of the general standards.
　　　　b. What factors are involved in the first general standard?
2–3.   What factors are important in determining whether an auditor is independent (a) in fact and (b) in appearance?
2–4.   What are the functions and potential advantages of audit committees?
2–5.   a. What is involved in the standard of due professional care?
　　　　b. How does this standard pertain to other categories of GAAS?
2–6.   What actions are necessary to be a prudent practitioner?
2–7.   What are the responsibilities of the AICPA Quality Control Review Division?
2–8.   Identify the nine elements of quality control and give the primary objective of each.
2–9.   What procedures should be used by a firm in determining whether to accept a new client?
2–10. What are the principal responsibilities of (a) the successor and (b) the predecessor auditor pertaining to communication between the two parties?
2–11. Indicate the importance and content of an engagement letter.
2–12. What are the common (a) objectives and (b) membership requirements of the SEC and Private Companies Practice Sections?
2–13. What sanctions may be imposed on firms that do not meet the quality control standards under the Division for CPA Firms?
2–14. Identify the three phases of the audit process and indicate the time frame when each is performed.
2–15. What steps are involved in audit planning?
2–16. What information is useful in audit planning?

2-17. What techniques may be used to acquire the essential information in planning?

2-18. a. Describe the nature and content of audit programs.
b. What purposes are served by audit programs?

2-19. Distinguish between interim and year-end work and indicate the primary activity associated with each.

2-20. What considerations are involved in audit supervision?

COMPREHENSIVE QUESTIONS

2-21. Four GAAS and nine quality control standards are included in this chapter. Listed below are items pertaining to one or both of these sets of standards.

1. Being unbiased during the audit. *Independence*
2. Preparing an audit program. *Planning*
3. Taking continuing professional education courses. *Competency*
4. Communicating with predecessor auditor before accepting engagement. *Due Care*
5. Being a prudent practitioner. *due Care*
6. Evaluating qualifications of audit personnel. *Competency*
7. Directing less qualified assistants. *due care or planning*
8. Assigning professional staff to engagement. *planning*
9. Scheduling the audit work. *planning*
10. Touring client operations.
11. Reviewing work done by assistants. *due care*
12. Designating an SEC expert for the engagement. *competency*
13. Employing top accounting graduates. *competency*
14. Obtaining help from a statistical sampling expert. *competency, due care*

Required
a. Indicate the essence of each of the first four GAAS.
b. Identify the auditing standard(s) that relate to each of the above items.
c. Identify the quality control element, if any, that relates to each item.

2-22. For many years, the financial and accounting community has recognized the importance of the use of audit committees and has endorsed their formation.
At this time, the use of audit committees has become widespread. Independent auditors have become increasingly involved with audit committees and consequently have become familiar with their nature and function.

Required
a. Describe what an audit committee is.
b. Identify the reasons why audit committees have been formed and are currently in operation.
c. What are the functions of an audit committee?

AICPA

2-23. Nine elements of quality control are identified in this chapter. Listed below are specific policies and procedures pertaining to quality control:

1. Keeping records of professional staff who have relatives in key client positions.
2. Designating one individual as an SEC or industry expert.
3. Reviewing working papers.
4. Using time budgets in determining manpower requirements and in scheduling field work.
5. Appraising periodically the competency of assistants.
6. Inquiring of bankers and lawyers as to the reputation of a proposed client.
7. Establishing standards of academic preparation and accomplishment at the entry level in the firm.

8. Requiring personnel to attend seminars.
9. Appointing review teams to inspect quality control practices in different offices within a firm.

Required

a. Identify the quality control element to which each policy and procedure relates.
b. Opposite your answer in (a), indicate one additional policy and procedure that pertains to the quality control element you have identified.

2–24. A CPA has been asked to audit the financial statements of a company for the first time. All preliminary verbal discussions and inquiries have been completed between the CPA, the company, the predecessor auditor, and all other necessary parties. The CPA is now preparing an engagement letter.

Required

a. List the items that should be included in the typical engagement letter in these circumstances.
b. Describe the benefits derived from preparing an engagement letter.
c. Who should prepare and sign the engagement letter?
d. When should the engagement letter be sent?
e. Why should the engagement letter be renewed periodically?

AICPA (adapted)

2–25. The CPA firm of Test & Check has been appointed auditors for the XYZ Corporation by the company's audit committee. The engagement is limited to making an audit of the company's financial statements. The audit fee is to be at the firm's regular per diem rates plus travel costs. To confirm the arrangements, Test & Check sends the following engagement letter.

March 10, 19X1

Mr. D. R. Brink, Controller
XYZ Corporation
Maintown, ME. 03491

Dear Mr. Brink:

This will confirm our understanding of the arrangements for our review of the financial statements of XYZ Corporation Inc., for the year ending December 31, 19X1.

We will examine the Company's balance sheet at December 31, 19X1, and the related statements of income, retained earnings, and changes in financial position for the year then ended, for the purpose of auditing them. Our examination will be in accordance with generally accepted auditing standards and will include such auditing procedures as we consider necessary to express an unqualified opinion.

These standards will include tests (by statistical sampling) of documentary evidence supporting the transactions recorded in the statements, tests of the physical existence of inventories, and direct confirmation of receivables and certain other assets and liabilities by correspondence with selected customers, creditors, legal counsel, and banks.

Although defalcations and similar irregularities should be uncovered by this type of examination, it is not designed for this purpose and we therefore cannot guarantee this result. We will, of course, report to you anything that looks suspicious to us during our examination.

Our fee for this examination will be on a cost plus basis, including travel costs. Invoices will be rendered every two weeks and are payable on presentation.

If this letter correctly expresses your understanding, please sign the enclosed copy and return it to us.

Very truly yours,

Test & Check, CPAs

M. E. Test

Partner

Approved:
By _____
Date _____

Required

List the deficiences in the engagement letter. For each deficiency, indicate the proper wording. Use the following format for your answer—do not write a proper engagement letter:

Deficiency	Proper Wording

2–26. The AICPA Division for CPA Firms provides for an SEC Practice Section and a Private Companies Practice Section.

Required
a. Identify the similarities in objectives between the two sections.
b. Enumerate the requirements of membership that are common to both sections.
c. Indicate the responsibilities and functions of the peer review teams that are common to both sections.
d. Identify the similarities in peer review objectives between the two sections.
e. Enumerate the types of sanctions that are applicable to both sections.

2–27. You are meeting with executives of Cooper Cosmetics Corporation to arrange your firm's engagement to examine the Corporation's financial statements for the year ending Decembere 31, 19X3. One executive suggests that the audit work be divided among three audit staff members, with one man examining asset accounts, a second examining liability accounts, and the third examining income and expense accounts in order to minimize audit time, avoid duplication of staff effort, and curtail interference with company operations.

Required
a. To what extent should a CPA follow the client's suggestions for the conduct of an audit? Discuss.
b. List and discuss the reasons why audit work should not be assigned solely according to asset, liability, and income and expense categories.

AICPA (adapted)

2–28. Johnson, Inc., a closely held company, wishes to engage Norr, CPA, to examine its annual financial statements. Johnson was generally pleased with the services provided by its prior CPA, Diggs, but thought the audit work performed was too detailed and interfered excessively with Johnson's normal office routines. Norr asked

Johnson to inform Diggs of the decision to change auditors but Johnson did not wish to do so.

Required
a. List and discuss the steps Norr should follow before accepting the engagement.
b. What additional procedures should Norr perform on this first-time engagement over and beyond those Norr would perform on the Johnson engagement of the following year?

AICPA

2–29. The audit process may be divided into three categories: planning the audit, performing the field work, and reporting the findings. Within these categories, the following specific steps must be performed in an audit engagement.

1. Evaluate evidence obtained.
2. Assign professional staff to engagement.
3. Form opinion, write and issue audit report.
4. Determine fairness of financial statements.
5. Prepare audit programs.
6. Obtain information about client's business and industry.
7. Study and evaluate internal control.
8. Verify account balances.
9. Schedule the work.

Required
a. List the number corresponding to each step and indicate the category to which it relates.
b. Indicate the sequence in which the steps are performed within each category.

2–30. The first standard of field work includes adequate planning of the work.

Required
a. What is the objective of audit planning?
b. What information about the client is essential in planning?
c. Identify the principal techniques used by the auditor to obtain the essential information?
d. Explain two specific types of information that can be obtained from each of the techniques identified in (c) above.

AICPA (adapted)

2–31. In late spring of 19X4, you are advised of a new assignment as in-charge accountant of your CPA firm's recurring annual audit of a major client, the Lancer Company. You are given the engagement letter for the audit covering the calendar year December 31, 19X4, and a list of personnel assigned to this engagement. It is your responsibility to plan and supervise the field work for the engagement.

Required
Discuss the necessary preparation and planning for the Lancer Company annual audit prior to beginning field work at the client's office. In your discussion, include the sources you should consult, the type of information you should seek, the preliminary plans and preparation you should make for the field work, and any actions you should take relative to the staff assigned to the engagement. Do not write an audit program.

AICPA

2–32. You are engaged in your second annual examination of the financial statements of the Claren Corporation, a medium-sized manufacturing company with 25 stockholders that manufactures optical instruments. During the audit the following matters come to your attention.

A new controller was employed six months ago. He also serves as office manager but apparently exercises little disciplinary control over his 15 subordinates, who include a cashier, two bookkeepers, a supply room attendant, and two technicians who show the company products in a factory salesroom attached to the office. The office staff seems to be continually talking about social matters, visiting, making personal telephone calls, or engaged in other private matters that are generally indicative of inefficiency. You know that the office has fallen about three weeks behind in its accounting work for the year. On numerous occasions you have been unable to obtain answers to questions that arose during the audit because the person who could supply the information was out of the office.

Required

a. Discuss what you would do when you found that you were frequently unable to obtain answers to questions because the person who could supply the information was out of the office.
b. Discuss your responsibility for drawing attention to the apparent general inefficiency of the office operations.
c. What steps would you take if you found numerous errors in the books?
d. What effect, if any, would the errors have upon your audit opinion?

2–33. In Figure 2-5, six phases or steps of an audit are identified in a time matrix.

Required

a. Indicate in tabular form the time dimensions of each step assuming a company has a fiscal year that ends on (1) February 28 and (2) September 30.
b. Is it permissible under GAAS to accept an engagement after the fiscal year has ended?
c. What advantages are derived from early appointment of the auditor?
d. How much of the audit can be performed at interim dates?

Case Study

2–34.* Sunny Energy Applications Co. sells solar-powered swimming pool heaters. Sunny contracts 100 percent of the work to other companies. As a new company, Sunny's balance sheet has total assets of $78,000, including $24,000 of "stock subscriptions receivable." The largest asset is $42,000 worth of "unrecovered development costs." The equity side of the balance sheet is made up of $78,000 of "Common Stock Subscribed."

The company is contemplating a public offering to raise $1 million. The shares to be sold to the public for the $1 million will represent 40 percent of the then issued and outstanding stock. There are two officers-employees of the company, Mike Whale and Willie Float. Whale and Float are former officers of Canadian Brass Co. Float is being sued by the SEC for misusing funds raised by Canadian Brass in a public offering. The funds were used as compensatory balances for loans to a Physics Inc. Physics Inc. was controlled by Float and is the predecessor of Sunny Energy Applications.

Canadian Brass is being sued by the SEC for reporting improper (exaggerated) income. Float was chief executive at the time. There are many organizations engaged in researching the feasibility of using solar energy. Most of the organizations are considerably larger and financially stronger than Sunny Energy. The company has not been granted any patents which would serve to protect it from competitors.

Required
a. What potential risks may be present in this engagement?
b. What specific auditing and accounting problems appear to exist?
c. What additional information do you feel you need to know about the company?
d. Do you believe the engagement should be accepted or rejected? Why?

3 Evidential Matter/ Working Papers

STUDY OBJECTIVES

The study objectives of this chapter are to acquire an understanding of the third standard of field work which pertains to audit evidence and the importance of working papers. To achieve these objectives, it is necessary for the reader to

- Understand the nature of evidential matter.
- Recognize the factors which affect the sufficiency and competency of evidential matter.
- Know the types of corroborating information available to the auditor.
- Comprehend the auditing procedures that may be used in gathering evidence.
- Realize the effects of evidential matter on the auditor's report.
- Know the nature and purpose of working papers.

As indicated in Chapter 1, the purpose of the ordinary examination is the expression of an opinion on the fairness of the client's financial statements. To have a basis for an opinion, the auditor must gather and evaluate evidence.

This chapter focuses on the third standard of field work, which requires the auditor to obtain sufficient competent evidential matter. The chapter is divided into three sections: (1) audit evidence, (2) obtaining and evaluating evidence, and (3) working papers.

Throughout this chapter, emphasis is given to the verification of account balances. The accumulation of evidence in making a study and evaluation of internal control, as required by the second standard of field work, is explained in Chapter 4.

AUDIT EVIDENCE

Nature of Evidential Matter

In auditing, evidential matter consists of underlying accounting data (e.g., the underlying accounting or financial records) and corroborating information available to the auditor.[1] The types of evidence in each category and the relationship of the categories to the third standard of field work are shown in Figure 3-1. In an electronic data processing (EDP) system, the underlying accounting data may consist of machine-readable media such as magnetic tapes and disks. The impact of the computer on audit evidence is explained in Chapter 5.

Both categories of evidential matter are required in making an examination in accordance with generally accepted auditing standards (GAAS). It should be obvious that underlying accounting data are indispensable, for they provide the basis for the client's financial statements. However, these records may not be reliable. Thus, it is imperative that the auditor obtain supportive evidence of the reliability of the financial records. Much of this evidence is available within the client organization, but recourse to knowledgeable persons outside the company is also necessary.

Evidential Matter and Financial Statement Assertions

As indicated in Chapter 1, auditing involves gathering and evaluating evidence about assertions. In financial statement audits, assertions are the representations of management that are presented in the financial statements. These assertions may be either general or specific. The former relate to the statements taken as a whole and include the representation that the financial statements are prepared in conformity with generally accepted accounting principles (GAAP). The latter relate to the individual accounts

---

[1] Auditing Standards Board, *Codification of Statements on Auditing Standards* (New York: American Institute of Certified Public Accountants, 1983), Auditing Section 326.13 (hereinafter referred to and cited as AU §).

Nature of Evidential Matter	Third Standard of Field Work

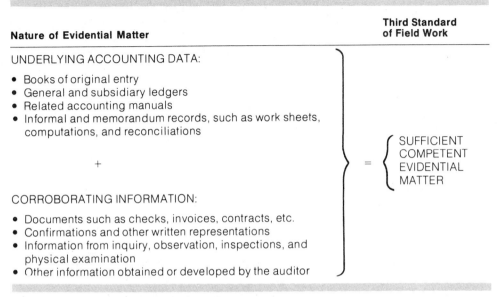

UNDERLYING ACCOUNTING DATA:

- Books of original entry
- General and subsidiary ledgers
- Related accounting manuals
- Informal and memorandum records, such as work sheets, computations, and reconciliations

+

CORROBORATING INFORMATION:

- Documents such as checks, invoices, contracts, etc.
- Confirmations and other written representations
- Information from inquiry, observation, inspections, and physical examination
- Other information obtained or developed by the auditor

= { SUFFICIENT COMPETENT EVIDENTIAL MATTER

FIGURE 3–1. Categories and Types of Evidential Matter

that are involved in the statements and include assertions that (1) cash and inventories exist, (2) notes payable are legal obligations, (3) sales are earned revenues, and (4) land is stated at historical (acquisition) cost.

An auditor normally does not obtain direct audit evidence in support of management's general assertions. Instead, he determines the fairness of the general assertions on (1) his knowledge and professional judgment and (2) audit evidence in support of the specific assertions that underlie management's overall representations. Thus, in the design and execution of the audit program for the verification of account balances, the auditor focuses on specific assertions pertaining to each account. Consideration is given to this aspect of audit evidence in Part III of this book.

Statement and Purpose of the Third Standard of Field Work

The third standard of field work states:

> Sufficient competent evidential matter is to be obtained through inspection, observation, inquiries, and confirmations to afford a reasonable basis for an opinion regarding the financial statements under examination.

Four possible courses of action that an auditor may use in obtaining evidential matter are identified in the third standard. These are examples of *auditing procedures*. At this point, it should be recognized that there are more than four auditing procedures available to the auditor. These and other procedures are explained later in the chapter. The standard also specifies that *sufficient* (i.e., enough) *competent* (i.e., reliable) evidential matter should be obtained to provide a reasonable (i.e., rational) basis for an opinion. Each of these key elements of the standard requires subjective judgment by the auditor in the specific audit engagement. Considerations that may influence the auditor's judgment are discussed below.

Sufficiency of Corroborating Information

This element of the third standard of field work pertains to the quantity of evidential matter. Considerations that may affect the auditor's judgment as to sufficiency include:

- Materiality.
- Risk.
- Economic factors.
- Size and characteristics of the population.

Materiality. Materiality refers to the relative importance of a transaction or an account balance to the financial statements under examination. A statement item is deemed to be material if knowledge of the item will affect the decision of the average intelligent reader of the financial statements. The auditor is expected to have more corroborating information for reaching a conclusion about material statement items than for immaterial items. In auditing, materiality is important in planning the examination, in doing the field work, and in reporting the findings. The auditor's consideration of materiality is a matter of professional judgment in the circumstances. In determining materiality, the auditor should consider both the qualitative and the quantitative aspects of the items.

Qualitative factors pertain primarily to the nature of an item. For example, an otherwise immaterial matter may become material when it (1) arises out of a possible conflict of interest, (2) may involve an illegal act, or (3) may be related to an irregularity.

Quantitatively, materiality is determined by the dollar significance of a financial statement item. For example, inventory in a retail company, such as J. C. Penney, is more important to the balance sheet and income statement than inventory in a service enterprise, such as American Airlines.

Percentage guidelines are often used in judging the financial statement importance of an item. The materiality criterion for income statement items is usually based on net income (or earnings per share). As a rule of thumb, an item is considered to be material if its effect is more than 10 percent of net income and immaterial if its effect is less than 5 percent. For balance sheet items, materiality is usually based on (1) the category to which the item belongs, such as current assets, (2) statement totals, or (3) key financial relationships, such as the current ratio.

The use of percentage guidelines contributes to greater consistency in determining the materiality of an item. However, the auditor should not use the guidelines as a substitute for professional judgment.

Risk. Risk pertains to the vulnerability of an item to misstatement. The amount of evidence required in a given case is proportional to the degree of risk associated with the validity and propriety of the account balance. For purposes of assessing risk, it is helpful to recognize that an account balance may result from

- Routine processing of transactions such as sales, purchases, and payroll.
- Nonroutine processing of transactions, such as those with affiliated companies, officers, and employees.
- Management judgments, such as those for product warranties, uncollectible receivables, and obsolete inventories.

The degree of risk associated with balances resulting from routine processing is inversely related to the effectiveness of the client's system of internal control. More evidence is needed by the auditor when controls are weak than when they are strong. Internal control procedures, however, may not extend to the processing of nonroutine transactions or to management judgments. The risk relating to nonroutine transactions depends on the existence and effectiveness of any specific controls. The degree of risk concerning management judgments depends largely on the integrity of management and any controls incorporated into the client's decision-making process.

Economic factors. An auditor works within economic limits which dictate that sufficient evidence must be obtained within a reasonable time and at reasonable cost. He is frequently faced with a decision as to whether the additional time and cost will produce commensurate benefits in terms of both the quantity and the quality of the evidence obtained. However, time and/or cost constraints alone are invalid reasons for not obtaining required evidence. In accepting audit engagements, an auditor should reject unreasonable client-imposed time and cost limitations. Such constraints are not conducive to making an examination in accordance with GAAS.

Population size and characteristics. Sampling is a practical necessity in the accumulation of evidential matter for many statement items. The size of a population refers to the number of items that comprise the total, as, for example, the number of credit sales transactions or the number of customer accounts in the accounts receivable ledger.

The characteristics of a population refer to the homogeneity or variability of the individual items that comprise the population. In the case of the customer accounts, one such factor is the range of the dollar amount of individual balances. The auditor may require a larger sample and more evidential matter for diverse populations than for uniform populations.

Competency of Evidential Matter

Both the competency (or reliability) of the underlying accounting data and corroborating information are involved in this aspect of the third standard of field work. The reliability of the accounting records is directly related to the effectiveness of the client's system of internal accounting control. Strong internal controls enhance the accuracy and reliability of the accounting records whereas weak internal controls often do not prevent or detect errors and irregularities in the accounting process, as is explained in Chapter 4.

The competency of corroborating information depends on many factors. The considerations that have the widest applicability in auditing are:

- Relevance.
- Source.
- Timeliness.
- Objectivity.

Relevance. This criterion means that the evidence must be pertinent to the auditor's decision. For example, if the objective is the quantity of goods on hand, the auditor can obtain relevant evidence by test counting the inventory. However, such evidence would not be relevant in determining whether the goods are owned by the client or their cost.

In executing an audit program, the auditor should be aware of the importance of this criterion. Unnecessary cost and time result when the auditor obtains irrelevant evidence. Moreover, such evidence may also lead to erroneous conclusions in forming an opinion on the client's financial statements. The importance of this criterion is highlighted in Parts II and III of this book where a framework of audit objectives is used to discuss auditing procedures and the resulting evidence obtained therefrom.

Source. The circumstances in which evidence is obtained affect the reliability of the evidence. The importance of this criterion can be illustrated by some examples. Suppose that as an auditor you seek evidence concerning the amount of cash on hand and the amount owed by customer X. For cash, you conclude that it should be counted. But by whom—you or the client? If you count it, you have direct personal knowledge of the amount on hand; if the client makes the count and gives you a report, you have indirect knowledge. Clearly, the former provides better evidence.

For the customer's balance, you can examine evidence within the client's organization, such as the shipping order and the duplicate sales invoice, or the customer could be asked to communicate directly to you the balance he owes. In this case, the latter evidence is considered to be more reliable because the respondent is a third party who is independent of the client. Moreover, the client is not able to alter the response.

For a third example, assume you are reviewing the bank reconciliation prepared by two different clients. For client A, the reconciliation is prepared by an internal auditor who is independent of the cashier and the accountant; for client B, it is prepared by the cashier who also serves as the company accountant. Greater credence would undoubtedly be given to the client A reconciliation because it was generated under a better system of internal control.

From these examples, it is possible to recognize the following presumptions about the effects of the source of the information on the reliability (competency) of evidential matter:

- When evidential matter can be obtained from independent sources outside an enterprise, it provides greater assurance of reliability for the purposes of an independent audit than that secured solely within the enterprise.
- When accounting data and financial statements are developed under satisfactory conditions of internal control, there is more assurance as to their reliability than when they are developed under unsatisfactory conditions of internal control.
- Direct personal knowledge of the independent auditor obtained through physical examination, observation, computation, and inspection is more persuasive than information obtained indirectly.[2]

Timeliness. This criterion relates to the date to which the evidence is applicable. The timeliness of the evidence is especially important in verifying current asset, current liability, and related income statement balances. For example, the auditor seeks evidence that the client has made a proper cutoff of cash, sales, and purchase transactions at the statement date. This task is facilitated when appropriate auditing procedures are applied at or near that date. Similarly, evidence obtained from physical counts at the balance sheet date provides better evidence of quantities on hand at that date than counts made at other times.

Objectivity. Evidence that is objective in nature is generally considered to be more reliable than evidence that is subjective. For example, evidence of the existence of tangible resources can be ascertained with a substantial degree of conclusiveness through physical inspection. Furthermore, evidence obtained from outside independent sources is considered to be more objective than evidence provided solely by the client.

In contrast, evidence in support of management's estimates of inventory obsolescence and product warranties may be largely subjective. In such case, the auditor should (1) consider the qualifications and integrity of the individual making the estimate, and (2) assess the appropriateness of the decision-making processes followed by the client in making the judgments.

Reasonable Basis

The auditor is not expected, or required, by the third standard of field work to have an absolute, certain, or guaranteed basis for an opinion. The requirement of a reasonable basis pertains to the overall level of assurance the auditor needs at the conclusion of the audit to express an opinion on the financial statements.

---

[2] Auditing Standards Board, *op. cit.,* AU § 326.18.

In executing an audit program, the auditor may quantify statistically the levels of assurance for individual items in the statements, as is explained in Chapter 11. It is not possible, however, to combine statistically the individual levels of assurance into an objective evaluation of overall reasonableness of the financial statements taken as a whole. Factors which influence the auditor's subjective decisions concerning reasonable basis include both professional and client considerations.

Professional considerations. Professional considerations contribute to a fairly uniform application of the quality and amount of evidence that is required. Statements on Auditing Standards (SAS) contain specific objectives to be attained during the course of an examination and provide guidance as to specific ways to achieve them. Auditors are required to justify any departure from these statements.

In the practice of public accounting, there are also two counterbalancing forces. On the one hand, competition among firms tends to make the individual firm cost- and fee-conscious. Accordingly, the firm is restrained from setting an inordinately high degree of assurance in a specific engagement since other firms may be able to perform the audit at less cost. On the other hand, the auditing firm is well aware that an inadequate basis for an opinion may result in lawsuits by those harmed by reliance on the auditor's report and sanctions by peer review committees.

Client considerations. Client considerations involve both internal and external factors. Internally, two overriding factors are the integrity of management and the existence of related party transactions. Management is responsible for the financial statement assertions, and it is also in a position to control the corroborating evidence and underlying accounting data supporting the statements. An auditor will clearly require more competent evidence when there is doubt as to the integrity of management.

Related party transactions are transactions where one of the participants is in a position to significantly influence the other participant to the extent that "arm's length" bargaining of terms and conditions is not possible. Such transactions include those between a parent company and its subsidiaries, and between a company and its management or principal stockholders. In making an examination in accordance with GAAS, the auditor is expected to be aware of the possible existence of material related party transactions. For related party transactions that are identified, the auditor should satisfy himself as to the substance of, and accounting for, such transactions, including financial statement disclosure.[3] Ordinarily, the auditor will require more competent evidence for identified related party transactions than for transactions between unrelated parties.

Externally, there are two factors. First, auditors generally believe that a higher overall level of assurance is needed for publicly held companies than for closely held companies. Not only are there more users of the auditor's

---

[3] Auditing Standards Board, *op. cit.,* AU § 335.01.

report in large corporations, but these users may rely entirely on audited statements in making investment decisions. Second, the threat of bankruptcy tends to raise the auditor's subjective evaluation of reasonable basis. In bankruptcy proceedings, creditors often seek financial relief by suing the auditors on the premise that the audited statements did not adequately forewarn them of the pending disaster. In such case, the auditor must be in a position to defend his opinion and the quality of his work.

Types of Corroborating Information

The principal types of corroborating information are:

- Physical evidence.
- Confirmations.
- Documentary evidence.
- Written representations.
- Mathematical evidence.
- Visual evidence.
- Oral evidence.
- Analytical evidence.

Each type of evidence is discussed separately below together with the circumstances where each is most relevant.

Physical Evidence

This form of evidence is widely used by the auditor in the verification of tangible asset balances. Physical evidence is obtained from physical examination of the resources. This type of evidence provides the auditor with direct personal knowledge of the existence of an item. Such evidence, however, does not establish the ownership, cost, or market value of the asset. Physical evidence will be helpful in determining quality (or condition) if the auditor is capable of making that determination. The representation of an outside expert on precious gems in a jewelry store audit would ordinarily be considered more reliable in evaluating quality than physical evidence obtained by the typical auditor.

Confirmations

Confirmations are a distinctive type of documentary evidence. They generally represent direct written responses by knowledgeable third parties to specific requests for financial information. When confirmations are obtained directly by the auditor, from third parties, they are generally considered to have a very high degree of reliability. Confirmations are especially useful in verifying the existence and accuracy of an account balance. It is common practice in an audit engagement to make extensive use of this form of evidence. The following are illustrative of the items that are frequently confirmed:

ITEM	KNOWLEDGEABLE RESPONDENT
Cash in bank	Bank
Accounts receivable	Individual customers
Inventory stored in public warehouse	Warehouse custodian
Bonds payable	Bond trustee
Lease terms	Lessor
Shares of common stock outstanding	Registrar

Documentary Evidence

This type of corroborating information includes checks, invoices, contracts, and minutes of meetings. Ordinarily, such documentation is contained in the client's files and is available to the auditor on request. The reliability of a document depends on the manner in which the document is created, how it is obtained by the auditor, and the nature of the document itself. Generalizations concerning the first two factors have already been indicated in the discussion of the competency of evidential matter.

Documentary evidence may be created outside the client organization or within it. Externally created documents may be sent directly to the auditor by the third party, or such documentation may be held by the client. The former are generally given a higher degree of reliability since the client does not have an opportunity to alter the documents.

Examples of third-party documentation that may be obtained directly by an auditor include bank statements and statements of escrow account balances held by banks. These documents will not become directly available to the auditor as a matter of course. They will be sent to the client, unless, by prearrangement, the client requests the preparer to send the document directly to the auditor. Illustrative of documents held by the client are customer purchase orders, suppliers' invoices, and tax bills.

The reliability of internally created documents depends on several factors. First is the distribution or circulation of the documents. Documents originated by the client that circulate outside the client organization are considered to be more reliable than documents that remain entirely within the company. The former include canceled checks and receipted bank deposit slips. The latter include time tickets and material requisition slips. Second is the quality of the system of internal control from which the documents are generated.

The nature of the document is important in appraising the probable existence of error or irregularity in the evidence. The amount on a manually prepared check, for example, is more easily altered than an amount that has been indelibly imprinted by a check-writing machine. Similarly, there is greater opportunity for a dishonest employee to create fictitious checks when black check forms are used than when prenumbered company checks are required.

Documentary evidence is extensively used in auditing. The auditor relies on documentation to establish the occurrence, terms, and propriety of exchange transactions, the ownership of assets, the claims of creditors, and the accuracy and completeness of the accounting records. Documentary evidence also plays a vital role in the auditor's study and evaluation of internal control, as is explained in Chapter 4.

Written Representations

A written representation is a signed statement by responsible and knowledgeable individuals about a particular account, circumstance, or event. Written representations are a form of documentary evidence. Such evidential matter may originate from within the client's organization or from external sources.

The auditor is required by GAAS to obtain certain written representations from management in meeting the third standard of field work.[4] Such representations are designed to document management's replies to inquiries made by the auditor during the audit engagement. Management representations, commonly presented in the form of a *rep letter,* may reveal information not shown in the accounting records such as the existence of contingencies that may require further investigation.

The reliability of a rep letter depends on the auditor's ability to corroborate the representations by other evidence. A rep letter is usually obtained near the end of the examination. An example of a rep letter is presented in Chapter 15 under the discussion of "Completing the Audit."

During the course of an audit, the auditor may also request written representations from outside experts. The independent auditor is not expected to possess the expertise of a lawyer in evaluating litigation pending against the client, a geologist in estimating the quantity of ore in a mine, or an appraiser of a fine arts collection. When such evidence is needed, the auditor may use the work of a specialist to obtain competent evidential matter.[5] The response may be received in the form of a letter, report, or other written communication. A relatively high degree of reliance may be placed on this type of documentation, especially when the response validates preliminary conclusions already formed by the auditor.

Mathematical Evidence

This type of evidence results from the auditor's computations or recomputations. Computations usually provide reliable evidence as to the accuracy of an amount determined by the client. This type of mathematical evidence may result from such routine tasks as checking the footings (totals) of journals and ledgers or from complicated calculations pertaining to pension

---

[4] Auditing Standards Board, *op. cit.,* AU § 333.01.
[5] Auditing Standards Board, *op. cit.,* AU § 336.04.

plans and earnings-per-share data. Mathematical evidence provides the auditor with direct personal knowledge of the arithmetical accuracy of an amount.

Visual Evidence

During the course of an examination, the auditor makes many observations. For example, he witnesses the performance of assigned responsibility and observes the security in a storeroom. This type of evidence enables the auditor to acquire direct personal knowledge concerning the matter at issue. The reliability of this evidence is limited only by the auditor's perception of what he observes.

Oral Evidence

During an examination, an auditor will make frequent oral inquiries of officers and employees of the client. Oral evidence is rarely reliable by itself. Its primary value to the auditor lies in corroborating other evidential matter and disclosing matters that may merit further investigation and documentation. Oral evidence may cover a broad range of topics, such as an interpretation of a board of directors' resolution, an explanation of the accounting treatment of a merger, and an evaluation of the collectibility of a customer's account. When an auditor uses oral evidence, it should be noted in the audit working papers. The auditor may ask management to confirm some oral data in its rep letter.

Analytical Evidence

This type of evidence involves the use of ratios and comparisons of client data with industry trends, general economic conditions, and prior and/or expected company results. Analytical evidence provides an indirect basis for supporting an inference as to the fairness of a specific financial statement item or relationship. The reliability of analytical evidence is largely dependent on the relevance of the comparable data. When industry trends and similar data provide a valid basis for comparison, the reliability of this type of evidence is enhanced.

As explained in Chapter 2, analytical data are useful in audit planning. Such data are also used in verifying account balances.

OBTAINING AND EVALUATING AUDIT EVIDENCE

Substantive Tests

The evidential matter required by the third standard of field work is obtained through two general classes of auditing procedures: (1) tests of details of transactions and balances and (2) analytical review procedures applied to financial information.[6] Collectively, these procedures are called *substantive tests*. The nature and purpose of these tests are explained below.

Tests of Transactions and Balances

These procedures are designed to obtain evidence as to the validity and propriety of the accounting treatment of transactions and balances. Conversely, their purpose is to determine the existence of any monetary errors (i.e., unintentional mistakes) or irregularities (i.e., deliberate distortions and misrepresentations) therein. A substantive test of a transaction occurs when a sales invoice is traced by the auditor to the accounting records to determine whether any monetary errors have occurred in journalizing and/or posting. Substantive tests of transactions may be performed during the year under audit or at or near the balance sheet date.

A substantive test of an account balance occurs, for example, when the auditor counts cash on hand to determine whether the amount of cash agrees with the recorded balance. Tests of balances are generally performed at or near the balance sheet date.

Analytical Review Procedures

Analytical review procedures are designed to verify the reasonableness of relationships among data and identify unusual fluctuations in such data. These procedures include:

- A comparison of the financial information with comparable information for corresponding previous period(s).
- A comparison of the financial information with anticipated results (e.g., budgets and forecasts).
- A study of the interrelationships of elements of financial information that would be expected to conform to a predictable pattern based on the entity's experience.
- A comparison of the financial information with information regarding the industry in which the entity operates.
- A study of interrelationships of financial information with relevant nonfinancial information.[7]

The foregoing may be performed in planning the audit, as explained in Chapter 2, during field work, and at or near the end of the examination (i.e., as an overall review). Analytical review procedures may involve the use of such measurement units as dollars, physical quantities, ratios, or percentages, and such techniques as trend analysis, graphs and charts, financial models, and regression analysis.

---

[6] Auditing Standards Board, *op. cit.,* AU § 318.01.
[7] Auditing Standards Board, *op. cit.,* AU § 318.06.

Analytical review procedures may be applied to (1) overall financial information of the entity, (2) financial data of subsidiaries, divisions, and segments, and (3) individual elements of financial information. The basic premise underlying analytical review procedures is that known relationships exist among data. Analytical evidence is provided by these procedures. When the results of the procedures confirm the reasonableness of the relationships, the auditor has additional corroborating information about account balances. When the reverse is true, the auditor ordinarily will require additional evidential matter in meeting the third standard of field work.

Auditing Procedures for Tests of Transactions and Balances

In making an examination in accordance with GAAS, the auditor is required to use the auditing procedures necessary in the circumstances. Auditing procedures are the acts performed by the auditor to obtain corroborating information. The procedures themselves are not evidence. The most widely used procedures in performing tests of transactions and balances are:

- Inspecting
- Observing
- Confirming
- Inquiring
- Retracing
- Recalculating
- Vouching
- Counting
- Scanning

Each procedure is discussed below. In the discussion, consideration will also be given to the types of circumstances to which each procedure is applicable.

Inspecting

Inspecting involves careful scrutiny or detailed examination of documents and physical resources. This procedure is extensively used in auditing. The inspecting of documents enables the auditor to assess the authenticity of the evidential matter or, conversely, the existence of alterations or questionable items. Examination of documents also permits a determination of the precise terms of invoices, contracts, and agreements. Through the inspection of physical resources, the auditor obtains direct personal knowledge of their existence and physical condition.

In using this procedure, the auditor seeks reasonable assurance that the document or tangible resource supports management's representations. However, the auditor is not expected to be an expert in determining the authenticity of endorsements on checks or a specialist in determining the quality of highly technical inventory components.

The inspection of documents provides a means for evaluating documentary evidence, whereas the inspection of tangible assets provides a means for evaluating physical evidence. Audit program instructions such as reviewing, reading and examining are synonymous with inspecting.

Observing

This auditing procedure pertains to watching or witnessing the performance of some activity. The activity may be the manner in which cash is safeguarded, vouchers are prepared and approved, and the care taken by the client in counting inventory. The subject matter of observation is personnel, procedures, and processes. From this observation, the auditor obtains direct personal knowledge of the activity in the form of visual evidence.

Confirming

Confirming is a form of inquiry that enables the auditor to obtain information directly from an independent source outside the client organization. In the usual case, the client makes the request of the outside party in writing, but the auditor controls the mailing of the inquiry. The request should include instructions requiring the recipient to send the response directly to the auditor. This auditing procedure produces confirmation evidence. It is extensively used in performing tests of account balances, and it may also be used in substantive tests of transactions.

Inquiring

This auditing procedure involves either oral or written inquiry by the auditor. Such inquiries may be made internally to management, as in the case of questions pertaining to the obsolescence of inventory items and the collectibility of receivables, or externally to lawyers concerning the probable outcome of litigation, and other specialists. Inquiry produces either oral evidence or evidence in the form of written representations.

Retracing

In retracing, the auditor begins with the document(s) created when the transaction is executed and proceeds to follow the evidence through the recording process. Thus, the auditor can trace a sales transaction from the receipt of the customer's order through the filling and shipping of the order, the billing of the customer, the journalizing and posting of the sale, and the summarizing and presenting of the transaction in the financial statements. This auditing procedure is extensively used in performing tests of transactions, and it is also applicable to tests of account balances. Retracing may provide a basis for determining the accuracy and completeness of the accounting records. The effectiveness of this procedure is enhanced when serially prenumbered documents are used by the client. Retracing pertains primarily to documentary evidence.

Recalculating

This procedure involves a reperformance of calculations and reconciliations made by the client. Recalculations may be made of amounts computed for depreciation, accrued interest, and unit price extensions on inventory summary sheets. In addition, the auditor will ordinarily verify the accuracy of totals on supporting schedules and reconciliations. Mathematical evidence is produced by this procedure.

Vouching

This procedure involves: (1) inspecting documents in support of transactions or financial data to determine their propriety and validity and (2) comparing the documents with the accounting records. In vouching, the auditor works from the accounting records back to the documentation that served as the basis for the entry. Notice that the direction of testing is opposite to that used in retracing. Vouching produces documentary evidence of the correctness of the accounting treatment of transactions and balances, or, conversely, of errors or irregularities therein. This procedure is extensively used.

Counting

The two most common applications of this procedure are: (1) the physical counting of tangible resources such as the amount of cash on hand and (2) accounting for all prenumbered documents. The first provides physical evidence of the quantity on hand and is used in tests of balances. The second may be used by the auditor to obtain evidence as to the completeness of the accounting records.

Scanning

The auditing procedure of scanning involves a less detailed level of scrutiny than inspection. Scanning may be described as the rapid review or *eyeballing* of documents, records, and schedules for the purpose of detecting unusual items or events that may require further audit investigation. For example, an audit program may require the auditor to scan (1) the June voucher register for unusual account classifications, and (2) additions to repairs expense for large expenditures.

Relationship of Audit Evidence and Auditing Procedures

During the course of an audit, the auditor will likely use each of the auditing procedures described above to obtain sufficient competent evidential matter.

The relationship between the types of evidential matter and auditing procedures is summarized in Figure 3-2. (Further consideration is given to these relationships in Part III of this book.)

Evaluation of Evidential Matter

The auditor should be objective, careful, and thorough in his evaluation of evidential matter. Proper evaluation of the evidence is essential to the preparation of a proper audit report. All relevant evidential matter should be considered by the auditor, regardless of whether it substantiates or negates management's financial statement assertions.

In evaluating evidence, the auditor should exercise care to limit the use of evidence to the specific assertion(s) to which it is pertinent. When this constraint is violated, an unwarranted inference is likely to occur. For example, it is not proper to infer from physical inspection of a plant asset that it is owned by the client. Similarly, the auditor should exercise care in interpreting evidential matter. This is especially true of analytical evidence where changed company operating conditions or unforeseen industry developments may negate relationships that previously were assumed to be reasonable.

The auditor should also recognize that relatively little evidential matter is absolutely conclusive. Because of economic constraints pertaining to the cost of obtaining evidence and the nature of financial statement assertions, it is usually unrealistic for the auditor to seek proof beyond all doubt. On the

Type of Evidence	Auditing Procedure	Illustrative Application of Auditing Procedure
Physical	Inspecting Counting	Inspect new warehouse Count cash on hand
Confirmation	Confirming	Confirm bank balance with bank
Documentary	Inspecting Retracing Vouching	Inspect (examine) bank statement Trace sales invoices to customers' ledger Vouch entries in check register to paid checks
Written Representations	Inquiring	Ask management for representation letter
Mathematical	Recalculating	Recompute accrued interest payable
Visual	Observing Scanning	Observe storeroom security Scan repairs expense for large expenditures
Oral	Inquiring	Ask storeroom supervisor about obsolete inventory items
Analytical	Analytical review	Compare sales with sales budget

FIGURE 3-2. Audit Evidence and Auditing Procedures

other hand, an auditor should not be satisfied with inconclusive or contradictory evidence. To have a reasonable basis for expressing an opinion, the auditor needs a preponderance (i.e., a consensus or majority) of persuasive evidence.

Effects on Auditor's Report

When the auditor has obtained sufficient competent evidential matter as required by the third standard of field work, an opinion ordinarily must be expressed on the fairness of the client's financial statements in conformity with GAAP. If the evidence supports an unqualified opinion, the auditor is able to issue a standard audit report.

However, when the auditor is unable to obtain a reasonable basis for an opinion on a material financial statement assertion, an opinion should be deferred until the necessary evidence is acquired, or a qualified opinion or disclaimer of opinion (no opinion) should be expressed on the financial statements. The choice between the latter alternatives depends on the auditor's judgment of the materiality of the assertion. The process of meeting the third standard of field work and determining the effects on the auditor's report is summarized in Figure 3-3.

WORKING PAPERS

Nature and Purpose of Working Papers

The auditor should prepare and maintain working papers. Working papers are the records kept by the auditor of the procedures applied, the tests performed, the information obtained, and the pertinent conclusions reached in the engagement.[8] Working papers provide

- The principal support for the auditor's report.
- Evidence that the examination was made in accordance with GAAS.
- A means for coordinating and supervising the examination.

Working papers should be tailored to meet the needs of the specific engagement.

Working Papers and Auditing Standards

Working papers have direct application to GAAS, as explained below.

General Standards

Working papers provide evidence of the auditor's technical training and proficiency by showing his knowledge of GAAP and his ability to apply

[8] Auditing Standards Board, *op. cit.*, AU § 339.03.

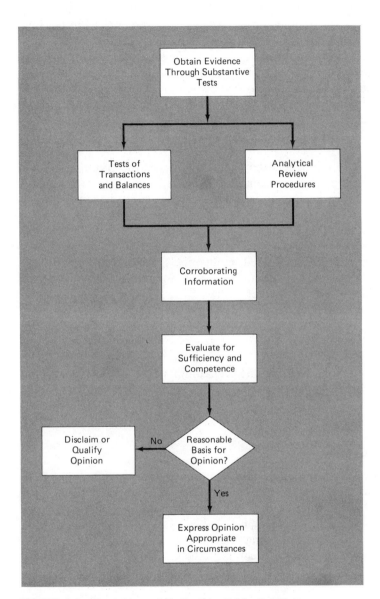

FIGURE 3-3. Obtaining and Evaluating Evidential Matter

auditing procedures applicable in the circumstances. Similarly, the conclusions reached by the auditor, as set forth in the working papers, help demonstrate the objectivity or independence of the auditor in his examination.

Working papers are especially important in meeting the standard of due care. The completeness of the working papers provides evidence of the care exercised by the auditor during his examination, and the content of the working papers reveals the scope of the work. On completion of the audit, the working papers should not contain any unresolved questions (other than those whose resolution depends on some future event). Unresolved questions could suggest the absence of due care during the examination. Working papers should provide evidence that each step of the audit program has been performed or an explanation of why a specified procedure was omitted and alternative methods employed.

Field Work Standards

A major use of working papers during the audit is in the coordination and control of the work by the manager and/or partner in charge of the engagement. Working papers also facilitate the review, at every level of supervision, of the work done. Accordingly, working papers are important in meeting the first standard of field work.

Working papers are indispensable in meeting the second and third standards of field work. As is explained in Chapter 4, the auditor's study and evaluation of internal control should be clearly documented in the working papers. As suggested in this chapter, working papers provide the means for documenting the evidential matter obtained during the examination.

Reporting Standards

Working papers not only facilitate the preparation of the auditor's report but represent the primary support for the auditor's opinion. The working papers should contain evidence pertaining to the conformity of the financial statements with GAAP consistently applied.

Types of Working Papers

There are many varieties and types of working papers an auditor accumulates during an examination. In most situations, working papers are classified into the following groupings: (1) audit plans and audit programs, (2) working trial balance, (3) schedules and analyses, (4) audit memoranda and documentation of corroborating information, and (5) adjusting and reclassifying entries. The nature of the items to be included in the first category is explained in Chapter 2. The other groupings are explained below.

Working Trial Balance

The working trial balance consists of a listing of each ledger account together with its balance at the end of the previous year under audit, its balance at the end of the current year under audit, and columns for adjusting entries, reclassifying entries, and the final balance for the current year. A partial working trial balance is illustrated in Figure 3-4.

The working trial balance may be prepared by the client or the auditor. When the former occurs, the auditor verifies the trial balance by footing the columns and tracing the account balances to the general ledger. A working

Prepared by: J.B.C Date: 2/10/X2
Reviewed by: a.R.C Date: 2/15/X2

Ouri, Inc.
Working Trial Balance – Balance Sheet
12/31/X1
AA-1

Work Paper Ref.	Account No.	Captions and Account Titles	Final Balance 12/31/X0	Ledger Balance 12/31/X1	Adjust Entries DR/(CR)	Reclass Entries DR/(CR)	Final Balance 12/31/X1
		Assets					
		Current					
A	110	Cash	392400	426700	(1) 50000		476700
B	150	Marketable Securities	52200	74400	(2)(12200)		62200
C	160	Receivables (NET)	1601400	1715300	(1)(50000)	(A) 10000	1675300
D	170	Inventories	2542500	2810200	(3)133000		2943200
E	180	Prepaid Expenses	24900	19500			19500
		Total Current	4615400	5046100			5176900
F	240	Long Term Investments	—	190000			190000
G	300	Property, Plant + Equipment (NET)	3146500	3310900			3310900
		Total	7762900	8547000	120800	10000	8677800
		Liabilities and Stockholders Equity					
		Current Liabilities					
M	400	Notes Payable	750000	825000			825000
N	410	Accounts Payable	2150400	2340300	(3)(133000)	(A)(10000)	2483300
O	420	Accrued Payables	210600	180500	(4)(8500)		189000
P	430	Income Taxes Payable	150000	170000			170000
		Total Current	3261000	3515800			3647300
R	500	Bonds Payable	1000000	1200000			1200000
S	600	Common Stock	2400000	2400000			2400000
T	700	Retained Earnings	1101900	1431200	(2) 12200 (4) 8500		1410500
		Total	7762900	8547000	(120800)	(10000)	8677800

FIGURE 3–4. Working Trial Balance Working Paper

trial balance is of paramount importance in the conduct of the audit. It provides a basis for controlling all of the individual working papers and for summarizing the data obtained during the course of the engagement. In addition, it is the connecting link between the general ledger and the financial statements.

Schedules and Analyses

In many audits, the terms *schedules* and *analyses* are used interchangeably. However, for purposes of illustration and explanation, it is possible to distinguish between the two types of working papers.

A schedule shows the composition of individual accounts and groups of accounts at a given point in time. For example, a schedule of marketable securities shows the specific types of securities that comprise the balance in the account at the statement date. In contrast, group schedules, also identified as *lead* or *summary schedules,* summarize the working paper data pertaining to a given type of statement item such as cash, receivables, etc. A lead schedule for cash is illustrated in Figure 3-5. Such schedules are common in audits of large companies. Group schedules serve as an intermediate summary before the data are transferred to the working trial balance.

An analysis of a ledger account shows all the changes in the account during the period covered by the financial statements. Account analyses may be made for any balance sheet or income statement account. In many instances, a single analysis may pertain to more than one account. For example, the analysis of notes receivable may also include interest receivable and interest earned, as illustrated in Figure 3-6. Each analysis should show the principal audit procedures used by the auditor.

Audit Memoranda and Corroborating Information

Audit memoranda refer to written data prepared by the auditor in narrative form. Memoranda may include comments on the performance of auditing procedures and conclusions reached from the audit work performed. Documentation of corroborating information includes (1) extracts of minutes of board of director meetings, (2) confirmation responses, (3) written representations from management and outsiders, and (4) copies of important contracts.

Adjusting and Reclassifying Entries

It is important to distinguish between adjusting entries and reclassifying entries. The former are expected to be recorded by the client; the latter are intended solely for the auditor's working papers. Adjusting entries are corrections of client errors of omission or commission or corrections resulting from misunderstandings or misinterpretations of GAAP. In contrast, reclassifying entries pertain to the proper financial statement presentation of a correct account balance.

To determine the reclassifying entry that is required, the auditor must ascertain the composition of the account balance. For example, if the balance of Bonds Payable includes some bonds due next year, those bonds should be reported as a current liability. The reclassification entry is (Dr) Bonds Payable and (Cr) Current Maturities of Bonds Payable. For another illustration, assume that the balance in Accounts Receivable includes some credit balances pertaining to customer advances. The reclassifying entry is (Dr) Accounts Receivable and (Cr) Customer's Advances, a liability account.

Adjusting and reclassifying entries, with accompanying explanations, should be summarized on separate lists in the working papers. The list of

FIGURE 3–5. Integrated Working Papers for Cash

Omni, Inc.
Notes Receivable and Interest
12/31/X1

C-4

Accounts: Notes 160, 161, and 450

Maker	Date Made	Date Due	Interest Rate	Face Amount	Notes Receivable				Interest			
					Bal 12/31/X0	Debits	Credits	Bal 12/31/X1	Accrued 12/31/X0	Earned 19X1	Collected 19X1	Accrued 12/31/X1
Coffman, Inc.	7/1/X0	4/30/X1	10%	250000	250000 √		25000 c	—	1250 √	1250 ⊘	2500 c	—
Morrison Bros	4/1/X0	9/15/X1	10%	300000	300000 √		30000 c	—	500 √	2500 ⊘	3000 c	—
Shirley and Son	4/1/X1	3/31/X2	12%	400000 √	—	40000		40000 ∧	—	3600 ⊘	—	3600
Warren Corporation	10/1/X1	9/30/X2	12%	200000 √	—	20000		200000 ∧	—	600 ⊘	—	600
					55000 √	60000	55000	600000 ∧	1750 √	7950	5500	4200 ∧
					F	F	F	FF TbC	F	F	F	FF TbC

√ Agreed to 12/31/X0 working papers
√ Confirmed with maker, no exceptions
√ Examined note during cash count
F Footed
FF Footed and crossfooted
∧ Traced to ledger balance
c Traced collections to cash receipts and deposit slips
⊘ Verified computations

FIGURE 3–6. Notes Receivable and Interest Working Paper

adjusting entries is usually labeled "proposed adjusting entries," since there frequently is a considerable amount of discussion and negotiation between the client and the auditor regarding proposed adjustments. The auditor should explain the entries to the client, where necessary, but not make the entries. To do so would technically make the auditor a company accountant rather than an independent auditor.

Both adjusting and reclassifying entries should pertain only to items which individually or collectively are material to the financial statements. In the working papers, each entry should be shown on (1) the schedule or analysis of the account, (2) the working trial balance, (3) the summary of adjusting or reclassifying entries, and (4) the lead schedules, if any, as summarized in Figure 3-5. To facilitate identification, adjusting entries may be numbered and reclassifying entries may be lettered.

Preparing Working Papers

There are a number of basic techniques that are widely used in preparing a working paper. These pertain to the mechanics of working paper preparation and include the following essential points:

Heading. Each working paper contains the name of the client, a descriptive title identifying the content of the working paper, such as *Bank Reconciliation—City National Bank,* and the balance sheet date or the period covered by the audit.

Index numbers. Each working paper is given an index number, such as A-1, B-2, etc., for identification purposes. In addition, there is *cross-referencing* of data both to and from other working papers to facilitate the flow of information.

Tick marks. Tick marks are symbols used by an auditor that provide a reference to a narrative explanation elsewhere in the working paper. The symbols are, in essence, the auditor's shorthand. Each tick mark or symbol must be accompanied by an explanation of the nature and extent of the work done.

Signature and dates. Both the preparer and reviewer should initial and date the working paper. The signatures establish responsibility for the work and the review.

Each of the basic techniques is illustrated in Figure 3-6.

Reviewing Working Papers

There are several levels in the review of working papers within a CPA firm. The first-level review is made by the preparer's supervisor, such as a senior or manager. This review occurs when the work on a specific segment of the audit has been completed. The reviewer is primarily interested in the work done, the evidence obtained, the judgment exercised, and the conclusions reached by the preparer of the working paper.

Other reviews are made of the working papers when all of the field work has been completed. These reviews are explained in Chapter 15 under "Completing the Audit."

Working Paper Files

Working papers are generally filed under two categories: (1) a permanent file and (2) a current file. The *permanent file* contains data that are expected to be useful to the auditor on many future engagements with the client. In contrast, the *current file* contains corroborating information pertaining to the execution of the current year's audit program.

Items typically found in the permanent file are:

- Copies of the articles of incorporation and bylaws.
- Chart of accounts and procedure manuals.
- Organization charts.
- Plant layout, manufacturing processes, and principal products.
- Terms of capital stock and bond issues.
- Copies of long-term contracts, such as leases, pension plans, and profit-sharing and bonus agreements.
- Summary of accounting principles used by the client.

Ownership and Custody of Working Papers

Working papers belong to the auditor. The auditor's ownership rights, however, are subject to constraints imposed by the auditor's own profession. The AICPA's Code of Professional Ethics stipulates that a CPA shall not disclose any confidential information obtained during the course of a professional engagement, except with the consent of the client.

Custody of the working papers rests with the auditor, and he is responsible for their safekeeping. Working papers included in the permanent file are retained indefinitely. Current working papers should be retained for as long as they are useful to the auditor in servicing his client or are needed to satisfy legal requirements for record retention. The statute of limitations rarely extends beyond six years.

CONCLUDING COMMENTS

Sufficient competent evidential matter cannot be measured in terms of audit hours worked or the number of working papers accumulated during the engagement. This determination requires the exercise of audit judgment. Every auditor, new or experienced, must make this evaluation for each segment of the audit to which he has been assigned. This responsibility begins on the first assignment of the first audit and continues in every engagement. The beginning auditor is well advised to work diligently and continuously on this important responsibility. The judgment exercised by an auditor must be documented. Working papers may prove to be a friend or foe of the auditor. Good working papers contribute to advancement within the firm and strengthen an auditor's defense in a lawsuit; poor working papers produce contrary results.

REVIEW QUESTIONS

3–1. Identify the two categories of evidential matter and indicate their relative importance to the third standard of field work.

3–2. a. What types of management assertions are made in financial statements?
b. Indicate the relationship of each type of assertion to audit evidence.

3–3. State the purpose of the third standard of field work.

3–4. What factors are relevant in determining the sufficiency of corroborating information?

3–5. What factors affect the competency of corroborating information?

3–6. a. Distinguish among (1) qualitative materiality, (2) quantitative materiality, and (3) risk.
b. What factors should be considered in assessing risk?

3–7. Identify the three presumptions concerning the competency of evidential matter.

3–8. a. An auditor is expected to have an absolute basis for the expression of an opinion. Do you agree? Why or why not?
b. What types of considerations are relevant concerning the basis for the auditor's opinion?

3–9. Identify the types of corroborating information that can be obtained by the auditor during an examination.

3–10. a. What are the objectives of a management representation letter?
b. Indicate the relationship of this form of evidence to generally accepted auditing standards.

3–11. What factors affect the reliability of documentary evidence?

3–12. Identify the two general classes of auditing procedures that are applicable to the third standard of field work and indicate the primary purpose(s) of each.

3–13. a. Enumerate the procedures that may be used in making an analytical review.
b. When may analytical review procedures be performed?

3–14. Identify the types of procedures that may be performed in making tests of transactions and balances.

3–15. a. What approach should the auditor take in evaluating evidence?
b. What restraints should be exercised in the evaluating process?

3–16. What effects will the failure to meet the third standard of field work have on the auditor and the auditor's standard report.

3–17. a. Define the term *working papers* and indicate their principal functions in auditing.
b. Enumerate the principal types of working papers.

3–18. Distinguish between (a) schedules and analyses and (b) adjusting and reclassifying entries.

3–19. Indicate the nature of the permanent working paper file and identify four types of data that would ordinarily be included in such a file.

3–20. Who owns and who should maintain custody of working papers?

COMPREHENSIVE QUESTIONS

3–21. The third GAAS of field work requires that the auditor obtain sufficient competent evidential matter to afford a reasonable basis for an opinion regarding the financial statements under examination. In considering what constitutes sufficient competent evidential matter, a distinction should be made between underlying accounting data and all corroborating information available to the auditor.

Required

a. Discuss the nature of evidential matter to be considered by the auditor in terms of the underlying accounting data, all corroborating information available to the auditor, and the methods by which the auditor tests or gathers competent evidential matter.
b. State the presumptions that can be made about the validity of evidential matter with respect to (1) corroborating information and (2) underlying accounting data.

AICPA (adapted)

3-22. In his examination of financial statements, the CPA is concerned with the examination and accumulation of accounting evidence.

Required

a. What is the objective of the CPA's examination and accumulation of accounting evidence during the course of his audit?
b. The source of the accounting evidence is of primary importance in the CPA's evaluation of its quality. Accounting evidence may be classified according to source. For example, one class originates within the client's organization, passes through the hands of third parties, and returns to the client, where it may be examined by the auditor. List the classifications of accounting evidence according to source, briefly discussing the effect of the source on the reliability of the evidence.
c. In evaluating the quality of the accounting evidence the CPA also considers factors other than the sources of the evidence. Briefly discuss these other factors.

AICPA

3-23. The concept of materiality is important to the CPA in the examination of financial statements and expression of opinion upon these statements.

Required

Discuss the following:

a. How are materiality (and immateriality) related to the proper presentation of financial statements?
b. In what ways will considerations of materiality affect the CPA in
   1. Developing an audit program?
   2. Performance of auditing procedures?
c. What factors and measures should the CPA consider in assessing the materiality of an exception to financial statement presentation?

AICPA

3-24. In his examination of financial statements, an auditor must judge the validity of the audit evidence he obtains.

Required

a. In the course of his examination, the auditor asks many questions of client officers and employees.
   1. Describe the factors that the auditor should consider in evaluating oral evidence provided by client officers and employees.
   2. Discuss the validity and limitations of oral evidence.
b. An auditor's examination may include computation of various balance-sheet and operating ratios for comparison to prior years and industry averages. Discuss the validity and limitations of ratio analysis.
c. In connection with his examination of the financial statements of a manufacturing

company, an auditor is observing the physical inventory of finished goods, which consists of expensive, highly complex electronic equipment. Discuss the validity and limitations of the audit evidence provided by this procedure.

AICPA

3-25. During the course of an examination, the auditor examines a wide variety of documentation. Listed below are some forms of documentary evidence and the source from which they are obtained:

1. Bank statement sent directly to the auditor by the bank.
2. Creditor monthly statement obtained from client's files.
3. Vouchers in client's unpaid voucher file.
4. Duplicate sales invoices in filled order file.
5. Time tickets filed in payroll department.
6. Credit memo in customer's file.
7. Material requisitions filed in storeroom.
8. Bank statement in client's files.
9. Invoices from suppliers attached to unpaid vouchers.
10. Paid checks returned with bank statement in (1) above.
11. Letter in customer file from collection agency on collectibility of balance.
12. Memo in customer file from treasurer authorizing the write-off of the account.

Required
a. Classify the evidence by source into one of four categories: (1) directly from outsiders, (2) indirectly from outsiders, (3) internal but validated externally, and (4) entirely internal.
b. Comment on the reliability of the four sources of evidence.

3-26. Analytical review procedures are extremely useful in auditing.

Required
a. Explain why analytical review procedures are considered substantive tests.
b. Explain how analytical review procedures may be useful in audit planning.
c. Identify the analytical review procedures which one might expect a CPA to utilize during an examination performed in accordance with generally accepted auditing standards.

AICPA (adapted)

3-27. A variety of specific audit procedures for obtaining audit evidence are listed below:

1. Inspect and count securities on hand.
2. Confirm inventories stored in public warehouses.
3. Obtain written report from a chemical engineer on grades of gasoline held as inventory by an oil company.
4. Recompute depreciation charges.
5. Learn about possible lawsuit during conversation with client's legal counsel during luncheon.
6. Compute and compare gross profit rates for the current and preceding years.
7. Examine certificates of title to delivery trucks purchased during the year.
8. Obtain letter from management on matters of audit interest.
9. Vouch sales journal entries to sales invoices.
10. Observe the client's count of cash on hand.
11. Review minute book for dividend authorizations.
12. Trace "paid" checks to check register entries.
13. Scan voucher register for unusual account classifications.

Required
a. Indicate the type of evidence obtained by each procedure.
b. List by number the types of evidence that are (1) obtained directly from independent sources outside the enterprise, and (2) obtained by the auditor's direct personal knowledge.

3–28. In meeting the third standard of field work, the auditor may perform (a) substantive tests of transactions, (b) substantive tests of balances, and (c) analytical review procedures. Below are listed specific audit procedures that fall within one of these categories:

1. Compare actual results with budget expectations.
2. Vouch entries in check register to "paid" checks.
3. Recalculate accrued interest payable.
4. Confirm customer balances.
5. Calculate inventory turnover ratios and compare with industry data.
6. Reconcile back accounts at year-end.
7. Vouch sales journal entries to sales invoices.
8. Count office supplies on hand at year-end.
9. Examine deeds of ownership for land purchased during year.
10. Obtain representation letter from management.
11. Scan postings to repair expense for evidence of charges that should be capitalized.
12. Ask storeroom supervisor about obsolete items.

Required
List the numbers of the foregoing procedures. For each procedure indicate the type of substantive test, and the type of evidence obtained. Use the following format for your answer:

Procedure No.	Type of Substantive Test	Type of Corroborating Information

3–29. Auditors frequently refer to the terms "standards" and "procedures." Standards deal with measures of the quality of the auditor's performance. Standards specifically refer to the ten GAAS. Procedures relate to those acts that are performed by the auditor while trying to gather evidence. Procedures specifically refer to the methods or techniques used by the auditor in the conduct of the examination.

Required
List the different types of procedures that an auditor would use during an examination of financial statements. For example, a type of procedure that an auditor would frequently use is the observation of activities and conditions. Do not discuss specific accounts.

AICPA (adapted)

3–30. An important part of every examination of financial statements is the preparation of working papers.

Required
a. Discuss the relationship of working papers to the standards of field work.
b. You are instructing an inexperienced staffman on his first auditing assignment. He is to examine an account. An analysis of the account has been prepared by the client for inclusion in the working papers. Prepare a list of the comments, commentaries, and notations that the staffman should make or have made on the account analysis to provide an adequate working paper as evidence of his examina-

tion. (Do not include a description of auditing procedures applicable to the account.)

AICPA (adapted)

3-31. The preparation of working papers is an integral part of a CPA's examination of financial statements. On a recurring engagement, a CPA reviews his audit programs and working papers from his prior examination while planning his current examination to determine their usefulness for the current engagement.

Required
a. 1. What are the purposes or functions of working papers?
   2. What records may be included in working papers?
b. What factors affect the CPA's judgment of the type and content of the working papers for a particular engagement?
c. To comply with GAAS, a CPA includes certain evidence in his working papers—for example, ''evidence that the engagement was planned and work of assistants was supervised and reviewed.'' What other evidence should a CPA include in audit working papers to comply with generally accepted auditing standards?

AICPA (adapted)

3-32. The accountant for the Rayan Co. is preparing financial statements for the year ended December 31. Your review of the accounting records discloses the need for the following adjusting and reclassifying entries.

1. Office Supplies has a balance of $2,400. An inventory at December 31 shows $1,100 of supplies on hand.
2. There are two insurance accounts in the trial balance, prepaid insurance—$9,200 and insurance expense—$2,800. Unexpired insurance at the statement date is $4,000.
3. All rent receipts were credited to rent income. At the end of the year, $4,000 of rentals are unearned.
4. The allowance for uncollectibles has a debit balance of $6,000. An aging schedule shows estimated uncollectibles of $14,000.
5. The balance in accounts payable is $122,400. Included in this amount is $12,400 of advance deposits made by Rayan Co. on future purchases.
6. The ledger shows interest receivable of $2,200 at the beginning of the year. All interest collections have been credited to interest revenue. At December 31 of the current year, accrued interest receivable totals $3,800.
7. A capital expenditure of $5,000 was debited to repairs expense on September 1. The annual rate of depreciation on the machinery is 10 percent.
8. Accounts receivable has a net balance of $118,400. This balance is net of customers with credit balances of $25,000.
9. Freight-in of $5,000 was debited to Freight-out.
10. Bonds payable has a balance of $550,000. Bonds maturing within the next year total $50,000.

Required
Journalize the adjusting and reclassifying entries. Identify the adjustments by number and the reclassifications by letter.

3-33.* During your work on the audit of the Jamaica Can Company, you discover the differences described below and note them in the working papers:
1. To verify the client accrual for wages payable, you took the gross wages for the week ending January 3, 19X0, and divided them by the number of working days in the week. You then multiplied this average daily wage by the number of working days that week in the client's year-end. The difference between your computation

and the amount the client recorded was $321. You considered this amount immaterial and no further work was done.

2. During your vouching of additions to plant buildings, you examined an invoice for repairs to the roof for $2,500 from the Dillon Fixit Shop. The charge should have been expensed.

3. During your scanning of customer balances receivable, you noticed that one item for $4,221 is over 180 days. The controller agreed the total should be written off because the customer is bankrupt. The client provided an allowance for doubtful accounts based on a percentage of sales.

4. You checked extensions on 20 percent of the dollar value of the client's manually prepared inventory summary and discovered differences of $418 (over client). You extrapolated the difference in accordance with your senior's instructions and came up with a difference of $2,090 (5 × $418).

5. Your review of the accounts payable listing revealed one rather large debit balance of $28,900. You examined shipping documents that indicated that your client had returned a defective batch of paint just prior to the balance sheet date.

Required

a. Prepare a summary schedule of audit differences using the following headings: Account Titles, Balance Sheet Dr and Cr, and Income Statement Dr and Cr.

b. Prepare, in good form, an adjusting journal entries working paper assuming each adjustment over $2,000 will be proposed to the client for booking.

3–34. As a staff assistant on the Portage Developers Corp. audit, you have been asked by your supervisor, Mary Reed, to prepare a cash summary or lead schedule for the working papers for the December 31, 19X0 cash balances. Portage Developers Corp. maintains a petty cash account and four checking accounts at local banks. At December 31, 19X0, the five accounts had a total balance of $3,645,486.28 consisting of

Account Title	Account Number	December 31, 19X0 Balance
Petty cash	101	$ 27,000.00
Payroll account, Eaton National Bank	102	1,322,750.00
General account, Eaton National Bank	103	1,631,342.20
Special account, Tanglewood Bank of Commerce	104	928,487.18
General account, Commercial Bank Corp.	105	(264,093.10)

Working paper documentation of the work done on these accounts have been indexed on working papers A1-A5, respectively.

During her review of the working papers, Mary Reed concludes that (1) the overdraft in the Commercial Bank Corp. account should be reclassified as a current liability and (2) that an adjusting entry should be made for a $20,000 payment by a customer on account that was properly included in deposits in transit to the Eaton National Bank general account, but not recorded on the books prior to December 31, 19X0.

Required

a. Prepare only the cash summary working paper. Use the following column headings: *Account Number, Account Title, Working Paper Reference 12/31/X0 Bal-*

ance per Books, Adjusting and Reclassifying Entries *Dr.* and *Cr.* and *12/31/X0 Final Balance.*

b. Below the summary totals, journalize the adjusting and reclassifying entries. Your firm uses numbers to identify adjusting entries and letters to identify reclassification entries.

CASE STUDY

3–35. The following schedule was prepared by staff accountant C. B. Sure on completing the verification of a December 31 client-prepared reconciliation of the City Bank General Account in the audit of Bold, Inc.

	A-1
BOLD, INC.	**Prepared by:** Client
#102 City Bank—Reconciliation	**Reviewed by:** C. B. Sure

Per bank		$62,765.18 ✔
Deposit in transit		1,452.20
Outstanding checks:		
87.10	619.75 ✔	
232.90 ✔	1,100.00 ✔	
17.20 ✔	472.19 ✔	(2,529.14)
Other (See AJE's 12 and 13 on cash lead Schedule A)		510.55
Reconciled balance		$62,198.79
✔ Verified		✔

As a senior on the job, you discuss the work done with Sure and determine:

1. The balance per bank agreed with the amount shown on the bank confirmation received directly from the bank.
2. The deposit in transit was traced to the January bank statement.
3. All outstanding checks were traced to the December check register.
4. Adjusting entry 12 was for the collection of a $515 non-interest bearing note by the bank; entry 13 was for December bank charges of $4.45.
5. The recorded balance per books at December 31 is $61,267.69.
6. In comparing "paid" checks with the check register, an error was discovered. Check number 2640 for $980 to a creditor was recorded by Bold, Inc. as $890. The bank paid the correct amount.
7. The final step, done on January 7, was to check the mathematical accuracy of the schedule.

Required

a. Prepare the bank reconciliation working paper in good form, showing adjusted balances per bank and per books.
b. Prepare the adjusting entries that presumably were made.
c. Prepare a cash lead schedule assuming (1) account number 101, Petty Cash $5,000 (working paper A-2—no adjustments) and (2) account number 103, City Bank—Payroll $20,000 (working paper A-3—no adjustment).
d. Prepare a partial working trial balance.

II Study and Evaluation of Internal Control

The study and evaluation of internal control are an essential part of an audit. Seven chapters are included in Part II.

In Chapter 4, attention is given to the basic features of internal control systems and to the nature and scope of the auditing standard that requires the auditor to make a study and evaluation of a client's system of internal control.

The succeeding two chapters expand on this requirement by considering the impact of electronic data processing (Chapter 5) and the applicability of statistical sampling (Chapter 6).

The remaining four chapters provide comprehensive coverage of internal control principles and the methodology for making a study and evaluation of internal control of specific classes of transactions within three transaction cycles—revenue, expenditure, and production.

4 Internal Control Principles and Review Concepts

STUDY OBJECTIVES

The study objectives of this chapter are to acquire an understanding of internal control systems and how the auditor makes a proper study and evaluation of internal control. To achieve these objectives, it is necessary for the reader to

- Know the meaning of internal accounting control.
- Understand the factors that contribute to a satisfactory internal accounting control environment.
- Understand the basic principles of internal accounting control.
- Know the steps required in making a study and evaluation of the client's internal control system.
- Comprehend the effects of the auditor's study and evaluation on substantive tests.

G enerally accepted auditing standards (GAAS) require the auditor to make a proper study and evaluation of the client's system of internal control. This chapter is divided into two major segments: (1) basic internal control considerations and (2) the methodology for meeting the second standard of field work.

BASIC CONSIDERATIONS

Nature and Importance of Internal Control

Insight into the nature of internal control can be obtained from the time-honored definition, which states:

> Internal control comprises the plan of organization and all of the coordinate methods and measures adopted within a business to safeguard its assets, check the accuracy and reliability of its accounting data, promote operational efficiency, and encourage adherence to prescribed managerial policies.[1]

This definition is broad in scope. It not only includes accounting and financial activities but extends to virtually every aspect of a company's operations. The importance of internal control to management and independent auditors has been recognized in the professional literature for many years. A 1947 American Institute of Certified Public Accountants (AICPA) publication cited the following factors as contributing to the constantly expanding recognition of the significance of internal control:

- The scope and size of the business entity has become so complex and widespread that management must rely on numerous reports and analyses to control operations effectively.
- The check and review inherent in a good system of internal control afford protection against human weaknesses and reduce the possibility that errors or irregularities will occur.
- It is impracticable for auditors to make audits of most companies within economic fee limitations without relying on the client's system of internal control.[2]

During the three decades following this publication even greater importance has been placed on internal control by management and independent auditors. In 1977, a new dimension was imposed with the passage of the Foreign Corrupt Practices Act. Under this Act, management and directors of companies subject to the reporting requirements of the Securities Exchange

---

[1] Auditing Standards Board, *Codification of Statements on Auditing Standards* (New York: American Institute of Certified Public Accountants, 1983), Auditing Section 320.09 (hereinafter referred to and cited as AU §).

[2] Committee on Auditing Procedure, *Internal Control* (New York: American Institute of Certified Public Accountants, 1947), p. 5.

Act of 1934, whether or not they operate outside the United States, are required to comply with antibribery and accounting standards provisions. The latter requires the maintenance of a satisfactory system of internal control. The Act is administered by the Securities and Exchange Commission (SEC), and management and directors who do not comply with the provisions are subject to fines, penalties, and/or imprisonment.

Administrative and Accounting Control

Two subdivisions of internal control are recognized in auditing—(1) administrative control and (2) accounting control:

> *Administrative control* includes, but is not limited to, the plan of organization and the procedures and records that are concerned with the decision processes leading to management's authorization of transactions . . . and is the starting point for establishing accounting control over transactions.[3]

> *Accounting control* comprises the plan of organization and procedures and records that are concerned with the safeguarding of assets and the reliability of financial records and consequently are designed to provide reasonable assurance that:
>
> a. Transactions are executed in accordance with management's general or specific authorization.
> b. Transactions are recorded as necessary (1) to permit preparation of financial statements in conformity with generally accepted accounting principles or any other criteria applicable to such statements and (2) to maintain accountability for assets.
> c. Access to assets is permitted only in accordance with management's authorization.
> d. The recorded accountability for assets is compared with the existing assets at reasonable intervals and appropriate action is taken with respect to any difference.[4]

The definition of *administrative control* indicates that these controls may extend beyond the process leading to the authorization of transactions. Such controls include the records used in evaluating personnel performance (such as the number of customers contacted by a salesman), in market analyses studies, and in quality control reports. These types of controls have little or no impact on a company's financial records. However, the definition also recognizes that the two subdivisions of internal control are not mutually exclusive because some administrative controls lead to the authorization of transactions, which is the starting point for accounting control.

The definition of accounting control focuses on two *broad objectives*: (1) the safeguarding of assets and (2) the reliability of financial records and *four operative objectives* (items a–d). Any administrative control that directly affects any of these aspects is considered to be an accounting control.

---

[3] Auditing Standards Board, *op. cit.*, AU § 320.27.
[4] Auditing Standards Board, *op. cit.*, AU § 320.28.

Clarifying Accounting Control

The auditor should have a thorough understanding of accounting control. Further clarification about the meaning of accounting control is given below.

Safeguarding of Assets

In a broad sense, the safeguarding of assets includes any precautionary measure taken by management to prevent something undesirable from happening to the company's resources. Such measures might apply to all losses, whether they result from "acts of God" or from bad business decisions. This interpretation extends considerably beyond the accounting process.

A narrower but more meaningful interpretation is to limit this element to the measures taken by management to protect the company from losses resulting from executing and recording transactions and from custody of the related assets. Losses, in such cases, may be due to either unintentional or intentional errors. Unintentional errors include "honest" mistakes, such as understatement of sales invoices by unknowingly applying incorrect unit prices and overpayment of employees by inadvertently using incorrect wage rates. Intentional errors are considered to be irregularities. They consist of defalcations (or embezzlements), which result in losses because of a breach of trust, and losses attributable to the falsification of records, such as overstating net income. In lay terms, an intentional error is generally associated with fraud.

Reliability of Financial Records

Financial records provide the basis for reporting (1) internally to management and (2) externally to stockholders and other interested parties. While both uses are important, it should be recognized that the auditor reports his findings to stockholders. Thus, for auditing purposes, the reliability of the financial records applies primarily to external reporting.

In this context, external reporting is broader than just financial statements. It includes all financial data in the annual report (financial highlights, comparative summaries, etc.) and other forms of financial reporting (interim reports and earnings releases). The term *financial records* is synonymous with the term *accounting records* in the scope paragraph of the auditor's standard report, *accounting data* in the time-honored definition of internal control, and *underlying accounting data* in the classification of evidential matter.

Reasonable Assurance

The establishment and maintenance of a system of internal accounting control is the responsibility of management. Management normally seeks reasonable, rather than absolute, assurance that the objectives of the system will be achieved. Two significant factors underlie this conclusion.

First is the recognition that the cost of the system should not exceed the benefits expected to be attained. The cost-benefit criterion is critical in the management decision-making process. This is complicated by the fact that the cost-benefit relationship involves estimates and judgments, rather than precise measurements. In airports, the cost of personal security surveillance for passengers was deemed to be worth the benefit of protection from hijackers and bombs. In contrast, managements of retail establishments, to date, have decided that a similar personal surveillance system is not worth the benefit of eliminating shoplifting losses. Many stores, however, have installed strategically located closed-circuit television cameras and electronic sensoring devices in an effort to cope with this problem.

Second is the realization that the control procedure should not have a significant adverse effect on efficiency or profitability. For example, a company could eliminate losses from bad checks by accepting only certified or cashiers' checks from customers. However, because of the possible adverse effect on sales, most companies believe that requiring identification from the check writer offers reasonable assurance against this type of loss.

Transactions

Transactions include exchanges of assets and services between a business enterprise and outside parties as well as the use and consumption of such assets and services within a company. Transactions constitute the basic components of business operations. Accordingly, they are the primary subject matter of accounting control.

The flow of transactions through a system of internal accounting control involves the authorization, execution, and recording of transactions and the accountability for resulting assets. The term *audit trail* is used when documents and accounting records exist for each step in the flow of transactions.

Different types of controls may be required for different types of transactions. Thus, the establishment of controls and the auditor's interest in them are centered on specific types or classes of transactions, such as sales, purchases, and so on. Moreover, the auditor is concerned about specific control procedures pertaining to each function (or step) involved in the flow of transactions for each class. For example, in executing credit sales in a manufacturing company, there should be controls in approving credit, filling and shipping the order, and billing the customer.

Limitations

All systems of internal accounting control are subject to inherent limitations. One limitation is the human factor which exists in most control procedures. The effectiveness of a specific control can be nullified by misunderstanding of instructions, carelessness, fatigue, and absenteeism. It is also possible for the effectiveness of a procedure to be minimized through deliberate circumvention by one employee or jointly by several employees. The latter situation is usually referred to as *collusion*.

A second limitation is that internal control procedures may not encompass all transactions. As explained in Chapter 3, internal control may not extend to nonroutine processing of transactions or to management's judgments involving accounting estimates.

In addition, it should be recognized that internal accounting control exists in a dynamic rather than a static business environment. Changed conditions, such as the resignation or retirement of a key employee or the installation of self-service by customers or "online, realtime" consoles in a computer system, may necessitate major modifications in existing controls. Consequently, special care should be taken in making projections as to the future effectiveness of a system solely on the basis of its current effectiveness.

Internal Accounting Control Environment

Each system of internal accounting control operates within a set of conditions or circumstances which collectively are referred to as the internal control environment. A good internal control environment complements prescribed control procedures whereas a poor environment adversely affects such controls. A company's internal control environment includes both external and internal factors. The former include prevailing economic, industry, and business conditions; the latter include:

- Management leadership.
- Organizational structure.
- Budgets and internal reports.
- Internal auditing.
- Personnel.
- Sound practices.
- Company circumstances.

These factors apply regardless of whether the method of data processing is manual, mechanical, or electronic.

Management Leadership

Management is responsible for establishing a favorable control environment within the organization. The board of directors, and particularly its audit committee and top management, should provide leadership in establishing an appropriate level of control consciousness. The communication of control policies, the frequency and extent of management's surveillance of the system, and management's disposition of exceptions to prescribed controls affect the potential effectiveness of a system.

The control environment is adversely affected when management fails to adhere to established control procedures or is unwilling to prescribe appropriate control procedures. Lack of adherence occurs, for example, when management directs subordinates to ignore prescribed controls and when top management elects to override existing controls.

Organizational Structure

An organizational structure contributes to a good internal control environment by providing an overall framework for planning, coordinating, and controlling operations. The organizational structure of a company involves (1) establishing the organizational independence of functional areas, divisions, and/or departments and (2) providing for the assignment of responsibility and delegation of authority within each organizational unit. The organizational structure of a company usually is depicted graphically in an organization chart. An organizational structure should also provide job descriptions for key positions within each unit.

To enable individuals to discharge their assigned responsibilities effectively, they should be knowledgeable about policies, procedures, and activities that directly and indirectly affect their duties. Appropriate communication of these factors is essential to developing an attitude of control consciousness throughout the organization.

Budgets and Internal Reports

Budgets make several contributions to a company's internal accounting control environment. They provide the means of formulating and communicating company objectives throughout the organization, and they furnish a basis for measuring performance against planned goals. The budgeting process should follow the divisions of responsibility set forth in the organizational structure of the company. Budgets should be updated periodically to reflect management's revised expectations resulting from changed operating conditions and other factors.

An effective system of internal reporting to all levels of management is essential to a sound control environment. When properly prepared and analyzed, internal reports provide a basis for evaluating performance and the manner in which delegated responsibility is being discharged. Internal reporting should be both regular and timely.

Internal Auditing

As explained in Chapter 1, internal auditing is an appraisal function. Internal auditing contributes to a good control environment through the monitoring of the functioning of prescribed control procedures. An effective internal audit function can assist management in exercising continuous supervision over the system. In addition, it can offer constructive suggestions for improving the system. A company's control environment is enhanced when internal auditors are independent of the units they audit and when they report or have direct access to the board of directors.

Personnel

Basic to a proper control environment are the quality and integrity of the personnel who must carry out the prescribed methods and procedures.

Dishonest and/or incompetent personnel can make most control procedures inoperative or ineffective. People in positions of responsibility, such as officers, department heads, managers, and cashiers, should be individuals who have both the training and the experience to discharge their assigned responsibilities efficiently and economically. On the one hand, it would be inefficient and injudicious to place an inexperienced accountant as the controller of a company; on the other hand, it would be uneconomical to use an experienced certified public accountant (CPA) as a bookkeeper. In addition to competency, personnel should have high personal and ethical standards.

The competence and integrity of personnel are largely dependent on a company's policies and procedures pertaining to hiring, training, compensation, performance evaluation, and promotions.

Sound Practices

Sound practices relate to miscellaneous measures taken by a company in creating a good control environment. The following are representative of practices that are widely used:

- Carrying fidelity insurance on personnel in positions of trust (this practice is commonly referred to as *bonding of employees*).
- Having a written *code of officer and employee conduct* pertaining to moral standards of behavior and prohibition against illegal acts.
- Having a clear-cut *conflict of interest policy* relating to actions that are incompatible with company objectives.
- Establishing a *mandatory vacation policy* for personnel in positions of trust.

Company Circumstances

This aspect of a company's environment pertains to such factors as: (1) the geographical dispersion of its operations, (2) the existence of wholly or partially owned subsidiaries, and (3) the recent acquisition of companies whose controls may not be comparable to the company's. These conditions suggest that there may be a lack of uniformity of controls throughout a company. This factor may be especially important in multinational companies with subsidiaries in foreign countries.

Internal Accounting Control Principles

To achieve the objectives of internal accounting control, a system should have certain essential features. The following six principles are basic to an effective system of accounting control:

- Segregation of functions.
- Authorization procedures.

- Documentation procedures.
- Accounting records and procedures.
- Physical controls.
- Independent internal verification.

Segregation of Functions

This basic principle applies to each of the four operative objectives and therefore is all pervasive. It involves the assignment of responsibility for a transaction in a manner such that the duties of one employee automatically provide a cross-check on the work of one or more other employees. The primary purpose of segregation of functions is the prevention and prompt detection of errors or irregularities in the performance of assigned responsibilities. Functions are considered to be incompatible from a control standpoint when it is possible for an individual to commit errors or irregularities in the normal course of his duties without detection by the system.

The primary application of this principle is that the responsibility for executing a transaction, recording the transaction, and custody of the assets resulting from the transaction should be assigned to different departments and individuals. For purchase transactions, for example, purchasing department personnel should make the purchase, accounting department personnel should record the goods received, and storeroom personnel should assume custody of goods received. Before recording the purchase, accounting personnel should ascertain that the purchase was authorized and that the goods ordered were received. The accounting entry, in turn, provides a basis of accountability for the goods in the storeroom.

The principle of segregation of duties also applies to the various steps involved in the execution of a transaction. Thus, in executing a sales transaction in a manufacturing company, different departments or individuals should be responsible for authorizing the sale, filling the order, shipping the goods, and billing the customer. Similarly, within the accounting department, different personnel should maintain the general ledger and the customers' subsidiary ledger.

Authorization Procedures

The purpose of this basic principle is to assure that transactions are authorized by management personnel acting within the scope of their authority. Authorizations may be general or specific. The former relates to the general conditions under which transactions are authorized, such as standard price lists for products and credit policies for charge sales. The latter relates to the granting of the authorization on a case-by-case basis. This may occur, for example, in nonroutine transactions, such as major capital expenditures and the issuing of capital stock. Specific authorization may also apply to routine transactions that exceed the limits prescribed in the general authorization, such as granting credit to a customer who does not meet specified credit conditions.

There is a difference between management's authorization of a transaction and employee approval. Acting within the scope of the authorized credit policies, for instance, credit department personnel can approve credit to individual customers.

Authorization procedures are also important in limiting access to assets. For example, only authorized personnel should have access to storage areas for tangible resources, such as inventories, cash, and marketable securities. Similarly, there should be restricted access to storage areas for unused forms, such as blank checks and vouchers, that may be used for improper disposition of assets. In addition, direct access to the accounting records should be restricted to authorized accounting personnel.

Documentation Procedures

Proper documentation is essential to effective internal accounting control. Documents provide evidence of the occurrence of transactions and the price, nature, and terms of the transactions. Invoices, checks, contracts, and time tickets are illustrative of common types of documents. When duly signed or stamped, documents also provide a basis for establishing responsibility for the executing and recording of transactions. Prenumbered documents are useful in maintaining control and accountability. For example, prenumbering helps to assure that (1) all transactions are recorded and (2) that no transactions are recorded more than once. When prenumbering exists, all voided documents should be retained.

Documentation procedures should provide for timely preparation of the document by operating personnel when transactions are executed. The recording of transactions is facilitated when documents are promptly forwarded to accounting. Documents should subsequently be filed in an orderly manner.

Accounting Records and Procedures

This basic principle focuses on the recording of transactions within the accounting department. The objectives of this control are (1) prompt preparation of accurate accounting records and (2) timely reporting of accounting data to users. Both an accounting procedures manual and a chart of accounts are important. A *chart of accounts* provides the basis for the classification of transactions and greatly facilitates the preparation of financial statements. In many companies, an accounting supervisor periodically reviews journal entries to evaluate the reasonableness of the account classifications.

Procedures should be established in accounting for the prompt processing of documents transmitted to accounting by operating personnel, including timely posting to subsidiary customer accounts. These procedures should also require accounting to sequentially journalize all serially prenumbered documents.

Physical Controls

Physical controls pertain to (1) security devices and measures for the safekeeping of assets, accounting records, and unused preprinted forms, and (2) the use of mechanical and electronic equipment in the execution and recording of transactions.

Security devices include on-site safeguards, such as fireproof safes and vaults, and enclosed (and locked) storerooms and warehouses, and off-site safeguards, such as bank deposit vaults and certified public warehouses. Security measures involve limiting access to storage areas to authorized personnel. Physical controls that pertain to the execution of transactions include both mechanical and electronic cash registers.

Independent Internal Verification

This basic principle of internal accounting control relates to reviewing the accuracy and propriety of an employee's work by another employee. For this principle to be effective, three conditions should exist:

- The review should be performed by an employee who is unrelated to, and independent of, the personnel who originally prepared the data or had custody of the related assets.
- The review should be made frequently either in total or on a sampling basis.
- Errors and exceptions should be promptly communicated to the employees involved for corrective action. Recurring and material inaccuracies and all improprieties should of course be reported to management.

Independent internal verification may involve comparing recorded accountability with existing assets (as in the case of a cash or inventory count), agreeing control accounts with their subsidiary records, and recalculating employee earnings or billings to customers by an individual who did not prepare the original data or have custody of the assets.

METHODOLOGY FOR MEETING THE SECOND STANDARD OF FIELD WORK

The Second Standard of Field Work

Now that the essential underlying information about internal accounting control has been explained, consideration can be given to the second generally accepted auditing standard of field work, which states:

> There is to be a proper study and evaluation of the existing internal control as a basis for reliance thereon and for the determination of the resultant extent of the tests to which auditing procedures are to be restricted.

Internal control systems are unique to each client since they are developed by different individuals with different skills, for different managements, and for different size companies utilizing different personnel, records, and data processing methods. Thus, the study of internal control systems cannot be standardized but must be tailored to the system used by the specific client.

Scope of the Standard

The auditor is required to make a study of the system in existence during the year being audited. Internal control systems can change significantly from year to year and even during the year as new controls are introduced and as personnel in key positions change. Thus, even in a long-standing ongoing relationship with a client, the auditor is required to study and evaluate the system each year.

The scope of the study extends to accounting controls, which include administrative controls that have a direct bearing on the financial statements. Thus, management's authorization of transactions should be included.

The evaluation of the system requires the exercise of professional judgment by the auditor in interpreting the information obtained from the study of the system.

Objectives of the Standard

The stated (and primary) objective of the standard is to ascertain the amount of reliance the auditor will place on the system in determining the extent to which other auditing procedures will be necessary in completing the engagement. The phrase "basis for reliance thereon" refers to specific aspects of the system and not to the system in its entirety. For example, the auditor wants to know the amount of reliance that can be placed on control procedures pertaining to the granting of credit in sales transactions. The phrase *for the determination of the resultant extent to which auditing procedures are to be restricted* implies that there is a relationship between the amount of reliance and the amount of additional work that will be needed. The auditing procedures referred to are the substantive tests of transactions and balances and analytical review procedures explained in Chapter 3.

In addition to the stated objective, the auditor's study and evaluation provide a basis for informing management about weaknesses in the system and making recommendations for improvement.

Overview of Methodology

The study of the system of internal accounting control consists of two major parts:

- A *review of the system* to obtain knowledge and understanding of the client's prescribed system.
- *Tests of compliance* to determine whether prescribed control procedures are in use and are operating as planned.

The review, in turn, is divided into phases. In the first or *preliminary phase,* the auditor seeks general knowledge about the client's internal control environment and accounting system. At the conclusion of the preliminary phase of the review, the auditor decides whether further study is likely to justify any restriction of substantive tests. If a negative answer results, the auditor proceeds directly to the design and execution of expanded substantive tests. If an affirmative answer results, the auditor continues to the second or *completion phase* of the review. In this part of the review, the auditor obtains specific knowledge of the design of the client's system of internal accounting control. At the conclusion of the completion phase of the review, the auditor makes a *preliminary evaluation* of prescribed controls.

The primary purpose of the preliminary evaluation is to identify specific control procedures that can be relied on in performing substantive tests, assuming satisfactory compliance with the prescribed procedures. If there are no controls that appear to be reliable, the auditor goes directly to the design and execution of expanded substantive tests.

For the controls that appear to be reliable, the auditor performs tests of compliance to determine whether the controls are in use and are operating as planned. Upon completing the tests of compliance, the auditor makes a *final evaluation*. This evaluation identifies the control procedures that can be relied on in performing restricted substantive tests. The courses of action and the decision points for the auditor in meeting the second standard of field work are shown in Figure 4-1. Observe that the auditor can discontinue the study and evaluation after either phase of the review. Note also that three decision paths will result in expanded substantive tests.

To satisfy GAAS with respect to the second standard of field work, the auditor is only required to perform the preliminary phase of the review. Further study of the system depends entirely on the auditor's judgment as to whether such effort will be cost beneficial in completing the audit. Each of the parts of the study and evaluation is explained more fully below.

Preliminary Phase of Review

In the preliminary phase of the review the auditor seeks information about (1) the internal control environment and (2) the flow of transactions through the accounting system. For the former, the auditor is interested in each of the environmental factors discussed earlier in this chapter. For the latter, he is interested in how transactions in each of the major classes are authorized, executed, and recorded, including the methods of data processing. In this phase of the review, the auditor needs only general knowledge. The auditor's preliminary understanding is usually obtained by inquiry, but it may also be acquired by review of documentation, observation, previous experience with the client, and reference to prior-year working papers.

At the conclusion of the preliminary phase of the review, the auditor must decide, for each of the major classes of transactions, whether to continue or to terminate his review. A decision to continue results when the auditor believes that (1) further study will likely justify some restriction of substantive tests and (2) the audit effort required to complete the review

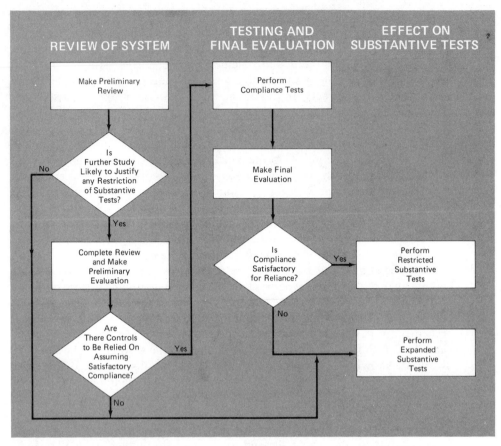

FIGURE 4–1. Overview of Methodology for the Study and Evaluation of Internal Accounting Control

and perform tests of compliance will not exceed the reduction in substantive tests that could be achieved by relying on internal accounting control. When both conditions do not exist, the auditor ends his review and proceeds to the design of expanded substantive tests that do not contemplate reliance on any control procedures. The auditor's decision, which requires professional judgment, should be documented in the working papers. However if the auditor plans no reliance on internal accounting control, he does not need to document his understanding of the client's system.

Completion Phase of Review

In this phase of the review, the auditor obtains specific knowledge and understanding of the client's prescribed control procedures as they pertain to particular classes of transactions or balances. In making the review, the auditor should consider the potential effectiveness of the prescribed controls, either individually or collectively, in preventing or detecting specific types of errors or irregularities. The completion phase of the review involves the following steps: (1) gathering information, (2) verifying the understanding, and (3) making a preliminary evaluation.

Gathering the Information

To facilitate the collection process, auditors traditionally have relied on questionnaires, and this approach is still widely used. A questionnaire consists of a series of questions relating to control procedures normally required to prevent or detect errors and irregularities that may occur for each type of transaction. The questions are usually phrased in a manner that results in either a "yes" or a "no" answer, with the former indicating that the necessary control procedure is prescribed by the client. Some firms have standardized questionnaires that are adaptable to many clients. A questionnaire provides a structured approach which minimizes the possibility of overlooking important aspects of the system. A further advantage is the ease with which a questionnaire can be completed. A completed questionnaire for Campus Theater is shown in Figure 4-2.

Prepared by: *C.J.A.* Date: *9/8/X1*
Reviewed by: *W.A.S.* Date: *9/15/X1*

INTERNAL ACCOUNTING CONTROL QUESTIONNAIRE
Cash Receipts Transactions

CLIENT: *Campus Theater*   AUDIT DATE: *12/31/X1*

Control Procedure	Yes	No	Remarks
1. Are prenumbered tickets used and subsequently accounted for?	✓		
2. Is there restricted access to rolls of unused tickets?	✓		
3. Is a ticket machine used in issuing tickets?	✓		
4. Are tickets voided upon admission of patrons?	✓		
5. Is there segregation of duties between the issuance of tickets and admission of patrons?	✓		
6. Is there an independent daily cash count and reconciliation with tickets issued?	✓		
7. Are cash receipts deposited in total daily?		✓	*cash is deposited every week.*

FIGURE 4–2. Internal Accounting Control Questionnaire: Cash Receipts Transactions

In recent years, many auditors have used flowcharts as one of the means of gathering information about accounting controls. A *flowchart* is a schematic diagram, using symbols and interconnecting lines, that portrays a system. In reviewing internal control, separate flowcharts are prepared for each type of transaction showing the applicable control procedures and the flow of data through the system. The fundamental techniques and principles of flowcharting are explained and illustrated in Appendix 4A at the end of this chapter. A flowchart enables the auditor to see the relationships that exist between controls and facilitates the identification of key controls.

In addition to completed questionnaires and flowcharts, auditors use narrative memoranda to document information obtained in the review. Narrative memoranda consist of a written description of the controls that are applicable to each class of transactions.

Verifying the Understanding

To reinforce his understanding of the information gathered from the various sources, the auditor may perform a *transaction walk-through review*. In this review, one or a few transactions within each of the major classes of transactions are traced through the audit trail of documents and accounting records, and the related accounting control procedures are observed. The primary purpose of a walk-through review is to verify (or clarify) the auditor's understanding of the flow of transactions through the client's system. However, some auditors consider the walk-through review to be part of the tests of compliance.

As a practical matter, a transaction walk-through review may start with any step in the execution and recording of a transaction so long as the complete sequence of steps performed and the persons performing them are identified. The transaction walk-through should be documented in the working papers.

Making a Preliminary Evaluation

An explanation of this step in the completion phase of the review requires a consideration of both the nature and purpose of this evaluation.

Nature. In making this evaluation, the auditor should

- Consider the errors and irregularities that could occur for each significant class of transactions and related assets.
- Identify the control procedures that should prevent or detect such occurrences.
- Determine whether the necessary procedures are prescribed in the client's system.

This approach recognizes that errors and irregularities are the converse of desired audit objectives.

In the first two steps, the auditor often uses generalized materials available within his firm. For example, the firm may have checklists that contain specific types of errors and irregularities, along with the control procedures that should prevent or detect them. The auditor then adapts the checklist, as necessary, to the particular client. This often provides the basis for developing an internal control questionnaire tailored to the specific client. The third step in the evaluation is accomplished through reviewing the client's system as described above.

Purpose. The primary purpose of this evaluation is to determine whether, assuming satisfactory compliance, specific procedures can be relied on by the auditor in performing substantive tests. A control is considered to be reliable when there is reasonable assurance that it will prevent or detect errors or irregularities pertaining to the particular class of transactions or balances. Professional judgment is indispensable in making this evaluation. The auditor may decide not to rely on a prescribed control procedure because

- The control procedure is unsatisfactory or unreliable for its intended purpose.
- There are other compensating controls that appear to be more reliable.
- The time and effort to test the control procedure are expected to be greater than the reduction in subsequent testing expected to be realized from such reliance.

A secondary purpose of this evaluation is to identify any weaknesses in prescribed controls that should be communicated to management. A weakness in internal accounting control is a condition in which the specific control procedures, or the degree of compliance with them, are not sufficient to achieve a specific control objective—that is, errors or irregularities may occur and not be detected within a timely period by employees in the normal course of performing their assigned functions.[5] A weakness may be immaterial or material. A material weakness exists when there is more than a relatively low risk that errors or irregularities, either individually or collectively, would have a material effect on the financial statements.

The working paper in Figure 4–3 illustrates the documentation of the auditor's preliminary evaluation. Each error or irregularity in this example is numbered to correspond with the questions shown in Figure 4–2. In Campus Theater, the auditor concludes that if compliance is satisfactory, all control procedures can be relied on in performing substantive tests, except for the control over the depositing of cash.

Tests of Compliance

Tests of compliance are performed to obtain reasonable assurance that controls expected to be relied on are in use and are operating as planned.

[5] Auditing Standards Board, *op. cit.*, AU § 642.30.

Prepared by: *R.A.K.*　　Date: *9/22/X1*
Reviewed by: *C.A.B.*　　Date: *9/25/X1*

Campus Theater
Preliminary Evaluation: Cash Receipts Transactions
12/31/X1

Errors and Irregularities	Necessary Control Procedure	Prescribed Control Procedure	Planned Reliance Yes	No
1. Tickets may be issued without accounting for the cash	Prenumbering of tickets	All tickets are prenumbered; theater manager accounts for tickets issued	✓	
2. Unused tickets may be stolen and sold for cash	Physical control and restricted access to storage area	Unused tickets are stored in a safe; manager has only access	✓	
3. Tickets may be issued out of sequence and cash may not be accounted for.	Mechanical equipment for issuing tickets	Ticket machines are used in issuing tickets	✓	
4. Doorperson could resell tickets or combine with cashier to resell tickets and keep the cash	Mutilation of tickets upon admission of patron	Doorperson tears tickets in half when admitting patrons	✓	
5. The cashier may collect cash and admit patron without issuing a ticket	Separation of functions in admissions	Cashier issues tickets; doorperson admits patrons with tickets	✓	
6. Cash may be over or short due to mistakes in making change	Independent daily cash count and reconciliation with tickets issued	Theater manager makes daily count and reconciliation	✓	
7. All cash receipts may not be deposited	Depositing total cash receipts daily	Cash receipts are deposited weekly		✓

FIGURE 4–3. Preliminary Evaluation Working Paper

This phase of the study of internal control does not extend to any control that will not be relied on in making substantive tests.

Nature

Compliance tests focus on the performance of prescribed procedures. They are generally performed during interim work and are concerned with three questions:

- Were the prescribed control procedures performed?
- How were the prescribed control procedures performed?
- By whom were the prescribed control procedures performed?[6]

The failure to perform a required procedure or the failure to perform it properly is referred to as an *exception,* an *occurrence,* or a *deviation.* Such terminology is superior to the use of the term *error,* for the lack of compliance only indicates that there may be an error in the accounting records. For example, the failure of a second person to verify the accuracy of a voucher is an exception, but the accounting record could still be correct if the first clerk has correctly prepared the document.

Three auditing procedures are commonly used in performing compliance tests:

- *Inquiring* of personnel concerning the performance of their duties.
- *Observing* personnel in the performance of their duties.
- *Inspecting* documentation for evidence of performance of control procedures.

Inquiring is designed to determine (1) the employee's understanding of his job, (2) the employee's performance in his job, and (3) the frequency, causes, and disposition of exceptions. The inability of the employee to answer inquiries may indicate that the employee is not performing or is improperly performing the prescribed control procedure. Observing the employee's work serves similar purposes. Ideally, this procedure should be performed without the employee's direct knowledge or on a surprise basis.

Inspecting (reviewing or examining) documentation is only applicable when there is an audit trail of performance in the form of documents that contain signatures and validation stamps. Thus, this procedure is not applicable to the accounting control principles of segregation of functions and physical controls. When inspection of documents is used, any document which fails to have evidence of performance of the control procedure is an exception, regardless of whether the document itself is correct.

---

[6] Auditing Standards Board, *op. cit.,* AU § 320.57.

Compliance Tests by Reperformance

In practice, some auditors test compliance with prescribed controls by reperforming the control procedure that was presumably performed by the employee. These same auditors maintain that this form of testing provides the best evidence of how well the control procedure is performed.

To illustrate reperformance, assume a control procedure requires a second clerk in the billing department to independently verify the correctness of unit selling prices on invoices by comparing them to an authorized price list. On doing so, the clerk initials a copy of the invoice to indicate performance. In testing compliance by reperformance, the auditor compares selling prices on invoices initialed by the clerk to the authorized price lists, and each instance of the use of incorrect prices is regarded as an exception. Thus, in this example, there would be two types of exceptions to prescribed control procedures: (1) invoices that do not have the employee's initials and (2) initialed invoices for which unit selling prices do not agree with the authorized price list.

Extent and Timing

Tests of compliance should be applied to control procedures used throughout the accounting period being audited because the financial statements show the results of transactions and events for the entire year. These tests, however, are often made during interim work which may be several months before the end of the accounting period. Such testing is acceptable under GAAS, if the auditor also determines that the control procedures are still functioning properly throughout the remainder of the period under audit. The nature and extent of additional compliance tests, if any, depend on such factors as the

- Effectiveness of the controls based on the interim tests.
- Length of the remaining period.
- Responses to inquiries concerning changes in controls and operating conditions during the remaining period.
- Results of tests made by internal auditors in the remaining period.
- Discovery of monetary errors in the accounts in the remaining period through substantive testing.[7]

The extent of compliance testing and the interpretation of results may be based entirely on the auditor's subjective judgment. Alternatively, the auditor's judgment may be based, in part, on statistical sampling. The use of statistical sampling in compliance testing is explained in Chapter 6.

[7] Auditing Standards Board, *op. cit.*, AU § 320.61.

CAMPUS THEATRE
AUDIT PROGRAM

TYPE OF TEST: Compliance   CLASS OF TRANSACTIONS: Cash Receipts

OBJECTIVE: Determine whether prescribed controls are operating as planned.

1. Examine tickets for prenumbering.
2. Observe storage of unused tickets and inquire about authorized access to safe.
3. Observe existence and use of ticket machines in issuing tickets.
4. Observe doorperson in admitting patrons.
5. Observe segregation of duties between cashier and doorperson.
6. Examine documentary evidence of daily cash counts and reconciliations with tickets issued.
7. Inquire of personnel and theater manager as to their performance of prescribed control procedures.

FIGURE 4–4. Audit Program: Compliance Tests of Cash Receipts Transactions

Audit Program

The audit program for compliance tests should state the audit objective(s) and identify the auditing procedures to be performed. An audit program for testing controls over cash receipts transactions in the Campus Theater is shown in Figure 4-4. Except for step 7, each test relates to the corresponding number of the prescribed control procedure in Figure 4-3 on which reliance is planned. The control over depositing cash is not tested for compliance in this example because the auditor does not intend to rely on this control. Step 6 of the audit program involves the examination of documentary evidence. When numerous documents are available for review, the auditor generally examines a representative sample. The results of compliance testing should be documented in the working papers.

Compliance Tests versus Substantive Tests of Transactions

Two types of tests are concerned with the details of transactions: (1) substantive tests, which are explained in Chapter 3, and (2) compliance tests. The primary purpose of each type of test and the field work standard to which each relates are as follows:

Type of Transaction Test	Primary Purpose	Field Work Standard
Compliance	Determine extent of compliance with prescribed accounting controls, or conversely, exceptions therefrom	Second
Substantive	Determine the validity and propriety of the accounting treatment of transactions, or conversely, monetary errors or irregularities therein	Third

Monetary errors may exist in the accounting records because of (1) incorrect journal entries (wrong amount, incorrect account title, or wrong accounting period), (2) incorrect postings, (3) incorrect summarization of accounts, (4) failing to record a transaction, or (5) recording a transaction more than once.

It is important to recognize that compliance tests relate to the second standard of field work whereas substantive tests pertain to the third standard of field work. Thus, exceptions to prescribed control procedures are used by the auditor in determining the reliance that can be placed on internal controls. In contrast, the existence of monetary errors will affect the auditor's decisions as to whether sufficient competent evidential matter has been obtained to have a reasonable basis for an opinion.

Dual Purpose Testing

Under dual purpose testing, the auditor simultaneously searches for exceptions to prescribed control procedures and monetary errors in the accounting records. Dual purpose testing is widely used in practice where there is documentary evidence of performance with prescribed controls because it is cost-efficient. When an exception or occurrence is discovered, the auditor also determines the amount of the resulting monetary error in the accounting records, if any. Conversely, if an auditor discovers a monetary error in the accounts, there is also a determination of whether there was noncompliance with a prescribed control procedure.

Final Evaluation of Controls

Upon completing the compliance tests, the auditor makes a final evaluation of the controls in the system. The nature and purpose of this evaluation are explained below.

Nature

This evaluation is similar to the preliminary evaluation. However, in making this evaluation, the auditor is primarily concerned with the deviations from prescribed control procedures discovered in compliance testing. Both a quantitative and a qualitative appraisal are required. On the one hand, the number of deviations found in a compliance test of a given control may be of such magnitude that there is reason to doubt that the control procedure can be relied upon. This might be true, for example, if many sales were made without credit approval. However, in order to judge the significance of occurrences, it usually is necessary to search for the underlying causes. Thus, the auditor may attach different importance to exceptions traceable to (1) a new employee, (2) a vacation replacement, and (3) an experienced regular employee. It is also essential to attempt to ascertain whether the failure to follow the prescribed control is attributable to unintentional or intentional mistakes. One instance of an occurrence or a pattern of occurrences that suggest the possibility of irregularities ordinarily will be more important in the auditor's evaluation than the frequency of occurrences.

Purpose

The purpose of this evaluation is to determine the extent to which the client's actual control procedures can be relied on in performing substantive tests. The auditor's judgment of reliance may be expressed in terms of the risk that errors and irregularities will not be detected by the client's controls. Three levels of risk may be identified:

- *Low*. The auditor expects few, if any, errors and no irregularities.
- *Moderate*. The auditor expects some immaterial errors and no irregularities.
- *High*. The auditor expects material errors or irregularities.

This evaluation is directed at the specific control procedures tested for each major class of transactions. The evaluation should be documented in the working papers. A useful format is to identify (1) strengths (effective controls), (2) weaknesses (ineffective or missing controls), (3) effects on substantive tests, and (4) matters to be communicated to management, if any. These four conclusions are vital in every audit engagement in which reliance is to be placed on internal accounting control. Figure 4-5 shows the evaluation of the control procedures in Campus Theater.

Determining Effects on Other Auditing Procedures

The second standard of field work does not permit the auditor to place complete reliance on internal control to the exclusion of other auditing procedures with respect to material amounts in the financial statements. This standard clearly is not an end in itself. It suggests a correlation of reliance on accounting controls with other auditing procedures rather than the elimination of other work by the auditor. The other auditing procedures referred to in the second standard of field work are substantive tests.

The ultimate purpose of the second standard of field work is to assist the auditor in obtaining a reasonable basis for an opinion on the client's financial statements as required by the third standard of field work.

In considering the interrelationship of these standards, it is useful to recognize that the auditor is concerned about two risks in an audit.

- The first risk is that material errors will occur in the accounting process by which the financial statements are developed.
- The second risk is that any material errors that occur will not be detected in the auditor's examination.[8]

---

[8] Auditing Standards Board, *op. cit.*, AU § 320.72.

Prepared by: *C.g.y.* Date: *10/22/X1*
Reviewed by: *W.A.S.* Date: *1/28/X1*

Campus Theater
Evaluation of Internal Control Over
Execution of Cash Receipts Transactions
12/31/X1

Strengths

1. *Admission tickets are prenumbered, and prices are posted.*
2. *Ticket machines are used to issue tickets.*
3. *Cashier/doorperson provide for segregation of duties.*
4. *Manager reconciles daily cash receipts with tickets issued.*

Weaknesses

Cash is deposited in the bank only once each week.

Effects on Substantive Tests

Extend tracing of daily cash receipts from daily cash counts to related deposit slips and the bank statement.

Management Communication

Indicate that the failure to deposit cash intact daily also makes cash vulnerable to theft. Suggest that the manager make daily deposits using the banks night depository vault.

FIGURE 4–5. Evaluation of Internal Control over Execution of Cash Receipts Transactions

The auditor relies on internal control to reduce the chance of material errors in the accounting process and on substantive tests to reduce the risk that material errors will go undetected. The relative weight to be given each factor is a matter for the auditor's professional judgment in the light of the circumstances. It should be recognized, however, that reliance on substantive tests may properly vary inversely with the reliance on internal accounting control.[9] The auditor's evaluation of accounting control may affect the nature, timing, or extent of substantive testing.

Nature

The nature of the test refers to the kind of auditing procedures to be performed. For example, in verifying the cash in bank account, it is customary to include the bank reconciliation in the audit evidence. When the auditor believes there is a low risk of errors in processing cash transactions, he may be satisfied to review the bank reconciliation prepared by the client. However, when the risk of errors is high, the auditor may deem it necessary to (1) obtain the bank statement directly from the bank and (2) prepare the bank reconciliation himself.

Timing

The extent of the auditor's reliance on internal control may affect the time when the testing is done. For example, when there is low risk of errors in processing sales transactions, a major portion of the examination of accounts receivable may be done several months prior to the end of the year. In contrast, when the risk of errors is high, most, if not all, of the examination is likely to be performed at or near the balance sheet date.

Extent

Internal control effectiveness may affect the degree or amount of testing to be performed. Thus, fewer customer accounts (a smaller sample) will be examined when the risk of errors in processing sales transactions is low than when the risk of errors is high.

OTHER CONSIDERATIONS

Required Communication of Material Weaknesses

During a financial statement audit, the auditor is required by GAAS to communicate any material weaknesses in internal accounting control that come to his attention to senior management and the board of directors (or its audit committee).[10] The communication should be made at the earliest practicable date following the completion of the examination.

In the communication, which may be oral or written, the auditor may offer suggestions for corrective action but this is not required. Further

[9] Auditing Standards Board, *op. cit.,* AU § 320.73.
[10] Auditing Standards Board, *op. cit.,* AU § 323.01.

consideration is given to this requirement in Chapter 15 under "Completing the Audit."

Using the Work of an Internal Auditor

The internal auditor performs an important management function, and his responsibilities often include the continuous monitoring of the company's system of internal control. It is necessary therefore to consider the effect of that aspect of an internal auditor's work on the independent auditor's study and evaluation of internal control.

The second standard of field work does not allow an independent auditor to substitute the work of an internal auditor for his own. However, the internal auditor's work pertaining to internal control may be used to supplement the external auditor's work. In determining the effect on his own procedures, the independent auditor should consider the competence and objectivity of the internal auditor and evaluate his work.[11]

The competence of an internal auditor can be ascertained by inquiring into his technical training, experience, and proficiency. The objectivity of an internal auditor can be evaluated by considering the organizational level to which he reports, both administratively and functionally, and by reviewing the substance of his reports. When he reports to the audit committee, he may have considerable independence. In evaluating the quality of the internal auditor's work, the independent auditor should examine, on a test basis, the audit programs and working papers of the work performed. In addition, he should personally test a portion of the internal auditor's work.

An internal auditor may provide direct assistance to an independent auditor in performing tests of compliance and substantive tests. In such cases, the external auditor should not only evaluate the competency and objectivity of the internal auditor but, to the extent considered necessary, supervise and test his work. Regardless of the extent of the work of the internal auditor, all judgments pertaining to both the study and the evaluation of internal control and the sufficiency and competency of evidential matter must be those of the independent auditor.

Reporting on Internal Control

Management may ask the auditor to issue a report on internal control based on the financial statement audit. This report and other reports on internal control are considered in Chapter 17.

CONCLUDING COMMENTS

The study and evaluation of internal accounting control are a vital part of field work in a financial statement audit. The basic principles of internal accounting control and the methodology described in this chapter to meet

[11] Auditing Standards Board, *op. cit.*, AU § 322.04.

this standard provide the framework for considering additional aspects of internal accounting control in future chapters. This consideration begins in the next chapter, where we explain the internal control implications of electronic data processing (EDP) systems.

APPENDIX 4A

Flowcharting

Auditors frequently use an internal control questionnaire or a narrative memorandum, or both, to document their understanding of relevant aspects of an internal control system. This documentation serves as the basis for the auditor's evaluation of the internal control system. Increasingly, auditors are supplementing the information derived from questionnaires or memoranda with flowcharts of their clients' systems. This is due, in part, to the pervasive use of flowcharts by clients with EDP systems.

A flowchart is a schematic representation of the flow of data through a sequence of operations performed in a system or subsystem. A flowchart is a particularly effective method of reflecting relationships among the various functions performed. A flowchart is not in itself an evaluation of a system; rather, it serves as the basis for the evaluation procedures. The evaluation process is facilitated by presenting evidence in a form more suitable for the kind of analysis performed by the auditor.

Flowcharts depicting internal control systems usually are prepared to portray only a portion of the relationships and transaction flows. For auditing purposes, flowcharts often are prepared for the major subsystems of a business, including the sales, cash receipts, purchases, cash disbursements, payroll, and production transactions. In practice, flowcharts range from very abbreviated portrayals of subsystems to very detailed portrayals, and employ a variety of symbols and techniques. The more commonly used symbols are shown in Figure 4A-1.

To be of maximum usefulness in the evaluation process, a flowchart should reveal the source, flow, and disposition of all important documents, including the locations of major files and records used in processing. Additionally, each operation or process comprising the subsystem should be depicted and identified with some function or department (e.g., purchasing, billing, or general accounting), or an individual performing the task (e.g., purchasing agent, billing clerk, or general ledger clerk). Segregation of functions may be indicated either by partitioning the flowchart into areas labeled by function, department, or individual, or by striping, a technique in which the function, department, or individual performing the task is shown in a stripe across the top of an operation or process symbol.

The use of these and other flowcharting conventions is demonstrated in many illustrative flowcharts in subsequent chapters of this book. For example, Figures 7-2 and 7-3 on pages 220 and 222, respectively, contain sample flowcharts for the execution and recording of sales transactions in a manual system. Figure 7-7 on page 230 presents a more abbreviated form of flowchart for the computerized processing of sales transactions.

Study of these flowcharts reveals a number of additional flowcharting conventions. Generally, the direction of flow is from top to bottom and from left to right. Figures 7-2 and 7-3 illustrate the use of connectors to enhance clarity by avoiding the need for long flow lines crossing through one or more partitions. On the other hand, in the more abbreviated flowchart in Figure 7-7, flow lines running between partitions have been used, omitting the need for connector symbols.

Flowcharting is a creative task, making it unlikely that any two people would draw flowcharts exactly alike for a given system. However, the following guidelines should prove helpful:

- Specify exactly what system or subsystem is to be portrayed in the flowchart.
- Collect the necessary information through interviews, observations, and review of documents.
- Visualize an organizational format for the flowchart (e.g., whether to use partitions or striping to indicate segregation of functions) and prepare a rough sketch.
- Prepare the flowchart in good form.
- Test the completeness and accuracy of the flowchart by walking a hypothetical transaction through the flowchart.
- Study the flowchart to detect internal accounting control strengths and weaknesses.

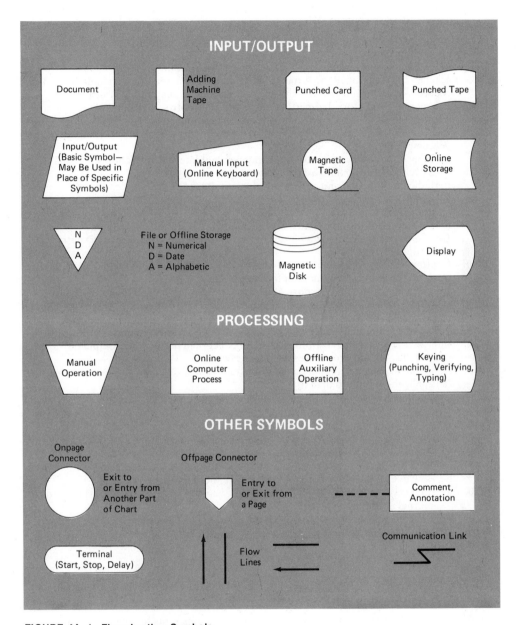

FIGURE 4A–1. Flowcharting Symbols

It should be emphasized that flowcharting is a means to an end, not an end in itself. The last item above is by far the most important, encompassing an analysis of what the flowchart reveals. From the flowchart and information obtained from questionnaires and other sources, the auditor should have ample knowledge to make an evaluation of the client's prescribed controls.

REVIEW QUESTIONS

4–1. What are the basic similarities and differences between administrative control and accounting control?

4–2. What are the four operative objectives of internal accounting control?

4–3. Explain the meaning of the terms (a) safeguarding of assets, (b) reliability of financial records, and (c) transactions, as these terms relate to accounting control.

4–4. Enumerate the factors that pertain to the internal control environment.

4–5. Identify the six basic principles of internal accounting control.

4–6. a. When is the assignment of duties among personnel deemed to be compatible? Incompatible?

 b. What conditions are important in independent internal verification?

4–7. a. State the second standard of field work.

 b. Indicate the scope and objectives of this standard.

4–8. a. Identify the parts and phases of the study of a system of internal accounting control.

 b. How much of the study must be completed in each audit engagement?

4–9. Distinguish between the two phases of the review of the system as to (a) nature, (b) method, and (c) purpose.

4–10. Contrast the advantages and disadvantages of using (a) questionnaires and (b) flowcharts in the completion phase of the review.

4–11. Describe the nature and purpose of a transaction walk-through review.

4–12. Indicate (a) the steps required in making a preliminary evaluation and (b) the method used by the auditor in performing each step.

4–13. What is the difference between a weakness and a material weakness?

4–14. Indicate (a) the three questions that are of concern in performing compliance tests and (b) the auditing procedures used in these tests.

4–15. Distinguish between compliance and substantive tests as to (a) primary purpose and (b) applicable standard of field work.

4–16. ''Compliance tests are normally performed during both interim and year-end work.'' Evaluate the accuracy of this statement.

4–17. What is meant by dual purpose testing?

4–18. Explain (a) the nature and purpose of the final evaluation of the system and (b) the levels of risk that may be identified.

4–19. a. What are the two risks that the auditor faces in an audit engagement?

 b. How does the auditor attempt to minimize these risks?

4–20. a. How may the work of the internal auditor be used in the study and evaluation of internal accounting control?

 b. What responsibilities do independent auditors have when they use the work of internal auditors?

COMPREHENSIVE QUESTIONS

4–21. An important procedure in the CPA's audit programs is his review of the client's system of internal control.

Required

 a. Distingush between accounting controls and administrative controls in a properly coordinated system of internal control.

 b. What bearing do these controls have on the work of the independent auditor?

 c. List the basic principles of a sound system of accounting control.

 d. Explain why the CPA is concerned about the separation of responsibilities for operating custodianship, financial custodianship, and controllership.

AICPA (adapted)

4–22. Jones, CPA, who has been engaged to examine the financial statements of Ajax Inc., is about to commence a study and evaluation of Ajax's system of internal control and is aware of the inherent limitations that should be considered.

Required
a. What are the objectives of a system of internal accounting control?
b. What are the reasonable assurances that are intended to be provided by the system of internal accounting control?
c. When considering the potential effectiveness of any system of internal accounting control what are the inherent limitations that should be recognized?

AICPA

4–23. As an audit manager, you find it necessary to provide an inexperienced assistant with an overview and an explanation of the auditor's study and evaluation of a client's system of internal accounting control.

Required
a. Present a flowchart of the auditor's study and evaluation of internal accounting control.
b. Explain the decision paths that may be followed with respect to substantive tests and indicate the effect of each path on the amount of substantive testing.
c. Explain the two conditions that normally justify a decision to complete the review.
d. Indicate the factors that might cause the auditor to forego compliance testing of prescribed controls.
e. Give the assistant an explanation of the manner in which the final evaluation of the system may be expressed.

4–24. Six principles of internal accounting control are identified in the chapter. Listed below are specific control procedures:

1. Cash registers are used for over-the-counter cash receipts.
2. Different individuals approve the payroll, write the payroll checks, and distribute the checks.
3. Checks are prenumbered.
4. Bank statements are independently reconciled each month.
5. Credit is approved by the credit department prior to sale.
6. A chart of accounts is maintained.
7. Inventory is stored in locked warehouses.
8. A voucher system is used.
9. Material requisitions are required to withdraw raw materials from the storeroom.
10. Control acounts and subsidiary ledgers are periodically agreed.

Required
a. Identify the internal control principle to which each procedure relates.
b. Identify two other procedures that apply to each internal control principle.

4–25. The Richmond Company, a client of your firm, has come to you with the following problem: It has three clerical employees who must perform the following functions:

1. Maintain general ledger.
2. Maintain accounts payable ledger.
3. Maintain accounts receivable ledger.
4. Prepare checks for signature.
5. Maintain disbursements journal.
6. Issue credits on returns and allowances.
7. Reconcile the bank account.
8. Handle and deposit cash receipts.

Required

Assuming that there is no problem as to the ability of any of the employees, the company requests your advice on assigning the above functions to the three employees in such a manner as to achieve the highest degree of internal control. It may be assumed that these employees will perform no other accounting functions than the ones listed and that any accounting functions not listed will be performed by persons other than these three employees.

a. State how you would recommend distributing the above functions among the three employees. Assume that, with the exception of the nominal jobs of the bank reconciliation and the issuance of credits on returns and allowances, all functions require an equal amount of time. (*Hint:* Give each employee a job title.)
b. List four possible unsatisfactory combinations of the above listed functions.

AICPA (adapted)

4–26. Adherence to GAAS requires, among other things, a proper study and evaluation of the existing internal control. The most common approaches to reviewing the system of internal control include the use of a questionnaire, preparation of a written description, preparation of a flowchart, and combinations of these methods.

Required

a. What is a CPA's objective in reviewing internal control for an opinion audit?
b. Discuss the advantages to a CPA of reviewing internal control by using
   1. An internal control questionnaire.
   2. The written description approach.
   3. A flowchart.
c. If after completing his description of internal control for an opinion audit he is satisfied that no material weaknesses in the client's internal control system exist, is it necessary to perform compliance tests? Explain.

AICPA (adapted)

4–27. For each of the following questions appearing on an internal accounting control questionnaire, assume that a ''No'' answer is given:

1. Is there separation of duties between the journalizing of transactions and posting to subsidiary ledgers?
2. Are cash registers used for cash receipts?
3. Is voucher preparation and check signing done by different individuals?
4. Are independent counts made of raw materials in storeroom?
5. Are all sales transactions authorized?
6. Are all bad debt write-offs authorized in writing?
7. Is access to storeroom restricted to storeroom personnel?
8. Are prenumbered checks accounted for in journalizing?
9. Are prenumbered vouchers used in processing purchases?
10. Are bank statements independently reconciled?
11. Is storeroom enclosed and locked?
12. Is a chart of accounts used in journalizing?

Required

a. Indicate the error or irregularity that could occur for each weakness.
b. Identify the internal control principle(s) involved in each situation.
c. Indicate by letter or by name (execution, recording, access, or comparison) the operative objective of internal accounting control to which the condition relates.

4–28. In your capacity as a staff assistant, you have worked on a number of audits during the year. Listed below are a list of possible internal control weaknesses that you have noted in your working papers:

1. A supermarket deposits cash intact every fourth day.

2. The cashier makes bank deposits, records cash transactions, and reconciles the bank statements.
3. The board of directors of a multinational company delegates the authorization of capital budgeting expenditures of less than $100,000 to the vice-president of manufacturing.
4. The reconciliation of the bank statement is made by a subsidiary ledger accounting clerk who does not have access to cash.
5. Office supplies in a large manufacturing company are stored in an unlocked closet in the office.
6. The write-off of bad debts is authorized by the accounts receivable clerk whenever a balance is 2 months past due.
7. Prenumbered receiving reports are not used in the receiving department.
8. The shipping department orally notifies the billing department of goods shipped.
9. Storeroom personnel and all foremen have access to the raw materials storeroom.
10. Monthly statements are not sent to customers.

Required
a. Classify the foregoing as (1) no weakness, (2) immaterial weakness, and (3) material weakness. Give the reasons for your answer.
b. For immaterial and material weaknesses indicate the internal control principle that has been violated.
c. Indicate your suggestions for eliminating any immaterial or material weaknesses.

4–29. The system of internal accounting control of the Trusty Company include the following control procedures:

1. An approved voucher is required for each check issued.
2. Two signatures are required on every check.
3. A supervisor makes daily cash register counts.
4. Overtime work must be approved by a supervisor.
5. Prenumbered sales invoices are used in billing.
6. A second clerk is required to verify the accuracy of each voucher.
7. Employee payroll records are kept in a locked file cabinet.
8. An accounting supervisor reviews journal entries periodically for reasonableness of account classifications.
9. Accounts receivable accounting personnel only make postings to the customers' ledger.
10. All vouchers must be stamped *paid* upon payment.
11. Only EDP equipment operators are allowed in the computer room.
12. A supervisor reconciles accounts receivable control with the customer ledger monthly.

Required
a. Indicate the internal control principle(s) applicable to each procedure.
b. Indicate an error or irregularity that could be prevented by each procedure.
c. Identify a compliance test that may be performed for each procedure.

4–30. The following is a list of prescribed accounting control procedures:

1. After the treasurer of the Ardent Company signs disbursement checks, the supporting data are returned to the accounting department, and the checks are given to his secretary for mailing.
2. The ticket-taker of a theater is required to tear each ticket presented for admission in half and present the stub to the patron.
3. The clerks of a department store are instructed to give the customer his cash register receipt along with the proper change.

4. The waitresses of the Elite Restaurant prepare the customer's check, which the customer then pays to the cashier. The waitresses are instructed not to make corrections on the check, but if an error is made to void the check and issue a new check. All voided checks are to be given to the manager at the end of the day.
5. The Larson Manufacturing Company prepares six copies of each purchase order. The third copy is sent to the receiving department to be used as a receiving memo, but the form is so designed that the quantity ordered does not print on this copy.
6. Hourly workers are required to punch clock cards.
7. A manager reconciles cash on hand with cash register readings daily.
8. An internal auditor reconciles the bank statements each month.
9. The credit department approves all credit sales.
10. Unused checks are stored in a safe under the custody of the treasurer.

Required

For each procedure indicate
a. The applicable internal control principle(s).
b. Identify the operative objective of accounting control to which the procedure relates.
c. Give an example of an error or irregularity that may be prevented.

4-31. At the Main Street Theater, the cashier, located in a box office at the entrance, receives cash from customers and operates a machine which ejects serially numbered tickets. To gain admission to the theater, a customer hands the ticket to a doorperson stationed some 50 feet from the box office at the entrance to the theater lobby. The doorperson tears the ticket in half, opens the door for the customer, and returns the stub to him. The other half of the ticket is dropped by the doorperson into a locked box.

Required

a. What internal controls are present in this phase of handling cash receipts?
b. What steps should be taken regularly by the manager or other supervisor to give maximum effectiveness to these controls?
c. Assume that the cashier and doorperson decided to collaborate in an effort to abstract cash receipts. What action might they take?
d. Continuing the assumption made in (c) above of collusion between the cashier and doorperson, what features of the control procedures would be likely to disclose the embezzlement?

AICPA

4-32. A description of some of the operating procedures of the Greystone Manufacturing Corporation is given in the succeeding paragraphs:

1. When materials are ordered, a duplicate of the purchase order is sent to the receiving department. When the materials are received, the receiving clerk records the receipt on the copy of the order, which is then sent to the accounting department to support the entry to Accounts Payable and to Purchases. The materials are then taken to stores where the quantity is entered on bin records.
2. Timecards of employees are sent to a data processing department which prepares punched cards for use in the preparation of payrolls, payroll checks, and labor cost distribution records. The payroll checks are compared with the payrolls and signed by an official of the company who returns them to the supervisor of the data processing department for distribution to employees.
3. A sales branch of the company has an office force consisting of the manager and two assistants. The branch has a local bank account in which it deposits cash receipts. Checks drawn on this account require the manager's signature or the signa-

ture of the treasurer of the company. Bank statements and paid checks are returned by the bank to the manager, who retains them in his files after making the reconciliation. Reports of disbursements are prepared by the manager and submitted to the home office on scheduled dates.

Required

For each of the activities described, you are to point out

a. The deficiencies, if any, in internal control, including an explanation of the errors or irregularities which might occur.

b. Recommendations for changes in procedures which would correct the existing weaknesses.

AICPA (adapted)

CASE STUDY

4–33.* Harlan, Inc., is a large, highly diversified organization engaged in feed and flour milling, the manufacture of plastic products, the manufacture of highly specialized machinery, and the operation of poultry hatcheries, farms, and processing plants. The company's facilities are located throughout the United States.

During the past several years, the company has been expanding the business through acquisitions, mergers, and natural growth of the original operations.

The company finances poultry growing operations of feed customers until the flocks are marketed. Poultry prices have been depressed for the past several years, and, as a result, large bad debt losses have been sustained. Many accounts are secured by collateral other than poultry and are not considered current assets.

Your review of the current internal controls and accounting procedures disclosed the following changes from prior years:

1. The company organized an internal audit staff during the year.
2. The internal audit staff is reconciling all bank accounts.
3. The company has instituted a procedure whereby divisions send the Home Office an "invoice apron" which lists the information required for payment of the invoices and the due date. The other invoices and other supporting data (e.g., receiving reports, purchase orders) remain at the receiving location.
4. Excess funds are now invested in short-term securities. The treasurer has sole authority for purchase and sale of the investments. Securities purchases are credited to a company account at a local brokerage house. The securities are held in the treasurer's name. All correspondence related to the investments is sent directly to the treasurer. He, in turn, forwards brokerage advices to the controller's office for recording in the accounts.
5. A physical inventory of office furniture and fixtures has been taken at the home office.

Discussions with company personnel and compliance testing disclosed the following information:

1. The company plans to discontinue extending credit to certain customers whose poultry raising operations have deteriorated to the point that their ability to repay the company is doubtful. It is anticipated that a large provision for doubtful accounts many be necessary to reduce these accounts to estimated realizable value on a forced realization basis (the company has second mortgages as collateral on many of the farms).
2. The tool crib inventory consists of a conglomeration of miscellaneous items, most of which are small quantities with very minor unit prices. This inventory totals $42,395.89 which is an insignificant portion of the total inventories.
3. The purchased parts stockroom at another plant is segregated from the production areas by a wire fence. While visiting this plant, you noted that the gate was left

open all day and access to the stockroom (which contains many valuable and easily concealed items) was available to any employee. The stockroom's perpetual inventory records were formerly checked by an employee who made periodic test counts. This employee has retired and has not been replaced. As a result, such counting has ceased. You expanded your tests in view of these situations and are satisfied that the perpetual records reasonably reflect the quantities on hand.

Required

a. Identify the environmental factors that impact on the company's internal accounting controls.
b. List identified strengths and weaknesses in Harlan's procedures.
c. From your list of weaknesses identify those you consider material and indicate your suggestions for improvement in your required communication to management.
d. Indicate the areas in which you would likely extend your substantive tests.

5 Auditing Electronic Data Processing Systems

STUDY OBJECTIVES

The study objectives in this chapter are to acquire an understanding of electronic data processing systems and their auditing implications. To achieve these objectives, it is necessary for the reader to

- Know the basic components of an EDP system.
- Comprehend the types of controls in an EDP system.
- Realize the similarities and differences in making a study and evaluation of internal control between an EDP and a manual system.
- Perceive the differences in performing compliance tests with and without the computer.
- Understand the audit impact of online realtime systems and computer service centers.
- Know the uses of the computer in obtaining audit evidence.

Electronic Data Processing (EDP) has been one of the most important technological developments in the latter half of the twentieth century. Computer installations now range in size from minicomputers used for limited applications, such as accounts receivable or payroll, to complex international financial communication networks. A company may elect to lease or own its computer system or to use outside, independent computer service centers to process accounting data. Thus, even a very small audit client may have some data processed electronically. Coupled with the greater use of computers in business has been a corresponding increase in computer-related frauds.

In this chapter consideration is given initially to the basic components and types of accounting controls in a computerized system. Then, attention is focused on the auditing implications of various kinds of EDP systems and computer service centers.

EDP SYSTEM COMPONENTS

The auditor should be familiar with the following components of an EDP system:

- Hardware.
- Software.
- Data files and processing methods.

Computer Hardware

Hardware is the physical equipment associated with the system. The basic hardware configuration consists of the central processing unit (CPU) and peripheral input and output devices. The principal hardware component is the CPU. It is composed of a control unit, an internal storage unit, and an arithmetic-logic unit. The control unit directs and coordinates the entire system, including the entry and removal of information from storage, and the routing of the data between storage and the arithmetic-logic unit. The internal storage unit, or computer "memory," stores the program instructions and the data to be processed. The arithmetic logic-unit is so named because it is capable of performing mathematical computations and certain logical operations.

Peripheral to the CPU are input devices, output devices, and auxiliary storage devices. Figure 5-1 illustrates common types of devices in each grouping.

Terminals are directly connected to the CPU. Generally they are located in remote locations. Keyboard printer terminals have keyboards similar to a typewriter that provide hard copy of the data being entered. Basic visual display terminals also have keyboards and show the data on a screen.

Character recognition devices consist of optical character recognition (OCR) and magnetic ink character recognition (MICR) devices. These devices read documents containing typed or coded characters and enter the data directly into the CPU or onto machine-readable media.

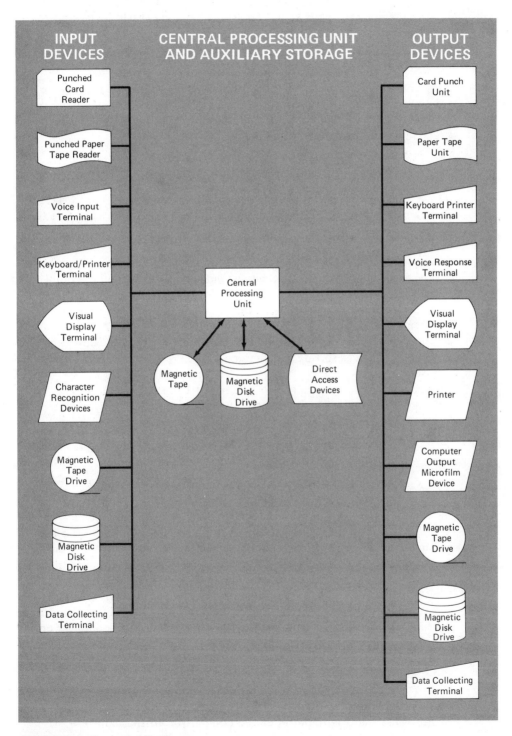

FIGURE 5–1. Computer Hardware

The printer is a widely used output device. It produces hard copy in the form of documents, reports, etc. Peripheral equipment in direct communication with the CPU is considered to be online.

Computer Software

This component consists of the programs and routines that facilitate the programming and operation of a computer. There are several kinds of computer software. Of particular interest to auditors are: (1) systems programs and (2) application programs.

Systems Programs

These programs, which sometimes are called *supervisory programs,* perform generalized functions for one or more application programs. There are three kinds of systems programs:

- *Operating systems* that (1) minimize the amount of human intervention in processing and (2) control, schedule, and maximize efficient use of the hardware.
- *Data-base management systems* that facilitate the processing and retrieval of file data in a data base environment.
- *Utility programs* (*routines*) that perform frequently required computer processes such as sorting and merging.

Systems programs generally are purchased from hardware suppliers and software companies. They are then adapted, as necessary, by each user to suit individual needs.

Application Programs

Application programs contain instructions that enable the user to perform data processing tasks appropriate for specific applications—such as payroll, inventory, and so on. These programs are generally written by the user of the equipment, but they may also be purchased from software vendors.

The instructions can be classified into four types: (1) input-output, (2) data movement, (3) arithmetic, and (4) logic. The input instruction enables the computer to read data from an appropriate input medium and store it in the computer memory. To get the data out of storage and onto an output medium, the output instruction must be provided. The data movement instruction allows a computer to move data from one storage location to another. Arithmetic instructions are used to specify the arithmetic operations and the data fields to be operated on. The basic concept of the logic instruction is the comparison of two sets of data in storage and the branching of the program to a particular step when a certain condition (equal, greater than, or less than) is found after the comparison of the data.

Data Files and Processing Methods

Data include transactions and related information that are entered into the system and stored, processed, or produced by the system. Input data may be processed in many forms (e.g., punched cards, magnetic tape, disk, diskette, and so on). Data may be stored on magnetic tape or disk devices.

Two types of data files are frequently mentioned in an EDP context: (1) a *master file* which contains the up-to-date information about a given class of data, such as the general ledger and the accounts receivable subsidiary ledger and (2) a transaction file which is a collection of individual transactions of a given type, such as the day's sales transactions. A transaction file is similar to a journal. File data in an EDP system are in machine-sensible form, which means that they usually can be read or changed only by using the computer.

There are two generally recognized methods by which data are processed in an EDP system: (1) sequential and (2) random. The choice of method is dependent on many factors, but the organization of the auxiliary permanent storage devices is a major consideration. When the file records are in sequence, as with punch cards and magnetic tape, transactions of a particular type, such as sales, must be sequenced before processing. For credit sales, it is customary to sequence by customer number because the accounts receivable master file is generally arranged in this manner. Normally, in sequential processing the entire file must be read by the computer each time any transactions are processed. In contrast, when file data do not have to be accessed in sequence, as in the case of magnetic disks, transactions can be processed in any order. With nonsequential processing, only the specific account in the file is read in processing the transaction. The difference between the two processing methods is graphically depicted in Figure 5-2.

INTERNAL CONTROL IN AN EDP SYSTEM

Most EDP systems involve a combination of manual and computer processing activities. In the usual case, separate control procedures are developed for each phase of the processing. As in a completely manual system, management has the responsibility for providing the control environment and for establishing and maintaining the system of internal control when EDP is used.

Internal Control Environment

The method of data processing may significantly affect the organizational structure and the control procedures necessary to meet the broad objectives of internal accounting control. Typically, EDP has a significant impact on internal control. In determining its effect on the control environment, the auditor should consider the following differences between manual and EDP activities:

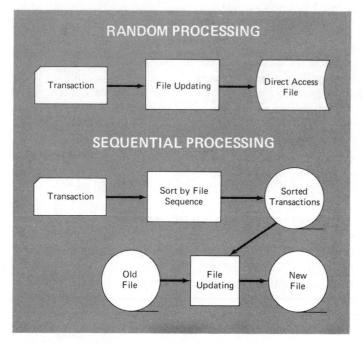

FIGURE 5–2. Random versus Sequential Processing

- There is often less documentary evidence of the performance of control procedures in computer systems than in manual systems.
- Information in manual systems is visible. In contrast, files and records in EDP systems are usually in machine-sensible form and cannot be read without a computer.
- The decrease of human involvement in EDP processing can obscure errors that might be observed in manual systems.
- Information in EDP systems may be more vulnerable to physical disaster, unauthorized manipulation, and mechanical malfunction than information in manual systems.
- Various functions may be concentrated in EDP systems, with a corresponding reduction in the traditional segregation of duties followed in manual systems.
- Changes in the system are often more difficult to implement and control in EDP systems than in manual systems.
- EDP systems can provide greater consistency in processing than manual systems because they uniformly subject all transactions to the same controls.

The concentration of functions within EDP systems tends to combine duties that would be incompatible in a manual system. For example, in the processing of payroll transactions, the computer may be programmed to compute gross and net earnings, record the payroll, update employee earning records, and prepare the payroll checks. If one individual performed these duties in a manual system, that person would be in a position to both perpetrate and conceal errors. The safeguard in an electronic system rests in the computer program. Once the program has been tested (debugged) and approved, that program will process transactions uniformly. The risk, from a control standpoint, is in the possibility of unauthorized changes in the program rather than the possibility of processing errors. It is for this reason that programming and machine operation should be separated.

Similarly, an individual should not be able to make unapproved changes in EDP data files. In the preceding payroll application, for example, an individual should not be able to add fictitious time reports or false pay rates to the file data, thereby causing the payroll program to process incorrect payroll checks. An individual who can make unapproved changes in systems programs or file data also performs incompatible functions. Where incompatible duties exist, other compensating controls should be provided.

A good control environment pertaining to EDP activities complements prescribed EDP control procedures whereas a poor environment may impede the effectiveness of such procedures. The auditor's evaluation of the control environment ordinarily will influence his study and evaluation of prescribed EDP controls.

Accounting Controls

There are two categories of accounting controls in a computerized system: general and application.

General controls pertain to the EDP environment and all EDP activities. These controls tend to be pervasive in their effect. Included within this category are the following specific controls.

- Organization and operation controls.
- Systems development and documentation controls.
- Hardware and systems software controls.
- Access controls.
- Data and procedural controls.[1]

Application controls relate to specific tasks to be performed by the computer. These controls are designed to provide reasonable assurance that the recording, processing, and reporting of data by EDP are properly performed. Included within this category of EDP controls are:

[1] Computer Services Executive Committee, Audit and Accounting Guide, *The Auditor's Study and Evaluation of Internal Control in EDP Systems* (New York: American Institute of Certified Public Accountants, 1977), p. 25.

- Input controls.
- Processing controls.
- Output controls.

Each of the specific types of controls is explained below.

Organization and Operation Controls

Organization and operation controls pertain to segregation of functions within the EDP department and between EDP and user departments. Weaknesses in these controls usually affect all EDP applications. The organizational structure shown in Figure 5-3 illustrates an arrangement which provides for clear-cut lines of authority and responsibility within the EDP department. The primary responsibilities for each position are as follows:

POSITION	PRIMARY RESPONSIBILITIES
EDP manager	Exercises overall control, develops short- and long-range plans, and approves systems
Systems analyst	Evaluates existing systems, designs new systems, outlines the systems, and prepares specifications for programmers
Programmer	Flowcharts logic of computer programs, develops and documents programs, and debugs programs
Computer operator	Operates the computer hardware and executes the program according to operating instructions
Data entry operator	Prepares data for processing by recording it on machine-readable media, e.g., by keying data onto magnetic tape
Librarian	Maintains custody of systems documentation, programs, and files
Data control group	Acts as liaison with user departments and monitors input, processing, and output

In small installations, the systems analysis and programming functions may be combined. However, the combining of these two functions with computer operating generally results in incompatible functions. When these three functions are performed by one individual, that person is in a position to both commit and conceal errors. A number of computer frauds have resulted when these duties were combined.

The EDP department should be organizationally independent of user departments. Thus, the EDP manager should report to an executive, such as the chief financial officer, who is not regularly involved in authorizing transactions for computer processing. In addition, EDP personnel should not correct errors unless they originate within EDP. For example, EDP can correct keypunching errors, but it should return a sales order with an invalid

FIGURE 5–3. Organizational Chart of an EDP Department

code number to sales for correction. Furthermore, EDP personnel should not authorize or initiate transactions or have custody of resulting assets. When the organizational plan does not provide for appropriate segregation of functions, the auditor may have serious doubts about the reliability of the results produced by the system.

Systems Development and Documentation Controls

Systems development controls relate to (1) review, testing, and approval of new systems, (2) control of program changes, and (3) documentation procedures. The following procedures are helpful in providing the necessary controls:

- Systems design should include representatives of user departments and, as appropriate, the accounting department and internal auditors.
- Each system should have written specifications that are reviewed and approved by management and the user department.
- Systems testing should be a cooperative effort of users and EDP personnel.
- The EDP manager, user personnel, and the appropriate level of management should give final approval to a new system before it is placed in normal operation.
- Program changes should be approved before implementation to determine whether they have been authorized, tested, and documented.[2]

Documentation controls pertain to the documents and records maintained by a company to describe computer processing activities. Adequate documentation is important to both management and the auditor. For management, documentation provides a basis for (1) reviewing the system, (2) training new personnel, and (3) maintaining and revising existing systems and programs. For the auditor, documentation provides the primary source of information about the flow of transactions through the system and the related accounting controls. Documentation includes:

[2] Computer Services Executive Committee, *op. cit.*, pp. 30-34.

- Descriptions and flowcharts of the systems and programs.
- Operating instructions for the computer operater.
- Control procedures to be followed by operators and users.
- Descriptions and samples of required inputs and outputs.

Hardware and Systems Software Controls

Modern computer technology has achieved a high degree of reliability in computer equipment. Contributing factors are the existence of built-in hardware control features and systems software controls that are designed to detect any malfunctioning of the equipment. This category of controls includes:

Dual read. Input data are read twice and the two readings are compared.

Parity check. Data are processed by the computer in arrays of bits (binary digits of 0 or 1). In addition to bits necessary to represent the numeric or alphabetic characters, a parity bit is added, when necessary, to make the sum of all the ''1'' bits always odd or even. As data are entered and ultimately transferred within the computer, the parity check is applied by the computer to assure that bits are not lost during the process.

Echo check. The echo check involves transmitting data received by an output device back to the source unit for comparison with the original data.

Read after write. The computer reads back the data after they have been recorded, either in storage or on the output device, and verifies the data by comparison with their original source.

To achieve maximum benefit from these controls (1) there should be a program of preventive maintenance on all hardware and (2) controls over changes in systems software should parallel the systems development and documentation controls described above.

Access Controls

Access controls should prevent unauthorized use of EDP equipment, data files, and computer programs. The specific controls include both physical and procedural safeguards.

Access to computer hardware should be limited to authorized individuals, such as computer operators. Physical safeguards include the housing of the equipment in an area that is separate from user departments. Access to the area should be restricted by guard services, door locks, or special keys. Procedural safeguards involve management review of computer utilization reports.

Access to data files and programs should be designed to prevent unauthorized use of such data. Physical controls exist in the form of a library and a librarian. Access to program documentation and data files should be limited to individuals authorized to process, maintain, or modify particular systems. Ordinarily, the librarian keeps a log of the use of files and programs.

Data and Procedural Controls

This category of general controls provides a framework for controlling daily computer operations, minimizing the likelihood of processing errors, and assuring the continuity of operations in the event of a physical disaster or computer failure.

The first two objectives are achieved through a control function performed by individuals or departments that are organizationally independent of computer operations. This responsibility is often assumed by the data control group within EDP. The control function involves

- Receiving and screening all data to be processed.
- Accounting for all input data.
- Following up on processing errors.
- Verifying the proper distribution of output.

The control of daily operations is facilitated by maintaining totals of input data and reconciling them with system-generated processing and output controls. Totals are usually obtained for batches of data, and a batch control transmittal ticket accompanies the data as they are processed.

The ability to maintain the continuity of computer operations involves (1) the use of off-premises storage for important files, programs, and documentation, (2) physical protection against environmental hazards, and (3) formal record retention plans. When sequential processing is used, a common method of records retention is the grandfather-father-son concept illustrated in Figure 5-4.

Under this concept, the new updated master file is the son. The master file utilized in the updating run which produced the son is the father, and the previous master file is the grandfather. To update these earlier master files, records of transactions for the current and prior periods also must be retained. In the event that the current computer master file is destroyed, the system then has the capability to replace it. Ideally, the three generations of files and the transaction files should be stored in separate locations to minimize the risk of losing all the files at one time.

Input Controls

Input controls are one type of application controls. They are of vital importance in an EPD system because most of the errors occur at this point. Input controls are designed to provide reasonable assurance that data received for processing have been (1) properly authorized, (2) converted into machine-

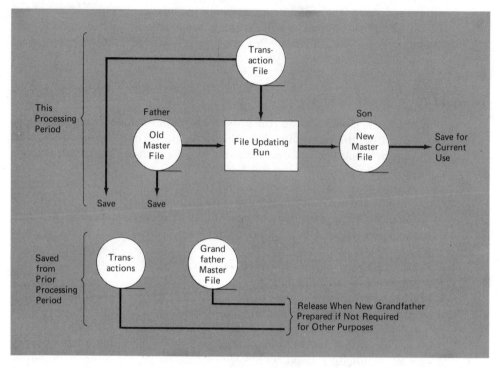

FIGURE 5–4. Grandfather-Father-Son in Magnetic Tape Files (Source: Gordon B. Davis, *Auditing and EDP* (New York: American Institute of Certified Public Accountants, 1968), p. 97.)

sensible form, and (3) subsequently accounted for.[3] These controls also include the rejection, correction, and resubmission of data that were initially incorrect.

Authorization

Each transaction entry should be properly authorized and approved in accordance with management's general or specific authorization. Where documents are individually processed, authorization is usually provided in the form of a signature or stamp on the source document; in contrast, when input data are assembled in batches, there ordinarily is user department approval of each batch of documents. In some cases, the computer performs the authorization function. For example, a purchase requisition is automatically initiated when inventory quantities are reduced to a specified reorder level. Control here occurs after the fact by review of the output by the data control group or by the user department.

[3] Auditing Standards Board, *Codification of Statements on Auditing Standards* (New York: American Institute of Certified Public Accountants, 1983), Auditing Section 321.08 (adapted) (hereinafter referred to and cited as AU §).

Conversion of Input Data

Controls over the conversion of data into machine-sensible form include the following techniques:[4]

Record counts. The transactions to be converted are counted. After conversion, the new records are counted and the total is compared to the original count.

Batch controls. After processing, a control total, for example, sales dollars, or hash total, such as the sum of all account numbers, for each batch is reconciled to the original control total.

Computer editing. The computer can perform a wide range of edit tests on input records, including tests of reasonableness (e.g., time cards exceeding a reasonable number of hours), cross-checks between files to verify relationships (e.g., the transaction is for an open account on the master file), and tests for nonnumeric data in a numeric field (i.e., the presence of alphabetic or special characters in a field that should contain numbers).

Verification. Data conversion is performed on a dual basis. After conversion, the two results are compared. This technique is used primarily in the keying of data for batch-oriented operations.

Additional controls that may be found in an online system are described in a later section of this chapter.

Subsequent Accountability

Controls are needed to ascertain that input data have not been lost, suppressed, added, duplicated, or otherwise changed during movement between processing steps or between departments. Transmittal controls, routing slips, and control totals are techniques that are frequently used for this purpose.

Error Correction

The correction and resubmission of incorrect data are vital to the accuracy of the accounting records. For example, if processing of a valid sales invoice is stopped because of an error, accounts receivable and sales will both be understated until the error is eliminated and the processing is completed. Errors should be corrected by those responsible for the mistake. Thus, errors in source documents should be corrected by user departments, whereas errors in conversion or movement of input data should be corrected by the EDP department. For control purposes, errors should be logged and

---

[4] Computer Services Executive Committee, *op. cit.,* p. 53.

their disposition should be periodically reviewed by the data control group.

Processing Controls

This class of application controls is designed to provide reasonable assurance that electronic data processing has been performed as intended for the particular application—that is, all transactions are processed as authorized, no authorized transactions are omitted, and no unauthorized transactions are added.[5]

Processing controls take a variety of forms. The most widely used techniques are as follows:

Control totals. Provision for accumulating control totals is written into the computer program to facilitate the balancing of input totals with processing totals for each run.

File identification labels. External labels permit visual identification of a file. Internal file labels are matched with specified operator instructions (or commands) incorporated into the computer program before processing can begin or be successfully completed.

Limit and reasonableness checks. This technique is similar to the computer editing of input data.

Before-and-after report. This report shows a summary of the contents of a master file before and after each update.

Output Controls

Output controls are designed to assure the accuracy of the processing result (such as account listings or displays, reports, magnetic files, invoices, or disbursement checks) and to assure that only authorized personnel receive the output.[6]

The accuracy of the processing result includes both updated machine-sensible files and printed output. This objective is met by the following:

Reconciliation of totals. Output totals that are generated by the computer programs are reconciled to input and processing totals by the data control group and user departments.

Comparison to source documents. Output data are subject to detailed comparison with source documents.

---

[5] Auditing Standards Board, *op. cit.*, AU § 321.08.
[6] *Ibid.*

Control over the distribution of output is usually maintained by the data control group. Special care should be exercised by this group over the distribution of confidential output. To facilitate control over the disposition of output, systems documentation should include a report distribution sheet.

METHODOLOGY FOR STUDYING AND EVALUATING EDP CONTROLS

There are both similarities and differences in making a study and evaluation of internal control between a manual and an EDP system.

Applicability of Generally Accepted Auditing Standards

All of the generally accepted auditing standards (GAAS) apply to an examination of financial statements prepared in accordance with generally accepted accounting principles (GAAP). This is true regardless of the method of data processing used by the client. The impact of a computerized data system on two of the standards merits special comment.

The first general standard states that the examination is to be made by individuals having adequate technical training and proficiency as an auditor. This means that the auditor must have sufficient expertise to understand and to evaluate the system. The extent of the knowledge depends on the complexity of the EDP system and the responsibilities the individual is assuming. The individual may be a (1) general audit staff member, (2) computer audit specialist, or (3) management advisory services EDP professional. A special American Institute of Certified Public Accountants (AICPA) task force has recommended the following knowledge about EDP for a general audit staff member:

- A basic knowledge of a computer system—its parts, functions, and capabilities.
- The ability to design, analyze, and flowchart a system of modest complexity.
- A general knowledge of a computer language sufficient to program a simple problem.
- An understanding of the control procedures and needed modification of auditing methods to audit using a computer.[7]

The other standard that merits comment is the second standard of field work relating to the auditor's study and evaluation of internal accounting control. The applicability of the standard is not affected by whether the EDP facilities used are those of the client or an outside third party.

---

[7] Adapted from *Information for CPA Candidates* (New York: American Institute of Certified Public Accountants, 1975), p. 7.

Overview of Methodology

The methodology for making a study and evaluation of internal controls in an EDP system is conceptually the same as in a manual system. For example, the steps and decision paths in Figure 4-3 for a manual system are identical with those applicable to a computer system. The methodology for an EDP system is as follows:

STEPS	DECISION PATHS
• Make preliminary review of accounting system and general and application controls to decide whether further study is justifiable	• Continue review or go to expanded substantive tests
• Complete review of general and application controls and make preliminary evaluation of prescribed controls	• Identify controls to be relied on, assuming satisfactory compliance, and proceed to compliance testing; or go to expanded substantive tests
• Perform compliance tests on controls to be relied on	
• Make final evaluation of control procedures	• For controls where compliance is satisfactory, go to restricted substantive tests; where compliance is not satisfactory, go to expanded substantive tests

Each of the steps and decision paths is explained below.

Reviewing the System

An auditor's review of a client's system of accounting control should encompass all significant and relevant manual, mechanical, and EDP activities and the interrelationship between EDP and user departments.[8] As in the case of a manual data processing system, the review consists of two phases: (1) preliminary and (2) completion.

Preliminary Phase of Review

In the preliminary phase of the review of EDP controls the auditor obtains information about three matters: (1) the flow of transactions through the system, (2) the extent to which EDP is used in each significant accounting application, and (3) the basic structure of accounting control within the client organization.[9] Significant accounting applications relate to classes of transactions, such as sales and payroll in a manufacturing company, that will materially affect the client's financial statements.

---

[8] Auditing Standards Board, *op. cit.*, AU § 321.24.
[9] Auditing Standards Board, *op. cit.*, AU § 321.25.

The preliminary review extends to both general controls and application controls. In this phase, the auditor relies primarily on inquiry, but knowledge may also be obtained by observation of the performance of control procedures and by reviewing organization charts, procedures manuals, and other documentation.

At the conclusion of the preliminary review, the auditor must decide whether further study is likely to justify any restriction of substantive tests. Basically, this is a "go" or "no go" decision. A "go" decision results in moving to the completion phase of the review. A "no go" decision terminates the review phase, and the auditor proceeds directly to substantive testing.

A decision to terminate the review may occur when

- EDP is not used in any significant accounting applications.
- EDP is used in significant accounting applications, but other auditing procedures (i.e., substantive tests) are more cost-efficient than performing compliance tests on the EDP controls.
- EDP controls in significant accounting applications are redundant because of other accounting controls, such as user department controls over input and output.
- EDP controls in significant accounting applications are too weak to rely on.[10]

Completion Phase of Review

In the completion phase of the review, the auditor is expected to expand on the knowledge about accounting controls obtained during the preliminary review through additional inquiry, observation, review of documentation, and transaction walk-through reviews. As in a manual system, the findings should be documented in the form of completed questionnaires, flowcharts, or narrative memoranda.

This phase of the review process begins with a review of general EDP controls pertaining to all significant accounting applications. In making this review, the auditor should obtain answers to such questions as the following:

- How does the organization of the data processing department provide adequate supervision and segregation of functions within EDP and between EDP and users?
- What procedures provide for control over systems development and access to systems documentation?
- What procedures provide for control over program and systems maintenance?

[10] Auditing Standards Board, *op. cit.*, AU § 321.26.

- What procedures provide control over computer operations, including access to data files and programs?
- What procedures, during the period under review, assured that file reconstruction and processing recoveries were complete?
- To what extent do internal auditors perform a review and evaluation of EDP activities?[11]

If material weaknesses are discovered in general controls, the auditor may terminate the review because general controls often have pervasive effects on application controls. However, when there are no material weaknesses in general controls, the auditor proceeds to complete his review of application controls pertaining to each significant accounting application. Thus, answers should be obtained to questions relating to the adequacy of prescribed EDP accounting controls over input, processing, and output. With respect to input data that were initially incorrect, for example, the auditor will ascertain whether

- User department errors are corrected in the initiating department.
- Such data are subsequently corrected and resubmitted.
- Error logs are kept of such data.

Making a Preliminary Evaluation. The nature and purpose of this evaluation of accounting controls in an EDP system is the same as in a manual system. For example, the auditor should (1) consider the types of errors and irregularities that could occur, (2) determine the control procedures that should prevent or detect such occurrences, and (3) determine whether the necessary control procedures are prescribed. Possible errors and irregularities and necessary control procedures relating to application controls are shown in Figure 5-5.

After completing this analysis, the auditor uses professional judgment to identify the control procedures to be relied on, assuming satisfactory compliance. A schematic presentation of the review of EDP accounting controls is provided in Figure 5-6.

Tests of Compliance

Tests of compliance are performed for the purpose of providing assurance that the internal control procedures that exist within the client's system are in use and are functioning as planned. For EDP control procedures that leave visible evidence of performance, the auditor inspects the document or record containing the evidence. An example is a file documenting the program changes for an EDP application and approval of the changes. Performance of some control procedures within the EDP activity leaves no visible evidence. Examples are input validation routines or processing controls designed to detect erroneous or invalid data. To test for the effectiveness of

---

[11] Computer Services Executive Committee, *op. cit.*, p. 16.

ERRORS AND IRREGULARITIES	NECESSARY CONTROL PROCEDURES
Input	
Valid data are incorrectly converted to machine-sensible form	Record counts Batch controls Computer editing Internal verification Data control monitoring
Properly converted input is lost, or duplicated, or distorted during handling	Transmittal controls Control totals
Detected erroneous data are not corrected and resubmitted for processing	Error logs Data control monitoring
Processing	
The wrong files are processed and updated	External file labels Internal file labels
Processing errors are made on valid input data	Control totals
Illogical or unreasonable input is processed	Limit and reasonableness tests Other logical tests
Output	
Output may be incorrect because of processing errors	Output control totals
Output may be incorrect because file revisions are unauthorized or approved changes are not made	Periodic comparisons of file data with source documents
Output is distributed to unauthorized users	Data control group monitoring Report distribution control sheet

FIGURE 5–5. Preliminary Evaluation Considerations: Application Controls

such controls, the auditor may examine transactions submitted for processing to determine that no transactions tested have unacceptable conditions or that the unacceptable conditions present were reported and appropriately resolved.

In an EDP system, the auditor's procedures for performing tests of compliance are determined by the adequacy of the audit trail. If sufficient printed output exists, the auditor may be able to follow ordinary manual audit procedures. In other cases, the auditor may need to use the computer to carry out these procedures.

Testing General Controls

The auditor must test all controls that are to be relied on in performing substantive tests. This includes both general and application controls. Tests

PRELIMINARY PHASE OF REVIEW

1. Obtain Knowledge
SCOPE
- Entire accounting system including both EDP and non-EDP segments
- Both EDP general and application controls
PURPOSE
- Understand flow of transactions in system
- Learn extent to which EDP is used in significant accounting applications
- Comprehend basic structure of accounting control
METHODS
- Same as manual system (i.e., inquiry, observation, review of documentation, etc.)

2. Make Decision
PURPOSE
- Determine significance of accounting controls within EDP in relation to entire system
- Determine extent of additional review of EDP accounting controls
METHOD
- Professional judgment
EFFECTS
- Cease further review of controls and proceed to substantive testing, or
- Continue to next phase of review

COMPLETION PHASE OF REVIEW

3. Expand Knowledge
SCOPE
- Both general and application controls
PURPOSE
- Expand knowledge obtained from preliminary review
METHODS
- More intensive use of techniques followed in making preliminary review

4. Make Preliminary Evaluation
SCOPE
- Both general and application controls
PURPOSE
- Identify controls on which reliance is planned
METHODS
- Same as manual (i.e., determination of errors or irregularities that could occur, etc.)
- Professional judgment

FIGURE 5–6. Schematic Presentation of Review of EDP Accounting Controls

of general controls consist primarily of inquiry, observation, and inspection of documentation. An illustrative audit program for testing of these controls is presented in Figure 5-7.

Testing Application Controls Without the Computer

If the processing application being tested is well documented and sufficient printed output exists or can be generated by the client, the auditor may decide to use audit procedures traditionally applied in a manual accounting system to test the existence and effectiveness of internal controls. This is done by using conventional source documents and printed output.

Auditing by testing input and output instead of the computer itself does not enable the auditor to detect program errors that do not show up in the output samples. Error listings generated by the processing function give evidence that a control does exist to detect such an error, but missing

---

AUDIT PROGRAM

TYPE OF TESTING: Compliance   **PURPOSE: Effectiveness of EDP general controls**

A. ORGANIZATION AND OPERATION CONTROLS ARE PROPERLY FUNCTIONING.

    1. Observe and make inquiries concerning segregation of functions between EDP and user departments and within EDP.
    2. Selectively test preprocessing, postprocessing, and programmed controls to determine if they provide for processing in accordance with management's authorization.

B. SYSTEMS DEVELOPMENT AND DOCUMENTATION CONTROLS ARE PROPERLY FUNCTIONING.

    1. Examine evidence for approval of new systems and programs and changes therein.
    2. Trace selected program changes to supporting documentation.
    3. Review results of tests to verify correctness of system and program changes.

C. HARDWARE AND SYSTEMS SOFTWARE CONTROLS ARE PROPERLY FUNCTIONING.

    1. Review and evaluate the hardware controls included in the operating system.
    2. Review documentation in support of systems software changes to ascertain whether prescribed procedures are being followed.
    3. Examine results of selected pretesting of software programs.

D. ACCESS CONTROLS ARE PROPERLY FUNCTIONING.

    1. Inquire of librarian as to compliance with procedures for controlling unauthorized access to programs and data files.
    2. Examine data files and program access records to test the library function as it applies to significant accounting applications.
    3. Observe procedures for limiting access to computer hardware.

E. DATA AND PROCEDURAL CONTROLS ARE PROPERLY FUNCTIONING.

    1. Review on a test basis reconciliations of control totals by the data control group.
    2. Selectively review computer operator manuals and observe whether prescribed procedures are being followed.
    3. Determine the extent, nature, and quality of internal auditing review of EDP activities.
    4. Observe distribution of computer output to ascertain that only authorized users receive copies.

SOURCE: Computer Services Executive Committee, *op. cit.,* pp. 25-40 (Adapted)

FIGURE 5–7. Audit Program: Compliance Tests of General Controls

controls are not revealed. Instead, the auditor must rely upon existing procedural and output controls to detect such omissions.

Auditing without the computer offers the following advantages:

- The auditor can use familiar manual system techniques.
- Recourse to the complexities of computer programs is unnecessary.[12]

The principal disadvantages of auditing without the computer are that the auditor may fail to utilize the capabilities of the computer in gathering audit evidence and cost savings in audit time and effort may not be realized.

---

[12] Davis, *op. cit.,* p. 136.

Testing Application Controls With the Computer

The auditor may find it advantageous to test programmed controls with the aid of the computer when

- A significant part of the internal control is embodied in a computer program.
- There are significant gaps in the visible audit trail.
- There are large volumes of records to be tested.[13]

To audit with the computer, it is necessary to use computer audit programs, or software. This software may be developed by the auditor, client, or independent suppliers. When client-developed programs are used, they must be tested and controlled by the auditor. The most common software currently in use for audit purposes is generalized audit software prepared by the auditor.

Generalized audit software commonly consists of individual computer programs, or routines, designed to perform a variety of functions. Typically, the software can perform all the normal data handling and processing functions provided by the client's own software. Information can be sorted, stratified, sampled, included or excluded, and summarized as desired. The software has the capability of processing transactions, updating master files for current transactions, generating printed reports, and performing data search and retrieval. Data files may be reviewed for completeness, reasonableness, and arithmetical accuracy. Using logic or edit checks, the data may be reviewed for validity, applying whatever criteria the auditor specifies. Because of the speed with which the computer operates, the auditor may be able to perform substantially more compliance testing than is possible with manual procedures. Generalized audit software may also be used in substantive testing, as explained later in the chapter.

Most generalized audit software packages allow the auditor to work with information from existing computer files. The auditor completes *specification forms* to define the processing requirements. These forms or other supporting documentation provide the auditor with instructions on how to utilize the functions available within the computer audit software. The auditor's instructions are then converted into machine-readable form and are processed by the audit software. The resulting output is turned over to the auditor.

Generalized audit software has the advantage of flexibility and wide application. Relatively little programming knowledge is required to use the software, and an auditor can become familiar with its use through as little as one week of training. The disadvantages of this type of software are its relatively high cost of development, the additional cost of updating the

---

[13] Davis, *op. cit.*, p. 161.

software as client's data processing systems change, and the fact that it cannot be used on all models of computers.

Once the auditor has obtained appropriate audit software, there are three methods of testing with the computer: (1) parallel simulation, (2) test data, and (3) integrated test facility (ITF).

Parallel simulation. In this approach (sometimes called *controlled reprocessing* or *modeling*), actual company data are reprocessed using an auditor controlled software program. Usually, the software is a generalized audit program prepared by the auditor. This method is so named because the software is designed to reproduce or simulate the client's processing of real data. A graphic portrayal of this approach is shown in Figure 5-8.

Parallel simulation may be performed at different times during the year under audit, and it may also be applied to the reprocessing of historical data. This approach does not contaminate client files, and it may be conducted at an independent computer facility.

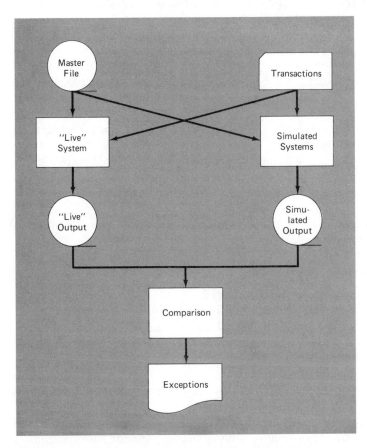

FIGURE 5–8. Flowchart of Parallel Simulation Process

This approach has the following advantages:

- Since real data are used, the auditor can verify the transactions by tracing them back to source documents and approvals.
- The size of the sample can be greatly expanded at relatively little additional cost.
- The auditor can independently run the test.

If the auditor does decide to use parallel simulation, care must be taken to determine that the data selected for simulation is representative of actual client transactions. It is also possible that the client's system may perform operations that are beyond the capacity of the generalized software program to simulate.

Test data. Under the test data approach (sometimes referred to as *test decks*), dummy transactions are prepared by the auditor and processed under auditor control by the client's computer program. The test data consist of one transaction for each valid or invalid condition the auditor wishes to test. For example, a payroll test deck may include both a valid and an invalid overtime pay condition. The output from processing the test data are then compared by the auditor with planned results to determine whether prescribed controls are operating as planned. This approach to testing is relatively simple, quick, and inexpensive. However, the method has the following major audit deficiencies:

- The client's program is tested only at a specific point in time rather than throughout the audit period.
- The method is only a test of the presence and functioning of controls in the program tested.
- There is no examination of documentation actually processed by the system.
- Computer operators know that test data are being run, which could reduce the validity of the output.
- The scope of the test is limited by the auditor's imagination and knowledge of the controls within the system.

Integrated test facility. This method of testing programmed controls requires the creation of a small subsystem (a minicompany) within the regular EDP system. This may be accomplished by creating dummy master files or by appending dummy master records to existing client files. Test data, specially coded to correspond to the dummy master files, are introduced into the system together with actual transactions. The test data should include all kinds of transaction errors and exceptions that may be encountered. In this manner, the test data are subjected to the same programmed controls as the actual data. For the subsystem, or dummy files, a separate set of outputs is produced. The results can be compared with those expected by the auditor.

The ITF method does have as a disadvantage the risk of potentially creating errors in client data. In addition, modifications may be necessary to client's programs in order to accommodate the dummy data.

Comparison of approaches. The primary differences between the parallel simulation and test data approaches are shown in Figure 5-9. The comparison of the output under each approach is done manually by the auditor. The integrated test facility technique combines features of each of these methods; both test data and actual transactions are processed simultaneously.

Irrespective of the choice among these three methods of testing the effectiveness of programmed controls, the procedures performed are analogous to the manual procedure of tracing transactions through all or selected components of the client's control system to determine the existence and effectiveness of selected accounting controls. Unlike the manual case, however, the procedures are performed by the computer and leave no visible trail. Only in the case of a transaction that does not satisfy a specific control incorporated into the program will an error message be generated. Audit programs for testing application controls for specific classes of transactions will be illustrated in Chapters 7–10.

Final Evaluation of Controls

After performing compliance tests, the auditor's evaluation of EDP accounting controls is conceptually the same as the corresponding evaluation of manual controls. As in a completely manual system, the evaluation will affect the nature, timing, and extent of the auditor's substantive tests.

FIGURE 5–9. Parallel Simulation versus Test Data Approach

OTHER CONSIDERATIONS

Online Realtime Systems

Online realtime (OLRT) systems are considered to be advanced EDP systems. The term *online* means that peripheral equipment or other computers are in direct communication with the CPU. *Realtime* exists when data processing is performed concurrently with the input activity and output is immediately available to the user. Data in online processing may originate at remote input terminals connected to the CPU by means of telephone or other communications lines. In OLRT processing, data are processed as entered and there is direct access to data stored on disk devices.

The reservation systems used by major commercial airlines are a good example of an OLRT system. Terminals in airports, ticket offices, and travel agencies are in direct communication with the CPU, which maintains a master reservations file for each flight. The turnaround time for determining the availability of space and making a reservation is almost instantaneous.

Figure 5-10 illustrates an OLRT system for a savings and loan company with branch offices. In the illustration, each branch cashier has an input-output device terminal. The transaction slip (deposit or withdrawal) provides a basis for subsequent reconciliation of computer control totals and cash on hand.

EDP Controls

The concepts of general and application controls discussed earlier in the chapter also are applicable to OLRT systems. The following major differences in an advanced system are highlighted below.

FIGURE 5–10. Online Realtime System

Access controls. In an OLRT system, many users have direct access to the CPU through remote input devices. Access often extends beyond company employees to outside agents and even to customers who have special keys, such as magnetic cards issued by banks, that activate the computer. To provide the necessary control, each user of a remote input device is given a key, code, or card which identifies the holder as an authorized user. Other access controls are:

- Locating terminals in areas that may be secured by locks, or providing locks on individual terminals.
- Utilizing computer call-back procedures if the telephone is used to dial the computer.
- Utilizing passwords that are checked by the computer before a person can enter a transaction.
- Restricting terminal operators to input or predetermined types of information.

Input controls. The authorization of a transaction in an OLRT system may not be traceable to a specific document. Direct input by a remote terminal, key, or card is an example. In such cases, the input should be logged at the CPU and/or at the originating terminal. Thus, the form but not the substance of the authorization changes. When source documents do exist, retrieval may be a problem because of the random processing and the filing of documents in the order in which they are received. While the task may be more time-consuming, the tracing to source documents is possible. Additional input controls are:

- Visual verification, or comparison of the converted data from the source document to a visual display.
- Key verification, by a second operator, of critical data fields (e.g., customer identification number, dollar amount of transaction).
- Editing by the computer of the completeness and reasonableness of the data entered.

Study and Evaluation of the System

It is possible to use test data to test the controls in an OLRT system. However, this approach is not widely used by auditors because of the contamination of file data and the difficulty of reversing the hypothetical data. Parallel simulation may also be used, but the availability of generalized audit software that can be used to simulate an OLRT system is very limited.

In lieu of traditional testing, the auditor often arranges for continuous monitoring of the system. Under this technique, an audit routine is added to the client's processing programs. Transactions entering the system are sampled at random intervals, and the output from the routine is used in testing the controls.

To provide for the integration of audit software into an OLRT system, *audit hook* capabilities must be built into the client's computer programs—both the operating and application programs—at the time they are created. Audit hooks are points in a program that allow *audit modules,* or programs, to be integrated into the system's normal processing activities. These audit modules provide the auditor with a means of selecting transactions possessing characteristics of interest to the auditor, such as a transaction of a certain kind, or an amount greater or lesser than a given value. Once a particular transaction has been identified as being of interest, a record of it can be retained by one of several methods. Two of these methods are tagging transactions and audit logs.

Tagging transactions. This method places an indicator, or tag, on the selected transaction. The presence of this tag enables the transaction to be traced through the system as it is being processed. The system must be programmed to provide for the creation of hard-copy printout of all paths followed by the transaction. Data with which the tagged transaction interacts at designated steps in the processing can be captured as well.

Audit log. An audit log is a record of certain processing activities. The log is used to record events as they occur at designated points in the system. Identified transactions or events are written onto a file available only to the auditor. The auditor can later print or use other techniques to analyze these records and make further tests as appropriate.

Other techniques for monitoring the processing of the system on a real-time basis also are available. Typically, they are variations of the methods previously described.

Computer Service Centers

Some companies use computer service centers to perform part, or all, of their data processing functions. The services offered by this kind of an outside organization normally include: (1) standard programs for specific functions, such as billing of sales or preparing the payroll, (2) standard industry programs such as time recording systems for legal firms, and (3) custom-made programs to meet the needs of individual users. A service center may also rent (or sell) computer time to customers who operate the computer with their own personnel.

Service Center Operations

Input data are furnished by the user either in the form of documents or in machine-readable form, such as diskette. File data are kept by the center, and processing is handled by one of the programs previously described. Output, in the form of documents and/or financial statements, is then provided for the user.

User Controls

When an outside service center is used, the user should adopt controls analogous to those that should exist if the data processing was performed within the company organization. For example, there should be input data controls, such as financial or quantity totals, document counts, and prenumbered forms. In addition, output documents, records, and statements should be reviewed. The user is generally responsible for record retention.

Auditing Implications

When service center processing is significant in the preparation of a client's financial statements, the auditor should include the service center in his study and evaluation of the internal control.

Because most service centers perform processing for a number of customers, it now is common for other independent auditors to review the system of controls at the center. Their report may be relied on by the auditor of the center's customers in evaluating his client's internal control. However, when the service center's activities are very material, such as the entire data processing operation, the auditor ordinarily should observe the service center's operations and use test data to test the adequacy of the controls at the center. In some cases, there is an adequate printed audit trail, enabling the auditor to evaluate internal control by auditing "around" the service center.

Using the Computer for Substantive Testing

The ability of the auditor to utilize the client's EDP equipment in the audit may significantly affect the evidential matter obtained during the examination. In comparison to an examination made without the computer, the use of such equipment may permit the accumulation of either the same quantity of evidence at less cost or more evidence at an economical cost. As in the case of compliance testing, use of the computer requires the auditor to have appropriate software, such as a generalized audit software package. Some of the audit tasks that are particularly suited to the computer are explained below.

Selecting and Printing Audit Samples

The computer can be programmed to select audit samples according to whatever criteria are specified by the auditor. These samples can be used for a variety of purposes. Individual customer accounts receivable accounts may be selected for confirmation, or the auditor may be interested in obtaining a listing of all items over a certain dollar amount. In examining supporting documentation for charges to a "repairs and maintenance expense" account, for example, the auditor may wish to specify a lower limit of $500. The samples selected may be based on multiple criteria. In the case of confirmation requests, the computer may also be used to print the confirmation letter as well as the envelope.

Testing Calculations and Making Computations

Another common use of the computer is to test the accuracy of computations in machine-readable data files. Tests of extensions, footings, or other computations may be performed. Inventory quantities may be extended by a unit cost and the amount of the inventory recalculated; individual customer accounts receivable records may be individually footed and a total of all accounts prepared. If client files contain sufficient information, the calculation of certain year-end adjusting entries also may be possible. Because of the speed with which computer processing is performed, recomputations can be performed on a more extensive basis than is practicable in a manual system.

Summarizing Data and Performing Analyses

The auditor frequently desires to have the client data reorganized in a manner that will suit a special purpose. For instance, the auditor may want to determine slow-moving inventory items, debit balances in accounts payable, or an aging of accounts receivable. Similarly, in performing analytical review procedures, the auditor may utilize the computer to compute desired ratios and other statistical data.

Comparing Audit Data with Company Records

Audited data resulting from work performed by the auditor may be compared with the information in a company's records. The audited data must, of course, first be converted into machine-readable form. Test counts made by the auditor of inventory quantities on hand may be keypunched and compared with the quantity shown on the perpetual inventory record or the quantity determined by the company as the result of a physical inventory count.

From these examples, it is apparent that the use of audit software for retrieving data from the client's system may greatly assist the auditor in accumulating evidence. This evidence directly assists the auditor in performing substantive tests of transactions and balances. The use of audit software for these purposes is limited only by the availability of client data files, the appropriate audit software, and the auditor's ingenuity.

CONCLUDING COMMENTS

The methodology of making a study and evaluation of internal accounting control in an EDP system is under continuing scrutiny within the accounting profession. Auditing methodology must keep pace with the increased sophistication of the computer.

This chapter has provided an introduction to the current "state of the art." Through practical experience and continuing professional education, the auditor of today must also be equipped to be the auditor of tomorrow. One conclusion appears indisputable—there will be more EDP systems in the future than there are today.

REVIEW QUESTIONS

5–1.   a. What is the principal hardware component in an EDP system?
b. What hardware components are peripheral to the principal hardware component?

5–2.   a. Explain the nature and functions of computer software.
b. Distinguish between systems programs and application programs.

5–3.   Identify the two types of file data and the two methods by which data are processed in an EDP system.

5–4.   Indicate four differences between EDP and manual systems that may affect the control environment.

5–5.   Distinguish between general and application controls and indicate the category of controls that is pervasive in its effect.

5–6.   a. Identify the customary positions in an EDP system.
b. Explain the primary applications of segregation of functions in an EDP system.

5–7.   a. What areas are related to systems development and documentation controls?
b. Why is documentation important to (1) management and (2) the auditor?

5–8.   a. Indicate the purpose of hardware and systems software controls.
b. Identify four kinds of hardware and systems software controls.

5–9.   a. Explain the purpose(s) and nature of access controls.
b. Identify the types of controls that may prevent unauthorized use of data files and programs.

5–10. a. Indicate the scope of data and procedural controls.
b. Describe the activities involved in the control function and identify the group that would perform this function.

5–11. Indicate the internal accounting control objectives for each of the three types of application controls.

5–12. a. Discuss the applicability of GAAS in auditing EDP accounting records.
b. Indicate the knowledge needed by a general audit staff member to meet the first general standard.

5–13. In the preliminary phase of the review, indicate (a) its scope, (b) the information desired, and (c) the procedures used.

5–14. Why may the auditor decide to terminate the review at the end of the preliminary phase?

5–15. What questions about the general controls are of interest to the auditor?

5–16. What are the advantages and disadvantages of auditing without the computer?

5–17. Contrast compliance testing by (a) parallel simulation, (b) test data, and (c) integrated test facility.

5–18. a. Explain the major differences in (1) access and (2) input controls in an OLRT system.
b. Identify the primary techniques for testing OLRT systems.

5–19. Explain the auditing implications of using computer service centers.

5–20. Identify the major uses of the computer in substantive testing.

COMPREHENSIVE QUESTIONS

5–21. Two categories and eight types of EDP accounting control procedures are identified in the chapter. Listed below are a number of specific control procedures:

1. EDP manager reports to chief financial officer.
2. Backup files.

3. Written approval of all program changes.
4. Physical controls for data files and programs.
5. Batch controls.
6. Reconciliation of output totals.
7. File identification labels.
8. Echo checks.
9. Limit and reasonableness checks.
10. Record counts.

Required

a. Indicate the category and type of control to which each procedure pertains.
b. Identify and explain one other control procedure for each of the eight types.

5–22. The plan or organization is an important aspect of an EDP activity.

Required

a. Diagram an appropriate structure for an EDP department.
b. Briefly describe the primary responsibilities of each individual or group identified in the diagram.
c. Indicate the conditions in an EDP structure that would result in incompatible functions.

5–23. When auditing an EDP accounting system, the independent auditor should have a general familiarity with the effects of the use of EDP on the various characteristics of accounting control and on the auditor's study and evaluation of such control. The independent auditor must be aware of those control procedures that are commonly referred to as "general" controls and those that are commonly referred to as "application" controls. General controls relate to all EDP activities and application controls relate to specific accounting tasks.

Required

a. What are the general controls that should exist in EDP-based accounting systems?
b. What are the purposes of each of the following categories of application controls?

1. Input controls.
2. Processing controls.
3. Output controls.

AICPA

5–24. Johnson, CPA, was engaged to examine the financial statements of Horizon Incorporated, which has its own computer installation. During the preliminary review, Johnson found that Horizon lacked proper segregation of the programming and operating functions. As a result, Johnson intensified the study and evaluation of the system of internal control surrounding the computer and concluded that the existing compensating general controls provided reasonable assurance that the objectives of the system of internal control were being met.

Required

a. In a properly functioning EDP environment, how is the separation of the programming and operating functions achieved?
b. What are the compensating general controls that Johnson most likely found? *Do not discuss hardware and application controls.*

AICPA

5–25. A well-designed management information system using EDP equipment will include methods of assuring that the data are appropriate to the situation and are accurate.

Required

a. Describe procedures that should exist in order to assure that the input data are accurate and appropriate.
b. Describe procedures that would assure that all data were processed and processed properly.
c. Describe procedures that would assure that the output data are accurate and appropriate.

CMA

5-26. The following five topics are part of the relevant body of knowledge for CPAs having field work or immediate supervisory responsibility in audits involving a computer:

1. EDP equipment and its capabilities.
2. Organization and management of the data processing function.
3. Characteristics of computer-based systems.
4. Fundamentals of computer programming.
5. Computer center operations.

CPAs who are responsible for computer audits should possess certain general knowledge with respect to each of these five topics. For example, on the subject of EDP equipment and its capabilities, the auditor should have a general understanding of computer equipment and should be familiar with the uses and capabilities of the central processor and the peripheral equipment.

Required

For each of the topics numbered 2 through 5 above, describe the general knowledge that should be possessed by those CPAs who are responsible for computer audits.

AICPA

5-27. The requirement to make a study and evaluation of internal control applies regardless of the method of data processing used by a company. However, the methodology of complying with this standard may be affected by the form of the data processing system.

Required

a. Describe the nature, purpose, and methods of the preliminary phase of the review.
b. Explain the purpose and methods of the completion phase of the review.
c. Identify the major differences and similarities between manual and EDP systems in making a study and evaluation of internal control.

5-28. You are performing an audit of the EDP function of a chemical company with about $150 million in annual sales. Your preliminary review discloses the following points:

1. The EDP manager reports to the director of accounting, who, in turn, reports to the controller. The controller reports to the treasurer, who is one of several vice presidents in the company. The EDP manager has made several unsuccessful requests to the director of accounting for another printer.
2. There is no written charter for the EDP function, but the EDP manager tells you that the primary objective is to get the accounting reports out on time.
3. Transaction tapes are used daily to update the master file and are then retired to the scratch tape area.
4. A third generation computer with large disk capacity was installed three years ago. The EDP activity previously used a second generation computer, and many of the programs written for that computer are used on the present equipment by means of an emulator.
5. You observe that the output from the computer runs is written on tape for printing at a later time. Some output tapes from several days' runs are waiting to be printed.

6. The EDP manager states that the CPU could handle at least twice the work currently being processed.

Required
a. Identify the defect inherent in each of the six conditions shown above.
b. Briefly describe the probable effect if the condition continues.
Note: On your answer sheet, show the defect, followed immediately by the probable effect, for each condition.

IIA

5–29. To test the effectiveness of general controls in an EDP system, the auditor may perform the following procedures:

1. Trace selected program changes to supporting documentation.
2. Review and evaluate the hardware controls included in the operating system.
3. Observe and make inquiries concerning segregation of functions between EDP and user departments and within EDP.
4. Selectively review computer operator manuals and observe whether prescribed procedures are being followed.
5. Inquire of librarian as to compliance with procedures for controlling unauthorized access to programs and data files.
6. Examine results of selected pretesting of software programs.
7. Examine evidence for approval of new systems and programs and changes therein.
8. Selectively test preprocessing, postprocessing, and programmed controls.
9. Review on a test basis reconciliations of control totals by the data control group.
10. Examine data files and program access records to test the library function as it applies to significant accounting applications.

Required
a. Indicate the type of general control to which each procedure relates.
b. Identify an error or irregularity that could occur if the procedure is lacking or is improperly functioning.

5–30. Listed below are a number of errors or irregularities pertaining to application controls in an EDP system:

1. An incorrect file is updated.
2. Output is distributed to unauthorized users.
3. Input data are duplicated during handling.
4. Processing errors are made on valid input data.
5. Valid data are improperly converted into machine-readable form.
6. Illogical or unreasonable input is processed.
7. Erroneous data are not corrected and resubmitted for processing.
8. Unauthorized data are converted into machine-sensible form.
9. Output control totals do not agree with input or processing controls.
10. Output data do not agree with original source documents.

Required
For each error or irregularity identify (a) the control procedures that should prevent or detect such occurrences and (b) the type of application controls (input, processing, and output) that is involved.

5–31. CPAs may audit "around" or "through" computers in examining financial statements of clients who use computers to process accounting data.

Required
a. Describe the auditing approach referred to as auditing "around" the computer.
b. Under what conditions does the CPA decide to audit "through" the computer instead of "around" the computer?
c. In auditing "through" the computer, the CPA may use a test deck.
   1. What is a test deck?
   2. Why does the CPA use a test deck?
d. How can the CPA satisfy himself that the computer program tapes presented to him are actually being used by the client to process its accounting data?

AICPA

5–32. You have been engaged by Central Savings and Loan Association to examine its financial statements for the year ended December 31, 19X1. The CPA who examined the financial statements at December 31, 19X0 rendered an unqualified opinion.

In January 19X1, the Association installed an online realtime computer system. Each teller in the Association's main office and seven branch offices has an online input-output terminal. Customers' mortgage payments and savings account deposits and withdrawals are recorded in the accounts by the computer from data input by the teller at the time of the transaction. The teller keys the proper account by account number and enters the information in the terminal keyboard to record the transaction. The accounting department at the main office has both punched card and typewriter input-output devices. The computer is housed at the main office.

In addition to servicing its own mortgage loans the Association acts as a mortgage servicing agency for three life insurance companies. In this latter activity the Association maintains mortgage records and serves as the collection and escrow agent for the mortgagees (the insurance companies), who pay a fee to the Association for these services.

Required
You would expect the Association to have certain internal controls in effect because an online realtime computer system is employed. List the internal controls which should be in effect solely because this system is employed, classifying them as
1. Those controls pertaining to input of information.
2. All other types of computer controls.

AICPA (adapted)

5–33. The independent auditor must evaluate a client's system of internal control to determine the extent to which various auditing procedures must be employed. A client who uses a computer should provide the CPA with a flowchart of the information processing system so the CPA can evaluate the control features in the system. Shown below is a simplified flowchart, such as a client might provide. Unfortunately, the client had only partially completed the flowchart when it was requested by you.

Required
a. Complete the flowchart shown on page 174.
b. Describe what each item in the flowchart indicates. When complete, your description should provide an explanation of the processing of the data involved. Your description should be in the following order:
   1. "Orders From Salesmen" to "Run 5."
   2. "From Mailroom" to "Run 5."
   3. "Run 5" through the remainder of the chart.

AICPA (adapted)

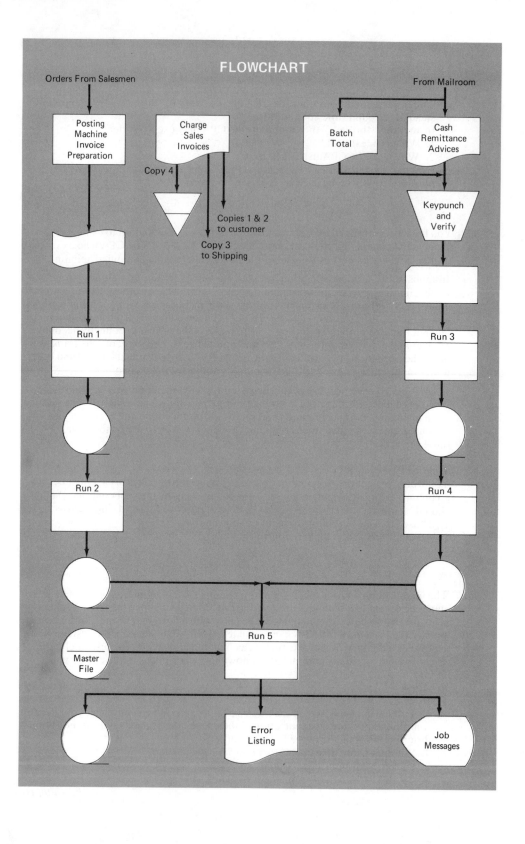

FLOWCHART

Orders From Salesmen

Posting
Machine
Invoice
Preparation

Charge
Sales
Invoices

Copy 4

Copies 1 & 2
to customer

Copy 3
to Shipping

From Mailroom

Batch
Total

Cash
Remittance
Advices

Keypunch
and
Verify

Run 1

Run 3

Run 2

Run 4

Master
File

Run 5

Error
Listing

Job
Messages

5–34. George Beemster, CPA, is examining the financial statements of the Louisville Sales Corporation, which recently installed an offline electronic computer. The following comments have been extracted from Mr. Beemster's notes on computer operations and the processing and control of shipping notices and customer invoices:

1. To minimize inconvenience Louisville converted without change its existing data processing system, which utilized tabulating equipment. The computer company supervised the conversion and has provided training to all computer department employees (except keypunch operators) in systems design, operations, and programming.
2. Each computer run is assigned to a specific employee, who is responsible for making program changes, running the program and answering questions. This procedure has the advantage of eliminating the need for records of computer operations because each employee is responsible for his own computer runs.
3. At least one computer department employee remains in the computer room during office hours, and only computer department employees have keys to the computer room.
4. System documentation consists of those materials furnished by the computer company—a set of record formats and program listings. These and the tape library are kept in a corner of the computer department.
5. The corporation considered the desirability of programmed controls but decided to retain the manual controls from its existing system.
6. Corporation products are shipped directly from public warehouses, which forward shipping notices to general accounting. There, a billing clerk enters the price of the item and accounts for the numerical sequence of shipping notices from each warehouse. The billing clerk also prepares daily adding machine tapes ("control tapes") of the units shipped and the unit prices.
7. Shipping notices and control tapes are forwarded to the computer department for keypunching and processing. Extensions are made on the computer. Output consists of invoices (in six copies) and a daily sales register. The daily sales register shows the aggregate totals of units shipped and unit prices, which the computer operator compares to the control tapes.
8. All copies of the invoice are returned to the billing clerk. The clerk mails three copies to the customer, forwards one copy to the warehouse, maintains one copy in a numerical file, and retains one copy in an open invoice file that serves as a detail accounts receivable record.

Required
a. Describe weaknesses in internal control over information and data flows and the procedures for processing shipping notices and customer invoices, and recommend improvements in these controls and processing procedures. Organize your answer sheets as follows:

Weakness	*Recommended Improvement*

b. Indicate which of the eight EDP controls is applicable to each weakness.
AICPA (adapted)

5–35. "The EDP function ran in a mode that courted disaster but left the EDP staff apparently isolated from knowledge of the fraud. An open shop functioned where a central staff developed and ran the primary programs for the business, but programmers in other departments such as actuarial could also write and run their own programs that had access to the live data base of insurance policies. The special processing required to carry out the fraud could have been done, and, it is claimed, was done by the programmers outside of the central EDP staff.

"It is also claimed that EDP management had proposed on numerous occasions the establishment of an internal audit group for the EDP environment, but it was always rejected by top management.

"The EDP staff also observed the external auditors from a revealing point of view. The auditors were apparently handed EDP listings of policy records printed from the master files and accepted them as documents of record since they had no capability or skills to directly access the master files in the system themselves. When the auditors happened to select a fake policy for confirmation, they were told that policy folder was in use by somebody in the company and would be available the next day.

"The way it worked was that Equity's head, Stanley Goldblum, set standards for growth in income, assets, and earnings. The desired quarterly and annual profits were relayed to Alan Green through Lewis and another executive. . . . Green would then go on the computer and crank out the necessary fictitious policies."†

Required
a. What controls were violated in this case?
b. As auditor of Equity Funding, how would you have reacted to the above?

5–36. "In late March, a programmer made a minor change in the program that was used to update the New York City Department of Social Services' master file. Because the revision was "trivial," the program was not tested. In the ensuing months, welfare recipients died, moved away, or lost their eligibility to receive further payments. Delete transactions were prepared in each case and processed as part of the normal master file update.

"The update program received both batch and online updates. Because of the program change, however, it no longer was able to handle both transactions. The "trivial" change caused the update program to ignore batch-entered deletions to the master file, so closed cases remained open.

"During April, May, and June, the printers on the system kept spewing out checks. After the checks were burst and stuffed into envelopes, they went winging on their way to dead men, people who were long gone from the city, and those no longer entitled to receive payments. Finally, field workers started to report payments on closed cases. By this time, $7,500,000 had been disbursed to people who should have been deleted from the files.

"Now it is possible to go back and find which checks should not have been written. Getting the money back is a different question. Most of the checks are in the low three figures. It cost $150 to file legal papers to bring suit for recovery of the funds. Collecting the $7,500,000 might end up costing $7,500,000 . . . .—Oh, well, it wasn't real money! It came out of the taxpayers' pockets!"††

Required
List the controls that would have prevented this fiasco from happening.

---

† Donn B. Parker, "Further Comment on the Equity Funding Insurance Fraud Case," *EDPACS*, January 1975, p. 16.
†† Donald L. Adams, "We Didn't Test the System But How Much Could We Lose? Would You Believe $7,500,000?" *EDPACS*, August 1974, p. 6.

CASE STUDY

5–37.* You have been assigned to the annual audit of Explosives, Inc. You contact the senior, Bob Good, as instructed and arrange a date to discuss the client and the current year's audit.

At your meeting with Good, the company and the current year's audit were discussed. During the discussion, Good emphasized that he wanted to take a good look at the data processing (DP) department. He had attended the firm's one-week course on computer auditing and felt strongly about the need for such review.

On the eighth day of the job, Bob received word that his immediate attention was needed on another job. He had performed most of the review in the DP department and wants you to complete it. Good left the following workpapers to help you complete the review of the DP department.

General Background

The DP department has evolved from a tab operation and currently uses IBM 360 equipment. The department is under the supervision of Gus Sampson, who has worked in it since its inception. He reports to the controller.

The department is located on the third floor of the east office wing. It shares office space with the research department and the general accounting department. The machines, however, are physically separated from the other departments by glass doors. The chemical mixing department is located just below on the second floor. The first floor houses the plant personnel department, various conference rooms, and other administrative offices.

The DP department services corporate accounting, the local plant, and three other plant locations elsewhere in the country. The department has an IBM 360/30 computer. Card input is used on most applications. There are two IBM card sorters which are used extensively to sort the card input. Cards are retained for at least one year.

Within the DP department, there are three groups, each with specific duties:
1. Keypunch.
2. Systems analysis.
3. Programming and operations.
Each group has its own supervisor who reports to the DP manager.

Computer Room Operations

All of the machine operators know the jobs they run quite well and have the knowledge to make changes in the operating procedures and programs when they encounter difficulties. This has greatly increased efficiency as less time is lost due to machine halts caused by program interruptions. Gus stated that because of the operators' familiarity with the various jobs, he doesn't have to devote much time to supervising them.

When asked about operating manuals for the operators, Gus replied it would be a waste of time to prepare them since the operators are so familiar with the programs and jobs. If a problem develops, an operator can simply look at a source program listing and make the necessary correction. Gus said he seldom reviewed any console sheets because of the confidence he had in his operators. He complained, however, about the accounting people always giving him bad data and then complaining about the output. "GIGO is the rule," he said.

During my tour of the computer room with Gus, I noticed that reels of tape, some with labels and some without, were in file racks, on tables, on top of equipment, and in the corner of the floor. In another corner, I noticed open boxes of various forms and payroll checks. I had expected to see only two or three operators in the computer room, but there were five or six people in it. When I asked Gus about these conditions, he said he had read all the books and publications on controlling the computer room and felt most of the alleged dangers were exaggerated. He trusted his employees and felt his shop was one of the best in the area. As for the additional people, he felt that too many people are mystified by the computer. Consequently, he maintains an open door policy so people can come in and see "what the monster is all about."

Programming Group

Information about this group was obtained from Betty James, the head programmer, who reports to Gus Sampson. The members of this group mainly write new programs and maintain current programs, about 75 percent of which were written years ago using a second generation (1401) programming language. These programs are currently being rewritten in a more modern and efficient language.

Documentation for the old programs and some of the new ones consists of source listings. The old programs were written by Gus, Betty, and a fellow who has left the company. Since Gus and Betty are still around, there hasn't been any need to prepare additional documentation. Betty said, however, that Gus has been thinking about developing documentation standards for all programs.

Betty mentioned numerous problems have arisen lately due to an operator or programmer making an undocumented "patch" in a program so the job can be run. Sometimes the change causes other errors to occur. Gus has attempted to stop the operators from making changes, but with the program cards being accessible to everyone, it has been impossible to enforce.

Required
a. Draw an organization chart of the EDP department.
b. For each of the eight EDP controls mentioned in the chapter discuss the weaknesses in the system and your recommendations for improvement.

6 | Audit Sampling in Compliance Testing

STUDY OBJECTIVES

The study objectives of this chapter are to obtain an understanding of the applicability of audit sampling in making a study and evaluation of internal control and the use of either statistical or nonstatistical sampling in compliance testing. To achieve these objectives, it is necessary for the reader to

- Comprehend the relationship of generally accepted auditing standards (GAAS) to audit sampling.
- Recognize the risks associated with audit sampling.
- Learn the essential steps in the design and execution of an attribute sampling plan for compliance tests.
- Understand the use of nonstatistical sampling in compliance testing.
- Be aware of the nature and purpose of discovery sampling in auditing.

In contemporary auditing, sampling is well established. The importance of audit sampling in current practice is underscored by the issuance in 1981 of SAS No. 39, *Audit Sampling,* and the subsequent publication of a proposed AICPA audit guide to assist auditors in implementing SAS No. 39.

This chapter explains the basic concepts of audit sampling and emphasizes the application of statistical sampling in compliance testing. The chapter is divided into four sections: (1) basic concepts (2) attribute sampling in compliance testing, (3) nonstatistical sampling in compliance testing, and (4) discovery sampling.

BASIC CONCEPTS OF AUDIT SAMPLING

Nature and Purpose of Audit Sampling

Audit sampling is the application of an audit procedure to less than 100 percent of the items within an account balance or class of transactions for the purpose of evaluating some characteristic of the balance or class.[1]

Audit sampling is applicable to both compliance and substantive testing. However, it is not equally applicable to all of the auditing procedures that may be used in performing these tests. For example, audit sampling is widely used in vouching, confirming, and retracing, but it is ordinarily not used in inquiry, observing, and analytical review procedures.

Risk and Audit Uncertainty

Both the second and third standards of field work contain an element of uncertainty. For example, the auditor's reliance on internal control affects the *extent of tests* to which other auditing procedures are to be restricted; in meeting the evidential matter standard, the auditor is required only to have a *reasonable basis* for an opinion.

The auditor is justified in accepting some uncertainty when the cost and time required to make a 100 percent examination of the data are, in his judgment, greater than the adverse consequences of possibly expressing an erroneous opinion from examining only a sample of the data. Since this is normally the case, sampling is widely used in auditing.

In Chapter 4, two audit risks are recognized: (1) the risk that material errors will occur in the accounting process that produces the financial statements, and (2) the risk that these errors will not be detected by the auditor's examination. In sampling, the combination of these two risks is referred to as *ultimate risk.*

Ultimate risk includes both uncertainties attributable to sampling (*sampling risk*) and uncertainties due to all other factors (*nonsampling risk*).

---

[1] Auditing Standards Board, *Codification of Statements on Auditing Standards* (New York: American Institute of Certified Public Accountants, 1983, Auditing Section 350.01). (Hereinafter referred to and cited as AU §).

Sampling Risk

This risk relates to the possibility that a properly drawn sample may not be representative of the population. Thus, the auditor's conclusion about internal control procedures or the details of transactions and balances based on the sample may be different from the conclusion that would result from the examination of the entire population. In performing compliance and substantive tests, the following types of sampling risk may occur:[2]

Compliance Testing

The risk of overreliance on internal accounting control is the risk that the sample supports the auditor's planned degree of reliance on the control when the true compliance rate does not justify such reliance.*
The risk of underreliance on internal accounting control is the risk that the sample does not support the auditor's planned degree of reliance on the control when the true compliance rate supports such reliance.**

Substantive Testing

The risk of incorrect acceptance is the risk that the sample supports the conclusion that the recorded account balance is not materially misstated when it is materially misstated.*
The risk of incorrect rejection is the risk that the sample supports the conclusion that the recorded account balance is materially misstated when it is not materially misstated.**

These risks have a significant impact on both the effectiveness and efficiency of the audit. The risk of overreliance and the risk of incorrect acceptance relate to audit effectiveness. When the auditor reaches either of these erroneous conclusions, his examination may not be sufficient to detect material errors and irregularities, and he may not have a reasonable basis for an opinion. In contrast, the risk of underreliance and incorrect rejection relate to the efficiency of the audit. When either of these erroneous conclusions are reached, the auditor will increase substantive tests unnecessarily. However, such effort will ordinarily lead ultimately to a correct conclusion, and the audit will nevertheless be effective.

Nonsampling Risk

This risk refers to the portion of ultimate risk that is not due to examining only a portion of the data. This risk results from (1) human mistakes, such as failing to recognize errors in documents in a sample, (2) applying auditing procedures inappropriate to the audit objective, and (3) misinterpreting the results of a sample. Nonsampling risk can never be mathematically measured. However, by proper planning and supervision and adherence to the

---

[2] Auditing Standards Board, *op. cit.,* AU § 350.12.
 * This risk is sometimes identified as the *beta* risk.
** This risk is sometimes identified as the *alpha* risk.

quality control standards described in Chapter 2, nonsampling risk can be held to a negligible level.

Nonstatistical and Statistical Sampling

In performing audit tests in accordance with GAAS, the auditor may use either nonstatistical or statistical sampling or both. Both types of sampling require the exercise of judgment in planning and executing the sampling plan and evaluating the results. Moreover, both types of sampling can provide sufficient evidential matter as required by the third standard of field work. Both types of audit sampling are also subject to some sampling and nonsampling risk. The critical difference between the two types of sampling is that the laws of probability are used to control sampling risk in statistical sampling.

The choice between the two types of sampling is based primarily on cost/benefit considerations. Nonstatistical sampling may be less costly than statistical sampling, but the benefits from statistical sampling may be significantly greater than nonstatistical sampling as explained below.

In nonstatistical sampling, the auditor determines sample size and evaluates sample results entirely on the basis of subjective criteria and his own experience. Thus, he may unknowingly use too large a sample in one area and too small a sample in another. To the extent that the sufficiency of audit evidence is based on a sample, the auditor may in turn obtain more (or less) evidence than is actually needed to have a reasonable basis for expressing an opinion. However, a properly designed nonstatistical sample may be just as effective as a statistical sample.

In statistical sampling, substantial costs may be required to train auditors in the use of statistics and in the design and implementation of the sampling plan. However, statistical sampling should benefit the auditor in (1) designing an efficient sample, (2) measuring the sufficiency of the evidence obtained, and (3) evaluating sample results.[3] Most importantly, statistical sampling enables the auditor to quantify and control sampling risk.

The choice of nonstatistical or statistical sampling does not directly affect the choice of auditing procedures to be applied to a sample. Moreover, it does not affect the competence of evidence obtained about individual sample items or the appropriate response by the auditor to errors found in sample items. These matters require the exercise of professional judgment. The relationship between nonstatistical and statistical sampling is graphically shown in Figure 6-1.

Audit Sampling Techniques

An auditor may use sampling to obtain information about many different characteristics of a population. However, most audit samples lead either to

---

[3] Statistical Sampling Subcommittee, Proposed Audit Guide *Audit Sampling,* (New York: American Institute of Certified Public Accountants 1982), p. 11. (Hereinafter referred to as *Audit Sampling Guide.*)

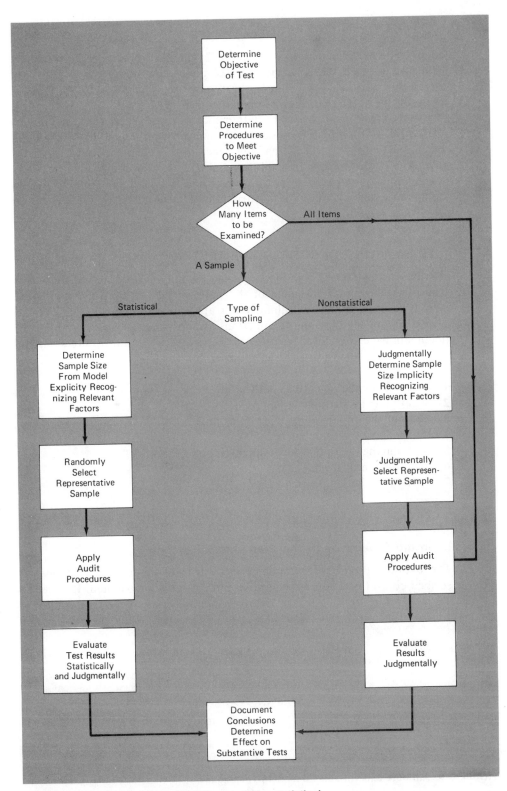

FIGURE 6–1. Audit Sampling: Statistical and Nonstatistical

an estimate of (1) an occurrence rate or (2) a dollar amount. When statistical sampling is used, these sampling techniques are identified as *attribute sampling* and *variables sampling,* respectively. The essential differences between these techniques are summarized in Figure 6-2.

There are several variations within each of these techniques, including a method of estimating the monetary amount of transactions involving compliance deviations. In the remaining pages of this chapter, consideration is given to (1) the steps in an attribute sampling plan for compliance tests, (2) the modifications in the approach when nonstatistical sampling is used in compliance testing, and (3) a variation of attribute sampling known as *discovery sampling.*

ATTRIBUTE SAMPLING IN COMPLIANCE TESTING

Attribute sampling for compliance tests generally is used only if there is a trail of documentary evidence of the performance of control procedures. This type of sampling is ordinarily not applicable to controls that depend primarily on segregation of functions or to controls that produce no documentary evidence of performance. The steps in an attribute sampling plan for compliance tests are as follows:

1. Determining the objectives of the plan.
2. Specifying the attributes of interest.
3. Defining the population and sampling unit.
4. Determining the sample size.
5. Determining the sample selection method.
6. Executing the sampling plan.
7. Evaluating the sample results.

Each of these steps should be documented in the working papers.

Determining the Objectives of the Plan

The overall purpose of compliance testing is to determine whether prescribed control procedures are in use and operating as planned. It is necessary, therefore, to identify the controls that are of interest to the auditor in

Sampling Technique	Type of Testing	Purpose
Attribute sampling	Compliance	Estimate the occurrence rate of deviations from prescribed control procedures in a population
Variables sampling	Substantive	Estimate the total dollar amount of a population or the dollar amount of error in a population

FIGURE 6–2. Attribute and Variables Sampling Techniques

terms of specific internal control objectives. For example, when the auditor is testing controls over the execution of sales transactions, the specific objectives may relate to the control procedures over granting credit, filling and shipping the order, and billing the customer.

Specifying the Attributes of Interest

On the basis of his knowledge of the internal control system, the auditor should be able to identify attributes that indicate compliance with the control procedure expected to be relied on in substantive testing. Attributes should be identified for each control procedure necessary to achieve the related specific internal control objective for the particular class of transactions. For example, if the control procedure requires credit department approval of credit prior to shipment, the attribute may be defined as "sales order with credit approval." Where the control procedure requires action by a specified individual, the attribute of interest is "approval of voucher by Jones."

Care should be exercised in specifying the attributes, since they provide the basis for the subsequent determination of the number of errors or occurrences (deviations) from prescribed procedures.

Figure 6-3 illustrates the attributes that may be tested in an attribute sampling plan to test controls over the execution of credit sales transactions. It is assumed in the example that the company prepares a sales order on receipt of the customer order.

Each attribute should relate to a control procedure upon which the auditor intends to rely. However, each attribute may not be of equal importance. In the example below, the auditor may consider credit approval to be more important than the verification of mathematical accuracy. The relative importance of each attribute should be considered in setting desired statisti-

Attribute	Description of Attribute
1	Authorization of sale by appropriate sales order department personnel
2	Sales order department verification of agreement of sales order with customer order as to quantities, descriptions, and prices
3	Credit approval by authorized credit department personnel
4	Shipping department verification of agreement of goods shipped with sales order
5	Billing department verification of agreement of sales invoice with shipping document
6	Billing department verification of agreement of sales invoice with sales order
7	Billing department verification of agreement of unit prices on sales invoice with specific price authorization and/or catalog or list prices
8	Billing department verification of mathematical accuracy of sales invoice

FIGURE 6-3. Attributes of Interest for Compliance Tests of Sales Transactions

cal objectives. Ordinarily, more stringent statistical parameters are set for the more critical controls.

The attributes in Figure 6-3 relate to documentary evidence of performance of a control procedure. In each case, the employee is expected to initial, sign, or stamp the document upon completing the control procedure. The auditor then obtains evidence of compliance with the control by reviewing (or inspecting) the documents for the initials, and so on.

Defining the Population and Sampling Unit

In compliance testing, the population is the class of transactions being tested. The auditor should determine that the population is appropriate for the objectives of the plan. For example, if the objective is whether all approved vouchers have been recorded, the population should be all approved vouchers, not all entries in the voucher register. If the voucher register were used as the population, unrecorded vouchers could not be included in the sample.

The identification of the population also includes a consideration of the population's homogeneity with respect to the control procedures to be tested. For example, cash disbursements may be stratified as to amount when there are significant differences in prescribed controls for disbursements over a specified dollar amount.

When there are multiple client locations, such as branches and divisions, the auditor may elect to regard each segment as a separate population. This choice would clearly be warranted when there are significantly different control procedures at each location. However, when the controls are similar throughout the organization and consolidated statements are prepared, one population for all locations may suffice.

The auditor is faced with a similar choice when the client has made a change in a control procedure during the year. If the auditor wishes to rely on both controls, the population should include transactions processed both before and after the change. However, if reliance is to be placed only on the new control, the population may be defined solely for transactions processed after the change.

It is not necessary in attribute sampling to know the exact size of the population. As will be shown later, population size has little or no effect on sample size. However, a reasonable approximation of population size may be needed when the population is relatively small.

The sampling unit is an individual element in the population. A sampling unit may be a document, a line item of a document, or a line item of a journal or register. It is imperative that the sampling unit be compatible with the objective of the test. For the voucher example above, the sampling unit should be the voucher. In contrast, if the objective is to determine the existence of improperly recorded transactions in the voucher register, the sampling unit should be the line item in the register.

The sampling unit may impact significantly on audit efficiency. Assume, for example, that sales invoices average four line items per invoice. If, in testing a control over pricing, the sampling unit is defined as the invoice, and sample size is 150, the auditor would have to test 600 items. In contrast, if the line item is the sampling unit, only 150 items would be tested for compliance.

Determining the Sample Size

The objective in determining sample size is to obtain a sample that will meet desired statistical objectives for each control procedure being tested. The factors that affect the determination of sample size are (1) acceptable level of risk of overreliance, (2) tolerable occurrence rate, (3) expected population occurrence rate, and (4) population size.

Acceptable Level of Risk of Overreliance

As explained earlier, two types of sampling risk are associated with internal control: (1) the risk of underreliance, which relates to the efficiency of the audit, and (2) the risk of overreliance, which relates to the effectiveness of the audit. Due to the potentially serious consequences associated with an ineffective audit, and because compliance testing may be the only source of evidence regarding deviations, the auditor desires to keep the risk of over-reliance at a low level.

In statistical sampling, the risk of overreliance must be stated explicitly. The level of acceptable risk has an inverse affect on sample size. Determining the appropriate sample size for varying levels of risk of overreliance and other factors may be accomplished by the use of tables like those illustrated later in Figure 6-4. The effects of varying levels of risk of overreliance on sample size can be seen by holding the other sample size factors constant. Assuming a tolerable occurrence rate of 5 percent, an expected population occurrence rate of 1 percent, and a large population, the following sample sizes result when sampling risk is changed:

Risk of Overreliance	Sample Size
10%	77
5	93
1	165

Most auditors either specify one level of risk of overreliance for all compliance tests or select 5 percent or 10 percent depending on the importance of the control.*

---

* The factor *reliability* or *confidence level* is sometimes used in attribute sampling. This factor is the complement of the risk of overreliance. Thus, a 5 percent risk of overreliance is the equivalent of specifying 95 percent reliability.

Tolerable Occurrence Rate

The tolerable occurrence rate is the maximum rate of deviations from a prescribed control procedure that an auditor is willing to accept and still rely on the control. In deciding on the tolerable rate, the auditor should consider the relationship of each occurrence to

- The accounting records being tested.
- Any related internal accounting control procedures.
- The purpose of the auditor's evaluation.[4]

The auditor should recognize that deviations from prescribed control procedures increase the *risk,* but not necessarily the number, of errors in the financial records. For example, the lack of approval on a voucher is a deviation, but the voucher may nevertheless pertain to a valid transaction that is properly recorded.

Related control procedures exist when there are compensating or auxiliary controls to a specified procedure. The significance of a deviation from the specified procedure, such as the approval of a voucher, is affected by the potential effectiveness of related controls, such as the review of supporting documentation by one (or more) authorized signers of company checks.

The purpose of the auditor's evaluation of internal control is to provide a basis for determining the extent to which other auditing procedures are to be restricted. As explained in Chapter 4, the auditor cannot entirely eliminate other auditing procedures. Thus, the auditor should recognize that other auditing procedures may detect errors or irregularities resulting from a deviation from prescribed control procedures.

Tolerable occurrence rate varies with the auditor's planned reliance on the control procedure—the greater the reliance, the lower the tolerable rate and vice versa. The following guidelines have been suggested in quantifying an acceptable range:[5]

Planned Reliance	*Tolerable Rate Range*
Substantial	2– 7%
Moderate	6–12
Limited	11–20

Tolerable rate has an inverse affect on sample size. The effect of tolerable rate on sample size, assuming a risk of overreliance of 5 percent, a zero expected population occurrence rate, and a large population is illustrated by the following:

---

[4] Auditing Standards Board, *op. cit.,* AU § 350.33.
[5] *Audit Sampling Guide, op. cit.,* p. 27.

Tolerable Rate Of Occurrence	Sample Size	Tolerable Rate Of Occurrence	Sample Size
2%	149	6%	49
4	74	8	36

Expected Population Occurrence Rate

The auditor uses one or more of the following to estimate the expected population rate for each control procedure.

- Last year's sample occurrence rate, adjusted judgmentally for current year changes in the control procedure.
- The current year's preliminary evaluation of internal control.
- The rate found in a preliminary sample of approximately 50 items.

If the expected occurrence rate is equal to or greater than the tolerable rate, the auditor cannot reasonably expect to rely on the controls. Thus, he should omit compliance testing and design substantive tests without any reliance on that control procedure.

The expected population occurrence rate has a significant effect on sample size. When the risk of overreliance and tolerable rate are held constant, increases and decreases from a given occurrence rate will result in larger and smaller sample sizes respectively. The effects of this factor on sample size are as follows assuming a 5 percent risk of overreliance, a 5 percent tolerable occurrence rate, and a large population:

Expected Population Occurrence Rate	Sample Size	Expected Population Occurrence Rate	Sample Size
0.0%	59	1.5%	124
1.0	93	2.0	181

These effects recognize that as the expected population occurrence rate approaches the tolerable occurrence rate, more precise information is needed and a larger sample size results.

Population Size

As previously explained, population size has little or no effect on sample size. Assuming a 5 percent risk of overreliance, a 5 percent tolerable occurrence rate, and a 1 percent expected population occurrence rate, the effects of changes in population size on sample size are as follows:[6]

[6] *Audit Sampling Guide, op. cit.*, p. 29.

Population Size	Sample Size	Population Size	Sample Size
100	64	2,000	92
500	87	5,000	93
1000	90	100,000	93

When the population is over 5,000 sampling units, it is appropriate in statistical sampling to consider the population as infinite. A large population will be assumed in all remaining examples and in end-of-chapter problems.

Sample Size Tables

When each of the factors affecting sample size has been quantified, sample size is determined objectively through the use of sample size tables like those shown in Figure 6-4. The tables are based on an upper occurrence limit (or one-tailed) approach because the auditor is concerned only that the actual population occurrence rate does not *exceed* the tolerable occurrence rate. To use the tables, is is necessary to

- Select the table that corresponds to the acceptable risk of overreliance.
- Locate the column that pertains to the specified tolerable occurrence rate.
- Locate the row that contains the expected population occurrence rate.
- Read the sample size from the intersection of the column and row determined in steps two and three.

Illustrative sample sizes are:

Risk of Overreliance	Tolerable Occurrence Rate	Expected Population Occurrence Rate	Sample Size
5%	4%	1.0%	156
5	6	2.0	127
10	5	1.0	77
10	6	2.0	88

Determining the Sample Selection Method

Once sample size has been determined, a method of selecting sampling units from the population must be chosen. Sample items should be selected in a manner that results in a sample that is representative of the population. Thus, all items in the population should have a chance of being selected. The principal selection methods used in attribute sampling are random number sampling and systematic sampling.

Random Number Sampling

To use random number sampling, the auditor must have a basis for relating a unique number to each item in the population. Then, either by reference to a

Statistical Sample Sizes for Compliance Testing (for large populations)

TABLE 1.   **5 Percent Risk of Overreliance**

Expected Population Occurrence Rate	TOLERABLE OCCURRENCE RATE								
	2%	3%	4%	5%	6%	7%	8%	9%	10%
0.00%	149	99	74	59	49	42	36	32	29
.50	*	157	117	93	78	66	58	51	46
1.00	*	*	156	93	78	66	58	51	46
1.50	*	*	192	124	103	66	58	51	46
2.00	*	*	*	181	127	88	77	68	46
2.50	*	*	*	*	150	109	77	68	61
3.00	*	*	*	*	195	129	95	84	61
4.00	*	*	*	*	*	*	146	100	89
5.00	*	*	*	*	*	*	*	158	116
6.00	*	*	*	*	*	*	*	*	179

TABLE 2.   **10 Percent Risk of Overreliance**

Expected Population Occurrence Rate	TOLERABLE OCCURRENCE RATE								
	2%	3%	4%	5%	6%	7%	8%	9%	10%
0.00%	114	76	57	45	38	32	28	25	22
.50	194	129	96	77	64	55	48	42	38
1.00	*	176	96	77	64	55	48	42	38
1.50	*	*	132	105	64	55	48	42	38
2.00	*	*	198	132	88	75	48	42	38
2.50	*	*	*	158	110	75	65	58	38
3.00	*	*	*	*	132	94	65	58	52
4.00	*	*	*	*	*	149	98	73	65
5.00	*	*	*	*	*	*	160	115	78
6.00	*	*	*	*	*	*	*	182	116

*Sample size is too large to be cost/effective for most audit applications.

FIGURE 6–4. Sample Size Tables. (SOURCE: *Audit Sampling Guide, op. cit.,* pp. 93–94 [adapted])

table of random numbers or to a computer program that generates random numbers, a selection of numbers can be made to choose the individual items that will make up the sample.

The use of random number tables is facilitated when the items in a population are consecutively numbered. In using tables, the auditor must (1) pick a starting point in the tables by making a "blind stab" or arbitrarily choosing a starting point, and (2) determine the direction or route (top to bottom, left to right, etc.) to be used in reading the tables. The route must be followed consistently and it should be fully documented in the audit working papers.

A random number table is shown in Figure 6-5. To illustrate its use, assume that a sample is desired from a population of sales invoices numbered 0001 to 4000. Assume further that the auditor elects to use the first set of four digits, to start with row 6 of column 1, and to read from top to bottom. In such case, the first four invoices in the sample would be numbers 0050, 3486, 2580, and 3942. Numbers 9287 and 7748 would be discarded because these digits do not correspond to the numbers in the population.

In using a random number table, it is possible that the same number may be drawn more than once. When the duplicate number is ignored (i.e., skipped), the auditor is said to be *sampling without replacement*. Statistical tables used by auditors to determine sample size, like those illustrated earlier in this chapter, are often based on sampling with replacement. As a practical matter, however, the auditor usually samples without replacement as no new information would be obtained from examining the same item twice. The use of tables based on sampling with replacement results in larger sample sizes and is therefore considered by auditors to be a conservative approach.

Most computer software packages offer a standard program that includes a random number generator. Such a program can provide a list of random numbers to fit any size sample. In addition, the generators can be programmed to produce numbers that correspond solely to numbers appearing in the population. Random number generators greatly expedite the process of obtaining the list of sample items.

Systematic Sampling

This method of selection consists of selecting every *n*th item in the population from one or more random starts. The interval between items is usually referred to as the *skip interval*. When a single random start is used, the interval can be computed by dividing the population size by the sample size. For example, when a sample of 400 is to be obtained from a population of 2,000, the skip interval is 5 (2,000/400), or every fifth item. The starting point

Row	Columns (1)	(2)	(3)	(4)	(5)
1	04734	39426	91035	54839	76873
2	10417	19688	83404	42038	48226
3	07514	48374	35658	38971	53779
4	52305	86925	16223	25946	90222
5	96357	11486	30102	82679	57983
6	92870	05921	65698	27993	86406
7	00500	75924	38803	05386	10072
8	34862	93784	52709	15370	96727
9	25809	21860	36790	76883	20435
10	77487	38419	20631	48694	12638

FIGURE 6–5. Partial Random Number Table

in this method of selection should be a number from a random number table that falls within the interval from 1 to 5.

A major advantage of systematic selection is that it may take less time than other selection methods. Once the interval and starting point are determined, selection of the sample can be started immediately. In addition, it is unnecessary to number the items in the population to use this method. The auditor (or the computer) simply counts every nth item. Thus, the method can be used when the data are in the form of punched cards, magnetic tapes, or ledger cards.

Whenever the auditor considers using systematic selection, he must be alert to the possibility of any cyclical pattern within the population coinciding with the skip interval. In that event, systematic selection could produce a nonrandom sample, and another selection method should be considered. Alternatively, he can minimize the chance of bias by picking multiple starting points for the selection process. When multiple random starting points are used, the skip interval, as determined earlier in this section, is multiplied by the number of random starts, thus keeping total sample size the same.

Executing the Sampling Plan

After the sampling plan has been designed, sample items are selected and examined to determine the nature and frequency of occurrences of deviations from prescribed control procedures.

When the sampling unit is a document, it is customary to select a quantity that is slightly larger than the required amount. The "extras" are used as replacements when voided, unused, or nonapplicable items are selected in the required sample. A nonapplicable item occurs when the sample item does not fit the definition of the deviation. For example, if the deviation is "a voucher not supported by a receiving report," a voucher for the payment of a monthly bill from a public utility would not be applicable because receiving reports are not prepared for such services. Thus, this voucher would be replaced by an extra in executing the sample plan.

An unused item refers to the selection of an item from a portion of the population that has not yet been used. This may occur when the auditor defines the population to include the entire year and the sampling plan is executed during interim work. In some cases, the auditor may not be able to apply planned auditing procedures to a sample item. For example, when a sample item cannot be located, the item should be counted as a deviation. The auditor may discontinue the sampling plan whenever the number of occurrences found in the sample will not support the planned reliance on the control procedure.

Evaluating the Sample Results

Deviations found in the sample must be tabulated, summarized, and evaluated. Professional judgment is required in the evaluation of the following factors leading to an overall conclusion.

Calculating the Sample Occurrence Rate

A sample occurrence rate for each control tested is calculated by dividing the number of occurrences found for each control by the sample size examined. This rate is the auditor's best estimate of the true occurrence rate in the population.

Determining the Upper Occurrence Limit

This limit indicates the maximum occurrence rate in the population based on the *number* of occurrences discovered in the sample. The upper limit is expressed as a percentage, which is sometimes alternately referred to as the *achieved upper precision limit* or *maximum population occurrence* or *deviation rate*.

The upper occurrence limit is determined from evaluation tables like those shown in Figure 6-6. To use the tables it is necessary to

- Select the table that corresponds to the acceptable risk of overreliance.
- Locate the column that contains the actual *number* of occurrences (not the occurrence rate) found in the sample.
- Locate the row that contains the sample size used. (If the sample size falls between two rows use the row with the smaller size.)
- Read the upper occurrence limit from the intersection of the column and row determined in steps two and three.

Illustrative upper occurrence limits are as follows:

Risk of Overreliance	Number of Occurrences	Sample Size	Upper Occurrence Limit
5%	1	100	4.7%
5	2	150	4.1
10	3	120	5.5
10	4	200	4.0

When the sample size used does not appear in the evaluation tables, the auditor may (1) use the largest sample size in the table not exceeding the actual sample size used, (2) interpolate, (3) obtain more extensive tables, or (4) use a computer program that will produce an upper occurrence limit for any sample size. The upper occurrence limits determined in this manner are used in assessing sampling risk.

Assessing the Sampling Risk

It will be recalled that sampling risk relates to the possibility that a properly drawn sample may nonetheless not be representative of the population. The upper occurrence limit represents the sample occurrence rate plus an allow-

Statistical Sample Results Evaluation Table for Compliance Tests

Upper Occurrence Limit
(for large populations)

TABLE 3. 5 Percent Risk of Overreliance

Sample Size	ACTUAL NUMBER OF OCCURRENCES FOUND								
	0	1	2	3	4	5	6	7	8
25	11.3	17.6	*	*	*	*	*	*	*
30	9.5	14.9	19.5	*	*	*	*	*	*
35	8.2	12.9	16.9	*	*	*	*	*	*
40	7.2	11.3	14.9	18.3	*	*	*	*	*
45	6.4	10.1	13.3	16.3	19.2	*	*	*	*
50	5.8	9.1	12.1	14.8	17.4	19.9	*	*	*
55	5.3	8.3	11.0	13.5	15.9	18.1	*	*	*
60	4.9	7.7	10.1	12.4	14.6	16.7	18.8	*	*
65	4.5	7.1	9.4	11.5	13.5	15.5	17.4	19.3	*
70	4.2	6.6	8.7	10.7	12.6	14.4	16.2	18.0	19.7
75	3.9	6.2	8.2	10.0	11.8	13.5	15.2	16.9	18.4
80	3.7	5.8	7.7	9.4	11.1	12.7	14.3	15.8	17.3
90	3.3	5.2	6.8	8.4	9.9	11.3	12.7	14.1	15.5
100	3.0	4.7	6.2	7.6	8.9	10.2	11.5	12.7	14.0
125	2.4	3.7	4.9	6.1	7.2	8.2	9.3	10.3	11.3
150	2.0	3.1	4.1	5.1	6.0	6.9	7.7	8.6	9.4
200	1.5	2.3	3.1	3.8	4.5	5.2	5.8	6.5	7.1

TABLE 4. 10 Percent Risk of Overreliance

Sample Size	ACTUAL NUMBER OF OCCURRENCES FOUND								
	0	1	2	3	4	5	6	7	8
20	10.9	18.1	*	*	*	*	*	*	*
25	8.8	14.7	19.9	*	*	*	*	*	*
30	7.4	12.4	16.8	*	*	*	*	*	*
35	6.4	10.7	14.5	18.1	*	*	*	*	*
40	5.6	9.4	12.8	15.9	19.0	*	*	*	*
45	5.0	8.4	11.4	14.2	17.0	19.6	*	*	*
50	4.5	7.6	10.3	12.9	15.4	17.8	*	*	*
55	4.1	6.9	9.4	11.7	14.0	16.2	18.4	*	*
60	3.8	6.3	8.6	10.8	12.9	14.9	16.9	18.8	*
70	3.2	5.4	7.4	9.3	11.1	12.8	14.6	16.2	17.9
80	2.8	4.8	6.5	8.3	9.7	11.3	12.8	14.3	15.7
90	2.5	4.3	5.8	7.3	8.7	10.1	11.4	12.7	14.0
100	2.3	3.8	5.2	6.6	7.8	9.1	10.3	11.5	12.7
120	1.9	3.2	4.4	5.5	6.6	7.6	8.6	9.6	10.6
160	1.4	2.4	3.3	4.1	4.9	5.7	6.5	7.2	8.0
200	1.1	1.9	2.6	3.3	4.0	4.6	5.2	5.8	6.4

* over 20%

FIGURE 6–6. Statistical Sample Evaluation Tables (SOURCE: *Audit Sampling Guide, op. cit.,* pp. 95–96 [adapted].)

ance for sampling risk based on the level of risk of overreliance specified. When tables are used to determine the upper occurrence limit, the allowance for sampling risk (sometimes referred to as *precision*) is determined deductively by subtracting the sample occurrence rate from the upper occurrence limit. For example, in the first case above, the sample occurrence rate is 1 percent (1/100) and the allowance for sampling risk is 3.7 percent (4.7% − 1.0%). The sample indicates that there is a 5 percent risk that the true population occurrence rate exceeds 4.7 percent. If the upper occurrence limit is greater than the tolerable rate specified in designing the sample, the results do not support relying on the control; otherwise the results support reliance.

Experience in working with the evaluation tables will reveal the validity of the following generalizations:

- Whenever the sample occurrence rate exceeds the expected occurrence rate used to determine sample size, the sample results do not support reliance on the control. This is true because the upper occurrence limit will exceed the tolerable rate for the specified risk of overreliance.
- Conversely, whenever the sample occurrence rate is less than or equal to the expected occurrence rate, the sample results support reliance because the corresponding upper occurrence limit will be less than or equal to the tolerable rate at the specified level of risk of overreliance.*

Thus, while the determination of the upper occurrence limit is not always necessary, the auditor ordinarily includes this information in his working papers. He may or may not calculate and include in his working papers the allowance for sampling risk.

Considering the Qualitative Aspects of Occurrences

It would be a mistake to conclude that the auditor is interested only in the frequency of the occurrences. Each deviation from a prescribed control procedure should be analyzed to determine its nature and cause. Occurrences may result from such factors as a new employee, an inexperienced replacement, an employee on vacation or sick leave, misunderstanding of instructions by new employees, incompetence, carelessness, and deliberate violation.

The auditor should also consider whether the exception may have a direct effect on the financial statements. For example, the failure of unit prices on a sales invoice to agree with authorized prices has an impact on the statements. In contrast, the absence of verification of the mathematical accuracy of an invoice that is mathematically correct does not indicate an error in the financial statements. A further consideration is whether the

---

* When the sample size determined from the tables in Figure 6-4 is rounded up or arbitrarily increased, these generalizations do not apply.

exception constitutes an irregularity. Nonsystematic occurrences are generally accidental and unintentional. However, a systematic pattern of exceptions may be the result of deliberate efforts to misrepresent or to conceal misappropriations. Obviously, occurrences that directly affect the financial statements or appear to be irregularities have greater audit significance.

Reaching an Overall Conclusion

The auditor uses the results of the sample and professional judgment to reach a conclusion as to the reliance to be placed on each of the control procedures that have been tested. When, in the auditor's judgment, the sample results do not support the planned reliance, the auditor ordinarily will have to modify the nature, timing, or extent of substantive tests, or if applicable, test other compensating controls for compliance.

Illustrative Case Study

In the audit of the Dexter Company, the auditor decides to use attribute sampling in compliance testing of sales transactions. The plan and the auditor's working papers are explained and illustrated below. This case study is divided into three parts: (1) the design of the sampling plan, (2) executing the plan, and (3) evaluating the results.

The *design of the sampling plan* involves the first five steps of the sampling plan. These are presented in the sample design section of the working paper in Figure 6-7. The objective of the plan, the sampling unit and population, and the sample selection method are identified at the top of the working paper. Then the attributes of interest are listed in column 1, and the factors used to determine sample size are specified in columns 2-4. In this plan, attributes 2 and 4 are considered less critical than the others; hence, the statistical parameters for these conditions are less stringent than for the more critical conditions. Sample sizes are next determined from the tables shown in Figure 6-4 and are entered in column 5. In the Dexter Company the auditor decides to round up sample sizes to provide extra units. These amounts are entered in column 6.

In *executing the plan,* the sample items are randomly selected, and the invoices are examined for each attribute. As occurrences of deviations are found, they are recorded and summarized on a worksheet as shown in Figure 6-8.

In *evaluating the results,* the number of occurrences of deviations from each attribute is entered in column 7 of Figure 6-7. Then the occurrence rates are computed and entered in column 8, and are compared with the corresponding expected population occurrence rates in column 4. In this case study, the sample rate for attribute 5 exceeds the expected rate. This enables us to foresee that the upper occurrence limit will exceed the tolerable rate for this attribute. Next, the auditor uses the evaluation tables in Figure 6-6 to determine the upper occurrence limit for each attribute. These results are entered in column 9. The upper occurrence limit is then compared with the

FIGURE 6-7. Statistical Sampling Plan Working Paper: Sample Design and Sample Results

tolerable rate for each attribute. When the upper occurrence limit exceeds the tolerable rate, the sample results to not support the auditor's planned reliance on the prescribed control. In the Dexter Company, as foreseen, attribute 5 again is the only exception. Finally, for illustrative purposes, the allowance for sampling risk (column 9 − column 8) is entered in column 10.

In order to form an overall conclusion about each control procedure, the auditor makes a qualitative assessment of the deviations to determine their nature, cause, and significance. This analysis is documented in the working papers as shown in Figure 6-9. Observe that this working paper also indi-

Prepared by: *C.J.A.*   Date: *10/6/X1*
Reviewed by: *R.C.P.*   Date: *10/9/X1*

Dexter Company
Sampling for Attributes — Execution of Sales Transactions
Occurrences Listing
12/30/X1

Invoice Number		Attribute								
		1	2	3	4	5	6	7	8	
A76504			√							
A76550						√				
A76720						√				
A76745							√			
A77001						√				
A77022								√		
A79268						√				
Total No. of Occurrences		0	1	0	0	4	1	1	0	
Sample Size		160	90	160	105	160	160	160	160	
Sample Occurrence Rate		0	1.1	0	0	2.5	.6	.6	0	

FIGURE 6–8. Occurrences Listing Working Paper

cates the effects of the deviations on substantive testing and whether any weaknesses should be reported to management.

In this case, the auditor concludes both the statistical evaluation and the qualitative assessment support planned reliance on all of the tested controls except the one related to attribute 5, which should be discussed with management. These conclusions are documented on the bottom of the working paper illustrated in Figure 6-7.

Prepared by: *C.J.H.*   Date: *10/6/X1*
Reviewed by: *R.C.P.*   Date: *10/9/X1*

Dexter Company
Sampling of Attributes — Execution of Sales Transactions,
Analysis of Sample Occurrences
12/31/X1

Attribute	Number of Occurrences	EXPLANATION OF OCCURRENCES	Effects on Substantive Tests	Management Letter
2	1	Verification of agreement of sales order and customers order not indicated but they did in fact agree.	None	No
5	4	Shipping documents not prepared because customers picked up orders. No receipts were obtained from customers.	Confirm 4 accounts where exceptions occurred; increase planned confirmation of other receivables by 10%.	Yes
6	1	Verification not indicated on two invoices involving backorders. Processing of backorders otherwise appropriate.	None	No
7	1	Evidence of verification not indicated on two invoices; however, in each case invoice price agreed with authorized price list.	None	No

FIGURE 6–9. Analysis of Sample Occurrences Working Paper

NONSTATISTICAL SAMPLING IN COMPLIANCE TESTING

As explained earlier, the auditor may use nonstatistical sampling in compliance testing. The steps involved in the design and execution of the sampling plan are similar regardless of the type of sampling. Similarly, the factors to be considered in determining sample size and in evaluating sample results are similar, although they may not be quantified and explicitly stated in nonstatistical applications. The major differences between nonstatistical and statistical sampling in performing the steps are summarized below.

Determining the Sample Size

As in statistical sampling applications, the major determinants of sample size in nonstatistical sampling are: (1) the acceptable risk of over-reliance, (2) the tolerable occurrence rate, and (3) the expected population occurrence rate for each attribute. In nonstatistical sampling, it is not necessary for the auditor to quantify these factors explicitly in determining sample size. However, he must implicitly quantify these factors and subjectively recognize the following effects on sample size of a change in one factor when other factors are held constant.

VARIABLE FACTOR	EFFECT ON SAMPLE SIZE
Decrease in risk of overreliance	Increase
Decrease in tolerable occurrence rate	Increase
Decrease in expected population occurrence rate	Decrease

The auditor may, but is not required to, use the information from statistical tables as a guide in determining sample size in a nonstatistical sample.

Determining the Sample Selection Method

In addition to random number and systematic sampling described earlier, the auditor may use block or haphazard sampling in selecting items in nonstatistical sampling.

Block Sampling

At one time, block sampling was the most common selection method. The method consists of selecting similar transactions occurring within a specified time period or grouping. For example, the sample may consist of all vouchers processed during a two-week period. If enough blocks are selected, this method of selection may be suitable in nonstatistical sampling. However, selection of a single block from a whole year's transactions is no longer considered appropriate in most circumstances.

Haphazard Sampling

This method involves selecting items at will, without regard to document number, amount (size), or other feature. For example, the auditor may haphazardly select a sample for 50 invoices from a file drawer. If bias is avoided in making the selections, the sample may be representative of the population.

Evaluating Sample Results

In nonstatistical samples, it is not possible to determine an upper occurrence limit or to quantify the sampling risk associated with a sample result. However, the auditor should relate the occurrence rate found in a sample to the corresponding tolerable occurrence rate considered in determining sample size. For example, if a sample occurrence rate of 1 percent is found for an attribute for which the tolerable rate was 7 percent, the auditor might view the difference of 6 percent as an adequate allowance for sampling risk and conclude that the sample provides an acceptably low level of risk of overreliance. On the other hand, if a sample occurrence rate of 5 percent is found for an attribute for which a tolerable rate of 6 percent was specified, the difference of 1 percent might be viewed as an inadequate allowance for sampling risk, resulting in an unacceptably high risk of overreliance. That is, the auditor is concerned that if, by chance, the sample occurrence rate is less than the specified maximum tolerable rate, the actual population occurrence rate may nonetheless exceed the tolerable rate.

In nonstatistical samples, the auditor uses his experience and professional judgment to reach an overall conclusion as to the amount of reliance that can be placed on each control procedure that has been tested. As is the case in evaluating statistical samples, the auditor gives consideration to the qualitative aspects of occurrences found in a sample, as well as to the frequency of such occurrences.

DISCOVERY SAMPLING

Nature and Purpose

Discovery sampling is a form of attribute sampling that is designed to locate at least one exception if the rate of occurrence in the population is at or above a specified rate. This method of sampling is used to search for critical occurrences that may indicate the existence of an irregularity. Discovery sampling is appropriate when the expected occurrence rate is quite low and the auditor wants a sample that will provide a specified chance to observe one occurrence.

Discovery sampling is useful when the auditor

- Is examining a large population composed of items that contain a very high proportion of audit risk.
- Suspects that irregularities have occurred.
- Seeks additional evidence in a given case to determine whether a known irregularity is an isolated occurrence or part of a recurring exception.

Discovery sampling generally is not used to find a "needle in the haystack" or a "once in a lifetime occurrence."

Design and Evaluation

In using discovery sampling, it is necessary to specify two statistical parameters: (1) the critical rate of occurrence and (2) the probability. The former refers to that rate of occurrence in the population that must be present (or exceeded) to provide the auditor with the desired probability of producing one example. Additionally, population size must be estimated to permit selection of an appropriate table for determining sample size. A discovery sampling table for use with populations over 10,000 is illustrated in Figure 6-10. Other tables are available for smaller population sizes.

To illustrate, assume a population of 14,000 in which you conclude that 70 or more occurrences would indicate a serious problem. Assume also that you wish to have a 90 percent probability of finding at least one occurrence if there are 70 or more. The critical rate of occurrence is 0.5 percent (70/14,000) and the sample size shown in the table is 460. It may be observed

**Probability in Percent of Including at
Least One Occurrence in a Sample
(for populations over 10,000)**

Sample Size	UPPER LIMIT ON CRITICAL RATE OF OCCURRENCES							
	0.01%	0.05%	0.1%	0.2%	0.3%	0.5%	1%	2%
50		2%	5%	9%	14%	22%	39%	64%
60	1%	3	6	11	16	26	45	70
70	1	3	7	13	19	30	51	76
80	1	4	8	15	21	33	55	80
90	1	4	9	16	24	36	60	84
100	1	5	10	18	26	39	63	87
120	1	6	11	21	30	45	70	91
140	1	7	13	24	34	50	76	94
160	2	8	15	27	38	55	80	96
200	2	10	18	33	45	63	87	98
240	2	11	21	38	51	70	91	99
300	3	14	26	45	59	78	95	99+
340	3	16	29	49	64	82	97	99+
400	4	18	33	55	70	87	98	99+
460	5	21	37	60	75	90	99	99+
500	5	22	39	63	78	92	99	99+
600	6	26	45	70	84	95	99+	99+
700	7	30	50	75	88	97	99+	99+
800	8	33	55	80	91	98	99+	99+
900	9	36	59	83	93	99	99+	99+
1,000	10	39	63	86	95	99	99+	99+
1,500	14	53	78	95	99	99+	99+	99+
2,000	18	63	86	98	99+	99+	99+	99+
2,500	22	71	92	99	99+	99+	99+	99+
3,000	26	78	95	99+	99+	99+	99+	99+

Courtesy of Ernst & Whinney (adapted).

FIGURE 6-10. Discovery Sampling Table

from Figure 6-10 that discovery sampling produces inordinate sample sizes when the critical rate of occurrence is less than 0.5 percent.

In the above example, if one occurrence is discovered in examining the randomly selected sample items, the auditor is 90 percent certain that a serious problem exists. Thus, the auditor would proceed to expand his examination of the population. In contrast, if no occurrences are found, the auditor can reach a conclusion as to the probability of the existence of a specified number of errors in the population. For example, the probability of fewer than 42 occurrences (a rate of less than 0.3 percent) is 75 percent, and the probability of an occurrence rate of less than 0.1 percent is 37 percent.

CONCLUDING COMMENTS

Audit sampling is well established in contemporary auditing. Both statistical and nonstatistical sampling may be used in performing compliance tests. The critical difference between the two types of sampling is that the laws of probability are used to control sampling risk in statistical sampling. Under either type of sampling, the auditor is primarily concerned about the risk of overreliance on internal accounting control. Further consideration is given to attribute sampling applications in Chapters 7-10.

REVIEW QUESTIONS

6-1. Why do the second and third standards of field work contain an element of uncertainty?

6-2. Distinguish between sampling risk and nonsampling risk.

6-3. Identify the types of sampling risk that may occur in auditing and identify the type of testing to which each risk pertains.

6-4. Indicate the impacts of the sampling risks on (a) audit effectiveness and (b) audit efficiency.

6-5. Explain the basic similarities and differences between nonstatistical and statistical sampling in audit testing.

6-6. Contrast nonstatistical and statistical sampling in regard to cost/benefit considerations.

6-7. a. Define an "attribute."
b. What evidence of performance should exist for attributes?

6-8. Identify four factors that may affect the auditor's identification of the population.

6-9. a. Define the sampling unit.
b. Identify the different kinds of sampling units that may be selected.

6-10. What factors affect the determination of sample size?

6-11. a. Does the auditor normally set the risk of overreliance high or low? Why?
b. What effect does this risk have on sample size?

6-12. a. Define the term "tolerable occurrence rate" and indicate the factors that should be considered in deciding on the tolerable rate.
b. What effect does this rate have on the sample size?

6-13. a. Indicate the information that may be used by the auditor to estimate the expected population occurrence rate.
b. What effect does this factor have on sample size?

6-14. Enumerate the steps that must be followed in determining sample size from sample size tables.

6-15. a. Identify and briefly explain the sample selection methods that may be used in statistical sampling.

    b. Using Figure 6-5, select the first five vouchers from a population of 7,000 vouchers prenumbered consecutively from number 1001 under each of the following assumptions:

Case	Start Row	Column	Digits to Be Used in Table	Selection Path
(1)	5	1	First 4	Top/bottom; left to right
(2)	10	2	Last 4	Bottom/top; right to left

6–16. a. Identify the three steps involved in quantitatively evaluating sample results.
    b. Indicate the steps involved in using the evaluation tables.

6–17. a. What factors should be considered in qualitatively evaluating sample results?
    b. What alternative courses of action should be considered when sample results do not support the auditor's planned reliance on a control procedure?

6–18. Contrast the method of (a) determining sample size and (b) evaluating sample results between a nonstatistical and a statistical sampling plan.

6–19. Distinguish between block and haphazard sampling selection, and identify the circumstances under which each method will produce a representative sample.

6–20. a. Describe the circumstances where discovery sampling may be useful in auditing.
    b. What factors are necessary to determine sample size in discovery sampling?

COMPREHENSIVE QUESTIONS

6–21. This problem focuses on the determination of sample sizes.

Required
    a. Given the constraints of a 7 percent tolerable occurrence rate, and an expected population occurrence rate of from 1 to 4 percent, indicate the specific combinations of these factors at both 5 and 10 percent levels of risk of overreliance that will result in sample sizes that will not be less than 125 or more than 200.
    b. At a 5 percent risk of overreliance, a 5 percent tolerable occurrence rate, and a 2 percent expected population occurrence rate, sample size is 181. Compute the new sample size for each of the following changes, assuming other factors are held constant.
        1. Increase tolerable occurrence rate to 6 percent.
        2. Decrease tolerable occurrence rate to 4 percent.
        3. Decrease expected population occurrence rate to 1 percent.
        4. Increase expected population occurrence rate to 2.5 percent.
        5. Increase risk of overreliance to 10 percent.

6–22. The use of statistical sampling techniques in an examination of financial statements does not eliminate judgmental decisions.

Required
    a. Identify and explain four areas where judgment may be exercised by a CPA in planning a statistical sampling test.
    b. Assume that a CPA's sample shows an unacceptable occurrence rate. Describe the various actions that he may take based upon this finding.
    c. A nonstratified sample of 80 accounts payable vouchers is to be selected from a population of 3,200. The vouchers are numbered consecutively from 1 to 3200 and are listed, 40 to a page, in the voucher register. Describe two different techniques for selecting a sample of vouchers for review.

AICPA (adapted)

6–23. An audit of inventory records disclosed that the population comprises 20,000 items of inventory. Units within the items vary from 30 to 750. The values of the units vary from 20¢ to $1,500. The auditor had estimated the error rate at not over 5 percent, and since a risk of overreliance of 5 percent and a tolerable rate of 8 percent was desired, the tables used showed a sample of 200 items. The selection was made from the north end of the storeroom, picking items having 100 or more units.

    In the test, 40 instances were found in which the number of units in stock varied by one or more units from the number shown on the inventory records.

    The report to management states that the auditor is 95 percent confident (5% risk of overreliance) that the number of records in the population which are in error is somewhere between 970 and 1030.

Required
Describe five errors in the auditor's techniques.

                                                      IIA

6–24. In the audit of the Joan Company the auditor specifies 10 attributes of interest. The statistical parameters for each condition and the number of occurrences found in the sample are as follows:

Attribute	Tolerable Occurrence Rate	Risk of Overreliance	Expected Population Occurrence Rate	Number of Sample Occurrences
1	4%	5%	1.00	2
2	3	5	.50	0
3	6	5	2.00	4
4	6	5	2.50	4
5	8	5	2.00	1
6	3	10	.50	0
7	4	10	1.50	2
8	5	10	1.50	1
9	6	10	2.50	2
10	7	10	3.00	4

Required
a. Assuming a large population, determine the sample size for each attribute.
b. Rounding sample size down to the nearest sample size in the tables in Figure 6-6, determine the upper occurrence limit for each attribute.
c. Assess the allowance for sampling risk for each attribute.
d. Identify the controls that can be relied on.
e. Identify the controls that cannot be relied on.
f. Indicate the range of tolerable rates for each of the three levels of auditor reliance on a control procedure.

6–25. In the development of an audit program it is determined that to achieve acceptable levels of the allowance for sampling risk and the risk of overreliance, a sample of 186 items from a population of 10,000 is adequate on a statistical basis.

Required
a. Briefly define each of the following terms used in the above statement:
    1. Population.
    2. Sample.
    3. Allowance for sampling risk.
    4. Risk of overreliance.
b. If the population is 100,000 and the specifications for allowance for sampling risk

and risk of overreliance are unchanged from the situation above for a population of 10,000, which of the following sample sizes could be expected to be statistically correct for the larger population: 186; 504; 3,000; 4,360? Justify your answer. (Your answer should be based on judgment and reasoning, rather than actual calculation.)

c. Statistical sampling techniques are being used in auditing. A sample is taken and analyzed to draw an inference or reach a conclusion about a population, but there is always a risk that the inference or conclusion may be incorrect. What value, then, is there in using statistical sampling techniques?

6–26. Mavis Stores had two billing clerks during the year. Snow worked three months and White worked nine months. As the auditor for Mavis Stores, Jones, CPA, uses attribute sampling to test clerical accuracy for the entire year, but due to the lack of internal verification, the system depends heavily upon the competence of the billing clerks. The quantity of bills per month is constant.

Required
a. Jones decided to treat the billing by Snow and White as two separate populations. Discuss the advisability of this approach, considering the circumstances.
b. Jones decided to use the same risk of overreliance, expected error rate, and tolerable occurrence rate for each population. Assuming he decided to select a sample of 200 to test Snow's work, approximately how large a sample is necessary to test White's?

AICPA (adapted)

6–27. In the Leo Company, 18,000 checks were issued during a designated period of time. Concern exists within management that some of these checks may be forgeries. As part of your regular audit engagement, you agree to use discovery sampling to test for such occurrences.

Required
a. Assuming you desire 95 percent probability of detecting at least one occurrence, determine sample size when the critical number of occurrences is (1) 54, (2) 90, and (3) 180.
b. Assuming no occurrences are found in the above samples, what is the probability that the number of occurrences is less than 18 in (1), less than 54 in (2), and less than 90 in (3)?

6–28. As the auditor for the Harns Company, you elect to use statistical sampling in performing tests of sales transactions. You decide to use shipping documents for the purpose of testing whether all shipments have been billed. The shipping document is selected as the sampling unit. There are 5,000 shipping documents in the population and you elect to use random sampling in drawing your sample. Pertinent data concerning attributes of interest are as follows:

Attribute	Tolerable Occurrence Rate (%)	Risk of Over-reliance (%)	Expected Population Occurrence Rate (%)
1. Prenumbered sales order for each shipping document	6	5	1.0
2. Prenumbered sales invoice for each shipping document	6	5	1.0
3. Agreement of details of shipping document with details of sales order	6	10	1.0

Attribute	Tolerable Occurrence Rate (%)	Risk of Over-reliance (%)	Expected Population Occurrence Rate (%)
4. Agreement of details of shipping document with details of sales invoice	5	5	1.0
5. Signature of shipping clerk on shipping document	6	10	2.0
6. Receipt from carrier attached to shipping document	7	10	.5

Assume that the results of the sample reveal the following number of occurrences for each attribute: (1) 2, (2) 0, (3) 2, (4) 2, (5) 1, (6) 1.

Required

a. Prepare a sampling plan worksheet using Figure 6-7 as an example (Round sample size per table up to next number ending in zero for sample size used; e.g., 78 to 80).
b. Statistically interpret the results of the sample.
c. Explain the alternative courses of action that are available to the auditor when the sample occurrence rate plus the allowance for sampling risk exceeds the tolerable occurrence rate.

6–29. The Tomlin Company's principal activity is buying milk from dairy farmers, processing the milk and delivering the milk to retail customers. You are engaged in auditing the sales transactions of the company and determine the following:

1. The company has 50 retail routes; each route consists of 100 to 200 accounts, the number that can be serviced by a driver in a day.
2. The driver enters cash collections from the day's deliveries to each customer directly on a statement form in record books maintained for each route. Mail remittances are posted in the route record books by office personnel. At the end of the month the statements are priced, extended and footed. Photocopies of the statements are prepared and left in the customers' milk boxes with the next milk delivery.
3. The statements are reviewed by the office manager, who prepares a monthly list for each route of accounts with 90-day balances or older. The list is used for intensive collection action.
4. The audit program used in prior audits for the selection of sales transactions for compliance tests stated: "Select two accounts from each route, one to be chosen by opening the route book at random and the other as the third account on each list of 90-day or older accounts. For each account selected, choose the latest transaction for testing."

Your review of sales transactions leads you to conclude that statistical sampling techniques may be applied to their examination.

Required

a. Since statistical sampling techniques do not relieve the CPA of his responsibilities in the exercise of his professional judgment, of what benefit are they to the CPA? Discuss.
b. Give the reasons why the audit procedure previously used for selection of sales transactions (as given in 4 above) would not produce a valid statistical sample.
c. Suggest two ways to select a valid statistical sample.
d. Assume that the Company has 10,000 sales transactions and that your statistical sampling disclosed 6 errors in a sample of 200 transactions. Is it reasonable to assume that 300 transactions in the entire population are in error? Explain.

6-30. In an attribute sampling plan for the Mid-East Sales Co., you examine 200 sales invoices. In your working papers, you make the following listing of possible exceptions to prescribed control procedures in the execution of the transactions:

Invoice Number	Prescribed Procedure	Findings
248	Written authorizations of sales by sales order department	Verbal notation authorization by phone by sales order department
333	Sales order verification of quantities and prices	No evidence of verification but quantities and prices are correct
377	Sales order verification of quantities and prices	No evidence of verification; quantities and prices are incorrect
472	Credit department authorization of credit	Evidence of credit department approval on invoice, but amount of invoice exceeds maximum credit limits of company
545	Shipping department verification of agreement of goods shipped with sales order	No shipping department verification but invoice agrees with sales order
617	Billing department verification of unit prices	Price verification indicated on invoice; by reperformance, you ascertain that the prices do not agree with price list in effect at time of sale
701	Billing department verification of mathematical accuracy of invoice	No verification of accuracy on invoice; by recalculation, you determine mathematical accuracy of invoice
719	Credit department authorization of credit	Credit department signature not on signature list; investigation discloses a new hire in credit whose name was not added to authorized list of signers
762	Billing department verification of invoice with sales order	No evidence of verification on invoice; investigation reveals that verification was done but employee forgot to initial invoice

Required

a. List the numbers of the foregoing items and indicate whether there is or is not a deviation from a prescribed procedure.

b. Briefly explain the reason for each answer.

6-31. You are now conducting your third annual audit of the financial statements of Elite Corporation for the year ended December 31, 19X1. You decide to employ unrestricted random number statistical sampling techniques in testing the effectiveness of the company's internal control procedures relating to sales invoices, which are all serially numbered. In prior years, after selecting one representative two-week period during the year, you tested all invoices issued during that period and resolved all of the errors which were found to your satisfaction.

Required

a. Explain the statistical procedure you would use to determine the size of the sample of sales invoices to be examined.

b. Once the sample size has been determined, how would you select the individual invoices to be included in the sample? Explain.

c. Would the use of statistical sampling procedures improve the examination of sales invoices as compared with the selection procedure used in prior years? Discuss.

6–32. You have made a review and preliminary evaluation of the Morgan Company's system of internal control, and based on this, you have designed a tentative audit program. Your next step is to perform compliance tests in order to confirm or challenge your evaluation.

A major area of compliance testing is cash disbursements. Monthly, the company processes an average of 360 vouchers, paying 600 invoices. Each voucher contains a copy of the check along with supporting documentation, such as vendor's invoices, purchase orders, and receiving reports.

You intend to examine a sample of vouchers using attribute estimation statistical sampling to evaluate compliance with several control procedures in which you are interested. The attributes for testing the controls are set forth in your audit program as:

1. Approval of account distribution.
2. Invoice and purchase order agreement.
3. Purchase order approval.
4. Purchase order and requisition agreement.
5. Invoice and receiving report agreement.
6. Discounts taken.
7. Invoice canceled after approval.
8. Approval of check request.

From experience, you expect a noncompliance rate of about 2 percent for attributes 1, 2, 5, and 6, and complete compliance with all others.

After consideration of a number of related audit steps, you decide on a tolerable occurrence rate for noncompliance of 6 percent for controls 1 through 6 and 3 percent for controls 7 and 8. A low risk of overreliance, 5 percent, is elected because compliance tests, as part of your review and evaluation of internal control, serve as the foundation for the greater part of the audit yet to come.

Required

a. What is the sampling unit and the population size?

b. Determine the appropriate sample size for each attribute.

c. Assume that on examining each sample item, given the sample sizes determined in part (b), you find that there were seven occurrences of inappropriate account distributions and two occurrences of invoices being paid after the discount date.

1. Determine the upper occurrence limit for each attribute. (Round sample size down to next largest value in evaluation tables).

2. State what impact these findings would have on the execution of the remainder of your audit program.

CASE STUDY

6–33.* The audit team has reviewed the internal accounting controls of Yates Company and has determined that it is cost beneficial to perform a compliance test on the *disbursement cycle*. The test will be restricted to inventory purchases. The results of this test will affect the nature, timing, and extent of the substantive test work related to inventory price tests.

The audit team has determined that they are willing to accept a 10 percent risk of overreliance.

The audit team has had many favorable results in performing this test in prior years, but the client has experienced a significant number of personnel changes this past year.

The audit team has asked you to provide them with a number of alternative sampling plans from which they could make a selection.

Required
a. Assuming that the number of occurrences expected is 1%, what is (1) the minimum sample size based on substantial planned reliance on internal control and (2) the maximum sample size based on moderate planned reliance.
b. If the audit team decides to place substantial reliance on the control procedure, what conclusions can the auditor make if the sample results show (1) three occurrences, and (2) one occurrence?
c. One of the attributes tested is "evidence of management approval of vendor's invoice." In your testing, you discover the following:
   1. The manager's initials are not present, although you observed the manager reviewing the documentation. There were no errors in information contained on the documents or in the invoice extensions.
   2. Management reviewed and approved the invoice and initialed the documents. However, the supporting documentation shows a difference in quantities received compared to the invoice, and no correction has been made.
   3. The invoice was reviewed and approved by management prior to payment. The manager's initials are present, and the auditor reviewed the steps performed and found no exceptions.

   Which of the foregoing, if any, represent an occurrence of a deviation from the control procedure?

7

Compliance Tests of Revenue Cycle: Sales Transactions

STUDY OBJECTIVES

The study objectives of this chapter are to acquire an understanding of internal control over sales transactions in the revenue cycle and the auditor's study and evaluation of these controls. To achieve these objectives, it is necessary for the reader to

- Know the meaning of the term *revenue cycle*.
- Recognize the applicability of internal control objectives to the revenue cycle.
- Comprehend how the principles of internal accounting control are applicable to sales transactions.
- Realize the methodology for reviewing, testing, and evaluating internal controls over sales transactions.
- Understand the application of statistical sampling in testing sales transactions.
- Perceive the methodology of testing the electronic data processing of sales transactions.

T his is the first of four consecutive chapters pertaining to systems of internal accounting control for specific classes of transactions. Each chapter contains a discussion of internal accounting control objectives and principles that are applicable to each class of transactions. Then attention is given to the auditor's study and evaluation of internal control, including case study applications of statistical sampling and electronic data processing (EDP).

Cycle Approach

Chapter 4 explained that transactions are the subject matter of internal control. Transactions may be grouped within a company by (1) operating units, such as divisions and departments, (2) functions, such as billing customers and preparing the payroll, or (3) cycles. In the context of internal control, *cycles* refer to the major areas of business activity within an entity. The cycle approach requires the identification of

- The major areas of activity.
- The major classes of transactions within the activity.
- The steps or functions associated with each class of transactions.

A cycle transcends differences in organizational structure among companies and permits the tracing of transactions from their inception to the ultimate effects on the financial statements of the entity. Cycles are widely used by management in designing systems of internal control and by auditors in studying and evaluating internal control. Accordingly, the cycle approach is used in this book.

The identification of major areas of business activity may be broad or narrow. For example, one company may elect to use a revenue cycle and include both sales and cash receipts within that grouping. In contrast, another company may decide to identify sales and cash receipts as separate cycles. While the identification of cycles may differ among entities, the cycles selected should include all repetitive transactions in which the entity normally engages. For purposes of discussion and illustration in this book, the following cycles and specific classes of transactions will be used:

CYCLE	PRINCIPAL CLASSES OF TRANSACTIONS	CHAPTER COVERAGE
Revenue	Sales (and cost of sales)	7
	Cash receipts and sales adjustments	8
Expenditure	Purchases and cash disbursements	9
	Payroll	10
Production	Manufacturing	10
Investing	Temporary and long-term investments	14
Financing	Long-term debt and capital stock	14

Internal Accounting Control Objectives

As explained in Chapter 4, there are four operative objectives of internal accounting control. To facilitate subsequent discussion, we will condense these into three objectives with the following text identifications and applicable internal control principles.

INTERNAL ACCOUNTING CONTROL OBJECTIVES	TEXT CLASSIFICATION AND IDENTIFICATION	PRIMARY INTERNAL CONTROL PRINCIPLES
Transactions are executed in accordance with management's general or specific authorization.	Transactions are properly executed.	Segregation of functions Authorization procedures Documentation procedures Physical controls Independent internal verification
Transactions are recoded as necessary (1) to permit preparation of financial statements in conformity with generally accepted accounting principles or any other criteria applicable to such statements and (2) to maintain accountability for assets.	Transactions are properly recorded.	Segregation of functions Accounting records and procedures Independent internal verification
Access to assets is permitted only in accordance with management's authorization. The recorded accountability for assets is compared with the existing assets at reasonable intervals and appropriate action is taken with respect to any differences.	Custody of assets is properly maintained.	Segregation of functions Authorization procedures Physical controls Independent internal verification

These three objectives will provide the framework for discussing (1) the basic features of accounting control over specific classes of transactions within a cycle and (2) the auditor's study and evaluation of internal controls for each of the classes.

Nature of the Revenue Cycle

An entity's revenue cycle consists of the activities relating to the exchange of goods and services with customers and to the collection of the revenue in cash. Different entities may have different sources of revenue. For example, merchandising and manufacturing companies have sales; doctors, attorneys, and CPAs have fees; theaters, sports arenas, and amusement parks have admissions; banks and financial institutions have interest and dividends; and mass transit companies and airlines have fares. The discussions and illustrations in this chapter are based on a merchandising company. However, much of the commentary can easily be adapted to other types of entities.

For a merchandising company, the classes of transactions in the revenue cycle include (1) sales, (2) sales adjustments (discounts, returns and allowances, and uncollectable accounts [provisions and write-offs]), and (3) cash receipts (collections on account and cash sales). Sales transactions are discussed in this chapter; the other classes of transactions are considered in Chapter 8.

Internal Control Environment

An organization plan that provides clear lines of authority and responsibility is an important aspect in the internal control environment over transactions in the revenue cycle. An organizational structure for a wholesale or mail order company is illustrated in Figure 7-1. In this example, billing is the responsibility of the vice president of sales. In some companies, billing is part of the controller's responsibility. A good control environment also requires

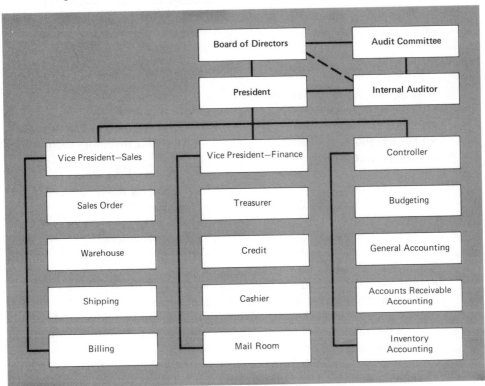

FIGURE 7–1. Organization Chart for Revenue Cycle

- Competent and trustworthy personnel.
- Monitoring of prescribed controls by internal auditing.
- Sales and cash budgets, with periodic comparisons of actual results with planned objectives.

INTERNAL CONTROL OVER SALES TRANSACTIONS

Basic Considerations

Sales may be made on a credit or cash basis. In a corner grocery store, all sales may be for cash in over-the-counter transactions. By contrast, national retailers such as Lord & Taylor, Montgomery Ward, and Sears, Roebuck have both cash and credit over-the-counter sales as well as mail order sales. The time period involved in executing the sales transaction may range from a matter of minutes in an over-the-counter sale in a retail store to days, weeks, and months in wholesaling and manufacturing companies. Attention in this chapter is directed primarily at credit sales transactions that require some time to process. Over-the-counter sales are considered in Chapter 8. Because the filling of a sales order requires the release of inventory, the costing of goods sold is considered to be a recording function associated with sales transactions. However, the internal controls associated with the acquisition and custody of inventory are discussed under the expenditure cycle.

The following matters are basic to an understanding of sales transactions in the revenue cycle:

Functions

Executing
- Accepting the customer's order.
- Approving credit.
- Filling the sales order.
- Shipping the sales order.
- Billing the customer.

Recording
- Journalizing and posting sales transactions.
- Updating the customers' ledger.
- Updating inventory records.

Custody
- Protecting the customers' ledger.
- Maintaining correctness of customer balances.

Common documents
- *Customer order.* A request for merchandise by a customer. It may be received directly from customers or through salespersons.
- *Sales order.* A form showing the description, quantity, and other data pertaining to a customer order. It serves as the basis for internal processing of the customer order by the seller.
- *Shipping document.* A form used to show the details and date of each shipment. It may be in the form of a *bill of lading,* which is a formal acknowledgment of the receipt of goods for delivery by a freight carrier.

- *Sales invoice.* A form stating the particulars of a sale, including the amount owed, terms, and date of sale. It is used to bill customers and provides the basis for recording the sale.
- *Daily sales summary.* A report showing total sales invoices issued during the day. It is used as a control device to assure that all invoices are recorded.
- *Customer monthly statement.* A report sent to each customer showing the beginning balance, transactions during the month, and the ending balance.

Accounting records
- *Book of original entry.* Sales journal (or register) with columns for both sales and cost of sales. It may also have columns for classifying sales by departments, product lines, and geographical location.
- *Subsidiary ledgers.* Customers' (or accounts receivable) and perpetual inventory records.
- *General ledger accounts.* Cash, accounts receivable, notes receivable, inventory, sales, and cost of sales.

File data
- *Approved customer file.* Contains a list of customers from whom orders may be accepted.
- *Customer credit file.* Shows the credit and collection history for each customer.
- *Catalogue and price list.* Shows authorized prices for goods offered for sale.
- *Customer order file.* Contains unfilled sales orders.
- *Customer account file.* Contains supporting documentation of postings to each customer's account.
- *Sales invoice file.* Holds copies of invoices sent to customers.

Materiality and Risk

Sales are the principal source of operating revenue for many business enterprises and a major component in the determination of net income. It is also common in merchandising and manufacturing companies for cost of sales to be the largest cost in the income measurement process. Numerous steps are involved in the execution and recording of sales transactions, and the volume of sales transactions is usually heavy. Consequently, errors or irregularities in amounts material to the financial statements could occur in the processing of sales transactions. The risk of such occurrences is inversely related to the effectiveness of the client's internal controls over sales transactions.

In order to assess this risk in a specific audit engagement, it is necessary for the auditor to study and evaluate the client's controls. When the auditor intends to rely on the controls in performing substantive tests of sales transaction balances, the review and testing of the controls are usually extensive.

Sales Transactions Are Properly Executed

Sales transactions are properly executed when (1) transactions are authorized by personnel acting within the scope of their authority and (2) executed transactions conform with the terms of the authorizations. The execution of sales transactions involves a sequence of functions or steps. It is desirable therefore to recognize specific accounting control objectives for each function as follows:

FUNCTION	SPECIFIC ACCOUNTING CONTROL OBJECTIVE
1. Accepting customer orders	Orders for sales or for services are accepted in accordance with management's authorized criteria
2. Approving credit	Credit is granted on basis of management's established credit policies and limits
3. Filling sales orders	Orders are filled or services rendered in accordance with approved sales orders
4. Shipping sales orders	Shipments are made on basis of approved sales orders
5. Billing customers	All shipments are billed at authorized prices and terms

The internal control principles applicable to the execution of sales transactions are explained below.

Authorization Procedures

The vice president of sales has the responsibility for general authorizations of selling prices, terms, and conditions of sales. Specific authorizations are necessary at four points: (1) granting credit, (2) setting prices and terms, (3) filling and shipping the order, and (4) billing the customer. These points are always present, whether in total or in condensed form. For example, in over-the-counter sales, filling and shipping may occur simultaneously, and the billing of the customer may result in an immediate payment of cash. Authorization procedures should provide for the (1) assignment of responsibility for authorizations and approvals to departments and/or individuals and (2) documentation of the action taken.

For over-the-counter credit sales, the credit department may issue company credit cards to customers which sales clerks are authorized to accept. In other cases, clerks may be permitted to accept national credit cards such as American Express, Visa, and MasterCard.

Segregation of Functions

Each of the functions involved in executing sales transactions should be assigned to different departments and/or individuals. Personnel participating in these functions should not record the transactions or have custody of the resulting receivables. Based on the organization chart in Figure 7-1, the assignment of responsibility for each function is as follows:

FUNCTION	DEPARTMENT	RELATED ACTIVITIES
1. Accepting customer orders	Sales Order	Receive orders, issue sales orders, trace customers to approved customer list, investigate acceptability of new customers, and maintain unfilled order file
2. Approving credit	Credit	Trace customers to credit files, indicate approval on sales orders, and maintain customer credit files
3. Filling sales orders	Warehouse	Maintain custody over inventory, fill orders per specifications, and initial filled sales orders
4. Shipping sales orders	Shipping	Agree goods for shipment with sales orders, pack and ship goods, prepare shipping documents, and obtain receipts from carriers
5. Billing customers	Billing	Match shipping documents with sales orders, bill customers at authorized prices and terms, prepare and mail sales invoices, and prepare batch or daily sales summaries of billings

It should also be recognized that the functions are completed in sequence. Thus, the order cannot be filled before credit is approved, and the customer is not billed before the goods are shipped. A flowchart of a manual system for executing sales transactions is shown in Figure 7-2.

Documentation Procedures

The essential source documents in executing sales transactions are the (1) *sales order*, (2) *shipping document (bill of lading)*, (3) *sales invoice*, and (4) *daily sales summary*. To achieve maximum accountability, the first three types of documents should be prenumbered and subsequently accounted for. The sales order and sales invoice should indicate the proper account classification and coding for each transaction.

Documentation procedures should provide for the prompt billing of customers. To achieve this objective, some companies require a billing depart-

FIGURE 7–2. Manual System for Executing Sales Transactions

ment supervisor to determine periodically that the billing date on invoices is not more than one business day later than the shipping date.

Physical Controls

Physical controls in the form of mechanical equipment are useful in executing sales transactions. The primary example is the use of a cash register to indicate the amount of over-the-counter sales. Another device is the autographic register to control the issuance of sales slips. This equipment contains prenumbered sales slips that are manually cranked through the machine as they are used. The original copy is given to the customer, and the duplicate is locked inside the register as evidence of the sale.

Independent Internal Verification

There are numerous opportunities for independent internal verification in executing sales transactions. For example, the shipping department is generally required to compare the goods received from the warehouse with the sales order before shipping the merchandise. In the billing department, the sales orders are matched with shipping documents before invoices are prepared. In addition, in a manual system, a second billing clerk verifies the correctness of each invoice before it is mailed, and accounts for all prenumbered sales invoices.

Sales Transactions Are Properly Recorded

To meet this operative internal control objective, the functions or steps in the recording of sales transactions must be properly performed. It is desirable therefore to recognize specific accounting control objectives and the assignment of responsibility for each function as follows:

FUNCTION	DEPARTMENT	SPECIFIC ACCOUNTING CONTROL OBJECTIVE
1. Journalizing and posting sales transactions	General Accounting	Only actual sales are recorded All actual sales are correctly journalized and posted as to amount, classification, and accounting period
2. Updating customers' ledger	Accounts Receivable Accounting	Sales are promptly and correctly posted to customer accounts
3. Updating inventory records	Inventory Accounting	Sales are promptly and correctly posted to inventory records

The internal control principles applicable to the recording of sales transactions are explained below.

Segregation of Functions

An appropriate segregation of functions is shown in the above tabulation. General Accounting Department personnel should not participate in the execution of sales transactions or have custody of the resulting assets. If the same employee bills the customer, records the sale, and maintains the accounts receivable ledger, that person could misstate the amount of the sale and conceal the error. Figure 7-3 illustrates a flowchart for the recording of sales transactions.

Accounting Records and Procedures

The source document for recording sales transactions is the sales invoice. Invoices should be journalized in the sales journal in numerical sequence.

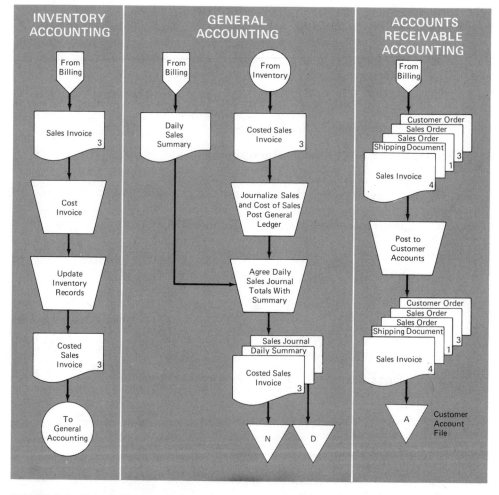

FIGURE 7-3. Manual System for Recording Sales Transactions

Postings to customer accounts and inventory records should be made directly from the invoices. Following posting to the customers' ledger, the invoice and supporting documentation are filed alphabetically in the customer account file. This file is often used extensively by the auditor in testing controls over sales transactions.

Independent Internal Verification

The completeness of daily sales journal entries can be internally verified by having a second accounting clerk (1) account for the numerical sequence of entries in the sales journal, and (2) establish the agreement of the daily sales summary with corresponding sales journal totals. In some companies, a supervisor reviews the journal entries periodically to verify the reasonableness of the account classifications.

Custody of Accounts Receivable Is Properly Maintained

As explained earlier, this operative objective pertains to limiting access to assets and comparing recorded accountability with existing assets. Both accounts receivable and cash may result from sales transactions. The former is considered here; the latter is discussed with cash receipts in the next chapter. For custody over accounts receivable, the functions and specific accounting control objectives are as follows:

FUNCTION	DEPARTMENT	SPECIFIC ACCOUNTING CONTROL OBJECTIVE
1. Protecting the customers' ledger	Accounts Receivable Accounting	Access to the customers' ledger is limited to authorized accounting personnel
2. Maintaining correctness of customer balances	Accounts Receivable Accounting	Recorded customer balances are independently verified with customers at reasonable intervals
	General Accounting	Customers' ledger is periodically agreed with accounts receivable control

The internal control principles applicable to these functions are explained below.

Physical Controls and Authorization Procedures

The customers' ledger should be kept in locked and fireproof files, and access should be restricted to authorized accounting personnel. Similarly, customer files should be locked to prevent unauthorized access to documentation that could be used to make unauthorized entries in customer accounts.

Segregation of Functions and Independent Internal Verification

Segregation of functions exists when individuals who have physical custody over the customers' ledger do not execute or record sales transactions. Independent internal verification occurs when an accounting department supervisor (1) controls the mailing of monthly statements to customers and the investigation of differences reported by customers, and (2) validates the agreement of accounts receivable control with the total of the customers' ledger each month.

STUDY AND EVALUATION OF INTERNAL CONTROL

The auditor's methodology for meeting the second standard of field work for sales transactions is identical with the steps and decision paths explained in Chapter 4.

Review of the Sales System

It will be recalled that the review consists of two phases: (1) preliminary and (2) completion. The preliminary review of sales pertains to the internal control environment and the flow of sales transactions through the accounting system. The completion phase relates to specific internal accounting controls prescribed in the sales system. The principal steps in the completion phase of the review of the controls over sales are described below.

Gathering Information

Information concerning specific controls over sales transactions is obtained through inquiry, observation, and review of documentation. A questionnaire for sales transactions is shown in Figure 7-4. The questions relate to control procedures that the auditor considers to be necessary for effective control over sales. Each question is referenced to a specific function. For example (E1) is the first function under executing (i.e., accepting customer orders); (R1) and (C1) refer to the first functions under recording and custody respectively. A "yes" answer to a question indicates that the client has the control; a "no" answer suggests a possible weakness in internal control over sales. The information gathered by the auditor should be documented in the form of flowcharts, in narrative memoranda, and in answers to questionnaires.

Making a Preliminary Evaluation

The primary purpose of this evaluation of sales transactions is to identify control procedures that can be relied on in performing substantive tests of sales transaction balances, assuming satisfactory compliance with the control procedures. The preliminary evaluation is made by (1) considering the errors and irregularities that could occur in performing each function,

CYCLE: Revenue	CLASS OF TRANSACTIONS: Sales

EXECUTING　　　　　　　　　　　　　　　　　　　　　　　　　　　　Yes　No

1. Are customer orders compared to an approved customer list? (E1)
2. Is a prenumbered sales order issued for each accepted customer order? (E1)
3. Is there internal verification of the agreement of sales order with customer order? (E1)
4. Are all credit sales approved prior to the sale? (E2)
5. Is a sales order required before an order is filled? (E3)
6. Is there internal verification of the goods in filling a sales order? (E3)
7. Are the goods compared with the sales order in shipping? (E4)
8. Is each shipment supported by a prenumbered shipping document? (E4)
9. Are shipping documents and sales orders compared in billing? (E5)
10. Are prenumbered sales invoices used in billing? (E5)
11. Is there internal verification of prices and mathematical accuracy of sales invoices? (E5)
12. Are daily sales summaries prepared and agreed to the invoices issued? (E5)

RECORDING

1. Are daily sales journal entries agreed to daily sales summaries (R1)
2. Are invoices journalized in numerical sequence? (R1)
3. Is there periodic review of the sales journal for reasonableness? (R1)
4. Are posting to the subsidiary ledgers made independent of journalizing and posting the general ledger? (R2, R3)

CUSTODY

1. Are there adequate physical controls over accounts receivable records? (C1)
2. Is there periodic independent reconciliation of accounts receivable control and the customers' ledger? (C2)
3. Is there independent mailing of monthly statements to customers? (C2)

FIGURE 7-4. Internal Control Questionnaire: Sales Transactions

(2) identifying the controls necessary to prevent or detect the occurrences, and (3) determining whether the necessary controls are prescribed by the client. A representative listing of possible errors and irregularities and necessary control procedures is shown in Figure 7-5.[1] Columns 2 and 3 of the form are based on generalized knowledge, adapted as needed by the auditor to the specific client. Information about prescribed controls over sales is obtained from step 1 of the completion phase of the review.

From a comparison of the necessary controls and the prescribed controls, the auditor makes a preliminary evaluation of the controls. If a necessary control is not prescribed or a prescribed control will not prevent the possible error or irregularity, the auditor looks for compensating controls or concludes that there is a weakness in the client's sales system. The auditor's evaluation should be fully documented in the working papers.

[1] Figure 4-3 shows two additional columns in the preliminary evaluation: Prescribed Controls and Reliance (Yes/No). These columns have been omitted here in the interest of simplification.

Function	Possible Errors and Irregularities	Necessary Control Procedures	Possible Compliance Tests
EXECUTING			
Accepting customer orders	The sales order may be incorrect as to quantities and types of goods	Internal verification of agreement of sales order with customer order	Examine evidence of verification
Approving credit	Sales may be made to customers who are poor credit risks	Approval of credit by credit department	Examine evidence of credit approval
Filling sales orders	Order specifications may not be met as to type and quantity	Internal verification of goods by warehouse and by shipping	Examine evidence of verification
Shipping goods	Goods may be shipped to unauthorized customers	Approved sales order for each shipment	Determine existence of approved sales order for each shipping document
Billing the customer	Some shipments may not be billed	Accounting for all prenumbered shipping documents and determining that each has a sales invoice	Examine evidence of internal verification and existence of a sales invoice for each shipping document
	Sales invoices may be incorrect as to prices and mathematical accuracy	Internal verification of accuracy of invoice	Examine evidence of internal verification
RECORDING			
Journalizing and posting of sales transactions	Invoices may not be journalized	Internal verification of agreement of sales journal entries with daily sales summaries	Review evidence of internal verification
Updating customers' ledger	Invoices may not be posted to customer accounts	Segregation of functions between general accounting and accounts receivable accounting	Observe segregation of functions
CUSTODY			
Protecting the customers' ledger	Customer accounts may be stolen	Customers' ledger is locked in safe and access is limited to authorized personnel	Observe storage; inquire as to access

(continued)

Function	Possible Errors and Irregularities	Necessary Control Procedures	Possible Compliance Tests
Maintaining correctness of customers' balances	Mathematical errors may be made in computing a customer's balance	Independent reconciliation of accounts receivable control and customers' ledger	Examine evidence of reconciliation
		Independent mailing of monthly statements to customers	Observe mailing of monthly statements

FIGURE 7-5. Preliminary Evaluation Considerations—Sales Transactions

Compliance Tests of Prescribed Controls

Based on his preliminary evaluation and the possible compliance tests shown in Figure 7-5, the auditor prepares the audit program for performing compliance tests on the controls to be relied on. As shown in the audit program in Figure 7-6, the objectives of the testing are to determine whether

---

TYPE OF TESTING: Compliance

CYCLE: Revenue

PURPOSE: Study and Evaluation of Internal Control

CLASS OF TRANSACTIONS: Sales

A. CONTROLS IN EXECUTING SALES TRANSACTIONS ARE OPERATING AS PLANNED.

1. Examine sample of sales invoices for
   - Approved sales order.
   - Evidence of agreement of sales order with customer order.
   - Evidence of credit approval.
   - Shipping department verification of agreement of goods to be shipped with sales order.
   - Accompanying shipping document and receipt from freight carrier.
   - Evidence of verification of prices and mathematical accuracy.
2. Observe segregation of functions in performing control procedures.
3. Inquire of personnel about performing control procedures.
4. Reperform selected control procedures to determine how well they were performed.

B. CONTROLS IN RECORDING SALES TRANSACTIONS ARE OPERATING AS PLANNED.

1. Examine evidence of verification of daily sales summaries with sales journal totals.
2. Examine evidence that all invoices are accounted for in journalizing.
3. Observe that accounting personnel do not execute sales transactions.
4. Observe segregation of duties between general ledger and customer ledger . accounting personnel.

C. CONTROLS OVER THE CUSTODY OF ACCOUNTS RECEIVABLE ARE OPERATING AS PLANNED.

1. Review evidence of independent reconciliations of accounts receivable control and the customers' ledger.
2. Observe mailing of monthly statements to customers.

FIGURE 7-6. Audit Program: Compliance Tests of Sales Transactions the controls pertaining to the execution and recording of sales transactions and to the custody of accounts receivable are operating as planned. This program includes each of the auditing procedures that are applicable to compliance tests: (1) review of documentation showing evidence of performance of control procedures, (2) observation of controls that do not leave an audit trail of documentation, (3) inquiry, and (4) reperformance of some controls.

Compliance tests should be applied to sales transactions for the entire year. Such tests, however, are usually made during interim work. This is permissible if the auditor also obtains evidence as to the functioning of the controls during the remainder of the year. The additional evidence may be acquired through inquiry, observation, and, if necessary, by additional testing.

In the program, the sampling unit is the sales invoice. By using this unit, the auditor can reach a conclusion as to whether the controls to assure that all billings have been shipped are operating effectively. Alternatively, the auditor could use the shipping document as the sampling unit to determine whether the controls to assure that all shipments have been billed are functioning properly.

Dual Purpose Testing

As explained in Chapter 4, the auditor may also perform substantive tests of transactions in conjunction with compliance tests. Substantive tests are designed to determine the validity and propriety of the accounting treatment of transactions and balances or, conversely, the existence of any monetary errors. Thus, while the sample of sales invoices is available for use, the auditor may perform the following substantive tests:

• Compare the amount, date, customer name, and account classification on the invoice with the corresponding sales journal entry for accuracy.
• Compare the same data with the corresponding postings to individual accounts in the customers' ledger for accuracy.

In addition, in reperforming the control procedures (step A4 of the audit program), the auditor accumulates the dollar amount of any monetary errors that are discovered. From these tests, the auditor can estimate the number, nature, and magnitude of monetary errors in the processing of sales transactions.

Final Evaluation of the Controls

This evaluation involves an analysis of the findings from compliance testing of prescribed controls. In making the analysis, the auditor considers both the number of deviations from prescribed control procedures and the causes of the deviations. The results of any substantive tests of transactions should also be considered in evaluating the controls. The existence of monetary errors in the accounting treatment of the transactions indicates that the system of internal control did not prevent or detect their occurrence.

The auditor then determines the effects of his evaluations of specific control procedures over sales transactions on the nature, timing, and extent of substantive tests over revenue cycle balances. For example, if there is moderate risk of errors in approving sales for credit, the auditor will apply more extensive substantive tests in determining the adequacy of the client's allowance for uncollectible accounts than when the risk of such errors is low. Substantive tests of revenue cycle balances are explained in Chapters 12 and 13.

STATISTICAL SAMPLING IN COMPLIANCE TESTING

As explained in Chapter 6, statistical sampling may be used in compliance testing. In that chapter, a comprehensive case study is presented in which statistical sampling is used in performing compliance tests of controls over sales transactions. The reader is encouraged to review that illustration at this time.

ELECTRONIC DATA PROCESSING

Many companies use electronic data processing in executing and recording sales transactions. To illustrate some of the effects of EDP on internal control and the auditor's study and evaluation of EDP controls, the following case study is presented.

Description of the System

For its sales transactions, the Joiner Company uses the computer to prepare the sales invoices, prepare the sales journal, and update customer account balances. Magnetic tape input is utilized and file data are maintained on magnetic tape and magnetic disk. A flowchart of the sales system is shown in Figure 7-7.

In the manual portion of the sales system, the key control procedures are (1) preparing batch totals in the billing department, (2) verifying and logging the totals in data control, and (3) keying and verifying the data in data entry.

As shown in Figure 7-7, there are two computer runs:

Run 1. In this run, the sales transaction tape is sorted by customer number and is then validated by the application of an *edit check* routine consisting of tests for completeness, validity, and reasonableness. The outputs of this run are the valid sales transaction tape and a report showing control totals and a listing of rejected transactions. The report is sent to data control, where the control totals are compared with the logged totals. In addition, data control assumes the responsibility for seeing that (1) the rejected transactions are corrected by the department making the error and (2) the corrected data are resubmitted for computer processing.

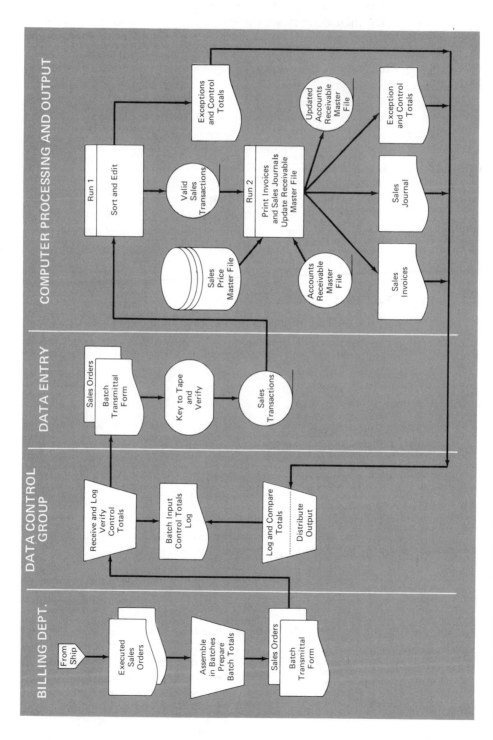

FIGURE 7-7. EDP System for Sales Transactions

Run 2. This run involves the processing of the valid transaction tape. As shown, both accounts receivable and sales price master files are used in the run. The price master file is on magnetic disk to facilitate access to the individual prices as the various products are encountered on the sales transaction tape. The outputs consist of an updated accounts receivable master file on magnetic tape and printouts of sales invoices, the sales journal, and a control and exception report. Each printout is forwarded to data control, where the totals are compared and the other outputs are distributed to the appropriate departments within the company.

A third run, the costing of the sales invoices and the updating of inventory records, is not included in the flowchart in the interest of simplification. Figure 7-7 shows only one aspect of updating the accounts receivable master file. The processing of a cash collections transaction tape with this file is illustrated in Chapter 8.

Study and Evaluation of EDP Controls

As explained in Chapter 5, the auditor must make a preliminary review of EDP controls. Thus, through observation and review of documentation, the auditor obtains information about (1) the flow of sales transactions through the accounting system, (2) the extent to which EDP is used in processing sales transactions, and (3) the basic structure of accounting control. The auditor may terminate his review at this point and design substantive tests that do not contemplate any reliance on EDP accounting controls. However, in the Joiner Company, the auditor decides to complete the review and perform compliance tests of the accounting controls expected to be relied on in substantive testing. The audit program for compliance testing of the application controls is shown in Figure 7-8. The program provides for the use of both test data and generalized audit software.

Use of test data. Test data are applicable to the testing of the program controls in run 1 and the program logic in run 2. For testing the proper functioning of the controls incorporated into the edit routine (program) of run 1, the auditor prepares both valid and invalid sales transaction test data. The latter include

• Missing or invalid customer number.
• Invalid product code.
• Incomplete customer name and address.
• Missing quantities.
• Abnormal (unrealistic) sales quantities.
• Alphabetical characters in numerical fields.

The data are keyed onto magnetic tape and run on the client's program. The error listing of invalid transactions is compared by the auditor with expected results. Any discrepancies are investigated for possible weaknesses in the controls of the edit routine.

TYPE OF TESTING: Compliance   **PURPOSE:** EDP Application
                                                                                 Controls
CYCLE: Revenue   **CLASS OF TRANSACTIONS:** Sales

A. INPUT CONTROLS ARE PROPERLY FUNCTIONING:

  1. Randomly select sample of executed sales orders and trace to sales invoices.
  2. Review, on test basis, the reconciliation of batched sales input totals with control totals in run 1.
  3. Selectively review exception listings of run 1 and investigate items that have remained uncleared for an unreasonably long time.
  4. Design and use test data to test program controls of edit routine in run 1.

B. PROCESSING CONTROLS ARE PROPERLY FUNCTIONING:

  1. Observe the procedures for reconciling control totals in run 2 and selectively trace control totals to related input controls.
  2. Review exception lists for unusual items and determine the disposition of rejected data.
  3. Use test data to test the program logic in the preparation of sales invoices, the sales journal, and updating the accounts receivable master file.
  4. Use generalized audit software to test master file data controls.

C. OUTPUT CONTROLS ARE PROPERLY FUNCTIONING:

  1. Review reconciliation of output controls with other control totals:
  2. Obtain printout of the two accounts receivable master files of run 2 and selectively reconcile changes in customer balances with sales invoices.

FIGURE 7–8. Audit Program: Compliance Tests of EDP Application Controls for Sales Transactions

For run 2, the auditor seeks evidence that the program controls pertaining to the decision steps and mathematical computations in the program are properly functioning. For this purpose, separate test data may be prepared or, alternatively, the valid test data that cleared the edit routine test of run 1 may be used. Test data for run 2 may include transactions that result in the use of recently changed unit sales prices and credit terms, discontinued product lines, and invalid pricing codes. As in the preceding test, the auditor compares the output of the test run with expected results and investigates any differences.

To be a valid test of a program, the auditor must make sure the program tested is actually used by the client. Thus, the auditor requests on a surprise basis, the client's program for sales from the librarian. The identification numbers on the program tapes are traced to program documentation in the library to assure that the client's regular programs are being obtained. The test data are then processed against a copy of the client's master file data under the auditor's supervision.

Use of generalized audit software. Generalized audit software is used in this example to test the reliability of the client's master file. The extent of this form of testing depends on the effectiveness of the general controls pertaining to file security and program changes. When such controls are strong and the foregoing compliance tests produce no exceptions, some auditors may not use this form of testing.

In the Joiner Company, the auditor decides to use the generalized audit software to test the accounts receivable master file. To do so, the auditor first obtains a copy of the file at the beginning of the day and updates it by processing the actual sales transactions for the day. The audit software is then used to compare the detail of the client's updated file with the updated file produced by the generalized audit software. Any differences are identified and printed out by the computer. Generalized audit software may also be used to select and print a sample of sales prices from the sales price master file. These prices can then be compared manually with the authorized prices established by the company and any differences noted. Differences found from the use of generalized audit software indicate that applicable control procedures are not operating as planned.

On completing the compliance tests of EDP general and application controls, the auditor evaluates the system and then determines the extent to which substantive tests of revenue cycle balances are to be restricted.

CONCLUDING COMMENTS

An entity's revenue cycle includes the activities in processing customer orders for goods and services and in achieving settlement of the selling price from the customer. The scope of the chapter has been limited to the sales transactions phase of the revenue cycle. Each of the operative objectives of internal accounting control and the six principles of internal control are applicable to sales transactions. In performing compliance tests of sales transactions, the auditor works extensively with the sales invoices. Either statistical or nonstatistical sampling may be used in performing compliance tests of sales transactions.

EDP methods may affect the nature of the control procedures and the audit trail of sales transactions. In a system that utilizes magnetic tape for both input and file data, the auditor may use test data in testing program controls and generalized audit software to test controls over updating master file data.

REVIEW QUESTIONS

7–1. Describe the nature of the revenue cycle and identify the classes of transactions that are part of this cycle.

7–2. State the framework of internal control objectives for revenue cycle transactions.

7–3. Indicate the functions that pertain to the executing and recording of sales transactions and custody of assets.

7–4. How important are sales transactions in terms of materiality and risk?

7–5. What are the specific accounting control objectives for each of the functions involved in executing sales transactions?

7–6. Indicate an appropriate segregation of duties among the departments involved in executing sales transactions.

7–7.   a. When are authorizations required in executing sales transactions?
           b. What forms of authorization exist in over-the-counter credit sales?
7–8.   a. Identify the specific internal accounting control objectives for each function associated with the recording of sales transactions.
           b. Indicate an appropriate segregation of duties for these functions.
7–9.   Indicate the flow of sales orders and sales invoices in the manual execution of sales transactions.
7–10. Indicate applications of the principle of independent internal verification to the recording of sales transactions.
7–11. a. What internal accounting control principles are applicable to the custody of assets in the revenue cycle?
           b. Indicate one application of each principle.
7–12. What is the purpose of making a preliminary evaluation of accounting controls over sales transactions?
7–13. Explain the relationship between the internal control questionnaire and the auditor's preliminary evaluation of sales transactions.
7–14. Identify the four types of audit procedures that may be used in performing compliance tests of sales transactions.
7–15. Contrast the purposes served by using (a) the sales invoice and (b) the shipping document in compliance testing.
7–16. Contrast the verifications made by (a) data control and (b) data entry in the case study.
7–17. Identify the control totals that are available to data control in the case study.
7–18. a. What objectives are served by the edit check routine in an EDP system?
           b. Identify three types of test data that may be used in an edit routine.
7–19. What precautions should the auditor take to make a valid test of a computer program?
7–20. How may test data and generalized audit software be used in compliance testing of EDP application controls over sales transactions?

COMPREHENSIVE QUESTIONS

7–21. The internal control questionnaire in Figure 7-4 includes the following questions:

1. Are all credit sales approved prior to sale?
2. Are customer orders compared to an approved customer list?
3. Is there internal verification of the goods in filling a sales order?
4. Are goods compared with sales order in shipping?
5. Are prenumbered sales invoices used in billing?
6. Is there internal verification of prices and mathematical accuracy of the sales invoices?
7. Are postings to the subsidiary ledgers made independent of journalizing and posting to the general ledger.
8. Are daily sales journal entries agreed to daily sales summaries?
9. Is there periodic independent reconciliation of accounts receivable control and the customers' ledger?
10. Are shipping documents and sales orders compared in billing?

Required
a. Identify the operative internal accounting control objective to which each question relates (i.e., executing, recording, or custody).
b. Identify the function and specific internal accounting control objective to which each question pertains.
c. Indicate the internal accounting control principle that is involved.
d. Identify an error or irregularity that may result from a No answer to each question. (Present your answer in tabular form, using separate columns for each of the four parts.)

7–22. The following control procedures over sales transactions are prescribed by the Harlan Company:

1. Credit department approval of credit sales.
2. Sales invoice for each shipping document.
3. Internal verification of prices, terms, and accuracy of sales invoice.
4. Prenumbered sales invoices.
5. Agreement of daily sales summaries with recorded entries.
6. Authorization of prices and terms.
7. Monthly statements independently mailed to customers.
8. Reconciliation of control accounts and subsidiary ledgers.
9. Sales orders agreed with customers orders.

Required

For each control procedure,
a. Indicate the function and the specific internal accounting control objective of each procedure.
b. Identify the internal accounting control principle that is involved.
c. Identify an error or irregularity that may be prevented or detected.
d. Indicate a compliance test that may be performed to determine whether each control is operating as prescribed. (Present your answer in tabular form.)

7–23. Assume the following exceptions to prescribed control procedures over sales transactions occurred in the Lane Company:

1. A shipment to a bona fide customer was not billed.
2. A sales invoice was correctly journalized but was not posted to the customer's account in the subsidiary ledger.
3. Sales were made at unauthorized prices.
4. A sales invoice was incorrectly footed, causing the sales entry and subsequent postings to be incorrect.
5. A sales order was incorrectly filled and shipped.
6. Sales were made to customers who were poor credit risks.
7. A sales invoice was not journalized.
8. A customer's records were stolen.
9. Sales entries were incorrectly classified.
10. A sales order shows incorrect quantities.

Required

a. Indicate the function and specific internal accounting control objective associated with each occurrence.
b. Indicate the control procedure(s) that could prevent or detect the occurrences.
c. Indicate a compliance test for each procedure in (b). (Present your answer in tabular form.)

7–24. A partially completed charge sales systems flowchart is shown on page 236. The flowchart depicts the charge sales activities of the Bottom Manufacturing Corporation.

A customer's purchase order is received and a six-part sales order is prepared therefrom. The six copies are initially distributed as follows:

Copy 1: Billing copy—to billing department.
Copy 2: Shipping copy—to shipping department.
Copy 3: Credit copy—to credit department.
Copy 4: Stock request copy—to credit department.
Copy 5: Customer copy—to customer.
Copy 6: Sales order copy—file in sales order department.

When each copy of the sales order reaches the applicable department or destination, it calls for specific internal control procedures and related documents. Some of the procedures and related documents are indicated on the flowchart. Other procedures and documents are labeled letters a to r.

Required
List the procedures or the internal documents that are labeled letters c to r in the flowchart of Bottom Manufacturing Corporation's charge sales system.

Organize your answer as follows (note that an explanation of the letters a and b which appear in the flowchart are entered as examples):

Flowchart Symbol Letter	*Procedures or Internal Document*
a	Prepare six-part sales order
b	File by order number

(AICPA)

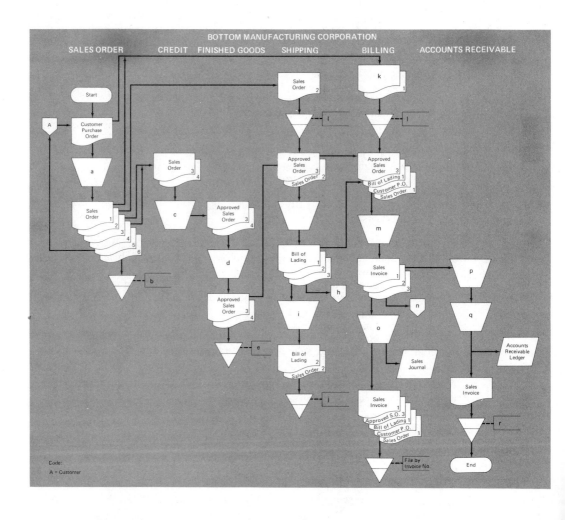

7-25. The customer billing function of the Robinson Company, a small paint manufacturer, is attended to by a receptionist, an accounts receivable clerk and a cashier who also serves as a secretary. The company's paint products are sold to wholesalers and retail stores.

The following describes *all* of the procedures performed by the employees of the Robinson Company pertaining to customer billings.

1. The mail is opened by the receptionist who gives the customers' purchase orders to the accounts receivable clerk. Fifteen to twenty orders are received each day. Under instructions to expedite the shipment of orders, the accounts receivable clerk at once prepares a five-copy sales invoice form which is distributed as follows:

   a. Copy 1 is the customer billing copy and is held by the accounts receivable clerk until notice of shipment is received.

   b. Copy 2 is the accounts receivable department copy and is held for ultimate posting of the accounts receivable records.

   c. Copies 3 and 4 are sent to the shipping department.

   d. Copy 5 is sent to the storeroom as authority for release of the goods to the shipping department.

2. After the paint ordered has been moved from the storeroom to the shipping department, the shipping department prepares the bills of lading and labels the cartons. Sales invoice copy 4 is inserted in a carton as a packing slip. After the trucker has picked up the shipment the customer's copy of the bill of lading and copy 3, on which are noted any undershipments, are returned to the accounts receivable clerk. The company does not "back order" in the event of undershipments; customers are expected to reorder the merchandise. The Robinson Company's copy of the bill of lading is filed by the shipping department.

3. When copy 3 and the customer's copy of the bill of lading are received by the accounts receivable clerk, copies 1 and 2 are completed by numbering them and inserting quantities shipped, unit prices, extensions, discounts, and totals. The accounts receivable clerk then mails copy 1 and the copy of the bill of lading to the customer. Copies 2 and 3 are stapled together.

4. The individual accounts receivable ledger cards are posted by the accounts receivable clerk by a bookkeeping machine procedure whereby the sales register is prepared as a carbon copy of the postings. Postings are made from copy 2, which is then filed, along with staple-attached copy 3, in numerical order. Monthly the general ledger clerk summarizes the sales register for posting to the general ledger accounts.

Required

a. Identify (1) errors and irregularities and (2) necessary control procedures. Organize your answer around the primary functions for sales transactions.

b. Which weaknesses, if any, do you consider material? Discuss.

AICPA (adapted)

7-26. Your examination of the financial statements of General Department Store, Inc. disclosed the following:

1. The store has 30,000 retail accounts which are billed monthly on a cycle basis. There are twenty billing cycle divisions of the subsidiary accounts receivable ledger, and accounts are apportioned alphabetically to the divisions.

2. All charge sales tickets, which are prenumbered, are microfilmed in batches for each day's sales. These sales tickets are then sorted into their respective cycle divisions, and adding machine tapes are prepared to arrive at the total daily sales for each division. The daily totals for the divisions are then combined for comparison with the grand daily total charge sales determined from cash register readings.

After the totals are balanced, the daily sales tickets are filed behind the related customer account cards in the respective cycle divisions.

3. Cycle control accounts for each division are maintained by postings of the tapes of daily sales.

4. At the cycle billing date the customers' transactions (sales, remittances, returns, and other adjustments) are posted to the accounts in the individual cycle. The billing machine used automatically accumulates six separate totals: previous balances, purchases, payments, returns, new balances, and overdue balances. After posting, the documents and the customers' statements are microfilmed and then mailed to the customer.

5. Within each division a trial balance of the accounts in the cycle, obtained as a by-product of the posting operation, is compared with the cycle control account.

6. Credit terms for regular accounts require payment within 10 days of receipt of the statement. A credit limit of $300 is set for all accounts.

7. Before the statements are mailed they are reviewed to determine which are past due. Accounts are considered past due if the full balance of the prior month has not been paid. Past due accounts are noted for subsequent collection effort by the credit department.

8. Receipts on account and customer account adjustments are accumulated and posted in a similar manner.

Required
List the audit procedures that you would apply to testing transactions of one billing cycle division. Confine your audit procedures to the sales tickets and charges to the accounts. Do not discuss the audit of cash receipts or customer account adjustments.

AICPA (adapted)

7–27. The Meyers Pharmaceutical Company, a drug manufacturer, has the following system for billing and recording accounts receivable:

1. An incoming customer's purchase order is received in the order department by a clerk who prepares a prenumbered company sales order form in which is inserted the pertinent information, such as the customer's name and address, customer's account number, quantity, and items ordered. After the sales order form has been prepared, the customer's purchase order is stapled to it.

2. The sales order form is then passed to the credit department for credit approval. Rough approximations of the billing values of the orders are made in the credit department for those accounts on which credit limitations are imposed. After investigation, approval of credit is noted on the form.

3. Next the sales order form is passed to the billing department, where a clerk types the customer's invoice on a billing machine that cross-multiplies the number of items and the unit price, then adds the automatically extended amounts for the total amounts of the invoice. The billing clerk determines the unit prices for the items from a list of billing prices.

The billing machine has registers that automatically accumulate daily totals of customer account numbers and invoice amounts to provide ''hash'' totals and control amounts. These totals, which are inserted in a daily record book, serve as predetermined batch totals for verification of computer imputs.

The billing is done on prenumbered, continuous, carbon-interleaved forms having the following designations:
a. ''Customer's copy.''
b. ''Sales department copy,'' for information purposes.
c. ''File copy.''
d. ''Shipping department copy,'' which serves as a shipping order. Bills of lading are also prepared as carbon copy by-products of the invoicing procedure.

4. The shipping department copy of the invoice and the bills of lading are then sent to the shipping department. After the order has been shipped, copies of the bill of lading are returned to the billing department. The shipping department copy of the invoice is filed in the shipping department.

5. In the billing department, one copy of the bill of lading is attached to the customer's copy of the invoice and both are mailed to the customer. The other copy of the bill of lading, together with the sales order form, is then stapled to the invoice file copy and filed in invoice numerical order.

6. A keypunch machine is connected to the billing machine so that punched cards are created during the preparation of the invoices. The punched cards then become the means by which the sales data are transmitted to a computer.

The punched cards are fed to the computer in batches. One day's accumulation of cards comprises a batch. After the punched cards have been processed by the computer, they are placed in files and held for about two years.

Required
List the procedures that a CPA would employ in his examination of his selected audit samples of the company's (1) typed invoices, including the source documents, and (2) punched cards.

(The listed procedures should be limited to the verification of the sales data being fed into the computer. Do not carry the procedures beyond the point at which the cards are ready to be fed to the computer.)

AICPA

7–28. Huron Company manufactures and sells eight major product lines with fifteen to twenty-five items in each product line. All sales are on credit, and orders are received by mail or telephone. Huron has a computer-based system that employs magnetic tape as a file medium.
All sales orders received during regular working hours are typed on Huron's own sales order form immediately. This typed form is the source document for the keypunching of a shipment or back-order card for each item ordered. These cards are employed in the after-hours processing at night to complete all necessary record keeping for the current day and to facilitate the shipment of goods the following day. In summary, an order received one day is to be processed that day and night and shipped the next day.

The daily processing which has to be accomplished at night includes the following activities:

1. Preparing the invoice to be sent to the customer at the time of shipment.
2. Updating accounts receivable file.
3. Updating finished goods inventory.
4. Listing of all items back-ordered and short.

Each month, the sales department would like to have a sales summary and analysis. At the end of each month, the monthly statements should be prepared and mailed to customers. Management also wants an aging of accounts receivable each month.

Required
a. Identify the master files which Huron should maintain in this system to provide for the daily processing. Indicate the data content which should be included in each file and the order in which each file should be maintained.
b. Prepare a systems flowchart of the daily processing required to update the finished goods inventory records and to produce the necessary inventory reports (assume that the necessary magnetic tape devices are available). Use the annotation sym-

bol to describe or explain any facts which cannot be detailed in the individual symbols.
c. Describe (1) the items that should appear in the monthly sales analysis report(s) the sales department should have and (2) the input data and master files that would have to be maintained to prepare these reports.

CMA (adapted)

7–29.* John Carr, controller for the General Corporation, provides you with the following information relative to the company's sales system:

The sales department prepares a six-part sales invoice form from the customer's order and files the order alphabetically by customer. Part 2 is sent to the credit department for approval; the remaining parts are held until credit is approved. After credit approval, the credit slip is returned to sales and filed with the customer's order. If credit is not approved, the customer is notified and the order is not processed. If approved, parts 1 (customer invoice) and 3 (accounting) are then sent to billing and held in a temporary customer file; part 4 is sent to shipping as a package slip; part 5 is sent to the warehouse as a stock request; and part 6 is sent to the customer to acknowledge the order.

The warehouse releases the goods and sends the stock request with the goods to shipping. In shipping, the goods are compared with the description on the stock request and units shipped are noted on this request and on the packing slip. Shipping then sends the packing slip with the goods to the customer. The stock request is sent to billing. For back-ordered items, a back-order report is prepared in billing after part 5 is returned from shipping. The report is sent to the sales department for preparation of a new sales invoice.

Billing enters the items shipped from the stock request on the customer invoice and accounting copy. Billing also makes extensions and checks them, compares prices to price list, and runs a tape of amounts on the accounting copies. The stock requests are filed numerically and numerical sequence is accounted for at this time. The customer invoice is sent to the customer.

The accounting copy is sent to accounting where it is posted to the customer ledger card and placed in the invoice file according to shipping date. A tape of invoices is also sent to accounting where the total is posted to the general ledger sales and accounts receivable control accounts. The total daily posting to customer ledger cards is balanced to the general ledger sales entry. The tape of invoices is discarded after balancing.

Required
Prepare a flowchart of the sales system.

7–30.* The Joppa Corporation's sales department receives each sales order (mail or phone), prepares the sales order form, and forwards a copy to the credit manager for credit approval. On indicating approval, the sales order copy is returned to the sales department, where the shipping order copy is sent to the shipping department for assembling the order. After the order is prepared for shipping, a prenumbered bill of lading is prepared for the shipment.

On shipment of the order, the shipping order copy is returned with a copy of the bill of lading to the sales department, where it is matched with the copy in the open sales order file. All the documents are forwarded to the accounting department.

From the information supplied by the sales department, the prenumbered sales invoices are prepared in the accounting department. Two copies are mailed to the customer and the invoice information is entered in detail in the sales journal. Invoice amounts are posted to the customers' accounts receivable cards at the same time they are entered in the sales journal. Totals from the sales journal are posted to the general ledger at month-end.

Required
a. List the procedures you would perform to compliance test the recorded sales.
b. Since this company maintains a file of unfilled sales orders in the sales department, list the recommendations you would give to the client for review of the file and pursuit of old unfilled sales orders.
c. Comment on the internal control system.

CASE STUDY

7-31.* The Alpha Company is a medium-size company which assembles robots from parts and subassemblies ordered to specification. All work done by outside processors is completed prior to the time the Alpha Company receives the component parts and/or subassemblies. These robots are sold to steel mills, automobile companies, and other manufacturing companies. Sales prices of the robots range from $8,000 to $25,000 depending upon their capacity, complexity, and variation from the standard model formats specified by the customer.

The company has been in operation approximately five years and has enjoyed increased gross revenue and earnings during each year. This year, sales are expected to be about $10 million and net income about $500,000.

In the past, we have always considered internal controls over sales and accounts receivable to be very reliable. This year you find that, for the first time, a significant portion (about 20 percent) of sales is composed of replacement parts for robots. Instead of employing the same sales and accounts receivable system as for sales of new robots, which system appears very reliable again this year, the following procedures are employed for sales of replacement parts:

> (The new procedures have been authorized by J.B. Brown, the vice-president of sales, to facilitate filling the replacement parts orders as expeditiously as possible so customers can minimize the "down time" of the Alpha robots in their plants. Brown believes very strongly that customers' satisfaction with Alpha robots depends to a large extent on the time required to repair the robots they have.)

Customers may telephone their replacement orders (which average about $150) to the sales order department, which orally transmits them to the shipping department, where the replacement parts inventory is stocked. The replacement parts inventory is not commingled with parts used in the assembly of new robots. The shipping department fills the order and prepares a scratch paper listing of the parts shipped, which is forwarded to the billing department. The billing department prepares a special three-part prenumbered sales invoice. It enters quantities from the memo received from the shipping department and prices from a current price list, makes extensions and footings, and mails the original after someone else in the department has completely checked it. The first copy is sent to the accounts receivable clerk for entry in the sales journal and on the accounts receivable ledger card and for filing in numerical order. The accounts receivable clerk frequently checks for missing invoice numbers and requests any missing invoices from the billing department. The second copy is sent to the sales order department for filing by customer.

Perpetual inventory records are not maintained for the replacement parts. However, a physical inventory of the replacement parts inventory is taken at the end of each month by a member of the controller's department assisted by someone from the shipping department.

Required
a. Identify the errors and irregularities that may occur in Alpha's system.
b. Opposite each items listed in a, indicate the necessary control procedures that may prevent or detect such occurrences.
c. Enumerate the compliance tests you would apply in testing sales of replacement parts transactions.

8 Compliance Tests of Revenue Cycle: Cash Receipts and Sales Adjustments Transactions

STUDY OBJECTIVES

The study objectives of this chapter are to acquire an understanding of internal controls over cash receipts and sales adjustments transactions and the auditor's study and evaluation of these controls. To achieve these objectives, it is necessary for the reader to

- Know how the principles of internal accounting control apply to cash receipts and sales adjustment transactions.
- Comprehend the audit programs for testing these transactions in the revenue cycle.
- Understand the application of statistical sampling to the testing of cash receipts transactions.
- Perceive the methodology of testing cash receipts transactions in an electronic data processing system.

This chapter completes the coverage of the revenue cycle. In the chapter, cash receipt transactions associated with the earning of revenues and sales adjustment transactions are considered. The format of the chapter parallels the approach used in the preceding chapter. Accordingly, consideration will be given first to the internal control environment, basic principles of internal control, and specific accounting control objectives. Then, attention is given to the study and evaluation of internal accounting control over cash receipts and sales adjustments, including applications of statistical sampling and electronic data processing (EDP).

INTERNAL CONTROL OVER CASH RECEIPTS AND SALES ADJUSTMENTS TRANSACTIONS

Basic Considerations

Cash receipts may result from a variety of sources. For example, cash receipts may result from revenue transactions, short- and long-term borrowing, issuance of capital stock, and the sale of marketable securities, long-term investments, and other assets. The scope of this chapter is limited to cash receipts from sales transactions. Such receipts include cash sales and collections from trade customers on credit sales. Other sources of cash receipts are discussed in the investing and financing cycles in Chapter 14.

Sales adjustments transactions include sales discounts, sales returns and allowances, and uncollectible accounts.

The following are basic to an understanding of cash receipts and sales adjustment transactions in the revenue cycle:

Functions
  Executing
- Receiving mail receipts.
- Receiving over-the-counter receipts.
- Aggregating total receipts.
- Depositing cash in bank.
- Granting cash discounts.
- Granting sales returns and allowances.
- Determining uncollectible accounts.

Recording
- Journalizing and posting cash receipts transactions.
- Journalizing and posting sales adjustments transactions.
- Updating the customers' ledger.

  Custody
- Protecting cash.
- Maintaining correctness of cash balances.
- Maintaining correctness of customer balances.

Common documents
- *Remittance advice*. A memo attached to or separate from a check indicating the item(s) paid by a check. If not sent by the customer, it usually is prepared by the recipient.

- *Check.* An order directing a bank to pay a specified sum of money to a payee on demand. Upon receipt, a check should be restrictively endorsed by stamp or signature *for deposit only.*
- *Cash register tape.* A chronological listing of cash receipts produced internally by the register of amounts registered by a cashier. The customer's copy is in the form of a *cash register receipt slip.*
- *Prelisting of cash receipts.* A detailed compilation of each cash remittance received through the mail.
- *Cash register reading.* A summary of total cash rung up on a register for a specified period of time such as a day. The reading is generally done by a supervisor.
- *Cash count sheet.* A listing of cash and checks in a register and a reconciliation of the total with the cash register reading.
- *Daily cash summary.* A report showing total mail and over-the-counter receipts for the day.
- *Bank deposit slip.* A listing of the detail and total cash deposited in the bank, as prepared by the depositor.
- *Bank statement.* A report by the bank sent to the depositor periodically (usually monthly). It shows the beginning and ending balances and transactions posted to the depositor's account.
- *Credit memo.* A notice to a customer issued by the seller granting credit for unsatisfactory merchandise.
- *Write-off authorization memo.* A notice used internally for writing off an uncollectible customer account.

Accounting records

- *Books of original entry.* Cash receipts journal and general journal.
- *Subsidiary ledgers.* Customers' ledger and perpetual inventory records.
- *General ledger accounts.* Cash, accounts receivable, notes receivable, inventory, sales, cost of sales, sales discounts, sales returns and allowances, allowance for uncollectible accounts, and uncollectible accounts expense.

File data

- *Customer account file.* Contains documentation of postings to each customer's account.

Internal Control Environment

The internal control environment described in Chapter 7 applies to all transactions in the revenue cycle. Additional comment is warranted here concerning the control environment for cash receipts transactions.

In the organization structure illustrated in Figure 7-1, the position of vice president of finance was shown. In most companies, this individual has the overall responsibility for cash management.

Responsibility for executing cash receipts transactions and custody of cash funds is usually delegated to departments or offices, such as the treasurer's office and the cashier's office. Personnel in these departments should be competent in the handling of cash transactions and should be knowledgeable of banks and banking practices.

When there is an internal auditing function within an entity, there can be independent monitoring of the receiving and depositing of cash receipts. Cash budgets play an important role in most companies' effective cash management. Monthly reports that compare actual results with budget expectations contribute to the control of cash.

Many companies bond employees who handle cash. Bonding involves the purchase of a fidelity insurance policy against loss of cash from theft and similar defalcations perpetrated by a dishonest employee. Before the insurer issues a policy or adds an employee to an existing policy, it generally makes an investigation as to the individual's honesty and integrity in previous positions. Bonding contributes to the control environment over cash receipts in two ways: (1) it may prevent the hiring of dishonest individuals, and (2) it serves as a deterrent to dishonesty because employees know that the insurance company may vigorously investigate and prosecute any dishonest act.

Other sound controls over cash receipts include (1) having employees who handle cash take vacations and (2) rotating their assigned duties periodically. The thrust of these controls is to deter dishonesty by making employees aware that they may not be able to permanently conceal their transgressions. Some bank embezzlements, for example, have been traced to the apparently dedicated employee who had the same job and did not take a vacation in 25 years.

Materiality and Risk

Cash is often referred to as the lifeblood of an entity because it is both the alpha and omega of a company's normal operating cycle. The inflow of cash from the revenue cycle is an important component of the flow of cash through an entity. In many companies, cash receipts transactions exceed all other classes of transactions in frequency and magnitude. These factors increase the likelihood of errors or irregularities in executing and recording cash receipts transactions. In addition, cash is the most liquid asset owned by an entity. Because of its intrinsic value as a medium of exchange and its high mobility, cash is very susceptible to theft and misappropriation. Most companies therefore have extensive internal controls over cash.

In order to assess the risk of errors and irregularities, it is necessary for the auditor to evaluate the client's controls over cash receipts. When the auditor intends to rely on the controls in performing substantive tests of resulting balances, the review and testing of internal controls may represent a significant portion of interim work in many audit engagements.

Cash Receipts Transactions are Properly Executed

The functions and specific accounting control objectives in executing cash receipts transactions are as follows.

FUNCTION	SPECIFIC ACCOUNTING CONTROL OBJECTIVE
1. Receiving mail receipts	Receipts are handled by authorized personnel and are promptly and accurately listed
2. Receiving over-the-counter receipts	Receipts are handled by authorized personnel and are promptly and correctly registered
3. Aggregating total receipts	Receipts are totaled, verified, and summarized by authorized personnel
4. Depositing cash	Receipts are promptly deposited intact in an authorized depository

The internal control principles applicable to the execution of these transactions are explained below.

Authorization Procedures

Authorization of cash receipts transactions embodies procedures for opening and closing bank accounts. The treasurer and/or the chief financial officer usually have this authority. It is also necessary to identify personnel who are authorized to handle cash. These may include all employees in the cashier's department, mail room employees who sort mail, and salespersons in retail companies who also have the authority to operate cash registers.

Segregation of Functions

The separation of duties in executing cash receipts transactions is indicated below.

FUNCTION	DEPARTMENT	RELATED ACTIVITIES
1. Receiving mail receipts	Mailroom	Prepare prelist of individual checks, prepare remittance advices if necessary, restrictively endorse checks
2. Receiving over-the-counter receipts	Sales	Make cash sales, ring up sales on cash register, restrictively endorse checks
	Cashier (Individual Cashiers)	Record collections from customers on cash registers, prepare remittance advices, restrictively endorse checks

(continued)

FUNCTION	DEPARTMENT	RELATED ACTIVITIES
3. Aggregating total cash received	Cashier (Supervisor)	Make cash register readings, make daily cash counts of registers, reconcile checks with prelists and remittance advices, prepare daily cash summary
4. Depositing cash in bank	Cashier (Supervisor)	Prepare bank deposit slip, make bank deposit
	Treasurer	Compare prelists and cash count sheets with daily cash summary, compare summary with bank deposit

In addition to a separation of functions between departments, this tabulation shows a separation of duties within the cashier's department. Many national retailers, for example, accept payments on account from customers only at the cashier's office. A flowchart of a manual system for executing mail receipts and over-the-counter cash sales is shown in Figure 8-1.

Documentation Procedures

A major concern in executing cash receipts transactions is the possible diversion of cash before there is any documentation of the receipt. Hence, control procedures should provide reasonable assurance that documentation is produced at the moment cash is received. For mail receipts, documentation consists of remittance advices, checks, and daily listings (technically called prelisting) of mail receipts. Upon receipt in the mail room, all checks should be restrictively endorsed for deposit only.

Documentation of over-the-counter receipts consists of *cash register tapes, checks,* and *remittance advices.* These documents are provided when the cash is received. Subsequently, the cashier's office will obtain cash register readings and prepare *cash count sheets, daily cash summaries,* and *bank deposit slips.* Responsibility for bank deposits is usually assigned to the cashier's office because all receipts are centralized at this location. Cash should be deposited in total (intact) daily for purposes of accountability, safekeeping, and good cash management. Consequently, the bank deposit should equal the total cash shown on the daily cash summary. Deposit slips are prepared in duplicate. One copy is retained by the bank and the other is validated by the bank and is then sent by the depositor to the treasurer's office. The details of the deposit (e.g., the individual checks) should be indicated on the slip or shown in a separate listing. Figure 8-1 shows the origin, routing, and disposition of the documents.

Physical Controls

In retail establishments, the use of cash registers is a vital accounting control procedure in executing cash receipts transactions.

The control features of a cash register include: (see p. 250)

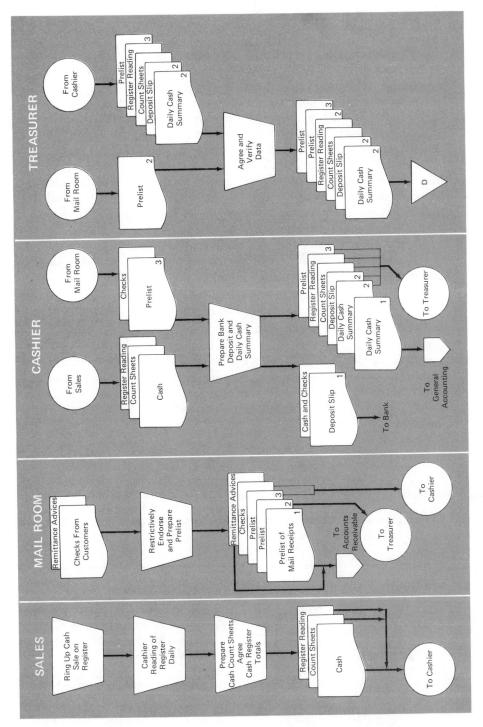

FIGURE 8-1. Manual System for Executing Cash Receipts Transactions

- Immediate visual display for the customer of the amount of the receipt.
- A printed receipt which is available to the customer.
- Locked-in totals of the day's receipts.

Electronically operated registers, often referred to as electronic point-of-sale (POS) systems, provide even greater control over the execution of register receipts. Such registers have the capability of "reading" the sales price from the price tags and automatically adding the sales tax. In addition, the registers can be utilized to perform a variety of control functions, such as updating accounts receivable and perpetual inventory records, and accumulating sales data by salesperson, product line, etc.

Companies with a large volume of mail receipts sometimes use a *lockbox system*. The lockbox is a post office box that is controlled by the company's bank. Under this type of security system, the bank picks up the mail daily, credits the company for the cash, and sends the remittance advices to the company. This system also expedites the depositing of checks, with the result that the company receives credit for them sooner.

Other examples of physical controls include coin machines in transit companies, automatic receptacles on interstate toll roads, ticket machines in theaters, and metered gas pumps in service stations.

Independent Internal Verification

For cash register receipts, each register is read (totaled) by a cashier department supervisor, and a reconciliation is made on cash count sheets of the total cash with the actual cash in the register. In the treasurer's office there should be daily comparisons of (1) prelists and cash register totals with the daily cash summary and (2) the summary with the corresponding duplicate deposit slip.

Cash Receipts Transactions Are Properly Recorded

The functions and accounting control objectives for recording cash receipts transactions are as follows:

FUNCTION	DEPARTMENT	SPECIFIC ACCOUNTING CONTROL OBJECTIVE
1. Journalizing and posting cash receipts transactions	General Accounting	Only valid cash receipts are recorded, and all valid receipts are correctly recorded as to amount, account classification, and accounting period
2. Updating customers' ledger	Accounts Receivable Accounting	Collections from customers are promptly and correctly posted to customer accounts

The internal control principles applicable to these functions are explained below.

Segregation of Functions

As in the case of sales transactions, there should be a separation of duties between journalizing and posting to the general ledger and updating the customers' ledger. In addition, accounting personnel should not participate in the execution of the transactions or have custody of the cash receipts.

Accounting Records and Procedures

The primary source documents for journalizing cash receipts transactions are the daily cash summaries and prelists. Postings to the customers' ledger are made directly from the prelists and accompanying remittance advices.

Independent Internal Verification

Applications of this principle include (1) agreeing remittance advices to prelists in accounts receivable accounting and (2) agreeing the prelist to the daily cash summary in general accounting as shown in the flowchart in Figure 8-2.

Custody of Cash Is Properly Maintained

The functions and specific accounting control objectives for proper custody of cash receipts are as follows:

FUNCTIONS	DEPARTMENT	SPECIFIC ACCOUNTING CONTROL OBJECTIVE
1. Protecting cash	Treasurer	Cash is stored in secure areas and access thereto is limited to authorized personnel
2. Maintaining correctness of cash balances	General Accounting	Recorded cash and bank balances are independently reconciled with cash on hand and in banks at reasonable intervals

The internal control principles applicable to these functions are explained below.

Physical Controls and Authorization Procedures

Because cash offers a great temptation for misappropriation, every effort should be made by a company to store cash (and checks) in a safe place from the moment it is received to its ultimate disposition. Direct physical access to cash held on company premises can be effectively limited by the use of

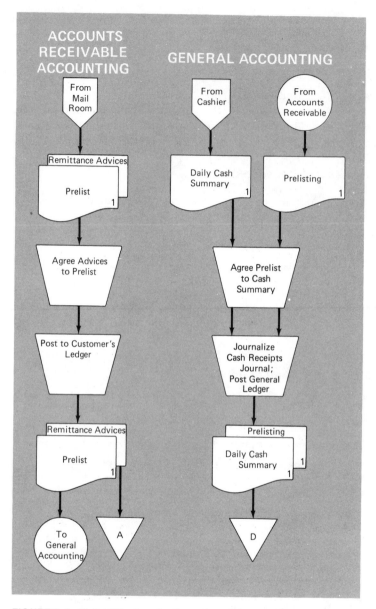

FIGURE 8–2. Manual System for Recording Cash Receipts Transactions

safes, vaults, and similar protective equipment. Access to such security devices should be restricted to authorized personnel only and be strictly enforced. Whenever possible, cash should be stored off premises, where the greater security of a bank can be utilized. All cash, except possibly small change and petty cash funds, should be deposited in the bank daily through regular or night depository facilities.

Segregation of Functions and Independent Internal Verification

Personnel responsible for the custody of cash on hand and in banks should not otherwise be involved in executing and recording cash receipts transactions.

Independent verifications of cash balances are generally made monthly. Recorded cash on hand and petty cash balances are compared with cash counts, and recorded bank balances are reconciled to balances shown on bank statements. These verifications should be made by personnel who have no other duties pertaining to cash receipts.

Sales Adjustments Transactions Are Properly Executed

The functions and specific accounting control objectives in executing sales adjustments transactions are as follows:

FUNCTION	SPECIFIC ACCOUNTING CONTROL OBJECTIVE
Granting cash discounts	Discounts are granted in accordance with authorized terms
Granting sales returns and allowances	Returns and allowances are granted in accordance with management's policies
Determining uncollectible accounts	Uncollectible accounts are determined on the basis of established criteria

The internal control principles applicable to the execution of these transactions are as follows.

Authorization Procedures

Authorization procedures usually provide for personnel in (1) the accounts receivable department to approve discounts, (2) the sales order department to grant credit for sales returns and allowances, and (3) the treasurer's department to approve the write-off of bad debts. Before approving a discount, the customer's remittance must be traced to the sales invoice in the customer account file for compliance with discount terms. Before approving other adjustments, there should be evidence in the form of a receiving report for returned goods, written communication from the customer requesting an allowance, or a collection agency report on the delinquent customer. Unauthorized sales adjustments result in improper credits to customer accounts and an understatement of the balance due.

Segregation of Functions

The segregation of functions for sales adjustments are tabulated below.

FUNCTION	DEPARTMENT	RELATED ACTIVITIES
Granting cash discounts	Accounts receivable accounting	Compare customer remittances with discount terms and indicate approval of discount
Granting sales returns and allowances	Sales	Evaluate requests for adjustments, review evidence of returned goods, and authorize issuance of credit memos
	Billing	Issue credit memos to customers
Determining uncollectible accounts	Treasurer	Review credit and collection history of delinquent customers, examine collection agency data, and issue write-off memos for bad accounts

Individuals performing these functions have incompatible duties if they have access to the customers' ledger and handle cash collections. In such case, they could make unauthorized credits to the accounts and pocket the collections when received.

Documentation Procedures

The approval of cash discounts should be indicated by accounts receivable on the prelists from the mail room and on the remittance advices from over-the-counter collections. Returns and allowances should be supported by credit memos, and write-offs of uncollectible accounts should be based on write-off memos. These documents should be prenumbered and subsequently accounted for.

Sales Adjustments Transactions Are Properly Recorded

The functions and internal control objectives in recording these transactions are as follows:

FUNCTION	DEPARTMENT	SPECIFIC ACCOUNTING CONTROL OBJECTIVE
Journalizing and posting sales adjustment transactions	General Accounting	Only valid sales adjustments are recorded
		Valid sales adjustments are correctly recorded as to amount, classification, and accounting period
Updating the customers' ledger	Accounts Receivable Accounting	Sales adjustments are promptly and correctly posted to customer accounts

The internal control principles of segregation of functions and accounting records and procedures are applicable to the recording of these transactions. As for other classes of transactions, all prenumbered documents should be accounted for in journalizing.

Custody of Assets Is Properly Maintained

The assets relating to sales adjustments transactions include cash and accounts receivable. The internal accounting control objectives and principles pertaining to the custody of these assets have already been explained.

STUDY AND EVALUATION OF INTERNAL CONTROL

The auditor's methodology for meeting the second standard of field work for cash receipts and sales adjustments transactions is identical with the steps described for sales transactions in Chapter 7.

Review of the Cash Receipts System

The auditor is required to make a preliminary review of the internal control environment and the flow of cash receipts transactions through the accounting system. A decision to complete the review is made when the auditor believes it will be cost-efficient to rely on the client's control procedures in performing substantive tests of resulting balances. The principal steps in the completion phase of review are explained below.

Gathering Information

In this step, the auditor seeks information about the specific control controls prescribed by the client. A questionnaire for cash receipts transactions is illustrated in Figure 8-3. As in the preceding chapter, the questions relate to necessary control procedures and they are referenced to specific functions. In addition to inquiry, the auditor may also obtain information about prescribed controls through observation and review of documentation.

CYCLE: Revenue   **CLASS OF TRANSACTIONS: Cash Receipts**

EXECUTING   Yes   No

1. Are prelists prepared for mail receipts? (E1)
2. Are checks restrictively endorsed on receipt? (E1, E2)
3. Are persons who handle cash prohibited from recording cash and making postings to the customers' ledger? (E1, E2)
4. Are cash registers used for over-the-counter receipts? (E2)
5. Is there periodic surveillance of cash register procedures? (E2)
6. Are prelists and checks independently reconciled with cash summaries? (E3)
7. Are cash registers read daily and reconciled to cash on hand? (E3)
8. Is cash deposited intact daily? (E4)
9. Do only authorized personnel make deposits? (E4)
10. Are deposits and daily cash summaries independently reconciled? (E4)

RECORDING

1. Are accounting personnel prohibited from handling cash? (R1)
2. Is there internal verification of the agreement of daily cash summaries and cash receipts journal entries? (R1)
3. Is there separation of duties between the journalizing of cash receipts transactions and posting to the customers' ledger? (R2)

CUSTODY

1. Is cash stored in safes or vaults prior to deposit? (C1)
2. Are periodic independent counts made of cash on hand? (C2)

FIGURE 8–3. Internal Control Questionnaire: Cash Receipts Transactions

Making a Preliminary Evaluation

A representative listing of errors and irregularities for cash receipts transactions and the control procedures considered necessary to prevent or detect their occurrence is shown in Figure 8-4. Then, using the knowledge about the client's prescribed controls obtained in step 1 of this review, the auditor makes a preliminary evaluation of each control. The auditor's preliminary evaluation should be documented in the working papers.

Lapping

Lapping is an irregularity that results in the deliberate misappropriation of cash receipts. It may involve either a temporary or a permanent abstraction of cash receipts for the personal use of the individual perpetrating the unauthorized act. Lapping is usually associated with collections from customers, but it may also involve other types of cash receipts. Conditions conducive to lapping exist when an individual who handles cash receipts also maintains the customers' ledger. The auditor should assess the likelihood of

Function	Possible Errors and Irregularities	Necessary Control Procedures	Possible Compliance Tests
EXECUTING			
Receiving mail receipts	Checks may be lost in the mailroom	Restrictive endorsement of checks upon receipt	Examine checks for endorsement
Receiving over-the-counter receipts	Cash sales may not be registered	Periodic surveillance of cash register procedures	Inquire of supervisors as to findings
	Errors may be made in making change	Daily cash register readings and cash counts by supervisors	Review cash count sheets
	Collections from customers may be misappropriated (lapping)	Segregation of functions of cash handling and recording	Observe segregation of functions
Aggregating total cash received	Accompanying checks may not agree with prelist from mailroom	Comparison of prelist with checks in cashiers department	Review evidence of comparison
Depositing cash in bank	Cash may not be deposited intact	Verification of agreement of deposit slip with daily cash summary	Review evidence of verification
RECORDING			
Journalizing and posting cash receipts transactions	Some receipts may not be recorded	Internal verification of agreement of cash receipts journal entries with daily cash summary	Examine evidence of verification
Updating customers' ledger	Recorded receipts may not be posted to customer accounts	Segregation of functions between journalizing and updating	Observe segregation of duties
CUSTODY			
Protecting cash	Cash may be stolen before being deposited	Storage of cash in vaults and safes	Observe storage security
Maintaining correctness of cash balances	Mathematical errors may be made in computing cash balances	Periodic independent comparisons of cash balances with cash on hand	Examine evidence of independent comparisons

FIGURE 8–4. Preliminary Evaluation Considerations: Cash Receipts Transactions

lapping when making a preliminary evaluation of controls over cash receipts by carefully considering the segregation of functions that exists in the receiving and recording of collections from customers.

To illustrate lapping, assume on a given day that cash register tapes totaled $600 and mail receipts opened by the lapper consisted of one payment on account by check for $200 from customer A. The lapper would proceed to abstract $200 in cash and destroy all evidence pertaining to the mail receipt except for the customer's check. The cash receipts journal entry would agree with the register tape ($600) and the deposit slip would show cash $400 and A's check for $200. These facts can be tablulated as follows:

ACTUAL RECEIPTS		DOCUMENTATION		CASH RECEIPTS JOURNAL ENTRY		BANK DEPOSIT SLIP	
Cash	$600	Cash tape	$600	Cash sales	$600	Cash	$400
A check	200		—		—	A check	200
	$800		$600		$600		$600

In an effort to conceal the shortage, the defrauder usually attempts to (1) keep bank and book amounts in daily agreement so that a bank reconciliation will not detect the irregularity and (2) correct the customer's account within three to four days of actual collection so that any discovered discrepancy in the customer's account can be explained as a delay in receiving the money or in posting. To accomplish the latter, the abstraction is shifted to another customer's account several days later as follows:

ACTUAL RECEIPTS		DOCUMENTATION		CASH RECEIPTS JOURNAL ENTRY		BANK DEPOSIT SLIP	
Cash	$500	Cash tape	$500	Cash sales	$500	Cash	$400
B check	300	A check	200	A check	200	B check	300
	$800		$700		$700		$700

The total shortage is now $300. Notice in both cases that the totals of the last two columns are in agreement. Thus, a comparison of totals will not detect lapping. However, a comparison of the details of the cash receipts journal entry with the details of the deposit slip will detect the shortage. If lapping exists at the balance sheet date, the confirmation of customer balances may also detect the irregularity.

Compliance Tests of Prescribed Controls

The auditor is required by GAAS to perform compliance tests of the controls expected to be relied on in substantive testing. In this case, the compliance tests are made to determine whether the prescribed controls over cash receipts transactions are operating as planned. An audit program is illustrated in Figure 8-5. This program includes most of the possible compliance tests shown in Figure 8-4.

In the program, daily cash summaries are used as the sampling unit in testing controls that leave a trail of documentary performance in the execution and recording of cash receipts transactions. The comparison of daily cash summary *totals* with the total amount shown on the daily deposit slip and the bank statement focuses on whether all receipts have been deposited intact daily. Any discrepancies in amount or time delays should be investigated. The comparison of the *details* of the deposit slip and the individual entries in the cash receipts journal is designed to detect lapping.

Final Evaluation of the Controls

Based on the results of compliance testing, the auditor determines the reliance that can be placed on specific control procedures in performing substantive tests. In making this determination, the auditor considers both the qualitative and the quantitative aspects of deviations from prescribed control procedures. The auditor subsequently determines the effects of his

---

TYPE OF TEST: Compliance   **PURPOSE: Study and Evaluation of Internal Control**
CYCLE: Revenue   **CLASS OF TRANSACTIONS: Cash Receipts**

A. CONTROLS IN EXECUTING CASH RECEIPTS TRANSACTIONS ARE OPERATING AS PLANNED

  1. Examine selected daily cash summaries for
    • Verification with prelists.
    • Verification with cash count sheets.
    • Verification with details and totals of daily deposit slips.
  2. Observe mail clerks and cashiers in performance of required control procedures.
  3. Inquire of supervisors as to the results of their surveillance of cash register procedures.
  4. Reperform verification procedures in step 1 for some cash summaries.

B. CONTROLS IN RECORDING CASH RECEIPTS TRANSACTIONS ARE OPERATING AS PLANNED

  1. Observe that only accounting personnel record cash receipts transactions.
  2. Examine above sample of daily cash summaries for evidence of agreement with daily cash receipts entries.
  3. Observe segregation of functions between journalizing of cash receipts and postings to customers' ledger.

C. CONTROLS OVER CUSTODY OF CASH ARE OPERATING AS PLANNED

  1. Observe storage of cash and means of limiting access to storage areas.
  2. Review evidence of periodic comparisons of cash balances with cash on hand.

FIGURE 8-5. Audit Program—Compliance Tests of Cash Receipts Transactions

evaluations on the nature, timing, and extent of substantive tests of account balances resulting from cash receipts and sales adjustments transactions.

STATISTICAL SAMPLING IN COMPLIANCE TESTING

Opportunities for the application of statistical sampling in compliance testing for cash receipts and sales adjustments transactions are more limited than for certain other classes of transactions. For example, several of the steps in the compliance testing program for cash receipts in Figure 8-5 involve inquiry about, or observation of, cash handling procedures. These procedures do not lend themselves to statistical sampling. Other steps in the program focus on the daily cash summaries as the sampling unit. Because this sampling unit relates to a small population (there would be a maximum of 365 summaries for the year in some companies), the attribute sampling tables in Chapter 6 (which are based on sampling from populations of 5,000 or more items) would not apply. While other tables and formulas are available for attribute sampling from small populations, auditors frequently use nonstatistical audit sampling in these circumstances.

Alternatively, a different sampling unit might be chosen for a specific compliance test. For example, step A1 in the audit program in Figure 8-7 in the EDP case study that follows specifies the customer remittance advice as the sampling unit. This would generally produce a population large enough to use the sampling theory and tables illustrated in Chapter 6. Such a sample could be selected by establishing correspondence between a random number table and prenumbered remittance advices, or by first randomly selecting daily prelists and then randomly selecting line items (remittances) on the prelists. Of course, appropriate selection of the sampling unit depends on the objective of the test.

In the compliance testing of sales adjustments transactions, a sample of remittance advices selected as described above could be examined for evidence of approval of any discounts taken. Also, statistical sampling of sales returns and allowances transactions could be performed where the volume of such transactions is large. This may occur, for example, for a national mail order company. The sampling unit would be the credit memo, and the attributes to be examined could include evidence of (1) the request for credit (customer letter), (2) a receiving report for the goods returned for credit, (3) internal verification of the credit memo, and (4) approval of credit by a supervisor.

ELECTRONIC DATA PROCESSING

Cash receipts transactions may be processed in an electronic system either by batch or online. Since many companies now use online processing, this system is used in the following case study.

Description of the System

The R. E. Birk Company uses the departments described earlier in this chapter (for the manual system) in processing cash receipts. Customer checks are received in the mailroom where they are endorsed and listed on a prelist. As shown in the flowchart in Figure 8-6, accounts receivable receives the checks, remittance advices, and a copy of the prelist from the mailroom. Authorized accounts receivable clerks then enter the receipts directly into the computer using display-type terminals. The input data are edited by the computer, and the accounts receivable clerk receives an immediate response of any incorrect data on the display screen.

As shown in the flowchart, there are two computer runs. In run 1, the input data are edited and sorted. The outputs of this run consist of a printed exception and control report and a valid cash receipts transaction tape. In run 2, the valid cash receipts transaction tape is processed. The outputs of this run are an updated accounts receivable master file in machine-readable form, a printed report of individual customer payments, an exception and control report, and three printouts pertaining to the recording and depositing of cash receipts.

Daily, accounts receivable makes a detailed comparison of the report of customer activity with the remittance advices and prelist. In addition, the cashier's department makes the bank deposit after agreeing the checks received from accounts receivable with the daily cash summary and prelist. Evidence of the cash activity and bank deposit is then sent to the treasurer's office.

Study and Evaluation of EDP Controls

The audit program for testing application controls over cash receipts transactions in Figure 8-7 is similar to the program presented in Figure 7-8. Input and output controls that leave a visible audit trail are tested by recourse to source documents and by reviewing reconciliations of batch and other control totals. The programmed controls in runs 1 and 2 do not leave an audit trail. Accordingly, the testing of controls is done through the computer using test data. Valid and invalid test data are prepared to test the limit and reasonableness checks incorporated within the cash receipts edit routines in run 1 and the program logic in run 2.

Based on the tests of general controls and the tests of application controls, the auditor proceeds to evaluate EDP controls over cash receipts transactions and determines the extent to which substantive tests of balances are to be restricted.

CONCLUDING COMMENTS

Cash receipts and sales adjustment transactions are integral parts of an entity's revenue cycle. The explanation of internal control principles appli-

FIGURE 8-6. EDP System for Cash Receipts

TYPE OF TEST: Compliance	PURPOSE: EDP application controls
CYCLE: Revenue	CLASS OF TRANSACTIONS: Cash receipts

A. INPUT CONTROLS ARE PROPERLY FUNCTIONING:

1. Randomly select sample of customer remittance advices and trace to recorded customer remittances.
2. Review, on test basis, the reconciliation of batched remittance input totals with control totals in run 1.
3. Selectively review exception listings of run 1 and investigate items that have remained uncleared for an unreasonably long time.
4. Design and use test data to test program controls of edit routine in run 1.

B. PROCESSING CONTROLS ARE PROPERLY FUNCTIONING:

1. Observe the procedures for reconciling control totals in run 2 and selectively trace control totals to related input controls.
2. Selectively review exception lists of run 2 for unusual items and determine the disposition of rejected data.
3. Use test data to test program controls in run 2.

C. OUTPUT CONTROLS ARE PROPERLY FUNCTIONING:

1. Review reconciliation of output controls of run 2 with other controls.
2. Obtain printout of the two accounts receivable master files of run 2 and selectively reconcile changes in customer balances with remittance advices.

FIGURE 8–7. Audit Program: Compliance Tests of EDP Application Controls for Cash Receipts Transactions

cable to these classes of transactions and the study and evaluation of internal control of cash receipts transactions completes the coverage of interim work on the revenue cycle.

In many engagements, the auditor places considerable emphasis on the review and compliance testing of control procedures over cash receipts transactions. The extent of reliance on these controls directly affects substantive testing of cash and accounts receivable balances. These tests are explained in Part III of this book.

REVIEW QUESTIONS

8–1. Indicate the scope of cash receipts and sales adjustments transactions in the revenue cycle.

8–2. What are the functions in executing and recording cash receipts transactions and in the custody of related assets?

8–3. Discuss the personnel and sound practices aspects of an internal control environment that relate to cash receipts transactions.

8–4. Indicate the relative importance of cash receipts transactions in the typical audit engagement.

8–5. Identify the specific internal accounting control objective and appropriate division of duties for each function involved in executing cash receipts transactions.

8–6. What authorizations are required in executing cash receipts transactions?

8–7. Describe the activities of each department that participates in the execution of cash receipts transactions.

8–8. Briefly discuss the use of cash registers, prelists, and daily cash summaries in controlling cash receipts.

8–9. Diagram the flow of data within the cashier's department when a company has both over-the-counter and mail receipts.

8–10. Identify the control procedures that offer reasonable assurance that cash receipts are deposited intact daily.

8–11. How does a lockbox system contribute to internal control over cash receipts?

8–12. What accounting control principles are applicable to the recording of cash receipts transactions?

8–13. Diagram the flow of data within general accounting in recording cash receipts transactions.

8–14. a. Indicate the specific accounting control objectives pertaining to the custody of cash receipts.
   b. Explain the applicability oı ϸhysical controls and authorization procedures to the custody of cash.

8–15. a. Identify the functions and the related department(s) involved in the execution of sales adjustments transactions.
   b. What types of documentation should exist for sales adjustments?

8–16. a. What is *lapping*?
   b. What internal control principle should prevent this irregularity?
   c. Identify an audit test that is useful in detecting lapping.

8–17. a. List the steps in the audit program for compliance testing of cash receipts transactions that involve a review of documentary evidence.
   b. Indicate the steps in the audit program that involve observation of control procedures.

8–18. Indicate the circumstances where statistical sampling may be used in compliance tests of (a) cash receipts and (b) sales adjustments transactions.

8–19. a. Identify the control(s) in the computer processing portion of Figure 8-6.
   b. Explain the controls in the cashier's and accounts receivable departments.

8–20. a. List the steps in the audit program for determining whether input controls are properly functioning.
   b. How may test data be used in the compliance testing of processing controls?

COMPREHENSIVE QUESTIONS

8–21. Jerome Paper Company engaged you to review its internal control system. Jerome does not prelist cash receipts before they are recorded and has other weaknesses in processing collections of trade receivables, the Company's largest asset. In discussing the matter with the controller, you find he is chiefly interested in economy when he assigns duties to the fifteen office personnel. He feels the main considerations are that the work be done by people who are most familiar with it, capable of doing it, and available when it has to be done.

The controller says he has excellent control over trade receivables because receivables are pledged as security for a continually renewable bank loan and the bank sends out positive confirmation requests occasionally, based on a list of pledged receivables furnished by the Company each week. You learn that the bank's internal auditor is satisfied if he gets an acceptable response on 70 percent of his requests.

Required
a. Explain how prelisting of cash receipts strengthens internal control over cash.
b. Assume that an employee handles cash receipts from trade customers before they are recorded. List the duties which that employee should not do to withhold from him the opportunity to conceal embezzlement of cash receipts.

AICPA

8-22. The internal control questionnaire in Figure 8-3 includes the following questions:

1. Are prelists prepared for mail receipts?
2. Are cash registers used for over-the-counter receipts?
3. Are cash registers read daily and reconciled to cash on hand?
4. Are deposits and daily cash summaries independently reconciled?
5. Is cash deposited intact daily?
6. Is there internal verification of the agreement of daily cash summaries and cash receipts journal entries?
7. Is there separation of duties between the journalizing of cash receipts transactions and posting to the customers' ledger?
8. Is cash stored in safes or vaults prior to deposit?
9. Are periodic independent counts made of cash on hand?

Required
a. Identify the operative internal control objective to which each question relates (i.e., executing, recording, or custody).
b. Identify the function and specific internal accounting control objective to which the question pertains.
c. Indicate the internal accounting control principle that is involved.
d. Identify an error or irregularity that may result from a "no" answer to each question. (Present your answer in tabular form.)

8-23. The following control procedures over cash receipts transactions are prescribed by the David Company:

1. Restrictive endorsement of checks upon receipt.
2. Daily cash register readings and cash counts by supervisors.
3. Daily cash deposits.
4. Internal verification of deposits and cash summaries by treasurer's office.
5. Internal verification of daily cash receipts journal entries with cash summaries.
6. Prelisting of remittances from customers in mail room.
7. Segregation of functions between general accounting and accounts receivable accounting.
8. Storing cash in vaults and safes prior to deposit.
9. A supervisor's review of entries for reasonableness of account classifications.

Required
a. Indicate the function and the specific internal accounting control objective served by each procedure.
b. Identify the internal accounting control principle that is involved.
c. Identify an error or irregularity that may be prevented or detected by the control procedure.
d. Indicate a compliance test that may be performed to determine whether each control procedure is operating as prescribed. (Present your answer in tabular form.)

8-24. Assume the following exceptions to prescribed control procedures over cash receipts transactions occurred in the Janz Company:

1. A mail remittance was misappropriated after receipt.
2. A cash sale was not registered.
3. Cash on hand was $5 short of the cash register reading due to errors in making change.
4. Recorded receipts were diverted to personal use before deposit.
5. The cash account was incorrectly footed.
6. A prelist receipt was not journalized.
7. A journalized collection was not posted to the customer's account.

8. Cash was stolen from the cashier's desk.
9. The accompanying checks did not agree with the prelist.
10. An actual deposit did not agree with the deposit slip.

Required
a. Indicate the function associated with each occurrence.
b. Indicate the control procedure(s) that could prevent or detect each occurrence.
c. Identify a compliance test that would determine whether each control indicated in b above is operating as planned. (Present your answer in tabular form.)

8–25.   This is a continuation of comprehensive question 7-25.

1. Since the Robinson Company is short of cash, the deposit of receipts is also expedited. The receptionist turns over all mail receipts and related correspondence to the accounts receivable clerk, who examines the checks and determines that the accompanying advices or correspondence contains enough detail to permit posting of the accounts. The accounts receivable clerk then endorses the checks and gives them to the cashier, who prepares the daily deposit. No currency is received in the mail and no paint is sold over the counter at the factory.
2. The accounts receivable clerk uses the advices or correspondence that accompanied the checks to post the accounts receivable ledger cards. The bookkeeping machine prepares a cash receipts register as a carbon copy of the postings. Monthly the general ledger clerk summarizes the cash receipts register for posting to the general ledger accounts. The accounts receivable clerk also corresponds with customers about unauthorized deductions for discounts, freight or advertising allowance, returns, etc. and prepares the appropriate credit memos. Disputed items of large amount are turned over to the sales manager for settlement. Each month, the accounts receivable clerk prepares a trial balance of the open accounts receivable and compares the resultant total with the general ledger control account for accounts receivable.

Required
a. Identify (1) errors and irregularities that could occur and (2) the necessary control procedures. Organize your answer around the primary functions for cash receipts transactions.
b. Which weaknesses, if any, do you consider material? Why?

AICPA (adapted)

8–26.   The town of Commuter Park operates a private parking lot near the railroad station for the benefit of town residents. The guard on duty issues annual prenumbered parking stickers to residents who submit an application form and show evidence of residency. The sticker is affixed to the auto and allows the resident to park anywhere in the lot for twelve hours if four quarters are placed in the parking meter. Applications are maintained in the guard office at the lot. The guard checks to see that only residents are using the lot and that no resident has parked without paying the required meter fee.

Once a week, the guard on duty, who has a master key for all meters, takes the coins from the meters and places them in a locked steel box. The guard delivers the box to the town storage building where it is opened, and the coins are manually counted by a storage department clerk who records the total cash counted on a "Weekly Cash Report." This report is sent to the town accounting department. The storage department clerk puts the cash in a safe and on the following day the cash is picked up by the town's treasurer who manually counts the cash again, prepares the bank deposit slip, and delivers the deposit to the bank. The deposit slip, authenticated by the bank teller, is sent to the accounting department where it is filed with the "Weekly Cash Report."

Required

Describe weaknesses in the existing system and recommend one or more improvements for each of the weaknesses to strengthen the internal control over the parking lot cash receipts. Organize your answer sheet as follows:

Weakness	*Recommended Improvement(s)*

AICPA

8-27. You have been asked by the board of trustees of a local church to review its accounting procedures. As a part of this review, you have prepared the following comments relating to the collections made at weekly services and record-keeping for members' pledges and contributions:

1. The church's board of trustees has delegated responsibility for financial management and audit of the financial records to the finance committee. This group prepares the annual budget and approves major disbursements but is not involved in collections or record-keeping. No audit has been considered necessary in recent years because the same trusted employee has kept church records and served as financial secretary for fifteen years.
2. The collection at the weekly service is taken by a team of ushers. The head usher counts the collection in the church following each service. He then places the collection and a notation of the amount counted in the church safe. Next morning the financial secretary opens the safe and counts the collection again. He withholds about $100 to meet cash expenditures during the coming week and deposits the remainder of the collection intact. In order to facilitate the deposit, members who contribute by check are asked to draw their checks to "cash."

Required

Describe the weaknesses and recommended improvements in procedures for collections made at weekly services. Organize your answer using the following format:

Weakness	*Recommended Improvement(s)*

AICPA (adapted)

8-28. The cashier of the Edgemont Company intercepted customer *A*'s check, payable to the company in the amount of $500, and deposited it in a bank account which was part of the company petty cash fund, of which he was custodian. He then drew a $500 check on the petty cash fund bank account payable to himself, signed it, and cashed it. At the end of the month, while processing the monthly statements to customers, he was able to change the statement to *A* so as to show that *A* had received credit for the $500 check that had been intercepted. Ten days later he made an entry in the cash received book which purported to record receipt of a remittance of $500 from *A*, thus restoring *A*'s account to its proper balance but overstating cash in bank. He covered the overstatement by omitting from the list of outstanding checks in the bank reconciliation two checks, the aggregate amount of which was $500.

Required

Enumerate the weaknesses in the existing system and recommend one or more improvements for each weakness to strengthen internal control over cash receipts. Organize your answer sheet as follows:

Weakness	*Recommended Improvement(s)*

AICPA (adapted)

8–29. In a large manufacturing organization supplying goods and services, several departments may be involved in the processing of customer complaints and the issuance of any resulting credit memos. Following is a list of such departments:

a. Receiving.
b. Sales.
c. Production.
d. Customer service.
e. Accounts receivable.

Required

Explain briefly the control function each of the departments above performs when processing complaints and issuing credit memos.

IIA

8–30. The Art Appreciation Society operates a museum for the benefit and enjoyment of the community. During hours when the museum is open to the public, two clerks who are positioned at the entrance collect a five-dollar admission fee from each nonmember patron. Members of the Art Appreciation Society are permitted to enter free of charge upon presentation of their membership cards.

At the end of the day one of the clerks delivers the proceeds to the treasurer. The treasurer counts the cash in the presence of the clerk and places it in a safe. Each Friday afternoon the treasurer and one of the clerks deliver all cash held in the safe to the bank and receive an authenticated deposit slip which provides the basis for the weekly entry in the cash receipts journal.

The board of directors of the Art Appreciation Society has identified a need to improve its system of internal control over cash admission fees. The board has determined that the cost of installing turnstiles or sales booths or otherwise altering the physical layout of the museum will greatly exceed any benefits which may be derived. However, the board has agreed that the sale of admission tickets must be an integral part of its improvement efforts.

Smith has been asked by the board of directors of the Art Appreciation Society to review the internal control over cash admission fees and provide suggestions for improvement.

Required

Indicate weaknesses in the existing system of internal control over cash admission fees which Smith should identify, and recommend one improvement for each of the weaknesses identified.

Organize the answer as indicated in the following illustrative example:

Weakness	Recommendation
1. There is no basis for establishing the documentation of the number of paying patrons.	1. Prenumbered admission tickets should be issued upon payment of the admission fee. *AICPA*

8-31. Charting, Inc., a new audit client of yours, processes its sales and cash receipts documents in the following manner:

1. *Payment on account.* The mail is opened each morning by a mail clerk in the sales department. The mail clerk prepares a remittance advice (showing customer and amount paid) if one is not received. The checks and remittance advices are then forwarded to the sales department supervisor, who reviews each check and forwards the checks and remittance advices to the accounting department supervisor.

The accounting department supervisor, who also functions as credit manager in approving new credit and all credit limits, reviews all checks for payments on past due accounts and then forwards the checks and remittance advices to the accounts receivable clerk, who arranges the advices in alphabetical order. The remittance advices are posted directly to the accounts receivable ledger cards. The checks are endorsed by stamp and totaled. The total is posted to the cash receipts journal. The remittance advices are filed chronologically.

After receiving the cash from the previous day's cash sales, the accounts receivable clerk prepares the daily deposit slip in triplicate. The third copy of the deposit slip is filed by date and the second copy and the original accompany the bank deposit.

2. *Sales.* Sales clerks prepare sales invoices in triplicate. The original and second copy are presented to the cashier. The third copy is retained by the sales clerk in the sales book. When the sale is for cash, the customer pays the sales clerk, who presents the money to the cashier with the invoice copies.

A credit sale is approved by the cashier from an approved credit list after the sales clerk prepares the three-part invoice. After receiving the cash or approving the invoice, the cashier validates the original copy of the sales invoice and gives it to the customer. At the end of each day, the cashier recaps the sales and cash received and forwards the cash and the second copy of all sales invoices to the accounts receivable clerk.

The accounts receivable clerk balances the cash received with cash sales invoices and prepares a daily sales summary. The credit sales invoices are posted to the accounts receivable ledger and then all invoices are sent to the inventory control clerk in the sales department for posting to the inventory control cards. After posting, the inventory control clerk files all invoices numerically. The accounts receivable clerk posts the daily sales summary to the cash receipts journal and sales journal and files the sales summaries by date.

The cash from cash sales is combined with the cash received on account to comprise the daily bank deposit.

3. *Bank deposits.* The bank validates the deposit slip and returns the second copy to the accounting department, where it is filed by date by the accounts receivable clerk.

Monthly bank statements are reconciled promptly by the accounting department supervisor and filed by date.

Required

You recognize that there are weaknesses in the existing system and believe a chart of information and document flows would be beneficial in evaluating this client's internal control in preparing for your examination of the financial statements. Complete the flowchart for sales and cash receipts of Charting, Inc. by labeling the appropriate symbols and indicating information flows on page 271. The chart is complete as to symbols and document flows.

AICPA

8–32.* PML Manufacturing, Inc., a privately held corporation, manufactures office equipment. The cash receipts portion of the revenue cycle is described below:

1. Mail is opened in the mailroom. Remittances (a check and a copy of the invoice) are separated.
2. A control list of checks is prepared and sent to the controller.
3. Checks are sent to the cashier and the remittance advices (copies of the invoices) to the accounts receivable department for posting.
4. Cashier 1 endorses the checks and prepares a duplicate deposit slip.
5. Cashier 2 compares the checks and deposit slips. He investigates any discrepancies and a messenger deposits the cash daily.
6. A messenger takes the deposit to the bank.
7. The messenger returns the validated duplicate deposit slip directly to the controller.
8. The controller reconciles the control list of checks and duplicate deposit slip and resolves any differences.
9. The controller files the reconciliation, duplicate deposit slip, and control list of checks received chronologically.

Required

Prepare a flowchart of the cash receipts procedures.

8–33. Your supervisor in the annual audit of the Milan Company asks you to design and execute an attribute sampling plan pertaining to the proper execution of sales returns and allowances. The population consists of 5,200 credit memos numbered consecutively beginning with number 830001.

Required

a. Using the additional information and instructions presented below, prepare a working paper similar to the one illustrated in Figure 6-7 to document the sampling plan.
   1. Identify four attributes to be examined in your sample.
   2. Determine an appropriate sample size for each attribute assuming the following:
      (a) You are willing to accept a 5 percent risk of overreliance for each attribute.
      (b) You are willing to accept the maximum tolerable rate for each attribute compatible with placing substantial reliance on the internal accounting controls.
      (c) You expect an occurrence rate of 1 percent for the first two attributes listed in (1) above and a rate of 2 percent for attributes 3 and 4.
   3. Assume that the sample size used and the number of occurrences found for each attribute were as follows:

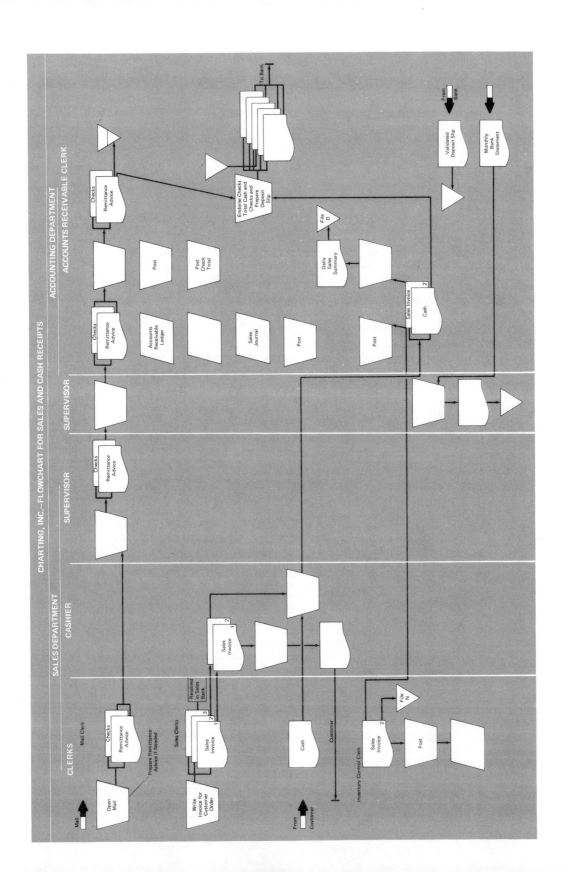

CHARTING, INC.—FLOWCHART FOR SALES AND CASH RECEIPTS

SALES DEPARTMENT

ACCOUNTING DEPARTMENT

CLERKS

CASHIER

SUPERVISOR

SUPERVISOR

ACCOUNTS RECEIVABLE CLERK

Mail Clerk

Mail

Open Mail

Checks
Remittance Advice

Prepare Remittance Advice If Needed

Sales Clerks

Write Invoice for Customer Order

Sales Invoice
1
2
3

Retained in Sales Bank

Sales Invoice
1
2

From Customer

Cash

Customer

Inventory Control Clerk

Sales Invoice
2

File N

Post

Checks
Remittance Advice

Checks
Remittance Advice

Checks
Remittance Advice

Accounts Receivable Ledger

Sales Journal

Post

Post

Post

Post Check Total

Post

Cash
2

Sales Invoice

Daily Sales Summary

File D

Endorse Checks Total Cash and Checks and Prepare Deposit Slip

To Bank

From Bank

Validated Deposit Slip

Monthly Bank Statement

Attribute	Sample Size Used	Number of Occurrences
1	75	1
2	75	2
3	100	0
4	100	3

For each attribute, determine the sample occurrence rate, the upper occurrence limit, and the allowance for sampling risk.

b. Comment on the results of your sample.

8–34. Until recently, Consolidated Electricity Company employed a batch processing system for recording the receipt of customer payments. The following narrative describes the procedures involved in this system.

The customer's payment and the remittance advice (a punch card) are received in the treasurer's office. An accounts receivable clerk in the treasurer's office keypunches the cash receipt into the remittance advice and forwards the card to the EDP department. The cash receipt is added to a control tape listing and then filed for deposit later in the day. When the deposit slips are received from EDP later in the day (approximately 2:30 P.M. each day), the cash receipts are removed from the file and deposited with the original deposit slip. The second copy of the deposit slip and the control tape are compared for accuracy before the deposit is made and then filed together.

In the EDP department, the remittance advices received from the treasurer's office are held until 2:00 P.M. daily. At that time the customer payments are processed to update the records on magnetic tape and to prepare a deposit slip in triplicate. During the update process, data are read, nondestructively, from the master accounts receivable tape, processed, and then recorded on a new master tape. The original and second copy of the deposit slip are forwarded to the treasurer's office. The old master tape (former accounts receivable file), the remittance advices (in customer number order), and the third copy of the deposit slip are stored and filed in a secure place. The updated accounts receivable master tape is maintained in the system for processing the next day.

Consolidated Electricity Company has revised and redesigned its computer system so that it has online capabilities. The new cash receipts procedures, described below, are designed to take advantage of the new system.

The customer's payment and remittance advice are received in the treasurer's office as before. A cathode ray tube terminal is located in the treasurer's office to enter the cash receipts. An operator keys in the customer's number and payment from the remittance advice and checks. The cash receipt is entered into the system once the operator has confirmed that the proper account and amount are displayed on the screen. The payment is then processed online against the accounts receivable file maintained on magnetic disk. The cash receipts are filed for deposit later in the day. The remittance advices are filed in the order they are processed; these cards will be kept until the next working day and then destroyed. The computer prints out a deposit slip in duplicate at 2:00 P.M. for all cash receipts since the last deposit. The deposit slips are forwarded to the treasurer's office. The cash receipts are removed from the file and deposited with the original deposit slip; the duplicate deposit slip is filed for further reference. At the close of business hours (5:00 P.M.) each day, the EDP department prepares a record of the current day's cash receipts activity on a magnetic tape. This tape is then stored in a secure place in the event of a systems malfunction; after ten working days, the tape is released for further use.

Required
a. Prepare a systems flowchart for the company's new online cash receipt procedures.
b. Have the new cash receipt procedures as designed and implemented by Consolidated Electric Company created any internal and systems control problems for the company? Explain your answer.

CMA (adapted)

CASE STUDY

8–35.* Empire Oil Company, an integrated oil company, operates throughout the United States.

Empire's treasury department is made up of two sections. One section handles cash receipts, and one section handles cash disbursements. The internal audit department approves all disbursements and reconciles all bank accounts.

Cash (includes currency, checks, and bank drafts) may be received in one of the following two ways:
1. In the home office directly from the customer.
2. In any one of 45 lockboxes maintained at various depository banks throughout the United States.

With regard to cash received in the home office, the mailroom forwards all mail addressed to the treasury department directly to the cash receipts section of that department unopened. Mail received with no department designation is opened by the mail room personnel. Any of this mail which contains cash is then forwarded directly to the cash receipts section.

With respect to cash received at lockboxes, daily the respective banks credit Empire's account and forward directly to the cash receipts section of the treasury department all remittance advices and a detailed listing showing the amount and source of the cash.

On receipt of the cash from the mailroom and data from the depository banks, the cash receipts section prepares a four-part form showing the date cash was received, the party from whom received, and the amount. After running an adding machine tape of the amounts and numbering the forms consecutively by day, one copy is furnished to the internal auditors who use it in connection with their bank reconciliations and the original and two copies are sent to the appropriate accounting sections (production and pipeline accounting, refining accounting, marketing accounting, etc.). These sections insert the general ledger account to be credited and return one copy to the cash receipts section. The accounting sections then see that the proper accounts are credited in the subsidiary ledgers (e.g., retail accounts receivable, for example).

The cash receipts section, upon receipt of the copies from the accounting sections, combines the copies with the remittance advices to make up the daily cash receipts vouchers. The vouchers are then forwarded to the computer department where the data are keypunched and fed into the system generating the general ledger.

Required
Evaluate the company's internal control over cash receipts transactions and indicate your recommendations for improvement.

9 Compliance Tests of Expenditure Cycle: Purchases and Cash Disbursements Transactions

STUDY OBJECTIVES

The study objectives of this chapter are to acquire an understanding of internal controls that are applicable to purchases and cash disbursements transactions in the expenditure cycle and the auditor's study and evaluation of these controls. To achieve these objectives, it is necessary for the reader to

- Recognize the internal control environment for the expenditure cycle.
- Be aware of the accounting control objectives pertaining to the expenditure cycle.
- Perceive the applicability of internal control principles to purchases and cash disbursements transactions.
- Comprehend the audit program for testing purchases and cash disbursements transactions.
- Understand the applicability of statistical sampling to purchases and cash disbursements transactions.
- Realize the impact of EDP on the testing of purchases and cash disbursements transactions.

This chapter begins with an explanation of the expenditure cycle and the internal control environment and objectives pertaining thereto. Then consideration is given to internal controls over purchases and cash disbursements transactions and to the study and evaluation of controls over these two classes of transactions. The organization and content of this chapter are similar to the preceding chapter pertaining to the revenue cycle.

Nature of the Expenditure Cycle

The expenditure cycle involves the activities associated with the acquisition of and payment for plant assets, goods and services, and labor. There are three major classes of transactions in this cycle: (1) purchasing, (2) cash disbursements, and (3) payroll. The first two classes of transactions are considered in this chapter; the third is discussed in Chapter 10.

This cycle does not include the acquisition of short- or long-term securities, the redemption of long-term debt, or the reacquisition of company capital stock. These transactions are considered to be part of the investing and financing cycles, respectively, and are explained in Chapter 14.

Internal Control Environment

The internal control environment in a company is influenced by the company's organizational structure, personnel, budgets and internal reports, internal auditing, and sound practices. An organization chart for the expenditure cycle is illustrated in Figure 9-1.

Both the competency and the integrity of personnel involved in purchases and cash disbursements transactions are important in creating a good internal accounting control environment. Purchasing agents, for example, may have direct personal interface with suppliers, and they may participate in extensive negotiations of price, quality specifications, and terms. Such personnel are frequently subjected to numerous pressures by solicitous vendors. In such cases, lack of integrity in a purchasing agent could lead to "kickbacks" from suppliers and the placing of purchase orders where the agent may have a vested interest. Similarly, dishonesty among receiving clerks and storeroom employees could lead to irregularities in the processing and safekeeping of goods received. Qualified and trustworthy personnel are equally important in the vouching and payment of purchases and the preparation and payment of the payroll.

Many companies prepare budgets for cash, capital expenditures, and repairs and maintenance expenses. Budget expectations should be compared with actual results periodically. Sound practices include the bonding of authorized check signers, custodians of petty cash funds, and storeroom employees.

Internal Control Objectives

For the expenditure cycle, the operative objectives of internal accounting control may be stated as follows:

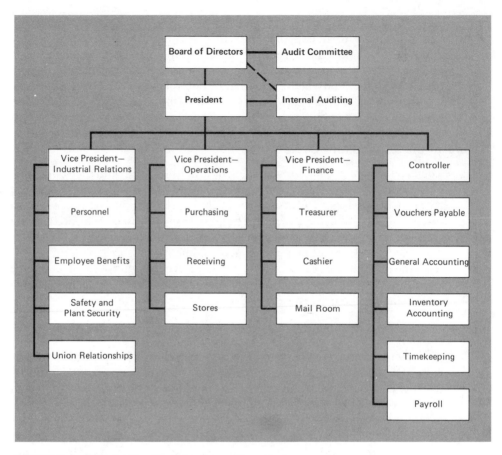

FIGURE 9-1. Organization Chart for Expenditure Cycle

- Expenditure cycle transactions (i.e., purchases, cash disbursements, and payroll) are properly executed.
- Expenditure cycle transactions are properly recorded.
- Custody of assets (i.e., inventories, plant assets, and prepayments) resulting from expenditure cycle transactions is properly maintained.

These three objectives will provide the framework for discussing (1) the basic features of accounting control over specific classes of transactions within the expenditure cycle and (2) the study and evaluation of internal control over expenditure cycle transactions.

INTERNAL CONTROL OVER PURCHASES AND CASH DISBURSEMENTS TRANSACTIONS

Basic Considerations

Purchasing (acquisition) and cash disbursements (payments) transactions involve the acquisition of goods and services from outsiders and the subsequent payment of the liabilities that have been incurred. The acquisition part of this cycle extends beyond the buying of merchandise for resale or raw materials for use in production. Purchasing also includes the methods and procedures that culminate in the acquisition of other assets (property, plant, equipment, intangibles, and prepayments) and myriad day-to-day operating expenses such as advertising, repairs, utilities, and insurance. Cash disbursement transactions, in turn, involve the process of preparing, signing, and mailing checks to vendors and providers of services for the benefits that have been received.

Throughout the chapter, emphasis is given to the acquisition of and payment for goods in a company that utilizes a voucher system for cash disbursements.

The following matters are basic to an understanding of purchases and cash disbursements transactions in the expenditure cycle:

Functions

Executing
- Requisitioning goods, other assets, and services.
- Ordering the items requested.
- Receiving the items ordered.
- Storing goods received for inventory.
- Preparing the payment voucher.
- Paying the liability.

Recording
- Journalizing and posting purchases and cash disbursements.
- Updating unpaid voucher file.
- Updating inventory records.

Custody
- Protecting inventory.
- Maintaining correctness of inventory records.

Common documents

- *Purchase requisition.* A written request made by an employee to purchasing to buy goods and services.
- *Purchase order.* A written offer by purchasing to another entity to purchase goods and services specified in the order.
- *Receiving report.* A report prepared upon the receipt of goods showing the kinds and quantities of goods received from vendors.
- *Vendor's invoice.* A form stating the items shipped or services rendered, the amount due, and the payment terms.
- *Voucher.* A form indicating the vendor, amount due, and payment date of purchases received. It is used internally as the authorization for recording and paying the liability.
- *Check.* A formal order to a bank to pay the payee the amount indicated on demand.
- *Remittance advice.* A memo stating the items being paid by a check.
- *Daily voucher summary.* A report of total vouchers processed during the day.
- *Daily check summary.* A report showing total checks issued during the day.

Accounting records

- *Books of original entry.* Voucher register, with multiple columns for debit accounts, and check register.
- *Subsidiary ledgers.* Creditors, plant and equipment, perpetual inventory, and manufacturing overhead.
- *General ledger accounts.* Cash, accounts payable, inventory, plant assets, manufacturing overhead control, and operating expenses.

File data

- *Unfilled purchase requisition file.* Contains copies of requisitions forwarded to purchasing that are open (unfilled).
- *Unfilled purchase order file.* Holds open purchase orders.
- *Approved vendor file.* Contains a list of vendors with whom orders may be placed.
- *Receiving report file.* Contains copies of receiving reports issued.
- *Unpaid voucher file.* Contains approved vouchers filed by date payment is due.
- *Paid voucher file.* Holds vouchers that have been paid.

Materiality and Risk

Purchasing and cash disbursements transactions affect more financial statement accounts than all the other cycles combined. On the balance sheet, these transactions directly affect every current asset account (except marketable securities and receivables), all plant and intangible assets, and accounts payable. The income statement effects are similarly pervasive.

Numerous functions are involved in executing and in recording these two classes of transactions and in maintaining custody over the resulting assets. Moreover, the volume of transactions is high. Thus, material errors and irregularities could occur in the processing of these transactions.

As previously explained, the risk of such occurrences is inversely related to the effectiveness of the client's system of internal control. To assess this risk, it is necessary for the auditor to make a study and evaluation of the client's controls. When the auditor intends to rely on the controls in performing substantive tests of expenditure cycle balances, the review and testing of the controls may be extensive.

Purchases and Cash Disbursements Transactions Are Properly Executed

These transactions in the expenditure cycle are properly executed when they are authorized by management and are executed in accordance with authorized terms. The execution of these two classes of transactions involves the following functions and specific accounting control objectives.

FUNCTION	SPECIFIC ACCOUNTING CONTROL OBJECTIVE
1. Requisitioning goods, other assets, and services	Requisitions are initiated and approved by authorized individuals
2. Ordering items requested	Purchase orders are properly executed as to price, quantity, and quality
3. Receiving items ordered	Goods received are counted, inspected, and agreed to purchase orders
4. Storing goods received for inventory	Goods received are added to inventory and properly safeguarded and accounted for
5. Preparing the payment voucher	Vouchers are for goods and services actually received and are correct as to amount, account classification, and payee
6. Paying the liability	Checks are supported by approved vouchers, are correct as to amount and payee, and are signed by authorized signers

The internal control principles applicable to these functions are explained below.

Authorization Procedures

Authorization is required at a number of control points: (1) initiating the request, (2) placing the order, (3) receiving the goods, and (4) paying the vendor. Most companies permit general authorizations for regular operating purposes. Such authorizations usually extend to purchases of inventory and raw materials when reorder points are reached, to normal repair and maintenance work, and to similar items. In contrast, company policy frequently requires specific authorization for capital expenditures and lease contracts. Operating within these policies, designated individuals are permitted to initiate purchase requests. Requisitions may be manually or electronically prepared. Each request should be signed by a supervisor who has budgetary responsibility for the category of expenditure.

The purchasing department has the authority to place (or issue) purchase orders for goods and services that have been requested. Before placing an order, purchasing should ascertain the best source of supply and for major items it should obtain competitive bids. A valid purchase order represents the authorization to receive incoming goods and services.

Authorization for payment of the goods and services originates in the vouchers payable department through the preparation of a voucher, and culminates in the signing of a check by authorized signers.

Segregation of Functions

The major functions involved in executing purchases and cash disbursements transactions should be assigned to different departments and individuals. Based on the organization chart in Figure 9-1, an appropriate segregation of functions is shown at bottom of this page. Under this plan, the work of one employee provides a check on the accuracy of the work of another. For example, the storeroom receipt for goods received confirms the receiving department's representation that the goods were received.

Documentation Procedures

Documentation is necessary for each of the major steps in the purchasing and cash disbursements functions. The key documents in ordering goods and services are the purchase requisition and the purchase order.

The requisition should specify the item(s) desired and be approved by a supervisor in the originating department. Because requisitions may originate in any department, they are rarely prenumbered. Purchase orders are prepared in the purchasing department. The orders should contain a precise description of the goods and services desired, quantities, price, and vendor name and address. Purchase orders should be prenumbered and signed by an authorized purchasing agent. The purchase order is sent to the vendor, and copies are distributed internally to receiving, vouchers payable, and the department that made the request. On the receiving department copy, the quantity ordered is generally obliterated so that receiving clerks will make careful counts of the goods received.

FUNCTION	DEPARTMENT	RELATED ACTIVITIES
1. Requisitioning goods, other assets, and services	Stores, Maintenance, Plant, etc.	Initiate and approve purchase requisitions
2. Ordering the items requested	Purchasing	Prepare, approve, and issue purchase orders; perform follow-up on unfilled orders
3. Receiving the items ordered	Receiving	Receive, count, and inspect goods and other assets received; deliver items received to initiating department; obtain signed receipt from initiator; prepare receiving reports
4. Storing goods received for inventory	Stores	Maintain custody of goods received for stock; acknowledge receipt of goods ordered
5. Preparing the payment voucher	Vouchers Payable	Prepare vouchers for payment; prepare daily voucher summary; maintain voucher files
6. Paying the liability	Treasurer	Prepare, sign, and mail checks to vendors, prepare daily check summary

Prenumbered receiving reports provide the documentation for goods and services received. In many companies, a purchase order must be on file before goods can be accepted. Receiving department personnel are expected to indicate the quantity and description of the goods and vendor name and address on the receiving report. On delivery of the goods to the initiating department, receiving clerks should obtain a signed receipt. In some cases, receipt may be indicated by initialing the receiving report.

The key documents in recording and paying the liability are the voucher and the check.

Voucher

There are many variations in voucher systems. A common arrangement is to prepare a separate document for the voucher. The preparation of a voucher involves the following control procedures:

- Establish the agreement of the vendor's invoice with the receiving report and purchase order.
- Determine the mathematical accuracy of the vendor's invoice.
- Indicate on the documents (or voucher) that the preceding verification steps have been performed.
- Prepare the voucher in duplicate and attach supporting documents (purchase order, receiving report, and vendor's invoice).
- Approve the voucher for payment by having an authorized person sign the voucher.

Other kinds of supporting documentation may be required when the voucher relates to services and other assets. In no case, however, should a voucher be approved without appropriate documentation. One copy of the voucher with supporting documentation attached is filed in an unpaid voucher file, and a copy is sent to accounting for recording.

Check

The issuance of checks is the responsibility of the treasurer's office. The control procedures for issuing checks include the following:

- The bank must be notified of the names of individuals authorized to sign checks, and samples of their signatures must be filed with the bank.
- Company imprinted and prenumbered checks should be used.
- Check-protection devices should be utilized in printing the amount of the check.
- Each check should be supported by an approved voucher and be accompanied by a remittance advice.
- Authorized check signers should review all supporting documentation before signing a check.
- Supporting documentation should be stamped, perforated, or otherwise mutilated after payment.
- The check signer, or last check signer when two signatures are required, should control the mailing of the check and remittance advice.
- No checks should be issued to "cash" or "bearer."

Daily summaries should be prepared of vouchers and checks for use in accounting. A flowchart for the execution of these two classes of transactions in the expenditure cycle is illustrated in Figure 9-2.

Physical Controls and Independent Internal Verification

One application of physical controls is enclosed and locked storerooms. Other applications include scales for weighing bulk materials and protective check-writing equipment in issuing checks.

Independent internal verification occurs when a second voucher clerk validates the accuracy and completeness of the voucher before it is approved by a supervisor. A similar review is sometimes required in the treasurer's department before the voucher is sent to the check signers.

Purchases and Cash Disbursements Transactions Are Properly Recorded

The functions and the specific accounting control objectives pertaining to the recording of these transactions are as follows:

FUNCTION	DEPARTMENT	SPECIFIC ACCOUNTING CONTROL OBJECTIVE
1. Journalizing and posting purchases and cash disbursements transactions	General Accounting	Purchases and cash disbursements are correctly journalized as to amount, account classification, and accounting period
2. Updating unpaid voucher file	Vouchers Payable	Unpaid vouchers are properly filed in an unpaid voucher file
3. Updating inventory records	Inventory Accounting	Purchases are promptly and correctly posted to perpetual inventory records

The internal control principles applicable to these functions are explained below.

Segregation of Functions

Accounting personnel who record these transactions should not participate in the execution of the transactions. Moreover, within accounting, individuals who journalize vouchers should not maintain the unpaid voucher file.

Accounting Records and Procedures

The primary source documents for the accounting entries are the approved voucher and the disbursement check. In journalizing vouchers, accounting personnel should review the reasonableness of the account classifications

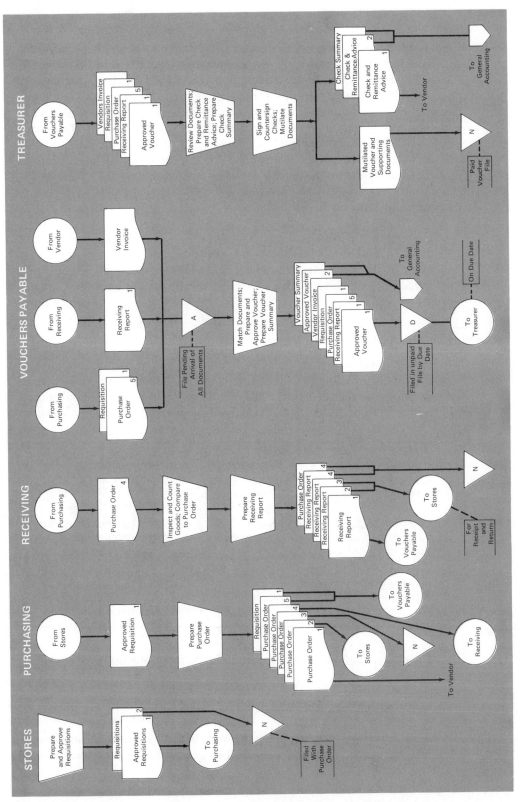

FIGURE 9–2. Manual System for Executing Purchases and Cash Disbursements Transactions

and trace any unusual items to the chart of accounts. Accounting procedures include the posting of purchases to inventory records directly from the voucher and the filing of the vouchers in an unpaid (tickler) voucher file.

The check register entries should agree with the data on the check. Special care should be exercised in recording checks issued near the end of the accounting period to assure that the checks are entered in the proper period. Checks do not represent disbursements until they are either mailed or delivered to the payee. A flowchart for the recording of purchases and cash disbursements transactions is shown in Figure 9-3.

Independent Internal Verification

Accounting receives daily summaries of vouchers and checks. As shown in Figure 9-3, these totals should be independently compared with the corresponding totals of the voucher and check registers respectively. Accounting personnel are expected to also verify the numerical sequencing of the entries.

Custody of Assets Is Properly Maintained

Inventory, plant assets, and cash in bank are among the major types of assets associated with the expenditure cycle. Consideration here is focused on inventories and cash in bank. The following functions and internal control objectives are applicable to the safeguarding of these assets.

FUNCTION	DEPARTMENT	SPECIFIC ACCOUNTING CONTROL OBJECTIVE
1. Protecting inventory	Stores	Access to inventory is restricted to authorized personnel
2. Maintaining correctness of inventory records	Inventory Accounting	Recorded balances are independently compared with existing assets at reasonable intervals
3. Maintaining correctness of cash in bank	General Accounting	Recorded balances are periodically independently reconciled with bank balances

The internal control principles pertaining to these functions are explained below.

Physical Controls and Authorization Procedures

Physical controls over inventory include locked storerooms and warehouses. Access to storage areas should be restricted to authorized personnel.

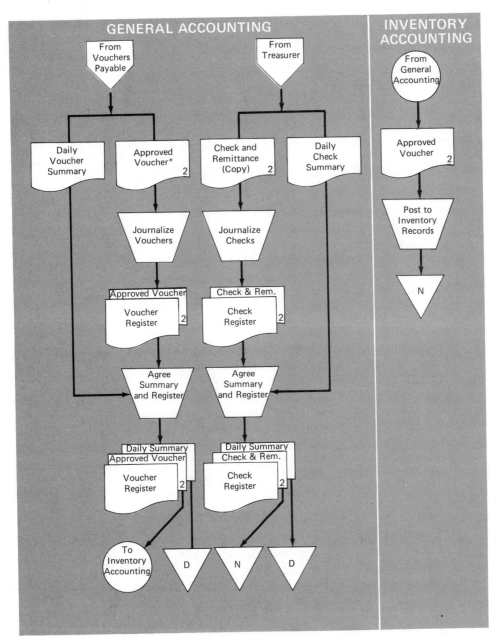

FIGURE 9–3. Manual System for Recording Purchases and Cash Disbursements Transactions

Independent Internal Verification and Segregation of Functions

Periodically, there should be an independent comparison of recorded inventory balances with existing assets. This comparison is often made on a cycle basis where designated segments are counted or inventoried on a rotating basis. Periodically, these records should also be reconciled to general ledger control accounts. Similarly, monthly bank reconciliations should be made by personnel not otherwise involved with executing or recording of checks.

STUDY AND EVALUATION OF INTERNAL CONTROL

The auditor's methodology for making a study and evaluation of controls over purchases and cash disbursements transactions involves the same steps and decision paths followed for other major classes of transactions.

Review of Purchases and Cash Disbursements Systems

As previously explained, the review consists of two phases: (1) preliminary and (2) completion. In this case, the preliminary review pertains to the internal control environment for expenditure cycle transactions and the flow of purchases and cash disbursements transactions through the accounting system. The completion phase relates to the client's prescribed internal accounting controls over these two classes of transactions. The essential steps in the completion phase of the review are described below.

Gathering Information

In obtaining information about prescribed controls over purchases and cash disbursements transactions, the auditor uses inquiry, observation, and review of documentation. Questionnaires for these transactions are shown in Figures 9-4 and 9-5. It will be recalled that the questions relate to specific control procedures considered by the auditor to be necessary for effective control. As in the preceding two chapters, each question is referenced to a specific function. The auditor's understanding of prescribed controls should be documented in the working papers in the form of flowcharts, in narrative memoranda, and in answers to questionnaires.

Making the Preliminary Evaluations

The primary purpose of the preliminary evaluations of purchases and cash disbursements transactions is to identify control procedures that can be relied on in making substantive tests of related balances, assuming satisfactory compliance. The evaluations are made by (1) considering the errors and irregularities that could occur in performing each function, (2) identifying the controls necessary to prevent or detect the occurrences, and (3) determining whether the necessary controls are prescribed by the client. Representative listings of errors and irregularities and necessary control procedures for each of these classes of transactions are shown in Figures 9-6 (page 289) and 9-7 (page 290). Columns 2 and 3 of each form are based on generalized knowledge about these transactions, adapted as necessary by the auditor to the specific client. Information concerning the prescribed controls over purchases and cash disbursements is obtained from the information gathering step of the review.

CYCLE: Expenditure		CLASS OF TRANSACTIONS: Purchases
	YES	NO

EXECUTING

1. Is an approved purchase requisition required for each purchase? (E1)
2. Is an authorized purchase order required for each purchase? (E2)
3. Are prenumbered purchase orders used and accounted for? (E2)
4. Is a purchase order required before receiving can accept a shipment? (E3)
5. Are goods counted, inspected, and compared with purchase order upon receipt? (E3)
6. Are prenumbered receiving reports used, accounted for, and signed by a receiving clerk? (E3)
7. Is a signed receipt obtained from storeroom upon delivery of goods by receiving? (E4)
8. Are purchase orders, receiving reports, and vendors' invoices matched in preparing vouchers? (E5)
9. Are vouchers internally verified for accuracy? (E5)

RECORDING

1. Is numerical sequence of vouchers followed in journalizing? (R1)
2. Are all issued vouchers accounted for in journalizing? (R1)
3. Are unpaid voucher file and perpetual inventory records independently maintained? (R2, R3)

CUSTODY

1. Are goods stored in locked areas with restricted access? (C1)
2. Are there periodic independent comparisons of inventory records with goods on hand? (C2)

FIGURE 9-4. Internal Control Questionnaire: Purchases Transactions

From a comparison of necessary and prescribed controls, the auditor makes a preliminary evaluation of the controls expected to be relied upon. If a necessary control is not prescribed, or a prescribed control does not appear adequate to prevent or detect the error or irregularity, the auditor considers the effect of the weakness on the remainder of the audit. He may, for example, look for compensating controls or proceed directly to the design of expanded substantive tests. The auditor's preliminary evaluations of the prescribed control procedures for each of these two classes of transactions should be documented in the working papers.

Compliance Tests of Prescribed Controls

Using the possible compliance tests shown in Figure 9-7, the auditor prepares the audit programs for determining whether the controls to be relied on are operating as planned. Illustrative audit programs for purchases and cash disbursements transactions are shown in Figures 9-8 and 9-9 (pages 291 and 292). Note that for controls that leave an audit trail of performance, the sampling unit for purchases is the voucher, and the sampling unit for cash

CYCLE: Expenditure	CLASS OF TRANSACTIONS: Cash Disbursements

EXECUTING*	YES	NO
1. Are all disbursements (except for petty cash) made by check?		
2. Are imprinted and prenumbered checks used?		
3. Is a check-protection device used in printing the check amount?		
4. Is each check supported by an approved voucher?		
5. Is supporting documentation mutilated after payment?		
6. Are two signatures required on each check?		
7. Does last check signer mail the check and remittance advice?		
8. Are there prohibitions against issuing checks to cash or bearer?		
9. Is the signing of blank checks prohibited?		
10. Is a daily summary of checks prepared?		

RECORDING

1. Are accounting personnel prohibited from signing checks? (R1)
2. Are daily summaries of checks compared with check register totals? (R1)

CUSTODY

1. Are there periodic independent reconciliations of bank accounts? (C3)

* All questions pertain to function E6, paying the liability.

FIGURE 9–5. Internal Control Questionnaire: Cash Disbursements Transactions

disbursements is the "paid" check. Both programs also include observation, inquiry, and reperformance. Alternatively, the purchase order or the receiving report could be used as the sampling unit for purchases.

Dual Purpose Testing

As previously explained, the auditor may decide to perform *dual purpose tests* during interim work. Thus, while the samples of vouchers and checks are available for use, the auditor may perform substantive tests of the details of the accounting treatment of the transactions. It will be recalled that the purpose of substantive tests of details is to ascertain the correctness of the accounts or conversely the existence of any monetary errors in the accounts. The tests for purchases and cash disbursements transactions may consist of the following:

• Compare the amount, date, payee, and account classification on the voucher with the corresponding data in the related voucher register entry for accuracy
• Compare the detailed data on the check with the details of the related check register entry for accuracy.

In addition, the auditor notes the monetary errors found in reperforming control procedures in step A4 of each audit program.

Function	Possible Errors and Irregularities	Necessary Control Procedures	Possible Compliance Tests
EXECUTING			
Requisitioning	Excess quantities of goods may be ordered	Review of requisitions for reasonableness by supervisor	Examine evidence of supervisor approval
Ordering	Purchases may be for unauthorized purposes	Approved purchase requisition for each purchase order	Examine purchase order for supporting requisition
Receiving	Receiving reports may be prepared for goods that were not ordered	Purchase order for each shipment	Examine receiving report for accompanying purchase order
	Goods received may be incorrectly counted	Storeroom count and signed receipt for goods received	Review evidence of storeroom receipt
Storing	Goods received may not be as ordered	Comparison of goods received with goods requisitioned	Review evidence of storeroom verification
Preparing the voucher	Vouchers may be prepared for goods that were unauthorized or not received	Matching purchase order, receiving report, and vendor's invoice for each voucher	Review voucher for evidence of supporting documents
	Vouchers may be incorrect as to payee and amount	Internal verification of voucher accuracy	Examine evidence of verification
RECORDING			
Journalizing and posting purchases transactions	Vouchers may be incorrectly classified	Supervisory review of entries for reasonableness	Inquire of supervisor concerning findings
Updating unpaid voucher file	A voucher may not be filed	Periodic reconciliation of accounts payable with unpaid vouchers	Review evidence of reconciliation
Updating inventory records	A purchase may not be posted to inventory records	Periodic reconciliation of control and subsidiary records	Review evidence of reconciliation
CUSTODY			
Protecting inventory	Inventory may be stolen	Locked storerooms	Observe storage security
Maintaining correctness of inventory records	A purchase may be posted to the wrong inventory card	Periodic independent comparisons of records with goods on hand	Review evidence of reconciliation; observe count

FIGURE 9–6. Preliminary Evaluation Considerations: Purchases Transactions

Function	Possible Errors and Irregularities	Necessary Control Procedures	Possible Compliance Tests
EXECUTING			
Paying the liability (review of documentation)	Voucher may be incomplete or lack supervisory approval	Review voucher for completeness and approval	Examine voucher for evidence of approval
	A voucher may be paid twice	Mutilation of voucher on payment	Examine "paid" vouchers for cancellation
Paying the liability (preparing and signing checks)	Checks may be incorrect as to payee and amount	Internal verification of checks with supporting voucher	Examine evidence of verification
Paying the liability (distributing checks)	Checks may be diverted to unauthorized payees	No checks payable to cash or bearer	Review checks for named payees
RECORDING			
Journalizing and posting cash disbursements	A check may not be recorded	Accounting for all prenumbered checks in journalizing	Review evidence of verification
CUSTODY			
Maintaining correctness of cash in bank	A mathematical error may be made in computing the bank balance	Periodic independent bank reconciliations	Review evidence of reconciliation

FIGURE 9–7. Preliminary Evaluation Considerations: Cash Disbursements Transactions

From these tests, the auditor can estimate the magnitude of monetary errors in the processing of purchases and cash disbursements transactions.

Final Evaluation of the Controls

The final evaluation of the controls is based on the results from compliance testing of these two classes of transactions. In analyzing the results, the auditor considers both the number of deviations from prescribed control procedures and the causes of the deviations. The auditor may express his reliance on the controls in terms of whether the risk of errors and irregularities in the processing of purchases and cash disbursements transactions is low, moderate, or high. The auditor then determines the effects of his evaluations of specific control procedures over these transactions on the nature, timing, and extent of substantive tests. For example, if there is moderate risk of errors in preparing vouchers, the auditor will perform more substantive tests on accounts payable balances than when the risk of such errors is low. Substantive tests of expenditure cycle balances are explained in Part III of this textbook.

TYPE OF TESTING: Compliance	PURPOSE: Study and Evaluation of Internal Control
CYCLE: Expenditure	CLASS OF TRANSACTIONS: Purchases

A. CONTROLS IN EXECUTING PURCHASES TRANSACTIONS ARE OPERATING AS PLANNED.

1. Examine sample of vouchers for the year to date for evidence of
   - Supporting documentation (purchase order, receiving report, and vendor's invoice).
   - Verification of agreement with supporting documentation.
   - Verification of mathematical accuracy.
   - Signed receipt from storeroom for goods received.
   - Supervisory approval of voucher.
2. Observe segregation of duties in performing control procedures.
3. Inquire of personnel about their performance of control procedures.
4. Reperform the verification procedures in (1) above on some vouchers.

B. CONTROLS IN RECORDING PURCHASES TRANSACTIONS ARE OPERATING AS PLANNED.

1. Examine a sample of daily voucher summaries for verification with daily voucher register entries.
2. Observe segregation of functions between general ledger accounting and inventory accounting.

C. CONTROLS OVER THE CUSTODY OF INVENTORY ARE OPERATING AS PLANNED.

1. Observe storage of inventory and means for restricting access to storeroom.
2. Review evidence of periodic inventory counts and reconciliations with inventory records.
3. Examine evidence of periodic agreement of inventory control with inventory records.

FIGURE 9-8. Audit Program: Compliance Tests of Purchases Transactions

STATISTICAL SAMPLING IN COMPLIANCE TESTING

Statistical sampling may be utilized in performing compliance tests of purchases and cash disbursements transactions. Each of the major steps in the design and implementation of an attribute sampling plan for purchase transactions for the Kemp Company is illustrated below.

Design of the Sampling Plan

In attribute sampling, the objectives of the test are usually expressed in terms of the proper execution or recording of transactions. In designing the sample, tests are made of the functions that relate to the overall objective of the plan. For this case study, the objective is execution of purchases transactions. The test includes the functions of ordering, receiving, and preparing the voucher. The sampling unit is the prenumbered voucher and the population consists of 18,000 vouchers. These elements of the sampling plan, together with the attributes corresponding to the controls the auditor wishes to test for reliance, are shown in the sample design section of the working paper in Figure 9-10.

TYPE OF TESTING: Compliance   **PURPOSE: Study and Evaluation of Internal Control**
CYCLE: Expenditure   **CLASS OF TRANSACTIONS: Cash Disbursements**

A. CONTROLS IN EXECUTING CASH DISBURSEMENTS TRANSACTIONS
     ARE OPERATING AS PLANNED.

    1. Examine sample of "paid" checks for the year to date for evidence of
        • Supporting approved voucher.
        • Verification of agreement of check with voucher.
        • Cancellation of voucher upon payment.
        • Signatures of authorized check signers.
        • Proper numerical sequencing of checks.
    2. Observe segregation of duties between voucher preparation and signing
       and mailing of checks.
    3. Inquire of personnel about their performance of control procedures.
    4. Reperform the control procedures in (1) above on some checks.

B. CONTROLS IN RECORDING CASH DISBURSEMENTS TRANSACTIONS ARE
     OPERATING AS PLANNED.

    1. Examine a sample of daily check summaries for evidence of verification with daily
       check register entries.
    2. Observe segregation of functions between accounting and treasurer's department.
    3. Inspect check register for numerical sequencing of checks.

C. CONTROLS OVER THE CUSTODY OF CASH IN BANK ARE OPERATING AS PLANNED.

    1. Examine evidence of periodic bank reconciliations.

FIGURE 9-9. Audit Program: Compliance Tests of Cash Disbursements Transactions

Because of the large volume of purchase transactions during the year and the significant impact of purchase transactions on a large number of accounts, the auditor wishes to place substantial reliance on the controls. Accordingly, he specifies tolerable occurrence rates of 7 percent or below for each attribute. A low risk of overreliance of 5 percent is specified for all of the tests. The auditor's past experience with this client is used in arriving at the expected population occurrence rates shown in column 4 of Figure 9-10. From these data, sample sizes are determined using the tables in Chapter 6 and entered in column 5. In this case, the auditor decides to round the sample sizes up by a few units, as shown in column 6, to provide for voided or invalid voucher numbers.

Executing the Plan

The sample items are randomly selected and the vouchers are examined for each attribute. Occurrences of deviations are recorded on a separate worksheet (not shown), and the frequency and percentage of occurrences for each attribute are entered in columns 7 and 8 of the sample results section of Figure 9-10.

Prepared by: C.G.A. Date: 8/2/X1
Reviewed by: R.C.P. Date: 8/14/X1

Kent Company
Sampling for Attribute — Purchase Transactions
12/31/X1

SAMPLE DESIGN

Objective: To determine whether official controls over the execution of purchase transactions are applied as described.

Sampling Unit and Population: Vouchers: Population = 18,200 — numbers 612,345–793,244.

Selection method: Random, using random number table with stated start.

(1) Attributes	(2) Risk-of-Over-reliance (%)	(3) Tolerable Occurrence Rate (%)	(4) Expected Population Occurrence Rate (%)	(5) Sample Size Per Table	(5) Sample Size Used	(7) Number of Occurrences Found	(8) Sample-Occurrence Rate (%)	(9) Upper-Occurrence Limit (%)	(10) Allowance for Sampling Risk (%)
1. Approval, purchase order indicating receipt, and vendor's invoice for each voucher.	5	5	1	93	100	1	1	4.7	3.7
2. Verification of agreement of invoice with supporting documentation.	5	7	2	88	90	1	1.1	5.2	4.1
3. Verification of mathematical accuracy of invoice.	5	7	2	88	90	1	1.1	5.2	4.1
4. Supervisory approval of voucher.	5	5	1	93	100	0	0	3.0	3.0

SAMPLE RESULTS

Sample results: All attributes were met. All occurrence rates were minor. Controls can be relied upon.

Management letter: None

FIGURE 9–10. Statistical Sampling Plan Working Paper: Compliance Tests of Purchase's Transactions

Evaluating the Results

In the concluding phase of the sampling plan, the auditor makes both a quantitative and qualitative assessment of the sample results. An upper occurrence limit is determined for each attribute using the tables in Chapter 6 and entered in column 9. The allowance for sampling risk (column 9 − column 8) may be calculated and entered in column 10.

Comparison of columns 9 and 3 reveals that the auditor's objective was met for each attribute. In each case, the upper occurrence limit is less than the tolerable rate. Thus, the auditor can conclude that at the specified risk of overreliance, the true but unknown population occurrence rate does not exceed the upper occurrence limit.

Further, qualitative assessment of the nature and causes of the occurrences of deviations produced no evidence of any irregularities or other serious problems. Thus, the auditor feels justified in concluding that the controls that were tested may be relied on for the purpose of determining substantive tests of related account balances.

ELECTRONIC DATA PROCESSING

EDP may be utilized in executing and recording purchases and cash disbursements transactions. A case study for purchases is presented below together with an explanation of the methodology for making tests of controls in the system.

Description of the System

In Huran Inc., the computer is used to process approved vouchers, disbursement checks, and related output. Input to the system is in the form of magnetic tape, and file data also are maintained on this medium. A flowchart of the major features of the system is presented in Figure 9-11.

As shown in the flowchart, data control verifies and logs the control totals received from vouchers payable. It then sends the vouchers and transmittal form to data entry where the vouchers are keypunched onto tape and verified. Next, the purchases transaction tape is forwarded to computer processing where it is used in two computer runs.

Run 1. This run involves editing the data for reasonableness and completeness, and balancing the data. From this run, a valid tape of purchases transactions is produced and a printout is made of erroneous data and control totals.

Run 2. As shown in Figure 9-11, this run involves the processing of the valid purchases transaction tape with the tapes of the accounts payable and inventory master files. The outputs from this run consist of printed reports of errors and control totals, the voucher register, and updated master file tapes.

The processing of checks also involves two computer runs.

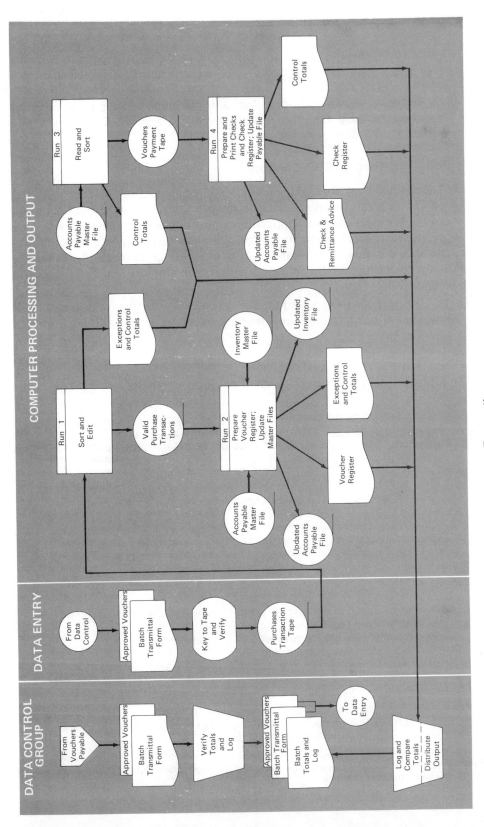

FIGURE 9–11. EDP System for Purchases and Cash Disbursements Transactions

Run 3. In this run, the accounts payable master file is read to identify the vouchers due for payment and to produce a vouchers payment tape.

Run 4. As shown in the flowchart, this run involves the processing of the vouchers payment tape to prepare the checks and check register and to update the accounts payable master file.

Study and Evaluation of EDP Controls

The methodology for making a study and evaluation of EDP controls over purchases transactions is similar to the procedures described in Chapters 7 and 8. Both general and application controls should be reviewed and compliance tests should be performed on all EDP controls on which reliance is to be placed in making substantive tests of resulting balances. An audit program for testing EDP application controls in this case study is shown in Figure 9-12.

The program provides for the use of test data in testing controls in the edit program of run 1 and the program logic in run 2. Invalid test data for run 1 may include:

- Missing or invalid vendor number.
- Missing or invalid purchases distribution code number.

TYPE OF TESTING: Compliance   **PURPOSE: EDP Application Controls**
CYCLE: Expenditure   **CLASS OF TRANSACTIONS: Purchases and Cash**
                                                                               Disbursements

---

A. INPUT CONTROLS ARE PROPERLY FUNCTIONING:

1. Review, on test basis, reconciliation of batch totals in data control with control totals in run 1.
2. Selectively review exception listings of run 1 and investigate uncleared items.
3. Prepare and use test data to test program controls in edit routine of run 1.
4. Select sample of entries in voucher register and vouch entries to source documents.

B. PROCESSING CONTROLS ARE PROPERLY FUNCTIONING:

1. Observe reconciling procedures over control data in runs 2-4 and selectively trace control totals to input controls.
2. Review error listings of run 2 and investigate unusual items.
3. Use test deck data to test program of run 2.
4. Use generalized audit software to test accounts payable and inventory master files.

C. OUTPUT CONTROLS ARE PROPERLY FUNCTIONING:

1. Review reconciliation of output controls with input controls.
2. On a test basis, obtain printouts of master files used in runs 2 and 4 and use source documents to reconcile the two sets of file data.

FIGURE 9–12. Audit Program: Compliance Tests of EDP Application Controls for Purchases and Cash Disbursements Transactions

- Missing dollar amount.
- Missing payment due date.
- Missing payment terms.
- Alphabetical characters in numerical field.

Both valid and invalid data may be used in testing the controls in run 2. The latter may consist of a purchase for a negative amount, a purchase with invalid pricing data, and a purchase for a zero amount.

Generalized audit software applications to the master files parallel those described in Chapter 7 for the accounts receivable master file. Thus, software can be used to randomly select a sample of inventory or vendor accounts and/or to make a reasonableness test of the entire file.

From evidence obtained in testing the system, the auditor proceeds to evaluate the EDP controls and determine the extent to which substantive tests of inventory and accounts payable balances are to be restricted.

CONCLUDING COMMENTS

An entity's expenditure cycle pertains to the acquisition and payment of plant assets, goods and services, and labor. The scope of this chapter has been limited to purchases and cash disbursements transactions. Each of the objectives and principles of internal control is applicable to these two classes of transactions. In performing compliance tests of transactions in a manual processing system, the auditor relies primarily on vouchers and paid checks. Compliance tests of the system may also involve statistical sampling and EDP.

Further attention is given to the expenditure cycle in the next chapter, where controls over payroll transactions are explained and illustrated.

REVIEW QUESTIONS

9–1. What classes of transactions are included in the expenditure cycle?

9–2. What departments report to (a) the vice president of operations and (b) the controller in the expenditure cycle?

9–3. What are the materiality and risks associated with purchases and cash disbursements transactions?

9–4. The purchasing aspect of this cycle extends only to the acquisition of inventory items, and cash disbursements applies to all payments. Discuss the validity of these assertions.

9–5. Identify the functions pertaining to the executing and the recording of purchases and cash disbursements transactions and custody of related assets.

9–6. Indicate the specific internal accounting control objectives and a proper departmental assignment of duties for the first four functions involved in executing purchase transactions.

9–7. a. What authorizations are necessary in executing purchases transactions?
b. What errors and irregularities may occur when these transactions are not authorized?

9–8. Describe the primary activities of (a) the receiving, (b) stores, and (c) vouchers payable departments in executing transactions.

9–9. Enumerate the steps in (a) preparing vouchers and (b) issuing checks.

9–10. What are the specific accounting control objectives for the three functions involved in recording purchases and cash disbursements?

9–11. Trace the flow of (a) purchase orders and (b) receiving reports in the flowchart in Figure 9-2.

9–12. Indicate the applicability of the internal control principle of independent internal verification to purchases and cash disbursements.

9–13. How may physical controls be used for these two classes of transactions?

9–14. a. List the steps in the audit program for compliance tests of purchases that involve the use of a sample.
   b. What sampling unit(s) other than vouchers might be used in compliance tests of purchases?

9–15. Identify the steps in the audit program for compliance tests of cash disbursements that involve observation and inquiry.

9–16. Explain the applicability of dual purpose testing to purchases and cash disbursements transactions.

9–17. a. Enumerate the specific steps in designing a statistical sampling plan for purchases transactions?
   b. Identify the steps in determining the sample results section of Figure 9-10.

9–18. Explain the nature of the magnetic tape symbols shown in Figure 9-11.

9–19. What aspects of the EDP system are subject to testing by the use of (a) test data and (b) generalized audit software?

9–20. Identify six types of invalid data that you might use in testing cash disbursements.

COMPREHENSIVE QUESTIONS

9–21. The following questions appear in Figures 9-4 and 9-5:

1. Are imprinted and prenumbered checks used?
2. Is each check supported by an approved voucher?
3. Is supporting documentation mutilated after payment?
4. Are two signatures required on each check?
5. Does last check signer mail the check and remittance advice?
6. Are there prohibitions against issuing checks to cash or bearer?
7. Is numerical sequence of vouchers followed in journalizing?
8. Are daily summaries of checks compared with check register totals?
9. Is an authorized purchase order required for each purchase?
10. Are goods counted, inspected, and compared with purchase order upon receipt?
11. Is a signed receipt obtained from storeroom or other recipient upon delivery of goods by receiving?
12. Are purchase orders, receiving reports, and vendors' invoices matched in preparing vouchers?
13. Are goods stored in locked areas with restricted access?

Required
a. Identify the internal accounting control objective to which each question relates (i.e., executing, recording, or custody).
b. Identify the function and specific internal control objective to which the question pertains.
c. Indicate the internal control principle that is involved.
d. Identify an error or irregularity that may result from a "no" answer to each question. (Present your answer in tabular form.)

9–22. The following control procedures over purchases and cash disbursements transactions are prescribed by the Merlin Company:

1. Approved purchase order for each purchase.

2. Prenumbered receiving report for goods received.
3. Signed receipt from preparer of purchase requisition upon acceptance of goods.
4. Matching of voucher with vendor's invoice.
5. Approved voucher for each check.
6. Cancellation of voucher upon payment.
7. Review of voucher and supporting documentation by check signers.
8. Reorder points for inventory items.

Required
a. Indicate the function served by each procedure.
b. Identify the internal accounting control principle that is involved.
c. Identify an error or irregularity that may be prevented or detected by the control procedure.
d. Indicate a compliance test that may be performed to determine whether the control procedure above is operating as prescribed. (Present your answer in tabular form.)

9–23. Assume the following exceptions to prescribed control procedures over purchases and cash disbursements transactions occurred in the Theor Company:

1. An unauthorized purchase requisition was processed.
2. The quantity of goods ordered exceeded the quantity stated on the approved purchase requisition.
3. Goods received were incorrectly counted and reported on a receiving report.
4. A voucher was prepared for goods and services that were not authorized.
5. A voucher was prepared for goods and services that were not received.
6. A check was issued for the goods received in 5 above.
7. A properly approved voucher was paid twice.
8. A check was made out for an incorrect amount.

Required
a. Indicate the function associated with each occurrence.
b. Identify the control procedure(s) that would prevent or detect the occurrences.
c. Identify a compliance test that would determine whether each control indicated in (b) above is operating as planned. (Present your answer in tabular form.)

9–24. Dunbar Camera Manufacturing, Inc., is a manufacturer of high-priced precision motion picture cameras in which the specifications of component parts are vital to the manufacturing process. Dunbar buys valuable camera lenses and large quantities of sheetmetal and screws. Screws and lenses are ordered by Dunbar and are billed by the vendors on a unit basis. Sheetmetal is ordered by Dunbar and is billed by the vendors on the basis of weight. The receiving clerk is responsible for documenting the quality and quantity of merchandise received.

A preliminary review of the system of internal control indicates that the following procedures are being followed:

1. *Receiving report*. Properly approved purchase orders, which are prenumbered, are filed numerically. The copy sent to the receiving clerk is an exact duplicate of the copy sent to the vendor. Receipts of merchandise are recorded on the duplicate copy by the receiving clerk.
2. *Sheetmetal*. The company receives sheetmetal by railroad. The railroad independently weighs the sheetmetal and reports the weight and date of receipt on a bill of lading (waybill), which accompanies all deliveries. The receiving clerk only checks the weight on the waybill to the purchase order.
3. *Screws*. The receiving clerk opens cartons containing screws, then inspects and weighs the contents. The weight is converted to number of units by means of con-

version charts. The receiving clerk then checks the computed quantity to the purchase order.

4. *Camera lenses*. Each camera lens is delivered in a separate corrugated carton. Cartons are counted as they are received by the receiving clerk and the number of cartons are checked to purchase orders.

Required

a. Explain why the internal control procedures as they apply individually to receiving reports and the receipt of sheetmetal, screws, and camera lenses are adequate or inadequate. Do not discuss recommendations for improvements.

b. What financial statement distortions may arise because of the inadequacies in Dunbar's system of internal control and how may they occur?

AICPA

9–25. Taylor, a CPA, has been engaged to audit the financial statements of University Books, Incorporated. University Books maintains a large revolving cash fund exclusively for the purpose of buying used books from students for cash. The cash fund is active all year because the nearby university offers a large variety of courses with varying starting and completion dates throughout the year.

Receipts are prepared for each purchase and reimbursement vouchers are periodically submitted.

Required

Construct an internal control questionnaire to be used in the evaluation of the system of internal control of University Books' buying segments revolving cash fund. The internal control questionnaire should elicit a yes or no response. *Do not discuss the internal controls over books that are purchased.*

AICPA

9–26. You are involved in an attribute sampling plan for testing the proper execution of vouchers in the Hickox Company. You elect to use the attributes shown in Figure 9-10 for testing, and decide on the following sample design specifications:

1. The risk of overreliance for each attribute test is 10 percent.
2. The tolerable occurrence rate is 6 percent for attributes 1 and 2 and 8 percent for attributes 3 and 4.
3. The expected occurrence rate is 1 percent for attributes 1 and 2 and 2 percent for attributes 3 and 4.

Your examination reveals the following number of occurrences, respectively, for attributes 1, 2, 3, and 4: 0, 1, 1, 3.

Required

a. Prepare a schedule showing details of the sample design and sample results.
b. Comment on your findings.

9–27. Long, CPA, has been engaged to examine and report on the financial statements of Maylou Corporation. During the review phase of the study of Maylou's system of internal accounting control over purchases, Long was given the document flowchart on page 301 for purchases.

Required

a. Identify the procedures, relating to purchase requisitions and purchase orders, that Long would expect to find if Maylou's system of internal accounting control over purchases is effective. For example, purchase orders are prepared only after giving proper consideration to the time to order and quantity to order. Do not comment on the effectiveness of the flow of documents as presented in the flow-chart or on separation of duties.

   b. What are the factors to consider in determining
      1. The time to order?
      2. The quantity to order?

AICPA

9–28. Western Meat Processing Company buys and processes livestock for sale to super-markets. In connection with the examination of the company's financial statements, you have prepared the following notes based on your review of inventory procedures:

    1. Each livestock buyer submits a daily report of his purchases to the plant superintendent. This report shows the dates of purchase and expected delivery; the vendor; and the number, weights, and type of livestock purchased. As shipments are received, any available plant employee counts the number of each type received and places a check mark beside this quantity on the buyer's report. When all shipments listed on the report have been received, the report is returned to the buyer.

    2. Vendors' invoices, after a clerical review, are sent to the appropriate buyer for approval and returned to the accounting department. A disbursement voucher and a check for the approved amount are prepared in the accounting department. Checks are forwarded to the treasurer for signature. The treasurer's office sends signed checks directly to the buyer for delivery to the vendor.

    3. Livestock carcasses are processed by lots. Each lot is assigned a number. At the end of each day a tally sheet reporting the lots processed, the number and type of animals in each lot, and the carcass weight is sent to the accounting department, where a perpetual inventory record of processed carcasses and their weights is maintained.

4. Processed carcasses are stored in a refrigerated cooler located in a small building adjacent to the employee parking lot. The cooler is locked when the plant is not open, and a company guard is on duty when the employees report for work and leave at the end of their shifts. Supermarket truck drivers wishing to pick up their orders have been instructed to contact someone in the plant if no one is in the cooler.

5. Substantial quantities of by-products are produced and stored, either in the cooler or elsewhere in the plant. By-products are initially accounted for as they are sold. At this time the sales manager prepares a two-part form: one copy serves as authorization to transfer the goods to the customer, and the other becomes the basis for billing the customer.

Required

For each of the numbered notes 1 to 5 above, indicate:

a. The operative internal accounting control objective that is applicable.
b. The control procedures that are prescribed.
c. The errors or irregularities that could occur.
d. The additional control procedures that are necessary to prevent the occurrences identified in (c) above.

AICPA (adapted)

9-29. During your examination of the financial statements of the Gary Manufacturing Company for the year ended December 31, 19X0, you find that at January 1, 19X0, the company had installed the following punched-card processing system for recording raw material purchases:

1. Vendors' invoices are sent directly to the accounts payable department by the mail department.
2. All supporting documents to the invoices are accumulated in the accounts payable department and attached to the invoices. After being checked and cash discounts computed, the invoices are accumulated in batches and adding machine tapes prepared of the net invoice amounts to provide input control totals. Then the batches of invoices and tapes are sent to the tabulating department.
3. In the tabulating department, keypunch operators prepare for each invoice an accounts payable punched card and one or more punched cards for the related debit distribution to several departmental inventories.
4. The invoice register is prepared by tab runs of the distribution cards and accounts payable cards. In this run, totals of distribution cards are compared by the tabulating machine with the amounts punched for the related accounts payable cards. Tab run subtotals by invoice batches are taken for checking to the input control totals.
5. The general ledger control account is posted monthly from the totals shown in the invoice register and all other journals.
6. By sorting, the distribution and accounts payable cards are separated. The distribution cards are filed for further processing. The accounts payable cards are sorted by due dates and tab runs prepared to determine cash requirements.
7. On the due dates, the accounts payable cards are processed to prepare combined check and remittance statements.
8. At the end of the month the accounts payable cards in the unpaid file are tabulated for comparison with the general ledger control account.

Required

a. Prepare a flowchart of the system.
b. List the audit procedures you would use to compliance test the system.

AICPA (adapted)

9–30. Kent County Grain and Milling Company decided to stimulate the sale of its flour by including a coupon, redeemable for fifty cents (50¢), in every 25- and 50-pound sack of flour produced subsequent to October 1, 19X0. The company contemplates that 150,000 coupons will be in the hands of customers before completion of the promotional campaign on March 31, 19X1.

On commencing your year-end work on January 10, 19X1 for the calendar year ending December 31, 19X0, the controller of Kent County Grain and Milling Company requested that you review the accounting records and the internal accounting controls applicable to the flour coupons.

In your review of the accounting records and the system of internal accounting controls, you learned the following:

1. A perpetual record of coupons received from the printer is entered from a copy of the receiving ticket, damaged coupons are reported orally by a line foreman, and coupons used are entered from a copy of the production report of sacks of flour packed. A summary of the perpetual record as of December 31, 19X0 is as follows:

Coupons received to date	150,000
Coupons damaged and destroyed	(2,000)
Coupons included in 25-pound sacks of flour	(50,000)
Coupons included in 50-pound sacks of flour	(25,000)
On hand per record	73,000

2. Unused coupons are kept in a storeroom with stationery and supplies and are readily accessible. No count of coupons within a package is made as they are received from the printers; however, the number of packages times the indicated amount in each package is recorded on a receiving ticket which is later agreed, in the office, with a copy of the vendor's invoice.
3. Coupons are sometimes damaged by the machinery which mechanically inserts them in the sacks. The production superintendent said that he thought that the line foreman destroyed these coupons. As previously mentioned, the number of damaged coupons are reported to the production superintendent orally each day by the foreman.
4. The line foreman takes a quantity of unused coupons from the storeroom each day based on scheduled production for that day.
5. Correspondence containing coupons mailed to the company for redemption is first opened in the mail department. The coupons are then sent to the cashier's department, where they are redeemed in cash out of a fund especially set up for that purpose. The cashier places a 50 cent piece in a self-addressed envelope, seals the envelope, and returns it to the mail department for ultimate disposition. The cashier stamps the coupon paid with the date of payment.
6. Once each week the cashier's coupon fund is reimbursed in the same manner as any other imprest fund.
7. Complaints from customers not receiving their 50 cent pieces are sent to the cashier for disposition.

You also learned that a physical inventory of unused coupons was taken on December 31, 19X0. It was found that 71,250 coupons were on hand. As of December 31, 19X0, flour containing 50,000 coupons had been sold to the company's retail outlets. In addition, by December 31, 19X0, 37,500 coupons had been redeemed and paid, and it was estimated that only 50 percent of the remaining coupons outstanding at that time would be redeemed.

Required
a. Prepare a memorandum to the controller as to weaknesses in his present control procedures in regard to handling redeemable coupons and your recommendations for improvement.

b. Prepare a journal entry setting up the company's liability for unredeemed coupons at December 31, 19X0. Show your method of computing the liability.

c. Identify the weaknesses, if any, you believe are material. Explain fully.

AICPA (adapted)

9–31. Anthony, CPA, prepared the flowchart on page 305, which portrays the raw materials purchasing function of one of Anthony's clients, a medium-size manufacturing company, from the preparation of initial documents through the vouching of invoices for payment in accounts payable. The flowchart was a portion of the work performed on the audit engagement to evaluate internal control.

Required

Identify and explain the systems and control weaknesses evident from the flowchart. Include the internal control weaknesses resulting from activities performed or not performed. All documents are prenumbered.

AICPA

9–32. You have completed an audit of activities within the purchasing department of Zale Company. The department employs thirty buyers, seven supervisors, a manager, and clerical personnel. Purchases total about $500 million a year. Your audit disclosed the following conditions:

1. The company has no formal rules on conflicts of interest. Your analysis produced evidence that one of the thirty buyers in the department owns a substantial interest in a major supplier and that he procures supplies averaging $50,000 a year from that supplier. The prices charged by the supplier are competitive.

2. Buyers select proposed sources without submitting the lists of bidders for review. Your tests disclosed no evidence that higher costs were incurred as a result of that practice.

3. Buyers who originate written requests for quotations from suppliers receive the suppliers' bids directly from the mailroom. In your test of 100 purchases based on competitive bids, you found that in 75 cases the low bidders were awarded the purchase orders.

4. Requests to purchase (requisitions) received in the purchasing department from other departments in the company must be signed by persons authorized to do so. Your examination of 200 such requests disclosed that three, all for small amounts, were not properly signed. The buyer who had issued all three orders honored the requests because he misunderstood the applicable procedure. The clerical personnel charged with reviewing such requests had given them to the buyer in error.

Required

For each of the four conditions, state

a. The risk, if any, which is incurred if each condition described above is permitted to continue.

b. The control, if any, you would recommend to prevent continuation of the condition described.

IIA

CASE STUDY

9–33.* The Daly Company feels that it has definite problems in its internal control functions, particularly in purchasing, receiving, and cash disbursements. Your firm has been engaged to review these areas and to report on its findings.

The company is involved in a highly specialized processing activity with annual gross sales of approximately $25,000,000. The nature of the business is such that not all

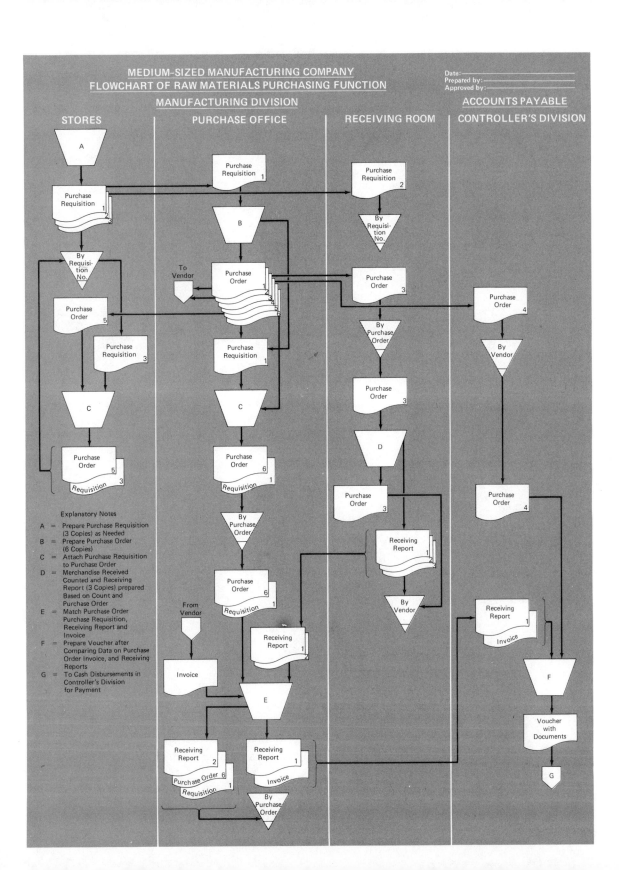

MEDIUM–SIZED MANUFACTURING COMPANY
FLOWCHART OF RAW MATERIALS PURCHASING FUNCTION

PURCHASING, RECEIVING & CASH DISBURSEMENTS FLOWCHART

purchases are received in one shipment and there are many back orders, causing a problem for the production department to meet raw material needs on a timely basis.

It has been agreed that no separation of the receiving and stores department is required.

The flowchart on page 306 (prepared by your assistant) illustrates and describes *all procedures* being performed. The departments are scattered throughout a large plant area.

Required
a. Prepare a listing of the strengths and weaknesses in the system of internal control over purchasing, receiving, and cash disbursements.
b. For each weakness, recommend one or more changes to improve the effectiveness of the control.

10

Compliance Tests of Payroll and Production Cycle Transactions

STUDY OBJECTIVES

The study objectives of this chapter are to acquire an understanding of internal control over payroll and manufacturing transactions and the auditor's study and evaluation of them. To achieve these objectives, it is necessary for the reader to

- Comprehend the internal control environment and principles that pertain to these two classes of transactions.
- Know the methodology for reviewing and testing the control procedures for these transactions.
- Understand the applicability of statistical sampling and electronic data processing in testing of payroll transactions.
- Perceive the nature of the production cycle.
- Be aware of the audit program for testing manufacturing transactions.

This is the fourth and final chapter that pertains exclusively to internal control and compliance testing. Two cycles are covered in the chapter. First, the coverage of the expenditure cycle is completed by focusing on payroll transactions. Second, the nature of the production cycle and manufacturing transactions in that cycle are considered.

INTERNAL CONTROL OVER PAYROLL TRANSACTIONS

Basic Considerations

Payroll transactions involve the events and transactions that pertain to executive and employee compensation. This class of transactions includes salaried personnel, hourly and incentive (piecework) wage earners, salespersons' commissions, executive bonuses, pensions and profit-sharing plans, vacation pay, employee benefits (e.g., health insurance), and payroll taxes. Attention in this chapter will be focused on hourly payrolls for employees.

Often, the processing of transactions in this part of the expenditure cycle has evolved into well-organized payroll systems that generally contain effective internal controls. In addition, the auditor is likely to find significant similarities in payroll systems among different companies, including wide application of electronic data processing (EDP).

The following are basic to an understanding of payroll transactions:

Functions

Executing
- Hiring employees.
- Authorizing payroll changes.
- Preparing attendance and timekeeping data.
- Preparing the payroll.
- Paying the payroll.
- Filing and paying payroll taxes.

Recording
- Journalizing and posting payroll transactions.
- Updating employee earnings records.
- Costing time tickets.

Custody
- Protecting payroll funds.
- Protecting payroll records.
- Maintaining correctness of payroll bank account(s).

Common documents

- *Personnel authorization.* A memo issued by personnel department indicating the hiring of an employee and each subsequent change in the employee's status for payroll purposes.
- *Clock card.* A form used by each employee to record hours worked daily during a pay period. It is used with time clocks that record the time on the card.

- *Time ticket*. A form used in timekeeping to record time worked by an employee on specific jobs. Time worked is often machine imprinted.
- *Payroll register*. A report showing each employee's name, gross earnings, payroll deductions, and net pay for a pay period. It provides the basis for paying employees.
- *Payroll summary*. A report showing total gross earnings, payroll deductions, and net pay for all employees for a pay period. It provides the basis for journalizing the payroll.
- *Payroll check*. An order drawn on a bank to pay an employee. It is accompanied by a detachable memo indicating gross earnings and payroll deductions.
- *Labor (cost) distribution summary*. A report showing the account classifications for gross factory earnings for each pay period.
- *Payroll tax returns*. Forms prescribed by taxing authorities for the filing of payroll tax returns.
- *Form W-2*. A form given to the employee and filed with the Internal Revenue Service showing annual earnings, federal income taxes withheld, and FICA taxes withheld.

Accounting records

- *Books of original entry*. General journal, voucher register, and check register or payroll check register.
- *Subsidiary ledgers*. Manufacturing overhead and work-in-process cost records.
- *General ledger accounts*. Salary and wages expense; factory labor; payroll taxes expense; salaries and wages payable; payroll taxes payable; accounts payable; cash in bank (payroll bank account); manufacturing overhead control.

File data

- *Employee personnel record*. Holds pertinent employment data for each employee and contains all personnel authorizations issued for the employee, job evaluations, and disciplinary actions, if any.
- *Employee earnings record*. Contains each employee's gross earnings, payroll deductions, and net pay for the year by pay periods.

Internal Control Environment

Overall responsibility for payroll administration is generally assigned to a vice president of industrial relations, labor, or manpower management. Departments that are of particular importance to payroll transactions are (1) personnel (2) timekeeping, and (3) payroll. Individuals in these departments should be knowledgeable about laws and regulations applicable to payroll transactions.

Internal auditing exercises surveillance over payroll practices and procedures. Payroll costs usually are subject to budget constraints and periodic reporting of actual and budgeted costs. Sound practices include the use of employee identification badges for employees.

Materiality and Risk

Employee compensation and payroll taxes are generally a major expense item for most companies in the determination of net income. Payroll costs are also important in the costing of work-in-process and finished-goods inventories in a manufacturing enterprise. The frequency and volume of payroll transactions make these transactions vulnerable to errors and irregularities. This is especially true when there are numerous employees who are paid on the basis of hourly, group, or incentive (piecework) rates. In addition, there is a potential for payroll fraud that results in the overstatement (padding) of the payroll and the subsequent disbursement of cash to unauthorized individuals.

In order to assess the risk associated with payroll transactions, it is necessary for the auditor to determine the effectiveness of the internal control procedures. When the auditor plans to rely on these controls in performing substantive tests of payroll balances, considerable audit effort may be required in reviewing and testing the control procedures.

Payroll Transactions Are Properly Executed

As in the case of other transactions, the execution of payroll transactions involves a series of functions. The functions, together with the related internal control objectives, are shown below.

Conceptually, the steps in executing payroll transactions are the same as executing the two classes of transactions described in the preceding chapter.

FUNCTION	SPECIFIC ACCOUNTING CONTROL OBJECTIVE
1. Hiring employees	Employees are hired in accordance with management's criteria
2. Authorizing payroll changes	Pay rates, payroll deductions, changes in job status, and terminations are properly authorized
3. Preparing attendance and timekeeping data	Appropriate records are maintained and time worked is properly approved
4. Preparing the payroll	Employee earnings and net pay are accurately determined on the basis of approved time data and authorized deductions
5. Paying the payroll	Payments of employee compensation are made to bona fide employees on the basis of approved and authorized data
6. Filing and paying payroll taxes	Payroll tax returns are correctly and promptly filed, and payments are made when due

For example, hiring of employees is analogous to ordering goods and services, attendance and timekeeping are comparable to receiving, and the vouching and paying functions are similar. The internal control principles applicable to executing payroll transactions are explained below.

Authorization Procedures

The personnel department plays a vital role in the authorization process. Its responsibility extends to each aspect of the employee's status: hiring, job classification, pay rate, payroll deductions, and termination. Authorization procedures should also be established for (1) approving time worked, (2) approving the payroll, and (3) paying the payroll. Time worked should be specifically approved by the employee's supervisor, the payroll should be approved by the head of the payroll department, and the approved payroll, in turn, provides the authorization for payment of the payroll.

Segregation of Functions

The functions involved in executing payroll transactions should be performed by different departments and individuals as shown below.

FUNCTION	DEPARTMENT	RELATED ACTIVITIES
1. Hiring employees	Personnel	Evaluate qualifications of applicants on basis of job description and hiring policies and issue employment authorization memos
2. Authorizing payroll changes	Personnel	Issue authorizations for pay rates, payroll deductions, transfers, and terminations; and maintain employee personnel records
3. Preparing attendance and timekeeping data	Timekeeping	Supervise clock card punching, prepare time tickets, and reconcile time ticket and clock card hours
4. Preparing the payroll	Payroll	Issue clock (time) cards, maintain attendance records, compute employee gross and net earnings, prepare payroll summary and payroll checks, and maintain employee earnings records
5. Paying the payroll	Vouchers Payable	Prepare voucher for payment of payroll
	Treasurer	Sign and distribute payroll checks
6. Filing and paying payroll taxes	Payroll	Prepare and file payroll tax returns
	Treasurer	Prepare and mail checks in payment of payroll taxes

A flowchart for the execution of payroll transactions is shown in Figure 10-1.

Documentation Procedures

Each step in executing payroll transactions should be documented. Personnel department authorization forms provide documentation of new hires, pay rates, job reclassifications, and terminations. For hourly employees, many companies use clock (time) cards and time tickets to accumulate time worked.

Preparation of the payroll involves calculating gross earnings, payroll deductions, and net pay for each employee based on authorized pay rates and approved time data. The computed amounts for each employee are then tabulated on a payroll register. When approved by a payroll supervisor, the register provides the basis for

- Posting of gross earnings and payroll deductions to the individual employee's earnings record maintained in payroll.
- Preparing a payroll summary of total gross earnings, payroll deductions, and net pay for the pay period which is sent to general accounting.
- Preparing individual payroll checks which are then sent to the treasurer's office for signature(s) and distribution to employees.

The payroll register constitutes the treasurer department's authority to pay employees. Payment is usually made in the form of prenumbered checks drawn either on the company's regular bank account or on a payroll bank account. Payroll checks should be distributed directly to employees, on proper identification, by treasurer department personnel. The checks should not be returned to payroll for distribution since the payroll department would then have control over both preparing and paying the payroll.

A termination notice (authorization) should be issued by the personnel department upon completion of an individual's employment. Prompt notification is vital in preventing terminated employees from continuing on the payroll. The subsequent diversion of payroll checks to such unauthorized individuals has characterized a number of payroll frauds.

Every company is expected to comply with legal requirements pertaining to filing payroll tax returns and paying payroll taxes. Ordinarily, the payroll department prepares the tax returns on forms provided by the taxing authority. When payment is due, a voucher is drawn and a check is issued.

Physical Controls and Independent Internal Verification

A common physical control is the use of time clocks for determining total hours worked. When such equipment is used, supervisors or security guards are often designated to observe the punching of the clocks by employees.

Independent internal verification applications include having a second payroll clerk validate (1) the accuracy of the computed payroll data for each

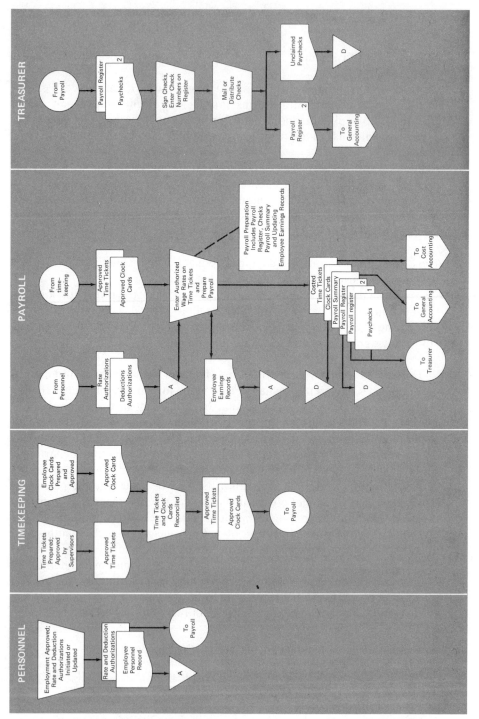

FIGURE 10-1. Manual System for Executing Payroll Transactions

employee, (2) the agreement of the amounts on the checks with corresponding amounts in the payroll register, and (3) the agreement of data on the tax returns with the data shown in the employee earnings records.

Payroll Transactions Are Properly Recorded

The functions in recording payroll transactions, an appropriate segregation of duties within the accounting department, and the related internal control objective are shown below.

FUNCTION	DEPARTMENT	SPECIFIC ACCOUNTING CONTROL OBJECTIVE
1. Journalizing and posting payroll transactions	General Accounting	Payroll data are correctly recorded as to amount, classification, and accounting period
2. Updating employee earnings records	Payroll Accounting	Employee earnings data for each pay period are correctly posted to the employee's earnings record
3. Costing time tickets	Payroll Accounting	Proper pay rates are correctly applied to each time ticket

The internal control principles applicable to the recording of payroll transactions are explained below.

Segregation of Functions

Proper separation of duties in accounting for payrolls is essential. Accounting personnel who record payroll transactions should not prepare or pay the payroll. In addition, personnel who maintain employee earnings records and cost time tickets should not journalize the payroll or post the transactions to the general ledger.

Accounting Records and Procedures

The accounting records consist of books of original entry, the payroll expense and payroll liability accounts in the general ledger, and employee earnings records. Payroll summaries provide the basis for journalizing the payroll, and vouchers and payroll checks furnish the data for recording payment of the payroll. Postings to the employee earnings records are made directly from the payroll registers. A flowchart for the recording of payroll transactions is shown in Figure 10-2.

Independent Internal Verification

There are several opportunities for this internal control principle in recording payroll transactions. Examples include (1) agreeing payroll and labor cost distribution summaries and payroll register totals in general accounting

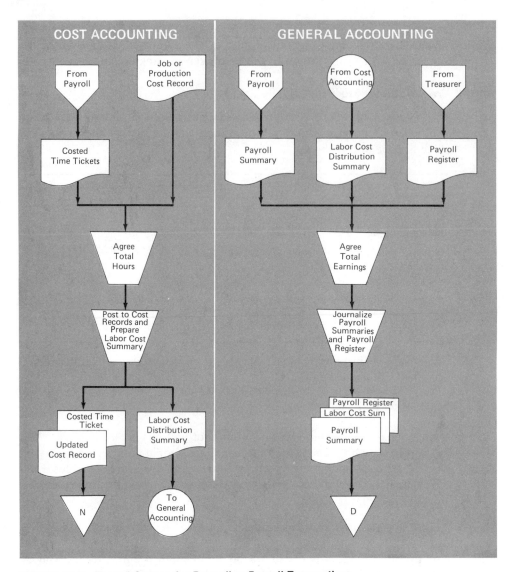

FIGURE 10–2. Manual System for Recording Payroll Transactions

and (2) reconciling costs shown on time tickets with postings to job or production cost records in cost accounting.

Custody of Payroll Funds Is Properly Maintained

Assets resulting from payroll transactions consist of payroll bank accounts and unclaimed wages. The following functions and specific accounting control objectives are applicable to maintaining proper custody over these assets:

FUNCTION	DEPARTMENT	SPECIFIC ACCOUNTING CONTROL OBJECTIVE
1. Protecting payroll funds	Treasurer	Access to payroll bank accounts and unclaimed wages is limited to authorized personnel
2. Protecting payroll records	Payroll	Access to payroll records is limited to authorized personnel
3. Maintaining correctness of payroll bank accounts	General Accounting	Recorded bank balances are independently compared with existing assets at reasonable intervals

The internal control principles applicable to these functions are explained below.

Physical Controls and Authorization Procedures

Physical controls include the security devices of a bank for the payroll bank account and vaults or safes for the storage of unclaimed wages. Physical controls are also needed to prevent indirect access to payroll funds. Thus, authorization forms, clock cards, and preprinted payroll checks should be stored with a responsible custodian and access should be restricted to authorized personnel. Employee earnings records should be filed in fireproof locked files and access should be restricted to authorized payroll department personnel.

Independent Internal Verification and Segregation of Functions

These principles apply primarily to the reconciliation of the payroll bank account per books with the balance reported on the payroll bank statement. Ordinarily, this is done monthly by personnel not otherwise involved with payroll transactions.

STUDY AND EVALUATION OF INTERNAL CONTROL

The auditor's methodology for meeting the second standard of field work for payroll transactions is identical with the steps described for purchases and cash disbursements transactions in Chapter 9.

Review of the Payroll System

When the auditor intends to rely on the client's control procedures over payroll transactions, it is necessary to perform both the preliminary and the completion phases of the review. The principal steps in the completion phase are explained below.

Gathering Information

Figure 10-3 illustrates an internal control questionnaire for payroll transactions. The questions, which are referenced to specific functions, relate to specific control procedures considered by the auditor to be necessary for effective control.

Making a Preliminary Evaluation

A representative listing of errors and irregularities in executing payroll transactions, and the control procedures necessary to prevent or detect them, is shown in Figure 10-4. Similar listings can be made for the recording of payroll transactions and for the custody of payroll funds. From a comparison of the necessary controls with the prescribed controls obtained earlier in the review, the auditor makes a preliminary evaluation of the controls in the payroll system. The auditor's preliminary evaluation should be documented in the working papers.

CYCLE: Expenditure   **CLASS OF TRANSACTIONS: Payroll**

EXECUTING   Yes | No

1. Are hirings authorized by personnel department? (E1)
2. Are pay rates, payroll deductions, and terminations authorized by the personnel department? (E2)
3. Are time clocks and clock cards used? (E3)
4. Is time clock punching supervised? (E3)
5. Is there supervisory approval of time worked by each employee? (E3)
6. Are time ticket hours reconciled to clock card hours daily? (E3)
7. Is there internal verification of accuracy of payroll computations? (E4)
8. Is there supervisory approval of the payroll? (E4)
9. Is there internal verification of payroll checks with payroll register data? (E5)
10. Are payroll checks signed and distributed by treasurer's office personnel? (E5)
11. Are payroll tax returns reconciled to employees earnings records? (E6)

RECORDING

1. Are personnel who journalize payroll transactions independent of those who prepare and pay the payroll? (R1)
2. Are changes in employee earnings records reconciled with payroll register data? (R2)
3. Are costed time tickets verified for proper rate and mathematical accuracy? (R3)

CUSTODY

1. Are unclaimed wages held by a treasurer's office employee? (C1)
2. Are personnel and employee earnings records kept in locked files? (C2)
3. Is payroll bank account periodically reconciled by an independent person? (C3)

FIGURE 10–3. Internal Control Questionnaire: Payroll Transactions

Function	Possible Errors and Irregularities	Necessary Control Procedures	Possible Compliance Tests
EXECUTING			
Hiring employees	An unauthorized employee may be added to the payroll records	Personnel department authorization for new employees	Examine personnel authorization for new employees
Authorizing payroll changes	A terminated employee may remain on payroll	Personnel department authorization of termination	Examine termination authorizations and trace to subsequent payroll
Attendance and timekeeping	An employee may punch more than one clock card	Surveillance of time clock punching	Observe surveillance and inquire as to number of exceptions
	Time ticket hours may be incorrect	Internal verification of agreement of time ticket and clock card hours	Examine evidence of verification
		Supervisor approval of hours worked	Review evidence of approval
Preparing the payroll	Mathematical errors may occur in calculating employees earnings and deductions	Internal verification of payroll calculations	Examine evidence of verification
Paying the payroll	Checks may be issued for incorrect amounts	Internal verification of checks with payroll register data	Review evidence of verification
	Checks may be distributed to unauthorized recipients	Segregation of functions between preparation and payment	Observe segregation of functions
		Employee identification upon distribution	Witness the distribution of the payroll
Filing and paying payroll taxes	An employee may be omitted from a tax return	Internal verification of tax return with employee earnings records	Examine evidence of verification

FIGURE 10-4. Preliminary Evaluation Considerations: Payroll Transactions

Compliance Tests of Prescribed Controls

When the auditor has identified controls that are expected to be relied on, it is necessary to perform compliance tests on these controls to determine whether they are operating as planned. An illustrative audit program for testing controls over payroll transactions is shown in Figure 10-5. Observe that the payroll check is used as the sampling unit in testing controls pertaining to the execution of payroll transactions. Alternatively, the line item in the payroll registers may be used in testing controls that leave an audit trail of documentary evidence. Compliance tests of payroll transactions should include personnel from each major accounting and functional classification, such as office, sales, factory, etc. In addition, each of the principal bases for computing compensation—hourly, salaried, and incentive—should be tested.

The witnessing of the distribution of a payroll is an important compliance test. In performing this procedure, the auditor should observe that

- Segregation of functions exists between the preparation and payment of the payroll.
- Each employee receives only one check.
- Each employee is identified by badge and/or signature.
- There is proper control and disposition of unclaimed checks.

TYPE OF TESTING: Compliance   **PURPOSE: Study and Evaluation of Internal Control**
CYCLE: Expenditure   **CLASS OF TRANSACTIONS: Payroll**

A. CONTROLS IN EXECUTING PAYROLL TRANSACTIONS ARE OPERATING AS PLANNED.

 1. For selected payroll checks for the year to date, examine for
  • Authorization of pay rates and deductions.
  • Supervisory approval of time worked.
  • Internal verification of payroll calculations.
  • Internal verification of check with payroll register.
  • Authorized signatures on check.
  • Employee endorsement of check.
 2. For pay periods from which checks are drawn, examine payroll registers for supervisory approval of payroll.
 3. Witness a distribution of a payroll.
 4. Observe clock card and timekeeping procedures.
 5. Inquire of personnel concerning performance of control procedures.
 6. Reperform verification procedures in Step 1 on some payroll checks.

B. CONTROLS IN RECORDING PAYROLL TRANSACTIONS ARE OPERATING AS PLANNED.

 1. Examine evidence of verification of payroll summaries with payroll entries.
 2. Examine evidence of periodic reconciliations of employee earnings records with payroll register data and tax returns.
 3. Examine sample of time tickets for verification of rates and calculations.

C. CONTROLS OVER THE CUSTODY OF PAYROLL FUNDS ARE OPERATING AS PLANNED.

 1. Observe controls over unclaimed wages.
 2. Examine evidence of payroll bank reconciliations.

FIGURE 10–5. Audit Program: Compliance Tests of Payroll Transactions

Final Evaluation of the Controls

Based on the results of compliance testing, the auditor evaluates the reliability of each control expected to be relied on. As previously explained, this determination involves a consideration of both the number and the causes of deviations from prescribed control procedures. This evaluation is then used to determine the nature, timing, and extent of substantive testing of payroll balances.

STATISTICAL SAMPLING IN COMPLIANCE TESTING

Payroll is another area in which attribute sampling can be utilized in performing compliance tests. The same steps that were illustrated in previous chapters to design, execute, and evaluate the sample are followed.

The objective of the sampling plan may be proper executing or proper recording or both. Sampling units may be payroll checks, clock cards, or line items in the payroll register. When the objective is the proper preparation of the payroll, the following attributes may be of interest in a sampling plan for hourly workers:

- Approval of time worked by supervisor.
- Verification of agreement of time tickets and clock cards.
- Verification of accuracy of payroll calculations.
- Authorization of pay rates and payroll deductions.

The auditor determines a sample size for each attribute by specifying (1) a tolerable occurrence rate, based on the extent of reliance to be placed on the related control, (2) an expected population occurrence rate, and (3) the desired risk of overreliance. The auditor then proceeds to randomly select the sample, examine the sample items, and statistically and qualitatively evaluate and interpret the sample results.

ELECTRONIC DATA PROCESSING

Electronic data processing of payroll transactions is very common. Since these transactions occur on a regular basis at the end of each payroll period, it is customary to use batch processing. However, it should also be recognized that numerous changes in pay rates, job classifications, and payroll deductions may occur during a payroll period. Accordingly, many companies provide the personnel department with direct access to the employee's personnel data master file maintained on the computer. A case study of a payroll system which has this direct access capability is described below.

Description of the System

In the Hart Company, the computer is used to perform three payroll functions: (1) preparing the payroll register, (2) preparing payroll checks, and (3) updating the employee earnings master file. Magnetic tape is used for input data and master files are maintained on magnetic disk. In addition, there is online input of personnel changes. A flowchart of the payroll system is shown in Figure 10-6.

The manual control procedures are similar to those described in earlier EDP case studies. These controls include the batch totals and the batch transmittal form in the payroll department, the review and verification of the batch totals in data control, and the verification of keypunched data in data entry.

As shown in Figure 10-6, the system provides for the updating of the personnel master file by direct access from online terminals and two computer runs.

Run 1. In this run, the payroll transactions are sorted by employee number and the data are verified by an *edit check* routine. The outputs consist of a valid payroll transaction tape and a control and exception report that is sent to data control.

Run 2. In this run the valid transactions data are processed using the Hart Company's payroll application program. The program is run using the personnel data master file, which contains current authorized pay rates and payroll deductions, and with the employee earnings master file, which contains earnings data for the year to date. The output of this run consists of an updated earnings master file in machine-readable form and printouts of payroll checks (with accompanying earnings and deductions data), the payroll register, and a control total and exception report. The checks are subsequently forwarded by data control to the treasurer's department for signing.

Study and Evaluation of EDP Controls

The methodology for making a study and evaluation of EDP controls in a payroll system is the same as described in earlier case studies. An audit program for testing the EDP application controls in the Hart Company is shown in Figure 10-7.

In testing the program controls in run 1, the auditor uses test data that contains invalid conditions such as:

* Missing or invalid employee number.
* Total hours per clock card not in agreement with hours on time tickets.
* Time tickets with invalid job numbers.
* Total hours that exceed a predetermined limit.

In testing the processing steps in run 2, the auditor uses test data to determine that the program controls are operating as planned for (1) calculating employee earnings and deductions, and (2) reporting as exceptions amounts that exceed predetermined limits.

In both tests, the test data are run using the client's regular programs,

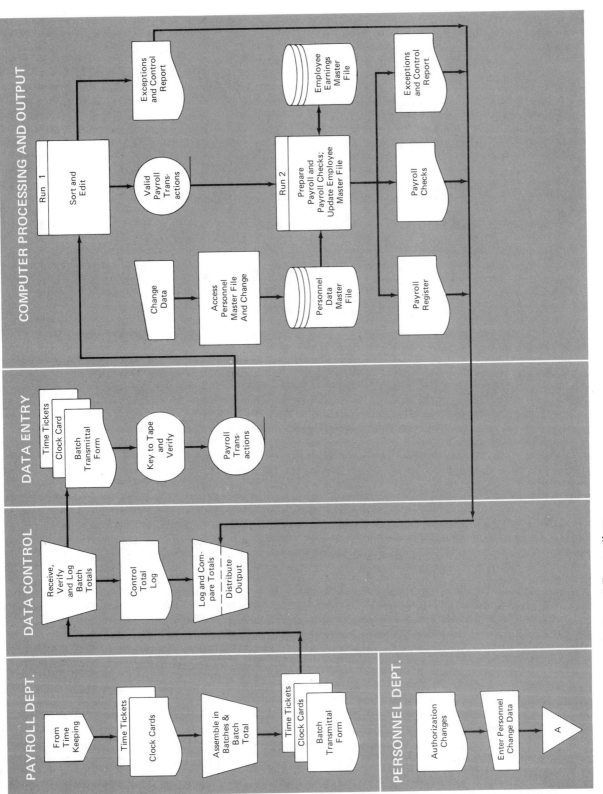

FIGURE 10–6. EDP System for Payroll Transactions

TYPE OF TESTING: Compliance   **PURPOSE: EDP Application Controls**
CYCLE: Expenditure   **CLASS OF TRANSACTIONS: Payroll**

A. INPUT CONTROLS ARE PROPERLY FUNCTIONING:

  1. Randomly select a sample of employee earnings in the payroll register and trace to source documents.
  2. Review, on test basis, reconciliation of batch totals in data control with control totals in run 1.
  3. Selectively review error listings of run 1 and investigate items to determine that they have been properly cleared.
  4. Design and use test data to test program controls of edit routine in run 1.

B. PROCESSING CONTROLS ARE PROPERLY FUNCTIONING:

  1. Observe the procedures for reconciling control totals in runs 1 and 2 and selectively trace control totals to related input controls.
  2. Review error lists for run 2 for unusual items and determine the disposition of rejected data.
  3. Use test data to test the program logic in run 2.
  4. Use generalized audit software to test master file data.

C. OUTPUT CONTROLS ARE PROPERLY FUNCTIONING:

  1. Review reconciliation of output controls with input controls.
  2. On a test basis, obtain printouts of employee earnings master files used in run 2 and use related payroll register data to reconcile changes in totals and to selectively account for changes in individual employee earnings data.

FIGURE 10–7. Audit Program: Compliance Tests of EDP Application Controls for Payroll Transactions

and the output of the test runs is manually compared by the auditor with the expected results.

The extent of testing of master files is dependent on the effectiveness of EDP general controls pertaining to file security and documentation of program changes. As shown in Figure 10-7, the auditor decides to test these files by using generalized audit software. For the personnel data file, a random sample of employees is obtained. The pay rates and deductions for these employees are printed out and are traced to source documents. The software program also is used to make a reasonableness test on pay rates in the personnel data file. Using the computer, the file is searched for abnormal pay rates, rate changes within specified time periods, and rate changes in excess of a specified percentage. The selection criteria are run against the file and the printout is manually traced to source documents by the auditor.

In using generalized audit software to test the employee earnings file for reasonableness, the selection criteria include excessive gross or net earnings, excessive income tax withholdings, and FICA withholdings in excess of the statutory maximum.

From evidence obtained from the compliance tests, the auditor determines the reliance that can be placed on EDP controls and their effect on the nature, timing, and extent of substantive tests of payroll balances.

THE PRODUCTION CYCLE

Nature of the Production Cycle

The production cycle relates to the conversion of raw materials into finished goods. This cycle includes production planning and control of the types and quantities of goods to be manufactured, the inventory levels to be maintained, and the transactions and events pertaining to the manufacturing process. Transactions in this cycle begin at the point where raw materials are requisitioned for production and end with the transfer of the manufactured product to finished goods. The accounting function associated with this cycle embraces a cost accounting system, which may include standard costs and perpetual inventory records.

The production cycle interfaces with both the expenditure and the revenue cycles. The former involves the acquisition of goods and services needed in production; the latter involves the custody and subsequent sale of finished goods.

Internal Control Environment

In the organizational structure of a manufacturing company, an officer with the title vice president of operations, manufacturing, or production usually has overall responsibility for production. This individual has line authority over the production planning and control department and each manufacturing department or division.

Personnel engaged in the production cycle include department or division heads, foremen, and factory workers. Production budgets are used to control the quantity and scheduling of production, and cost budgets and standard costs are frequently used to control manufacturing costs.

Internal Control Objectives

For the production cycle, the operative objectives of internal accounting control are as follows:

- Production cycle transactions (i.e., manufacturing transactions) are properly executed.
- Production cycle transactions are properly recorded.
- Custody of assets (i.e., work in process) is properly maintained.

These three objectives provide the framework for discussing (1) the basic features of accounting control over manufacturing transactions in this cycle and (2) the study and evaluation of internal control over these transactions.

INTERNAL CONTROL OVER MANUFACTURING TRANSACTIONS

Basic Considerations

The following are basic to an understanding of the events and transactions pertaining to the manufacturing transactions in the production cycle:

Functions

Executing
- Issuing production orders
- Requisitioning raw materials
- Processing raw materials
- Transferring completed work to finished goods

Recording
- Journalizing and posting manufacturing transactions
- Updating work-in-process records

Custody
- Protecting work in process
- Maintaining correctness of work-in-process records

Common documents

- *Production order.* A form indicating the quantity and kind of goods to be manufactured. An order may pertain to a job order or to a continuous process.
- *Bill of materials.* A listing of raw material components for a particular product. In some cases, the listing is included in the production order.
- *Materials requisition.* A memo to the storeroom requesting the release of materials for use on an approved production order.
- *Routing ticket.* A notice accompanying the transfer of work in process between departments and to finished goods.
- *Daily activity reports.* Separate reports showing raw materials and direct labor used during the day.

Accounting records

- *Books of original entry.* General journal and voucher register.
- *Subsidiary ledgers.* Work-in-process records and manufacturing overhead records.
- *General ledger accounts.* Raw materials, work in process, finished goods, manufacturing overhead, over- or underabsorbed overhead, and standard cost variances.

Materiality and Risk

In a manufacturing company, inventories and cost of goods manufactured and sold are usually material to the company's financial position and results of operations. Transactions in the production cycle occur with a high degree of frequency. Thus, there is a potential risk of errors and irregularities in executing and recording manufacturing transactions and in maintaining custody of work-in-process inventories. A company's system of internal control over manufacturing transactions should provide for both *physical control* over the goods and *cost control* over manufacturing costs.

As for other major classes of transactions, it is necessary for the auditor to (1) study and evaluate the client's controls in order to assess the audit risk in the particular engagement, and (2) test the controls when reliance on them is planned in performing substantive tests.

Manufacturing Transactions Are Properly Executed

The functions and specific accounting control objectives in executing manufacturing transactions are as follows:

FUNCTION	SPECIFIC ACCOUNTING CONTROL OBJECTIVE
1. Issuing production orders	Orders are issued in accordance with management's established criteria
2. Issuing raw materials	Materials are issued on the basis of approved materials requisitions
3. Processing of raw materials	Production is based on authorized production orders
4. Transferring completed work to finished goods	Transfers are properly authorized

The internal control principles applicable to these functions are explained below.

Authorization Procedures

The production planning and control department has the responsibility to authorize production. Both general and specific authorizations may occur. The former usually involve production for stock, the latter pertain to tailor-made customer orders. Evidence of authorization is provided by production orders, which then serve as the basis for incurring materials and labor costs.

Before an order for stock items (inventory) is released for production, a supervisor in production control should determine that (1) the quantities requested are compatible with established reorder quantities and with production budgets, and (2) existing quantities are at the reorder level.

During the production process, the movement of goods between departments and into the finished goods warehouse should be authorized.

Segregation of Functions

An appropriate separation of duties for manufacturing transactions is as follows:

FUNCTION	DEPARTMENT	RELATED ACTIVITIES
1. Issuing production orders	Production Planning and Control	Prepare and approve product specifications, schedule production, and issue production orders
2. Issuing raw materials	Raw Materials Stores	Release raw materials, obtain materials requisitions for each issue, and prepare batch or daily totals of materials issued
3. Processing raw materials	Manufacturing (fabricating, enameling, assembling)	Apply direct labor, prepare time tickets, and prepare control totals of labor usage
4. Transferring work to finished goods	Manufacturing	Prepare routing ticket and obtain receipt from finished goods

Documentation Procedures

The production order is a key document in the production cycle. The orders should be prenumbered and signed by a supervisor. For custom-made items, the orders should be accompanied by a detailed bill of materials. During production, documentation procedures should (1) provide evidence of direct materials and direct labor usage, (2) create a basis for physical control of the goods, and (3) permit the determination of accurate production cost data.

Materials requisitions serve as the authorization for the release of materials from the storeroom. For control purposes they should be prenumbered and storeroom personnel should prepare daily or batch totals of materials issued. *Time tickets* provide the documentation for direct labor usage, and timekeeping should prepare control totals of hours worked.

Routing tickets provide the basis for control over the movement of goods through the production process. The tickets should be initialed by the transferring department, signed by the department that is accepting the goods, and forwarded to accounting. Routing tickets should be prenumbered and filed with the production order.

Transfers to finished goods are documented by the completed production order and a routing ticket signed by personnel in the finished goods warehouse upon receipt of the goods.

Independent Internal Verification

This principle is applicable in accounting for prenumbered documents and in comparing the daily activity reports with corresponding materials requisitions and time tickets.

Manufacturing Transactions Are Properly Recorded

The functions and specific accounting control objectives in recording manufacturing transactions are as follows:

FUNCTION	DEPARTMENT	SPECIFIC ACCOUNTING CONTROL OBJECTIVE
1. Journalizing and posting manufacturing transactions	General Accounting	All manufacturing transactions are correctly recorded as to amount, classification, and accounting period
2. Updating work-in-process records	Cost Accounting	Work-in-process records are accurately updated on a timely basis

The internal control principles applicable to these functions are explained below.

Authorization procedures

Authorizations are necessary in establishing manufacturing overhead (burden) rates and in setting standard costs. Similarly, all revisions of these data should be formally authorized.

Segregation of functions

Adherence to the assignment of departmental responsibilities indicated above should provide for proper segregation of functions in recording. In addition, there should be a separation of duties between these departments and payroll and inventory accounting.

Accounting Records and Procedures

This principle serves the following purposes in this cycle:

- Costing direct materials and direct labor.
- Assigning manufacturing overhead to production.
- Recording the transfer of costs between departments.
- Determining the cost of work-in-process inventories.

Direct materials costs are obtained through the costing of materials requisitions. Direct labor costs are derived from the costing of time tickets. Manufacturing overhead costs are usually based on predetermined burden rates. When standard costs are used, variance accounts are used for each of the manufacturing cost elements. In a job order system, the subsidiary work-in-process ledger consists of individual job cost sheets. Entries for the transfer of costs between departments should parallel the physical movement of the goods through the manufacturing process. The costing of ending work in process is obtained from job and production cost records.

Custody of Work in Process Is Properly Maintained

This objective pertains to limited access to work in process and to the comparison of work in process records with existing assets. The functions and specific internal accounting control objectives are as follows:

FUNCTION	DEPARTMENT	SPECIFIC ACCOUNTING CONTROL OBJECTIVE
1. Protecting work in process	Manufacturing	Access to work in process is limited to authorized personnel
2. Maintaining correctness of work-in-process records	General Accounting	Work in process is periodically reconciled with unfinished cost records

The internal control principles applicable to these objectives are explained below.

Physical Controls and Authorization Procedures

Wherever possible, work in process should be stored in locked areas and access thereto should be limited to authorized personnel. Physical controls over work in various stages of completion on an assembly line may consist of surveillance by supervisory personnel and tagging of the goods.

CYCLE: Production   **CLASS OF TRANSACTIONS: Manufacturing**

	Yes	No
EXECUTING		
1. Are prenumbered production orders used and accounted for? (E1)		
2. Are production orders approved by a supervisor? (E1)		
3. Are materials requisitions required before materials can be released from stores? (E2)		
4. Are batch or daily totals of materials usage prepared by stores? (E2)		
5. Are time tickets prepared for direct labor incurred? (E3)		
6. Are batch or daily totals of direct labor hours reconciled with time ticket hours? (E3)		
7. Do routing tickets accompany the transfer of goods? (E4)		
8. Is receipt obtained from transferee when goods are transferred? (E4)		
RECORDING		
1. Is there segregation of functions between general accounting and cost accounting? (R1)		
2. Are verifications made of the agreement of daily entries with labor cost distribution summary? (R1)		
3. Is there internal verification of correct application of burden rates on job cost sheets? (R2)		
CUSTODY		
1. Is each production order tagged during production? (C1)		
2. Is work in process periodically reconciled with unfinished job cost sheets? (C2)		

FIGURE 10–8. Internal Control Questionnaire: Manufacturing Transactions

Function	Possible Errors and Irregularities	Necessary Control Procedures	Possible Compliance Test
EXECUTING			
Issuing production orders	Excessive quantities of stock items may be authorized for production	Supervisory approval of each order	Review evidence of approval
Issuing raw materials	The wrong materials may be requisitioned for custom-made items	Bill of materials; supervisory approval of requisitions	Determine existence of bill of materials; review approval
Processing raw materials	Excessive production costs may be incurred	Cost budgets for each order and periodic comparison of actual and budgeted cost	Review budget reports
Transferring completed work to finished goods	Goods may be lost during transfer	Routing ticket and receipt from finished goods on delivery	Examine routing tickets and receipts
RECORDING			
Journalizing and posting	Direct labor may be charged to manufacturing overhead	Internal verification of daily entry with factory labor summary	Review evidence of verification
Updating work-in-process records	An incorrect burden rate may be used in costing a job order	Verification of authorized rate and mathematical accuracy	Review evidence of authorization and verification
CUSTODY			
Protecting work in process	Goods may be lost or stolen in production	Tagging of work and storage in locked areas	Inspect physical controls
Maintaining correctness of work-in-process records	Job cost sheets may be incorrectly posted	Periodic reconciliation of control and subsidiary records	Review reconciliations

FIGURE 10–9. Preliminary Evaluation Considerations: Manufacturing Transactions

Segregation of Functions and Independent Internal Verification

Personnel responsible for the custody of work in process should not record manufacturing transactions. Independent internal verification involves periodic comparison of work-in-process control with unfinished job and production cost records by personnel who have no incompatible duties.

STUDY AND EVALUATION OF INTERNAL CONTROL

The auditor's methodology for meeting the second standard of field work for manufacturing transactions is the same as for other major classes of transactions.

TYPE OF TESTING: Compliance   **PURPOSE: Study and Evaluation of Internal Control**
CYCLE: Production   **CLASS OF TRANSACTIONS: Manufacturing**

A. CONTROLS IN EXECUTING MANUFACTURING TRANSACTIONS ARE OPERATING AS PLANNED.

    1. Examine selected production orders for evidence of
       • Proper authorization.
       • Signed receipt for goods from finished goods.
    2. Examine evidence of internal verification of daily activity reports of materials and direct labor usage.
    3. Observe and make inquiries of employees in performance of control procedures.

B. CONTROLS IN RECORDING MANUFACTURING TRANSACTIONS ARE OPERATING AS PLANNED.

    1. Review budget and standard cost variance reports.
    2. Review evidence of reconciliation of usage reports with materials requisitions and time tickets.

C. CONTROLS OVER THE CUSTODY OF WORK IN PROCESS ARE OPERATING AS PLANNED.

    1. Observe physical controls over work in process.
    2. Examine evidence of periodic reconciliations of work in process with uncompleted production cost records.

FIGURE 10–10. Audit Program: Compliance Tests of Manufacturing Transactions

Review of the system

A questionnaire that may be used in gathering information about prescribed controls over manufacturing transactions is shown in Figure 10-8. As in previous examples, the questions relate to necessary control procedures and are referenced to specific functions.

A representative listing of errors and irregularities is shown in Figure 10-9. From a comparison of necessary controls and prescribed controls, the auditor makes a preliminary evaluation of the specific controls in the client's system.

Compliance Tests of Prescribed Controls

An audit program for compliance testing of manufacturing transactions is illustrated in Figure 10-10. In this program, the production order is used as the sampling unit. Alternatively, the sampling unit may be the job cost sheet or the production cost report.

Final Evaluation of the Controls

Based on the results of compliance testing, the auditor makes a final evaluation of the controls over manufacturing transactions. The auditor then determines the effects of his evaluation on the nature, timing, and extent of substantive tests of production cycle balances.

CONCLUDING COMMENTS

The seven chapters pertaining to the study and evaluation of internal control have now been completed. These chapters have explained and illustrated the auditor's responsibilities and methodology for meeting the second standard of field work.

While the study and evaluation of internal control is a vital part of the typical audit engagement, it must be remembered that this auditing standard is not an end in itself. GAAS dictate that there is a correlation between the effectiveness of internal controls and the extent to which substantive tests are to be restricted.

Part III, which follows, considers the substantive tests that may be performed in verifying account balances.

REVIEW QUESTIONS

10-1. What are the functions in (a) executing, (b) recording, and (c) custody of payroll transactions?

10-2. Briefly explain the materiality and risk associated with payroll transactions.

10-3. Indicate the specific internal accounting control objectives in (a) hiring, (b) preparing the payroll, and (c) paying the payroll.

10-4. What authorizations are required for payroll transactions? For each authorization identify the department or individual who should make the authorization.

10-5. Explain the primary activities of the (a) timekeeping and (b) payroll departments.

10-6. Distinguish between a payroll summary and a payroll register, and indicate the principal uses of each.

10-7. Diagram the flow of payroll data within (a) the timekeeping and (b) the payroll departments.

10-8. Diagram the flow of payroll data within general accounting.

10-9. What control procedures should be prescribed and followed for proper custody over assets pertaining to payroll transactions?

10-10. Explain the applicability of independent internal verification to (a) executing payroll transactions and (b) custody of payroll funds.

10-11. Describe the steps of the audit program for compliance testing payroll transactions in a manual system that uses a sample of documents.

10-12. What controls should be observed in witnessing the distribution of a payroll?

10-13. What attributes may be identified in using statistical sampling in performing compliance tests of payroll transactions?

10-14. a. Identify the computer runs that are illustrated in Figure 10-6.
b. Which run(s) may be tested by the use of test data?

10-15. Explain the nature of the production cycle.

10-16. Identify the departments reporting to the vice president of operations.

10-17. Enumerate the functions related to the production cycle.

10-18. Indicate the specific accounting control objectives for each function in the execution of manufacturing transactions.

10-19. Indicate the purposes served by production orders in the production cycle.

10-20. What purposes are served by accounting records and procedures in the production cycle?

COMPREHENSIVE QUESTIONS

10-21. The following questions are included in Figure 10-3:

1. Are pay rates, payroll deductions, and terminations authorized by the personnel department?
2. Are time clocks and clock cards used?

3. Is there supervisory approval of time worked by each employee?
4. Is there internal verification of accuracy of payroll computations?
5. Is there supervisory approval of the payroll?
6. Are payroll checks signed and distributed by treasurer office personnel?
7. Is there internal verification of payroll checks with payroll register data?
8. Are costed time tickets verified for proper rate and mathematical accuracy?
9. Are unclaimed wages controlled by a treasurer's office employee?
10. Are personnel and employee earnings records kept in locked files?

Required
a. Identify the internal accounting control operative objective to which each question relates (i.e., executing, recording, or custody).
b. Identify the function and specific accounting control objective to which the question pertains.
c. Indicate the internal control principle that is involved.
d. Identify an error or irregularity that may result from a "no" answer to each question. (Present your answer in tabular form.)

10–22. The following control procedures over payroll transactions are prescribed by the Hahn Company:

1. Operating department requisition for each hiring.
2. Personnel department authorizations for termination of employment.
3. Employee authorizations for payroll deductions.
4. Supervised clock card punching.
5. Internal verification of agreement of payroll checks and payroll register.
6. Distribution of payroll checks by individual who did not prepare payroll.
7. Internal verification of payroll summaries and payroll entries.
8. Supervisor approval of time tickets.

Required
a. Indicate the function served by each procedure.
b. Identify an error or irregularity that may be prevented or detected by the control procedure.
c. Indicate a compliance test that may be performed to determine whether each control procedure above is operating as prescribed. (Present your answer in tabular form.)

10–23. Assume the following exceptions to prescribed control procedures over payroll transactions occurred in the Haze Company:

1. A fictitious employee is on the payroll.
2. A fictitious pay rate is used in calculating an employee's gross earnings.
3. An employee is paid for unauthorized overtime hours.
4. A mathematical error is made in computing an employee's net earnings.
5. A payroll check is issued for an incorrect amount.
6. A payroll check is distributed to an unauthorized recipient.
7. An employee's time tickets do not agree with clock card hours.
8. A terminated employee is not removed from the payroll.

Required
a. Indicate function and the specific internal accounting control objective associated with each occurrence.
b. Indicate the control procedure(s) that could prevent or detect the occurrences.
c. Identify a compliance test that would determine whether the controls indicated in (b) above are operating as planned. (Present your answer in tabular form.)

10-24. In the Sumet Company, two employees were terminated for falsifying their time records. The two employees had altered overtime hours on their time cards after their supervisors had approved the hours actually worked.

Several years ago, the company discontinued the use of time clocks. Since then, the plant supervisors have been responsible for manually posting the time cards and approving the hours for which their employees should be paid. The postings are usually entered in pencil by the supervisors or their secretaries. After the postings for the week are complete, the time cards are approved and placed in the mail racks outside the supervisors' offices for pickup by the timekeepers. Sometimes the timekeepers do not pick up the time cards promptly.

Required
Assuming the company does not wish to return to using time clocks, give three recommendations to prevent recurrence of the situation described above. For each recommendation, indicate how it will deter fraudulent reporting of hours worked.

IIA

10-25. The Kowal Manufacturing Company employs about fifty production workers and has the following payroll procedures.

The factory foreman interviews applicants and on the basis of the interview either hires or rejects the applicants. When the applicant is hired he prepares a W-4 form (Employee's Withholding Exemption Certificate) and gives it to the foreman. The foreman writes the hourly rate of pay for the new employee in the corner of the W-4 form and then gives the form to a payroll clerk as notice that the worker has been employed. The foreman verbally advises the payroll department of rate adjustments.

A supply of blank time cards is kept in a box near the entrance to the factory. Each worker takes a time card on Monday morning, fills in his name, and notes in pencil on the time card his daily arrival and departure times. At the end of the week, the workers drop the time cards in a box near the door to the factory.

The completed time cards are taken from the box on Monday morning by a payroll clerk. Two payroll clerks divide the cards alphabetically between them, one taking the A to L section of the payroll and the other taking the M to Z section. Each clerk is fully responsible for her section of the payroll. She computes the gross pay, deductions, and net pay, posts the details to the employee's earnings records, and prepares and numbers the payroll checks. Employees are automatically removed from the payroll when they fail to turn in a time card.

The payroll checks are manually signed by the chief accountant and given to the foreman. The foreman distributes the checks to the workers in the factory and arranges for the delivery of the checks to the workers who are absent. The payroll bank account is reconciled by the chief accountant, who also prepares the various quarterly and annual payroll tax reports.

Required
a. Identify the errors or irregularities that may occur in the Kowal Company's procedures.
b. For each error or irregularity in (a) above, give your recommended improvements.

AICPA (adapted)

10-26. In connection with his examination of the financial statements of the Olympia Manufacturing Company, a CPA is reviewing procedures for accumulating direct labor hours. He learns that all production is by job order and that all employees are paid hourly wages, with time-and-one-half for overtime hours.

Olympia's direct labor hour input process for payroll and job cost determination is summarized in the flowchart on page 336:

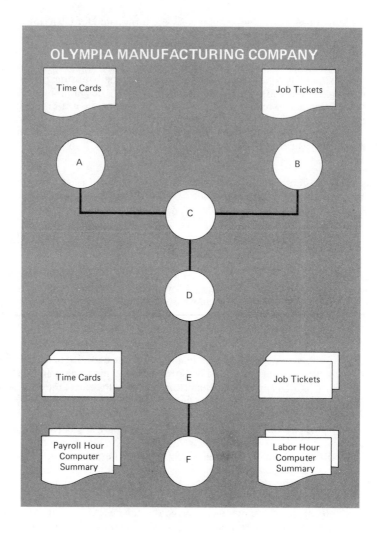

Steps A and C are performed in timekeeping, step B in the factory operating departments, step D in payroll audit and control, step E in data preparation (keypunch), and step F in computer operations.

Required

For each input processing step A through F:

a. List the possible errors or discrepancies that may occur.

b. Cite the corresponding control procedure for each error or discrepancy.

Note: Your discussion of Olympia's procedures should be limited to the input process for direct labor hours, as shown in steps A through F in the flowchart. Do not discuss personnel procedures for hiring, promotion, termination, and pay rate authorization. In step F do not discuss equipment, computer program, and general computer operational controls.

Organize your answer for each input-processing step as follows:

Step	Possible Errors or Discrepancies	Control Procedures

AICPA

10–27. You are reviewing the working papers containing a narrative description of the Tenney Corporation's factory payroll system. A portion of that narrative is as follows:

> Factory employees punch time clock cards each day when entering or leaving the shop. At the end of each week, the timekeeping department collects the time cards and prepares duplicate batch control slips by department showing total hours and number of employees. The time cards and original batch control slips are sent to the payroll accounting section. The second copies of the batch control slips are filed by date.
>
> In the payroll accounting section, payroll transaction cards are keypunched from the information on the time cards, and a batch total card is keypunched from the batch control slip. The time cards and batch control slips are then filed by batch for possible reference. The payroll transaction cards and batch total card are sent to data processing, where they are sorted by employee number within batch. Each batch is edited by a computer program which checks the validity of employee number against a master employee tape file and the total hours and number of employees against the batch total card. A detail printout by batch and employee number is produced which indicates batches that do not balance and invalid employee numbers. This printout is returned to payroll accounting to resolve all differences.

In searching for documentation you found a flowchart of the payroll system which included all appropriate symbols but was only partially labeled. The portion of this flowchart described by the above narrative appears on page 338.

Required
a. Number your answer 1 through 17. Next to the corresponding number of your answer, supply the appropriate labeling (document name, process description, or file order) applicable to each numbered symbol on the flowchart.
b. Flowcharts are one of the aids an auditor may use to determine and evaluate a client's internal control system. List advantages of using flowcharts in this context.

AICPA

10–28. The Generous Loan Company has 100 branch loan offices. Each office has a manager and four or five subordinates who are employed by the manager. Branch managers prepare the weekly payroll, including their own salaries, and pay employees from cash on hand. The employee signs the payroll sheet signifying receipt of his salary. Hours worked by hourly personnel are inserted in the payroll sheet from time cards prepared by the employees and approved by the manager.

The weekly payroll sheets are sent to the home office along with other accounting statements and reports. The home office compiles employee earnings records and prepares all federal and state salary reports from the weekly payroll sheets.

Salaries are established by home office job evaluation schedules. Salary adjustments, promotions, and transfers of full-time employees are approved by a home office salary committee based upon the recommendations of branch managers and area supervisors. Branch managers advise the salary committee of new full-time em-

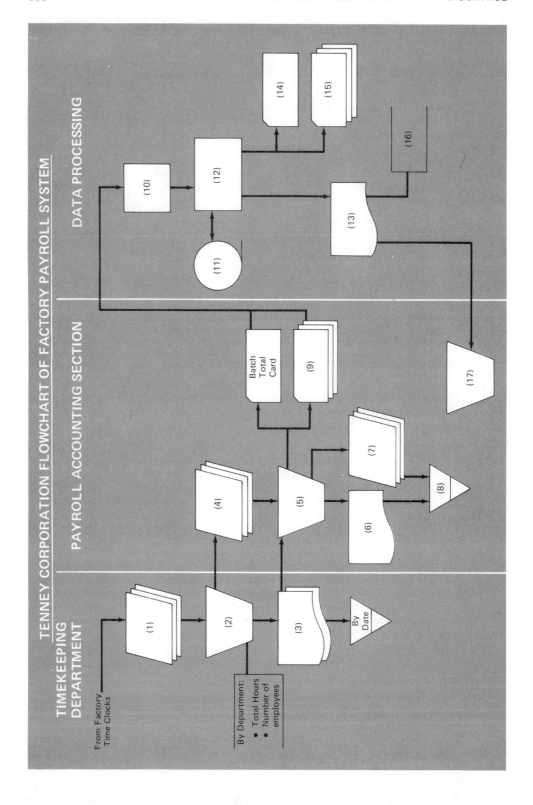

TENNEY CORPORATION FLOWCHART OF FACTORY PAYROLL SYSTEM

ployees and terminations. Part-time and temporary employees are hired without referral to the salary committee.

Required
a. Based on your review of the system, how might payroll funds be diverted?
b. Indicate your recommendations for improvement.
c. Do you believe any weaknesses in the system are material? Explain.

AICPA (adapted)

10–29. You are engaged in auditing the financial statements of Henry Brown, a large independent contractor. All employees are paid in cash because Brown believes this arrangement reduces clerical expenses and is preferred by his employees.

During the audit, you find in the petty cash fund approximately $200, of which $185 is stated to be unclaimed wages. Further investigation reveals that Brown has installed the procedure of putting any unclaimed wages in the petty cash fund so that the cash can be used for disbursements. When the claimant to the wages appears, he is paid from the petty cash fund. Brown contends that this procedure reduces the number of checks drawn to replenish the petty cash fund and centers the responsibility for all cash on hand in one person inasmuch as the petty cash custodian distributes the pay envelopes.

Required
a. Does Brown's system provide proper internal control of unclaimed wages? Explain fully.
b. Because Brown insists on paying salaries in cash, what procedures would you recommend to provide better internal control over unclaimed wages?

AICPA

10–30. As part of the audit of Manor Company, you are assigned to review and test the payroll transactions of the Galena plant. Your tests show that all numerical items were accurate. The proper hourly rates were used and the wages and deductions were calculated correctly. The payroll register was properly footed, totaled, and posted.

Various plant personnel were interviewed to ascertain the payroll procedures being used in the department. You determine that

1. The payroll clerk receives the time cards from the various department supervisors at the end of each pay period, checks the employee's hourly rate against information provided by the personnel department, and records the regular and overtime hours for each employee.
2. The payroll clerk sends the time cards to the plant's data processing department for compilation and processing.
3. The data processing department returns the time cards with the printed checks and payroll register to the payroll clerk upon completion of the processing.
4. The payroll clerk verifies the hourly rate and hours worked for each employee by comparing the detail in the payroll register to the time cards.
5. If errors are found, the payroll clerk voids the computer-generated check, prepares another check for the correct amount, and adjusts the payroll register accordingly.
6. The payroll clerk obtains the plant signature plate from the accounting departing and signs the payroll checks.
7. An employee of the personnel department picks up the checks and holds them until they are delivered to the department supervisors for distribution to the employees.

Required

a. Identify the shortcomings in the payroll procedures used in the payroll department of the Galena plant and suggest corrective action.

b. Identify the weaknesses, if any, that you believe are material and the reasons why.

CMA (adapted)

10–31. The Vane Corporation is a manufacturing concern which has been in business for the past eighteen years. During this period, the company has grown from a very small family-owned operation to a medium-sized manufacturing concern with several departments. Despite this growth, a substantial number of the procedures employed by Vane Corp. have been in effect since the business was started. Just recently Vane Corp. has computerized its payroll function.

The payroll function operates in the following manner. Each worker picks up a weekly time card on Monday morning and writes in his name and identification number. These blank cards are kept near the factory entrance. The workers write on the time card the time of their daily arrival and departure. On the following Monday the factory foremen collect the completed time cards for the previous week and send them to data processing.

In data processing, the time cards are used to prepare the weekly time file. This file is processed with the master payroll file, which is maintained on magnetic tape according to worker identification number. The checks are written by the computer on the regular checking account and imprinted with the treasurer's signature. After the payroll file is updated and the checks are prepared, the checks are sent to the factory foremen, who distribute them to the workers or hold them for the workers to pick up later if they are absent.

The foremen notify data processing of new employees and terminations. Any changes in hourly pay rate or any other changes affecting payroll are usually communicated to data processing by the foremen.

The workers also complete a job time ticket for each individual job they work on each day. The job time tickets are collected daily and sent to cost accounting, where they are used to prepare a cost distribution analysis.

Further analysis of the payroll function reveals the following:

1. A worker's gross wages never exceed $300 per week.
2. Raises never exceed $0.55 per hour for the factory workers.
3. No more than 20 hours of overtime is allowed each week.
4. The factory employs 150 workers in ten departments.

The payroll function has not been operating smoothly for some time, but even more problems have surfaced since the payroll was computerized. The foremen have indicated that they would like a weekly report indicating worker tardiness, absenteeism, and idle time, so they can determine the amount of productive time lost and the reason for the lost time. The following errors and inconsistencies have been encountered in the past few pay periods:

1. A worker's paycheck was not processed properly, because he had transposed two numbers in his identification number when he filled out his time card.
2. A worker was issued a check for $1,531.80 when it should have been $153.81.
3. One worker's paycheck was not written, and this error was not detected until the paychecks for that department were distributed by the foreman.
4. Part of the master payroll file was destroyed when the tape reel was inadvertently mounted on the wrong tape drive and used as a scratch tape. Data processing attempted to reestablish the destroyed portion from original source documents and other records.
5. One worker received a paycheck for an amount considerably larger than he should have. Further investigation revealed that 84 had been punched instead of 48 for hours worked.

6. Several records on the master payroll file were skipped and not included on the updated master payroll file. This was not detected for several pay periods.
7. In processing nonroutine changes a computer operator included a pay rate increase for one of his friends in the factory. This was discovered by chance by another employee.

Required
Identify the control weaknesses in the payroll procedure and in the computer processing as it is now conducted by the Vane Corp. Recommend the changes necessary to correct the system. Arrange your answer in the following columnar format:

Control Weakness	*Recommendations*

CMA

10–32. A CPA's audit working papers contain a narrative description of a segment of the Croyden Factory, Inc., payroll system and the flowchart on page 342:

NARRATIVE

The internal control system with respect to the personnel department is well functioning and is not included in the accompanying flowchart.

At the beginning of each work week, payroll clerk No. 1 reviews the payroll department files to determine the employment status of factory employees and then prepares time cards and distributes them as each individual arrives at work. This payroll clerk, who is also responsible for custody of the signature stamp machine, verifies the identity of each payee before delivering signed checks to the foreman.

At the end of each work week the foreman distributes payroll checks for the preceding work week. Concurrent with this activity, the foreman reviews the current week's employee time cards, notes the regular and overtime hours worked on a summary form, and initials the aforementioned time cards. The foreman then delivers all time cards and unclaimed payroll checks to payroll clerk No. 2.

Required
a. Based upon the narrative and accompanying flowchart, what are the weaknesses in the system of internal control?
b. Based upon the narrative and accompanying flowchart, what inquiries should be made with respect to clarifying the existence of possible additional weaknesses in the system of internal control?
Note: Do not discuss the internal control system of the personnel department.

10–33. The prescribed control procedures over manufacturing transactions in the Adrian Company are as follows:

1. Bills of materials for each production order.
2. Authorized production order for each job or process.
3. Approved materials requisition slips.
4. Approved time tickets.
5. Signed receipts from transferee upon movement of goods.

Required
a. Indicate the specific internal accounting control objective served by each procedure.

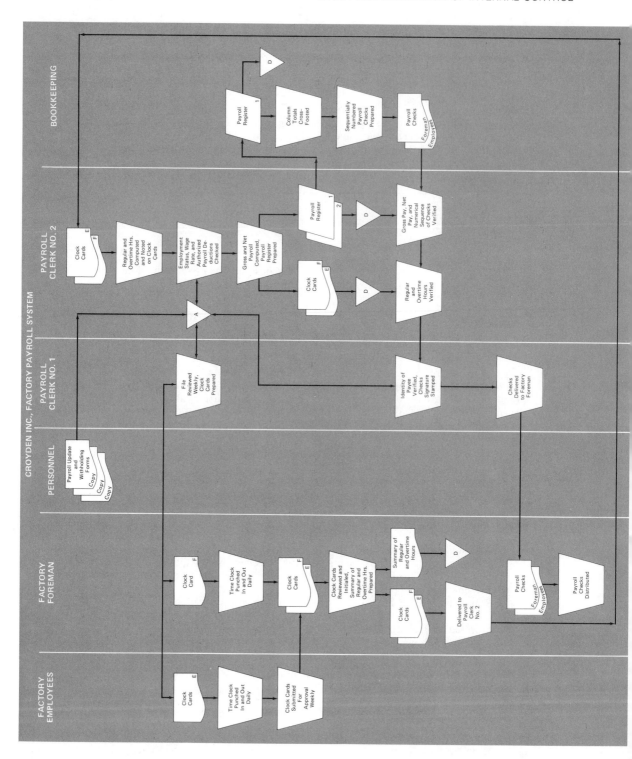

CROYDEN INC., FACTORY PAYROLL SYSTEM

b. Identify the internal accounting control principle that is involved.

c. Identify an error or irregularity that may be prevented or detected by the control procedure.

d. Indicate a compliance test that may be performed to determine whether each control procedure is operating as prescribed. (Present your answer in tabular form.)

10-34. The following errors or irregularities could occur in the executing and recording of manufacturing transactions and in the safeguarding of work in process in the Leslie Company:

1. Materials may be released from the storeroom without proper authorization.
2. Excessive production costs may be incurred during a month.
3. Direct labor assigned to production may be unauthorized.
4. Work in process may be stolen.
5. Work-in-process control may not agree with subsidiary cost records.
6. Work in process may be lost when transferred to another department.

Required

a. Indicate the function and specific internal accounting control objective associated with each occurrence.

b. Indicate the control procedure(s) that could prevent or detect the occurrences.

c. Identify the compliance tests that would determine whether each control indicated in (b) above are operating as planned. (Present your answer in tabular form.)

10-35. You have been engaged by the management of Alden, Inc. to review its internal control over the purchase, receipt, storage, and issue of raw materials. You have prepared the following comments which describe Alden's procedures:

1. Raw materials, which consist mainly of high-cost electronic components, are kept in a locked storeroom. Storeroom personnel include a supervisor and four clerks. All are well trained, competent, and adequately bonded. Raw materials are removed from the storeroom only upon written or oral authorization of one of the production foremen.

2. There are no perpetual-inventory records; hence, the storeroom clerks do not keep records of goods received or issued. To compensate for the lack of perpetual records, a physical inventory count is taken monthly by the storeroom clerks who are well supervised. Appropriate procedures are followed in making the inventory count.

3. After the physical count, the storeroom supervisor matches quantities counted against a predetermined reorder level. If the count for a given part is below the reorder level, the supervisor enters the part number on a materials requisition list and sends this list to the accounts payable clerk. The accounts payable clerk prepares a purchase order for a predetermined reorder quantity for each part and mails the purchase order to the vendor from whom the part was last purchased.

4. When ordered materials arrive at Alden, they are received by the storeroom clerks. The clerks count the merchandise and agree the counts to the shipper's bill of lading. All vendors' bills of lading are initialed, dated, and filed in the storeroom to serve as receiving reports.

Required

a. Describe the weaknesses in internal control and recommend improvements of Alden's procedures for the purchase, receipt, storage, and issue of raw materials. Organize your answer sheet as follows:

Weaknesses	*Recommended Improvements*

b. Do you believe any of the weaknesses are material? Explain.

AICPA (adapted)

CASE STUDY

10–36. The Jameson Company produces a variety of chemical products for use by plastics manufacturers. The plant operates on two shifts, five days per week with maintenance work performed on the third shift and on Saturdays as required.

An audit conducted by the staff of the new corporate internal audit department has recently been completed and the comments on inventory control were not favorable. Audit comments were particularly directed to the control of raw material ingredients and maintenance materials.

Raw material ingredients are received at the back of the plant, signed for by one of the employees of the batching department, and stored near the location of the initial batching process. Receiving tallies are given to the supervisor during the day and he forwards the tallies to the inventory control department at the end of the day. The inventory control department calculates ingredient usage using weekly reports of actual production and standard formulas. Physical inventories are taken quarterly. Purchase requisitions are prepared by the inventory control department and rush orders are frequent. In spite of the need for rush orders the production superintendent regularly gets memos from the controller stating that there must be excess inventory because the ingredient inventory dollar value is too high.

Maintenance parts and supplies are received and stored in a storeroom. There is a storeroom clerk on each of the operating shifts. Storeroom requisitions are to be filled out for everything taken from the storeroom; however, this practice is not always followed. The storeroom is not locked when the clerk is out because of the need to get parts quickly. The storeroom is also open during the third shift for the maintenance crews to get parts as needed. Purchase requisitions are prepared by the storeroom clerk and physical inventory is taken on a cycle count basis. Rush orders are frequent.

Required
a. Identify the weaknesses in Jameson Company's internal control procedures used for (1) ingredients inventory and (2) maintenance material and supplies inventory.
b. Recommend improvements which should be instituted for each of these areas.

CMA

III

Verification of Account Balances

The verification of account balances relates to substantive tests performed by the auditor at or near the balance sheet date. In practice, as in this book, the verification of balances follows the study and evaluation of internal control.

There are five chapters in this section. Chapter 11 describes the use of statistical and nonstatistical sampling in verifying account balances. Chapters 12-14 explain and illustrate the audit objectives and methodology for substantive tests of balances resulting from specific transactions within a given cycle. The final chapter discusses the steps the auditor takes in verifying income statement balances and in completing the audit.

11 | Audit Sampling in Substantive Testing

STUDY OBJECTIVES

The study objectives of this chapter are to obtain an understanding of the applicability of audit sampling in substantive testing and the use of either statistical or nonstatistical sampling in tests of transactions and balances. To achieve these objectives, it is necessary for the reader to:

- Know the basic concepts of audit sampling that are applicable to substantive testing.
- Comprehend the two statistical approaches that may be used by the auditor.
- Learn the essential steps in the design and execution of a probability-proportional-to-size sampling plan.
- Realize the considerations and steps involved with each of the classical variables sampling plan techniques.
- Understand the use of nonstatistical sampling in substantive testing.

T he basic concepts of audit sampling and the application of sampling in compliance
testing are explained in Chapter 6. This chapter considers the use of audit
sampling in substantive testing. The chapter is divided into four sections: (1)
basic concepts, (2) probability-proportional-to-size sampling, (3) classical
variables sampling, and (4) nonstatistical sampling.

BASIC CONCEPTS

Nature and Purpose

As explained in Chapter 6, audit sampling is the application of auditing
procedures to less than 100 percent of the items within a population, such as
an account balance or class of transactions, for the purpose of evaluating
some characteristic of the population. Whereas attribute sampling is used to
obtain information about the rate of occurrence of deviations from prescribed controls, the audit sampling in this chapter is used to obtain information about the correctness of monetary amounts. Thus, it serves the purpose
of substantive tests, which is to obtain evidence as to the validity and
propriety of the accounting treatment of transactions and balances, or conversely, of errors or irregularities therein.

Sampling plans for substantive tests may be designed to (1) test the
reasonableness of a recorded amount (for example, the book value of
accounts receivable) or (2) make an independent estimate of some amount
(for example, to price an inventory for which no recorded book value
exists). The emphasis in this chapter is on testing the reasonableness of
recorded amounts.

Risk and Audit Uncertainty

The auditor is justified in accepting some uncertainty in substantive testing
when the cost and time required to make a 100 percent examination of items
in a population are, in his judgment, greater than the adverse consequences
of expressing an erroneous opinion from examining only a sample of the
data.

Audit sampling in substantive testing is subject to both sampling risk and
nonsampling risk. As explained in Chapter 6, the sampling risks associated
with substantive testing are:

- The *risk of incorrect acceptance* (sometimes referred to as the beta risk) is
  the risk that the sample supports the conclusion that the recorded account
  balance is not materially misstated when it is materially misstated.
- The *risk of incorrect rejection* (sometimes referred to as the alpha risk) is
  the risk that the sample supports the conclusion that the recorded account
  balance is materially misstated when it is not materially misstated.[1]

---

[1] Auditing Standards Board, *Codification of Statements of Auditing Standards* (New York:
American Institute of Certified Public Accountants, 1983), Auditing Section 350.12 (hereinafter
referred to and cited as AU §).

It will be recalled that the risk of incorrect acceptance relates to the effectiveness of the audit, whereas the risk of incorrect rejection relates to audit efficiency.

Statistical Sampling Approaches

Two statistical sampling approaches may be used by the auditor in substantive testing: (1) probability-proportional-to-size (PPS) sampling and (2) classical variables sampling.

The fundamental difference between the two approaches is that PPS sampling is based on attribute sampling theory, while classical variables sampling is based on normal distribution theory. Each approach can provide sufficient evidence under the third standard of field work. However, in certain circumstances, as described in this chapter, one approach may be more practical and appropriate in meeting the auditor's objective than the other.

The principal circumstances affecting the choice between the two approaches are tabulated in Figure 11-1. It may be observed for example, that PPS sampling may be more appropriate when (1) the number of units in, and the variability of, the population are unknown, (2) the population contains only debit balances, (3) only a few errors of overstatement are expected, and (4) computer assistance is not available.

	APPROPRIATE SAMPLING APPROACH	
Sampling Application Circumstances	**PPS**	**Classical Variables**
AVAILABILITY OF INFORMATION		
Book values for sampling units not available		X
Number of units in population unknown at start of sampling	X	
Variability of population unknown	X	
CHARACTERISTICS OF POPULATION UNITS		
Existence of zero or credit balances		X
EXPECTATIONS REGARDING ERRORS		
Expect few errors of overstatement only	X	
Expect many errors or errors of both under- and overstatement		X
EASE OF APPLICATION		
Computer assistance not available	X	

FIGURE 11–1. Circumstances Affecting Selection of Sampling Approach for Substantive Testing

PROBABILITY-PROPORTIONAL-TO-SIZE-SAMPLING[2]

PPS sampling is an approach that uses attribute sampling theory to express a conclusion in dollar amounts rather than as a rate of occurrence. This form of sampling may be used in the substantive testing of both transactions and balances.

PPS is primarily applicable in testing transactions and balances for overstatement. It may be especially useful in tests of:

- Receivables when unapplied credits to customer accounts are insignificant
- Investment securities
- Inventory price tests when few differences are anticipated
- Plant asset additions[3]

PPS sampling may not be the most cost-effective approach for receivables and inventories when the above conditions are not met and where the primary objective is to independently estimate the value of a class of transactions or balances.

Sampling Plan

The steps in a PPS sampling plan are similar but not identical to those used in attribute sampling. The steps are:

- Determining the objectives of the plan
- Defining the population and sampling unit
- Determining the sample size
- Determining the sample selection method
- Executing the sampling plan
- Evaluating the sample results

The considerations involved in executing these steps are explained below and a case study is used to illustrate each step. The auditor should document each step in his working papers.

Determining the Objectives of the Plan

The most common objective of PPS sampling plans is to test the reasonableness of a recorded account balance. To illustrate this application, it is

---

[2] There are three variations of PPS sampling: (1) dollar unit sampling (DUS), (2) cumulative monetary amount (CMA), and (3) combined attribute variables (CAV) sampling. The distinctions among these variations are beyond the scope of this text.

[3] Statistical Sampling Subcommittee, *Proposed Audit Guide: Audit Sampling,* (New York: American Institute of Certified Public Accountants, 1982), p. 61. (Hereinafter referred to as *Audit Sampling Guide.*)

assumed that the auditor's objective is to obtain evidence about the book value of trade accounts receivable of the Harris Company.

Defining the Population and Sampling Unit

The population consists of the class of transactions or the account balance to be tested. For each population the auditor should decide whether all of the items should be included. For example, four populations are possible when the population is based on account balances in the customers' ledger: that is all balances, debit balances, credit balances, and zero balances.

The sampling unit in PPS sampling is the individual dollar. Thus, the population is considered to be a *number* of dollars equal to the total dollar amount of the population. Each dollar in the population is given an equal chance of being selected in the sample. While individual dollars are the basis for sample selection, the auditor does not actually examine individual dollars in the population. Rather he examines the account, transaction, document, or line item associated with the dollar selected. Individual dollars selected for a sample are sometimes thought of as hooks that upon selection snag or bring in the entire item with which they are associated. The item snagged (account, document, etc.) is known as a *logical sampling unit*.

It is this feature that gives PPS sampling its name. The more dollars associated with a logical unit, the greater its chance of being snagged. Thus, the likelihood of selection is proportional to its size. This feature is also responsible for two limitations of PPS sampling. In testing receivables, for example, zero balances should be excluded from the population because such balances have no chance of being selected in the sample. Similarly, PPS sampling is not suitable in testing liabilities for understatement since the more a balance is understated the less is its chance of being included in the sample.

The auditor chooses a logical sampling unit compatible with the nature of the audit procedures to be performed. If, for example, the auditor intends to seek confirmation of customer account balances, he would ordinarily choose the customer account as the logical unit. Alternatively, the auditor might choose to seek confirmation of specific transactions with customers rather than the account balance. In that case he might choose customer invoices as the logical unit.

The auditor selects the sample items from a physical representation of the population such as a computer printout of customer balances. Before selecting the sample, the auditor should determine that the physical representation is complete. This may be done by reconciling the printout to a control account balance or a control total.

For the Harris Company, (1) the population is defined as customer accounts with debit balances, (2) the aggregate book value of these accounts is $600,000, (3) the customer account is defined as the logical sampling unit, and (4) the printout from which the accounts are to be selected has been reconciled to the control account and to the $600,000 figure used in (2) above.

Determining Sample Size

The formula for determining sample size in PPS sampling is:

$$n = \frac{BV \times RF}{TE - (AE \times EF)}$$

where

BV = book value of population tested
RF = reliability factor for the specified risk of incorrect acceptance
TE = tolerable error
AE = anticipated error
EF = expansion factor for anticipated error

Each of these factors is explained below.

Book Value of Population Tested

The book value specified in determining sample size must relate precisely to the definition of the population as described in the preceding section. The amount of the book value has a direct effect on sample size—the larger the book value being tested, the larger the sample size.

Reliability Factor for Specified Risk of Incorrect Acceptance

In specifying an acceptable level of risk of incorrect acceptance, the auditor should consider (1) the level of ultimate risk that he is willing to take that a material error in the account will go undetected, (2) the degree of assurance obtained from reliance on internal accounting controls, and (3) the results of other auditing procedures including analytical review. For example, if he concludes that substantial reliance can be placed on internal controls, and if other auditing procedures provide some assurance about the fairness of the book value being tested, he will be willing to accept a higher risk of incorrect acceptance for the PPS sample, perhaps up to 30 percent. If little reliance can be placed on the controls, and if other procedures provide little assurance about the account being tested, then greater assurance must be obtained from the test and the auditor will specify a low risk of incorrect acceptance, perhaps as low as 5 percent. Experience and professional judgment must be used in making these determinations.[4] The risk of incorrect acceptance has an inverse effect on sample size—the lower the specified risk, the larger the sample size.

The reliability factor (RF) for this risk is obtained from Table 1 of Figure 11-2. It is based on the risk of incorrect acceptance specified by the auditor and *zero number of overstatement errors*, regardless of the number of errors

---

[4] A model for relating the risk components in an audit is presented in Appendix A of this chapter.

PROBABILITY-PROPORTIONAL-TO-SIZE SAMPLING TABLES

TABLE 1. Reliability Factors for Errors of Overstatement

Risk of Incorrect Acceptance

Number of Overstatement Errors	1%	5%	10%	15%	20%	25%	30%	37%	50%
0	4.61	3.00	2.30	1.90	1.61	1.39	1.20	1.00	.69
1	6.64	4.74	3.89	3.37	2.99	2.69	2.44	2.15	1.69
2	8.41	6.30	5.32	4.72	4.28	3.92	3.62	3.27	2.69
3	10.05	7.75	6.68	6.01	5.52	5.11	4.76	4.37	3.69
4	11.60	9.15	7.99	7.27	6.72	6.27	5.89	5.46	4.69
5	13.11	10.51	9.27	8.49	7.91	7.42	7.01	6.54	5.69
6	14.57	11.84	10.53	9.70	9.08	8.56	8.11	7.61	6.69
7	16.00	13.15	11.77	10.90	10.23	9.68	9.21	8.68	7.69
8	17.40	14.43	12.99	12.08	11.38	10.80	10.30	9.74	8.69
9	18.78	15.71	14.21	13.25	12.52	11.91	11.39	10.80	9.69
10	20.14	16.96	15.41	14.41	13.65	13.02	12.47	11.86	10.69
11	21.49	18.21	16.60	15.57	14.78	14.12	13.55	12.91	11.69
12	22.82	19.44	17.78	16.71	15.90	15.22	14.62	13.96	12.69
13	24.14	20.67	18.96	17.86	17.01	16.31	15.70	15.01	13.69
14	25.45	21.89	20.13	19.00	18.13	17.40	16.77	16.06	14.69
15	26.74	23.10	21.29	20.13	19.23	18.49	17.83	17.11	15.69
16	28.03	24.30	22.45	21.26	20.34	19.57	18.90	18.16	16.69
17	29.31	25.50	23.61	22.38	21.44	20.65	19.96	19.21	17.69
18	30.58	26.69	24.76	23.50	22.54	21.73	21.02	20.26	18.69
19	31.85	27.88	25.90	24.62	23.63	22.81	22.08	21.31	19.69
20	33.10	29.06	27.05	25.74	24.73	23.88	23.14	22.35	20.69

TABLE 2. Expansion Factors for Expected Errors

Risk of Incorrect Acceptance

	1%	5%	10%	15%	20%	25%	30%	37%	50%
Factor	1.9	1.6	1.5	1.4	1.3	1.25	1.2	1.15	1.0

FIGURE 11-2. Reliability and Expansion Factors for PPS Sampling (SOURCE: Audit Sampling Guide, p. 101.)

anticipated. In the Harris Company, the auditor specifies a 5 percent risk of incorrect acceptance. Thus, the reliability factor is 3.0.

Tolerable Error

The tolerable error reflects the auditor's judgment about the maximum misstatement that may occur in an account balance without causing the financial statements to be materially misstated. He seeks assurance from a sample that the projected error in the population plus an allowance for sampling risk does not exceed this amount.

The relationship between the tolerable error and sample size is inverse—the smaller the tolerable error, the larger the sample size. For the Harris sample, the auditor specifies a tolerable error equal to 5 percent of the book value, or $30,000.

Anticipated Error and Expansion Factor

In PPS sampling the auditor does not explicitly control the risk of incorrect rejection. He does so indirectly, however, by specifying the anticipated error, which is inversely related to the risk of incorrect rejection and directly related to sample size. The auditor uses his prior experience and knowledge of the client and professional judgment in determining an amount for anticipated error. He must bear in mind that an excessively high anticipated error will unnecessarily increase sample size while too low an estimate will result in a high risk of incorrect rejection. For the Harris Company, the auditor specifies anticipated error of $6,000.

The expansion factor is required only when errors are anticipated. It is obtained from Table 2 of Figure 11-2 using the auditor's specified risk of incorrect acceptance. Thus, in the Harris case, this factor is 1.6. The effect of anticipated error and the factor are then subtracted from tolerable error in computing sample size.

Calculation of Sample Size

The factors for determining sample size in the Harris Company are: $BV = $600,000$, $RF = 3.0$, $TE = $30,000$, $AE = $6,000$, and $EF = 1.6$. Thus, sample size is 88, computed as follows:

$$n = \frac{\$600,000 \times 3.0}{\$30,000 - (\$6,000 \times 1.6)} = 88$$

Determining the Sample Selection Method

The most common selection method used in PPS sampling is systematic selection. This method divides the total population of dollars into equal groups or intervals of dollars. A logical unit is then systematically selected from each interval. Thus, a sampling interval must be calculated as follows:

$$SI = \frac{BV}{n}$$

In the Harris Company, the sampling interval is $6,818 ($600,000 ÷ 88).

The initial step in the selection process is to pick a random number between 1 and 6,818. The auditor then selects the logical unit that contains every 6,818th dollar thereafter in the population. Assuming a 5,000 random number start, the first four sample items in the Harris Company are selected as shown in Figure 11-3. Observe that a sample of individual dollars results in the selection of the entire balance associated with the logical unit. The

Logical Unit	Book Value	Cumulative Balance	Dollar Unit Selected	Book Value of Sample Item
001	$1,200	$ 1,200		
002	6,043	7,243	5,000	$6,043
003	2,190	9,433		
004	3,275	12,708	11,818	3,275
005	980	13,688		
006	1,647	15,335		
007	4,260	19,595	18,636	4,260
008	480	20,075		
009	7,150	27,225	25,454	7,150
Total	$600,000			

FIGURE 11–3. Systematic Selection Process

process also leads to the selection of all logical units that are equal to or greater than the skip interval. The use of a computer program facilitates the selection process. However, it is also possible to do the selecting manually with the aid of an adding machine.

Executing the Sampling Plan

In this phase of the plan the auditor applies appropriate auditing procedures to determine an audited value for each logical unit included in the sample. In the Harris sample this includes obtaining confirmations for as many sample units as possible and applying alternative procedures when no response is received to the confirmation request.

Where differences occur, the auditor records both the book and audited values in his working papers. This information is then used to project the total error in the population as explained in the next section.

Evaluating the Sample Results

In evaluating the results of the sample, the auditor considers (1) the projected error determined from the sample, (2) the allowance for sampling risk, and (3) the upper error limit. Item (3) is the sum of items (1) and (2). These factors are analogous to the sample occurrence rate, allowance for sampling risk, and upper occurrence limit used in evaluating the results of an attribute sampling plan, as discussed in Chapter 6. However, in PPS sampling, each factor is expressed as a dollar amount rather than as a percentage. The evaluation process differs depending on whether any errors are found in the sample.

No Errors

The error results of the sample are used to project the error in the population. When no errors are discovered in the sample, the projected error is zero dollars. Moreover, the allowance for sampling risk will equal the upper error limit, which will always be equal to or less than the tolerable error specified in designing the sample. Accordingly, when no errors are found, the auditor can ordinarily conclude, without making additional calculations, that the book value of the population is not overstated by more than the tolerable error at the specified risk of incorrect acceptance.

If no errors are found in the sample when some were anticipated in the sample design, the auditor may wish to express a more precise conclusion about the population by calculating the allowance for sampling risk. When no errors are found, this risk factor consists of one component sometimes referred to as *basic precision* (*BP*). The amount is obtained by multiplying the reliability factor (*RF*) for zero errors at the specified risk of incorrect acceptance times the sampling interval (*SI*). In the Harris Company, basic precision is $20,454 computed as follows:

$$BP = RF \times SI$$
$$= 3.0 \times \$6,818$$
$$= \$20,454$$

Since projected error is zero, this amount is also equal to the upper error limit, which is less than the $30,000 tolerable error specified in the sample design. Thus, the auditor may now state that the book value for the population is not overstated by more than $20,454 at the 5 percent risk of incorrect acceptance.

Some Errors

If errors are found in the sample, the auditor must calculate both the projected error in the population and the allowance for sampling risk in order to determine the upper error limit for overstatement errors. The upper error limit is then compared with tolerable error.

Projected population error. A projected error amount is calculated for each logical unit containing an error. These amounts are then summed to arrive at the projected error for the entire population. The projected error is calculated differently for (1) logical units with book values less than the sampling interval, and (2) logical units with book values equal to or greater than the sampling interval.

For *each* logical unit with a book value less than the sampling interval that contains an error, a tainting percentage and projected error are calculated as follows:

Tainting percentage = (book value − audit value) ÷ book value
Projected error   = tainting percentage × sampling interval

The calculations recognize that each logical unit included in the sample represents one sampling interval of the dollars in the population book value. Thus, the degree to which a logical unit is "tainted" with error is projected to all of the dollars in the sampling interval it represents.

For each logical unit equal to or greater than the sampling interval, the projected error is the amount of error found in the unit (book value − audit value). Since the logical unit itself is equal to or greater than the sampling interval, a tainting percentage to project the error to the interval is unnecessary. However, the actual amounts of such errors are used in arriving at the projected error for the population as a whole.

To illustrate, assume the PPS sample of the Harris Company's accounts receivable revealed the following errors:

Book Value (BV)	Audit Value (AV)	Tainting Percentage (TP = (BV − AV)/BV)	Sampling Interval (SI)	Projected Error (TP × SI) or (BV − AV)
$ 950	$ 855	10	$6,818	$ 682
2,500	−0−	100	6,818	6,818
7,650	6,885	N/A*	N/A*	765
5,300	5,035	5	6,818	341
8,000	−0−	N/A*	N/A*	8,000
$24,400	$12,775			$16,606

* Logical unit is greater than sampling interval; therefore, projected error equals actual error (BV − AV).

Note that the first, second, and fourth logical units containing errors have book values less than the sampling interval. Accordingly, tainting percentages have been calculated and used to determine the projected errors. The third and fifth units have book values greater than the sampling interval. Therefore, the projected error for each is the difference between the book value and the audit value. The total error in the sample is $11,625 ($24,400 − $12,775) and the total projected error in the population is $16,606.

Allowance for sampling risk. The allowance for sampling risk for samples containing errors has two components: (1) basic precision, and (2) an incremental allowance resulting from the errors. The calculation of basic precision is the same as explained previously for no errors. Thus, in the Harris Company the amount of this component is again $20,454.

To calculate the incremental allowance for sampling risk, the auditor must consider separately the logical units with book values less than the sampling interval and those with book values equal to or greater than the sampling interval. Since *all* logical units equal to or greater than the sampling interval will have been examined, there is no sampling risk associated with them. Accordingly, calculation of the incremental allowance involves only errors related to logical units with book values less than the sampling interval.

Calculation of the incremental allowance involves the following steps:

- Determining the appropriate incremental change in reliability factors.
- Ranking the projected errors for *logical units less than the sampling interval* from highest to lowest.
- Multiplying the ranked projected errors by the appropriate factor and summing the products.

The following tabulation illustrates the first step:

5% RISK OF INCORRECT ACCEPTANCE

Number of Overstatement Errors	Reliability Factor	Incremental Change in Reliability Factor	Incremental Change in Reliability Factor Minus One
0	3.00	—	—
1	4.74	1.74	.74
2	6.30	1.56	.56
3	7.75	1.45	.45
4	9.15	1.40	.40

The data in the first two columns above are taken from Table 1 of Figure 11-2 for the specified risk of incorrect acceptance (5 percent in this illustration). Each entry in the third column is the reliability factor on the same line less the reliability factor on the previous line. The column four factors are obtained by subtracting one from each of the column three factors.

The second and third steps are illustrated below.

Ranked Projected Errors	Incremental Change in Reliability Factor Minus One	Incremental Allowance for Sampling Risk
$6,818	.74	$5,045
682	.56	382
341	.45	153
		$5,580

Observe (1) that only the projected errors for logical units less than the sampling interval are ranked and (2) that the appropriate reliability factor is obtained from column four of the preceding tabulation. The incremental allowances for the projected errors are then added to determine the total incremental allowance of $5,580. Thus, the total allowance for sampling risk in the Harris Company is $26,034 computed as follows:

Basic precision	$20,454
Incremental allowance for projected errors	5,580
Total allowance for sampling risk	$26,034

Upper error limit for overstatement errors. The upper error limit equals the sum of the projected errors plus the allowance for sampling risk. For the Harris sample, the upper error limit is:

Projected errors	$16,606
Allowance for sampling risk	26,034
Upper error limit	$42,640

Thus, the auditor may conclude that there is a 5 percent risk that the book value is overstated by $42,640 or more.

Generally, if the upper error limit is less than the tolerable error, the sample results support the conclusion that the population book value is not misstated by more than the tolerable error at the specified risk of incorrect acceptance. In the Harris sample, the upper error limit exceeds the tolerable error of $30,000 specified in designing the sample. When this occurs the auditor should consider several possible reasons and alternative courses of action. These matters are discussed below in the section on *Reaching an Overall Conclusion.* However, whether the upper error limit is less than, equal to, or greater than the tolerable error, certain qualitative considerations should be made prior to reaching an overall conclusion.

Qualitative considerations. As in attribute sampling, in addition to evaluating the frequncy and amounts of monetary misstatements the auditor should consider the qualitative aspects of errors. For example, he should consider the nature and cause of misstatements such as whether they (1) are differences in principle or in application, (2) are errors or irregularities, or (3) are due to misunderstanding of instructions or to carelessness. He should also consider the relationship of misstatements to other phases of the audit. For example, if errors are discovered in substantive tests in amounts or frequency greater than implied by the degree of reliance initially placed on internal accounting control, the auditor should consider whether the planned reliance is still appropriate.

Reaching an overall conclusion. The auditor uses professional judgment in combining evidence from several sources to reach an overall conclusion as to the fairness of an account balance. When (1) the results of a PPS sample reveal the upper error limit to be less than the tolerable error, (2) the results of other substantive tests do not contradict this finding, and (3) analysis of the qualitative considerations reveals no evidence of irregularities, or other significant problems, the auditor can generally conclude that the population is not materially misstated. When any of these conditions do not hold, the auditor must use professional judgment in deciding on the appropriate course of action.

If the upper error limit is greater than the tolerable error, the auditor should consider the following possible reasons and actions:

- The sample is not representative of the population. The auditor might suspect this is the case when all other related evidence suggests the population is fairly stated. In this case the auditor might examine additional sampling units or perform alternative procedures to determine whether the population is misstated.[5]
- The amount of anticipated error specified in designing the sample may not have been large enough relative to tolerable error to adequately limit the allowance for sampling risk. That is, the population may not be misstated by more than the tolerable error, but because the amount of error in the population is greater than anticipated, more precise information is needed from the sample. If the auditor believes this situation pertains, he may examine additional sampling units and reevaluate or perform alternative auditing procedures to determine whether the population is misstated by more than the tolerable error.
- The population may be misstated by more than the tolerable error. If the auditor believes this to be the case, he may request the client to investigate the errors and, if appropriate, adjust the book value.

As a result of any of these courses of action the client's book value might be adjusted. If the upper error limit after adjustment is less than the tolerable error, the sample results would support the conclusion that the population, as adjusted, is not misstated by more than the tolerable error at the specified risk of incorrect acceptance. For example, in the Harris sample two receivables with book values of $2,500 and $8,000 were found to have audited values of zero. If these accounts were written off, the projected error for the population would be reduced by $6,818 + $8,000 = $14,818. Additionally, the incremental allowance for sampling risk related to the $2,500 receivable would be eliminated, further reducing the upper error limit below the $30,000 tolerable error specified in designing the sample.

The working paper in Figure 11-4 illustrates how the manual application of PPS sampling in the audit of the Harris Company's receivables may be documented. When a computer is used in selecting and evaluating the sample results, much of the important information is documented in the form of a computer printout.

Advantages and Disadvantages of PPS Sampling

In making a decision as to the use of this approach in audit sampling, the auditor should be aware of the advantages and disadvantages of PPS sampling. The advantages of PPS sampling are:

---

[5] A simple method of expanding the sample is to divide the sampling interval in half. This will produce a sample containing all of the units in the original sample plus an equal number of additional units. Other methods of expanding the sample size are beyond the scope of this text.

Harris Company
Accounts Receivable—Test of Details
12/31/X1

Prepared by: R.O.S. Date: 1/15/X2
Reviewed by: C.M.B. Date: 1/25/X2

B-2

PPS SAMPLING PLAN WORKSHEET

SAMPLE DESIGN

Objective: To test reasonableness of aggregate book value of customer accounts (debit balances).

Population: Total book value of customer accounts with debit balances on computer listing prepared from master file.

Logical Sampling Unit: Customer account

Sample Size:

Book Value of Population	$600,000 (BV)
Risk of Incorrect Acceptance	.05
Corresponding Reliability Factor (from Figure 11-2)	3.0 (RF)
Tolerable Error	$30,000 (TE)
Anticipated Error	$6,000 (AE)
Expansion Factor (from Figure 11-2)	1.6 (EF)

$$n = \frac{BV \times RF}{TE - (AE \times EF)} = \frac{\$600,000 \times 3.0}{\$30,000 - (\$6,000 \times 1.6)} = 88$$

Sample Selection— Systematic Method

Sampling Interval $= BV \div n = \$600,000 \div 88 = \$6,818$

Random Start $= \$3,185$

Execution of Sampling Plan:

Logical Units Selected Listed on W/P: B-3

Audit Procedures: Audit values obtained for each logical unit in sample by mail confirmation or application of alternative procedures.

SAMPLE RESULTS

Projected Error:

Book Value (BV)	Audit Value (AV)	Tainting Percentage (TP = (BV − AV)/BV)	Sampling Interval or (SI)	Projected Error (TP × SI) or (BV − AV)
$950	$855	.10	$6,818	$682
2,500	-0-	1.00	6,818	6,818
7,650	6,885	N/A	N/A	765
5,300	5,035	.05	N/A	341
8,000	-0-	N/A	6,818	8,000
$24,400	$12,775			$16,606

Allowance for Sampling Risk:

Basic Precision = Sampling Interval × Reliability Factor

$$\$6,818 \times 3.0 = \$20,454$$

Incremental Allowance:

Ranked Projected Errors	Incremental Change in Reliability Factor Minus One	Incremental Allowance for Sampling Risk
$6,818	.74 (4.74−3.0−1)	$5,045
682	.56 (6.30−4.74−1)	382
341	.45 (7.75−6.30−1)	153
	Total = Basic Precision + Incremental Allowance	$5,580

Upper Error Limit:

Projected Error	$16,606
Allowance for Sampling Risk	26,034
Upper Error Limit	$42,640

Conclusion: Upper error limit of $42,640 exceeds tolerable error of $30,000. Discussed errors found with client. Client agreed to write off two customer accounts with book values of $2,500 and $8,000, respectively, both of which have audit values of zero. This places the upper error limit at $22,777 which is below tolerable error. See adjusting entry on W/P PBC-1. Conclude: Total customer accounts with debit balances as adjusted is fairly stated.

FIGURE 11-4. PPS Sampling Plan Working Paper

- It is generally easier to use than classical variables sampling because the auditor can calculate sample sizes and evaluate sample results by hand or with the assistance of tables.
- The size of a PPS sample is not based on any measure of the estimated variation of audited values.
- PPS sampling automatically results in a stratified sample because items are selected in proportion to their dollar values.
- PPS systematic sample selection automatically identifies any item that is individually significant if its value exceeds an upper monetary cutoff.
- If the auditor expects no errors, PPS sampling will usually result in a smaller sample size than under classical variables sampling.
- A PPS sample can be designed more easily and sample selection may begin before the complete population is available.

In contrast, PPS sampling has the following disadvantages:

- It includes an assumption that the audited value of a sampling unit should not be less than zero or greater than book value. When overstatements are anticipated where the audited value will be less than zero, special design considerations may be required.
- If understatements are identified in the sample, the evaluation of the sample may require special considerations.
- The selection of zero balances or balances of a different sign requires special consideration.
- PPS evaluation may overstate the allowance for sampling risk when errors are found in the sample. As a result, the auditor may be more likely to reject an acceptable book value for the population.
- As the expected number of errors increases, the appropriate sample size increases. Thus a larger sample size may result than under classical variables sampling.[6]

Professional judgment should be exercised by the auditor in determining the appropriateness of this approach in a given audit circumstance.

CLASSICAL VARIABLES SAMPLING

As explained earlier, the auditor may use a classical variables sampling approach in substantive testing. Under this approach, normal distribution theory is used in evaluating the characteristics of a population based on the results of a sample drawn from the population.

Classical variables sampling may be useful to the auditor when the audit objective relates to either the possible under- or overstatement of an account balance and in circumstances when PPS sampling is not cost-efficient.

[6] *Audit Sampling Guide, op. cit.,* p. 59-61.

Types of Sampling Techniques

There are three techniques (or methods) that may be used in classical variables sampling: (1) mean-per-unit (MPU), (2) difference, and (3) ratio. The auditor should consider the following constraints in selecting the technique that is most appropriate in the circumstances:

- *The ability to design a stratified sample.* Stratification may significantly reduce sample size under the MPU method but may not materially affect sample size under the difference or ratio methods.
- *The expected number of differences between audited and book values.* A minimum number of differences must exist between these values in the sample to use either the difference or ratio methods.
- *The available information.* In the MPU method, the total number of items in the population must be known. The audited value for each sampling unit must also be known in each of the methods. In addition, the book value of each sampling unit must be known in ratio and difference estimation.[7]

When all of the constraints can be satisfied by any of the methods, the auditor ordinarily will prefer either difference or ratio estimation because these methods generally require a smaller sample size than the MPU method. Thus, they are more cost efficient in meeting the auditor's objectives.

The sampling plan for each method involves the same steps required in PPS sampling. However, as explained below, there are some variations in the way some of the steps are performed among the three methods.

Mean-per-Unit (MPU) Estimation[8]

This technique involves determination of an audited value for each item in the sample. An average of these audited values is then calculated and multiplied by the number of units in the population to obtain an estimate of the total population value. An allowance for sampling risk associated with this estimate is then calculated for use in evaluating the sample results.

Determining the Objectives of the Plan

The objective of an MPU sampling plan may be to test the reasonableness of a recorded account balance or to develop an independent estimate of an amount where no recorded book value is available. For illustrative purposes, it is assumed that a test is to be made of the recorded value of loans receivable in the Ace Finance Company.

---

[7] *Audit Sampling Guide, op. cit.* p. 79 (adapted).
[8] This technique is sometimes referred to as the *simple extension* method.

Defining the Population and Sampling Unit

In defining the population, the auditor should consider the nature of the items comprising the population and whether all items should be eligible for inclusion in the sample. It is not necessary, however, to verify that the book values for the individual items sum to the total recorded book value of the population because this value is not a variable in MPU calculations.

The sampling unit should be compatible with the nature of the audit procedure(s) to be performed. In MPU sampling, physical units (accounts, documents, and line items in a journal) are the basis for selection, not individual dollars.

For the Ace Finance Company: (1) the population is defined as 3,000 small loans receivable, (2) the recorded book value of these receivables is $1,340,000, (3) individual loans are defined as the sampling unit, and (4) the physical representation from which sample items are selected is a computer printout listing all loans receivable.

Determining the Sample Size

The following factors determine sample size in an MPU estimation sample:

- Population size (number of units)
- Estimated population standard deviation
- Tolerable error
- Risk of incorrect rejection
- Risk of incorrect acceptance
- Allowance for sampling risk

Population size. It is critical to have accurate knowledge of the number of units in the population since this factor enters into the calculation of both the sample size and sample results. Population size is directly related to sample size—that is, the larger the population, the larger the sample size required. As noted above, the population for the Ace Finance Company consists of 3,000 loans receivable.

Estimated population standard deviation. In MPU estimation, the sample size required to achieve specified statistical objectives is related directly to the variability of the characteristic of interest, which is the audited values of the sample items. The measure of variability used is the standard deviation. Since the standard deviation of the audited values for the sample items is not known before the sample is selected, it must be estimated.

There are three ways of estimating this factor. First, in a recurring engagement, the standard deviation found in the preceding audit may be used to estimate the deviation for the current year. Second, the standard deviation can be estimated from available book values. Third, the auditor can take a small presample of 30 to 50 items and base the estimate of the current year's population standard deviation on the audited values of these sample items. When this is done, the presample may be made a part of the final sample. Computer programs for MPU estimation sampling include a routine to calculate the estimated standard deviation.

The formula for calculating the standard deviation is:

$$S_{x_j} = \sqrt{\sum_{j=1}^{n} \frac{(x_j - \bar{x})^2}{n - 1}}$$

where

$\displaystyle\sum_{j=1}^{n}$ = sum of sample values; $j = 1$ means summary should begin with first item and n means that the summary should end with the last item in the sample

x_j = audit values of individual sample items

$\bar{x}$ = mean of the audit values of sample items

n = number of items audited

A primary concern of the auditor in MPU sampling is whether the population should be stratified because sample size increases as the variability of the population increases.[9] In fact, a change in the variability of a population affects sample size by the square of the relative change. For example, when the variation in the population changes from 100 to 200, the sample size required to meet the same statistical objectives would increase by a multiple of four (2^2). The optimal number of strata depends on the tradeoff of the additional costs of dividing the population against the cost savings resulting from smaller sample sizes. When stratification is not feasible, the auditor may be able to use either the difference or ratio techniques.

The Ace Finance Company limits loans to a maximum of $500 per customer. The auditor, therefore, concludes that there is no need to stratify the population of loans receivable. Based on last year's audit, the auditor estimates a standard deviation of $100.

Tolerable error. As in PPS sampling, tolerable error reflects the auditor's judgment concerning the maximum misstatement that may occur in an account balance without causing the financial statements to be materially misstated. Some auditors and computer programs use the term *materiality* (or *material amount*) as an alternative for tolerable error. As is to be expected, tolerable error has an inverse effect on sample size. For example, a smaller tolerable error will result in a larger sample size. For the Ace Finance Company, the auditor specifies a tolerable error of $60,000.

---

[9] Stratified sampling involves dividing the population into relatively homogeneous groups or strata, sampling separately from each stratum, and then combining sample results for each stratum to evaluate the total sample. This is most practical when computer assistance is available. To simplify subsequent illustrations in this chapter, unstratified samples are used.

Risk of incorrect rejection. This factor permits the auditor to control the risk that the sample results will support the conclusion that the recorded account balance is materially misstated when it is not. The principal consequence of this risk is the potential incurrence of additional costs associated with expanded audit procedures following the initial rejection. However, the auditing procedures should ultimately result in the conclusion that the balance is not materially misstated.

If the auditor specifies a very low risk of incorrect rejection, the size and cost of performing the initial sample will be larger. Therefore, the auditor should use his experience and knowledge of the client to specify an appropriate risk of incorrect rejection to balance the costs associated with the initial sample and the potential costs of later expanding the sample.

In some computer software programs, the auditor inputs the risk of incorrect rejection directly as a percentage figure. Other programs require the auditor to input a *confidence* or *reliability* level, which is the complement of the risk of incorrect rejection. In either case, the computer then converts the percentage into an appropriate standard normal deviate or U_R factor for use in calculating the sample size. If the sample size is being calculated manually, a U_R factor for the specified risk of incorrect rejection is obtained from the table in Figure 11-5.

The auditor decides to specify a 5 percent risk of incorrect rejection in the Ace Finance Company. Thus, the U_R factor is 1.96.

Risk of incorrect acceptance. The factors to be considered by the auditor in specifying this risk are the same as in PPS sampling. The risk of incorrect acceptance of a materially misstated balance is ordinarily specified in the range of from 5 to 30 percent, depending on the auditor's reliance on internal control and the results of other substantive tests. In Ace Finance, the auditor specifies a 20% risk of incorrect acceptance.

Allowance for sampling risk. The allowance for sampling risk (sometimes referred to as "desired precision") is derived from the following formula:

$$A = R \times TE$$

Risk of Incorrect Rejection	Standard Normal Deviate (U_R Factor)	Corresponding Confidence or Reliability Level*
.30	±1.04	.70
.25	±1.15	.75
.20	±1.28	.80
.15	±1.44	.85
.10	±1.64	.90
.05	±1.96	.95
.01	±2.58	.99

* For information purposes only.

FIGURE 11–5. Selected Risk of Incorrect Rejection Percentages and Corresponding Standard Normal Deviates or U_R Factors

where

A = desired or planned allowance for sampling risk
R = ratio of desired allowance for sampling risk to tolerable error
TE = tolerable error

The ratio is based on the specified risks of incorrect acceptance and incorrect rejection. The amount of the ratio is obtained from the table shown in Figure 11-6. For example, if the aforementioned risks are set at 20 percent and 10 percent, respectively, the R factor is .661. In the Ace Finance Company, the foregoing risks have been specified at 20 percent and 5 percent. Thus, the R factor is .70. This factor is then applied to the tolerable error of $60,000 to produce an allowance for sampling risk of $42,000.

Sample size formula. The following formula is used to determine sample size for an MPU estimation sample:

$$n = \left(\frac{N \cdot S_{x_j} \cdot U_R}{A} \right)^2$$

where

N = population size
S_{x_j} = estimated population standard deviation
U_R = the standard normal deviate for the desired risk of incorrect rejection
A = desired or planned allowance for sampling risk

In the Ace Finance Company, these four factors are 3,000, $100, 1.96, and $42,000, respectively. Thus, sample size is 196 computed as follows:

$$n = \left(\frac{3,000 \times \$100 \times 1.96}{\$42,000} \right)^2 = 196$$

Risk of Incorrect Acceptance	Risk of Incorrect Rejection			
	.20	.10	.05	.01
.01	.355	.413	.457	.525
.025	.395	.456	.500	.568
.05	.437	.500	.543	.609
.075	.471	.532	.576	.641
.10	.500	.561	.605	.668
.15	.511	.612	.653	.712
.20	.603	.661	.700	.753
.25	.653	.708	.742	.791
.30	.707	.756	.787	.829
.35	.766	.808	.834	.868
.40	.831	.863	.883	.908
.45	.907	.926	.937	.952
.50	1.000	1.000	1.000	1.000

FIGURE 11-6. Ratio of Desired Allowance for Sampling Risk to Tolerable Error (SOURCE: *Audit Sampling Guide*, p. 100.)

This formula assumes sampling with replacement (i.e., an item once selected is put back into the population and is eligible for selection again). When sampling without replacement, a finite correction factor is recommended when the relationship between n (sample size) and N (population size) is greater than .05. The adjusted sample size (n') is determined as follows:

$$n' = \frac{n}{1 + \dfrac{n}{N}}$$

Since n/N is greater than .05 (196 ÷ 3000 = .065) in Ace Finance, the adjusted sample size is:

$$n' = \frac{196}{1 + \dfrac{196}{3000}} = 184$$

Determining the Sample Selection Method

Either the simple random number selection method or the systematic selection method may be used in selecting the sample under the MPU method. For the Ace Finance Company, the auditor decides to use a computer random number generator to identify the 184 loan receivable accounts to be examined.

Executing the Sampling Plan

The execution phase of an MPU estimation sampling plan includes the following steps:

- Performing appropriate auditing procedures to determine an audit value for each sample item.
- Calculating the following statistics based on the sample data:
  - the average of the audit sample values ($\bar{x}$)
  - the standard deviation of the audit sample values (S_{x_j})

The average and standard deviation statistics for the sample may be computed manually or by a computer.

For the Ace Finance sample, the sum of the audit values is assumed to be $81,328, resulting in an average audit value of $442 ($81,328 ÷ 184). The standard deviation of the audit values is assumed to be $90.

Evaluating the Sample Results

To evaluate the results of an MPU estimation sampling plan, the auditor calculates:

- The estimated total population value
- The achieved allowance for sampling risk, sometimes referred to as achieved precision
- A range equal to the estimated total population value ± the achieved allowance for sampling risk.

The estimated total population value ($\hat{X}$) is calculated as follows:

$$\hat{X} = N \cdot \bar{x}$$

Thus, the estimated total population value for Ace Finance Company's 3,000 loans receivable is:

$$\hat{X} = 3000 \times \$442 = \$1,326,000$$

The achieved allowance for sampling risk, as distinguished from the desired allowance specified in determining sample size, is calculated as follows:

$$A' = N \cdot U_R \cdot \frac{S_{x_j} \cdot \sqrt{1 - \dfrac{n}{N}}}{\sqrt{n}}$$

where S_{x_j} is the standard deviation of the audit sample values. Thus, for Ace Finance, A' is $37,803:

$$A' = 3000 \times 1.96 \times \frac{\$90 \sqrt{1 - \dfrac{184}{3000}}}{\sqrt{184}} = \$37,803$$

Note that the adjusted sample size (n') is substituted for (n) in the formula when the finite correction factor is used in determining sample size.

Evaluation when achieved allowance for sampling risk is not greater than planned allowance. If the achieved allowance for sampling risk (A') is no greater than the planned allowance (A), the auditor calculates a range (sometimes referred to as the precision interval) as follows:

$$\hat{X} \pm A'$$

If the recorded book value falls within this range, the sample results support the conclusion that the book value is not materially misstated at a risk of incorrect acceptance not exceeding that specified in designing the sample.

The achieved allowance for sampling risk for the Ace Finance Company is $37,803, which is less than the planned allowance of $42,000. Therefore, the range is

$$\hat{X} \pm A' = \$1,326,000 \pm \$37,803$$
$$= \$1,288,197 \text{ to } \$1,363,803$$

Since the total book value, $1,340,000, falls within this interval, the sample

results support the conclusion that the book value is not materially misstated.

In some cases the book value may fall outside the range because the
achieved allowance is significantly smaller than the planned allowance. If
this occurs and the difference between the book value and the far end of the
range is less than the specified tolerable error, the sample results support the
book value of the population. For example, if the achieved allowance in Ace
Finance Company is $12,000, the range becomes $1,314,000 to $1,338,000
and the book value ($1,340,000) falls outside the precision interval. The
difference between the book value and the far end of the range is $26,000
($1,340,000 $-$ $1,314,000). Since this is less than the tolerable error of
$42,000, the book value is supported.

An alternate decision rule that the auditor may use when A' is less than A
focuses on the projected error (*PE*) in the population. *PE* is equal to the
absolute value of the difference between the estimated total population value
and the total book value (*BV*). If *PE* plus the achieved allowance for
sampling risk (A') is less than tolerable error (*TE*), the sample results
support the book value. For Ace Finance, *PE* is $14,000 ($1,340,000 $-$
$1,326,000) and A' in the original example was $37,803. Thus, *PE* plus A' is
$51,803 ($14,000 + $37,803). Since this sum is less than tolerable error of
$60,000, the book value is supported.

***Evaluation when achieved allowance for sampling risk is greater than
planned allowance.*** When A' is greater than A, there is a greater chance that
the book value will fall within the range $\hat{X} \pm A'$. However, the achieved risk
of incorrect acceptance associated with this interval will exceed the auditor's planned level. To hold the risk of incorrect acceptance to the planned
level, an adjusted achieved allowance for sampling risk (A'') is calculated
using the following formula:

$$A'' = A' + TE \left(1 - \frac{A'}{A}\right)$$

The adjusted achieved allowance is then substituted for the achieved allowance in applying the range and projected error decision rules discussed
above. For example, if A' is $43,000 in Ace Finance, the computations for A''
and the range are:

$$A'' = \$43,000 + \$60,000 \left(1 - \frac{\$43,000}{\$42,000}\right)$$
$$= \$41,571$$
$$\hat{X} \pm A'' = \$1,326,000 \pm \$41,571$$
$$= \$1,284,429 \text{ to } \$1,367,571$$

Since the book value, $1,340,000, falls within the range, it is supported by
the sample. Similarly, using the projected error decision rule, since the
projected error plus the adjusted achieved allowance ($14,000 + $41,571 =
$55,571) is less than the tolerable error ($60,000), the book value is supported.

Qualitative considerations. Prior to reaching an overall conclusion, the auditor should consider the qualitative aspects of the sample results. These considerations relate to the nature and cause of errors found and are the same as those discussed for PPS sampling on page 359.

Reaching an overall conclusion. When either the auditor's quantitative (statistical) or qualitative assessments of sample results do not support the conclusion that the population is fairly stated, he should use professional judgment in deciding on an appropriate course of action. The possible causes and actions are as follows:

CAUSES	ACTIONS
1. The sample is not representative of the population.	Expand the sample and reevaluate the results.
2. The achieved allowance for sampling risk may be larger than the desired allowance because the sample size was too small.	Same as above.
3. The population book value may be misstated by more than tolerable error.	Have client investigate and, if warranted, adjust the book value and reevaluate the sample results.

To illustrate the third possibility, assume the book value for the Ace Finance Company's loans receivable was $1,380,000 instead of $1,340,000, and that the computed range is the same as above ($1,288,197 to $1,363,803). The minimum adjustment necessary for the auditor to be able to accept the book value as being fairly stated is a credit of $31,803. This adjustment would reduce the book value to $1,348,197 ($1,380,000 − $31,803), which is equal to the far end of the range plus tolerable error ($1,288,197 + $60,000 = $1,348,197). These relationships are shown graphically in Figure 11-7.

The working paper in Figure 11-8 summarizes the steps performed in designing, executing, and evaluating the MPU sampling plan to test the book value of Ace Finance Company's loans receivable and illustrates how these steps can be documented.

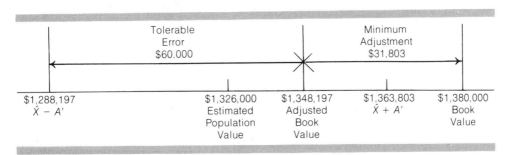

FIGURE 11-7. Minimum Adjustment for Materially Misstated Book Value

Ace Finance Company
Loans Receivable — Test of Details
12/31/X1

Prepared by: WCA Date: 1/11/X2
Reviewed by: RAJ Date: 1/15/X2

B4

MEAN-PER-UNIT SAMPLING PLAN WORKSHEET

SAMPLE DESIGN

Objective: To test reasonableness of recorded book value for loans receivable.

Population: 3,000 loans receivable on computer listing — prepared from master file.

Sampling Unit: Individual loans receivable

Sample Size:

Population Size	3,000 (N)
Estimated Standard Deviation	100 (S_{xj})
Tolerable Error	$60,000 (TE)
Risk of Incorrect Rejection	.05
Corresponding U_R Factor (from Fig. 11-5)	1.96 (U_R)
Risk of Incorrect Acceptance	.20
Ratio of Desired Allowance for Sampling Risk to Tolerable Error (from Figure 11-6)	.70 (R)
Desired Allowance for Sampling Risk (= R × TE)	$42,000 (A)

$$n = \left(\frac{N \cdot S_{xj} \cdot U_R}{A} \right)^2 = \left(\frac{3,000 \times \$100 \times 1.96}{\$42,000} \right)^2 = 196$$

$$n' = \frac{n}{1 + \frac{n}{N}} = \frac{196}{1 + \frac{196}{3000}} = 184$$

Sample Selection: Simple random number sampling using computer random generator to identify 184 loans receivable by loan number; sample loans listed on W/P B-5.

Execution of Sampling Plan: Audit value obtained for each sample loan by confirmation or alternative procedures and shown on W/P B-5. Sum of audit values: $81,328; mean $442; standard deviation of audit values: $90.

SAMPLE RESULTS

Estimated Total Population Value:

$$\bar{X} = N \cdot \bar{x} = 3,000 \times \$442 = \$1,326,000$$

Achieved Allowance for Sampling Risk:

$$A' = N \cdot U_R \cdot \frac{S_{xj}}{\sqrt{n}} \sqrt{1 - \frac{n}{N}} = 3,000 \times 1.96 \times \frac{\$90}{\sqrt{184}} \sqrt{\frac{1-184}{3000}}$$

$$A' = \$37,803$$

If A″ > A, calculate A″ and substitute for A′ below:

$$A'' = A' + TE \left(1 - \frac{A'}{A} \right) =$$

Range or Precision Interval:

$$\bar{X} \pm A' = \$1,326,000 \pm \$37,803$$
$$= \$1,288,197 \text{ to } \$1,363,803$$

Conclusion: Total book value of $1,340,000 falls within calculated precision interval. Sample results support conclusion that loans receivable not misstated by more than tolerable error.

FIGURE 11–8. Mean-Per-Unit Sampling Plan Working Paper

Difference Estimation

In difference estimation sampling, an audit value is determined for each sample item and subtracted from the item's book value. These differences, which may be negative, zero, or positive, are then summed and the sum is divided by the number of items in the sample to obtain an average difference. The average difference is multiplied by the number of units in the population to project the total difference or error in the population. The total projected error is then added to (if positive) or subtracted from (if negative) the total book value to arrive at an estimated total value for the population. An allowance for sampling risk is then calculated based on the variability of the differences between the audit and book values for the individual sample items.

Three conditions are indispensable in using this technique:

- The book value of each population item must be known.
- The total book value of the population must be known and correspond to the sum of the book values of the individual items.
- More than a few differences between audit and book values must be expected.

As explained below, the calculation of the allowance for sampling risk in difference estimation is based on the variability of the differences in the sample. Without a sufficient number of differences, the variability measure is unreliable. The minimum number of differences is a matter of audit judgment. Among statisticians the minimum number varies considerably, ranging from 20 to 50.

The steps in performing difference estimation are explained in the following sections. The Ace Finance Company loans receivable case study is used again to highlight the similarities and differences between the MPU and difference estimation techniques.

Determining the Objectives and Defining the Population and Sampling Unit

Since book values must be known in difference estimation, this method can be used only to test the reasonableness of a recorded amount. Other considerations relevant to these steps are the same as in MPU sampling. Accordingly, the following assumptions for the Ace Finance Company in the MPU illustration are continued: (1) population = 3,000 loans receivable, (2) book value of population = $1,340,000, and (3) sampling unit = the individual loan.

Determining the Sample Size

The same factors are required in determining sample size for MPU and difference estimation samples, with one exception. In difference estimation, the estimated standard deviation of the differences between audited and book values is used rather than the estimated standard deviation of the audited values themselves. The auditor may base this estimate on the results of the prior year's sample, or on the differences found in a presample in the current audit. As stated above, the estimate may be unreliable if it is based on too few differences.

Changes are required in the formulas used earlier in MPU estimation for computing the standard deviation and sample size. In the standard deviation formula (p. 365), the following substitutions in symbols are required:

- S_{d_j} (estimated standard deviation of population differences) for S_{x_j}
- d_j (differences between audit and book values of individual sample items) for x_j
- $\bar{d}$ (mean of the differences between audit and book values for the sample items) for $\bar{x}$.

In the sample size formula (p. 367), S_{d_j} is substituted for S_{x_j}

For the Ace Finance Company, the auditor estimates that S_{d_j} is $70. Other assumptions continued from the MPU illustration are: $N = 3,000$; $TE = \$60,000$; risk of incorrect rejection $= .05$ ($U_R = 1.96$); risk of incorrect acceptance $= .20$; and $A = \$42,000$. Therefore, sample size is 96 items, computed as follows:

$$n = \left(\frac{N \cdot U_R \cdot S_{d_j}}{A} \right)^2 = \left(\frac{3,000 \times 1.96 \times \$70}{\$42,000} \right)^2 = 96$$

Observe that the sample size is considerably smaller than the sample size of 196 in the MPU example. This is due to the fact that the estimated standard deviation of the differences between audit and book values is smaller than the estimated standard deviation of the audit values used in the MPU illustration. In this example, an adjustment of the sample size by a finite correction factor is unnecessary because n/N is less than .05 ($96 \div 3,000 = .032$).

Determining the Sample Selection Method

The performance of this step is the same in both MPU and difference estimation.

Executing the Sampling Plan

The initial step in executing the sampling plan is to determine the audited value for each sample item. Thus, this is the same as in MPU sampling. However, then the following steps occur:

- Subtract the audited value from the book value of the sample item. The difference may be positive, negative, or zero.
- Sum the differences of the individual samples items (Σ_{d_j})

- Divide the sum of the differences by the number of items in the sample to obtain the average (or mean) difference ($\bar{d}$).
- Compute the standard deviation of the sample differences (S_{d_j}).

In our case study, the following sample results are assumed: $\Sigma_{d_j} = \$-480$, $\bar{d} = \$-5$, and $S_{d_j} = \$68$.

Evaluating the Sample Results

In difference estimation the total projected difference ($\hat{D}$) in the population is first determined as follows:

$$\hat{D} = N \times \bar{d}$$

Therefore,

$$\hat{D} = 3,000 \times (\$-5) = \$-15,000$$

The negative sign indicates the projected error is an overstatement.

The estimated total population value is then determined as follows:

$$\hat{X} = BV + \hat{D}$$

Thus,

$$\hat{X} = \$1,340,000 + (\$-15,000) = \$1,325,000$$

In computing the achieved allowance for sampling risk, it is necessary to substitute the standard deviation of the population differences (S_{d_j}) for the standard deviation of the population (S_{x_j}). The formula is

$$A' = N \cdot U_R \cdot \frac{S_{d_j}\sqrt{1 - \dfrac{n}{N}}}{\sqrt{n}}$$

Thus, in the case study the achieved allowance is $40,150 computed as follows:

$$A' = 3,000 \times 1.96 \times \frac{\$68\sqrt{1 - \dfrac{96}{3,000}}}{\sqrt{96}} = \$40,150$$

Because A' ($40,150) is less than TE ($42,000), the auditor computes the range:

$$\hat{X} \pm A' = \$1,325,000 \pm \$40,150$$
$$= \$1,284,850 \text{ to } \$1,365,150$$

Since the range includes the book value, $1,340,000, the sample results support the conclusion that the book value of loans receivable is not materially misstated.

Note that the auditor reaches the same conclusion under both the MPU and the difference techniques. However, both in this case and in practice, this result normally can be obtained from a significantly smaller sample under difference estimation than under MPU.

Ratio Estimation

In ratio estimation sampling, the auditor determines an audit value for each item in the sample. A ratio is then calculated by dividing the sum of the audit values by the sum of the book values for the sample items. This ratio is multiplied by the total book value to arrive at an estimate of the total population value. An allowance for sampling risk is then calculated based on the variability of the ratios of the audit and book values for the individual sample items. The conditions for using ratio estimation are the same as those for difference estimation. The choice between ratio and difference estimation depends primarily on whether there is any correlation between the amount of the individual differences and their book values. When the differences are closely proportional to book value (i.e., the amount of the differences tend to increase as book values increase), ratio estimation will require a smaller sample size and therefore be more efficient. Computer programs are available that permit the auditor to input book and audit values for a presample to determine the sample size under both difference and ratio estimation. The auditor can then choose the technique that appears most efficient in the circumstances. The steps in ratio estimation are the same as in difference estimation except as explained below.

Executing the Sampling Plan

This aspect of the sampling plan is the same as in difference estimation except that after an audit value for each sample item has been determined, it is necessary to:

- Calculate the ratio of the audit and book value for each item.
- Calculate the ratio of the sums of the audit and book values for the sample items.
- Compute the standard deviation of the ratios of the sample items.

Evaluating the Results

In ratio estimation the estimated total population value is derived from the following formula:

$$\hat{X} = BV \times R$$

The symbol R in this formula is the ratio of the sums of the audit and book values of the sample items. For example, if the sums of the audit and book values of the sample items in the Ace Finance Company are $196,000 and $200,000, respectively, the ratio is 98 percent and the estimated value of the population is $1,313,200 ($1,340,000 × 98 percent).

The formula for determining the achieved allowance for sampling risk is the same as in difference estimation, except the standard deviation of the individual ratios in the sample is substituted for the standard deviation of the differences. The standard deviation of ratios is an extremely cumbersome calculation, and it is rarely done in practice without the assistance of a computer program. Accordingly, manual calculation of this factor is not illustrated.

Once the estimated total population value and achieved allowance for sampling risk are computed, the sample results are assessed quantitatively and qualitatively in the same manner as for MPU or difference estimation.

Advantages and Disadvantages of Classical Variables Sampling

Now that classical variables sampling has been explained, it is possible to evaluate this statistical approach. The principal advantages of this approach in audit sampling are:

- If there are a large number of differences between book and audit values, the auditor's objectives may be met with a smaller sample size than in PPS sampling.
- The samples may be easier to expand if that becomes necessary.
- Zero balances and different sign balances do not require special design considerations.[10]

The disadvantages of classical variables sampling should also be recognized. They consist primarily of the following:

- Classical variables sampling is more complex than PPS sampling; generally, an auditor needs the assistance of computer programs to design an efficient sample and to evaluate sample results.
- To determine sample size, the auditor must have an estimate of the standard deviation of the characteristic of interest in the population.[11]

The auditor should use professional judgment in selecting the approach that is most appropriate in the circumstances.

NONSTATISTICAL SAMPLING IN SUBSTANTIVE TESTING

As explained earlier, the auditor may choose to use nonstatistical sampling in certain substantive testing applications. The major differences between statistical and nonstatistical sampling are in the steps for determining sample size and in evaluating sample results. These steps are often perceived as being more objective or rigorous in statistical sampling and more subjective and judgmental in nonstatistical samples. However, judgment is also re-

---

[10] *Audit Sampling Guide, op. cit.*, p. 76.
[11] *Audit Sampling Guide, op. cit.*, p. 77.

quired in statistical applications, and certain relationships considered explicitly in statistical samples may be helpful in designing and evaluating nonstatistical samples.

Determining Sample Size

Careful consideration of sample design must be made to achieve efficient and effective samples. This is accomplished in statistical samples through explicit specification of key factors and relating them through mathematical models. Consideration of the same factors in nonstatistical samples may help to produce more efficient and effective samples, even if the factors are not explicitly quantified. For example, the auditor should consider the following relationships:

FACTOR	EFFECT ON SAMPLE SIZE
Population size	Small direct effect
Variation in the population	Direct
Tolerable error	Inverse
Expected error	Direct
Risk of incorrect acceptance	Inverse
Risk of incorrect rejection	Inverse

Careful subjective analysis of these factors in a particular circumstance, combined with the auditor's experience and judgment, should result in a sample size that is more appropriate than an arbitrarily determined sample size. The auditor may, but is not required to, consult statistical tables or models in evaluating the appropriateness of judgmentally determined sample sizes.

Evaluating Sample Results

In nonstatistical as well as statistical sampling, the auditor should (1) project the error found in the sample to the population, and (2) consider the sampling risk in evaluating sample results.

Two acceptable methods of projecting the error are:

- Divide the total dollar amount of error in the sample by the fraction of total dollars from the population included in the sample.
- Multiply the average difference between audit and book values for sample items by the number of units in the population.

In nonstatistical samples, the auditor cannot calculate an allowance for sampling risk for specific, measurable levels of risk of incorrect acceptance and rejection. However, he may view the difference between the projected amount and tolerable error as an allowance for sampling risk. If tolerable error exceeds projected error by a large amount, he may be reasonably assured that there is an acceptably low sampling risk that the true error exceeds tolerable error. If the difference between tolerable and projected error is quite small, he may conclude there is an unacceptably high sampling risk that the true error exceeds the tolerable error.

The number and size of errors found in the sample relative to expected errors are also helpful in assessing sampling risk. For example, if the sample is carefully designed and the number and size of errors found do not exceed his expectations, the auditor can generally conclude that there is an acceptably low risk that actual error exceeds tolerable error.

When the results of a nonstatistical sample do not appear to support the book value, the auditor may (1) examine additional sample units and reevaluate, (2) apply alternative auditing procedures and reevaluate, or (3) ask the client to investigate and, if appropriate, make an adjustment. As in statistical sampling, prior to reaching an overall conclusion, consideration should be given to the qualitative characteristics of errors as well as the frequency and amounts of errors.

CONCLUDING COMMENTS

Audit sampling is widely used in substantive testing. Both statistical and nonstatistical audit sampling can provide the auditor with sufficient evidence to have a reasonable basis for an opinion. The use of statistical sampling has increased significantly in practice in recent years, and this trend can be expected to continue in the future. In the next two chapters, additional applications of PPS and classical variables sampling will be explained and illustrated.

APPENDIX 11A

Relating the Risk Components in Audit Sampling to Substantive Testing

The appendix to AU. Section 350 contains the following model for expressing the general relationship of ultimate risk to other risk components in an audit.[12]

$$UR = IC \times AR \times TD$$

where

UR = the allowable ultimate risk that monetary errors equal to tolerable error might remain undetected in the account balance or class of transactions after the auditor has completed all audit procedures deemed necessary

IC = the auditor's assessment of the risk that, given that errors equal to tolerable error occur, the system of internal accounting control fails to detect them

AR = the auditor's assessment of the risk that analytical review procedures and other relevant substantive tests would fail to detect the errors, given that the errors occur and are not detected by the system of internal accounting control

TD = the allowable risk of incorrect acceptance for the substantive test of details, given that the errors occur and are not detected by the system of internal accounting control or analytical review procedures and other relevant substantive tests

The model is not intended to be a mathematical formula. It may, however, be helpful to the auditor in making his subjective evaluations of the factors in the model. The assessment of the risk for each factor involves a considerable amount of subjectivity and the exercise of professional judgment. Ultimate risk is generally set at 5 or 10 percent. The following guidelines have been developed to assist the auditor in making explicit judgments of the risk associated with IC and AR:[13]

Internal Accounting Control (IC)		Analytical Review and Other Relevant Substantive Tests (AR)	
Reliance	*Risk Factor*	*Effectiveness*	*Risk Factor*
Substantial	10–30%	Very	10–40%
Moderate	20–70%	Moderate	30–60%
Limited or none	60–100%	Marginal or none	50–100%

The relationships expressed in the model may be useful to the auditor in planning his substantive tests of details. For example, if the auditor concludes that UR = 5 percent, IC = 30 percent, and AR = 50 percent, the risk of incorrect acceptance for the test of details is 33 percent, computed as follows:

$$TD = \frac{UR}{IC \times AR} = \frac{(.05)}{(.30)\,(.50)} = 33\%$$

In analyzing this result, the auditor may decide that the performance of another relevant substantive test may lower the risk for AR to 30 percent. In such case, the risk of incorrect acceptance for the test of details becomes 55% $\left(\dfrac{(.05)}{(.30)\,(.30)} \right)$. The auditor then must decide whether the cost of the additional auditing procedure is warranted by the cost saving that will result from the reduction in sample size for the planned test of details.

---

[12] *Auditing Standards Board, op. cit.,* AU § 350. Appendix, par. 4.
[13] *Audit Sampling Guide, op. cit.,* p. 106.

REVIEW QUESTIONS

11–1. Identify the two major statistical sampling approaches used in substantive testing and indicate the fundamental difference between them.

11–2. Explain two purposes for which sampling plans for substantive tests may be designed.

11–3. Explain the meaning of the following terms: (1) ultimate risk, (2) risk of incorrect rejection, and (3) risk of incorrect acceptance.

11–4. a. What effect does the availability of information about the following have on selecting an appropriate sampling approach for a substantive test?
   1. Book values for population items.
   2. Number of units in the population.
   3. Variability of the population items.
   b. What effect does the auditor's expectations about errors have on selecting a sampling approach for substantive tests?

11–5. Explain the difference between the sampling unit and the logical sampling unit in a PPS sample.

11–6. Explain why units with zero and credit balances require special consideration when using PPS sampling.

11–7. a. Give the formula for calculating sample size in PPS sampling.
   b. Explain what each element in the formula represents and how a change in that element, other things constant, affects sample size.

11–8. What role does the specification of anticipated error play in designing a PPS sample?

11–9. What three factors are considered in evaluating a PPS sample?

11–10. What are the two components of the allowance for sampling risk for PPS samples?

11–11. Explain the terms *tainting percentage* and *projected error* as they pertain to individual items in a PPS sample.

11–12. Identify three classical variables sampling techniques used in substantive testing.

11–13. a. Give the formula for determining sample size in a mean-per-unit sampling plan.
   b. Explain what each element in the formula represents.
   c. How does the formula differ for (1) difference estimation and (2) ratio estimation?

11–14. How is the risk of incorrect acceptance controlled in classical variables sampling plans?

11–15. Explain three ways of estimating the standard deviation for a mean-per-unit sampling plan.

11–16. Describe briefly the technique by which the estimated total population value is determined under (1) mean-per-unit, (2) difference, and (3) ratio estimation sampling.

11–17. Explain the role of each of the following in a classical variables sampling plan:
   1. Planned allowance for sampling risk.
   2. Achieved allowance for sampling risk.
   3. Adjusted achieved allowance for sampling risk.

11–18. What alternatives exist when sample results do not support the book value?

11–19. Why do the difference and ratio estimation techniques generally produce more efficient samples than mean-per-unit estimation?

11–20. Describe two acceptable methods for projecting the error found in nonstatistical samples.

COMPREHENSIVE QUESTIONS

11–21. You have completed a pricing test of the Grapefruit Computer Company's inventory using a PPS sampling plan. The sample design for your test of the $5,000,000 inventory (book value) specified a risk of incorrect acceptance of 10 percent and a tolerable error of $400,000. You anticipated not more than $50,000 of error in the inventory due to an excellent internal controls.

Required

a. What size sample should you have examined?
b. What was your sampling interval?
c. Assuming no errors were found in the sample, what is your conclusion (state as precisely as possible)?
d. Assuming the sample yielded a projected error of $20,000, and a total allowance for sampling risk of $48,000, what conclusion might you draw from the sample?

11–22. Assume the following errors were found in a PPS sample:

Sample Item	Book Value	Audit Value
1	$ 450	0
2	640	$ 512
3	1,800	0
4	2,400	1,800
5	2,700	2,430

Required

a. Calculate the projected error assuming:

   1. The sampling interval was $1,500.
   2. The sampling interval was $2,500.

b. If a risk of incorrect acceptance of 10 percent was specified in the sample design, the sampling interval was $2,000, and five errors were found as enumerated above, calculate:

   1. Basic precision.
   2. The incremental allowance for sampling risk.
   3. The upper error limit.

c. If tolerable error was $35,000 and anticipated error was $5,000, what conclusion would you reach based on your results in (b) above?

11–23. You decide to use statistical sampling to test the reasonableness of the recorded book value of the Key West Company's accounts receivable. Because the company's internal accounting controls over accounts receivable have been evaluated by you as excellent, and because you believe few errors will be found, you decide to use probability-proportional-to-size sampling. The company has 2,500 customer accounts with a total book value of $1,500,000. You decide $75,000 is the maximum tolerable misstatement and anticipate that there may be $20,000 of error in the population. You wish to limit the risk of incorrect acceptance to 5 percent. It is your intention to seek positive confirmation of accounts included in your sample and to apply alternative procedures to accounts for which no reply is received.

Required

a. Compute the sample size.
b. Compute the sampling interval.
c. Assume the following errors were found in the sample:
   Calculate:

Sample Item	Book Value	Audit Value
1	$ 750	$ 675
2	500	0
3	16,000	15,200
4	15,000	0

    1. Projected error.
    2. Allowance for sampling risk.
    3. Upper error limit.
  d. State your conclusion based on the results in (c) above.

11–24. Four different populations and related statistical objectives are:

Population	Population Size	Estimated Standard Deviation	Risk of Incorrect Rejection	Allowance for Sampling Risk
A	5,000	$15	5%	$10,000
B	10,000	20	1	50,000
C	8,000	12	10	24,000
D	7,500	32	5	30,000

Required
a. Compute the sample size for each population for a mean-per-unit sampling plan.
b. Assuming the standard deviation of the sample values is 20 percent lower than the estimated standard deviation (rounded to the nearest dollar), compute the achieved allowance for sampling risk (A') for each population.
c. Assuming planned allowance for sampling risk equal to 80 percent of tolerable error, compute adjusted allowance for sampling risk.

11–25. Data pertaining to four populations are presented below:

	1	2	3	4
Book value	$13,650,000	$21,000,000	$9,000,000	$12,000,000
Tolerable error	900,000	1,200,000	500,000	750,000
Planned allowance for sampling risk	600,000	800,000	300,000	500,000
Population estimate	13,000,000	22,000,000	8,500,000	11,750,000
Achieved allowance for sampling risk	400,000	600,000	150,000	350,000

Required
a. Compute the adjusted allowance for sampling risk (A'') and the range about the population estimate.
b. Indicate whether the statistical evidence supports fair statement.

11–26.* Data relative to three sampling plans are presented below:

	1	2	3
Tolerable error	$100,000	$120,000	$150,000
Size of population	5,000	6,000	8,000
Risk of incorrect rejection	5%	10%	5%
Estimated population standard deviation	$75	$100	$120
Risks that errors accumulating to greater than tolerable error will not be detected by:			
Internal control	40%	50%	40%
Analytical review and other substantive procedures (excluding test of details)	85%	25%	50%
Desired ultimate risk	5%	5%	5%

Required
Calculate sample size in each of the plans. Show computations.

11–27. An audit client has an inventory of 10,000 head of beef cattle (steers). The steers were purchased at various dates and varying prices. In view of the dollar amounts involved, $200,000 is considered to be a material amount. A risk of incorrect rejection of 5 percent and a risk of incorrect acceptance of 10 percent are acceptable. The estimated standard deviation of the population is $105. The book value is $2,860,000.

Required
a. Compute the sample size for a mean-per-unit sample.
b. Without prejudice to your answer in (a), assume that a sample of 200 produced an average audit value of $275 with a standard deviation of $100. Is the account fairly stated?

11–28. This question is designed to test your knowledge of sampling risks in classical variables sampling plans.

Required
a. Will your resulting sample size be larger or smaller if the risk of internal control not detecting material errors is 10 percent rather than 50 percent, when all other factors are equal?
b. Will your sample be larger or smaller if you specify a risk of incorrect acceptance of 50 percent for a test of details rather than 11 percent?
c. If you desire risk of incorrect rejection of 5 percent and risk of incorrect acceptance of 15 percent, what amount should your planned allowance for sampling risk be when tolerable error is $100,000?
d. If the achieved allowance for sampling risk is greater than the planned allowance, then the actual risk of incorrect acceptance is (greater/less) than the planned risk?
e. Assuming tolerable error is $200,000, the planned risks of incorrect rejection and acceptance are 5 and 20 percent, respectively, and the achieved allowance for sampling risk is $155,000, calculate the adjusted achieved allowance for sampling risk.

11–29. A contractor has 1,515 homes in various states of construction. From a random presample of 50 homes, you determine that the estimated population standard deviation is $2,000. On the basis of audit risk and other factors, you set desired allowance for sampling risk at $240,000 and desired risk of incorrect rejection at 10 percent.

Required
a. Determine sample size, assuming mean-per-unit sampling with replacement.
b. What would sample size be if the standard deviation was increased to $3,000?
c. Assume the auditor elects to limit sample size to 330 in the interest of cost efficiencies. What risk of incorrect rejection can be achieved if desired allowance for sampling risk remains at $240,000 and the standard deviation remains at $2,000?
d. What allowance for sampling risk results if the risk of incorrect rejection is held at 10 percent and sample size is 330?
e. Redo part (a) above assuming sampling without replacement.

11–30. The following facts pertain to a difference estimation sampling plan:

1. Objective is to determine whether book value is fairly stated.
2. Population consists of 4,000 customer accounts.
3. Book value of accounts receivable is $2.65 million.
4. The preliminary estimated standard deviation of the differences used to determine sample size is $140.
5. Tolerable error is $80,000.
6. Ultimate risk is 5 percent.
7. Risk of incorrect rejection is 5 percent.
8. Planned allowance for sampling risk is $59,360.
9. Sample size is 315.
10. Audit value of the sample items is $206,955 and book value is $208,687.50.
11. The standard deviation of the sample differences is $160.

Required
a. Verify the sample size indicated above in item 9.
b. What risk of incorrect acceptance is implicit in the sample design?
c. Compute achieved allowance for sampling risk. Is this consistent with the planned risk of incorrect acceptance? Why or why not? If not, compute the adjusted allowance.
d. Is book value fairly stated?
e. Assume that instead of being $2.65 million, the book value of accounts receivable is $2.75 million. Would your conclusion differ from your answer to (d) above? What course of action would you take?

11–31. You desire to evaluate the reasonableness of the book value of the inventory of your client, Drew, Inc. You satisfied yourself earlier as to inventory quantities. During the examination of the pricing and extension of the inventory, the following data were gathered using a difference estimation sampling plan and sampling with replacement:

1. Total items in inventory	12,700
2. Total book value of inventory	$1,270,000
3. Total items in the sample (*n*)	400
4. Total book value of sample items	$40,000
5. Total audit value of sample items	$38,400
6. Standard deviation of sample item differences	$28
7. Tolerable error	$70,000
8. Risk of incorrect rejection	5%
9. Risk of incorrect acceptance	20%

Required
a. Based on the sample results, what is the estimate of the total value of the inventory? Show computations in good form where appropriate.

b. What statistical conclusion can be reached regarding the estimated total inventory value calculated in (a) above?

c. Independent of your answers to parts (a) and (b), assume that the book value of Drew's inventory is $1.7 million, and based on the sample results the estimated total value of the inventory is $1.69 million. Discuss the audit and statistical considerations the auditor must evaluate before deciding whether the sampling results support acceptance of the book value as a fair presentation of Drew's inventory. Do the results support fair statement in this case?

11–32. The Hard Finance Company has 3,000 loans outstanding at a recorded book value of $980,000. As the auditor on this engagement, Mary Jones selects a sample of 300 loans for vouching. These loans have a reported book value of $96,000 and an audited value of $94,000.

Required
Compute the estimated total value of the loans by (1) mean-per-unit estimation, (2) difference estimation, and (3) ratio estimation.

11–33. * The following data apply to four different populations:

	A	B	C	D
Risk that errors or irregularities accumulating to greater than tolerable error will not be detected by:				
Internal control	30%	50%	100%	10%
Analytical review and other substantive audit procedures (excluding test of details)	50%	50%	100%	30%
Tolerable error	$100,000	$150,000	$200,000	$300,000

Required
a. Using the model in Appendix A, determine an appropriate risk of incorrect acceptance for each population.

b. Calculate the planned allowance for sampling risk for each population, assuming the auditor uses a mean-per-unit sampling plan with a risk of incorrect rejection of 5 percent in each case.

11–34. * In planning the audit of accounts receivable, you decide to select accounts for confirmation using a variables estimation sampling plan. A major reason for your decision is the advantage of being able to measure and control the risks involved. You recall that auditing literature describes ultimate risk as a combination of two separate risks: (1) that material errors will occur in the accounting process by which the financial statements are developed, and (2) that any material errors that occur will not be detected in the auditor's examination.

Required
a. How does this description of risk relate to the following expression in the context of the variables sampling application described above?

$$UR = IC \times TD \times AR$$

b. What guidelines are available for specifying the amount of ultimate risk?

CASE STUDY

11–35. Fairview Publishing Company, incorporated in 19X4, is a small, closely held publisher of high school textbooks. A local accounting firm has reviewed the preparation of the financial statements, performed certain audit procedures, and prepared the tax returns for many years. The accountants' report has always contained a disclaimer of opinion, because the stockholders would not permit confirmation of receivables or observation of inventories.

The company plans to "go public" in about three years. In anticipation of this, they engaged you in May to perform an audit for the year ended June 30.

The company's first fiscal quarter is usually the most profitable; the last quarter is usually a break-even situation.

The company has a job order cost system for determining its unit cost prices for each textbook. If a book has not been ordered by any customer for 12 months, it is "no valued," scrapped, and discontinued. Only a minimal quantity is maintained of each title until a firm order is received. The company expects that it has no more than $3,000 inventory of any one title.

You have completed your year-end inventory work and found the client's perpetual records were remarkably accurate with respect to quantities, unit prices, and extensions. No errors were located, and it was concluded that the perpetual records can be relied on for beginning inventory quantities.

However, as to the beginning inventory amount, the client is not able to produce a listing with detail sufficient to provide any audit trail. They can find only an adding machine tape to support the recorded amount, $1,405,165. The tape is in no particular order.

At June 30 of the prior year, the company had exactly 1,000 different titles in inventory. This agrees with the number of entries on the tape and with the number of perpetual records having a quantity at the beginning of the current year.

In this case, $150,000 is considered the tolerable error.

The risks that errors accumulating to greater than tolerable error will not be detected by (1) internal controls and (2) by analytical review and substantive tests other than this test of details are 25 and 50 percent, respectively. The ultimate risk is 5 percent.

A 5 percent risk of incorrect rejection is also viewed as acceptable. Based on this year's inventory, the standard deviation should approximate $635 and you have decided to use one stratum.

Required
a. What is the nature and objective of the test?
b. Compute the risk of incorrect acceptance.
c. What planned allowance for sampling risk should be used in determining sample size? (Round down to nearest $10,000.)
d. Calculate sample size (without replacement) using the estimated standard deviation of $635 and the planned allowance determined in (c) above.
e. Assuming the sample produces an audited value of sample items of $123,954 and a standard deviation of $662, calculate (1) the estimated total population value and (2) the achieved allowance for sampling risk.
f. Compute adjusted achieved allowance.
g. Interpret the results of the sample.

12

Substantive Tests of Cash and Revenue Cycle Balances

STUDY OBJECTIVES

The study objectives of this chapter are to acquire an understanding of the specific substantive tests used by the auditor to verify cash balances and receivables balances resulting from the revenue cycle. To achieve these objectives, it is necessary for the reader to

- Know the audit objectives for substantive tests of balances.
- Comprehend the audit program for verifying cash and receivables balances.
- Understand the nature of the auditing procedures designed to determine whether all cash transactions have been recorded.
- Be aware of the auditor's responsibilities in performing the required audit procedure of confirming accounts receivable.
- Know how statistical sampling and electronic data processing can be used in verifying accounts receivable.

Specific substantive tests of account balances are considered in this chapter. First, attention is given to the verification of year-end cash balances that result from the revenue and expenditure cycles. Second, the verification of receivables balances resulting from the revenue cycle is discussed. A brief explanation of tests of balances and audit objectives for these tests precedes the main focus of the chapter.

Nature and Scope of Tests of Balances

To have a reasonable basis for an opinion on the client's financial statements, the auditor must obtain sufficient competent evidential matter. Such evidence is obtained through substantive tests. As explained in Chapter 3, these tests take one of three forms: (1) tests of details of transactions, which often are performed concurrently with compliance tests during interim work, (2) tests of balances, and (3) analytical review procedures. When substantive tests are performed at or near the balance sheet date they are directed at the verification of the account balance. Hence, the single designation "tests of balances" is used in these chapters in referring to year-end substantive tests.

Tests of balances are explained within the context of account balances that result from specific classes of transactions within a cycle except in the case of cash and inventories. Both of these accounts are affected by more than one cycle. Cash is discussed in this chapter; inventories are considered with expenditure and production cycle balances in Chapter 13. Tests of balances are sometimes referred to as *direct* tests of balances.

Throughout Part II of this book, emphasis is frequently given to the fact that the purpose of the auditor's study and evaluation of internal accounting control is to determine the resultant extent to which auditing procedures are to be restricted. Thus, the design of an audit program for tests of balances (i.e., the nature, timing, and extent of such tests) must be based on the effectiveness of the client's control procedures pertaining to specific classes of transactions within a cycle.

In the typical audit engagement, the following approaches are often taken in designing audit programs for tests of balances:

- When internal controls over a specific class of transactions are effective, tests of balances are applied to resulting balance sheet account balances and reliance is placed primarily on internal controls and analytical review procedures for related income statement account balances.
- When internal controls over a specific class of transactions are not tested or cannot be relied upon, tests of balances are applied to both resulting balance sheet and income statement account balances.

It should also be recognized that evidence obtained from substantive tests of transactions made during interim work may affect subsequent tests of balances. The foregoing approaches will be recognized in the illustrative audit programs for tests of balances.

Management Assertions and Audit Objectives for Tests of Balances

As explained in Chapter 3, management assertions are the representations made by management in the financial statements. These assertions may be general or specific. The former pertain to the assertion that the financial statements are fairly presented in conformity with generally accepted accounting principles (GAAP). The latter relate to representations concerning the elements or components of the statements. The specific assertions made in financial statements may be classified into the following categories: (1) existence or occurrence, (2) completeness, (3) rights and obligations, (4) valuation or allocation, and (5) statement presentation and disclosure.[1]

Management's assertions can be translated into corresponding categories of audit objectives. The general audit objective is to express an opinion as to whether the client's financial statements, taken as a whole, are presented fairly in conformity with GAAP. Specific audit objectives, in turn, relate to verifying each of the specific assertions. In performing tests of balances, the auditor works with specific audit objectives for individual account balances. From the evidence obtained, the auditor reaches a conclusion as to whether he has a reasonable basis for an opinion on the financial statements taken as a whole.

In auditing, one other specific objective is frequently used—clerical accuracy. Thus, the following framework of audit objectives will be used for tests of balances: (1) clerical accuracy, (2) existence or occurrence, (3) completeness, (4) rights and obligations, (5) valuation or allocation, and (6) statement presentation and disclosure.

Clerical Accuracy

It is axiomatic that the financial statements should agree with the underlying accounting records. The objective of clerical accuracy pertains to the mathematical correctness of the accounting records and the client's supporting schedules as of the date the substantive tests are to be performed. This objective involves: (1) footing and cross-footing journals, registers, schedules, and trial balances, (2) tracing postings from the journals to general ledger accounts, (3) agreeing the totals of schedules with ledger balances, and (4) ascertaining the agreement of control accounts and subsidiary ledgers. Attention is focused on the latter two aspects in tests of balances in these chapters. The auditing procedures of retracing and recalculating are

---

[1] Auditing Standards Board, *Codification of Statements on Auditing Standards* (New York: American Institute of Certified Public Accountants, 1983), Auditing Section 326.03 (hereinafter referred to and cited as AU §).

applicable to this objective. Many auditors regard this objective as a prerequisite for meeting the other objectives.

Existence or Occurrence

This objective is two-dimensional. First, it requires the auditor to determine whether assets and liabilities and owners' equities exist as of a given point in time. Second, it relates to whether income statement transactions have actually occurred.

A variety of auditing procedures are used to establish existence. For tangible assets, such as cash on hand and inventories, the procedures include physical inspection, observation, and counting; for other types of assets, liabilities, and owners' equity, confirmation with knowledgeable outsiders, and inspection of supporting documents are used. In obtaining evidence as to existence, the auditor should recognize that the major audit risks are that assets may be overstated and liabilities may be understated. Similarly, in obtaining evidence as to occurrence, the auditor may perceive the major audit risks to be the overstatement of revenues and the understatement of expenses.

Completeness

The primary purpose of this objective is to establish whether all transactions that should have been recorded by the client are included in the accounts. The failure to include all transactions may result from neglecting to make an entry or from making an entry in the wrong accounting period. Evidence obtained by the auditor from the study and evaluation of internal control is important in meeting this objective.

Auditing procedures for completeness generally are performed at or near the date the balances are being verified. The procedures of inspection of documents, tracing and vouching of transactions, and analytical review are helpful in meeting this objective.

Rights and Obligations

This objective requires the auditor to obtain evidence that the client has rights to existing assets and that existing liability and owners' equity claims against the entity are valid. Ordinarily, rights to assets result from ownership and creditor claims are legal obligations. However, it should be recognized that a capitalized lease is an asset even though ownership resides with the lessor. Similarly, accrued but unfunded pension costs are liabilities but not legal obligations.

The auditing procedures of confirmation, inquiry, and inspection of documents are utilized in establishing the existence of rights and obligations. For this objective, documentation may include certificates of deposits, title registrations for delivery trucks, and legal contracts.

Valuation or Allocation

The valuation or allocation objective relates to whether financial statement elements are stated at the proper amount. This objective focuses primarily on the cost, matching, and consistency principles (or concepts) of accounting. Thus, it is concerned with (1) original cost, (2) net realizable values, (3) cost allocations, (4) accruals, (5) estimates, and (6) consistency in the application of accounting principles.

The auditing procedures of inspection of documents, observation, vouching, inquiry, and recalculation are important in obtaining evidence as to proper valuation or allocation.

Statement Presentation and Disclosure

It is imperative that account balances are properly presented in the financial statements and that accompanying disclosures are adequate. Presentation pertains to the identification, classification, and arrangement of items in a financial statement. For example, a temporary investment is identified as a marketable security, classified as a current asset, and shown immediately after cash on hand and cash in bank.

Disclosure relates to descriptions of material and relevant facts in the body of the statements and in accompanying notes thereto. Required disclosures are set forth in authoritative accounting pronouncements.

In performing tests of balances to meet this objective, the auditing procedures include inspection of documents, confirmation, and inquiry for data such as liens, contingencies, and restrictions that may require disclosure in the statements. The auditor then compares the financial statement presentation and disclosures with GAAP.

Summary of Objectives

A summary of the six audit objectives for tests of balances and the primary auditing procedures applicable to each is found on page 393. From this listing, it should be evident that a given auditing procedure may be applicable to more than one objective. For example, inspection applies to four and confirmation to three of the objectives. The auditing procedures used in tests of balances produce all the forms of audit evidence explained in Chapter 3.

It should also be recognized that the objectives are interrelated. For example, satisfaction of the completeness objective for an asset account also contributes to the achievement of the existence, rights, and valuation objectives. While there may be some variations, audit programs are generally designed and executed to meet these six audit objectives.

TESTS OF CASH BALANCES

The starting point in the design of the audit program for testing cash balances is the auditor's evaluation of internal control procedures over cash receipts and cash disbursements transactions: As described in Chapters 8 and 9, the

AUDIT OBJECTIVE	PURPOSE OF OBJECTIVE	PRIMARY AUDITING PROCEDURES
Clerical accuracy	Establish the mathematical accuracy of accounting records and agreement of records with supporting schedules	Recalculating, retracing
Existence or occurrence	Determine the existence of balance sheet items, and the occurrence of revenue and expense transactions	Physical inspection, observing, counting, confirming, inspection of documents
Completeness	Determine that all transactions that should have been recorded are recorded in the accounts	Inspecting, retracing, analytical review, vouching
Rights and obligations	Verify client rights to existing assets and the validity of liability and owners' equity claims on existing assets	Confirming, inquiring, inspecting, vouching
Valuation or allocation	Ascertain that statement items are stated at proper amounts	Inspecting, inquiring, recalculating, vouching
Statement presentation and disclosure	Determine appropriateness of the presentation of statement items and the adequacy of accompanying disclosures	Inspecting, confirming, inquiring

auditor's reliance on controls over these two classes of transactions will affect the nature, timing, and extent of the tests of cash balances. When substantial reliance on internal control over cash transactions is justified, the extent of testing can be reduced and many of the procedures can be performed prior to the balance sheet date.

Cash balances include cash on hand, cash in bank, and miscellaneous balances such as plant expansion funds and bond sinking funds. Attention here is centered on the first two types of cash balances.

An audit program for tests of cash balances is shown in Figure 12-1. Some of the procedures shown in the program may satisfy more than one audit objective, but they are listed alongside the objective they most typically satisfy. Some of the audit objectives are combined because of the nature of cash.

The audit procedures for cash result in evidential matter that has a high degree of reliability because much of the corroborating information is obtained through (1) the auditor's direct personal knowledge and (2) direct communication from independent sources outside the enterprise. Each procedure is explained below within the framework of the six audit objectives.

TYPE OF TEST: Substantive   **PURPOSE: Validity and Propriety of Balances**
CYCLE: Revenue and Expenditure   **ACCOUNTS: Cash on Hand and Cash in Bank**

A. CLERICAL ACCURACY:

    1. Foot cash journals and schedules.
    2. Reconcile schedules with ledger balances.

B. EXISTENCE OR OCCURRENCE, RIGHTS AND OBLIGATIONS, AND VALUATION
   OR ALLOCATION:

    1. Count cash on hand.
    2. Confirm bank balances.

C. COMPLETENESS:

    1. Perform cash cutoff test.
    2. Examine or prepare bank reconciliations.
    3. Obtain and use bank cutoff statements.
    4. Trace bank transfers.
    5. Prepare proof of cash.
    6. Make analytical review.

D. STATEMENT PRESENTATION AND DISCLOSURE:

    1. Make inquiries and review documentation for cash restrictions and liens.
    2. Compare statement presentation and disclosures with GAAP.

FIGURE 12–1. Audit Program: Cash Balances

Clerical Accuracy

The starting point in the verification of cash is to foot any client schedules that are to be included in the audit working papers. A common schedule is a bank reconciliation. For this objective, the mathematical accuracy of the reconciliation including subtotals, such as total outstanding checks, is validated by recalculation. The balance per books shown in the reconciliation is also agreed to the ledger balance.

Existence or Occurrence, Rights and Obligations, and Valuation or Allocation

The auditor's primary concern under these objectives is whether the client has all the cash it claims to have. This involves the comparison of recorded cash balances with cash on hand and cash in banks. As shown in the audit program, two audit procedures are directed at these objectives.

Count Cash on Hand

Undeposited cash receipts, change funds, and petty cash funds are ordinarily considered to be cash on hand. To properly perform this test, the auditor should

- Control all cash and negotiable instruments held by the client until all funds have been counted.
- Insist that the custodian of the cash be present throughout the count.
- Obtain a signed receipt from the custodian on return of the funds to the client.
- Ascertain that all undeposited checks are payable to the order of the client, either directly or through endorsement.

The control of all funds is designed to prevent transfers by the client of counted funds to uncounted funds. The sealing of funds and the use of additional auditors are often required when cash is held in many locations. The safeguards pertaining to the custodian serve to minimize the possibility, in the event of a shortage, of the client claiming that all cash was intact when released to the auditor for counting.

Confirm Bank Balances

It is customary for the auditor to confirm cash on deposit with banks as of the balance sheet date. A completed standard bank confirmation form request used in this test is illustrated in Figure 12-2. It may be noted that the request includes not only the cash balances on deposit, but also direct and indirect obligations to the bank, contingent liabilities, and security agreements.

The confirmation request is prepared in duplicate and signed by an authorized check signer of the client. Both copies are sent to the bank, and the original is returned to the auditor. To assure the competency of the evidence from this procedure, the auditor should personally mail the request in his own return address envelope and the response should be returned directly to the auditor by the bank.

Bank confirmation requests should be sent to all banks in which the client has an account, including those that may have a zero balance at the end of the year. Such communication may disclose the existence of a balance in the account and/or obligations and contingencies to the bank.

The auditor uses the confirmation responses in reconciling bank and book balances, in verifying loans, and in determining the existence of restrictions on cash and of contingencies such as notes receivable discounted.

The terms of bank loans and the establishment of a line of credit with a bank may require the borrower to maintain a cash balance equal to an agreed-on percentage of the amount borrowed or a specified dollar amount. The required minimum balance is referred to as a *compensating balance*. The American Institute of Certified Public Accountants (AICPA) has developed a special form for confirming compensating balance agreements. Because of the specific data requested, the confirmation should be sent separately to the loan officer of the bank and not be included with the regular bank confirmation request.

STANDARD BANK CONFIRMATION INQUIRY
Approved 1966 by
AMERICAN INSTITUTE OF CERTIFIED PUBLIC ACCOUNTANTS
and
BANK ADMINISTRATION INSTITUTE (FORMERLY NABAC)

```
┌─────────────────────────┐
│      O R I G I N A L     │
│  To be mailed to accountant │
└─────────────────────────┘
```

December 20 19 *X1*

Your completion of the following report will be sincerely appreciated. IF THE ANSWER TO ANY ITEM IS "NONE," PLEASE SO STATE. Kindly mail it in the enclosed stamped, addressed envelope *direct* to the accountant named below.

Report from   Yours truly,

Bates Company
(ACCOUNT NAME PER BANK RECORDS)

(Bank) *City Bank*

10 Monroe Street   By *C. A. Merten, Tres.*
Authorized Signature

Midtown, Indiana

Bank customer should check here if confirmation of bank balances only (item 1) is desired.

NOTE—If the space provided is inadequate, please enter totals hereon and attach a statement giving full details as called for by the columnar headings below.

Accountant *Reddy + Abel*
4 Court Street
Urban, Michigan

1. At the close of business on *December 31* 19 *X1* our records showed the following balance(s) to the **credit** of the above named customer. In the event that we could readily ascertain whether there were any balances to the credit of the customer not designated in this request, the appropriate information is given below.

AMOUNT	ACCOUNT NAME	ACCOUNT NUMBER	Subject to Withdrawal by Check?	Interest Bearing? Give Rate
$ 120,262.47	General	12345-642	yes	no
$ 5,000.00	Payroll	12345-643	yes	no

2. The customer was directly liable to us in respect of loans, acceptances, etc., at the close of business on that date in the total amount of $_____, as follows:

AMOUNT	DATE OF LOAN OR DISCOUNT	DUE DATE	INTEREST Rate	INTEREST Paid to	DESCRIPTION OF LIABILITY, COLLATERAL, SECURITY INTERESTS, LIENS, ENDORSERS, ETC.
$ 120,000	8/1/X1	2/1/X2	15	N/A	Unsecured
$ 80,000	12/1/X1	6/1/X2	15	N/A	Unsecured

3. The customer was contingently liable as endorser of notes discounted and/or as guarantor at the close of business on that date in the total amount of $ *none*, as below:

AMOUNT	NAME OF MAKER	DATE OF NOTE	DUE DATE	REMARKS
$				

4. Other direct or contingent liabilities, open letters of credit, and relative collateral, were

None

5. Security agreements under the Uniform Commercial Code or any other agreements providing for restrictions, not noted above, were as follows (if officially recorded, indicate date and office in which filed):

None

Date *January 9* 19 *X2*

Yours truly, (Bank) *City Bank*

By *Nancy L. Springer, V.P.*
Authorized Signature

Additional copies of this form are available from the American Institute of CPAs, 1211 Avenue of the Americas, New York, N. Y. 10036

FIGURE 12–2. Standard Bank Confirmation Request Form

Completeness

This objective relates to whether the client's cash balances include all cash transactions that should be recorded. As shown in Figure 12-1, there are six audit procedures that pertain to completeness.

Perform Cash Cutoff Test

A prompt cutoff of cash receipts and cash disbursements at the end of the year is essential to the proper statement of cash on the balance sheet and the overall fairness of the client's financial statements.

Evidence concerning the accuracy of the cutoff can be obtained by personal observation and a review of internally created documentation. If an auditor can be present at all client locations on the balance sheet date, it is possible by personal observation to ascertain that all cash received prior to the close of business is included in cash on hand or in deposits in transit. Furthermore, the auditor can personally determine the last check written and mailed by the client. Subsequent tracing of this evidence to the accounting records will verify the accuracy of the cash cutoff.

As an alternative to physical observation, the auditor can generally obtain satisfactory evidence of a prompt cutoff by (1) reviewing the source documents pertaining to cash receipts and cash disbursements for several days before and after the balance sheet date, and (2) determining whether they are recorded in the proper accounting period. The use of a bank cutoff statement, described below, is also helpful in determining whether a proper cash cutoff has been made.

Examine or Prepare Bank Reconciliations

Most companies reconcile their bank and book balances monthly. When the reconciliations are done independently, and reviewed by internal auditors, the auditor may only need to review the client's reconciliation at the end of the year. The review should include:

- Tracing bank balances to the bank confirmation responses.
- Verifying the validity of the reconciling items such as deposits in transit and outstanding checks.
- Scanning the bank statements for erasures and alterations.

A client-prepared reconciliation is shown in Figure 12-3. The auditor should also substantiate the propriety of the adjusting entries, if any, and determine whether the client has recorded them.

When internal accounting control is weak, the auditor may prepare the bank reconciliation. Normally, the bank statement and accompanying data

FIGURE 12–3. Client-Prepared Bank Reconciliation

(e.g., paid checks, debit memos, etc.) will be in the possession of the client and therefore some alterations could have been made. To eliminate this possibility, the client can be asked to instruct the bank to send the year-end bank statement directly to the auditor.

The evidence provided by a bank reconciliation alone is generally not considered to be sufficient to verify the balance of cash in bank because of the uncertainties concerning two of the most important reconciling items: (1) deposits in transit and (2) outstanding checks. Such evidence is obtainable only by tracing these items into the bank statement in the next accounting period. The procedure of obtaining a bank cutoff statement is designed, in part, for this purpose. When the cutoff statement procedures validate these and other reconciling items, the reliance that an auditor can place on a bank reconciliation is significantly enhanced.

Obtain and Use Bank Cutoff Statements

A bank cutoff statement is a bank statement as of a date subsequent to the date of the balance sheet. The date should be at a point in time that will permit most of the year-end outstanding checks to clear the bank. Usually, the date is seven to ten business days following the end of the client's fiscal year in areas where most of the banks are members of the Federal Reserve System and ten days or longer in areas where this is not the case.

The client must request the cutoff statement from the bank and instruct that it be sent directly to the auditor. On receipt of the cutoff statement, with enclosed canceled checks and bank memoranda, the auditor should

- Trace all prior year dated checks to the outstanding checks listed on the bank reconciliation.
- Trace deposits in transit on the bank reconciliation to deposits on the cutoff statement.
- Scan the cutoff statement and enclosed data for unusual items.

The tracing of checks is designed to verify the list of outstanding checks. In this step, the auditor may also find that a prior period check not on the list of outstanding checks has cleared the bank and that some of the checks listed as outstanding have not cleared the bank. The former may be indicative of an irregularity known as kiting, which is explained on page 400; the latter may be due to delays in (1) mailing the checks by the payer, (2) depositing the checks by the payees, and (3) processing the checks by the bank. The auditor should investigate any unusual circumstances.

When the aggregate effect of uncleared checks is material, it may be indicative of an irregularity known as *window dressing,* which is a deliberate attempt to overstate a company's short-term solvency.[2] In such case, the auditor should trace the uncleared checks to the check register and supporting documentation and, if necessary, make inquiries of the treasurer.

The tracing of deposits in transit to the cutoff statement is normally a relatively simple matter since the first deposit on the cutoff statement should be the deposit in transit shown on the reconciliation. When this is not the case, the auditor should determine the underlying circumstances for the time lag from the treasurer and verify his explanations.

In scanning the cutoff statement for unusual items, the auditor should be

---

[2] Assume at the balance sheet date, the client's balances show current assets of $800,000 and current liabilities of $400,000. If $100,000 of checks to short-term creditors have been prematurely entered, the correct totals are current assets of $900,000 and current liabilities of $500,000, which results in a 1.8-to-1 current ratio instead of the reported 2-to-1.

alert for such items as unrecorded bank debits and credits and bank errors and corrections.

Inasmuch as the cutoff statement is obtained directly by the auditor from an independent source outside the client's organization, it provides a high degree of competent corroborating information as to the validity of the year-end bank reconciliation and the amount of cash in bank at the statement date.

Trace Bank Transfers

Many entities maintain accounts with more than one bank. A company with multiple bank accounts may make authorized transfers of money between bank accounts. For example, money may be transferred from a general bank account to a payroll bank account for payroll checks that are to be distributed on payday. When a bank transfer occurs, several days (called the *float period*) generally will elapse before the check clears the bank on which it is drawn. Thus, cash on deposit per bank records will be overstated during this period because the check will be included in the balance of the bank in which it is deposited and will not be deducted from the bank on which it is drawn. Bank transfers may also result in a misstatement of the bank balance per books if the disbursement and receipt are not recorded in the same accounting period.

Intentionally recording a bank transfer as a deposit in the receiving bank while failing to show a deduction from the bank account on which the transfer check is drawn is an irregularity known as *kiting*. Kiting may be used to conceal a cash shortage or to overstate cash in bank at the statement date.

An auditor requires evidence as to the validity of bank transfers or conversely, of errors or irregularities therein. This is obtained by preparing a schedule of these checks issued at or near the end of the client's fiscal year. Data for the schedule are obtained from an analysis of the cash entries per books and applicable bank and cutoff bank statements. The schedule lists all transfer checks and shows the dates that the checks were recorded by the client and the bank, as illustrated in Figure 12-4.

Assuming all checks are dated and issued on December 31, check 4100 in Figure 12-4 has been handled properly since both book entries were made in December and both bank entries occurred in January. This check would be listed as an outstanding check in reconciling the general bank account at December 31 and as a deposit in transit in reconciling the payroll bank account. Check 4275 illustrates a transfer check in transit at the closing date. Cash per books is understated $10,000 since the check has been deducted from the balance per books by the issuer in December but has not been added to the Branch #1 account per books by the depositor until January. Thus, an adjusting entry is required at December 31 to increase the branch balance per books.

Bates Company
Bank Transfer Schedule —
12/31/X1
A-2

Bank Accounts			Amount of check	Disbursement Date		Receipt Date	
Ck.#	From	To		Books	Bank	Books	Bank
4100	General	Payroll	50000	12/31	1/3	12/31	1/2
4275	General	Branch #1	10000	12/31	1/4	1/2	1/2
4280	General	Branch #I	20000	1/2	1/2	12/31	12/31
B403	Branch #4	General	5000	1/2	1/3	1/3	12/31

FIGURE 12–4. Bank Transfer Schedule

Checks 4280 and B403 illustrate the likelihood of kiting because these December checks were not recorded as disbursements per books until January even though they were deposited in December. Check 4280 results in a $20,000 overstatement of cash in bank because the receipt per books occurred in December, but the corresponding book deduction was not made until January. Check B403 may illustrate an attempt to conceal a cash shortage since the deposit occurred in December presumably to permit reconcilement of bank and book balances, and all other entries were made in January.

Kiting is possible when weaknesses in internal accounting control allow one individual to issue and record checks (i.e., improper segregation of functions), or there is collusion between the individuals who are responsible for the two functions. In addition to tracing bank transfers, kiting may be detected by (1) obtaining and using a bank cutoff statement because the kited check clearing in January will not appear on the list of outstanding checks for December and (2) performing a cash cutoff test since the last check issued in December will not be recorded in the check register.

Prepare Proof of Cash

A *proof of cash* is a simultaneous reconciliation of bank transactions and balances with corresponding data per books for a specified period of time. This substantive test is generally prepared only when the auditor has concluded that internal control over cash is weak. As illustrated in Figure 12-5, a proof of cash permits a reconciliation of four bank and book items: beginning balances, cash receipts transactions, cash disbursements transactions, and ending balances. The illustrated format may be extended to show the "true cash" balance by adding (or subtracting) book adjustments from the ending balance per books.

The following steps are helpful in preparing a proof of cash:

• Obtain the bank and book totals from the bank statement and cash in bank account, respectively.
• Obtain the beginning and ending balance reconciling items from the bank reconciliations at the designated dates.
• Determine the reconciling items for the two middle columns by analysis.

All reconciling items in the schedule are attributable to either negating (for purposes of reconciliation only) items recorded by the bank that have not been recorded on the books or recognizing items recorded on the books that have not been recorded by the bank. In Figure 12-5, for example, the deposit in transit on November 30 is subtracted from December bank receipts because that deposit is not included in the December receipts per books. In contrast, deposits in transit on December 31 are added to receipts per bank and to the ending bank balance because this amount has been recorded on the books but not by the bank.

The occurrence of a dishonored customer check sometimes proves to be troublesome in preparing a proof of cash. When the bank receives notice of "not sufficient funds" (NSF) from the customer's bank, it issues a debit memorandum (often referred to as an *NSF charge*) which is posted as a debit on the depositor's bank statement to cancel the credit that was made when the check was originally deposited. The action taken by the depositor on notification of dishonor determines the effect on the proof of cash. The disposition of the NSF check in Figure 12-5 is based on the fact that the depositor made no entry upon notification and that the check was not redeposited prior to December 31.

The failure of any of the four columns of a proof of cash to reconcile is indicative of an unexplained error or irregularity which should be investigated by the auditor.

Prepared by: *W.C.R.*   Date: *1/12/X2*
Reviewed by: *W.K.S.*   Date: *1/16/X2*

Bates Company
Proof of Cash for December
12/31/X1

Acc. # 110 City Bank—General   A-3

	Balance 11/30/X1	Receipts	Disbursements	Balance 12/31/X1
Per bank statement	115261 40	912274 60	907273 53	120262 47
Deposit in transit:				
Beginning (11/30)	21320 81 √	(21320 81)		
Ending (12/31)		26269 94		26269 94 θ
Outstanding checks:				
Beginning (11/30)	(27264 45) φ		(27264 45)	
Ending (12/31)			25174 49 θ	(25174 49)
Other items:				
NSF check			(200 00) ʅ	200 00
Per books	109317 76 ✗	917223 73 ✗	904983 57 ✗	121557 92 ✗
	F	F	F	FF

√   Traced to December bank statement

✗   Traced to cash in bank account

ʅ   Examined debit memo

φ   Agrees with list of outstanding checks

F   Footed

FF Footed and crossfooted

θ   Traced to January cutoff bank statement

FIGURE 12–5. Proof of Cash Working Paper

Make Analytical Review

Cash is seldom directly interrelated with other accounts. Thus, the opportunities for analytical reviews of cash balances are limited. It is possible, however, to compare the proportion of current assets represented by cash this year with preceding years. Another test is to compare the cash balances with budget expectations and to review monthly cash budget variance reports if such data are available. Any significant fluctuations and questionable items normally will require further inquiry and investigation to determine whether all cash transactions have been recorded.

Statement Presentation and Disclosure

Cash should be properly presented in the balance sheet and appropriate disclosure should be made of any restrictions on the use of cash.

When compensating balances exist, any cash balances legally restricted under loan or line of credit agreements should be segregated on the balance sheet and classified according to the appropriate classification of the related debt. In addition, supplementary disclosures, in the form of notes to the financial statements, must be made of pertinent provisions of the agreement such as the rate of interest, maximum limit of short-term borrowing, and repayment terms. A bank overdraft is normally reported as a current liability.

The auditor determines the appropriateness of the statement presentation from a review of the draft of the client's statements, and the evidence obtained from the foregoing substantive tests. For example, the response from a bank confirmation may indicate the existence of restrictions on the use of cash funds. In addition, the auditor should review the corporate minutes and loan agreements for evidence of cash restrictions, and make inquiry of management.

TESTS OF RECEIVABLES BALANCES

The nature, timing, and extent of substantive tests of receivables balances depend on the auditor's evaluation of internal controls of sales and cash receipts transactions in the revenue cycle, as described in Chapters 7 and 8.

For example, if the auditor has determined that controls over credit approval are weak, additional tests of the allowance for uncollectibles account may be necessary. In contrast, when controls over billings are strong, the auditor may confirm accounts receivable one or two months prior to the balance sheet date. An audit program for accounts receivable, notes receivable, and the allowance for uncollectibles is illustrated in Figure 12-6. In this program, the audit objectives of existence and rights are combined.

The auditor relies primarily on evidential matter obtained from confirmations in meeting the existence and rights objectives. Corroborating information for the other objectives is obtained largely from documentation originating within the client organization.

Clerical Accuracy

The starting point for tests of accounts receivable and the allowance for uncollectible accounts is an aged trial balance of individual customer balances prepared by the client. The components (transactions) comprising the balance are aged by the length of time the obligation has been outstanding (unpaid) at the balance sheet date. An aged trial balance, which is illustrated

TYPE OF TEST: Substantive CYCLE: Revenue	PURPOSE: Validity and Propriety of Balances ACCOUNTS: Notes and Accounts Receivable and Allowable for Uncollectible Accounts

A. CLERICAL ACCURACY:

    1. Foot supporting schedules.
    2. Reconcile general ledger balances with schedules and subsidiary ledger totals.

B. EXISTENCE OR OCCURRENCE AND RIGHTS AND OBLIGATIONS:

    1. Inspect notes on hand.
    2. Confirm accounts receivable.
    3. Confirm notes receivable.
    4. Review documentation in client's files.

C. COMPLETENESS:

    1. Perform sales and sales returns cutoff test.
    2. Make analytical review.

D. VALUATION OR ALLOCATION:

    1. Examine subsequent collections.
    2. Review documentation and schedules pertaining to collectibility.
    3. Recalculate interest earned and accrued.

E. STATEMENT PRESENTATION AND DISCLOSURE:

    1. Make inquiries and review documentation concerning assigning, pledging, or factoring (selling) accounts receivable and the discounting of notes receivable.
    2. Compare statement presentation and disclosures with GAAP.

FIGURE 12–6. Audit Program: Receivables Balances

in Figure 12-7, may be manually or electronically prepared and compared to the control account balance.

The auditor should verify the accuracy of the aged trial balance. This is done by recalculating the totals of the schedule, tracing selected customer balances in the trial balance to the subsidiary ledger, and tracing unpaid invoices to sales transaction dates.

Since all customer balances are included, the aged trial balance is used extensively in performing other tests of balances. For example, as shown in Figure 12-7, it may be used in confirming accounts receivable. The aged trial balance may also enable the auditor to identify balances that should be reclassified, such as customers with credit balances and amounts due from officers and affiliated companies.

It is customary for the client to also prepare a schedule of notes and interest receivable, as shown in Figure 3-6 on page 90. The accuracy of this listing is verified by footing the schedules and reconciling the total to the general ledger balance. This schedule is used to simultaneously verify accrued interest receivable and interest revenue.

(PBC)

Bates Company—Accounts Receivable—Trade
Aged Trial Balance
12/31/x1

Prepared by: O.C.C. Date: 1/15/x2
Reviewed by: P.A.R. Date: 1/20/x2

B-1

Acct. #140

Account Name	Past Due Over 90 days	Over 60 days	Over 30 days	Current	Conf. #	Balance per Books 12/31/x1	Adjustments	Balance per Audit 12/31/x1	Cash Received 1/x2
Ace Engineering		2329.09	2016.14	11875.90	1	C 16421.08	√	16421.08	12621.29
Applied Devices			15938.89	27901.11	2	C 43940.00	√	43940.00	29460.00
Astro Electric			71.22	8207.95		8143.17	√	8143.17	71.22
Barry Manufacturing	1088.92	793.12	3120500	92106		5858.10	√	5858.10	9324
Best Electronics	50110	7309.50	3094801	21444.25	3	C 63199.86	√	63199.86	2621060
Carothers, Inc.			3813.76	861730		12493.06	√	12493.06	3913760
Columbia Corporation				439218		4392.18	√	4392.18	
Delta Manufacturing			739.57	29533.88		30293.45	√	30293.45	
EMC		(461.01)	10487.26	16179476	4	C 18504000	√	13504.00	17248.24
General Electric		1241.27	20000.63	8901715	5	C 11823.14	√	11823.14	76328.41
Harvey Radio			110203	4752160		56235.63	√	56235.63	110203
R+L Industries			330737	631487		9621.74	√	9621.74	362137
Instrumentation Corp.	261587	170916	170465	741134		10822.35	√	10822.35	341.01
Jet Air		20928.00	15435446	56536.88	6	(E) 86852.1	(14162) (7)	85267.00	27532.87
Lavalle Electric		119872	131314	17167.04	7	C 1432.86	√	1432.86	119872
Houston Industries		301245	7362368	48573.99	8	C 24543.77	√	24543.77	39935.42
Lester Electronics	131510	1757743	924599	524816	9	C 17176.40	√	17176.40	306633
Nelson, Inc.		3516.20	608603	214325	10	16850.39	√	16850.39	651603
Oak City Electronics	382149	4777808	5936.89	950008		C 35926.71	√	35926.71	8539.57
Orbital Products			907565			10406.13	√	10406.13	90545
Progress Electronics				301790		301790	√	301790	
Rohr Corp.		571.02	620162	9724.14	11	10496.78	√	10496.78	71824.28
SEG, Inc.		1654.80	3121016	8565525	12	C 13432.81	√	13432.81	131200
W+M Mfg. Corp.		1904.65	2126678	28389.69	13	C 32461.12	√	32461.12	161093
Vario Corp.	91498	2861105	987443	135180		27111.96	√	27111.96	114898
Miscellaneous			192026	1571.18		(E) 176.54		176.54	
	5545.55	613.17.50	16053728	3921.364.1		6195.367.4	(14162)	6182120.53	267207.71

(E) To Record Credit Memo - Issued 1/12/x2

C Confirmed
√ Traced to subledger - Verified Aging
√ Footed
∅ Traced to CR Journal and Examined Remittance Advice
ϰ Unable to Confirm
∅ Correction of Error in Aging Schedule

ATE (7) See B-16   Per Subsidiary Retained 1/31/x2
C. Accounts Retained Re. (14162)

FIGURE 12–7. Aged Trial Balance Working Paper

Existence or Occurrence and Rights and Obligations

These objectives relate to whether recorded receivables are owned by the client and represent valid claims against customers. Four auditing procedures apply to these objectives.

Inspect Notes on Hand

The auditor should inspect all notes in the possession of the client. This procedure should occur simultaneously with the count of cash and marketable securities. In examining notes receivable, the auditor compares the terms and face value of the instrument with the client's records and with the schedule of notes and interest that normally is prepared by the client for the auditor. The auditor should also be alert for notes held beyond their maturity dates, notes bearing abnormal interest rates, and nontrade notes such as those issued by officers and affiliated companies. The existence of any of these factors should be indicated in the working papers in determining the collectibility of the notes and the appropriate statement presentation.

The auditor is expected to ascertain that the notes are made out to the client or are endorsed to the client. Similarly, the auditor also inspects any collateral held by the client as security for a note. If the collateral is in the form of securities, it should be examined to obtain evidence that the debtor has legal title.

Confirm Accounts Receivable

Confirmation of accounts receivable involves direct written communication between the individual customers and the auditor. Through confirmation, the auditor obtains evidence as to the existence of the customer and the accuracy of the balance due from the customer. A confirmation is not a request for payment. Consequently, this procedure is not directed at evidence as to the collectibility or net realizable value of the claim. Confirmation responses, however, may reveal previously paid items and disputed items that affect the proper valuation of the claim. Relevant considerations in performing this procedure are as follows:

Practicability and reasonableness. The confirmation of accounts is a generally accepted auditing procedure whenever (1) the receivables are material to a company's financial position or results of operations and (2) it is practicable and reasonable to do so. In auditing, *practicable* means capable of being done with available means or with reason or prudence; *reasonable* means sensible in the light of prevailing circumstances. In virtually all cases, it will be practicable and reasonable for the auditor to perform this procedure.

However, there are two circumstances in which the auditor may be unable to confirm accounts receivable. First, debtors may be unable to confirm if they use voucher systems that show the amount owed on individual transactions but not the total amount owed to one creditor. This is generally true of governmental agencies. In some cases, the auditor may be able to overcome this problem by confirming individual transactions rather than balances. Second, the client may prohibit the auditor from confirming any or certain accounts receivables. Complete prohibition represents a serious limitation on the scope of the auditor's examination that generally will result in a disclaimer of opinion on the financial statements. The effect of partial prohibition should be evaluated on the basis of management's reasons therefor and whether the auditor can satisfy himself by other auditing procedures.

Form of confirmation. There are two forms of confirmation request: (1) the *positive* form, which requires the debtor to respond whether or not the balance shown is correct, and (2) the *negative* form, which requires the debtor to respond only when the amount shown is incorrect. The two forms are illustrated in Figures 12-8 and 12-9. The positive confirmation request is usually made in the form of a separate letter, but it may be in the form of a stamp on the customer's monthly statement. In contrast, the negative request is usually in the form of a stamp. The positive form generally produces the better evidence, because under the negative form, the failure to receive a response can only lead to a presumption that the balance is correct, whereas the customer may have overlooked the request or neglected to return an exception.

National Mine Service
Box 131
Indiana, Pennsylvania 15701

This request is being sent to you to enable our independent auditors to confirm the correctness of our records. It is not a request for payment.

Our records on <u>December 31, 19X1</u> showed an amount of <u>$64,457.36</u> receivable from you. Please confirm whether this agrees with your records on that date by signing and returning this form direct to our auditors. An addressed envelope is enclosed for this purpose. If you find any difference please report details direct to our auditors in the space provided below.

a. B. Smart
_____
Controller

The above amount is correct ☐. The above amount is incorrect for the following reasons: ____

_____

_____

_____
(Individual or Company Name)

By: _____

Conf. No. 6

FIGURE 12–8. Positive Confirmation Request: Letter Form

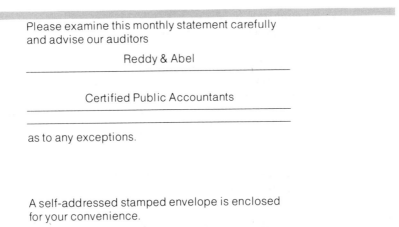

Please examine this monthly statement carefully
and advise our auditors

Reddy & Abel

_____

Certified Public Accountants

_____
_____

as to any exceptions.

A self-addressed stamped envelope is enclosed
for your convenience.

THIS IS NOT A REQUEST FOR PAYMENT

FIGURE 12–9. Negative Confirmation Request: Stamp Form

The form of the confirmation request rests with the auditor. In reaching this decision, the auditor considers the effectiveness of the client's internal accounting controls and the composition of the customers' accounts. The positive form is preferred when internal control is weak (i.e., there appears to be opportunity for errors or irregularities to occur) or individual account balances are relatively large. When the reverse is true, the negative form may be used.

Frequently, a combination of the two forms is used in a single engagement. For example, in the audit of a public utility, the auditor may elect to use the negative form for residential customers and the positive form for commercial customers. When the positive form is used, the auditor should generally follow up with a second and sometimes an additional request to those debtors that fail to reply.[3]

Timing and extent of requests. The confirmation date and the number of responses to be requested are decisions that must be made by the auditor. Confirmation may be requested as of the balance sheet date or a month or two before the statement date, if internal controls are effective. In the latter case, the auditor is expected to perform other substantive tests of transactions from the confirmation date to the balance sheet date. In addition, the auditor may elect to reconfirm balances at year end which have changed significantly since the confirmation date. Accounts to be confirmed may be programmed on the computer, chosen from random number tables, or selected by the auditor on a judgmental basis. The sample should be sufficiently representative to justify valid generalizations about the entire population of receivables.

[3] Auditing Standards Board, *op. cit.*, AU § 331.08.

Controlling the requests. The auditor must control every step in the confirmation process. This means

- Ascertaining that the amount, name, and address on the confirmation agree with the corresponding data in the customer's account.
- Maintaining custody of the confirmations until they are mailed.
- Using his own return address envelopes for the confirmations.
- Personally depositing the requests in the mail.
- Insisting that the returns be sent directly to the auditor.

Client assistance can be used in the preparation of the requests provided the foregoing controls are observed.

Disposition of responses. Confirmation responses will inevitably contain some exceptions. The auditor should describe all exceptions in the working papers. Exceptions may be attributable to in-transit items at the confirmation date, items in dispute, errors, and irregularities. All differences should be investigated by the auditor, and their resolution should be indicated in the working papers.

When insufficient responses are received or when numerous exceptions are found, the auditor may be unable to issue a standard audit report, unless the auditing procedures of reviewing documentation in the customer's account file and examining collections subsequent to the examination date are more extensively applied. These procedures are explained later in the chapter.

Confirm Notes Receivable

The auditor normally uses the positive form of confirmation for notes and acceptances receivable. Confirmations are sent to both the maker of the instrument and any party that is currently holding the note for the client. The request to the maker should include verification of the terms, last interest payment date, balance due, and a description of any collateral. The confirmation to holders is designed to determine the existence of the note and the attendant circumstances pertaining thereto. Notes may be held by others for collection or because they have been discounted, sold, renewed, dishonored, or pledged.

Review Documentation in Client's Files

The customer account file maintained by the client should contain such documents as customer orders, shipping documents, sales invoices, credit memoranda, and correspondence. These documents provide evidence as to the existence of the receivable. This procedure may be used to supplement confirmation procedures when no response is obtained from a positive confirmation and when the negative form of confirmation is used.

Completeness

This objective relates to whether all accounts receivable transactions that should be recorded are recorded. The substantive tests applicable to this objective consist of the cash cutoff test described earlier in this chapter and the following procedures.

Perform Sales and Sales Returns Cutoff Test

The sales cutoff test is designed to obtain reasonable assurance that (1) sales and accounts receivable are recorded in the accounting period in which the goods are shipped and (2) the corresponding entries for inventories and cost of goods sold are made in the same period.

The basis for recognizing sales normally is the date of shipment, but when goods are shipped F.O.B. (free on board) destination, the seller may arbitrarily add several days to the shipping date, since legal title does not pass in such case until the buyer receives the goods. The sales cutoff test usually is made as of the balance sheet date. The test involves:

- Examining shipping documents for several days before and after the cutoff date to determine the date and terms of shipment.
- Tracing shipping documents to the sales and inventory records to establish that the entries were made in the correct accounting period.
- Inspecting invoices for a period of time before and after the cutoff date to ascertain the validity and propriety of the shipments and corresponding entries.
- Inquiring of management as to any direct shipments by outside suppliers to customers and determining the appropriateness of related entries.

If internal control is weak, the auditor should be alert for the possibility of fictitious sales. For example, unordered goods may be shipped to a regular customer shortly before the statement date, with the subsequent return not made and booked until the following period. When evidence obtained from the sales cutoff indicates material errors in recording year-end sales, the auditor should request the client to make the necessary adjustments.

The sales returns cutoff test involves: (1) reviewing the receiving report on goods returned, and (2) retracing the credit memos to recorded entries shortly before and after the balance sheet date. Sales shipped prior to the end of the year but returned after year-end should be deducted from sales.

Make Analytical Review

The reasonableness of receivables and sales balances should be tested by analytical review procedures. Comparisons of sales data with sales results for prior periods, budget expectations for the current year, and industry trends will provide analytical evidence of the reasonableness of sales. In addition, physical data that are functionally related to sales may be studied to corroborate sales totals. For example, production volume such as kilowatt hours of electricity and new car or truck units manufactured may, through the application of average selling prices, provide evidence as to the reasonableness of total sales. Any unusual fluctuations and questionable items should be investigated by the auditor.

Valuation or Allocation

For receivables balances, this objective includes verifying gross claims against debtors, collectibility of receivables, uncollectible accounts expense, and interest earned on notes receivable. There are three audit procedures that are applicable to this objective.

Examine Subsequent Collections

The best evidence of collectibility is the receipt of payment from the customer. Prior to actual receipt, the collectibility of an account can only be estimated. Between the balance sheet date and the conclusion of the auditor's examination, collections on the prior year's receivables may be received by the client. The matching of such collections back to balances outstanding at the statement date establishes the collectibility of the accounts.

In performing this test, the auditor should recognize the possible adverse implications of collections that cannot be matched to specific transactions or balances. For example, a round sum amount may, on investigation, reveal items in dispute, and token payments on large balances may indicate financial instability on the part of the customer.

Review Documentation and Schedules Pertaining to Collectibility

Receivables should be stated on the balance sheet at net realizable value. This value for notes receivable is determined by the collectibility of the instrument or, in the event of default, by the value of the collateral held. In evaluating collectibility, the auditor usually looks for evidence that might adversely affect the client's ability to obtain collection at the due date. One source is to examine the schedule of notes receivable for past due notes, and notes that have been frequently renewed. Inquiry of the credit manager may also be helpful.

The schedule of notes should indicate the existence of any collateral which may be in the form of securities or negotiable warehouse receipts. The auditor should ascertain the current realizable value of the collateral at the statement date. When securities are widely traded current market prices can be obtained from published prices or from a broker. Similarly, the value of the warehouse receipts may be obtained from market quotations of the merchandise pertaining thereto.

For accounts receivable, the aged trial balance is the starting point in determining the adequacy of the allowance account. The auditor should review the percentages used for each of the current and past due categories for reasonableness. In addition, for past-due accounts, the auditor should

- Examine correspondence in the debtor's file.
- Review published annual financial statements.
- Make inquiries of outside agencies, such as Dun & Bradstreet, as to the customer's credit rating.
- Review correspondence between the client and outside collection agencies as to the status of accounts turned over for collection.
- Discuss the collectibility of the account with appropriate management personnel.

From the foregoing, it should be apparent that substantial evidence is generally available to the auditor in making a determination of the reasonableness of the allowance for uncollectible accounts. It is neither necessary nor desirable for the auditor to place too much reliance on the opinion of the credit manager or other client personnel in making this decision. An analysis of an allowance account is illustrated in Figure 12-10.

Recalculate Interest Earned and Accrued

The auditor obtains evidence of interest rates and interest dates by inspecting the notes. Verification of interest earned and accrued is achieved by reperformance of the client's interest calculations shown on the schedule of notes receivable. When a client, such as a financial institution, has numerous notes, the recomputations can be made on a test basis. The auditor should also verify accrued interest receivable and interest collected. The former requires recourse to the date and terms of the note. The latter involves a review of cash receipts records and supporting documentation.

Statement Presentation and Disclosure

The auditor is required to determine whether receivables are properly identified, classified, and disclosed in the financial statements. The existence of contingencies and pledges of notes should be disclosed in the statements. Data pertaining to these matters are obtained from confirming notes held by others, bank confirmation responses, and inquiries of management.

For accounts receivable, a scanning of the aged trial balance may reveal items that may require separate identification and classification. For example, credit balances may warrant reclassification as current liabilities and receivables from employees, officers, affiliated companies, and related parties should be specifically identified if material. The existence of liens and assignments indicated by a review of the minutes and inquiry of management should be properly disclosed.

Equal consideration must be given by the auditor to the client's presentation of sales and net sales. Proper presentation of sales may include report-

Prepared by: _M.Q.Y._ Date: _1/18/X2_
Reviewed by: _P.A.K._ Date: _1/24/X2_

Bates Company
Allowance for Uncollectible Accounts
Acc. #122   12/31/X1   B-3

Balance 1/1/X1		5000 00	Ø
Accounts Written Off:			
Penn Central	535 10		∨
Dudley Inc.	460 90		∨
P+L Corp.	287 09		
		(1283 09)	
Balance Per Books 12/31/X1		3716 91	L
Add AJE ⑧ See Below		1283 09	
Audited Balance 12/31/X1		5000 00	
		To Ø	
Possible Uncollectible Accounts			
1. Barry Mfg. - Amount has been in dispute since 6/10.			
Resolution unsure. Customer claims goods not			
mfgd. to specifications.			
2. Progress Electronics - Co. filed for Chap. 11 bankruptcy		1088 92	
on 1/10/X1. Examined corresp. and it appears			
maximum recoverable will be 10% and that is			
doubtful.			
3. Miscellaneous small amounts on which Bates		3017 90	
has decided they will not pursue collection.			
		190 36	
Total possible uncollectible accounts		4297 18	
Based on the above information, it appears that an			
allowance for uncollectible accounts of $5000 is			
reasonable and should cover any potential			
losses on outstanding A/R at 12/31/X1 the following			
adjustment is proposed.			
⑧			
DR. General and Admin. Expenses (420)	1283 09		
CR. Allowance for uncollectible A/c's (122)		1283 09	
To adjust allowance to required amount			
A5			
∨ Examined correspondence - company is currently in			
chapter 11 bankruptcy - expected return is max of 5%			
per discussions with client + copies of plans of arrangement.			
Ø Agrees with ending balance in prior year w/p's.			

FIGURE 12–10. Allowance for Uncollectible Accounts Working Paper

ing of sales by segments, departments, and product lines. It is essential that sales be reported on a consistent basis.

Statistical Sampling of Receivables Balances

Both probability-proportional-to-size and classical variables sampling plans are frequently used in the audit of receivable balances and may also be used in the audit of sales, sales adjustments, and other revenue accounts such as interest or lease income. The remainder of this section presents a case study involving the use of statistical sampling in the audit of the Porter Company's trade accounts receivable. Using the approach developed in Chapter 11, each step in designing, executing, and evaluating the sample is explained.

Determining the Objectives of the Plan

The objective of the sample is to test the reasonableness of the total recorded book value of Porter's receivables. Because the evaluation of related internal controls and the results of other substantive tests suggest that errors of both under and overstatement may occur with some frequency, it is decided to use the difference estimation technique.

Defining the Population and Sampling Unit

The population consists of 1,000 customer accounts with a total recorded book value of $985,500. The auditor obtains a computer listing of these accounts and satisfies himself as to its completeness and that the individual account book values sum to the total recorded book value. Since confirmation of customer account balances will be the primary audit procedure performed on the sample items, the individual customer account is designated as the sampling unit.

Determining Sample Size

To determine sample size, the auditor specifies the following:

- population size $(N) = 1,000$
- estimated standard deviation of the differences $(S_{d_j}) = \$105$
- risk of incorrect rejection = .05
- risk of incorrect acceptance = .05
- tolerable error = $40,000

The estimated standard deviation is based on the results of the prior year's audit. The risks of incorrect rejection and acceptance are set at a low level because, as noted above, little assurance is available from other procedures. Additionally, if material errors are found in the sample, the auditor wants the sample to be sufficiently reliable to serve as the basis for proposing the minimum required adjustment to the book value. The specified tolerable error represents the maximum misstatement allowable in the control account that will still permit the auditor to conclude that the balance is fairly stated.

For the specified risks of incorrect rejection and acceptance, the auditor determines the ratio, R, of desired allowance for sampling risk to tolerable error, TE, from a table like the one in Figure 11-6. In this case, the ratio is .543. The desired allowance for sampling risk, A, is then calculated as follows:

$$A = R \times TE$$
$$= .543 \times \$40,000$$
$$= \$21,720$$

After determining the appropriate U_R factor for the specified risk of incorrect rejection ($U_R = 1.96$ for .05 from Figure 11-5), the auditor determines sample size as follows:

$$n = \left(\frac{N \times U_R \times S_{d_j}}{A} \right)^2 = \left(\frac{1,000 \times 1.96 \times \$105}{\$21,720} \right)^2 = 90$$

Since n/N (90/1,000) is greater than .05, the adjusted sample size for sampling without replacement is determined as follows:

$$n' = \frac{n}{1 + \dfrac{n}{N}} = \frac{90}{1 + \dfrac{90}{1,000}} = 83$$

Determining the Sample Selection Method

The auditor uses a random number table to obtain 83 random numbers to use in manually selecting a simple random number sample from the customer accounts listing.

Executing the Sampling Plan

First and second confirmation requests are sent and alternative auditing procedures are performed for all non-replies to obtain an audited value for each of the 83 sample items. The difference between the audited and book value for each item as well as the average difference, $\bar{d}$, and the standard deviation of the differences, S_{d_j}, are calculated. In this case study, $\bar{d}$ is assumed to be $\$-35$ and S_{d_j} is assumed to be $\$112$. These statistics are then used in evaluating the sample results.

Evaluating the Sample Results

The auditor calculates (1) the total projected error, $\hat{D}$, (2) the total estimated population value, $\hat{X}$, and (3) the achieved allowance for sampling risk, A'. He then calculates the range about the estimated total value. These computations are shown below:

Estimated total projected error

$$\hat{D} = N \times \bar{d} = 1,000 \times \$-35 = \$-35,000$$

Estimated total population value

$$\hat{X} = BV + \hat{D} = \$985,500 + (\$-35,000)$$
$$= \$950,500$$

Achieved allowance for sampling risk

$$A' = N \times U_R \times \frac{S_{d_j}\sqrt{1 - \dfrac{n}{N}}}{\sqrt{n}} = 1,000 \times 1.96 \times \frac{\$112\sqrt{1 - \dfrac{83}{1,000}}}{\sqrt{83}}$$

$$= \$23,073$$

Since A' ($23,073) is greater than A ($21,720), the auditor calculates an adjusted achieved allowance for sampling risk as follows:

$$A'' = A' + TE\left(1 - \frac{A'}{A}\right)$$

$$= \$23,073 + \$40,000\left(1 - \frac{\$23,073}{\$21,720}\right)$$

$$= \$20,581$$

He then calculates the range

$$\hat{X} \pm A'' = \$950,500 \pm \$20,581$$
$$= \$929,919 \text{ to } \$971,081$$

Since the total book value, $985,500, does not fall within the computed range, the sample results support the conclusion that the account is misstated by more than tolerable error.

After reviewing the nature and amounts of differences in the sample, and after considering the results of other tests and the qualitative aspects of the errors, the auditor concludes that a minimum adjustment of $15,581 (credit) is required. This is the amount required to reduce the book value to an amount equal to the far end of the range plus tolerable error (i.e., $985,500 − ($929,919 + $40,000) = $15,581). He arranges a meeting with the client to work out the details of any adjustment.

Computer-Assisted Tests of Accounts Receivable Balances

When a client maintains its accounts receivable records by EDP, the auditor may use the computer to assist in performing substantive tests on the accounts receivable balances. This is possible if the auditor has appropriate generalized audit software or a program tailormade for the client.

In this case illustration, it is assumed that the client's master file of accounts receivable is maintained in magnetic tape form. In addition to updating the file for revenue cycle transactions, the client's program provides for monthly printouts of an aged trial balance and monthly statements for customers.

There are two widely used computer-assisted applications in testing accounts receivable balances: (1) verifying the accuracy of the accounts receivable aged trial balance and (2) preparing confirmation requests. These applications, which are illustrated in Figure 12-11, are explained below.

Verify Accuracy of Aged Trial Balance

The auditor may use a generalized audit software package to verify the accuracy of the aged trial balance. To accomplish this objective, the auditor first inputs the audit selection criteria in Figure 12-11 that are desired in the test. The auditor then runs a program that copies the accounts receivable

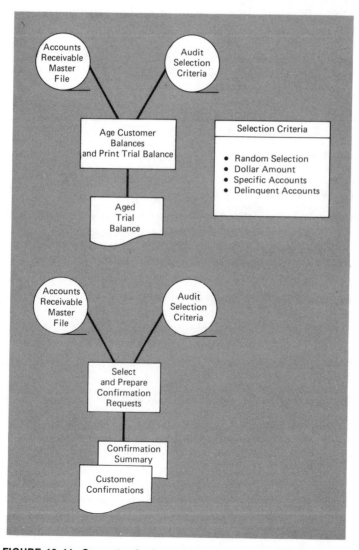

FIGURE 12–11. Computer-Assisted Tests of Accounts Receivables Balances

master file and converts it onto a tape in a format that is compatible with the software package. The auditor proceeds to process the tape with the specified audit selection criteria using the software package (program). The printed output is compared by the auditor with accounts receivable control and the aged trial balance is analyzed as part of the auditor's input in determining the adequacy of the allowance for doubtful accounts.

A further test is to compare the details of the aged trial balance from the auditor's run with the details of the client's EDP aged trial balance for the same date. The auditor may also trace individual balances shown on the auditor's trial balance to documentation in the customer's account file and to customer monthly statements.

Prepare Confirmation Requests *

In this application, a generalized software package is used to select the customer accounts for confirmation. As in the preceding example, the auditor must input the desired audit selection criteria, convert the master file to tape in a format compatible with the software package, and process the data using the software program. The printouts of this application are the confirmation requests and summary data used by the auditor for control purposes.

In addition to these two applications, the computer may be used to accumulate other data that may be of interest to the auditor such as account balances that (1) exceed credit limits and (2) have unusual activity, as, for example, the payment of a recent bill before paying an earlier billing.

CONCLUDING COMMENTS

The audit objectives in performing substantive tests of account balances apply to all cycles. These objectives consist of (1) clerical accuracy, (2) existence or occurrence, (3) completeness, (4) rights and obligations, (5) valuation or allocation, and (6) statement presentation and disclosure. The verification of cash and receivables balances comprises an important part of the auditor's substantive tests of balances in a typical audit engagement. Simultaneous cash counts, bank confirmations, and cash cutoff procedures are essential audit procedures for cash balances. In addition, the confirmation of receivables is a required auditing procedure under GAAS.

REVIEW QUESTIONS

12–1.   Describe the nature and scope of tests of balances.
12–2.   Identify and briefly explain the primary purpose of the audit objectives that are applicable to tests of balances.
12–3.   What audit procedures are required to verify the (a) existence or occurrence and (b) completeness of cash balances?

12–4. What precautions should be taken by the auditor in (a) counting cash on hand and (b) confirming bank balances?

12–5. Identify the five types of information included in a standard bank confirmation.

12–6. How reliable is a bank reconciliation in terms of audit evidence? Briefly defend your answer.

12–7. a. What safeguards must be taken by the auditor in obtaining and using a bank cutoff statement?

   b. What steps should be taken by the auditor after he has received a cutoff statement?

12–8. What steps are involved in performing a cash cutoff test?

12–9. a. Define and illustrate *kiting*.

   b. How can kiting be prevented and detected?

12–10. a. Explain the purpose of a proof of cash.

   b. What circumstance generally results in the preparation of a proof of cash?

12–11. List four cash items that require special classification and disclosure. For each item indicate the required statement presentation.

12–12. Identify the audit procedures in tests of receivable balances that satisfy the audit objectives of (a) existence and occurrence and (b) completeness.

12–13. In confirming receivables, what conditions (a) may make it impracticable or unreasonable for the auditor to perform this test, (b) should be considered by the auditor in determining the form of the confirmation request, and (c) are relevant to the auditor in determining the timing and extent of the requests?

12–14. What precautions should the auditor take in confirming accounts receivables?

12–15. When the auditor is unable to confirm accounts receivable, indicate (a) the alternative procedures he may perform and (b) the effects on his audit report.

12–16. For an aged trial balance prepared by the client, explain (a) the auditor's responsibilities and (b) the specific types of data he may obtain therefrom.

12–17. How does the auditor perform a sales cutoff test?

12–18. What is the best evidence of the collectibility of an account?

12–19. How does the auditor establish the reasonableness of the allowance for uncollectible accounts?

12–20. What specific assistance can a computer provide in verifying accounts receivable balances?

COMPREHENSIVE QUESTIONS

12–21. As the senior auditor on the audit of the Elles Company for the year ending December 31, you discover the following errors in cash working papers prepared by your assistants:

1. Compensating bank balances were overlooked.
2. Kiting was missed.
3. Several December 31 checks were not recorded as disbursements until January. These checks are not listed as outstanding on the December 31 bank reconciliation.
4. The petty cash on hand was $25 short of the imprest fund balance.
5. The December cash disbursements journal included the checks issued January 2 and 3.
6. Several mathematical errors were made in the client's December bank reconciliation schedule.
7. The December 31 bank balance shown on the reconciliation schedule was incorrect.
8. A contingent liability on a discounted note receivable was missed.

Required
a. Identify the test of balances that should have detected each error.

    b. For each error, indicate the applicable audit objective.

    c. Indicate the type of evidence obtained by each audit procedure.

12–22. Lingham Company's fiscal year ends on April 30, and the company's certified public accountant, Sanders & Stein, conducts the annual audit during May and June. Sanders & Stein has prepared audit procedures for the different phases of the audit engagement with Lingham Company. Included among the audit program steps for cash on deposit with the Union State Bank are the following:

    1. Obtain a bank confirmation as of April 30, 19X0, directly from Union State Bank.

    2. Prepare a proof of cash for the month of April 19X0.

    3. Obtain a cutoff bank statement directly from Union State Bank for a fifteen-day period (May 15) subsequent to the close of operations on April 30, 19X0.

Required

    a. Why should Sanders & Stein obtain a bank confirmation directly from the Union State Bank?

    b. What is a "proof of cash" and why is it important in the audit of the cash in the bank account?

    c. What is the purpose of obtaining a cutoff bank statement for a fifteen-day period after the end of Lingham Company's fiscal year?

CMA

12–23. The Patricia Company had poor internal control over its cash transactions. Facts about its cash position at November 30, 19X0 were as follows:

The cashbook showed a balance of $18,901.62, which included undeposited receipts. A credit of $100 on the bank's records did not appear on the books of the company. The balance per bank statement was $15,550. Outstanding checks were: #62 for $116.25, #183 for $150, #284 for $253.25, #8621 for $190.71, #8623 for $206.80, and #8632 for $145.28.

The cashier abstracted all undeposited receipts in excess of $3,794.41 and prepared the following reconciliation:

Balance per books, November 30, 19X0		$18,901.62
Add: Outstanding checks:		
8621	$190.71	
8623	206.80	
8632	145.28	442.79
		$19,344.41
Less: undeposited receipts		3,794.41
Balance per bank, November 30, 19X0		$15,550.00
Deduct: unrecorded credit		100.00
True cash, November 30, 19X0		$15,450.00

Required

    a. Prepare a working paper showing how much the cashier abstracted.

    b. How did he attempt to conceal his theft?

    c. Using only the information given, name two specific features of internal control which were apparently lacking.

AICPA

12–24. You are the in-charge accountant examining the financial statements of the Gutzler Company for the year ended December 31, 19X0. During late October 19X0 you, with the help of Gutzler's controller, completed an internal control questionnaire and prepared the appropriate memoranda describing Gutzler's accounting procedures. Your comments relative to cash receipts are as follows:

All cash receipts are sent directly to the accounts receivable clerk with no processing by the mail department. The accounts receivable clerk keeps the cash receipts journal, prepares the bank deposit slip in duplicate, posts from the deposit slip to the subsidiary accounts receivable ledger, and mails the deposit to the bank.

The controller receives the validated deposit slips directly (unopened) from the bank. He also receives the monthly bank statement directly (unopened) from the bank and promptly reconciles it.

At the end of each month, the accounts receivable clerk notifies the general ledger clerk by journal voucher of the monthly totals of the cash receipts journal for posting to the general ledger.

Each month, with regard to the general ledger cash account, the general ledger clerk makes an entry to record the total debits to cash from the cash receipts journal. In addition, the general ledger clerk on occasion makes debit entries in the general ledger cash account from sources other than the cash receipts journal (e.g., funds borrowed from the bank).

Certain standard auditing procedures which are listed below have already been performed by you in the audit of cash receipts. The extent to which these procedures were performed is not relevant to the question.

1. Total and cross-total all columns in the cash receipts journal.
2. Trace postings from the cash receipts journal to the general ledger.
3. Examine remittance advices and related correspondence to support entries in the cash receipts journal.

Required
Considering Gutzler's internal control over cash receipts and standard auditing procedures already performed, list all other auditing procedures and reasons therefor which should be performed to obtain sufficient audit evidence regarding cash receipts. Do not discuss the procedures for cash disbursements and cash balances. Also do not discuss the extent to which any of the procedures are to be performed. Assume adequate controls exist to assure that all sales transactions are recorded. Organize your answer sheet as follows:

Other Audit Procedures	*Reason for Other Audit Procedures*

AICPA

12–25. The LMN Company maintains three bank accounts: City Bank—Regular, City Bank—Payroll, and Metro Bank—Special. Your analysis of cash disbursements records for the period June 23 to July 6 reveals the bank transfers:

Check No.	Date of Check	Bank Drawn On	Payee	Amount
2476	June 23	Regular	Payroll	$100,000
2890	June 25	Regular	Payroll	200,000
3140	June 28	Regular	Special	100,000
A1006	June 29	Special	Payroll	50,000
A1245	June 30	Special	Regular	25,000
3402	June 30	Regular	Special	125,000

You determine the following facts about each of the first five checks: (1) the date of the cash disbursements journal entry is the same as the date of the check, (2) the payee receives the check two days later, (3) the payee records and deposits the check on the day it is received, and (4) it takes five days for a deposited check to clear banking channels and be paid by the bank on which it is drawn. Check 3402 was not recorded as a disbursement until July 1. This check was picked up by the payee on the date it was issued and it was included in the payees after-hours bank deposit on June 30.

Required
a. What are the purposes of the audit of bank transfers?
b. Prepare a bank transfer schedule as of June 30 using the format illustrated in Figure 12-4.
c. Prepare separate adjusting entries for any checks that require adjustment.
d. In the reconciliations for the three bank accounts, indicate the check numbers that should appear as (1) an outstanding check or (2) a deposit in transit.
e. Which check(s) may be indicative of kiting?

12–26. The following information was obtained in an audit of the cash account of Tuck Company as of December 31, 19X0. Assume that the CPA has satisfied himself as to the validity of the cash book, the bank statements, and the returned checks, except as noted.

1. The bookkeeper's bank reconciliation at November 30, 19X0:

Balance per bank statement		$ 19,400
Add deposit in transit		1,100
Total		$ 20,500
Less: outstanding checks		
#2540	$140	
1501	750	
1503	480	
1504	800	
1505	30	2,300
Balance per books		$ 18,200

2. A summary of the bank statement for December 19X0:

Balance brought forward	$ 19,400
Deposits	148,700
	$168,100
Charges	132,500
Balance, December 31, 19X0	$ 35,600

3. A summary of the cash book for December 19X0 before adjustments.

Balance brought forward	$ 18,200
Receipts	149,690
	$167,890
Disbursements	124,885
Balance, December 31, 19X0	$ 43,005

4. Included with the canceled checks returned with the December bank statement were the following:

Number	Date of Check	Amount of Check	Comment
1501	November 28, 19X0	$ 75	This check was in payment of an invoice for $750 and was recorded in the cash book as $750.
1503	November 28, 19X0	$580	This check was in payment of an invoice for $580 and was recorded in the cash book as $580.
1523	December 5, 19X0	$150	Examination of this check revealed that it was unsigned. A discussion with the client disclosed that it had been mailed inadvertently before it was signed. The check was endorsed and deposited by the payee and processed by the bank even though it was a legal nullity. The check was recorded in the cash disbursements.
1528	December 12, 19X0	$800	This check replaced 1504 that was returned by the payee because it was mutilated. Check 1504 was not cancelled on the books.
——	December 19, 19X0	$200	This was a counter check drawn at the bank by the president of the Company as a cash advance for travel expense. The president overlooked informing the bookkeeper about the check.
——	December 20, 19X0	$300	The drawer of this check was the Tucker Company.
1535	December 20, 19X0	$350	This check had been labeled NSF and returned to the payee because the bank had erroneously believed that the check was drawn by the Luck Company. Subsequently the payee was advised to redeposit the check.
1575	January 5, 19X0	$10,000	This check was given to the payee on December 30, 19X0 as a postdated check with the understanding that it would not be deposited until January 5. The check was not recorded on the books in December.

5. The Tuck Company discounted its own sixty-day note for $9,000 with the bank on December 1, 19X0. The discount rate was 6 percent. The bookkeeper recorded the proceeds as a cash receipt at the face value of the note.
6. The bookkeeper records customers' dishonored checks as a reduction of cash receipts. When the dishonored checks are redeposited they are recorded as a regular cash receipt. Two NSF checks for $180 and $220 were returned by the bank during December. The $180 check was redeposited but the $220 check was still on hand at December 31. Cancellations of Tuck Company checks are recorded by a reduction of cash disbursements.
7. December bank charges were $20. In addition a $10 service charge was made in

December for the collection of a foreign draft in November. These charges were not recorded on the books.
8. Check 2540 listed in the November outstanding checks was drawn three years ago. Since the payee cannot be located, the president of Tuck Company agreed to the CPA's suggestion that the check be written back into the accounts by a journal entry.
9. Outstanding checks at December 31, 19X0 totaled $4,000 excluding checks 2540 and 1504.
10. The bank had recorded a deposit of $2,400 on January 2, 19X1. The bookkeeper had recorded this deposit on the books on December 31, 19X0 and then mailed the deposit to the bank.

Required
Prepare a four-column reconciliation (''proof of cash'') of the cash receipts and cash disbursements recorded on the bank statement and on the Company's books for the month of December 19X0. Use the format illustrated in this chapter.

AICPA (adapted)

12–27. Dodge, CPA, is examining the financial statements of a manufacturing company with a significant amount of trade accounts receivable. Dodge is satisfied that the accounts are properly summarized and classified and that allocations, reclassifications, and valuations are made in accordance with GAAP. Dodge is planning to use accounts receivable confirmation requests to satisfy the third standard of field work as to trade accounts receivable.

Required
a. Identify and describe the two forms of accounts receivable confirmation requests and indicate what factors Dodge will consider in determining when to use each.
b. Assume Dodge has received a satisfactory response to the confirmation requests. Describe how Dodge could evaluate collectibility of the trade accounts receivable.

AICPA

12–28. The following situations were not discovered in the audit of Pars Company by an inexperienced staff assistant:

1. Several accounts were incorrectly aged on the client's aging schedule.
2. Interest earned on notes receivable was incorrectly accrued.
3. A note reported to be held by a bank for collection is fictitious.
4. Four year-end sales are recorded in the wrong accounting period.
5. The customers' ledger totals are correct but balances in some individual customers' accounts are incorrect.
6. Errors were made in journalizing sales invoices.
7. The allowance for uncollectible accounts is understated.
8. Two notes on hand were not owned or endorsed to Pars Company.
9. The accounts receivable turnover ratio is unreasonable.
10. The contingent liability pertaining to the discounting of a note receivable was not disclosed.

Required
a. Identify the test of balances that should have detected each situation.
b. For each situation indicate the relevant audit objective.
c. Indicate the type of corroborating information obtained by each audit procedure.

12–29. Jerome and Gerard, Certified Public Accountants, are preparing for the annual audit of the Fordham Office Machine Company. Several procedures which are included in the audit program pertaining to accounts receivable and sales are summarized below:

1. Evaluate internal controls relating to accounts receivable and sales.
2. Obtain and analyze an aged trial balance of accounts receivable; indicate any collections subsequent to the balance sheet date.
3. Confirm accounts receivable by direct written communication with customers.
4. Evaluate the adequacy of the allowance for uncollectible accounts.
5. Review the year-end cutoff of sales and cash collections.
6. Examine all phases of several sales transactions and subsequent cash collections selected at random.

Required
a. What are the auditor's objectives in performing each procedure?
b. What is meant by "year-end cutoff of sales" (5 in the summarized audit program above), and why is it important that the "year-end cutoff of sales" be reviewed by the auditor?

CMA (adapted)

12–30. You have been assigned to the first examination of the accounts of The Chicago Company for the year ending March 31, 19X1. The accounts receivable were circularized at December 31, 19X0 and at that date the receivables consisted of approximately 200 accounts with balances totaling $956,750. Seventy-five of these accounts with balances totaling $650,725 were selected for circularization. All but twenty of the confirmation requests have been returned; thirty were signed without comments, fourteen had minor differences which have been cleared satisfactorily while eleven confirmations had the following comments:

1. We are sorry but we cannot answer your request for confirmation of our account as the PDQ Company uses an accounts payable voucher system.
2. The balance of $1,050 was paid on December 23, 19X0.
3. The above balance of $7,750 was paid on January 5, 19X1.
4. The above balance has been paid.
5. We do not owe you anything at December 31, 19X0 as the goods, represented by your invoice dated December 30, 19X0, number 25,050, in the amount of $11,550, were received on January 5, 19X1 on FOB destination terms.
6. An advance payment of $2,500 made by us in November 19X0 should cover the two invoices totaling $1,350 shown on the statement attached.
7. We never received these goods.
8. We are contesting the propriety of this $12,525 charge. We think the charge is excessive.
9. Amount okay. As the goods have been shipped to us on consignment we will remit payment upon selling the goods.
10. The $10,000, representing a deposit under a lease, will be applied against the rent due to us during 19X3, the last year of the lease.
11. Your credit dated December 5, 19X0 in the amount of $440 cancels the above balance.

Required
What steps would you take to clear satisfactorily each of the above eleven comments?

AICPA

12–31. The Fox Company has been using 0.05 percent of net sales in providing for uncollectible accounts. The provision, however, has been inadequate since the allowance account shows a debit balance of $1,272 on December 31, 19X0 before making the annual provision for bad debts.

On December 31, 19X0, the Fox Company decides to switch to the aging method. On this date, the trial balance shows accounts receivable of $74,000. This total includes $15,000 of past due accounts and $3,000 of customer credit balances. Further investigation reveals that $4,000 of past due accounts represent advances to officers and $2,000 of past-due accounts are worthless. In addition, it is found that the cashbook was held open until January 2, 19X1 with the result that $5,000 of January collections on current accounts were entered as December cash receipts. Management estimates that past-due accounts are 10 percent uncollectible and current accounts are 2 percent uncollectible.

Required
a. Compute the bad debt provision at December 31, 19X0 under the aging method. Show computations.
b. Prepare the adjusting entries required at December 31, 19X0.

12-32. You are engaged to perform an audit of the Wilcox Corp. for the year ended December 31, 19X0.

Only merchandise shipped by the Wilcox Corporation to customers up to and including December 30, 19X0 has been eliminated from inventory. The inventory as determined by physical inventory count has been recorded on the books by the company's controller. No perpetual inventory records are maintained. All sales are made on an F.O.B. shipping point basis. You are to assume that all purchase invoices have been correctly recorded.

The following lists of sales invoices are entered in the sales journal for the months of December 19X0 and January 19X1, respectively.

Sales Invoice Amount	Sales Invoice Date	Cost of Merchandise Sold	Date Shipped
		December	
a. $ 3,000	Dec. 21	$2,000	Dec. 31
b. 2,000	Dec. 31	800	Nov. 3
c. 1,000	Dec. 29	600	Dec. 30
d. 4,000	Dec. 31	2,400	Jan. 3
e. 10,000	Dec. 30	5,600	Dec. 29 (shipped to consignee)
		January	
f. $ 6,000	Dec. 31	$4,000	Dec. 30
g. 4,000	Jan. 2	2,300	Jan. 2
h. 8,000	Jan. 3	5,500	Dec. 31

Required
Record necessary adjusting journal entries at December 31, in connection with the foregoing data.

AICPA

12-33. As the in-charge auditor, you begin your field work to examine the December 31 financial statements of a client on January 5, knowing that you must leave temporarily for another engagement on January 7 after outlining the audit program for your assistant. Before leaving, you inquire about the assistant's progress in his examination of notes receivable. Among other things, he shows you a working paper listing the makers' names, the due dates, the interest rates, and amounts of seventeen outstanding notes receivable totaling $100,000. The working paper contains the following notations:

1. Reviewed system of internal control and found it to be satisfactory.
2. Total of $100,000 agrees with general ledger control account.
3. Traced listing of notes to sales journal.

The assistant also informs you that he is preparing to request positive confirmation of the amounts of all outstanding notes receivable and that no other audit work has been performed in the examination of notes receivable and interest arising from equipment sales. There were no outstanding accounts receivable for equipment sales at the end of the year.

You ask your assistant to examine all notes receivable on hand before you leave. He returns in thirty minutes from the office safe where the notes are kept and reports that notes on hand total only $75,000.

Required
List the possible explanations that you would expect from the client for the $25,000 difference. (Eliminate fraud or misappropriation from your consideration.) Indicate beside each explanation the audit procedures you would apply to determine if each explanation is correct.

AICPA

12–34. Data relevant to the audit of accounts receivable in two companies are tabulated below:

	Company X	Company Y
Client's book value	$99,000	$190,000
Population size	1,000	2,000
Desired risk of incorrect acceptance	20%	30%
Desired risk of incorrect rejection	10%	5%
Tolerable error	$ 9,900	$ 9,000
Estimated standard deviation	$ 50	$ 25

Required
a. Compute the required sample size for each company with replacement.
b. Compute the required sample size for each company without replacement.
c. Ignoring your answers in (a) and (b) above, assume that 169 customer accounts were selected for confirmation in Company X. If the total audited value of this sample is $16,900 and its standard deviation is $52, may the auditor conclude that book value is fairly stated?
d. Again ignoring your answers in (a) and (b) above, assume that 225 customer accounts were selected for confirmation in Company Y. If the mean of the audited sample values is $100 and the sample standard deviation $30, may the auditor conclude that the book value is fairly stated?

12–35. An auditor is conducting an examination of the financial statements of a wholesale appliance distributor. The distributor supplies appliances to hundreds of individual customers in the metropolitan area. The distributor maintains detail accounts receivable records on a computer disk. At the end of each business day, the customer account file is updated. Each customer record in the computer file contains the following data:

1. Customer account number.
2. Address.
3. Open (unpaid) invoices at the beginning of the month, by invoice number and date.
4. Sales during the current month, by invoice number and date.

5. Individual cash receipts during the current month.
6. Date of last sale.
7. Date of last cash receipt.
8. Total sales during the year.

The auditor is planning to confirm selected accounts receivable as of the end of the current month. The auditor will have available a computer tape of the data on the accounts receivable master file on the date that the company regularly sends monthly statements to its customers. The auditor also has a general purpose software package.

Required
The auditor is planning to perform the customary audit procedures involved in the verification of accounts receivable. Identify the basic procedures to be performed and describe how the use of the general purpose software package and the tape of the accounts receivable file data might be helpful to the auditor in performing such auditing procedures. Organize your answer as follows:

Basic Receivable Auditing Procedure	*How General Purpose Computer Software Package and Tape of Accounts Receivable Data Might Be Helpful*

AICPA

CASE STUDY

12–36. * The Ohio River Authority is an instrumentality of the state created to control, store, and preserve the waters of the Ohio River within its reservoirs and to regulate the flow therefrom to develop hydroelectric energy and to provide water for irrigation and to conserve and protect the soil along its watershed.

The board of directors of the authority has selected us as auditors for the year ended June 30, 19X1. The interim work is completed in March and the review of operating procedures and tests of internal control have enabled you to determine the following:

1. The Authority has three branch offices, all located within a 300 mile radius of the home office, to conduct operations in their respective districts. The functions of these branches include the installation and servicing of power facilities, meter reading, billing, maintaining detail customers' ledgers, receiving collections on accounts receivable, and the preparation of various daily reports which are forwarded to the home office accounting department for entry to the general ledger accounts.

2. The Authority maintains separate departments under the supervision of responsible employees for each of the following functions: (a) meter installation, (b) meter reading, (c) billing and posting receivables ledgers, (d) cash collections, (e) credit approval and follow-up, (f) accounting.

3. The employees of the home office accounting department function as internal auditors and perform an audit of each branch office at least once every two years. The internal audits are comprehensive but do not include circularization of accounts receivable, bank balances, or outstanding liabilities.

4. Sales of primary power at wholesale rates and power sales to most of the larger commercial and industrial customers are billed at rates established under con-

tracts with the customers. All sales of irrigation water are charged to customers at contract rates.

5. The number of customers served, classified according to major income statement captions, are: wholesale 50, retail-residential 9,000, retail-commercial 1600, and water 150.

6. Revenues from irrigation water contracts are based on a standard rate per acre as stated in the contract, regardless of the amount of water used for irrigation during the growing season from April to September. The Authority accrues this income monthly and bills the farmer at the end of the growing season.

7. The Authority requires all power customers to put up a deposit prior to installation of the power meters. Residential consumers must deposit $5; deposits of other customers range from $5 to $100. Bad debts are infrequent and, after deducting deposits, have been minor in the past.

8. Total kilowatt hours of electric energy sales are accounted in the same classifications used for revenue in the income statement.

9. Accounts receivable substantially turn over every month.

10. Our internal control work did not disclose any significant exceptions in recording transactions or safeguarding assets.

11. Excerpts from financial statements audited by another CPA firm one year ago are as follows:

	Balance Sheet			*Income Statement*	
Cash	$277,710		Sales of primary power:		
Accounts Receivable:			Wholesale		
Customer electrical	401,823		Municipalities	$1,802,516	
Accrued irrigation contracts	141,825		Rural coops	954,919	
Notes receivable	484		Other utilities	759,160	
Allowance for uncollectible accounts	(584)		Retail Commercial	771,565	
Total assets	37,306,309		Residential	345,045	
Customer deposits	(57,226)		Other operating revenues		
			Sales of water	280,460	
			Fees—operating coops	131,699	
			Other	32,209	
			Net income	1,263,700	

These data are comparable to the current year's statements prepared by the Authority.

Required

1. What procedures will be used in confirming accounts receivable? Indicate when confirmations will be mailed, what type of confirmations will be used, how many accounts will be circularized, and how control of detail account balances will be established.

2. What methods should be utilized to determine the adequacy of the bad debt allowance?

3. What audit steps should be performed to determine that the revenue reported on the income statement is reasonable?

13 Tests of Revenue, Expenditure, and Production Cycle Balances

STUDY OBJECTIVES

The study objectives of this chapter are to acquire an understanding of substantive tests of balances that are applicable to inventories, plant assets, and current liabilities associated with an entity's expenditure and production cycles. To achieve these objectives, it is necessary for the reader to

- Comprehend the audit programs for verifying inventory, plant assets, and current liability balances.
- Recognize the auditor's responsibilities in performing the required audit procedure of observing the client's inventory taking.
- Perceive the major differences in auditing current assets and plant assets.
- Realize the differences in audit risk and in auditing procedures between current assets and current liabilities.
- Know the application of statistical sampling and electronic data processing to tests of inventory balances.

The explanation of substantive tests of balances is continued in this chapter. Attention is focused primarily on three types of accounts as being representative of material account balances resulting from transactions in the expenditure and production cycles. These accounts are (1) inventories, (2) plant assets, and (3) accounts payable. The form and arrangement of the chapter are similar to that used in Chapter 12.

TESTS OF INVENTORY BALANCES

Inventories include goods held for sale to customers, goods in the process of production, and materials and supplies expected to be used or consumed in production. The term *merchandise inventory* is usually applied to goods held for sale by a retailer or wholesaler when such goods have been acquired in a condition for resale. The terms *raw materials, work in process, finished goods,* and *factory supplies* are generally used in referring to the inventories of a manufacturing company. In this chapter, the term *inventories* will be used as an all-inclusive designation for all of the foregoing terms.

The examination of inventories requires careful planning and a very substantial investment in audit time, cost, and effort. The audit program for tests of inventory balances is directly related to the results of the auditor's tests of internal accounting control procedures in the revenue, expenditure, and production cycles. For example, weak physical controls over inventory storage may lead to more extensive tests of quantities on hand at the statement date. Conversely, effective controls over the costing of perpetual inventory records may result in a reduction of inventory pricing tests during year-end work. The primary tests of inventory balances are shown in Figure 13-1. Each of the tests is explained below within the framework of the audit objectives.

Clerical Accuracy

Tests for mechanical accuracy include footing of inventory schedules and summaries. In addition, the balances in inventory accounts are reconciled with the totals of inventory summaries and perpetual inventory records. The accuracy of pricing extensions on the inventory summaries is also verified as part of this objective.

Existence or Occurrence

This objective relates to management's assertions as to the physical existence of the inventory and the occurrence of purchases and manufacturing transactions. Tests of balances are the primary source of evidence for existence, whereas reliance on internal accounting control generally constitutes the major support for occurrence. There are two auditing procedures for this objective.

Observe Client's Inventory Taking

The observation of inventories has been a generally accepted auditing procedure for over forty years. This procedure is required whenever inventories

TYPE OF TEST: Substantive	PURPOSE: Validity and Propriety of Balances
CYCLE: Expenditure and production	ACCOUNTS: Inventories

A. CLERICAL ACCURACY:

  1. Verify accuracy of inventory schedules and summaries.
  2. Reconcile general ledger control with inventory records and schedules.

B. EXISTENCE OR OCCURRENCE:

  1. Observe client's inventory taking.
  2. Confirm inventories in public warehouses.

C. COMPLETENESS:

  1. Perform purchases and purchases returns cutoff tests.
  2. Make analytical review.

D. RIGHTS AND OBLIGATIONS:

  1. Make inquiries of management regarding ownership.
  2. Examine consignment agreements.
  3. Review purchase commitments.

E. VALUATION OR ALLOCATION:

  1. Review data pertaining to inventory quality.
  2. Vouch and test inventory pricing.
  3. Review entries to cost of goods sold.

F. STATEMENT PRESENTATION AND DISCLOSURE:

  1. Make inquiries of management as to pledging of inventories.
  2. Compare statement presentation and disclosure with GAAP.

FIGURE 13–1. Audit Program: Inventory Balances

are material to a company's financial statements and it is practicable and reasonable to do so. The observation of inventories may prove to be inconvenient, time-consuming, and difficult for the auditor but it is seldom impracticable and unreasonable.

In performing this auditing procedure, the auditor is expected to (1) observe the taking of the inventory by the client, (2) make some test counts of inventory quantities, and (3) make inquiries of the client concerning the inventories. The auditor has no responsibility to take or supervise the taking of the inventory. From this auditing procedure, the auditor obtains direct knowledge of the effectiveness of the client's inventory taking and the measure of reliance which may be placed on management's assertions as to the quantities and physical condition of the inventories.[1] In some cases, outside inventory specialists may be hired by the client to take the inventory. When this occurs, the auditor must be present to observe their counts.

[1] Auditing Standards Board, *Codification of Statements on Auditing Standards* (New York: American Institute of Certified Public Accountants, 1983), Auditing Section 331.09 (hereinafter referred to and cited as AU §).

The primary audit considerations applicable to this required procedure are as follows:

Timing and extent of the test. The timing of an inventory observation depends on the client's inventory system and the effectiveness of internal accounting control. In a periodic inventory system, quantities are determined by a physical count, and all counts are made as of a specific date. The date should be at or near the balance sheet date, and the auditor should ordinarily be present on the specific date.

In a perpetual inventory system, physical counts may be taken and compared to inventory records at interim dates. When the perpetual records are well kept and comparisons with physical counts are made periodically by the client, the auditor should be present to observe a representative sample of such counts. In such case, this procedure may occur either during or after the end of the period under audit. In companies where inventories are at multiple locations, the auditor's observations ordinarily should encompass all significant inventory locations.

Inventory-taking plans. The taking of a physical inventory by a client is usually done according to a plan or a list of instructions. The client's instructions should include such matters as the

- Names of employees responsible for supervising the inventory taking.
- Date of the counts.
- Locations to be counted.
- Detailed instructions on how the counts are to be made.
- Use and control of prenumbered inventory tags and summary (compilation) sheets.
- Provisions for handling the receipt, shipment, and movement of goods during the counts if such activity is unavoidable.
- Segregation or identification of goods not owned.

The auditor should review and evaluate the client's inventory-taking plans well in advance of the counting date. With ample lead time, the client should be able to respond favorably to suggested modifications in the plans before the count is begun. It is common for the auditor to assist the client in designing an inventory-taking plan that will facilitate both the taking and the observing of the inventory.

Advance planning must be done by the auditor if an inventory observation is to be done efficiently and effectively. An experienced auditor usually has the responsibility for planning the procedure, determining the manpower needs, and assigning members of the audit team to specific locations. Each observer should be provided with a copy of the client's inventory plans and written instructions of his duties.

Performing the test. In observing inventories, the auditor should

- Scrutinize the care with which client employees are following the inventory plan.
- See that all merchandise is tagged and no items are double tagged.
- Determine that prenumbered inventory tags and compilation sheets are properly controlled.
- Make some test counts and trace quantities to compilation sheets.
- Be alert for empty containers and for hollow squares (empty spaces) that may exist when goods are stacked in solid formations.
- Watch for damaged and obsolete inventory items.
- Appraise the general condition of the inventory.
- Identify the last receiving and shipping documents used and determine that goods received during the count are properly segregated.
- Inquire about the existence of slow-moving inventory items.

The extent of the auditor's test counts depends in part on the care exercised by client employees in taking the inventory and the nature and composition of the inventory. Ordinarily, the auditor will stratify the inventory items in order to include the items of highest dollar value in the count and take a representative sample of other items. Recourse to perpetual inventory records is helpful in identifying the high-value items and in selecting the sample items.

In making test counts, the auditor should record the count and give a complete and accurate description of the item (identification number, unit of measurement, location, etc.) in the working papers as shown in Figure 13-2. Such data are essential for the auditor's comparison of the test counts with the client's counts, and the subsequent tracing of the counts to inventory summary sheets and perpetual inventory records. Any differences in any of the comparisons should be investigated by the auditor. The test counts and related comparisons provide the auditor with evidence of the existence of the inventory and the accuracy of the client's counts, inventory compilation sheets, and perpetual inventory records.

Upon conclusion of the observation procedure, a designated member of the audit team should prepare an overall summary. The summary should include a description of such matters as (1) departures from the client's inventory-taking plan, (2) the extent of test counts and any material discrepancies resulting therefrom, and (3) conclusions as to the accuracy of the counts and the general condition of the inventory.

Inventories determined by statistical sampling. A company may have inventory controls or use methods of determining inventories, such as statistical sampling, that do not require an annual physical count of every item of inventory. Such methods do not relieve the auditor of the responsibility to observe the taking of inventories. It is still necessary to observe such counts

Prepared by: *CJ.A.*   Date: *1/8/x2*
Reviewed by: *R.C.P.*   Date: *1/11/x2*

Highlift Company
Raw Materials Test Counts,   F-2
12/31/X1

Tag No.	Inventory Sheet No.	Inventory Number	Inventory Description	Count Client	Count Audit	Difference
6531	15	1-42-003	Back Plate	125 ✓	125	
8340	18	1-83-012	1/4" Copper Plate	93 ✓	93	
1483	24	2-11-004	Single End Wire	1321 yds ✓	1325 yds.	4 yds.
4486	26	2-28-811	Copper Tubing	220 ft ✓	220 ft.	
3334	48	4-26-204	Side Plate	424 ✓	424	
8502	64	7-44-310	1/2" Copper Wire	276 ft ✓	276 ft.	
8844	68	7-72-460	3/8" Copper Wire	419 ft ✓	419 ft.	
6295	92	3-48-260	Front Plate	96 ✓	69	27

Each difference was corrected by the client. The net effect of the corrections was to increase inventory by $840. Total inventory values for which test counts were made and traced to inventory summaries without exception = $26,460 or 22% of the total. In my opinion, errors were immaterial.

✓ = Traced to client's inventory summary sheets (F-4) noting corrections for all differences.

FIGURE 13–2. Inventory Test Counts Working Paper

as deemed necessary in the circumstances. In addition, the auditor must obtain evidence as to the appropriateness of the method used to determine inventory quantities. When statistical sampling methods are used by the client, the auditor must ascertain that (1) the sampling plan has statistical validity, (2) it has been properly applied, and (3) the results in terms of precision and reliability are reasonable in the circumstances.[2]

[2] Auditing Standards Board, *op. cit.,* AU § 331.11.

Alternative substantive tests for ending inventories. When inventories are material and the auditor does not observe the inventory at or near the year-end:

- Tests of the accounting records alone will not be sufficient as to quantities.
- It will always be necessary for the auditor to make, or observe, some physical counts of the inventory and to apply appropriate tests of intervening transactions.[3]

This language is unequivocal; the observation (or counting) of the inventory can be postponed, but it cannot be eliminated. The auditor must obtain some physical evidence pertaining to ending inventories in order to comply with generally accepted auditing standards (GAAS). In addition, the auditor should review the records of any counts made by the client.

Observation of beginning inventories. In order to express an unqualified opinion on the income statement, the auditor must observe the taking of both the beginning and ending inventories. On a continuing audit engagement, this requirement is met by observing the ending inventory of each year. However, in the initial audit of an established company, the auditor may either be appointed after the beginning inventory was taken or be asked to report on the financial statements of one or more prior periods. In such circumstances, it is clearly impracticable and unreasonable for the auditor to have observed the inventory taking, and GAAS permit the auditor to verify the inventories by other auditing procedures.

When the client has been audited by another firm of independent auditors in the prior period(s), the other procedures may include a review of the predecessor auditor's report and/or working papers and a review of the client's inventory summaries for the prior period(s). If the client has not been audited previously, the auditor may be able to obtain audit satisfaction by reviewing the summaries of any client counts, testing prior inventory transactions, and applying gross profit tests to the inventories. Such procedures are only appropriate when the auditor is able to verify the validity and propriety of the ending inventory for the period under audit.[4]

Effects on auditor's report. When inventories have been observed, the auditor may be able to issue a standard audit report. This is also permissible when the auditor has used alternative substantive tests to verify the existence of the beginning inventory. However, when sufficient evidence has not been obtained as to the existence of beginning inventories or the auditor is unable to observe the taking of ending inventories, the auditor is precluded from issuing a standard audit report. The specific effects on the auditor's report are considered in Chapter 16.

---

[3] Auditing Standards Board, *op. cit.,* AU § 331.12.
[4] Auditing Standards Board, *op. cit.,* AU § 331.13.

Confirm Inventories in Public Warehouses

When client inventories are stored in public warehouses or with other outside custodians, the auditor should obtain evidence as to the existence of the inventory by direct communication with the custodian. This type of evidence is deemed to be sufficient except when the amounts involved represent a significant proportion of total or current assets. When this is the case, the auditor must obtain additional evidence through one or more of the following supplemental procedures:

- Discussing with the client his investigation of the reputation, financial standing, and control procedures of the warehouse.
- Reviewing the client's control procedures concerning the performance of the warehouse, such as comparisons of quantities shown on warehouse statements with the client's records.
- Observing counts made by warehouse personnel if practicable and reasonable.
- Confirming with lenders (on a test basis, where appropriate) any warehouse receipts pledged as collateral.
- Obtaining the report of the independent auditor on the financial statements of the custodian expressing an opinion on the warehouseman's system of internal accounting control relevant to the custody of goods.[5]

Inspection of warehouse receipts held by the client may also provide evidence of goods stored in a public warehouse, but such evidence alone is not sufficient.

Completeness

This objective is directed at whether all of the company's inventories are recorded. The following tests of balances are used to obtain evidence as to the completeness of inventory balances.

Perform Purchases and Purchases Returns Cutoff Tests

A purchase cutoff test is performed to obtain evidence that all goods owned by the client at the balance sheet date are included in inventory and that the related liability is recorded. Legal title to goods in transit is determined by whether shipping terms are F.O.B. (free on board) shipping point or destination.

The cutoff period extends from several days before the balance sheet date to several days after. For this five- to seven-day period, the auditor examines evidence that year-end purchases have been recorded in the proper account-

---

[5] Auditing Standards Board, *op. cit.*, AU § 331.14 (adapted).

ing period. The test involves tracing of receiving reports to voucher register entries and vouching recorded entries to receiving reports and vendors' invoices.

Any material cutoff errors should be proposed for correction by the client. This test should include inventory in transit from branches, divisions, and affiliates of the client as well as shipments from vendors.

A similar test is made of purchases returns to determine that inventory and the related payables are relieved of the cost of the returned goods in the proper period.

Make Analytical Review

The auditor performs analytical review procedures to obtain evidence as to the reasonableness and completeness of inventory balances. Three quantitative relationships that are frequently computed and compared with corresponding data for the preceding year are: (1) the gross profit percentage (gross profit ÷ net sales), (2) inventory turnover ratios (cost of goods sold ÷ average inventory), and (3) number of days' sales in inventories (360 ÷ inventory turnover). In addition, it is customary to compare inventory amounts with internal client data such as budgets and with external data such as industry statistics.

When the comparisons produce normal or expected results, the auditor has additional corroborating evidence. In contrast, when unusual relationships or fluctuations are found, the auditor should make further investigations. For example, an abnormally low gross profit rate could result from an understatement of ending inventory or improper purchases and sales cutoffs.

Rights and Obligations

This objective relates to whether inventories are owned by the client and whether any binding commitments exist for the future purchase of goods. Three auditing procedures are applicable to this objective.

Make Inquiries of Management Regarding Ownership

Since title to goods purchased passes to the buyer no later than when the goods are received, there is a presumption that goods on hand are owned by the client. Support for this presumption is obtained by tracing purchases to vendors' invoices, payment vouchers, and paid checks.

However, goods on hand may be held for customers, at their request, after a sale has occurred, and goods may be held on consignment. Thus, management is requested to segregate goods not owned during the inventory taking. In addition, the auditor usually requests a written assertion on ownership of inventories in the client representation letter. This letter is illustrated in Chapter 15.

Examine Consignment Agreements

Under consignment agreements, title to the goods remains with the owner (i.e., the consignor). Thus, goods held on consignment should not be included in the holder's (i.e., the consignee's) physical inventory count or reported as inventory in the balance sheet.

The auditor should inquire of management as to any goods held on consignment. When consignments exist, the agreement should be examined for terms and conditions. In addition, as indicated under the observation of the client's inventory taking, the auditor should ascertain that goods not owned by the client are properly segregated and excluded from the physical count.

If the client has shipped goods on consignment, the auditor should review the documentation to determine that goods held by the consignee are included in the consignor's inventory at the balance sheet date.

Review Purchase Commitments

Inquiry of management is used to determine the existence of binding contracts for future purchases of goods. When such commitments exist, the auditor should examine the terms of the contracts and evaluate the propriety of the company's accounting and reporting thereof. An important test is to compare the contract prices with the supplier's current selling price for the items. If the former exceeds the latter and the difference is not covered by a binding sales contract on the items, a loss has occurred. When material losses exist on purchase commitments, they should be recognized in the statements, together with disclosure of the attendant circumstances.

Valuation or Allocation

The proper valuation of inventories and cost of goods sold is vital to the overall fairness of financial statements. This objective relates to the cost and net realizable value of the inventory. Three tests of balances are applicable to the valuation of inventories and cost of goods sold.

Review Data Pertaining to Inventory Quality

The auditor's responsibility for quality is limited to that of a reasonably informed observer. This means that the auditor is expected to determine whether the inventory appears to be in condition for sale, use, or consumption and whether there are any obsolete, slow-moving, or damaged goods. The auditor obtains evidence of general condition or obsolescence by

- Observing the client's inventory taking.
- Scanning perpetual inventory records for slow-moving items.
- Reviewing quality control production reports.
- Making inquiries of client.

When the evidence suggests a decline in the utility of the goods, appropriate write-down below cost is required by GAAP.

When client representations as to the nature of the inventory pertain to highly technical matters, the auditor may require the assistance of an outside expert. This might occur, for example, in an oil company with different grades of gasoline and motor oil, or in a jewelry store with different carat diamonds and different jeweled watches. As explained in Chapter 3, the auditor may use the work of a specialist as an audit procedure to obtain competent evidential matter, providing he is satisfied as to the qualifications and independence of the expert.

Vouch and Test Inventory Pricing

This verification procedure consists of two steps:

- Determining the propriety and consistency of the client's pricing (costing) of inventory quantities.
- Tracing unit costs used by the client to supporting documentation.

A review of perpetual inventory records and inquiry of the client should enable the auditor to determine both the basis (historical cost) and costing methods (first in, first out [FIFO], last in, first out [LIFO], etc.) used in pricing inventory quantities. The consistency of the pricing, in turn, can be established by recourse to last year's working papers on a recurring audit and/or to the prior year's financial statements. This step in the verification of pricing includes a review of the pricing of obsolete and damaged goods to ascertain that they are not valued in excess of net realizable value at the statement date.

Evidence in support of unit costs varies with the nature of the inventory. For items purchased for resale, use, or consumption (merchandise inventory, raw materials, and supplies), costs should be traced to representative vendor invoices. When the lower of cost or market method is used, the auditor must verify both cost and market. The current replacement cost of an item may be obtained (1) from purchases made at or near the balance sheet date, or (2) by inquiries of suppliers.

The nature and extent of the auditor's pricing tests of work in progress and finished goods depend on the reliability of the client's cost accounting records and the methods used by the client in accumulating such costs. The methods should be reviewed by the auditor for propriety and for the accuracy and consistency of application.

Review Entries to Cost of Goods Sold

Considerable evidence as to the propriety, accuracy, and consistency of costs assigned to cost of goods sold is obtained from tests of sales, purchases, and manufacturing transactions and by substantive tests of inventory balances. Direct tests of cost of goods may be limited to (1) scanning entries for possible errors and (2) performing analytical review procedures. When the client uses standard costs, the auditor should determine the underlying causes of variances in order to evaluate the propriety of the accounting treatment. In some cases, an overall adjustment of cost of goods sold and ending inventory may be warranted.

Statement Presentation and Disclosure

It is customary to identify the major inventory categories in the balance sheet and the cost of goods sold in the income statement. In addition, there should be disclosure of the inventory costing method(s) used, the pledging of inventories, and the existence of major purchase commitments.

Evidence pertaining to statement presentation and disclosure is provided by the substantive tests described above. Further evidence may be obtained, as needed, from a review of the minutes of board of directors meetings, inquiries of management, and the examination of any binding purchase commitments. Based on the evidence and a comparison of the client's financial statements with applicable accounting pronouncements, the auditor determines the propriety of the presentation and disclosures.

Statistical Sampling of Inventory Balances

The expenditure and production cycles offer many opportunities for implementing statistical sampling. A primary application chosen for illustration in the following case study is an audit of inventory balances. Each step in designing, executing, and evaluating the sampling plan for the audit of the Henson Company's inventory balance is explained.

Determining the Objectives of the Plan

The objective is to test the reasonableness of the recorded book value for Henson's inventory. Having already tested quantities, the auditor is concerned primarily with testing prices and extensions in this sample. Internal controls over inventory transactions have been found to be strong, and prior year's audits have revealed few errors in the inventory balance. Because of this, and since the auditor is concerned primarily with overstatement errors, he decides to use probability-proportional-to-size sampling.

Defining the Population and Sampling Unit

The population consists of 2,000 different inventory items, with a total recorded book value of $4,500,000. A computer listing is obtained showing quantity, price, and extended dollar value for each item. As a test of the completeness of the listing, it is footed and agreed to the total recorded book value. The logical sampling unit is lines on the inventory listing representing different stock items.

Determining Sample Size

To determine an appropriate sample size, the auditor specifies the risk of incorrect acceptance, tolerable error, and anticipated error. He sets the risk of incorrect acceptance at .20, which reflects the good internal control situation and assurance gained from other audit procedures including analytical review. He decides tolerable error is $45,000. While he expects few errors, he wishes to hold down the risk of incorrect rejection; therefore he specifies an anticipated error of $10,000. From tables like those in Figure 11-2, he next obtains the reliability factor for the .20 risk of incorrect acceptance and zero errors, and the corresponding expansion factor for the anticipated error. These are 1.61 and 1.3, respectively. He then calculates sample size as follows:

$$n = \frac{BV \times RF}{TE - (AE \times EF)} = \frac{\$4,500,000 \times 1.61}{\$45,000 - (\$10,000 \times 1.3)} = 226$$

Determining the Sample Selection Method

Systematic selection is used based on a sampling interval calculated as follows:

$$SI = \frac{BV}{n} = \frac{\$4,500,000}{226} = \$19,911$$

Thus, the logical unit associated with every 19,911th dollar will be included in the sample.

Executing the Sampling Plan

The primary auditing procedures performed on the sample items are (1) testing the price to recent invoices, and (2) testing the accuracy of the extension of quantity times price. A list of errors showing both book and audited values is made. Only two errors are found.

Evaluating Sample Results

To evaluate the sample, the auditor calculates the projected error and an allowance for sampling risk. He then compares the sum of these to tolerable error. The calculation of the projected errors is shown below:

Book Value (BV)	Audit Value (AV)	Tainting Percentage [$TP = (BV - AV)/BV$]	Sampling Interval (SI)	Projected Error ($TP \times SI$) or ($BV - AV$)
$10,000	$9,000	10	$19,911	$1,991
8,000	7,600	5	19,911	996
			Total	$2,987

The calculation of the allowance for sampling risk includes two components as follows:

$$\text{Basic precision} = \text{sampling interval} \times \text{reliability factor}$$
$$= \$19,911 \times 1.61 = \$32,057$$

Incremental Allowance =

Ranked Projected Errors	Incremental Change in Reliability Factor Minus One	Incremental Allowance for Sampling Risk
$1,991	1.38 (2.99 − 1.61)	$2,748
996	1.29 (4.28 − 2.99)	1,285
	Total	$4,033

Thus, the total allowance for sampling risk is $36,090 ($32,057 + $4,033). Adding this to the total projected error of $2,987 produces an achieved upper error limit of $39,077. Since this amount is less than the tolerable error of $45,000, the sample results support the conclusion that the recorded book value of the inventory is fairly stated at the levels of risk specified.

Computer-Assisted Tests of Inventory Balances

When the client maintains perpetual inventory records by electronic data processing (EDP), the auditor may use the computer to perform substantive tests of inventory balances. This is possible if the auditor has the appropriate software.

In this illustration, it is assumed that the client's master file of merchandise inventory is maintained on magnetic tape. The file includes the inventory part number, warehouse location, unit cost, and the quantity on hand. In addition to updating the file for sales in the revenue cycle and purchases in the expenditure cycle, the client's programs provide for a monthly printout of the quantity, unit cost, and total cost for each inventory item and the total cost of inventories on hand.

There are two widely used computer-assisted applications in testing inventory balances: (1) selecting items for test counts and (2) verifying inventory pricing. These applications, which are illustrated in Figure 13-3, are explained below.

Select Items for Test Counts

In order to use the computer in performing this substantive test, the auditor inputs the desired audit selection criteria, such as (1) all inventory items with a balance over a specified dollar amount and (2) a random selection of remaining items. Using the appropriate software program, the criteria are then run with the client's master file to obtain a printout of items for test count.

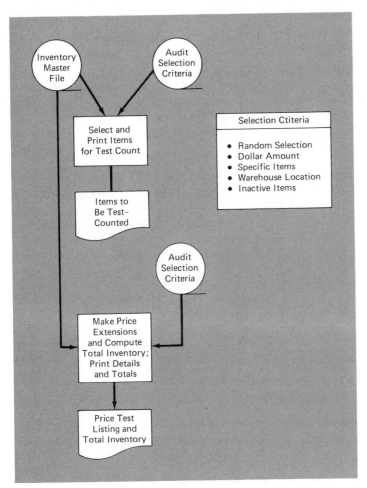

FIGURE 13–3. Computer-Assisted Tests of Inventory Balances

Verify Inventory Pricing

Computer assistance in performing this test of inventory balances extends to the verification of both the total cost of the inventory and the cost of selected individual units. The first objective is achieved by using a software package that performs a price-times-quantity calculation for each inventory item and computes a total dollar value for goods on hand. If inventory is stored in different locations, the audit criteria may specify totals for each location. The auditor then compares the totals with the client's data, and differences are investigated.

The procedure for verifying the cost of individual units of inventory is similar to the technique described above for test counts. Audit selection criteria in this case may also include slow-moving items and items normally subject to frequent price fluctuations. The printout of this run is a listing of individual items of inventory that are traced to source documents for verification of unit costs.

The computer may also be used to identify excess quantities, compare inventory balances between two points in time, and determine the effects of possible changes in inventory costing methods.

TESTS OF PLANT ASSET BALANCES

Plant assets consist of tangible resources that are held for use in operations. This category on the balance sheet includes: (1) land, buildings, equipment, furniture, and fixtures, (2) leaseholds, and (3) accumulated depreciation. The principal related income accounts are depreciation expense, repairs expense, and rent on operating leases.

Plant assets often represent the largest component of total assets on the balance sheet, and expenses associated with plant assets are material factors in the determination of net income.

Comparison with Audit of Current Assets

The time required to perform substantive tests of plant assets is significantly less than the time required to verify current assets. This is due to the following factors:

- Fewer transactions occur.
- Plant assets are less vulnerable to misappropriation.
- Confirmation of plant assets and observation of inventories of plant assets are not required.

The auditor also has considerably more flexibility in scheduling tests of plant asset balances as they do not need to be performed at or near the balance sheet date.

Initial Audit Engagement

The auditor's substantive tests will be much more extensive in his initial audit of a client than in a repeat engagement. In the first audit, evidence must be obtained as to the propriety of the beginning balances in the accounts and the ownership of the assets comprising the balances. When the client has previously been audited by another independent auditor, the acquisition of such evidence is facilitated when the successor auditor is able to review the predecessor auditor's working papers. However, if the client has not been previously audited, the auditor must undertake the investigation of the balances and the ownership of major units of plant currently in service. Information concerning beginning balances in an initial audit is usually summarized and kept in the auditor's permanent working papers.

Recurring Audit Engagement

Tests of plant asset balances depend on whether any reliance is to be placed on internal accounting control. Where there are few plant asset transactions, the auditor usually decides to make only a preliminary review of internal controls and to make extensive tests of plant asset balances. In contrast, when there are numerous plant asset transactions, the auditor normally will complete his review of the controls, and perform compliance tests of the controls expected to be relied upon. This may be done as part of evaluating the controls over purchases transactions in the expenditure cycle or separately within that cycle. Ordinarily, the auditor will use separate testing because plant asset acquisitions will not occur with enough frequency to assure satisfactory audit coverage through the testing of purchases transactions.

In a recurring engagement the auditor concentrates on the current year's transactions because the balances at the beginning of the year have been validated through the preceding year's audit. Heavy reliance is placed on documentary evidence in verifying asset balances and on mathematical evidence in verifying accumulated depreciation. An audit program for plant assets is shown in Figure 13-4.

Clerical Accuracy

This objective is met by footing plant asset and depreciation schedules, and reconciling general ledger balances with subsidiary ledgers and supporting schedules. An auditor's schedule for plant assets and accumulated depreciation is illustrated in Figure 13-5.

Existence or Occurrence

This objective relates to the physical existence of plant assets at the balance sheet date and the occurrence of related income statement transactions. The auditing procedures of physical inspection and examination of documents are used in completing the two tests of balances applicable to this objective.

Inspect Plant Additions

Information on plant additions may be obtained from an analysis of plant accounts, an examination of plant asset schedules, a review of the minutes of board of directors meetings, and inquiry of management. The inspection of plant assets acquired during the year enables the auditor to obtain direct personal knowledge of their existence.

Physical inspection may allow the auditor to acquire other corroborating information. For example, during the inspection, the auditor can make inquiry concerning the disposition of the retired unit, if any, and the incurrence of installation, testing, and other costs to make the new facility ready for its intended use.

When a complete physical inventory of plant assets is taken by the client, the auditor is not required to observe it. However, a review of the inventory

---

TYPE OF TESTS: Substantive   **PURPOSE: Validity and Propriety of Balances**
CYCLE: Expenditure   **ACCOUNTS: Plant Assets**

A. CLERICAL ACCURACY:

    1. Foot plant asset schedules.
    2. Reconcile general ledger balances with subsidiary ledgers and supporting schedules.

B. EXISTENCE OR OCCURRENCE:

    1. Inspect plant additions.
    2. Review documentation in client's files.

C. COMPLETENESS:

    1. Make plant tour.
    2. Make analytical review.

D. RIGHTS AND OBLIGATIONS:

    1. Inspect documentation of ownership.
    2. Examine lease contracts.

E. VALUATION OR ALLOCATION:

    1. Vouch entries to plant asset accounts.
    2. Analyze entries to repairs expense.
    3. Review entries to accumulated depreciation.

F. STATEMENT PRESENTATION AND DISCLOSURE:

    1. Make inquiries of management and review documentation for pledging of plant assets.
    2. Compare statement presentation and disclosures with GAAP.

FIGURE 13–4. Audit Program: Plant Asset Balances

compilation may reveal the existence of unrecorded plant assets or the failure to remove retired assets from the records.

Review Documentation in Client's Files

The client's files should contain numerous documents that relate to this objective. Evidence of existence may take the form of completed construction contracts, receiving reports, certificates of title, tax bills, and insurance policies. Support for occurrence may be found in vendor invoices, vouchers, "paid" checks, and work orders pertaining to repairs expense.

Completeness

The completeness objective is designed to determine that all plant asset transactions are recorded. This objective is met through (1) making cash disbursements and purchases cutoff tests, and (2) performing the following tests of plant assets.

Daylight Company
Property, Plant and Equipment and Accumulated Depreciation
Lead Schedule
12/31/X1

Prepared by: CJH   Date: 2/4/X2
Reviewed by: RCP   Date: 2/12/X2

G

W/P Ref.	Acc. No.	Account Title	Asset Cost Balance 12/31/X0	Additions	Disposals	Adjustments DR(CR) 12/31/X1	Balance 12/31/X1	Accumulated Depreciation Balance 12/31/X1	Previous	Disposals	Adjustments DR(CR)	Balance 12/31/X1
G-1	301	Land	4,500,000 ✓				4,500,000					
G-2	302	Buildings	2,108,000 ✓	125,000			2,208,000	3,797,420	843,320		② (1,000)	462,740
G-3	303	Machinery and Equipment	3,757,250 ✓	920,000	370,000	② (25,000)	4,332,250	10,774,210	3,529,10	172,500	② 1,000	1,255,620
G-4	304	Furniture and Fixtures	853,400 ✓	144,000	110,000	② 25,000	887,400	2,174,50	43,250	21,000		239,700
			7,603,650	1,249,000	480,000	-0-	7,937,650	14,671,100	480,480	193,500	-0-	1,958,080
			F	F	F	F	FF	F	F	F	F	FF

✓ - Traced to general ledger and 12/31/X0 working papers
F - Footed
FF - Footed and crossfooted

FIGURE 13-5. Plant Asset and Accumulated Depreciation Schedule

Make Plant Tour

The auditor generally makes a tour of the client's operating facilities. Through a plant tour, the auditor obtains direct personal knowledge of the types of machinery and equipment in use and the condition of the plant. The auditor should be alert for obsolete or damaged units, major new additions, and construction, betterments, and repair work in progress. Such items should be noted and traced to the accounting records.

Make Analytical Review

A number of analytical review procedures can be performed by the auditor to obtain evidence as to the completeness of plant asset accounts and related income statement accounts. For example, comparisons may be made of expenditures with budget expectations and prior-year results. When repairs expenses are significantly below budget, unrecorded expenses may exist or such expenses may have been improperly classified as capital expenditures.

Rights and Obligations

Rights to plant assets may exist through ownership and from lease contracts. Lease contracts, in turn, may represent an obligation of the entity. Two procedures are applicable to this objective.

Inspect Documentation of Ownership

The ownership of vehicles may be established by examining certificates of title, registration certificates, and insurance policies. For equipment, furniture, and fixtures, the "paid" invoice may be the best evidence of ownership. Evidence of ownership in real property is found in deeds, title insurance policies, property tax bills, mortgage payment receipts, and fire insurance policies. Verification of ownership in real property can also be substantiated by a review of public records. When this form of additional evidence is desired, the auditor may seek the help of an attorney.

Examine Lease Contracts

Lease agreements convey to a lessor the right to use property, plant, or equipment, usually for a specified period of time. For accounting purposes, leases may be classified as either capital leases or as operating leases. The auditor should read the lease agreement to determine the proper accounting classification of the lease in accordance with *Financial Accounting Standards Board* pronouncements. When a capital lease exists, both an asset and a liability should be recognized in the accounts and statements.

Valuation or Allocation

This objective pertains to the cost and net book value of plant assets on the balance sheet, and the amounts reported for depreciation and related plant asset expenses in the income statement. Vouching, recalculation, and scanning are the primary audit procedures used in performing the three tests of balances applicable to valuation or allocation.

Vouch Entries to Plant Asset Accounts

All additions should be supported by documentary evidence in the form of authorizations in the minutes, vouchers, invoices, contracts, and canceled checks. The recorded amounts should be vouched to supporting documentation. If there are numerous transactions, the vouching may be done on a test basis. In performing this test, the auditor ascertains that appropriate accounting recognition has been given to installation, freight, and similar costs. For construction in progress, the auditor may review the contract and documentation in support of construction costs.

When plant assets are acquired under a capital lease, the cost of the property and the related liability should be recorded at the present value of the future minimum lease payments. The accuracy of the client's determination of the present value of the lease liability should also be verified by recomputation.

Evidence of sales, retirements, and trade-ins should be available to the auditor in the form of cash remittance advices, written authorizations and sales agreements. Such documentation should be carefully examined to determine the accuracy and propriety of the accounting records, including the recognition of gain or loss, if any.

The following procedures may also be useful to the auditor in determining whether all retirements have been recorded:

- Analyze the miscellaneous revenue account for proceeds from sales of plant assets.
- Investigate disposition of facilities associated with discontinued product lines and operations.
- Trace retirement work orders and authorizations for retirements to the accounting records.
- Review insurance policies for termination or reductions of coverage.
- Make inquiry of management as to retirements.

Plant additions and retirements may be traced to schedules of changes prepared by the client. The schedules should show balances and changes by major classifications or functional groupings.

Analyze Entries to Repairs Expense

The auditor's objectives in performing this test are to determine the propriety and consistency of the charges to repairs expense. Propriety involves a consideration of whether the client has made appropriate distinctions between capital and repair expenditures. Accordingly, the auditor should scan the individual charges to identify those which are sufficiently material to be capitalized. For these items, the auditor should examine supporting documentation, such as the vendor's invoice, company work order, and management authorization to determine the propriety of the charge or the need for an adjusting entry.

Consistency involves a determination of whether the company's criteria for distinguishing between capital and revenue expenditures is the same as in the preceding year.

Review Entries to Accumulated Depreciation

In meeting the valuation or allocation objective for accumulated depreciation, the auditor seeks evidence as to the reasonableness, consistency, and accuracy of depreciation charges. An essential starting point for the auditor in making this test is to ascertain the depreciation methods used by the client during the year under examination. The identity of the methods can be obtained from a review of depreciation schedules prepared by the client and inquiry of the client. The auditor must then determine whether the methods currently in use are consistent with the preceding year. On a recurring audit, this can be established by a review of last year's working papers.

Determination of the reasonableness of depreciation provisions involves a consideration of such factors as (1) the client's past history in estimating useful lives, and (2) the remaining useful lives of existing assets.

The auditor's verification of accuracy is achieved through recalculation. Ordinarily, this is done on a selective basis by recomputing the depreciation on major assets and testing depreciation taken on additions and retirements during the year.

Statement Presentation and Disclosure

The financial statements, or the notes thereto, should show the following information for property, plant, and equipment:

- Depreciation expense for the period.
- Balances of major classes of depreciable assets, by nature or function, at the balance sheet date.
- Accumulated depreciation, either by major classes of depreciable assets or in total, at the balance sheet date.
- A general description of the method or methods used in computing depreciation with respect to major classes of depreciable assets.[6]

Property pledged as security for loans should be disclosed. Information as to pledging may be obtained from reviewing the minutes and long-term

---

[6] Accounting Principles Board, *APB Opinion No. 12, Omnibus Opinion* (New York: American Institute of Certified Public Accountants, 1967).

contractual agreements, by confirming debt agreements, and through inquiries of management. The appropriateness of the client's disclosures related to assets under lease can be determined by recourse to the authoritative accounting pronouncements and the related lease agreements.

Companies meeting certain size requirements are required to disclose certain information on the effects of changing prices in annual reports to stockholders. The auditor should make inquiries of management and compare the data with other relevant information to determine whether the disclosures are in conformity with GAAP.

TESTS OF CURRENT LIABILITY BALANCES

The expenditure cycle produces many current liability balances including accounts payable, wages payable, and payroll taxes payable. These accounts will be used to illustrate substantive testing of current liability balances.

Comparison with Tests of Asset Balances

Current liabilities are significant in evaluating an entity's short-term solvency. These accounts are as vulnerable to errors and irregularities as current assets. Similarly, deliberate misrepresentation of financial position could occur as frequently with liabilities as with assets. However, the manner of the actions and the techniques of concealment differ significantly. In most misrepresentations, it is presumed that the client desires to report a financial position that is better than the true condition. Thus, the client may *overstate assets* and/or *understate liabilities*.

To overstate assets, the client will have to either record a legitimate transaction improperly or create and record a fictitious transaction. In either case, the irregularity is a matter of record and the auditor's examination of assets might detect the impropriety. In contrast, to understate liabilities, personnel can destroy all evidence pertaining to the transaction that created the obligation or can merely forget to record the transaction. In either case, the error is not a matter of accounting record and the auditor's examination may not detect the error. In the design and execution of an audit program for liabilities, the auditor must be constantly alert to the possibility of understatement of obligations by the client.

Audit Program

The nature, timing, and extent of substantive tests of current liability account balances depends on the auditor's reliance on internal control over expenditure cycle transactions. When controls are not tested for compliance, the auditor must perform extensive substantive tests. When controls are tested for compliance, the auditor may reduce the amount of substantive testing. An audit program for testing these balances is shown in Figure 13-6. Primary attention is given in the program to accounts payable.

TYPE OF TEST: Substantive   **PURPOSE:** Validity and Propriety of Balances
CYCLE: Expenditure   **ACCOUNTS:** Accounts Payable, Wages
      and Production   Payable, and Payroll Taxes Payable

A. CLERICAL ACCURACY:

   1. Foot schedule of individual creditor balances.
   2. Reconcile accounts payable with supporting schedule and creditors' ledger totals.

B. EXISTENCE OR OCCURRENCE, COMPLETENESS, AND RIGHTS AND
   OBLIGATIONS:

   1. Review documentation in client's files.
   2. Confirm accounts payable.
   3. Examine subsequent payments to creditors.
   4. Search for unrecorded accounts payable.
   5. Make analytical review.

C. VALUATION OR ALLOCATION:

   1. Vouch accounts payable schedule.
   2. Recalculate accrued wages and payroll taxes payable.

D. STATEMENT PRESENTATION AND DISCLOSURE:

   1. Make inquiries and review documentation as to purchase commitments and contract
      terms.
   2. Compare statement presentation and disclosure with GAAP.

FIGURE 13–6. Audit Program: Current Liability Balances

A comparison of the accounts payable portion of this program with the program for accounts receivable in Chapter 12 will show many similarities. This is understandable since an account payable on the records of the buyer is an account receivable on the books of the seller. However, there is a major difference in executing the two programs. For accounts receivable, the tests of balances focus on the possibility of overstatement, whereas for accounts payable the auditor is concerned about the possibility of understatement. It should also be recognized that there is more externally created documentation for accounts payable than for accounts receivable. It will be recalled that external sources of evidence are generally assumed to have greater reliability than internally created evidence. The impact of these differences should be recognized in the following explanation of the specific audit procedures.

Clerical Accuracy

The starting point for substantive tests of accounts payable is a schedule (or listing) of amounts owed to specific creditors. Ordinarily, the schedule is prepared by the client from the unpaid voucher file or the creditors' subsidiary ledger. The auditor must verify the accuracy of the manual or computerized listing by refooting the schedule and reconciling the total with the ledger balance. In addition, the auditor selectively tests the items on the schedule with the unpaid file or creditor subsidiary ledger.

The auditor scrutinizes the listing of payables for debit balances and amounts owed to subsidiary companies and other nontrade creditors. When material, such items should be identified for subsequent investigation.

Existence or Occurrence, Completeness, and Rights and Obligations

The auditor's principal concern with these objectives is to determine that all obligations of the entity are reported in the financial statements. In addition to the purchase cutoff test described earlier in this chapter, there are five procedures that pertain to these objectives.

Review Documentation in Client's Files

The client's files should contain various documents that support the validity of creditor claims against assets. These include documentation required under a voucher system (i.e., purchase order, receiving report, and vendor's invoice). In addition, it should be possible to examine creditor monthly statements received by the client.

Confirm Accounts Payable

Unlike the confirmation of accounts receivable, the confirmation of accounts payable is not required. This procedure is optional because (1) confirmation offers no assurance that unrecorded payables will be discovered, and (2) external evidence in the form of invoices and vendor monthly statements should be available to substantiate the balances. Confirmation of accounts payable is recommended when internal controls are weak, there are individual creditors with relatively large balances, and when a company is experiencing difficulties in meeting its obligations.

When confirmation is to be undertaken, accounts with zero or small balances should be among those selected for confirmation because they may be more understated than accounts with large balances. In addition, confirmations should be sent to major vendors who (1) were used in the prior year but not in the current year, and (2) do not send monthly statements. The positive form should be used in making the confirmation request as illustrated in Figure 13-7. It may be observed that the confirmation does not specify the amount due. In confirming a payable, the auditor prefers to have the creditor indicate the amount due because that is the amount that is reconciled to the client's records. As in the case of confirming accounts receivable, the auditor must control the preparation and mailing of the requests and should receive the responses directly from the respondent.

Examine Subsequent Payments to Creditors

This test is similar to the tracing of collections from customers subsequent to the statement date. This test is scheduled toward the end of field work in order to enhance the opportunity of obtaining evidence concerning unre-

---

HIGHLIFT COMPANY
P.O. Box 1777
Cleveland, Ohio 39087

January 4, 19X1

Supplier, Inc.
2001 Lakeview Drive
Cleveland, Ohio 39089

Dear Sir or Madam:

Will you please send directly to our auditors, Reddy & Abel, Certified Public Accountants, an itemized statement of the amount owed to you by us at the close of business December 31, 19X0? Will you please also supply the following information:

Amount not yet due $ _____
Amount past due $ _____
Amount of purchase commitments $ _____
Description of any collateral held _____
_____

A business reply envelope addressed to our auditors is enclosed. A prompt reply will be very much appreciated.

Very truly yours,

C. J. Owens
_____
Controller
Highlift Company

FIGURE 13–7. Accounts Payable Confirmation

corded debts that existed at the statement date. The test consists of tracing vouchers or checks issued after the statement date to the list of payables at the balance sheet date. The comparison should enable the auditor to identify

- Large disbursements that clearly relate to the list of payables or to liabilities incurred subsequent to the statement date.
- Large disbursements pertaining to the prior period not included in the list of payables.
- Significant listed balances that remain unpaid.

The latter two items should be investigated by the auditor. A payment not on the list indicates the possibility of unrecorded liabilities, whereas unpaid items may be attributable to items in dispute, misplaced vouchers, errors in recording transactions, or items not due for payment.

Search for Unrecorded Accounts Payable

This test supplements other substantive procedures pertaining to accounts payable. It consists of a specific investigation to discover the existence of any significant vendors' invoices that are unrecorded at the statement date. The search usually occurs after the results of other tests are evaluated. In making a search, the auditor may also obtain evidence that an invoice or voucher has been recorded in the wrong accounting period. The procedures used by the auditor in this test may include, but are not necessarily limited to, the following:

- Inquire of accounting and purchasing personnel concerning unrecorded invoices that are being held for approval or further information such as a requested allowance for damaged goods.
- Investigate unmatched purchase orders, receiving reports, and invoices that may indicate the incurrence of a liability as of the balance sheet date.
- Review capital budgets, work orders, and construction contracts for unrecorded amounts.

Any unrecorded liabilities that have a material effect on financial position or the results of operations should be proposed to the client for adjustment.

Make Analytical Review

Analytical review tests of accounts payable may include ratios of the average number of days payables are outstanding, an analysis of lost discounts, and comparisons with budget expectations and prior year's balances. Any unusual fluctuations and relationships should be investigated by the auditor.

Valuation or Allocation

The objective of valuation or allocation relates to the amount of the liability and the related cost or expense. Relatively few problems are encountered by the auditor in meeting this objective. There are two procedures that are applicable to this objective.

Vouch Accounts Payable Schedule

Previous procedures in the audit program have established the clerical accuracy, existence, and completeness of amounts owed to creditors at the balance sheet date. This procedure is directed at the proper valuation of the obligation. To achieve this objective, amounts owed to creditors shown in the schedule of accounts payable are vouched to supporting documentation. When a voucher system is used by the client, the documentation should be attached to the voucher in the unpaid voucher file at the balance sheet date. Thus, this audit test is facilitated when it is done at or near the statement date. When such a system is not used, the creditor's account file should contain the supporting documentation.

Recalculate Accrued Wages and Payroll Taxes Payable

A variety of adjusting entries may be made by a company for compensation owed to officers and employees at the balance sheet date. Accruals may pertain to commissions, bonuses, vacation pay, sick leave pay, and other benefits. The auditor seeks evidence as to the correctness of the accrual. This is done by reviewing documentation in support of the entry and by recalculating the amount accrued.

Similarly, the auditor should trace accrued payroll taxes to tax returns and verify the amount by recalculation.

Statement Presentation and Disclosure

Each major type of obligation, such as accounts payable, accrued expenses payable, and taxes payable should be identified in the current liability section. For short-term notes payable, there should also be disclosure of interest rates, and the existence of any assets pledged as collateral. Evidence pertaining to this objective may be obtained through inquiries of management and a review of debt contracts. The auditor then compares the statement presentation and disclosures with GAAP.

CONCLUDING COMMENTS

Inventory, plant asset, and current liability balances associated with specific transaction cycles offer myriad challenges for the auditor. Observation of the physical inventory is a generally accepted auditing procedure, and pricing and cutoff tests are often extensive. In an initial engagement of an established client, additional work is required for plant assets to establish existence or occurrence, rights and obligations, and valuation or allocation. In recurring audits, primary attention is given to the vouching of entries to plant asset accounts and verifying the reasonableness, accuracy, and consistency of depreciation. For current liabilities, the auditor's primary risk is that creditor claims are understated. Considerable reliance is placed on examination of documents in the verification of current liability balances.

REVIEW QUESTIONS

13-1. Identify the audit procedures that enable an auditor to verify the (a) existence or occurrence and (b) valuation or allocation objectives for inventory balances.

13-2. For the observation of inventories, indicate (a) when this test is required, (b) the steps to be performed, and (c) the timing and extent of the test.

13-3. Identify the items that should be (a) included in the inventory-taking plan and (b) covered in observing inventories.

13-4. When statistical sampling methods are used in determining inventories, what additional requirements must be met by the auditor?

13-5. What alternative procedures are available to the auditor when he is unable to observe (a) the ending inventory and (b) the beginning inventory?

13-6. Why is it necessary for the auditor to make tests of the client's inventory counts?

13–7.   What procedures are required when inventories stored in a public warehouse are material?

13–8.   a. Explain the auditor's responsibility for the quality and condition of the inventory.
          b. Indicate how the auditor can discover obsolete and slow-moving items.

13–9.   What steps are involved in verifying inventory pricing?

13–10.   a. What information is required to determine sample size in a PPS variables sampling plan of inventory balances?
          b. Assuming the auditor has calculated the projected error in the population, what additional information is required to determine the achieved upper error limit?

13–11.   What data and program(s) are needed to use the computer in an inventory pricing test?

13–12.   What are the principal differences between the audit of plant assets and current assets?

13–13.   What audit procedures are performed to determine (a) rights and obligations and (b) valuation or allocation of plant assets?

13–14.   Identify the relationships that may be used in making an analytical review of property, plant, and equipment.

13–15.   What procedures may be helpful in determining whether all plant asset retirements have been recorded?

13–16.   What factors are involved in determining whether a company has been consistent in recording repair and maintenance expenditures?

13–17.   Identify the principal differences between tests of asset balances and tests of current liability balances.

13–18.   a. What audit procedures are used to verify the existence or occurrence and completeness of accounts payable?
          b. How may the auditor obtain evidence as to the valuation and completeness of accrued wages payable?

13–19.   What purposes are served by examining payments to creditors subsequent to the statement date?

13–20.   What procedures are useful to the auditor in searching for unrecorded accounts payable?

COMPREHENSIVE QUESTIONS

13–21.   In performing tests of balances on inventory balances, the auditor should recognize that the following potential errors may occur or exist:

1. All inventory items are not counted or tagged.
2. Extension errors are made on the client's inventory summaries.
3. Purchases received near the balance sheet date may be included in the physical count but may not be booked.
4. Obsolete and damaged goods may not be recognized.
5. Inventory stored in a public warehouse may not exist.
6. Client personnel may incorrectly count the inventory.
7. The lower of cost or market method may be incorrectly applied.
8. Empty containers or hollow squares may be included in the inventory.
9. Goods held on consignment may be included as inventory.
10. Losses on purchases commitments may not be recognized.

Required
a. Identify the audit procedure that should enable the auditor to detect each error.
b. Indicate the audit objective to which the audit procedure relates.
c. Identify the type of evidential matter obtained by the audit procedure.

13–22. Often an important aspect of a CPA's examination of financial statements is his observation of the taking of the physical inventory.

Required
a. What are the general objectives or purposes of the CPA's observation of the taking of the physical inventory? (Do not discuss the procedures or techniques involved in making the observation.)
b. For what purposes does the CPA make and record test counts of inventory quantities during his observation of the taking of the physical inventory? Discuss.
c. A number of companies employ outside service companies which specialize in counting, pricing, extending, and footing inventories. These service companies usually furnish a certificate attesting to the value of the inventory.

Assuming that the service company took the inventory on the balance sheet date,

1. How much reliance, if any, can the CPA place on the inventory certificate of outside specialists? Discuss.
2. What effect, if any, would the inventory certificate of outside specialists have upon the type of report the CPA would render? Discuss.
3. What reference, if any, would the CPA make to the certificate of outside specialists in his audit report?

AICPA

13–23. In connection with his examination of the financial statements of Knutson Products Co., an assembler of home appliances, for the year ended May 31, 19X0, Ray Abel, CPA, is reviewing with Knutson's controller the plans for a physical inventory at the Company warehouse on May 31. (*Note:* In answering the two parts of this question do not discuss procedures for the physical inventory of work in process, inventory pricing, or other audit steps not directly related to the physical inventory taking.)

1. Finished appliances, unassembled parts, and supplies are stored in the warehouse, which is attached to Knutson's assembly plant. The plant will operate during the count. On May 30, 19X0, the warehouse will deliver to the plant the estimated quantities of unassembled parts and supplies required for May 31 production, but there may be emergency requisitions on May 31. During the count the warehouse will continue to receive parts and supplies and to ship finished appliances. However, appliances completed on May 31 will be held in the plant until after the physical inventory.
2. Warehouse employees will join with accounting department employees in counting the inventory. The inventory takers will use a tag system.

Required
a. What procedures should the company establish to insure that the inventory count includes all items that should be included and that nothing is counted twice?
b. What instructions should the company give to the inventory takers?

AICPA

13–24. Ace Corporation does not conduct a complete annual physical count of purchased parts and supplies in its principal warehouse but uses statistical sampling instead to estimate the year-end inventory. Ace maintains a perpetual inventory record of parts and supplies and believes that statistical sampling is highly effective in determining inventory values and is sufficiently reliable to make a physical count of each item of inventory unnecessary.

Required
a. Identify the audit procedures that should be used by the independent auditor that change or are in addition to normal required audit procedures when a client

utilizes statistical sampling to determine inventory value and does not conduct a 100 percent annual physical count of inventory items.

   b. List the normal audit procedures that should be performed to verify physical quantities whenever a client conducts a periodic physical count of all or part of its inventory.

AICPA (adapted)

13-25. Your audit client, Household Appliances, Inc. operates a retail store in the center of town. Because of lack of storage space Household keeps inventory that is not on display in a public warehouse outside of town. The warehouseman receives inventory from suppliers and, on request from your client by a shipping advice or telephone call, delivers merchandise to customers or to the retail outlet.

The accounts are maintained at the retail store by a bookkeeper. Each month the warehouseman sends to the bookkeeper a quantity report indicating opening balance, receipts, deliveries, and ending balance. The bookkeeper compares book quantities on hand at month-end with the warehouseman's report and adjusts his books to agree with the report. No physical counts of the merchandise at the warehouse were made by your client during the year.

You are now preparing for your examination of the current year's financial statements in this recurring engagement. Last year, you rendered an unqualified opinion.

Required
   a. Prepare an audit program for the observation of the physical inventory of Household Appliances, Inc. (1) at the retail outlet and (2) at the warehouse.
   b. As part of your examination would you verify inventory quantities at the warehouse by means of

      1. A warehouse confirmation? Why?
      2. Test counts of inventory at the warehouse? Why?

   c. Since the bookkeeper adjusts books to quantities shown on the warehouseman's report each month, what significance would you attach to the year-end adjustments if they were substantial? Discuss.

AICPA

13-26. Decker, CPA, is performing an examination of the financial statements of Allright Wholesale Sales, Inc., for the year ended December 31, 19X0. Allright has been in business for many years and has never had its financial statements audited. Decker has gained satisfaction with respect to the ending inventory and is considering alternative audit procedures to gain satisfaction with respect to management's representations concerning the beginning inventory, which was not observed.

Allright sells only one product (bottled brand X beer) and maintains perpetual inventory records. In addition, Allrights takes physical inventory counts monthly. Decker has already confirmed purchases with the manufacturer and has decided to concentrate on evaluating the reliability of perpetual inventory records and performing analytical review procedures to the extent that prior years' unaudited records will enable such procedures to be performed.

Required
What are the audit tests, including analytical review procedures, which Decker should apply in evaluating the reliability of perpetual inventory records and gaining satisfaction with respect to the January 1, 19X0, inventory?

AICPA

13-27. As auditor for the Court Company, you decide to use variables sampling to estimate the total cost of an inventory of 1,150 items which has a net book value of $260,400. The auditor decides to use a sampling plan that will provide a risk of 5% that a fairly stated book value is not rejected as being materially misstated. Based on past experience, it is believed that the standard deviation of the population is $120. The audit estimate is to be made with a tolerable error of $25,000 and a risk of incorrect acceptance of 10 percent.

Required
a. Calculate the required sample size, assuming sampling without replacement.
b. Without prejudice to your answer in (a), assume a sample of 130 with a total audited value of $28,600 and a standard deviation of $120. Compute the achieved allowance for sampling risk.
c. Is the book value fairly stated? Explain.

13–28. In auditing the annual physical inventory being taken by employees in the Sutter Company, you decide to use PPS sampling for variables to estimate the cost of the inventory. Thus far, the following information has been compiled:

Book value of inventory	$2,078,534
Tolerable error	$200,000
Population size	6,511
Estimated standard deviation	$100
Desired risk of incorrect acceptance	10%
Anticipated error	$50,000

Required
a. Calculate the necessary sample size.
b. Ignore the answer to (a) above. Instead, assume that 121 items in inventory are selected for physical count, tests of pricing and other appropriate audit procedures. Assume that the total projected error of this sample is $36,300 and that the allowance for sampling risk is $149,500. May the auditor conclude that the book value of the inventory is fairly stated?

13–29. An auditor is conducting an examination of the financial statements of a wholesale cosmetics distributor with an inventory consisting of thousands of individual items. The distributor keeps its inventory in its own distribution center and in two public warehouses. An inventory computer file is maintained on a computer disk and at the end of each day the file is updated. Each record of the inventory file contains the following data:

1. Item number.
2. Location of item.
3. Description of item.
4. Quantity on hand.
5. Cost per item.
6. Date of last purchase.
7. Date of last sale.
8. Quantity sold during year.

The auditor is planning to observe the distributor's physical count of inventories as of a given date. The auditor will have available a computer tape of the data on the inventory file on the date of the physical count and a general purpose computer software package.

Required
The auditor is planning to perform basic inventory auditing procedures. Identify the basic inventory auditing procedures and describe how the use of the general purpose software package and the tape of the inventory file data might be helpful to the auditor in performing such auditing procedures. Organize your answer as follows:

Basic Inventory Auditing Procedure	How General Purpose Computer Software Package and Tape of the Inventory File Data Might Be Helpful
1. Observe the physical count, making and recording test counts where applicable.	Determining which items are to be test counted by selecting a random sample of a representative number of items from the inventory file as of the date of the physical count.

AICPA

13-30. Rivers, CPA, is the auditor for a manufacturing company with a balance sheet that includes the caption "Property, Plant & Equipment." Rivers has been asked by the company's management if audit adjustments or reclassifications are required for the following material items that have been included in or excluded from "Property, Plant & Equipment":

1. A tract of land was acquired during the year. The land is the future site of the client's new headquarters, which will be constructed in the following year. Commissions were paid to the real estate agent used to acquire the land, and expenditures were made to relocate the previous owner's equipment. These commissions and expenditures were expensed and are excluded from "Property, Plant & Equipment."
2. Clearing costs were incurred to make the land ready for construction. These costs were included in "Property, Plant & Equipment."
3. During the land clearing process, timber and gravel were recovered and sold. The proceeds from the sale were recorded as other income and are excluded from "Property, Plant & Equipment."
4. A group of machines was purchased under a royalty agreement which provides royalty payments based on units of production from the machines. The cost of the machines, freight costs, unloading charges, and royalty payments were capitalized and are included in "Property, Plant & Equipment."

Required
a. Identify the audit objectives for "Property, Plant & Equipment" and indicate the principal audit procedures pertaining to each.
b. Indicate whether each of the items numbered 1 to 4 above requires one or more audit adjustments or reclassifications, and explain why such adjustments or reclassifications are required or not required. Organize your answer as follows:

Item Number	Is Audit Adjustment or Reclassification Required?		Reasons Why Audit Adjustment or Reclassification Is Required or Not Required
	Yes or No		

AICPA (adapted)

13-31. In connection with the annual examination of Johnson Corporation, you have been assigned to audit the fixed assets. The company maintains a detailed property ledger for all fixed assets. You prepared an audit program for the balances of property, plant, and equipment but have yet to prepare one for accumulated depreciation and depreciation expense.

Required

Prepare a separate comprehensive audit program for the accumulated depreciation and depreciation expense accounts.

AICPA

13–32. You are engaged in the examination of the financial statements of the Ute Corporation for the year ended December 31, 19X3. The following schedules for the property, plant, and equipment and related allowance for depreciation accounts have been prepared by the client. You have checked your prior year's audit working papers.

Ute Corp.
Analysis of Property, Plant and Equipment and Related
Allowance for Depreciation Accounts
Year Ended December 31, 19X3

Assets

Description	Final 12/31/X2	Addi-tions	Retire-ments	Per Books 12/31/X3
Land	$ 22,500	$ 5,000		$ 27,500
Buildings	120,000	17,500		137,500
Machinery and equipment	385,000	40,400	$26,000	399,400
	$527,500	$62,900	$26,000	$564,400

Allowance for Depreciation

Description	Final 12/31/X2	Addi-tions*	Retire-ments	Per Books 12/31/X3
Buildings	$ 60,000	$ 5,150		$ 65,150
Machinery and equipment	173,250	39,220		212,470
	$233,250	$44,370		$277,620

* Depreciation expense for the year.

Your examination reveals the following information:

1. All equipment is depreciated on the straight line basis (no salvage value taken into consideration) based on the following estimated lives: buildings, 25 years; all other items, 10 years. The company's policy is to take one-half year's depreciation on all asset acquisitions and disposals during the year.
2. On April 1, the company entered into a ten-year lease contract for a die casting machine with annual rentals of $5,000 payable in advance every April 1. The lease is cancellable by either party (sixty days' written notice is required) and there is no option to renew the lease or buy the equipment at the end of the lease. The estimated useful life of the machine is ten years with no salvage value. The company recorded the die casting machine in the machinery and equipment account at $40,400, the present discounted value at the date of the lease, and $2,020, applicable to the machine, has been included in depreciation expense for the year.
3. The company completed the construction of a wing on the plant building on June 30. The useful life of the building was not extended by this addition. The lowest

construction bid received was $17,500, the amount recorded in the Buildings account. Company personnel were used to construct the addition at a cost of $16,000 (materials, $7,500; labor, $5,500; and overhead, $3,000).

4. On August 18, $5,000 was paid for paving and fencing a portion of land owned by the company and used as a parking lot for employees. The expenditure was charged to the Land account.

5. The amount shown in the machinery and equipment asset retirement column represents cash received on September 5 upon disposal of a machine purchased in July 19X1 for $48,000. The bookkeeper recorded depreciation expense of $3,500 on this machine in 19X3.

6. Crux City donated land and building appraised at $10,000 and $40,000 respectively to the Ute Corporation for a plant. On September 1, the company began operating the plant. Since no costs were involved, the bookkeeper made no entry for the above transaction.

Required

a. Prepare the formal adjusting journal entries that you would suggest at December 31, 19X3 to adjust the accounts for the above transactions. Disregard income tax implications. The books have not been closed. Computations should be rounded off to the nearest dollar.

b. Prepare a schedule for property, plant, and equipment and accumulated depreciation using the working paper reference *P*.

AICPA (adapted)

13–33. Mincin, CPA, is the auditor of the Raleigh Corporation. Mincin is considering the audit work to be performed in the accounts payable area for the current year's engagement.

The prior year's papers show that confirmation requests were mailed to 100 of Raleigh's 1,000 suppliers. The selected suppliers were based on Mincin's sample that was designated to select accounts with large dollar balances. A substantial number of hours were spent by Raleigh and Mincin resolving relatively minor differences between the confirmation replies and Raleigh's accounting records. Alternate audit procedures were used for those suppliers who did not respond to the confirmation requests.

Required

a. Identify the accounts payable audit objectives that Mincin must consider in determining the audit procedures to be followed.

b. Identify situations when Mincin should use accounts payable confirmations and discuss whether Mincin is required to use them.

c. Discuss why the use of large dollar balances as the basis for selecting accounts payable for confirmation might not be the most efficient approach and indicate what more efficient procedures could be followed when selecting accounts payable for confirmation.

AICPA

13–34. You were in the final stages of your examination of the financial statements of Ozine Corporation for the year ended December 31, 19X0 when you were consulted by the Corporation's president who believes there is no point in your examining the 19X1 voucher register and testing data in support of 19X1 entries. He stated that (a) bills pertaining to 19X0 which were received too late to be included in the December voucher register were recorded as of the year-end by the Corporation by journal entry, (b) the internal auditor made tests after the year-end, and (c) he would furnish you with a letter certifying that there were no unrecorded liabilities.

Required

a. Should a CPA's test for unrecorded liabilities be affected by the fact that the client made a journal entry to record 19X0 bills which were received late? Explain.

b. Should a CPA's test for unrecorded liabilities be affected by the fact that a letter is obtained in which a responsible management official certifies that to the best of his knowledge all liabilities have been recorded? Explain.

c. Should a CPA's test for unrecorded liabilities be eliminated or reduced because of the internal audit tests? Explain.

d. Assume that the Corporation, which handled some government contracts, had no internal auditor but that an auditor for a federal agency spent three weeks auditing the records and was just completing his work at this time. How would the CPA's unrecorded liability test be affected by the work of the auditor for a federal agency?

e. What sources in addition to the 19X1 voucher register should the CPA consider to locate possible unrecorded liabilities?

AICPA

13–35.* Your client, Special Cases, Inc., took its physical inventory at November 30, one month before its December 31 year-end.

The client compiled the inventory as of November 30 and "carried forward" the inventory amounts to December 31.

You were present at the taking of the physical inventory and you satisfied yourself that the inventory was properly counted. All goods received up to and including November 30 were counted. Listings prepared at the time of your observation have been traced to the compiled inventory and no differences were noted. The compiled physical inventory at November 30 amounted to $582,000.

At the time of your observation and from subsequent review of the company's records, you have obtained the following cutoff information:

Receipts (Part No.)	Amount	Received	Invoice Date	Date Recorded
3795	$15,000	11/29	11/21	12/1
4683	24,000	11/30	11/29	11/30
2904	15,000	11/25	11/17	11/27
1316X	1,200	12/1	11/30	12/10
1781	3,500	11/30	11/28	12/3
1415	1,600	12/1	11/29	11/30

The following shows the activity in the raw material inventory account from November 30 to December 31:

	Dr.	Cr.
Balance at November 30	$625,000	
Adjustment to physical inventory		$ 43,000
Purchases—Part No. 3795	15,000	
3612	25,000	
1781	3,500	
1316X	1,200	
4714	21,500	
Relief of inventory for material transferred to work in process		117,000
Balance at December 31	531,200	

Required

a. List those procedures you would employ in testing an inventory "carryforward."

b. List the adjustments, if any, that should be made at December 31. Compute the actual difference between the book and physical inventory at November 30.

c. State why it is desirable to test the shipping and receiving cutoff at November 30 and December 31.

d. List any internal control weaknesses noted from the facts presented.

CASE STUDY

13–36.* Your firm has been engaged to examine the financial statements of Brown Appliances, Inc. for the year ended December 31. The company manufactures major appliances sold to the general public through dealers and distributors.

You are to audit the trade accounts payable of a division of Brown Appliances, Inc. The trade accounts payable of this division aggregate $2.5 million, which is 60 percent of total accounts payable. Accounts payable total 40 percent of total liabilities and 30 percent of total liabilities and stockholders' equity. Net income for the year is $3 million.

Excerpts from the internal control memorandum follow:

"Invoices from suppliers are received in the purchasing department, where they are matched with receiving reports and checked to the applicable purchase order for quantities and pricing. Invoices and receiving reports are then forwarded to the accounting department for clerical checking and final approval for payment.

"On the payment date (the seventh working day of the month), invoices with attached receiving reports are separated into two groups: one group of invoices with receiving reports dated in the prior month, the other group with receiving reports dated in the current month. The check register is then prepared, with each group having a separate total and check number sequence. The accounts payable for monthly financial statement purposes is the total of the check register for invoices with receiving reports dated in the prior month. A voucher register is not maintained.

"The purchasing department holds unmatched receiving reports and unmatched invoices.

"Cutoff procedures as established by the company appear adequate; however, the company makes it a practice not to record inventory in transit.

"Vendors' statements received by the company are forwarded to a clerk in the accounting department. The clerk does not check all charges appearing on the vendors' statements, but does reconcile all old outstanding charges appearing thereon."

An accounts payable listing has been prepared by the company for the auditors. As explained above, this listing was prepared from the check register of December charges paid in January, and shows vendor, check number, invoice date, date paid, and amount. A quick review of the listing reveals the following:

1. January-dated invoices amounting to $200,000 appear on the listing payable to Talley and Park Advertising Agency, for advertising to appear in *Better Homes and Gardens* magazine in February and March. This was included in the year-end accounts payable listing at the request of the vice-president of advertising because he said he wanted to more closely match advertising department budgeted expenses with actual expenditures for the year. The distribution was made to advertising expense.

2. Amounts appear on the listing as payments for payrolls, payroll taxes, other taxes, and profit-sharing plans.
3. No amounts appear on the listing for legal or accounting services.

Required

Discuss the problems and procedures involved in auditing this company's accounts payable. Specifically discuss (a) the auditing procedures you would use in your examination and (b) the adjustments you would recommend to be made to the accounts payable listing.

14 Substantive Tests of Investing and Financing Cycle Balances

STUDY OBJECTIVES

The study objectives of this chapter are to acquire an understanding of transactions in the investing and financing cycles and the auditor's responsibilities for reviewing internal controls and examining account balances in these cycles. To achieve these objectives, it is necessary for the reader to

- Understand the transactions that are included in the investing and financing cycles.
- Comprehend the internal accounting control objectives and principles applicable to each cycle.
- Realize the applicability of the second standard of field work to these cycles.
- Know the audit procedures that are applicable to the verification of investing and financing cycle balances.

T hree cycles have been discussed in this book: revenue, expenditure, and production. The remaining cycles to be considered are the investing cycle and the financing cycle. These cycles embrace the major nonoperating activities of many companies.

The format of this chapter differs from the preceding tests of balances chapters. First, brief consideration is given to internal control principles and the study and evaluation of internal control. Then, comprehensive attention is directed to substantive tests of account balances. Each cycle is discussed separately.

THE INVESTING CYCLE

An entity's investing cycle pertains to the activities relating to the ownership of securities issued by other entities. The securities may be in the form of certificates of deposit (CDs), preferred and common stock, or corporate and government bonds. Consideration will be given here only to investments in common stock and corporate bonds held either as a short- or long-term investment.

Basic Considerations

The following are basic to an understanding of the events and transactions in this cycle:

Functions

Executing
- Purchasing securities
- Receiving periodic revenue
- Selling securities

Recording
- Journalizing and posting transactions
- Updating investment ledger

Custody
- Protecting securities
- Maintaining correctness of investment balances

Common documents

- *Stock certificate.* An engraved form showing the number of shares of stock owned by a shareholder in a corporation.

- *Bond certificate.* An engraved form showing the number of bonds owned by a bondholder.
- *Bond indenture.* A contract stating the terms of the bond issue between the bondholder and the issuing entity.
- *Broker's advice.* A statement from a broker specifying the details of an investing transaction.

Accounting records

- *Books of original entry.* General journal, cash receipts journal, voucher register, and check register.
- *Subsidiary ledger.* Investments (or securities).
- *General ledger accounts.* Marketable securities, investments in stock (or bonds), interest revenue, dividend revenue, earnings from investments under equity method, gains (losses) on sales of securities.[1]

Materiality and Risk

Marketable securities held as short-term investments often are material to a company's short-term solvency, but income from such securities is seldom significant to the results of operations of an industrial or commercial company. Securities held as long-term investments may be material to both the balance sheet and income statement. The risk of errors or irregularities in investing transactions is generally low because of infrequent transactions and the participation of one or more company officers in executing the transactions.

The following discussion of internal control, compliance tests, and substantive tests applies equally to marketable securities and long-term investments in securities, except as specifically indicated.

Internal Accounting Control Objectives

The three operative objectives of internal accounting control are applicable to the investing cycle. It will be recalled that these objectives consist of proper (1) executing of transactions, (2) recording of transactions, and (3) custody of assets. The assignment of departmental responsibility and specific control objectives for each function in this cycle are as follows:

---

[1] Financial Accounting Standards Board, *Statement of Financial Accounting Standards No. 12, Accounting for Certain Marketable Securities* (Stamford: Financial Accounting Standards Board, 1975) (hereinafter referred to and cited as *FASB Statement No. 12*). *FASB Statement No. 12* requires additional accounts in reporting marketable equity securities at the lower of aggregate cost or market.

FUNCTION	DEPARTMENT	SPECIFIC ACCOUNTING CONTROL OBJECTIVE
Executing		
Purchasing securities	Treasurer	Purchases are made in accordance with management's authorizations
Receiving periodic revenue	Cashier	Dividend and interest checks are promptly deposited intact
Selling securities	Treasurer	Sales are made in accordance with management's authorizations
Recording		
Journalizing and posting transactions	General Accounting	Transactions and events are correctly recorded as to amount, classification, and accounting period
Updating investment ledger	Investment Ledger Accounting	Transactions are promptly and correctly posted to individual accounts
Custody		
Protecting securities	Treasurer	Access to securities is restricted to authorized personnel
Maintaining correctness of investment balances	General Accounting	Recorded balances are compared with existing assets at reasonable intervals

The basic features of internal accounting control are explained below.

Securities Transactions Are Properly Executed

Three principles of internal control are applicable in executing these transactions.

Authorization procedures. The purchase and sale of securities may be executed on specific authorization of the board of directors. In such case, the corporate minutes should include the authorization. If authorization is delegated by the board of directors, it usually is assigned to a corporate officer, such as the treasurer or vice president of finance. Evidence of such authorizations should be in writing and signed by the officer.

Segregation of functions. The separation of duties in executing transactions, is illustrated above. Controls over the receipt of periodic revenue follows the procedures described for cash receipts in Chapter 8.

Documentation procedures. Documentation of purchases of securities includes authorizations, broker's advices, paid vouchers, canceled checks, and the stock or bond certificates. The latter should be in the name of the company rather than in the name of the custodian. For sales of securities, authorizations, broker's advices, and cash remittance advices should be available. The latter form of documentation should also be present for the receipt of cash dividends and interest.

Securities Transactions Are Properly Recorded

The internal control principles applicable to this objective are as follows.

Segregation of functions. Accounting personnel who record investment transactions should not perform any other functions pertaining to such transactions. In addition, personnel who journalize and post transactions to the general ledger should not update the investment ledger.

Accounting records and procedures. When a client has an investment portfolio, it is preferable to have an investment subsidiary ledger with an account for each security. For large portfolios, the subsidiary ledger may be maintained by electronic data processing (EDP).

Custody of Securities Is Properly Maintained

There are four internal control principles that apply to this objective.

Physical controls and authorization procedures. Because securities are vulnerable to theft and misappropriation, physical controls should be used in protecting these assets. Securities should be kept in a safe place, such as in a bank safety deposit box or with an independent custodian. Direct access to storage areas should be limited to authorized personnel only. Many companies also require the presence of two responsible persons when there is direct access to a safety deposit box in order to prevent unauthorized removal of securities. To minimize the likelihood of unauthorized indirect access to securities, every withdrawal request should be in writing and be signed by two company officers, each acting within the scope of his authority.

Independent internal verification and segregation of functions. The principle of independent internal verification is also applicable to this objective. Periodically, securities owned by a company should be counted and compared with the accounting records by personnel who do not have other duties pertaining to the securities.

Study and Evaluation of Internal Control

As in the case of other major classes of transactions, the auditor must make a preliminary review of the flow of transactions through the accounting system. When there are few investment transactions, the auditor may decide to proceed directly to substantive tests of investment balances after meeting this requirement. This decision may be based on cost-benefit considerations rather than on the absence of effective controls. When a client has an extensive investment portfolio and numerous transactions, the auditor may decide to complete his review of internal control and perform compliance tests on the controls expected to be relied upon.

Substantive Tests of Investment Balances

An audit program for testing account balances in the investing cycle is shown in Figure 14-1. A discussion of the audit procedures is given below.

Clerical Accuracy

As in the case of other account balances, this objective is met by verifying the mechanical accuracy of supporting schedules and reconciling data on the schedules with ledger data. A client-prepared schedule for the investing cycle is a listing of securities owned at the statement date.

Existence or Occurrence and Rights and Obligations

The auditor is expected to obtain evidence of the (1) existence of securities at or near the balance sheet date, (2) ownership of the securities, and (3) occurrence of securities transactions during the year. The audit procedures applicable to this objective are as follows:

Inspect and count securities on hand. This test ordinarily is performed simultaneously with the auditor's count of cash and other negotiable instruments. As in the case of cash, (1) the custodian of the securities should be present throughout the count, (2) a receipt should be obtained from the custodian when the securities are returned, and (3) all securities should be controlled by the auditor until the count is completed.

In inspecting securities, the auditor should observe such matters as the certificate number on the document, name of owner (which should be the client, either directly or through endorsement), description of the security, number of shares of stock, par or face value, and name of issuer. These data should be recorded as part of the auditor's analysis of the investment account. Figure 14-2 illustrates an audit working paper for marketable equity securities. For securities purchased in prior years, the data should be compared with those shown on last year's audit working papers. A lack of agreement between the certificate numbers may be indicative of unauthorized transactions for those securities.

Securities on hand may be stored for safekeeping in several different locations. In such case, either simultaneous counts should be made at the locations or the securities should be kept under seal until all locations have been counted. For example, banks will generally seal a safety deposit box at the client's request and will confirm to the auditor that there was no access to the box during the counting period. When the count is not made on or within a day of the balance sheet, the auditor should prepare a reconciliation from the date of count to the statement date by reviewing the intervening security transactions.

Confirm securities held by others. Securities held by outsiders for safekeeping must be positively confirmed by the auditor. Confirmations should be requested as of the date securities held by the client are counted. The confirmation process for securities is identical with the steps required in confirming receivables. Thus, the auditor must control the mailings and receive the responses directly from the custodian. The data confirmed are the same as the data that should be noted by the auditor when he is able to inspect the securities

Securities may also be held by creditors as collateral against loans or be placed in escrow by court order. In such cases, the confirmation should be sent to the indicated custodian.

Examine documentation in client's files. This test is directed primarily at the occurrence of security transactions. Documentation in the files relative to this objective includes broker's advices, vouchers, "paid" checks, and remittance advices for dividends and interest.

TYPE OF TEST: Substantive CYCLE: Investing	PURPOSE: Validity and Propriety of Balances ACCOUNTS: Marketable Securities, Long-term Investments, and Related Income Statement Accounts

A. CLERICAL ACCURACY:

　1. Foot schedules of securities.
　2. Reconcile general ledger balances with data on schedules.

B. EXISTENCE OR OCCURRENCE AND RIGHTS AND OBLIGATIONS:

　1. Inspect and count securities on hand.
　2. Confirm securities held by others.
　3. Examine documentation in client's files.

C. COMPLETENESS:

　1. Make analytical review.

D. VALUATION OR ALLOCATION:

　1. Vouch entries in investment accounts.
　2. Recalculate revenue earned.
　3. Review documentation concerning market values.

E. STATEMENT PRESENTATION AND DISCLOSURE:

　1. Make inquiries of management and review documentation as to pledging.
　2. Compare statement presentation with GAAP.

FIGURE 14–1. Audit Program: Investment Cycle Balances

Acct. # 415 and 425

Williams Company
Marketable Equity Securities
12/31/X1

Prepared by: O.E.B. Date: 1/3/X2
Reviewed by: R.C.L. Date: 1/10/X2

#2

Description	Cert. No.	Date Acquired	No. of Shares	Cost per Share	Balance 1/1/X1	Purchases	Sales	Balance 12/31/X1	Market Price Per Share	Market Price Total 12/31/X1	Div. Income
√ Atwood Mfg. Co.	C21779	9/21/X0	800	22	19800 √			19800 ∧	27.50 ∧	22050 ∧	675
√ Metropolitan Edison Co.	M82931	9/21/X0	500	33.20	16600 √		16600 ∅	∧	—	—	126.75
√ Pacific Power, Inc.	51942	2/4/X1	200	18.50		37000 ∅		37000 ∧	17.00 ∧	3400 ∧	—
√ Warrington Corp.	7393G	7/8/X0	400	27.25	10900 √			10900 ∧	29.00 ∧	11700 ∧	120
					59500 √	19800 √	16600	42700 ∅		61350 ∧	2792
					F	F	F	FF		F	F
								✗			✗

√ – Examined stock certificate or obtained Trust Co.
√ – Traced to prior year work paper
✗ – Traced to general ledger balance
F – Footed
FF – Crossfooted
∧ – Extension checked
∅ – Traced to broker advices and board of directors authorization
– Per market quotation in 1/2/X2 Wall Street Journal
D – Dividend rates checked to Standard and Poor; Dividends received traced to cash receipts journal

Aggregate market exceeded aggregate cost of securities at both beginning and end of year.
Therefore, no allowance for declines in market value.

FIGURE 14–2. Marketable Equity Securities Working Paper

Completeness

All investing cycle transactions that have occurred should be recorded in the accounts and statements. The auditor generally relies on cutoff tests of cash transactions to meet this objective. In some cases, the auditor may also use analytical review.

Make analytical review. This review may involve the interrelationship of specific accounts and/or comparisons with budget expectations and prior year's results. Account relationships involve the reconciliation of bond interest revenue with interest rates on bonds held as an investment. The investigation of unreconciliable items and unusual fluctuations may reveal unrecorded transactions.

Valuation or Allocation

This audit objective relates to the cost and carrying value of short- and long-term investments and the propriety of related income statement amounts. The audit tests used in meeting the valuation or allocation objective are explained below.

Vouch entries in investment accounts. The starting point in vouching is to establish the cost of securities. This is done by reference to broker's advices, invoices, and paid checks. Subsequently, the auditor should vouch all changes in carrying value.

Common stock held as a long-term investment may be accounted for under either the cost method or the equity method of accounting. When an investor either directly or indirectly owns 20 percent or more of the voting stock of an investee there is a presumption that, in the absence of evidence to the contrary, the investor has the ability to exercise significant influence over the investee.[2] In such cases, the equity method of accounting should be used by the investor.

To obtain evidence as to the ability of the investor's management to exercise significant influence over the investee, the auditor should make inquiry of management and determine the circumstances that support management's conclusion. When an investor accounts for a long-term investment in common stock contrary to the applicable presumption, the auditor should obtain evidence that the presumption has been overcome. In addition, he should determine that appropriate disclosure is made in the financial statements.

For investments accounted for under the equity method, audited financial statements of the investee generally constitute sufficient evidential mat-

[2] Accounting Principles Board, *APB Opinion No. 18, The Equity Method of Accounting for Investments in Common Stock* (New York: American Institute of Certified Public Accountants, 1971).

ter as to the underlying net assets and the results of operations of the investee. Audited financial statements also represent competent evidence for investments in bonds and similar debt obligations.[3]

Recalculate revenue earned. Income from investments is verified by documentary evidence and by recalculation. Dividends on all stocks listed on stock exchanges and many others are included in dividends record books published by many investment services. The auditor can independently verify the dividend revenue by reference to the declaration date, amount, and payment date shown in the record book.

Interest earned and interest collected on investments in bonds can be verified by examining the interest rates and payment dates indicated in the bond indenture. In addition, the auditor also reviews the client's amortization schedule for bond premium and discount and recalculates the amount amortized, if any. The verification of these accounts is usually incorporated into the schedule of investments, as illustrated in Figure 14-2.

Review documentation concerning market values. Marketable equity securities, such as common stock, should be valued at the lower of aggregate cost or market,[4] and marketable debt securities, such as government and corporate bonds, should be stated at the lower of cost or a permanent decline in market value. The value of securities at the balance sheet date may be obtained from market quotations. The auditor should verify market quotations by reference to published security prices on stock exchanges. If published data are not available, the auditor should obtain direct confirmation from an independent broker.

When market quotations are based on a reasonably broad and active market, they ordinarily constitute sufficient competent evidential matter as to the current market value of the securities.

Statement Presentation and Disclosure

The proper presentation of investments in securities in the financial statements requires:

- Identification and classification of the different types of investments in the balance sheet.
- Recognition of realized revenues, gains, and losses in the income statement.
- Recognition of allowance for market declines and unrealized gains and losses associated therewith.
- Disclosure of the basis and methods of accounting used.
- Disclosure of liens, if any.

---

[3] Auditing Standards Board, *Codification of Statements on Auditing Standards* (New York: American Institute of Certified Public Accountants, 1983), Auditing Section 332.05 (hereinafter referred to and cited as AU §).

[4] *FASB Statement No. 12, op. cit.*

The substantive tests described above should provide evidence of the first four items. The inspection of the minutes and loan agreements should reveal the existence of liens. In addition, the auditor should make inquiries of management as to its intent in holding the securities. On the basis of the evidence obtained, the auditor determines whether the proposed statement presentations and disclosures are appropriate.

THE FINANCING CYCLE

An entity's financing cycle consists of transactions pertaining to the acquisition of capital funds through issuance of long-term debt and capital stock and the subsequent redemption or reacquisition of these securities. Long-term debt includes borrowings from notes, mortgages, and bonds; capital stock includes preferred and common stock. The issuance of bonds and common stock typically represents the primary sources of capital funds. Accordingly, attention will be directed primarily on these two sources of financing.

Basic Considerations

The following are basic to an understanding of the events and transactions in the financing cycle:

Functions

  Executing
- Issuing bonds and capital stock
- Paying bond interest and cash dividends
- Redeeming and reacquiring bonds and capital stock

  Recording
- Journalizing and posting transactions
- Updating subsidiary ledgers

  Custody
- Maintaining correctness of debt and equity balances

Accounting records

- *Subsidiary ledgers*. Bondholders' and stockholders'.
- *General ledger accounts*. Bonds payable, premium (discount) on bonds, interest expense, gain (loss) on retirement of bonds, preferred stock, common stock, treasury stock, paid-in capital, retained earnings, dividends, and dividends payable.

The common documents and books of original entry pertaining to the financing cycle are similar to those described for the investing cycle.

Materiality and Risk

There is considerable variation in the importance of long-term debt to the fair presentation of financial position. In some major corporations, long-term debt is immaterial to total liabilities and stockholders' equity, whereas, in many public utilities, such liabilities may represent more than 50 percent of the total claims on corporate assets. Stockholders' equity clearly is a material component of a balance sheet. The income statement effects of financing cycle transactions for a manufacturing company are generally immaterial, whereas the effect of dividends on the retained earnings statement is often material. The disclosure requirements for long-term debt and stockholders' equity are usually significant.

The risk of errors or irregularities in executing and recording financing cycle transactions is usually low. In many companies these transactions occur infrequently, except for the payment of dividends and interest which are handled by outside agents. In addition, board of director authorizations are required for most transactions, and company officers participate in their execution.

Internal Accounting Control Objectives

Each of the operative objectives of internal accounting control is applicable to the financing cycle. In order to meet these objectives, it is useful to identify the following specific accounting control objectives and assignment of responsibility for each function in the cycle:

FUNCTION	DEPARTMENT	SPECIFIC ACCOUNTING CONTROL OBJECTIVE
Executing		
Issuing bonds and capital stock	Treasurer	Issues are made in accordance with board of directors authorizations and legal requirements, and proceeds are promptly deposited intact
Paying bond interest and cash dividends	Treasurer	Payments are made to proper payees in accordance with board of directors or management authorizations
Redeeming and reacquiring bonds and capital stock	Treasurer	Transactions are executed in accordance with board of directors authorizations
Recording		
Journalizing and posting transactions	General Accounting	Transactions are correctly recorded as to amount, classification, and accounting period
Updating subsidiary ledgers	Corporate Secretary	Transactions are correctly posted to individual accounts
Custody		
Maintaining correctness of debt and equity balances	General Accounting	Recorded balances are reconciled with subsidiary ledgers at reasonable intervals

Bond and Capital Stock Transactions Are Properly Executed

The following internal control principles are applicable to this objective.

Authorization procedures. Formal authorization procedures are followed in the issuance of bonds and capital stock. Board of directors authorization is required in each case; in addition, stockholder approval is usually required for new stock issues. The certificates must be signed by one or two corporate officers. Board of directors authorization also precedes the reacquisition of bonds that is not in accordance with the terms of the issue, reacquisition of capital stock, and the declaration of dividends.

Payments of interest and dividends ordinarily are subject to the controls over cash disbursements procedures described in Chapter 9.

Segregation of functions. Full adherence to this internal control principle occurs in executing financing cycle transactions. Responsibility for executing the authorizations frequently is assigned to a corporate officer, such as the treasurer, who does not participate in the recording of the transactions.

For bond issues, a trustee, usually either a bank or a trust company, frequently acts as an independent third party to protect the respective interests of the bondholders and the issuing corporation.

For a publicly held company, additional compliance with this principle exists through the use of an outside registrar and transfer agent for capital stock issues and transfers. These agents are usually banks or trust companies which have the experience, competent personnel, and facilities to assure maximum efficiency and control over capital stock transactions. The primary responsibility of a registrar is to verify that stock is issued in accordance with the articles of incorporation, statutory requirements, and the formal authorizations of the board of directors. When a registrar is not used, these responsibilities are assumed by corporate legal staff or counsel. The registrar maintains records of total shares authorized, issued and canceled. Every new certificate is prepared and recorded by the registrar.

A stock transfer agent maintains detailed records of each shareholder's stock ownership and records the transfers of stock ownership among shareholders. The transfer agent assists corporate officers in seeing that each stock transfer meets regulatory requirements. Another arrangement that contributes to effective internal control is the use of an outside independent agent, such as a bank, for the payment of bond interest and dividends.

Documentation procedures. Documentation of financing cycle transactions takes a variety of forms. Each type of security issue is based on a formal written contract that stipulates the terms of the issue. Evidence of authorizations is found in the minutes. Proceeds of issues are evidenced by brokers' advices and cash remittance advices. Payments of interest and dividends are supported by paid vouchers and canceled checks. These forms of evidence are also available for reacquisitions of bonds and capital stock.

In addition, the redemption of bonds should be evidenced by a cremation certificate which signifies that the original certificate has been destroyed. The stock certificates and stubs for stock retired should be clearly marked canceled and the canceled certificate should be attached to the stub.

Bond and Capital Stock Transactions Are Properly Recorded

The internal control principles applicable to this objective are as follows:

Segregation of Functions. Accounting personnel who record financing transactions should not execute them. For bond issues, a bond register should be maintained showing the bonds held by each bondholder. The register may be kept by the issuing corporation or by a bond registrar. For capital stock issues, a stockholders' ledger should be maintained. In a small company, the corporate secretary has this responsibility; in a large company, a stock transfer agent performs this function.

Accounting records and procedures. As indicated above subsidiary ledgers should be maintained for both bonds and capital stock. In recording capital stock transactions, a proper distinction must be maintained between paid-in and accumulated capital.

Custody of Assets Is Properly Maintained

The internal controls principles applicable to this objective are the same as those described for the investing cycle.

Physical controls and authorization procedures. Physical controls in the form of safes and safety deposit boxes should be used to store bond cremation certificates, treasury stock, and the stock certificate book. Such facilities may also be employed to safeguard unissued bond and stock certificates from unauthorized use. Responsibility for restricting access should be assigned to a company officer.

Independent internal verification and segregation of functions. Periodically, there should be independent internal verification of the agreement of capital stock with the stockholders' ledger. Similarly, there should be periodic reconciliations of bonds issued with bond certificate stubs, and the number of shares of treasury stock with the treasury stock account. These comparisons are facilitated when outside independent agents are involved.

Study and Evaluation of Internal Control

The auditor's responsibilities under the second standard of field work for the financing cycle are comparable to those described earlier in this chapter for the investing cycle. Thus, the auditor may elect to forego completing the review of the system and rely entirely on substantive tests in verifying financial cycle balances. The use of outside independent agents in keeping the subsidiary ledgers and in paying interest and dividends often reduces the need for the auditor to rely on the client's controls.

Substantive Tests of Long-Term Debt Balances

From an auditing standpoint, notes payable, mortgages payable, and bonds payable have similar characteristics. Generally, these forms of debt (1) involve interest-bearing contractual agreements, (2) require approval by the board of directors, and (3) may be secured by the pledging of collateral. Ordinarily, a company will have infrequent transactions pertaining to long-term debt, but the amount per transaction may be material. Tests of balances may occur before or after the balance-sheet date. The primary tests of long-term debt balances and the audit objectives to which they pertain are shown in Figure 14-3. The tests are explained below within the framework of the audit objectives.

Clerical Accuracy

The starting points in the testing of balances are to verify the mathematical accuracy of supporting schedules by footing the schedules and reconciling data on the schedule with general ledger balances. A common schedule is a listing of the number of bonds held by registered owners prepared by the bond trustee. The schedule is footed and the total is compared with bonds issued and outstanding.

TYPE OF TEST: Substantive **PURPOSE: Validity and Propriety of Balances**
CYCLE: Financing **ACCOUNTS: Long-term Debt and Interest Expense**

A. CLERICAL ACCURACY:

   1. Foot supporting schedules.
   2. Reconcile general ledger with supporting schedules.

B. EXISTENCE OR OCCURRENCE AND RIGHTS AND OBLIGATIONS:

   1. Review authorizations and contracts.
   2. Confirm debt.

C. COMPLETENESS:

   1. Make analytical review.

D. VALUATION OR ALLOCATION:

   1. Vouch entries to long-term debt.
   2. Recalculate interest expense.

E. STATEMENT PRESENTATION AND DISCLOSURE:

   1. Makes inquiries and review documentation for restrictions and liens.
   2. Compare statement presentation with GAAP.

FIGURE 14-3. Audit Program: Tests of Long-Term Debt Balances

Existence or Occurrence and Rights and Obligations

Tests of balances for these audit objectives are designed to provide evidence that (1) recorded long-term debt exists at the balance sheet date, (2) long-term debt transactions have actually occurred, and (3) long-term debt represents a legal obligation. The following tests of balances are applicable to these objectives:

Review authorizations and contracts. The authority of a corporation to enter into a contractual agreement to borrow money through the issuance or incurrence of long-term debt rests with the board of directors. Accordingly, evidence of authorizations should be found in the minutes of board meetings. Normally, the auditor only reviews the authorizations that have occurred during the year under audit, since evidence of the authorizations for debt outstanding at the beginning of the year should be in the permanent working paper file.

Authorization for the debt issue should include reference to the applicable sections of the corporate bylaws that pertain to such financing. It may also include the opinion of the company's legal counsel as to the legality of the debt. Further support for existence is obtained by a review of debt contracts and periodic reports received from trustees.

Vouchers, paid checks, and reports of independent paying agencies provide evidence of the occurrence of interest transactions.

Confirm debt. The auditor generally confirms the long-term debt with lenders or trustees of the instruments. The purposes of the confirmation are to obtain evidence as to the existence and terms of the debt and discover any unrecorded liabilities. Notes payable to banks in which the client has an account are confirmed as part of the confirmation of bank balances. Other notes are confirmed with the holders by separate letter. Such requests should be made by the client and mailed by the auditor. The existence of mortgages and bonds payable normally can be confirmed directly with the trustee. Each confirmation should include a request for the current status of the debt and current year's transactions. All confirmation responses should be compared to the records and any differences should be investigated.

Completeness

This objective focuses on the possible understatement of long-term debt and interest expense. The audit tests for completeness include the confirmation of long-term debt, described above, and analytical review.

Make analytical review. As in the case of investment balances, this test may involve individual account balances. For example, bond interest expense divided by bonds outstanding should equal or approximate the contractual rate of interest on the bonds. When this result is not obtained, investigation may reveal unrecorded transactions.

The computation of ratios may also be useful. For example, the debt-to-equity ratio and the number of times bond interest is earned can be calculated for the current year and compared with budget expectations and prior years' results. Any major fluctuations should be investigated.

Valuation or Allocation

The points of concern in this objective are the carrying value of long-term debt and the accuracy of interest expense. Two tests of balances are applicable to this objective:

Vouch long-term debt entries. For bonds, the auditor should obtain evidence as to both the face value and net proceeds of the obligation at the date of issue. Issuances of debt instruments should be traced to cash receipts as evidenced by brokers' advices. Payments on principal of long-term debt can be verified by an examination of vouchers and canceled checks; payments in full can be validated by an inspection of the canceled instrument and, in the case of bonds, a cremation certificate. When installment payments are involved, their propriety can be traced to repayment schedules. Bonds may also be converted into stock. Evidence of such transactions is available in the form of canceled bond certificates and the issuance of related stock certificates.

From the evidence obtained, the auditor should be able to determine the validity and propriety of the accounting treatment of the transactions. Special care should be exercised in ascertaining that net proceeds were properly allocated to principal, accrued interest, and discount or premium. Similarly, the auditor must determine that gains or losses and carrying values were properly recognized on payment.

Recalculate interest expense. Evidence of interest expense and accrued interest payable is easily obtainable by the auditor. The auditor reperforms the client's interest calculations and traces interest payments to supporting vouchers, canceled checks, and confirmation responses. Accrued interest, in turn, is verified by identifying the last interest payment date and recalculating the amount booked by the client. Interest expense should be reconciled to the debt contract to which it relates and any unreconcilable items should be investigated.

Where bond interest coupons are involved, the auditor can examine the cancelled coupons and reconcile them to the amount paid. When bonds were originally sold at a premium or discount, the auditor should review the client's amortization schedule and verify the recorded amount of amortization by recalculation.

Audit working papers, such as the analysis of notes payable and interest in Figure 14-4, are used in verifying long-term debt balances.

N-3

Prepared by: CJM Date: 1/24/X2
Reviewed by: RCP Date: 1/30/X2

Willow Company
Long-term Notes Payable and Accrued Interest
12/31/X1

Acc #'s 220, 225, 445

Description	Notes Payable Balance 1/1/X1	Additions	Payments	Balance 12/31/X1	Balance 1/1/X1	Interest Payable Expense	Payments	Balance 12/31/X1
10% note payable to Culver National Bank, due 7/1/X3 per year at 7/1/X3 ①	30,000 n √		10,000 ○	20,000 ⓒ √	1,500 ○ √	2,500 Ⓑ	3,000 ⓒ	1,000
9% note payable to First Trust Company due 9/1/X3 ②		25,000 √ ○		25,000 ⓒ √		7,500 Ⓐ		7,500
Totals	30,000 F	25,000 F	10,000 F	45,000 FF To W/4	15,000 F	3,250 F To S-1	30,000 F	17,500 X FF To W/4

① Long-term investments in stock of Alter Company and Baley Co. pledged as security. See confirmation received from bank A-4.

② Land and building pledged as security. See confirmation received from bank A-5.

u Traced to prior year work papers.

A Traced to ledger @ 12/31/X1

ⓒ Confirmed by bank – see A-4 and A-5

√ Examined copy of note

○ Traced to cash journals and supporting documentation

Ⓐ Recomputed interest expense – no exception

F Footed

FF Crossfooted

FIGURE 14–4. Notes and Interest Payable Working Paper

Statement Presentation and Disclosure

In evaluating the appropriateness of the client's classification of long-term debt, the auditor should be aware of applicable Financial Accounting Standards Board (FASB) pronouncements. The auditor meets this objective through inspection of the debt contract, confirmation with trustees, and inquiry of management.

Substantive Tests of Stockholders' Equity Balances

As in the case of long-term debt, capital stock transactions in the financing cycle may be verified at any convenient time during the audit engagement. An audit program for tests of these balances is shown in Figure 14-5. Each of these tests of balances is explained below within the framework of the six audit objectives. As in the case of bonds, the verification of the current year's capital stock transactions receives priority in executing the audit program.

Clerical Accuracy

An essential starting point in the verification of stockholders' equity balances is to establish the accuracy of supporting schedules. This is done by footing the schedules and reconciling the data on the schedules to the ledger balances. For a small company without a registrar and transfer agent, a common schedule is a trial balance of the stockholders' ledger. Total shares shown in the schedule should agree with the shares outstanding in the capital stock account.

Existence or Occurrence

For balance sheet accounts, this objective relates to the validity of recorded stockholders' equity balances; for transactions, such as those pertaining to the issuance of stock, the acquisition of treasury stock, and the payment of dividends, the objective is to determine whether the transactions actually occurred. Several tests of balances are used by the auditor in meeting this objective.

Review authorizations and terms of stock issue. All stock issues, stock reacquisitions, and dividend declarations should be authorized by the board of directors. Accordingly, a review of the minutes should provide evidence of stockholders' equity transactions authorized during the year. In some cases, the minutes also contain information as to the legality of the authorized action.

Different classes of stock may contain restriction provisions or convey preferences in dividend declarations and liquidation. The auditor should examine each issue for such terms and make appropriate notation in the working papers.

TYPE OF TEST: Substantive   **PURPOSE: Validity and Propriety of Balances**
CYCLE: Financing   **ACCOUNTS: Stockholders' Equity**

A. CLERICAL ACCURACY:

   1. Foot supporting schedules.
   2. Reconcile data on schedules to ledger balances.

B. EXISTENCE OR OCCURRENCE:

   1. Review authorizations and terms of stock issues.
   2. Confirm shares outstanding with registrar and transfer agents.
   3. Inspect stock certificate book.
   4. Inspect certificates of shares held in treasury.
   5. Review documentation in client's files.

C. COMPLETENESS:

   1. Make analytical review.

D. RIGHTS AND OBLIGATIONS:

   1. Make inquiries of legal counsel.
   2. Review articles of incorporation and bylaws.

E. VALUATION OR ALLOCATION:

   1. Vouch capital stock entries.
   2. Vouch dividend payments.
   3. Vouch entries to retained earnings.

F. STATEMENT PRESENTATION AND DISCLOSURE:

   1. Review minutes of board of directors' meetings for stock options and dividend restrictions.
   2. Compare statement presentation with GAAP.

FIGURE 14–5. Audit Program: Stockholders' Equity Balances

Confirm shares outstanding with registrar and transfer agent. When the client uses a registrar, the auditor should confirm total shares authorized, issued, and outstanding at the balance sheet date with the registrar. Confirmation with the transfer agent, in turn, provides evidence of shares held by each stockholder.

Inspect stock certificate book. This test is required when the client serves as its own transfer agent. Several steps are involved in the test. First, the auditor should examine the stock certificate book to determine that (1) stubs for shares issued and outstanding have been properly filled out, (2) canceled certificates are attached to original stubs, and (3) all unissued certificates are intact.

Second, the auditor should ascertain that the changes during the year have been correctly recorded in the individual stockholders' accounts in the subsidiary ledger. When there are numerous issuances and cancellations, this comparison may be done on a test basis.

Third, the auditor should reconcile the total shares issued and outstanding as shown in the stock certificate book with total shares reported in the stockholders' ledger and capital stock accounts.

Inspect certificates of shares held in treasury. If capital stock is held in the treasury, the auditor should count the certificates at the same time other securities are counted. Ideally, the count should be made at the balance sheet date. If this is not possible, there must be a reconciliation from the date of the count to the balance sheet date. The number of shares held should also be agreed to the shares shown in the treasury stock account. In inspecting the certificates, the auditor should note in the working papers the number of shares acquired during the year for subsequent tracing to the cash records.

Review documentation in client's files. This test relates primarily to the occurrence of stockholders' equity transactions. Documentation in the client's files that provides evidence of occurrence includes remittance advices of cash proceeds from stock issues, payment vouchers for treasury stock acquisitions, and dividend checks for the payment of dividends.

Completeness

The completeness objective is directed at whether recorded stockholders' equity accounts reflect all data that should be recorded. Evidence for this objective ordinarily is obtained from the procedures previously described under existence or occurrence. In some cases, these procedures may be supplemented by analytical review.

Make analytical review. A number of analytical review procedures may be performed to establish the completeness of capital stock accounts. For example, the auditor may compute for the current year (1) book value per share of stock, (2) return on shareholders' equity, (3) dividend payout ratio, and (4) the price-earnings ratio, and compare the data with prior years' results. When analysis indicates unusual fluctuations or questionable items, they should be investigated by the auditor.

Rights and Obligations

Management's assertions about the rights and obligations pertain to whether capital stock was legally issued and whether shareholders have a legal claim on corporate assets at the balance sheet date. Evidence of the legality of a stock issue and any changes in capitalization may be obtained through inquiry of the client's legal counsel. The attorney's response preferably should be in writing. A review of the articles of incorporation and bylaws should also reveal the right of the entity to authorize and to execute the stockholders' equity transactions.

Valuation or Allocation

This objective pertains to the proper statement amounts for stockholders' equity balances. For these balances, the valuation objective includes maintaining a proper distinction between paid-in capital and retained earnings in recording stock transactions. Evidence concerning this objective is obtained primarily through the vouching of recorded entries.

Vouch capital stock entries. Each change in a capital stock account should be traced to supporting documentation. For a new issue of stock, the auditor can examine remittance advices of the cash proceeds from the issue. The proceeds should be traced to the cash receipt records and to capital stock and other paid-in capital accounts. If the consideration for the shares was other than cash, the auditor should carefully examine the basis for the valuation, such as the market value of the consideration received or given. For the shares issued, market quotations may be useful in determining the propriety of the valuation; when the value of the property received is used, an appraisal may be necessary. An analysis of a capital stock account is illustrated in Figure 14-6. Similar analyses are prepared for treasury stock and other stockholders' equity accounts.

The auditor should exercise care in determining the propriety of the accounting treatment for shares issued as part of stock option, stock warrant, or stock conversion plans or in connection with a stock split. Documentation of the cost of treasury stock should be available to the auditor in the form of authorizations in the minutes, disbursement vouchers, and canceled checks.

Vouch dividend payments. All dividend distributions should be authorized by the board of directors. The auditor should inspect the minutes for authorization and note the amount per share and the date of record. In determining the propriety of the distribution, the auditor should

- Establish that preferential or other rights of stockholders and any restrictions on dividend distributions have been recognized.
- Establish the number of shares outstanding on the date of record and verify the accuracy of the total dividend declaration by recalculation.
- Ascertain the propriety of the entry to record the declaration.
- Trace dividend payments to canceled checks and other documentation.

Vouch Entries to Retained Earnings. Each entry to retained earnings except the posting of net income (or net loss), should be vouched to supporting documentation. Entries for dividend declarations and retained earnings appropriations are traced to the minute book. The client is also expected to furnish support for any prior-period adjustments. Vouching enables the auditor to ascertain whether (1) a proper distinction has been made between paid-in capital and retained earnings, and (2) applicable legal and contractual requirements have been met.

Prepared by: *Q.E.R.*   **Date:** *1/12/x2*
Reviewed by: *R.C.P.*   **Date:** *1/19/x2*

Willens Company   *P-2*
Capital Stock $100 par

Acc. # 600	12/31/X1			
	Shares			
	Authorized	Issued and Outstanding	Amount	
Balances, 1/1/X1	10000 ✓	5000 ✓	500000 ✓	
Shares issued at par for cash on 4/1/X1		1000 ʼн	100000 нø	
Balances, 12/31/X1	10000	6000 C	600000	To-P/

✓ - Traced to prior years working papers
ʼн - Traced to approval per minutes of Board of Directors meeting on 3/20/X1
ø - Traced proceeds to cash receipts
C - Confirmed by First Trust Company, transfer agent for the company - See P-3

Reviewed minutes of all Board of Directors meetings for evidence of capital stock transactions. Only reference was to transaction of 4/1/X1 as per above.

FIGURE 14-6. Capital Stock Working Paper

Statement Presentation and Disclosure

APB Opinion No. 12 provides that disclosure of changes in the separate accounts comprising stockholders' equity is required to make the financial statements sufficiently informative. Such disclosure may be made in the basic statements and notes thereto or be presented in a separate statement.

Disclosures related to the equity section include details of stock option plans, dividends in arrears, par or stated value, and dividend and liquidation preferences. The auditor meets this audit objective by a review of evidence obtained from the foregoing tests and from a review of the corporate minutes for provisions and agreements affecting the stockholders' equity accounts. In reviewing the minutes, the auditor should note whether any shares of stock have been reserved for stock option or similar plans, commitments for future issuance of stock in the purchase of or merger with another company, and restrictions limiting dividend payments or requiring minimum working capital requirements. Relevant evidence may also be obtained from discussions and/or communications with legal counsel.

CONCLUDING COMMENTS

Internal accounting controls over transactions in the investing and financing cycles are generally strong because of infrequent transactions, officer participation in the transactions, and the use of outside custodians and independent agents. In the typical audit engagement, it is relatively easy for the auditor to obtain sufficient competent evidential matter concerning investment, long-term debt, and stockholders' equity accounts by direct tests of such balances.

REVIEW QUESTIONS

14–1. Indicate the functions associated with the investing cycle.

14–2. Evaluate the materiality and risk for investing cycle balances.

14–3. Explain the specific internal accounting control objectives for the functions identified in (1) above.

14–4. What internal accounting control principles are applicable to (a) executing and (b) recording securities transactions?

14–5. Identify the internal control principles that relate to the custody of securities.

14–6. Indicate the alternative decision paths the auditor may take in making a study and evaluation of internal control over investment transactions, and explain the circumstances when each choice is justified.

14–7. What precautions should be taken by the auditor in inspecting and counting securities on hand?

14–8. What data should be shown in the working papers concerning securities?

14–9. Indicate the form and timing of confirming securities held by outside custodians.

14–10. What audit procedures are useful in verifying the (a) existence or occurrence and rights and obligations and (b) valuation or allocation of investment balances?

14–11. What evidence is available to the auditor in determining (a) "market" when securities are accounted for on the cost basis and (b) the value of underlying net assets when securities are accounted for under the equity method?

14–12. What supplemental disclosures in notes to financial statements are required for investments in securities?

14–13. Identify (a) the functions and (b) the specific internal accounting control objectives for financing cycle transactions.

14–14. Briefly explain the application of (a) authorization procedures and (b) segregation of functions to the proper execution of transactions in the financing cycle.

14–15. What audit procedures are useful in verifying (a) existence or occurrence, (b) completeness, and (c) valuation or allocation of long-term debt balances?

14–16. What purposes are served in confirming debt with holders?

14–17. What specific relationships may be determined in making an analytical review of long-term debt balances?

14–18. What audit procedures may be employed to establish the (a) existence or occurrence and (b) rights and obligations of stockholders' equity balances?

14–19. What procedures are required in vouching dividend payments?

14–20. What procedures are used in determining whether there is proper statement presentation and disclosure of stockholder equity items?

COMPREHENSIVE QUESTIONS

14–21. You have been assigned to the examination of the "investments" account of one of your firm's older clients, the *D* Co. During the prior year, your client received more than $1 million from the sale of all of its stock in a subsidiary. The proceeds from this sale were promptly invested in time certificates of deposit (CDs) having various maturities. More than one year has elapsed since the sale of the stock, and your client continues to invest the funds in CDs. Investment decisions are made by the company treasurer, who also is responsible for custody of the CDs.

During the current year, the *D*'s treasurer obtained $100,000 from the surrender of a CD at maturity and invested the proceeds in another six-month certificate having an interest rate of 10 percent. This transaction was recorded on the books of the company as being for a CD bearing an interest rate of 8 percent. At the end of the six months, the treasurer redeemed this CD for its $105,000 maturity value. On the books of the company, the transaction was recorded as having been for $104,000, and the treasurer deposited that amount in the company's bank account prior to reinvesting the proceeds in another security.

Required
a. What internal controls could have prevented or permitted detection of the treasurer's action?
b. What audit procedures could you perform to discover this irregularity?

14–22. You have been assigned to examine the "Long-term Investments" account of the Richard Company, a new audit client of your firm, for the current year. The client's records show an investment of $75,000 for 750 shares of the common stock of one of its major suppliers of raw materials. This amount is approximately 8 percent of your client's total current assets. You learn that the supplier has 15,000 shares of common stock issued and outstanding. The supplier does not publish financial statements for the general public and its stock has no recently quoted market value.

As a part of your audit of the long-term investment account, you examine the stock certificate for 750 shares, the paid check for $75,000 issued for this stock, and determine that the transaction was approved by your client's board of directors.

Required
a. Have you accumulated sufficient, competent evidence for this account? Explain.
b. Identify any additional auditing procedures that should be performed.

14–23. In verifying investing cycle balances, the auditor should recognize that the following errors may occur or exist:

1. A mathematical error is made in accruing interest earned.
2. A 25 percent common stock investment in an affiliated company is accounted for on the cost basis.
3. Securities held by an outside custodian are in the treasurer's name.
4. Securities on hand at the beginning of the year are diverted to personal use in July and are replaced in December.
5. An authorized purchase is recorded at cost and the broker's fee is expensed.

6. Ten shares of stock reported to be on hand are missing.
7. Marketable equitable securities are reported at cost, which is above market.
8. The schedule of marketable securities does not reconcile to the general ledger account.
9. Gain on a sale of securities is reported net of taxes.
10. Securities pledged as collateral on a bank loan are not disclosed.

Required
a. Identify the audit procedure that should enable the auditor to detect each error.
b. Indicate the audit objective to which the audit procedure relates.
c. Identify the type of evidential matter obtained by the audit procedure.

14–24. As a result of highly profitable operations over a number of years, Eastern Manufacturing Corporation accumulated a substantial investment portfolio. In his examination of the financial statements for the year ended December 31, 19X0, the following information came to the attention of the corporation's CPA:

1. The manufacturing operations of the corporation resulted in an operating loss for the year.
2. In 19X0, the corporation placed the securities making up the investment portfolio with a financial institution which will serve as custodian of the securities. Formerly, the securities were kept in the corporation's safe deposit box in the local bank.
3. On December 22, 19X0, the corporation sold and then repurchased on the same day a number of securities that had appreciated greatly in value. Management stated that the purpose of the sale and repurchases was to establish a higher cost and book value for the securities and to avoid the reporting of a loss for the year.

Required
a. List the objectives of the CPA's examination of the investment account.
b. Under what conditions would the CPA accept a confirmation of the securities on hand from the custodian in lieu of inspecting and counting the securities himself?
c. What disclosure, if any, of the sale and repurchase of the securities would the CPA recommend for the financial statements?

AICPA

14–25. In connection with his examination of the financial statements of Belasco Chemicals, Inc., Kenneth Mack, CPA, is considering the necessity of inspecting marketable securities on the balance sheet date, May 31, 19X1 or at some other date. The marketable securities held by Belasco include negotiable bearer bonds, which are kept in a safe in the treasurer's office, and miscellaneous stocks and bonds kept in a safe deposit box at The Merchants Bank. Both the negotiable bearer bonds and the miscellaneous stocks and bonds are material to proper presentation of Belasco's financial position.

Required
a. What are the factors that Mr. Mack should consider in determining the necessity for inspecting these securities on May 31, 19X1, as opposed to other dates?
b. Assume that Mr. Mack plans to send a member of his staff to Belasco's offices and The Merchants Bank on May 31, 19X1, to make the securities inspection. What instructions should he give to his staff member as to the conduct of the inspection and the evidence to be included in the audit working papers? (*Note:* Do not discuss the valuation of securities, the income from securities, or the examination of information contained in the books and records of the company.)
c. Assume that Mack finds it impracticable to send a member of his staff to Belasco's

offices and The Merchants Bank on May 31, 19X1. What alternative procedures may he employ to assure himself that the Company had physical possession of its marketable securities on May 31, 19X1, if the securities are inspected (1) May 28, 19X1? (2) June 5, 19X1?

AICPA

14–26. As part of his examination of the financial statements of the Marlborough Corporation for the year ended March 31, 19X1, Marion Romito, CPA, is reviewing the balance-sheet presentation of a $1.2 million advance to Franklin Olds, Marlborough's president. The advance, which represents 50 percent of current assets and 10 percent of total assets, was made during the year ended March 31, 19X1. It has been described in the balance sheet as "miscellaneous accounts receivable" and classified as a current asset.

Olds informs the CPA that he has used the proceeds of the advance to purchase 35,000 shares of Marlborough's common stock, in order to forestall a take-over raid on the company. He is reluctant to have his association with the advance described in the financial statements because he does not have voting control and fears that this will "just give the raiders ammunition."

Olds offers the following four-point program as an alternative to further disclosure:

1. Have the advance approved by the board of directors. (This can be done expeditiously because a majority of the board members are officers of the company.)
2. Prepare a demand note payable to the company with interest of 7.5 percent (the average bank rate paid by the company).
3. Furnish an endorsement of the stock to the company as collateral for the loan. (During the year under audit, despite the fact that earnings did not increase, the market price of Marlborough common rose from $20 to $40 per share. The stock has maintained its $40 per share market price subsequent to year-end.)
4. Obtain a written opinion from the company attorney supporting the legality of the company's advance and the use of the proceeds.

Required
a. Discuss the proper balance-sheet classifications of the advance to Olds and other appropriate disclosures in the financial statements and footnotes.
b. Discuss each point of Olds' four-point program as to whether or not it is desirable and as to whether or not it is an alternative to further disclosure.
c. If Olds refuses to permit further disclosure, what action(s) should the CPA take? Discuss.
d. In his discussion with the CPA, Olds warns that the raiders, if successful, probably will appoint new auditors. What consideration should the CPA give to this factor? Explain.

AICPA

14–27. The schedule on page 496 was prepared by the controller of World Manufacturing Inc. for use by the independent auditors during their examination of World's year-end financial statements. All procedures performed by the audit assistant were noted in the "Legend" section at the bottom. The schedule was properly initialed, dated, and indexed, and then submitted to a senior member of the audit staff for review. Internal control was reviewed and is considered to be satisfactory.

Required
a. What information that is essential to the audit of marketable securities is missing from this schedule?
b. What are the essential audit procedures that were not noted as having been performed by the audit assistant?

AICPA

World Manufacturing Inc.
Marketable Securities
Year Ended December 31, 19X1

Description of Security	%	Yr. Due	Serial No.	Face value of bonds	Gen. ledger 1/1	Purch. in 19X1	Sold in 19X1	Cost	Gen. ledger 12/31	12/31 market	Pay date(s)	Amt. rec.	Accruals 12/31
Corp. Bonds													
A	6	91	21-7	10,000	9,400a				9,400	9,100	1/15	300b,d	275
D	4	83	73-0	30,000	27,500a				27,500	26,220	7/15	300b,d	100
G	9	98	16-4	5,000	4,000a				4,000	5,080	12/1	1,200b,d	188
Rc	5	85	08-2	70,000	66,000a		57,000b	66,000			8/1	450b,d	
Sc	10	99	07-4	100,000		100,000e			100,000	101,250	7/1	5,000b,d	5,000
					106,900	100,000	57,000	66,000	140,900	141,650		7,250	5,563
					a,f	f	f	f	f,g	f		f	f
Stocks													
P 1,000 shs. Common			1,044		7,500a				7,500	7,600	3/1 / 6/1 / 9/1 / 12/1	750b,d / 750b,d / 750b,d / 750b,d	250
U 50 shs. Common			8,530		9,700a				9,700	9,800	2/1 / 8/1	800b,d / 800b,d	667
					17,200				17,200	17,400		4,600	917
					a,f				f,g	f		f	f

Legends and comments relative to above

a = Beginning balances agreed to 19X0 working papers
b = Traced to cash receipts
c = Minutes examined (purchase and sales approved by the board of directors)
d = Agreed to 1099 (tax form)
e = Confirmed by tracing to broker's advice
f = Totals footed
g = Agreed to general ledger

14–28. You were engaged to examine the financial statements of Ronlyn Corporation for the year ended June 30.

On May 1, the Corporation borrowed $500,000 from Second National Bank to finance plant expansion. The long-term note agreement provided for the annual payment of principal and interest over five years. The existing plant was pledged as security for the loan.

Due to unexpected difficulties in acquiring the building site, the plant expansion had not begun at June 30. To make use of the borrowed funds, management decided to invest in stocks and bonds, and on May 16, the $500,000 was invested in securities.

Required
a. What are the audit objectives in the examination of long-term debt?
b. Prepare an audit program for the examination of the long-term note agreement between Ronlyn and Second National Bank.
c. How could you verify the security position of Ronlyn at June 30?
d. In your audit of investments, how would you

   1. Verify the dividend or interest income recorded?
   2. Determine market value?
   3. Establish the authority for security purchases?

AICPA

14–29. The following transactions and events relate to financing cycle transactions:

   1. Declare cash dividend on common stock.
   2. Issue bonds.
   3. Pay bond interest.
   4. Purchase 500 shares of treasury stock.
   5. Pay cash dividend declared in 1 above.
   6. Issue additional common stock for cash.
   7. Accrue bond interest payable at year-end.
   8. Redeem outstanding bonds.
   9. Establish appropriation for bond retirement.
   10. Announce a 2-for-1 stock split.

Required
a. Identify the substantive test(s) that will be useful in verifying each transaction or event.
b. For each procedure in (a) indicate the type of audit evidence obtained.

14–30. The following covenants are extracted from the indenture of a bond issue. The indenture provides that failure to comply with its terms in any respect automatically advances the due date of the loan to the date of noncompliance (the regular due date is twenty years hence):

   1. "The debtor company shall endeavor to maintain a working capital ratio of 2 to 1 at all times, and, in any fiscal year following a failure to maintain said ratio, the company shall restrict compensation of officers to a total of $100,000. Officers for this purpose shall include Chairman of the Board of Directors, President, all Vice Presidents, Secretary, and Treasurer."
   2. "The debtor company shall keep all property which is security for this debt insured against loss by fire to the extent of 100 percent of its actual value. Policies of insurance comprising this protection shall be filed with the trustee."
   3. "The debtor company shall pay all taxes legally assessed against property which is security for this debt within the time provided by law for payment without pen-

alty, and shall deposit receipted tax bills or equally acceptable evidence of payment of same with the trustee.''

4. ''A sinking fund shall be deposited with the trustee by semiannual payments of $300,000, from which the trustee shall, in his discretion, purchase bonds of this issue.''

Required
a. Indicate the audit procedures you would perform for each covenant.
b. Comment on any disclosure requirements that you believe are necessary.

AICPA

14–31. You have been assigned to the examination of the capital stock of *A* Company. As a result of your review of changes in the account for the year, you have identified the following transactions:

1. Cancellation of treasury stock.
2. Issuance of a 5 percent stock dividend.
3. Issuance of capital stock in exchange for land wanted as a site for possible future expansion.
4. Issuance of ten shares of $25 par common stock having a market price of $125 per share in exchange for a $1,000 convertible bond.

Required
State the audit procedures you would use to gather evidence in support of the propriety of the above transactions.

14–32. The Eaton Company was incorporated July 10, 19*X*0, with an authorized capital as follows:

1. Common stock, Class A, 20,000 shares, par value $25 per share.
2. Common stock, Class B, 100,000 shares, par value $5 per share.

The capital stock account in the general ledger is credited with only one item in the year 19*X*0. This represents capital stock sold for cash, at par, as follows:

1. Class A, 12,000 shares.
2. Class B, 60,000 shares.

The sum of open certificate stubs in the stock certificate books at December 31, 19*X*0 indicates that 82,000 shares of stock were outstanding.

Required
a. State possible explanations for this apparent discrepancy.
b. State the procedures you would perform to determine the cause of the discrepancy.

AICPA

14–33. You are engaged in doing the audit of a corporation whose records have not previously been audited by you. The corporation has both an independent transfer agent and a registrar for its capital stock. The transfer agent maintains the record of stockholders and the registrar checks that there is no overissue of stock. Signatures of both are required to validate certificates.

It has been proposed that confirmations be obtained from both the transfer agent and the registrar as to the stock outstanding at balance-sheet date. If such confirmations agree with the books, no additional work is to be performed as to capital stock.

Required
If you agree that obtaining the confirmations as suggested would be sufficient in this case, give the justification for your position. If you do not agree, state specifically all additional steps you would take and explain your reason for taking them.

AICPA

14-34. You are a CPA engaged in an examination of the financial statements of Pate Corporation for the year ended December 31, 19X3. The financial statements and records of Pate Corporation have not been audited by a CPA in prior years.

The stockholders' equity section of Pate Corporation's balance sheet at December 31, 19X3 follows:

Stockholders' equity

Capital stock—10,000 shares at $10 par value authorized; 5,000 shares issued and outstanding	$ 50,000
Capital contributed in excess of par value of capital stock	32,580
Retained earnings	47,320
Total stockholders' equity	$129,900

Pate Corporation was founded in 19X0. The corporation has ten stockholders and serves as its own registrar and transfer agent. There are no capital stock subscription contracts in effect.

Required
a. Prepare the detailed audit program for the examination of the three accounts comprising the Stockholders' Equity section of Pate Corporation's balance sheet. (Do not include in the audit program the verification of the results of the current year's operations.)
b. After every other figure on the balance sheet has been audited by the CPA, it might appear that the retained earnings figure is a balancing figure and requires no further verification. Why does the CPA verify retained earnings as he does the other figures on the balance sheet? Discuss.

AICPA

CASE STUDY

14-35.* The Jones Company, located in Chicago, has been your client for many years. The company manufactures light machinery and has a calendar year closing. At December 31, 19X1 and 19X0 the following items appeared in the accounts applicable to marketable and investment securities. All investments in securities are carried on the books at cost and represent approximately 8 percent of total assets. Income from securities represents approximately 3 percent of income before federal income tax.

Balance sheet accounts:	19X0	19X1
U.S. government certificates of indebtedness 3% series D dated May 15, 19X0, due May 15, 19X2	$300,000	$300,000
Marketable securities:		
50 shares of AP Company	5,000	5,000
100 shares of UC Corporation	—	8,000
75 shares of IC Corporation	12,000	—
Investment in a 60% owned subsidiary—SUB, Inc.	50,000	50,000
Accrued interest income	1,125	1,125
Income statement accounts:		
Interest income	9,000	9,000
Gain (loss) on sale of securities	(2,000)	3,000
Dividend income	13,000	14,000

During 19X1, there were fourteen purchases and sales of marketable securities. The U.S. Government securities shown above are held at the Utah Banking Company.

The AP Company securities are held in the Jones Company's safe and the UC Corporation securities are in a safety deposit box at the Chicago Bank Company, which is the company's bank. Access to the company's safe is limited to the treasurer or his assistant. Access to the safety deposit box is limited to any two of the treasurer, the assistant treasurer, or the controller. The securities of SUB, Inc. are also held by the Chicago Bank Company as collateral for a loan which the Jones Company has outstanding. SUB, Inc. has a June 30 closing and is audited by your firm.

Your tests of internal control indicate unusual strengths in the areas of cash receipts and cash disbursements. The treasurer is responsible for the physical control of securities while the controller is responsible for the recording of all transactions affecting securities. An assistant to the assistant controller maintains an investment ledger which shows the name of each investment, the number of shares held or the face value of bonds, the date of purchase and sale, if applicable, the cost, the physical location of the securities and the income thereon. This person prepares monthly statements of securities on hand showing their description and cost. All purchases and sales of securities are authorized by the company's finance committee. The following audit program has been prepared for the examination of securities at December 31, 19X1.

1. *U.S. Government securities:*
   a. Prepare a schedule of the securities at December 31, 19X1.
   b. Obtain direct confirmation from the Utah Banking Company as to description and amount of securities held.
   c. Trace the confirmation to the schedule and so indicate.
   d. Verify the interest earned for the year and accrued interest receivable at December 31, 19X1.
   e. Trace the appropriate totals to the general ledger accounts.
2. *Marketable securities:*
   a. Prepare an analysis of the securities account for the year under audit, including the market value of the securities at December 31, 19X1.
   b. Count AP Company securities at the company's office at the close of business on December 31, 19X1. Inspection of the securities should be in the presence of client's representative. Note the time of count, name of client's representative, and name of the auditor on the count sheet. Accompanied by the client's representative, inspect the UC Corporation securities at the Chicago Bank Company. Inspection should be completed at the close of business on December 31, 19X1. The same information should be shown on this count sheet as is indicated to be appropriate for the count sheet mentioned above. The count sheets should show the number of shares, the full name of security and the type of security (preferred or common shares).
   c. Vouch purchases and sales by reference to brokers' advices. Compare authorizations of the finance committee to the schedule.
   d. Compare dividends received for the year with a published dividend record.
   e. Verify the recorded gain or loss on sale of securities.
   f. Trace the appropriate totals on the schedule to the general ledger accounts.
3. *Investment in 60% owned subsidiary—SUB, Inc.:*
   a. Request the Chicago Bank Company to confirm that it holds the securities for SUB, Inc. as collateral for a loan. The amount payable to the bank may be confirmed concurrently.
   b. Review the monthly statements of SUB, Inc. since your latest examination and compare them with the audited statements at June 30. Obtain an explanation of all unusual transactions and fluctuations.
   c. Discuss the December 31, 19X1 financial statements with the management of the company. Inquire as to material amounts not recorded.
   d. Establish that the intercompany accounts are in agreement at December 31.

e. Record the company's equity in the net assets and net income of SUB, Inc. at December 31, 19X1.

Required
a. List the audit procedures that you believe are appropriate and identify the audit objective(s) to which each procedure relates.
b. List the audit procedures that you believe are inappropriate and give the reasons for your conclusion.

15 | Tests of Income Statement Balances/ Completing the Audit

STUDY OBJECTIVES

The study objectives of this chapter are to acquire an understanding of the methodology for verifying income statement balances and the auditor's responsibilities in completing the audit. To achieve these objectives, it is necessary for the reader to

- Realize the audit approach in verifying income statement balances.
- Perceive the nature of direct tests of income statement accounts.
- Become aware of the primary procedures involved in completing the field work.
- Be knowledgeable of the steps involved in evaluating the findings.
- Comprehend the nature and extent of the auditor's postaudit responsibilities

As the title suggests, this chapter consists of two major sections. The first involves substantive tests of revenue and expense account balances; the second covers specific responsibilities that must be met by the auditor in completing the audit examination. Near the end of the chapter, brief consideration is also given to the auditor's postaudit responsibilities.

SUBSTANTIVE TESTS OF REVENUE AND EXPENSE BALANCES

Materiality and Risk

Generally accepted auditing standards (GAAS) apply equally to both the income statement and balance sheet. For example, the auditor must have a reasonable basis for expressing an opinion on the fairness of the client's income statement representations and disclosures. Indeed, since many users of financial data currently attach more importance to the results of operations than to financial position, it may be concluded that the auditor's examination of revenue and expense accounts should be more comprehensive than his examination of asset, liability, and owners' equity accounts.

The risk associated with the income statement relates to the susceptibility of expense and revenue accounts to errors or misstatement. In assessing the risk, the auditor should recognize that income statement balances may result from (1) routine processing of transactions such as sales and purchases, (2) nonroutine transactions such as officers' bonuses or extraordinary events, and (3) management judgments such as those for product warranties and uncollectible receivables. As explained in Chapter 3, the degree of risk for routine transactions is inversely related to the effectiveness of the client's system of internal control. For nonroutine transactions and management judgments, the degree of risk depends on the existence of specific controls that may be applicable.

Approach to Verification of Income Statement Balances

The verification of expense and revenue accounts is an integral, rather than a separate, part of the auditor's examination. It will be recalled, for example, that compliance tests involve both balance sheet and income statement accounts, and many of the substantive tests discussed in Chapters 12–14 pertain to both financial statements.

The auditor's basic approach to substantive testing of balances is explained in Chapter 12. The application of this approach to income statement balances may be stated as follows:

- When internal controls can be relied on, obtain evidence on income and expense balances primarily through analytical review procedures.
- When internal controls are not tested or are found to be unreliable, perform direct tests of income statement balances.

The auditor's approach in verifying expense and revenue accounts is cost efficient in terms of the overall audit process and is in accordance with GAAS.

Direct Tests of Income Statement Balances

In performing direct tests of income statement balances, five of the six audit objectives identified in Chapter 12 are applicable:

AUDIT OBJECTIVE	APPLICABILITY TO INCOME STATEMENT ACCOUNTS
Clerical accuracy	Schedules supporting revenue and expense balances are mathematically correct and agree with ledger balances
Existence or occurrence	Transactions affecting statement accounts actually occurred during the year
Completeness	Income statement balances include all transactions that should be recorded
Valuation or allocation	Income statement items are stated at proper amounts
Statement presentation and disclosure	Income statement items are properly identified, presented, and classified, and accompanying disclosures are adequate

In addition to the circumstances described in the preceding section, direct testing of expense and revenue accounts also occurs when (1) analytical review procedures reveal unusual relationships or fluctuations in the accounts, and (2) the accounts require special analysis and disclosure.

Accounts Requiring Analysis

Accounts in this category include miscellaneous expense, travel and entertainment expense, and legal expense. Different problems of analysis exist in these accounts. Miscellaneous expense, for example, may contain authorized expenditures that should be charged to other income statement accounts. In contrast, travel and entertainment expense may contain unauthorized expenditures that are for personal rather than for business purposes. Legal expenses are analyzed for proper identification of losses due to legal suits and for expenditures that may reveal the existence of contingencies.

In applying tests of balances to the first two types of expenses, the auditor ordinarily will vouch selected transactions to supporting documents. For legal expense, a 100 percent review of entries is common.

Accounts Requiring Disclosure

Accounts in this grouping include officers' salaries, executive bonuses, and charitable contributions. Information concerning these accounts is generally required in filing tax returns with the Internal Revenue Service (IRS) and in filing reports with the Securities and Exchange Commission (SEC). An audit working paper for officers' salaries is illustrated in Figure 15-1. Schedules of these accounts are generally prepared by the client.

The extent of the direct testing by the auditor will depend on the reliance that can be placed on internal control and the materiality of the amounts. Direct testing is also done on information that must be specifically disclosed in the income statement. This includes segment information and earnings per share data. The objective of applying auditing procedures to these data is to obtain a reasonable basis for determining if the data are presented in conformity with authoritative pronouncements.

S-4

Prepared by: _A.E.R._ Date: _1/5/X3_
Reviewed by: _R.C.P._ Date: _1/18/X2_

Rogel Company
Officers' Salaries
Acc. # 500   12/31/X2

	Gross Salaries		
	19X2	19X1	19X0
F.J. Curtis, President	85000 ✓	80000	75000
J.W. Nielson, V.P. Purchasing	65000 ✓	58000	50000
S.A. Powers, Secretary	34000 ✓	25000	20000
R.M. Nichols, Controller	52000 ✓	44000	40000
E.J. Jarvis, Treasurer	50000 ✓	42000	36000
Total charged to General and Administrative Exp. (S-3)	286000 ✓	249000	221000
P.J. Spencer, V.P. Sales charged to Selling Exp. (S-2)	58000 ✓	52000	45000
J.E. Sperry, V.P. Production charged to Factory Ohd. (S-1)	65000 ✓	58000	50000
Totals	409000 ✓X	359000	316000
	F	F	F

✓ = Agreed to salaries approved by Board of Directors per minutes of meeting held on 12/20/X2.

F = Footed

X = Traced to General Ledger.

FIGURE 15-1. Officers' Salaries Working Paper

COMPLETING THE AUDIT

Many facets of interim and year-end field work have been discussed in the previous chapters of this book. Attention here is focused on the procedures that the auditor normally performs in completing the audit. For convenience of discussion, the material is subdivided into two categories: (1) completing the field work and (2) evaluating the findings. The completion of field work is directed primarily at general tests that pertain to the objective of obtaining sufficient competent evidential matter. The evaluation of findings includes formulating an opinion on the financial statements and determining whether quality control standards have been met. The specific steps in each category are tabulated below:

COMPLETION OF FIELD WORK	EVALUATION OF FINDINGS
• Make subsequent events review • Make inquiry of client's lawyer • Identify and examine related party transactions • Obtain client representation letter • Make overall analytical review • Make general review of statement of changes in financial position	• Formulate an opinion on financial statements • Complete review of working papers • Make technical review of financial statements • Make independent in-house review of working papers • Make required communication of material weaknesses in internal accounting control • Prepare and issue management letter

Make Subsequent Events Review

The auditor's responsibility for assessing the fairness of the client's financial statements is not limited to an examination of events that occur prior to the date of the balance sheet. The auditor also has specified responsibilities for events that occur after the balance sheet date. These events are called *subsequent events.* As shown in Figure 15-2, the time frame for a subsequent event extends from the balance sheet date to the issuance of the auditor's report. Figure 15-2 also identifies a *subsequent events period,* which extends from the balance sheet date to the end of field work. During this period, the auditor is required under GAAS to discover and evaluate any subsequent events that may have a material effect on the financial statements being reported on. As explained more fully later in the chapter, the auditor has no responsibility to discover subsequent events that occur between the end of field work and the issuance of the report.

Types of Events

There are two types of subsequent events:

Type 1 consists of those events that provide additional evidence with respect to conditions that existed at the date of the balance sheet and affect the estimates inherent in the process of preparing financial statements.

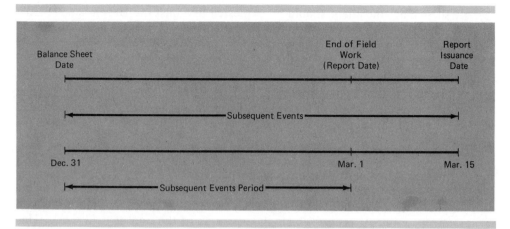

FIGURE 15–2. Subsequent Events Time Dimensions

Type 2 consists of those events that provide evidence with respect to conditions that did not exist at the date of the balance sheet but arose subsequent to that date.[1]

Type 1 events require *adjustment* of the financial statements; Type 2 events require *disclosure* in the statements, or in very material cases, by attaching pro-forma (as if) data to the financial statements. The following examples are illustrative of the two types of events:

TYPE 1	TYPE 2
Realization of recorded year-end assets, such as receivables and inventories, at a different amount than recorded	Issuance of long-term debt or equity capital stock
	Purchase of a business
Settlement of recorded year-end estimated liabilities, such as litigation and product warranties, at a different amount than recorded	Casualty losses resulting from fire or flood

An example may help in distinguishing between the two types of events. Assume that a major customer becomes bankrupt on February 1, 19X1 and that the client considered the customer's balance to be totally collectible in making its estimate of potential uncollectible accounts in its December 31, 19X0 statements. If, on review of the subsequent event, the auditor determines that the bankruptcy was attributable to the customer's deteriorating financial position that existed (but was unknown to the client) at the balance

---

[1] Auditing Standards Board, *Codification of Statements on Auditing Standards* (New York: American Institute of Certified Public Accountants, 1983), Auditing Sections 560.03, 560.05 (Hereinafter referred to and cited as AU §).

sheet date, the client should be requested to adjust the December 31, 19X0 statements for the loss prior to their issuance. If, on the other hand, the auditor determines that the customer was financially sound at December 31 and the bankruptcy resulted from a fire or similar catastrophe that occurred after the balance sheet date, only disclosure in the notes to the December 31 statements is needed. Ordinarily, Type 1 events require adjustment because they typically represent conditions that have accumulated over an extended period of time.

Auditor's Responsibility for Subsequent Events

The auditor should identify and evaluate subsequent events up to the date of the auditor's report which should be as of the end of field work. This responsibility is discharged in two ways: (1) by being alert for subsequent events in performing year-end substantive tests such as cutoff tests and the search for unrecorded liabilities and (2) by performing the following specific auditing procedures at or near the completion of field work:

- Read the latest available interim financial statements and compare them with the statements being reported on and make other comparisons appropriate in circumstances.
- Inquire of management having responsibility for financial and accounting matters as to
    - Any substantial contingent liabilities or commitments listed at the balance sheet date or date of inquiry.
    - Any significant changes in capital stock, long-term debt, or working capital to the date of inquiry.
    - The current status of items previously accounted for on the basis of tentative, preliminary, or inconclusive data.
    - Whether any unusual adjustments have been made since the balance sheet date.
- Read minutes of meetings of directors, stockholders, and other appropriate committees.
- Inquire of client's legal counsel concerning litigation, claims, and assessments.
- Obtain letter of representation from client about subsequent events that would, in its opinion, require adjustment or disclosure.
- Make additional inquiries or perform additional procedures considered necessary in the circumstances.[2]

The procedures pertaining to legal counsel and the representation letter are explained later in the chapter.

---

[2] Auditing Standards Board, *op. cit.*, AU § 560.12.

Effects on Auditor's Report

Improper treatment of subsequent events will require modification of the auditor's standard report when the effect on the financial statements is material. Depending on materiality, either a qualified or adverse opinion should be issued, as is explained in Chapter 16.

Make Inquiry of Client's Lawyer

In performing an examination in accordance with generally accepted auditing standards (GAAS), the auditor must determine whether litigations, claims, and assessments (LCA) are reported in conformity with GAAP. Each of these matters is included under the term *loss contingencies* in *FASB Statement No. 5, Accounting for Contingencies*. Loss contingencies should be recorded in the financial statements when (1) the loss is *probable* and (2) the amount of the loss can be reasonably estimated. Disclosure may be warranted when there is only a *possibility* of a loss to the enterprise or the amount of the probable loss cannot be reasonably estimated.

Audit Considerations

With respect to LCA, the auditor should obtain evidential matter as to

- The existence of a condition, situation, or set of circumstances indicating an uncertainty as to the possible loss to an entity arising from litigation, claims, and assessments.
- The period in which the underlying cause for legal action occurred.
- The degree of probability of an unfavorable outcome.
- The amount or range of potential loss.[3]

LCA should be under the direct purview of management. In such cases, management represents the primary source of information about the existence of such matters. Thus, the auditor should obtain from management (1) a description and evaluation concerning LCA that existed at the balance sheet date and (2) assurance from management, preferably in writing, of the existence of any unasserted claims. Other auditing procedures such as the reading of the minutes of directors meetings and a review of contracts and loan agreements may also disclose LCA.

The auditor should examine supporting documentation in the client's files pertaining to all such matters that have come to his attention. It should be recognized, however, that the auditor normally does not possess sufficient legal skills to make an informed judgment on all such matters. Accordingly, the auditor needs the assistance of an outside specialist. A letter of audit inquiry to the client's outside legal counsel is the auditor's primary means of obtaining corroborating information as to management's assertions concerning LCA.

[3] Auditing Standards Board, *op. cit.*, AU § 337.04.

Form and Content of Inquiry

A letter of audit inquiry is illustrated in Figure 15-3. It should be sent by management to each lawyer who has been engaged and who has devoted substantive attention during the year to either pending or threatened LCA or to unasserted claims and ·assessments that management believes would result in an unfavorable outcome if asserted. The letter should ask the lawyer to respond directly to the auditor.

XYZ CORPORATION
Midtown, Texas 48100

[Name and Address of Legal Counsel]

Dear Sirs:

In connection with an examination of our financial statements at [balance sheet date] and for the [period] then ended, management of the Company has prepared, and furnished to our auditors [name and address of auditors], a description and evaluation of certain contingencies, including those set forth below involving matters with respect to which you have been engaged and to which you have devoted substantive attention on behalf of the Company in the form of legal consultation or representation. These contingencies are regarded by management of the Company as material for this purpose. Your response should include matters that existed at [balance sheet date] and during the period from that date to the date of your response.

Pending or Threatened Litigation
[Description Provided]

Unasserted Claims and Assessments
[Description Provided]

Please furnish to our auditors such explanation, if any, that you consider necessary to supplement the foregoing information, including an explanation of those matters as to which your views may differ from those stated and an identification of the omission of any contingencies or a statement that the list of such matters is complete.

We understand that whenever, in the course of performing legal services for us with respect to a matter recognized to involve an unasserted possible claim or assessment that may call for financial statement disclosure, if you have formed a professional conclusion that we should disclose or consider disclosure concerning such possible claim or assessment, as a matter of professional responsibility to us, you will so advise us and will consult with us concerning the question of such disclosure and the applicable requirements of *Statement of Financial Accounting Standards No. 5*. Please specifically confirm to our auditors that our understanding is correct.

Please specifically identify the nature of and reasons for any limitation on your response. A return envelope is enclosed for your reply.

Very truly yours,

_____
Signature of Client

FIGURE 15–3. Letter of Audit Inquiry (SOURCE: Auditing Standards Board, *op. cit.,* AU § 337A.01.)

When the lawyer refuses to respond or if he has not given enough attention to items to be able to respond, it may be necessary for the auditor to modify his report.

Identify and Examine Related Party Transactions

A related party transaction occurs when the relationship between the transacting parties may not permit one of the parties to pursue fully its own separate interests. Examples include transactions (1) between a parent company and its subsidiary, (2) between or among subsidiaries of a common parent, or (3) between a company and its executive officers. An examination made in accordance with GAAS cannot assure that all related party transactions will be discovered. However, the auditor is required to

- Be aware of the possibility that material related party transactions may have occurred.
- Apply procedures that may identify such transactions.
- Determine whether identified related party transactions are properly accounted for, including the appropriateness of financial statement disclosures.

Related party transactions may be discovered through auditing procedures normally performed in an examination. In addition, the auditor should consider applying additional procedures that are specifically directed to related party transactions. These include reviewing (1) the board of director minutes for the authorization of such transactions, (2) conflict-of-interest statements obtained by the company from its management, and (3) related party information submitted in filings with regulatory commissions such as the SEC.[4]

In examining identified related party transactions, the auditor is not expected to determine whether a particular transaction would have occurred if the parties had not been related; or, assuming the transaction did take place, what the exchange price and terms would have been.[5] He is required, however, to determine the substance of the transactions and their effect on the financial statements. To obtain sufficient competent evidential matter about related party transactions, the auditor's procedures should extend beyond inquiry of management.

Obtain Client Representation Letter

The auditor is required to obtain certain written representations from management in meeting the third standard of field work. Client representations are commonly referred to as *rep letters*. The objectives of written representations from management are to

---

[4] Auditing Standards Board, *op. cit.*, AU § 335.13.
[5] Auditing Standards Board, *op. cit.*, AU § 335.18.

- Confirm oral representations given to the auditor.
- Document the continuing appropriateness of such representations.
- Reduce the possibility of misunderstandings concerning management's representations.
- Impress upon management that it has the primary responsibility for the financial statements.

A rep letter complements other auditing procedures, and it may bring to light matters not otherwise discovered by the auditor.

Written representations from management may be limited to matters that either individually or collectively are considered to be material to the financial statements. Such representations should be prepared on the client's stationery, addressed to the auditor, signed by appropriate officers and employees, and dated as of the date of the auditor's report. In many audits, the auditor will draft the representations which subsequently become the responsibility of the individual who signs the letter.

Content of Representation Letter

The professional literature identifies twenty items that may be included in a rep letter. A partial listing is as follows:

- Acknowledgment of management's responsibility for the financial statements.
- Completeness and availability of the accounting records and minutes of meetings of stockholders, directors, and audit committees.
- Absence of unrecorded transactions and errors and irregularities in the financial statements.
- Compliance with (or violations of) laws and regulations.
- Existence (or nonexistence) of compensating balances, related party transactions, contingencies, and losses from contractual commitments.
- Information concerning subsequent events.
- Management's plans or intentions that may affect the carrying value or classification of assets and liabilities.[6]

Representations concerning the foregoing matters normally should be signed by the chief executive officer and the chief financial officer. A rep letter is illustrated in Figure 15-4.

Effects of Representation Letter

A rep letter is not a substitute for any auditing procedures necessary to provide a reasonable basis for an opinion on the financial statements. The

[6] Auditing Standards Board, *op. cit.,* AU § 333.04.

(To the Independent Auditor:)

In connection with your examination of the (identification of financial statements) of (name of client) as of (date) and for the (period of examination) for the purpose of expressing an opinion as to whether the (consolidated) financial statements present fairly the financial position, results of operations, and changes in financial position of (name of client) in conformity with generally accepted accounting principles (other comprehensive basis of accounting), we confirm, to the best of our knowledge and belief, the following representations made to you during your examination.

1. We are responsible for the fair presentation in the (consolidated) financial statements of financial position, results of operations, and changes in financial position in conformity with generally accepted accounting principles (other comprehensive basis of accounting).

2. We have made available to you all—
   a. Financial records and related data.
   b. Minutes of the meetings of stockholders, directors, and committees of directors, or summaries of actions of recent meetings for which minutes have not yet been prepared.

3. There have been no—
   a. Irregularities involving management or employees who have significant roles in the system of internal accounting control.
   b. Irregularities involving other employees that could have a material effect on the financial statements.
   c. Communications from regulatory agencies concerning noncompliance with, or deficiencies in, financial reporting practices that could have a material effect on the financial statements.

4. We have no plans or intentions that may materially affect the carrying value or classification of assets and liabilities.

5. The following have been properly recorded or disclosed in the financial statements:
   a. Related party transactions and related amounts receivable or payable, including sales, purchases, loans, transfers, leasing arrangements, and guarantees.
   b. Capital stock repurchase options or agreements or capital stock reserved for options, warrants, conversions, or other requirements.
   c. Arrangements with financial institutions involving compensating balances or other arrangements involving restrictions on cash balances and line-of-credit or similar arrangements.
   d. Agreements to repurchase assets previously sold.

6. There are no—
   a. Violations or possible violations of laws or regulations whose affects should be considered for disclosure in the financial statements or as a basis for recording a loss contingency.
   b. Other material liabilities or gain or loss contingencies that are required to be accrued or disclosed by *Statement of Financial Accounting Standards No. 5.*

7. There are no unasserted claims or assessments that our lawyer has advised us are probable of assertion and must be disclosed in accordance with *Statement of Financial Accounting Standards No. 5.*

8. There are no material transactions that have not been properly recorded in the accounting records underlying the financial statements.

9. Provision, when material, has been made to reduce excess or obsolete inventories to their estimated net realizable value.

10. The company has satisfactory title to all owned assets, and there are no liens or encumbrances on such assets nor has any asset been pledged.

11. Provision has been made for any material loss to be sustained in the fulfillment of, or from inability to fulfill, any sales commitments.

12. Provision has been made for any material loss to be sustained as a result of purchase commitments for inventory quantities in excess of normal requirements or at prices in excess of the prevailing market prices.

13. We have complied with all aspects of contractual agreements that would have a material effect on the financial statements in the event of noncompliance.

14. No events have occurred subsequent to the balance sheet date that would require adjustment to, or disclosure in, the financial statements.

(Signature of Chief Executive
Officer and Title)

(Signature of Chief Financial
Officer and Title)

FIGURE 15–4. Client Representation Letter (SOURCE: Auditing Standards Board, *op. cit.,* AU § 333A.05.)

representation is a form of documentary evidence. Such evidence is judged to have relatively low reliability because of possible management bias.

The refusal of management to furnish a written representation constitutes a limitation on the scope of the auditor's examination that may preclude the issuance of a standard audit report. A scope limitation may also exist when the auditor is not able to perform audit procedures considered necessary in the circumstances to verify essential data in the management representation letter.

Make Overall Analytical Review

The objective of the typical audit engagement is the expression of an opinion on the fairness of the financial statements taken as a whole. It is essential therefore for the auditor to apply overall analytical review procedures to the final draft of the client's financial statements. In making overall analytical review tests, the auditor may emphasize statement categories and totals. Analytical review procedures that may be performed at the end of the year include the following:

- Compare financial statement subtotals and totals with corresponding prior period amounts and with current year budget expectations.
- Calculate relevant ratios and compare with (1) prior year and current year budgeted ratios, and (2) current year ratios of major competitors or composite industry data.
- Compare nonfinancial data, e.g., sales volume, production volume, and number of employees by location, with prior year and current year planned activity.
- Compare common-size statements to similar statements of prior years.

Both systematic comparison (i.e., comparison of current-year data with budgeted or forecast data for the same period and with actual results of one or more preceding periods) and an analysis of interrelationships should be made. In addition, comparisons of data, such as gross profit margin and net income, with similar industry data may be helpful in judging the fairness of the overall results. Key financial relationships, such as the current ratio, debt-to-equity ratio, book value per share of common stock, and rates of return on assets and common stock equity, are often calculated and systematically compared with other data.

An overall analytical review provides the auditor with a final opportunity to evaluate the reasonableness of the financial statements or conversely to investigate any unusual fluctuations and questionable items.

Make General Review of Statement of Changes in Financial Position

The statement of changes in financial position is a basic financial statement. Thus, the auditor is required to express an opinion on the fairness of its presentation. Ordinarily, it is not necessary for the auditor to perform substantive tests on specific items in the statement because the evidence from tests of income statement and balance sheet accounts should provide sufficient verification for the items. It is usually necessary, however, for the auditor to perform the general steps shown in Figure 15-5.

The auditor should recognize that substantial flexibility in form, content, and terminology is permitted in the statement of changes in financial position. For example, replacing working capital with cash in expressing the changes in financial position is considered to be a reclassification rather than a change in an accounting principle.[7] When changes in the method of presentation materially affect the comparability of the statements, they should be disclosed in the statements and the prior year's statements should be restated using the new method. If this is done, the auditor can issue a standard audit report.

Formulate an Opinion on Financial Statements

During the course of an audit engagement, a variety of audit tests is performed. These tests often are performed by staff personnel whose participation in the audit may be limited to a few areas or accounts. As the tests for each functional area or statement item are completed, the staff auditor is expected to summarize the findings. These findings may include the identification of monetary errors and proposed adjustments.

It is necessary in completing the audit for the separate findings to be summarized and evaluated for the purpose of expressing an opinion on the financial statements taken as a whole. The ultimate responsibility for these

---

General Review of Statement of Changes in Financial Position

1. Verify the clerical accuracy of the statement by recalculation.
2. Ascertain that the statement format (e.g., concept of funds) is the most informative in the circumstances.
3. Ascertain that the statement discloses all important aspects of the company's financing and investing activities.
4. Determine that the statement discloses the important sources and uses of cash (or working capital).
5. Ascertain that the format correctly and prominently shows funds provided from or used by operations and funds provided from or used by extraordinary items.
6. Verify that the statement is based on the balances shown in the audited financial statements at the beginning and end of the period covered by the audit.
7. Establish that a statement of changes in financial position is presented for each period for which an income statement is presented.
8. Trace, match, or agree statement amounts to like amounts in other financial statements and/or in the working papers.
9. Ascertain that the term "funds" used in the presentation is consistent with prior years.
10. Establish that a comparative schedule of working capital elements is presented.

FIGURE 15-5. Audit Program: Statement of Changes in Financial Position

[7] Auditing Standards Board, *op. cit.*, AU § 420.15.

steps rests with the partner in charge of the engagement. In some cases, audit managers make the initial determinations which are then carefully reviewed by the partner.

The summarization of monetary errors is objective; the formulation of an opinion is subjective. Before reaching a final decision on the opinion, a conference is held with the client. At this meeting, the auditor reports his findings orally and attempts to provide rationale for proposed adjustments and/or additional disclosures. Management, in turn, may attempt to defend its position. In the end, agreement is generally reached on the changes to be made and the auditor can proceed to issue a standard audit report. Where such an agreement is not obtained, the auditor may not be able to issue an unqualified opinion.

Communication of the auditor's opinion is made through an audit report. Audit reports are explained in Chapters 16 and 17.

Complete Review of Working Papers

In Chapter 3, the first-level review of working papers by a supervisor is explained. It will be recalled that the review is made to evaluate the work done, the evidence obtained, and the conclusions reached by the preparer of the working paper. Additional reviews of the working papers are made at the end of field work. The following illustrates the various levels of review that may be made in completing the audit.

REVIEWER	NATURE AND PURPOSE(S) OF REVIEW
Manager	Reviews working papers prepared by seniors and reviews some or all of the working papers reviewed by seniors.
Partner in charge of engagement	Reviews working papers prepared by managers and reviews other working papers on a selective basis to (1) evaluate work done and (2) determine if the working papers support the auditor's opinion.

A working paper review guide (or checklist) is used in many firms to facilitate the review process. A checklist of 30 to 40 items, with questions such as those shown in Figure 15-6, is typical.

Make Technical Review of Financial Statements

Many public accounting firms have detailed financial statement checklists that are completed by the auditor who performs the initial review or drafts the financial statements. The completed checklist is then reviewed by the manager and/or partner in charge of the engagement. Prior to the release of the audit report on a publicly held client, there may also be a technical review of the statements by an independent partner.

The checklists include matters pertaining to the form and content of each of the basic financial statements as well as to required disclosures. Most firms now have separate checklists for SEC and non-SEC clients. The

Do the working papers contain evidence of proper planning and supervision?	☐
Are all open points cleared and all questions answered?	☐
Are overall evaluations of internal controls included in the working papers?	☐
Is there documentation of tests and evaluation of the internal audit function, and of the nature and extent of reliance thereon?	☐
Are written conclusions as to the audit work for each significant account or group of related accounts included in the working papers?	☐
Do the working papers contain a summary of significant matters relative to audit procedures or financial statement presentation which were brought to the attention of the partner or principal by the manager?	☐

FIGURE 15–6. Partial Working Paper Review Checklist

completed checklist and the findings of the reviewers should be included in the working papers.

Make Independent In-House Review of Working Papers

The quality control procedures for many firms require an independent "cold" review before issuance of the audit report. A "cold" review of the audit working papers is made by one or more partners who have not otherwise participated in the audit engagement. The rationale is that this review may detect shortcomings in the working papers that were missed in earlier reviews. Thus, this review provides additional assurance that all GAAS have been met.

Make Required Communication of Material Weaknesses in Internal Accounting Control

As briefly explained in Chapter 4, the auditor is required to communicate material weaknesses in internal accounting control to senior management and the board of directors (or its audit committee) that have come to his attention during the audit engagement. It will be recalled that a *material weakness* is a condition where there is more than a relatively low risk that errors or irregularities, in amounts material to the financial statements, may occur and not be detected within a timely period by employees in the normal course of performing their assigned functions.

The communication, which may be oral or written, should be made at the earliest practicable date following the completion of the auditor's study and evaluation of internal accounting control or his entire examination. A suggested form of written communication issued at the conclusion of an audit engagement is illustrated in Chapter 17.

In the absence of material weaknesses, the auditor is not required to communicate that fact. When there are material weaknesses for which management believes corrective action is not practicable, the auditor may limit his communication to a summary of such weaknesses and a statement to the effect that correction is impracticable. The auditor may include in his communication comments concerning corrective action that has been taken or is in process. In addition, an auditor may elect to disclose immaterial weaknesses in internal accounting control. The auditor's communication on material weaknesses in internal accounting control may be issued separately or be incorporated in a management letter. The auditor's communication on internal accounting control may be useful to management in its evaluation of compliance with the internal accounting control provisions of the Foreign Corrupt Practices Act. Because of its importance in this regard, extra care should be exercised by the auditor in identifying a weakness as material.

Prepare and Issue Management Letter

During the course of an audit engagement, auditors observe many facets of the client's business organization and operations. At the conclusion of an examination, many auditors believe it is desirable to write a letter to management which contains recommendations for improving the efficiency and effectiveness of those matters which were noticed during the course of the audit. The issuance of such letters has become an integral part of the services rendered by many auditors to their clients. A management letter tangibly demonstrates the auditors continuing interest in the welfare and future of the client.

The audit plan should contain a separate section on management letters. Where feasible the plan should indicate areas of the client's operations and controls that might be included in management letters. It should also suggest the possible assistance of tax and management services personnel in the audit and the timing of their participation.

Matters that are relevant to management letters should be noted in the audit working papers as the audit progresses to insure that they are not overlooked. Subsequently, the working papers should provide adequate documentation of the management letter comments. Such support will also be useful in any discussions with management about the comments.

Management letters should be carefully prepared, well-organized, and written in a constructive tone. Prompt issuance of the letters creates a favorable impression and may encourage both an early and positive response by management.

Management letters may include comments on

- Internal accounting control weaknesses that are not considered to be material.
- The accounting and information system, including EDP.
- Administrative controls pertaining to achieving the objectives of the organization.
- Management of resources such as cash, inventories, and investments.
- Tax-related matters.

An example of a management letter is shown in Figure 15-7.

REDDY & ABEL
Certified Public Accountants
4 Court Street
Urban, Michigan 48206

March 31, 19X1

Dear Mr. Jones:

Our examination of the financial statements of OYE Inc. for the year ended December 31, 19X0 has disclosed certain opportunities for improvements in your organization and operations. Items which we believe should be brought to your attention are set forth below.

Internal Accounting Control

One individual is both the cashier and the custodian of marketable securities. We believe these duties should be segregated between two employees in order to minimize the possibility of unauthorized purchases and sales of marketable securities.

Data Processing

Because of the size of the Company and the widespread geographic location of its operating entities, we believe you should begin to develop a long range data processing plan. Without such a plan, the Company might find itself in the position of utilizing several service bureaus, developing noncoordinated procedures, or possibly acquiring small pieces of equipment at outlying locations which are not compatible.

Administrative Controls

Common stock

As in the prior years, there is no effective means to control the number of stock certificates outstanding. We recommend that all stock certificates outstanding be assigned a permanent number and that new certificates be issued from a stub-type stock book using prenumbered certificates. Periodically, the open stubs in the stock book should be reconciled to shares outstanding.

Insurance coverage

The Company presently carries life insurance coverage on the President. We recommend that life insurance coverage be considered for other executives vital to the Company's continued success.

Tax Matters

Sales tax on property and equipment purchases

Sales taxes paid on purchases of property and equipment are capitalized in the financial statements and tax returns. Such taxes can be deducted for tax purposes.

This letter is issued solely for the information of the Company's management; it should not be presented or quoted to anyone outside the Company. We would be pleased to discuss the matters reported or to answer any questions you may have at your convenience.

Yours very truly,

Reddy & Abel

Reddy & Abel
Certified Public Accountants

FIGURE 15-7. Management Letter

POSTAUDIT RESPONSIBILITIES

This section pertains to the auditor's responsibilities following the completion of field work. It includes a consideration of

- Subsequent events occurring between the date and issuance of the auditor's report.
- The discovery after issuing the audit report of facts that were unknown at issuance.

Responsibility for Subsequent Events Occurring After Completion of Field Work but Before Issuance of Report

As shown in Figure 15-2, a time interval of one to two weeks may elapse between the end of field work and the actual issuance of the audit report. The auditor has no responsibility to make any inquiry or to perform any auditing procedures during this time period to discover any material subsequent events.[8] However, if knowledge of such an event comes to the auditor's attention, he should consider whether there should be disclosure in or adjustment of the financial statements for the event. When adjustment is required and management appropriately modifies the statements, the auditor may issue a standard audit report. When required disclosure is made by management, the auditor may also issue a standard report providing the report is *redated* to coincide with the date of the subsequent event. Alternatively, the auditor may *dual date* the audit report. Under this course of action, the original date is retained except for the dating of the subsequent event. For example, dual dating might say:

> February 28, 19X1, except for the information in Note X for which the date is March 7, 19X1.

Dual dating is the most common practice because redating of the entire report extends the auditor's overall responsibility beyond the completion of field work. Under redating, the auditor should extend his subsequent events review procedures to the later date. If management refuses to make the necessary changes for the event, the auditor should qualify his opinion and dual-date his report.

Responsibility for Postaudit Discovery of Facts Existing at Date of Audit Report

Postaudit discovery relates to the time period after the issuance date of the audit report. In Figure 15-2, the time period begins after March 15. The fact, in this case, is not limited to the occurrence of a subsequent event. The event, in this instance, may have occurred prior to the balance sheet date or between that date and the date of the audit report, but the auditor does

---

[8] Auditing Standards Board, *op. cit.,* AU § 530.02.

not become aware of that fact until after the audit report has been issued. Examples include the postaudit discovery of fraud or a flaw in legal title that negates ownership of property.

The auditor has no responsibility for the postaudit discovery of facts existing (but unknown) at the date of the audit report. However, if (1) the auditor becomes aware of such facts and (2) the facts may have affected the report that was issued, the auditor is required to ascertain the reliability of the information. When the investigation confirms the existence of the fact and the auditor believes the information is important to those relying or likely to rely on the financial statements, the auditor should take steps to prevent future reliance on the audit report.

The preferred result is the preparation of revised statements by the client and the issuance of a revised audit report as soon as practicable. If the client refuses to disclose the newly discovered facts, the auditor should notify each member of the board of directors of such refusal and take the following steps to prevent further reliance on his report:

- Notify the client that the audit report must no longer be associated with the financial statements.
- Notify the regulatory agencies having jurisdiction over the client that the report should no longer be relied on.
- Notify (generally vià the regulatory agency) each individual known to be relying on the statements that the report should no longer be relied on.[9]

CONCLUDING COMMENTS

This chapter completes the explanation of substantive tests of account balances and the auditor's responsibilities in completing the audit. When considered in concert with Parts I and I₋ of this book, six of the ten GAAS have been explained. We now proceed to Part IV, where in-depth consideration is given to the four reporting standards and other auditor responsibilities.

REVIEW QUESTIONS

15–1. Evaluate revenue and expense balances in regard to materiality and risk.

15–2. Identify the steps involved in the auditor's approach to verifying income statement balances.

15–3. Indicate the specific applicability of the audit objectives to revenue and expense balances.

15–4. Indicate the types of disclosures that may necessitate direct testing of income statement balances.

15–5. What are the two types of activities that pertain to completing the audit?

15–6. a. What is meant by the term *subsequent events?*
b. Identify the two types of subsequent events and the criteria used in distinguishing between them.

[9] Auditing Standards Board, *op. cit.*, AU § 561.08.

15–7. a. What is the auditor's responsibility for subsequent events?
b. How does he discharge this responsibility?

15–8. What specific procedures should be performed to ascertain the existence of subsequent events?

15–9. What information should the auditor obtain about litigation, claims, and assessments (LCA)?

15–10. a. Can an examination in accordance with GAAS be expected to discover all related party transactions? Discuss.
b. What approach is followed by the auditor in discovering related party transactions?

15–11. a. What objectives are met by a client representation letter?
b. What effect may a "rep" letter have on the auditor's examination and audit report?

15–12. Identify four items that may be included in a representation letter.

15–13. a. What factors should be emphasized in making an overall analytical review?
b. What purpose is served by an overall analytical review?

15–14. The auditor must examine the specific items in the statement of changes in financial position. Do you agree? Why or why not?

15–15. Who are the principal recipients of the auditor's required communication of material weaknesses in internal accounting control?

15–16. Indicate the form and timing of the auditor's communication of material weaknesses in internal accounting control.

15–17. a. What purpose is served by management letters?
b. List the types of data that may be included in management letters.

15–18. What is the auditor's responsibility for subsequent events occurring after completion of field work but before issuance of his audit report?

15–19. What is meant by dual dating an audit report?

15–20. a. What responsibility does the auditor have for the postaudit discovery of facts existing at the date of his report?
b. Identify the steps the auditor should take when the client refuses to make disclosure of the newly discovered facts.

COMPREHENSIVE QUESTIONS

15–21. Windek, a CPA, is nearing the completion of an examination of the financial statements of Jubilee, Inc., for the year ended December 31, 19X0. Windek is currently concerned with ascertaining the occurrence of subsequent events that may require adjustment or disclosure essential to a fair presentation in conformity with generally accepted accounting principles.

Required
a. Briefly explain what is meant by the phrase "subsequent event."
b. How do those subsequent events which require financial statement adjustment differ from those that require financial statement disclosure?
c. What are the procedures which should be performed in order to ascertain the occurrence of subsequent events?

AICPA

15–22. In connection with your examination of the financial statements of Olars Manufacturing Corporation for the year ended December 31, 19X0, your post-balance-sheet-date review disclosed the following items:

1. January 3, 19X1: The state government approved a plan for the construction of an express highway. The plan will result in the appropriation of a portion of the land area owned by Olars Manufacturing Corporation. Construction will begin in late 19X1. No estimate of the condemnation award is available.

2. January 4, 19X1: The funds for a $25,000 loan to the Corporation made by Mr. Olars on July 15, 19X0 were obtained by him by a loan on his personal life insurance policy. The loan was recorded in the account Loan from Officers. Mr. Olars' source of the funds was not disclosed in the Company records. The Corporation pays the premiums on the life insurance policy and Mrs. Olars, wife of the president, is the beneficiary of the policy.

3. January 7, 19X1: The mineral content of a shipment of ore en route on December 31, 19X0 was determined to be 72%. The shipment was recorded at year end at an estimated content of 50% by a debit to Raw Material Inventory and a credit to Accounts Payable in the amount of $20,600. The final liability to the vendor is based on the actual mineral content of the shipment.

4. January 15, 19X1: Culminating a series of personal disagreements between Mr. Olars, the president, and his brother-in-law, the treasurer, the latter resigned, effective immediately, under an agreement whereby the Corporation would purchase his 10% stock ownership at book value as of December 31, 19X0. Payment is to be made in two equal amounts in cash on April 1 and October 1, 19X1. In December the treasurer had obtained a divorce from his wife, who was Mr. Olars' sister.

5. January 31, 19X1: As a result of reduced sales, production was curtailed in mid-January and some workers were laid off. On February 5, 19X1 all the remaining workers went on strike. To date the strike is unsettled.

6. February 10, 19X1: A contract was signed whereby Mammoth Enterprises purchased from Olars Manufacturing Corporation all of the latter's fixed assets (including rights to receive the proceeds of any property condemnation), inventories, and the right to conduct business under the name "Olars Manufacturing Division." The effective date of the transfer will be March 1, 19X1. The sale price was $500,000 subject to adjustment following the taking of a physical inventory. Important factors contributing to the decision to enter into the contract were the policy of the board of directors of Mammoth Industries to diversify the firm's activities and the report of a survey conducted by an independent market appraisal firm which revealed a declining market for Olars products.

Required

Assume that the above items came to your attention prior to completion of your audit work on February 15, 19X1 and that you will render an audit report. For *each* of the above items:

a. Give the audit procedures, if any, that would have brought the item to your attention. Indicate other sources of information that may have revealed the item.

b. Discuss the disclosure that you would recommend for the item, listing all details that you would suggest should be disclosed. Indicate those items or details, if any, that should not be disclosed. Give your reasons for recommending or not recommending disclosure of the items or details.

AICPA

15–23. In connection with his examination of Flowmeter, Inc., for the year ended December 31, 19X0, Hirsch, CPA, is aware that certain events and transactions that took place after December 31, 19X0 but before he issues his report dated February 28, 19X1, may affect the company's financial statements.

The following material events or transactions have come to his attention.

1. On January 3, 19X1, Flowmeter, Inc., received a shipment of raw materials from Canada. The materials had been ordered in October 19X0 and shipped FOB shipping point in November 19X0.

2. On January 15, 19X1, the company settled and paid a personal injury claim of a

former employee as the result of an accident which occurred in March 19X0. The company had not previously recorded a liability for the claim.

3. On January 25, 19X1, the company agreed to purchase for cash the outstanding stock of Porter Electrical Co. The acquisition is likely to double the sales volume of Flowmeter, Inc.

4. On February 1, 19X1, a plant owned by Flowmeter, Inc., was damaged by a flood resulting in an uninsured loss of inventory.

5. On February 5, 19X1, Flowmeter, Inc., issued and sold to the general public $2,000,000 in convertible bonds.

Required

For each of the above events or transactions, indicate the audit procedures that should have brought the item to the attention of the auditor, and the form of disclosure in the financial statements including the reasons for such disclosures. Organize your answer in the following format:

Item No.	Audit Procedures	Required Disclosure or Entry and Reasons

AICPA

15–24.* During an audit engagement an auditor is expected to communicate with lawyers concerning claims, litigation, and assessments. Listed below are five situations regarding LCA. The last clause or sentence of each case states a conclusion:

1. If the client's lawyer is silent on certain aspects of an attorney's letter request, the auditor may infer the response is complete.

2. Letters of audit inquiry ask for the lawyer's evaluation of the probable outcome of matters reported in his response. If the lawyer's response doesn't contain this evaluation, the auditor should conclude the scope of his examination has been restricted.

3. The Top Dollar Corporation is involved in litigation where the potential liability is so great that an unfavorable judgment at or near the claimed amount would seriously impair its operations. This is how the company's attorneys answered the legal confirmation request:

> While no assurance can be given as to the outcome of this action, based upon the facts known by us to date, in the confidence of the attorney/client relationship and otherwise, and our understanding of the present law, we believe the company has good and meritorious defense to the claims asserted against it and should prevail.

On this basis, the independent auditor may issue an unqualified opinion.

4. In situations where the auditor has orally discussed matters involving litigation with the client's legal counsel and has obtained his oral opinion on the outcome of disputed matters, it is not necessary to obtain written confirmation of these oral opinions if the auditor has summarized the attorney's opinion in a memo to the working papers.

5. For the past ten years, XYZ Company has used the services of JJH&I for its primary legal advice and in many significant matters of litigation. 95% of JJH&I's legal fees originate from services performed for XYZ Company. At December 31, JJH&I was handling litigation involving great potential liability to the company and has now responded to the auditor's letter of inquiry. Assuming full disclosure, complete reliance can be placed on this response.

Required
For each case indicate whether you agree or disagree with the conclusion and the reason(s) therefor.

15–25. During an audit engagement Harper, CPA, has satisfactorily completed an examination of accounts payable and other liabilities and now plans to determine whether there are any loss contingencies arising from litigation, claims, or assessments.

Required
What are the audit procedures that Harper should follow with respect to the existence of loss contingencies arising from litigation, claims, and assessments? Do not discuss reporting requirements.

AICPA

15–26. In your audit of the Learned Corporation you request a management "rep" letter. You are particularly interested in management's representations on

1. Irregularities involving management or employees.
2. Minutes of directors' meetings.
3. Compliance with laws and regulations.
4. Completeness of the accounting records.
5. Net realizable value of inventories.
6. Ownership of assets.

Required
Using Figure 15-4 as an example, prepare a rep letter in good form covering the points listed above.

15–27. In auditing the financial statements of a manufacturing company that were prepared from data processed by electronic data processing equipment, the CPA has found that his traditional "audit trail" has been obscured. As a result the CPA may place increased emphasis upon overall checks of the data under audit. These overall checks, which are also applied in auditing visibly posted accounting records, include the computation of ratios, which are compared to prior year ratios or to industrywide norms. Examples of such overall checks or ratios are the computation of the rate of inventory turnover and the computation of the number of days' sales in receivables.

Required
a. Discuss the advantages to the CPA of the use of ratios as overall checks in an audit.
b. In addition to the computations given above, list the ratios that a CPA may compute during an audit as overall checks on balance sheet accounts and related nominal accounts. For each ratio listed name the two (or more) accounts used in its computation.
c. When a CPA discovers that there has been a significant change in a ratio when compared to the prior year's ratio, he considers the possible reasons for the change. Give the possible reasons for the following significant changes in ratios:

1. The rate of inventory turnover (ratio of cost of sales and average inventory) has decreased from the prior year's rate.
2. The number of days' sales in receivables (ratio of average daily accounts receivable and sales) has increased over the prior year.

AICPA

15–28. Annette, CPA, is conducting the 19X0 audit of the financial statements of Johnson Company and has been given the following statement of changes in financial position:

Johnson Company
Statement of Changes in Financial Position
For the Year Ended December 31, 19X0
(in thousands)

Funds provided from operations:

Net income from operations	$46,000
Add or (deduct) items not requiring outlay of working capital in the current period:	
Depreciation	5,500
Deferred income taxes	1,500
Investment in unconsolidated subsidiary (net of cash dividends paid)	(1,700)*
From operations prior to extraordinary loss	51,300
Extraordinary loss	(13,000)
From operations after extraordinary loss	38,300
Proceeds from exercise of stock options	2,700*
Total	$41,000

Funds used:

Cash dividends paid on comon and preferred stock	$15,000*
Increase in long-term investments (net of allowance)	3,000 ⎫
Allowance for unrealized losses on noncurrent marketable equity securities	5,000 ⎬*
Increase in working capital	18,000
Total	$41,000

Changes in Working Capital—Increase (Decrease):

Cash and short-term investments	$ (9,000)
Accounts receivable	17,000
Inventories	18,000
Accounts payable and accrued liabilities	(7,000)
Other current assets and liabilities	(1,000)
Increase in working capital	$18,000

Annette has completed necessary auditing procedures on the balance sheet, income statement, and statement of stockholders' equity and is satisfied that these statements are fairly presented with adequate disclosures in the statements and the footnotes. Annette has not yet examined the statement of changes in financial position.

Required
a. What general steps should be followed by Annette to examine the statement of changes in financial position of the Johnson Company? Do not discuss the presentation or verification of any specific item on the statement.
b. What additional specific steps should be followed by Annette to verify each of the four items marked with an asterisk (*) on the statement of changes in financial position of the Johnson Company?

AICPA

15–29. The major result of a financial audit conducted by an independent accountant is the expression of an opinion by the auditor on the fairness of the financial statements. While the auditor's report containing the opinion is the best known report issued by the independent auditor, other reports are often prepared during the course of a normal audit. One such report is the management letter (informal report).

Required

a. What is the purpose of a management letter?

b. Identify the major types of information that are likely to be covered in a management letter. Support your answer with a detailed example of one of the types identified above.

CMA

15–30. Tuloak Manufacturing Company is a small manufacturer of oak porch swings. It was organized as a proprietorship by its current president and majority stockholder, Samuel Lawten. Tuloak was incorporated in 19X0 when growth of the company necessitated the raising of additional capital.

The accounting system of Tuloak is quite simple. The system has evolved over the years in response to external reporting requirements, and a strong emphasis has not been placed on internal control. The firm's relatively small size (49 employees) also makes effective internal control more difficult than in a larger firm.

The CPA firm of Deber & Associates has been hired to perform the audit of Tuloak for fiscal year ending October 31, 19X0. This is the first time that Deber has been engaged to audit Tuloak's financial statements. The partner-in-charge of the audit has reminded his staff that material weaknesses in internal control must be communicated to audit clients. The partner has concluded that a management letter should be issued to Tuloak following the audit for the year ended October 31, 19X0. The management letter sent by Deber to Tuloak is reproduced below.

Upon receipt of the management letter, Mr. Lawten asked his chief accountant, Charles Earl, to respond to the management letter. The response prepared by Mr. Earl is shown on the next page.

Deber & Associates, CPAs
Oak Park, North Carolina

Samuel Lawten, President
Tuloak Manufacturing Company

In connection with our audit of the financial statements of Tuloak Manufacturing Company of October 31, 19X0, we reviewed various internal procedures and controls of the company in order to plan the scope of the audit. We did not make a comprehensive review for the purpose of submitting detailed recommendations. However, as a result of our review, we did observe certain areas where material weaknesses in internal controls and procedure exist. These weaknesses are itemized below and should be corrected.

Cash. Control over cash disbursements for purchases of materials is inadequate due to the fact that creditor checks are prepared by the accounts payable bookkeeper, later signed by the treasurer, then returned to the accounts payable bookkeeper for mailing to creditors.

We recommend that the checks be mailed by the treasurer rather than by the accounts payable bookkeeper.

Accounts Receivable. The extension of credit to customers is approved by the sales manager, who also authorizes the write-off of delinquent accounts.

We recommend that the write-off of delinquent accounts be approved by the chief accountant.

Inventory. Purchases of raw materials are made only upon receipt of a purchase requisition signed by the production supervisor. When shipments of raw materials are received, a receiving report is signed by any available production worker in the vicinity of the receiving dock.

We recommend that the production supervisor be the only employee permitted to sign the receiving report; then the supervisor will know that the materials requisitioned have arrived.

Marketable Securities. Stock certificates related to marketable securities are kept in Mr. Lawten's office desk drawer to facilitate prompt settlement when the expected holding period is relatively short.

We recommend that all stock certificates be held in a bank safety deposit box accessible only to Mr. Lawten.

Payroll. Hourly production workers are required to punch in on a mechanical time clock each morning, then punch out at the end of the day. Presumably, they take a one-hour lunch break. Occasionally, a worker might not return from lunch, have a friend punch his card at the end of the day, and receive a full day's pay for a half-day's work.

To prevent this from happening in the future, we recommend that each employee be required to punch out and back in for lunch and that each supervisor initial the daily time cards of each employee under his/her control, thereby verifying the presence of workers for the full day.

Sincerely,

_____

Deber & Associates

Memorandum

TO: Samuel Lawten, President
FROM: Charles Earl, Chief Accountant
SUBJECT: Response to management letter from Deber & Associates

Pursuant to your request, I am writing this memo in response to the management letter of our independent accountants, Deber & Associates. My comments related to each of their recommendations are presented below.

Cash. I do not believe that the change in procedure recommended is necessary because the accounts payable bookkeeper cannot possibly benefit from handling the signed checks made payable to our material suppliers. Each check is supported by an approved purchase requisition, purchase order, receiving report, and vendor's invoice.

Accounts Receivable. The current system of having the sales manager approve the write-off of delinquent accounts is preferable because the sales manager is more familiar with each of the customers having delinquent accounts and thus can more accurately determine the appropriate time to write off their accounts. In addition, as chief accountant I should not be required to approve the write-off of accounts which I am responsible for maintaining.

Inventory. The auditors' recommendation that the production supervisor alone sign receiving reports is impractical because the supervisor is often supervising employees physically removed from the vicinity of the receiving dock. Such a requirement would reduce the production supervisor's effectiveness. I suggest we continue with the present system of receiving report approvals.

Marketable Securities. All stock certificates related to marketable securities are registered in the company name so putting such certificates in a bank safety deposit box is unnecessary. In addition, your desk drawer may be locked, and the advantage of convenient access more than offsets any improvement in control.

Payroll. The recommendation that hourly production workers punch out and back in for their lunch breaks would necessitate new time cards to accommodate twice as many clock entries as are currently required. In addition, if an employee is going to miss a half day's work by having a friend punch his or her card at the end of the day under the current system, only one additional erroneous entry will be required by the friend after lunch under the proposed system.

Required

For each of the weaknesses of internal controls and procedures identified by Deber & Associates, discuss whether

a. The weakness identified by Deber & Associates is substantive and should be brought to Tuloak's attention.

b. The recommendation proposed by Deber & Associates is a reasonable and appropriate solution.

c. The response of Charles Earl of Tuloak Manufacturing Company is satisfactory under the circumstances.

CMA

15–31.   The fiscal year of the Eddy Company ends on December 31. Your audit report, dated February 26, is to be delivered to the client on March 9. Listed below are events that occur or are discovered from the date of the balance sheet to June 30 of the following year:

1. Jan. 15 Inventory is sold at a price below December 31 net realizable value.
2. Jan. 20 A major customer becomes bankrupt from net losses.
3. Jan. 31 The board of directors authorizes the acquisition of a company as a subsidiary.
4. Feb. 10 A fire destroys a major company warehouse.
5. Feb. 25 A lawsuit is decided against the company for an accident that occurred on October 10. The damages are three times higher than estimated on December 31.
6. Feb. 28 The board of directors authorizes a 2-for-1 stock split.
7. Mar. 7 A foreign government expropriates a major foreign subsidiary following the unexpected overthrow of the government.
8. Mar. 31 A court rules that a minority group is the rightful legal owner of land on which an operating division is located.

Required

a. Identify each event as a (1) subsequent event requiring adjustment, (2) subsequent event requiring disclosure, (3) subsequent event occurring after field work but before issuance of report, or (4) postaudit discovery of facts existing at date of report.

b. Explain your audit responsibilities for each of the categories in (a).

c. Indicate how you would obtain knowledge of each of the eight items.

d. What additional responsibilities does an auditor have for item (a4) above if the client refuses to make required disclosures?

CASE STUDY

15–32.* On June 15, you were assigned to the current year's audit of Castle Petroleum Company. The company is a large, progressive oil company operating in the United States and fifteen foreign countries. Last year, gross sales were $600 million and net income was $60 million. Total assets approximated $850 million at December 31 of the preceding year.

The controller is responsible for maintaining the financial records of the company, preparing and interpreting financial statements, preparing federal and state tax returns, studying and establishing systems and procedures, formulating depreciation policies, coordinating matters between the company and the independent public accountants, and certain other matters. The treasurer's department is the custodian of cash and securities and is responsible for collecting cash receipts, disbursing funds, preparing cash forecasts and budgets, and maintaining friendly relations with bankers and underwriters.

Your review and tests of internal control during interim work disclose the following:

1. No accounting manual is maintained to provide descriptions of the approximately 450 accounts. However, a chart of accounts showing account number, name, and sub-codings is used. Periodically, bulletins on special accounting problems are issued. A suggestion that a descriptive accounting manual be maintained was incorporated in your firm's management letter two years ago. The controller has indicated that such a manual is probably desirable, but you find that no effort has been made to develop one.
2. No listing is prepared of checks received in the mailroom and subsequently forwarded to the cash receipts section. All letters are opened by the mailroom unless it is obvious that a check is enclosed. If an envelope appears to contain a check, it is forwarded to the cash receipts section unopened. Approximately 250 check remittances are received each day. Receipts in cash are minor.
3. During your several visits to the treasurer's department, you note that the check signing machines are left unlocked at noon. Virtually all checks are signed by machine. The number of signatures recorded by the machines are investigated. At all times, blank checks are locked in a filing cabinet located in the same room with the check signing machines; the key to the cabinet is hidden in an unlocked desk drawer.
4. The company generally attempts to do most of its purchasing through the purchasing department located at the home office. However, to prevent the closing down of plants or drilling sites, field personnel are authorized to make emergency purchases. Company policy requires that the employee making the purchase obtain a counter order slip (COS). The COS then is routed to the district supervisor for approval and submission to the purchasing department at the home office. The purchasing department then prepares a confirming purchase order (CPO) for each COS instructing the vendor to invoice Castle Petroleum Company. The CPO is mailed to the vendor. Approximately 125,000 CPOs are prepared each year.
5. For years, the company has prepared annual budgets for each operating department and at year-end the actual results have been compared and variances investigated. The budgets are prepared by the treasurer and are reviewed and approved by the board of directors.
6. Capital expenditure proposals are accompanied by a calculation of the payback period. Subsequent savings are compared to those forecast in an effort to improve forecasting ability.

Required

Prepare a draft of a management letter which you believe is appropriate. If you exclude any of the above, give your reasons.

IV Reporting and Other Responsibilities

In this, the concluding part of this book, attention is directed at the reporting standards and the responsibilities imposed on the auditor by the profession, the courts, and the Securities and Exchange Commission. There are five chapters in this part.

The first two chapters relate to the auditor's reporting function. Chapter 16 focuses exclusively on audit reports in the typical audit engagement. Chapter 17 considers other types of audit reports and communications resulting from other types of professional services.

The final three chapters explain the responsibilities of the auditor in (1) meeting the rules of professional conduct established by the public accounting profession, (2) recognizing the potential legal liabilities in the practice of public accounting, and (3) complying with the requirements of the Securities and Exchange Commission in rendering professional services to SEC clients.

16 Reporting on Audited Financial Statements

STUDY OBJECTIVES

The study objectives of this chapter are to acquire an understanding of the four reporting standards and the circumstances that require a modification of the auditor's standard report. To achieve these objectives, it is necessary for the reader to

- Know the four reporting standards.
- Realize the requisites for issuing a standard audit report.
- Recognize the circumstances that result in a modification of the auditor's standard report.
- Perceive the effects of each type of circumstance on the form and content of the auditor's report.

The final phase of the auditing process is reporting the findings. In the preparation and issuance of a report on audited financial statements, the auditor must comply with the four reporting standards. Each of these generally accepted auditing standards (GAAS) is explained and illustrated in this chapter. In addition, consideration will be given to circumstances that may cause the auditor to modify the standard audit report.

Throughout this chapter, it will be assumed that management is asserting that the financial statements are prepared in conformity with generally accepted accounting principles (GAAP).

STANDARDS OF REPORTING

Statement of the Reporting Standards

The four reporting standards are as follows:

- The report shall state whether the financial statements are presented in accordance with generally accepted accounting principles.
- The report shall state whether such principles have been consistently observed in the current period in relation to the preceding period.
- Informative disclosures in the financial statements are to be regarded as reasonably adequate unless otherwise stated in the report.
- The report shall contain either an expression of opinion regarding the financial statements, taken as a whole, or an assertion to the effect that an opinion cannot be expressed. When an overall opinion cannot be expressed, the reasons therefor should be stated. In all cases where an auditor's name is associated with financial statements, the report should contain a clear-cut indication of the character of the auditor's examination, if any, and the degree of responsibility he is taking.[1]

The first three reporting standards are discussed in due course. For the present, attention is focused on the fourth reporting standard.

The Fourth Reporting Standard

The objective of the fourth standard is to prevent misinterpretation of the degree of responsibility the auditor is assuming when his name is associated with financial statements.[2] This standard directly influences the form, content, and language of the auditor's report.

---

[1] Auditing Standards Board, *Codification of Statements on Auditing Standards* (New York: American Institute of Certified Public Accountants, 1983), Auditing Section 150.02 (hereinafter referred to and cited as AU §).

[2] Auditing Standards Board, *op. cit.,* AU § 509.05.

Expressing or Denying an Opinion

This standard requires the auditor to express an opinion or to assert that an opinion cannot be expressed. In the latter case, the reasons therefor should be stated in the auditor's report. There are four types of opinions that may be expressed—unqualified, qualified, adverse, or disclaimer (no opinion).

Financial Statements

The financial statements referred to in this standard apply to a single statement, such as a balance sheet, as well as to a complete set of basic statements (balance sheet, income statement, retained earnings statement, and statement of changes in financial position). In some cases, the basic statements may be accompanied by a statement of changes in stockholders' equity accounts. The financial statements may be individual company statements, consolidated statements, and statements of one or more prior periods that are presented on a comparative basis with those of the current period. The auditor's opinion must be expressed (or denied) in terms of the financial statement(s) that have been examined as set forth in the scope paragraph of the auditor's report.

Reference in the fourth standard of reporting to the statements "taken as a whole" is important to the auditor in several ways. First, it means that the auditor's opinion should pertain to what the individual statement, in its entirety, purports to present. For the balance sheet, this is financial position; for the income statement, it is results of operations, etc. The auditor is not expected to express an opinion on individual components or categories of the individual statement in the ordinary audit engagement. Second, "taken as a whole" does not mean that the auditor is prohibited from expressing different opinions on the statements included in a complete set of financial statements. It is possible, for example, to express an unqualified opinion on the balance sheet and another type of opinion on the income statement and the statement of changes in financial position. Different opinions within a given set of basic financial statements are rare.

Character of Auditor's Examination

Along with the expression (or denial) of an opinion regarding the financial statements, the auditor is required to include in his report a clear-cut indication of the character of the examination. The nature of the examination is described in the second sentence of the scope paragraph of the auditor's report through the phrases "in accordance with generally accepted auditing standards," "tests of the accounting records," and "such other auditing procedures as we considered necessary in the circumstances." In lay terms, these phrases can be interpreted to mean that the examination was made according to established professional standards, which included selective testing of the accounting records and the application of appropriate auditing procedures.

The primary frame of reference for an examination is generally accepted auditing standards (GAAS), and any depatures from these standards must be indicated in the scope paragraph of the auditor's report. When an examination has not been made, the scope paragraph should clearly indicate this fact and there should be no reference to auditing standards.

Association with Financial Statements

A certified public accountant may be associated with audited or unaudited financial statements. The concern in this chapter is with audited financial statements. A CPA is associated with audited financial statements when he has been engaged to examine the statements in accordance with GAAS and has applied auditing procedures to such statements. Association also exists when a CPA consents to the use of his name in a report, document, or written communication containing audited financial statements.

Degree of Responsibility

The final requirement of the fourth reporting standard is that the auditor must indicate the degree of responsibility that is being taken for the examination and the opinion. This is done through such wording as "we have examined," "our examination," "procedures we considered necessary," and "in our opinion." The use of these words without qualification means that the auditor is assuming full or complete responsibility for the work done and for the opinion rendered. When more than one auditor is involved in the examination and each auditor assumes responsibility only for his own work and his own opinion, both the scope and opinion paragraphs must indicate the divided responsibility that exists.

The Auditor's Standard Report

The auditor's standard report was introduced in Chapter 1. Recall that it consisted of a scope (or opening) paragraph, an opinion (or closing) paragraph, and standardized language. The language of the report varies slightly depending on whether the auditor is reporting on financial statements for one year or for two or more years, as illustrated in Figure 16-1 and Figure 1-2 on page 17.

We have examined the balance sheet of X Company as of [at] December 31, 19XX, and the related statements of income, retained earnings and changes in financial position for the year then ended. Our examination was made in accordance with generally accepted auditing standards and, accordingly, included such tests of the accounting records and such other auditing procedures as we considered necessary in the circumstances.

In our opinion, the financial statements referred to above present fairly the financial position of X Company as of [at] December 31, 19XX, and the results of its operations and the changes in its financial position for the year then ended, in conformity with generally accepted accounting principles applied on a basis consistent with that of the preceding year.

FIGURE 16–1. Standard Report: Single-year Financial Statements (SOURCE: Auditing Standards Board, op. cit., AU § 509.07.)

The report is normally addressed to the individuals or groups that appointed the auditors. For a corporate client, this is the board of directors and/or stockholders; for unincorporated clients, the addressee is the partners or proprietor.

The auditor's standard report should be dated as of the completion of field work. The signature on the report is generally in the firm name because the firm assumes responsibility for the work and the findings of its professional staff.

Types of Audit Opinions

There are four types of opinions that may be expressed on audited financial statements:

- An *unqualified opinion* states that the financial statements present fairly financial position, results of operations, and changes in financial position in conformity with GAAP consistently applied. *use when there is uncertainty*
- A *qualified opinion* states that, "except for" or "subject to" the effects of the matter to which the qualification relates, the financial statements present fairly . . . consistently applied.
- An *adverse opinion* states that the financial statements do not present fairly . . . in conformity with GAAP.
- A *disclaimer of opinion* states that the auditor does not express an opinion on the financial statements.

The auditor's judgment concerning the "fairness" of the overall presentation of financial statements is applied within the framework of generally accepted accounting principles. Without that framework, the auditor would not have a uniform standard for making a judgment.[3]

In deciding on the appropriate opinion, the auditor considers the following questions:

- Was (were) the examination(s) made in accordance with GAAS? *qualified disclaimer*
- Are the financial statements prepared in conformity with GAAP, which include adequate disclosures (first and third standards of reporting)? *qualified adverse*
- Have GAAP been applied on a consistent basis (second standard of reporting)? *even good changes get qualified reports*
- Are the financial statements unaffected by any unusual uncertainties?

Materiality should be considered in answering these questions. A negative answer should be given only when an exception pertains to a matter that has a material effect on the financial statements. With due recognition to materiality, the auditor may

- Express an unqualified opinion when affirmative answers are given to each of the questions.
- Express a qualified opinion when a negative answer is given to one or

---

[3] Auditing Standards Board, op. cit., AU § 411.03.

more of the questions and the effect does not prevent the financial statements, taken as a whole, from being in conformity with GAAP. The most frequent causes of qualified opinions are lack of consistency and the existence of unusual uncertainties.

- Express an adverse opinion when a negative answer is given to the second question, and the effect prevents the statements, taken as a whole, from being in conformity with GAAP.
- Disclaim an opinion when a negative answer is necessary for the first or fourth question, and it is not possible to determine whether the financial statements are in conformity with GAAP.

The effects on the auditor's opinion of negative answers to the foregoing questions are tabulated below:

EXCEPTION	QUALIFIED	ADVERSE	DISCLAIMER
Examination not in accordance with generally accepted auditing standards	X*		X
Nonconformity with GAAP, which includes adequate disclosure	X	X	
Inconsistency	X		
Unusual uncertainties	X		X

* If the auditor is not independent in making the examination, a disclaimer of opinion is required.

An analysis of these effects reveals three instances where alternative opinions are possible. For exceptions to GAAS and unusual uncertainties, the auditor may issue a qualified opinion or disclaim an opinion; for lack of conformity with GAAP, the auditor may issue either a qualified or adverse opinion. In general, the more material the matter in question, the more likely the auditor will elect to disclaim an opinion for the first and fourth exceptions and express an adverse opinion for the second exception.

Effects of Other than Unqualified Opinions on the Auditor's Report

The issuance of a qualified or adverse opinion or the denial of an opinion on the fairness of a client's financial statements is a significant development that requires a change in both the form and content of the auditor's standard report. Accordingly, except for an opinion qualified because of inconsistency, the auditor should use one or more explanatory paragraphs to explain the substantive reasons for the opinion being expressed (or denied). The additional paragraph(s) should be between the scope and opinion paragraphs and be referred to in the opinion paragraph.

When the auditor issues other than an unqualified opinion, the following changes in the wording of the opinion paragraph are required:

OPINION	LANGUAGE
Qualified	
• Other than for inconsistency and uncertainties	In our opinion, *except for* . . .
• For inconsistency	*except for* . . . (inserted at end of paragraph)
• For uncertainties	In our opinion, *subject to* . . .
Adverse	In our opinion, *because of* . . . , the financial statements *do not* present fairly . . .
Disclaimer	*Because of* . . . , *we are* unable to *express an opinion on the fairness of* . . .

When a qualified opinion or disclaimer of opinion is due to noncompliance with GAAS, the scope paragraph is modified by adding the following at the end of the second sentence: "except as explained in the following paragraph."

CIRCUMSTANCES RESULTING IN DEPARTURE FROM THE AUDITOR'S STANDARD REPORT

Types of Circumstances

A departure from the auditor's standard report occurs when there is a substantive change in the wording or form of the report. The following circumstances will result in substantive changes in the standard report:

- The scope of the auditor's examination is affected by conditions that preclude the application of one or more auditing procedures he considers necessary in the circumstances.
- The auditor's opinion is based in part on the report of another auditor.
- The financial statements are affected by a departure from a generally accepted accounting principle.
- The financial statements are affected by a departure from an accounting principle promulgated by the body designated by the AICPA Council to establish such principles.
- Accounting principles have not been applied consistently.
- The financial statements are affected by uncertainties concerning future events, the outcome of which is not susceptible of reasonable estimation at the date of the auditor's report.
- The auditor wishes to emphasize a matter regarding the financial statements.[4]

Each of the circumstances is explained below. In addition, actual reports are used in most cases to illustrate the report that is appropriate.

[4] Auditing Standards Board, *op. cit.,* AU § 509.09.

Scope Limitation

In an examination made in accordance with GAAS, the auditor is able to perform all auditing procedures considered necessary in the circumstances. From these procedures, it is expected that the auditor will obtain sufficient competent evidential matter to have a reasonable basis for expressing an opinion on the financial statements. When the auditor cannot perform the necessary procedures or the procedures do not provide sufficient evidence, the auditor is said to have a *scope limitation.*

A scope limitation may be imposed by the client or result from circumstances. Client restrictions may include refusal to (1) permit confirmation of receivables, (2) sign a client representation letter, or (3) authorize inquiry with the client's outside legal counsel. Restrictions attributable to circumstances may extend to the timing of procedures, such as appointment too late to perform procedures considered necessary in the circumstances, and to inadequate client records.

A scope limitation does not exist when the auditor is engaged to make an examination on only one financial statement and not the others, provided he can perform all the procedures he considers necessary in the circumstances. Such an engagement simply involves limited reporting objectives. For example, if the engagement extends only to the balance sheet and the auditor examines that statement in accordance with GAAS, a standard audit report may be issued on the balance sheet.

Effects on Auditor's Report

When a scope limitation exists, the auditor should

- Indicate the scope limitation in the scope paragraph of his report.
- Give the substantive reasons for the limitation in an explanatory paragraph.
- Express a qualified opinion or a disclaimer of opinion in the opinion paragraph.

The importance of the missing evidence and the materiality of the effects of the item(s) in question on the financial statements are factors the auditor should consider in deciding whether to qualify or disclaim an opinion. When the scope limitation extends to many financial statement items, there is a greater probability that a disclaimer of opinion will be necessary. The wording of the opinion paragraph should refer to the potential effects on the financial statements of the items for which the auditor has not obtained audit satisfaction, rather than to the scope limitation itself, because the auditor's opinion relates to the financial statements. A scope limitation resulting in a qualified opinion is illustrated in Figure 16-2. When the scope limitation is attributable to a client-imposed restriction, the auditor generally should disclaim an opinion on the financial statements.

To the Board of Directors and Shareholders of Atlas Incorporated:

We have examined the consolidated balance sheets of Atlas Incorporated and subsidiaries as of December 31, 1982 and 1981, and the related consolidated statements of operations, stockholders' equity, and changes in financial position for each of the three years in the period ended December 31, 1982. Our examinations were made in accordance with generally accepted auditing standards and, accordingly, included such tests of the accounting records and such other auditing procedures as we considered necessary in the circumstances, except as explained in the following paragraph.

As discussed in Note 4 of the Notes to Consolidated Financial Statements, Atlas Incorporated recognized certain adjustments, principally a $4.2 million inventory write-down in 1982. Sufficient documentary evidence could not be examined, or other reliable tests made, to determine the full extent to which these adjustments in the aggregate may affect prior years.

In our opinion, except for the effect on the consolidated statements of operations, stockholders' equity, and changes in financial position of the matter described in the preceding paragraph, the consolidated financial statements referred to above present fairly the financial position of Atlas Incorporated and subsidiaries at December 31, 1982 and 1981, and the results of their operations and the changes in their financial position for each of the three years in the period ended December 31, 1982, in conformity with generally accepted accounting principles applied on a consistent basis.

Reddy & Abel

FIGURE 16-2. Auditor's Report Qualified Because of Scope Limitation

Part of Examination Made by Other Independent Auditors

When a client has one or more subsidiaries, divisions, or branches, it may be necessary for more than one auditing firm to participate in the examination. Assume, for example, that a client with its major operations located in the Midwest has a West Coast branch and a foreign subsidiary. The branch operation is audited by an established local firm on the West Coast, and the subsidiary is audited by a foreign national firm. When two or more auditing firms are involved in an examination, one firm should be the principal auditor. This decision should be based on such factors as the relative amount and significance of the work done and the extent of the firms' knowledge of the overall statements. In this example, the firm auditing the Midwest operations would be the principle auditor.

The principal auditor must then decide whether he is willing to assume responsibility for the work of the other auditors insofar as it relates to the client's statements taken as a whole. If the principal auditor accepts this responsibility, no reference should be made in the audit report to the other auditors' examination. However, if the principal auditor is not willing to assume this responsibility, the fourth standard of reporting requires that reference be made to the other auditors in the auditor's report. Such action is necessary to indicate the shared responsibility that exists among the auditors for both the examination and the expression of an opinion on the financial statements.

Decision Not to Make Reference

If the principal auditor is able to obtain satisfaction as to the (1) independence and professional reputation of the other auditors and (2) scope and quality of the other auditors' examination, reference to the other auditors ordinarily is not made. The principal auditor would be able to reach this decision when

- The other auditors are associated or correspondent firms whose work is well known to the principal auditor.
- The work is performed under the principal auditor's guidance and control.
- The principal auditor reviews the audit programs and working papers of the other auditors.

The principal auditor may also elect not to make reference to another auditor if the portion of the financial statements examined by the other auditor is not material to the financial statements taken as a whole.

Decision to Make Reference

The principal auditor may decide to make reference to another auditor when the foregoing factors are not present. Regardless of other considerations, the principal auditor may also decide to make reference whenever the portion of the financial statements examined by another auditor is material to the financial statements taken as a whole.

The principal auditor is required under this decision to make inquiries concerning the independence and professional reputation of the other auditor. In cases where the other firm's primary practice is in a foreign country, the principal auditor should also communicate with the other auditor to ascertain his familiarity with GAAS and GAAP in the United States.

Effects on Auditor's Report

A standard audit report is issued when the principal auditor decides not to make reference to the other auditor(s). Mention of the other auditor(s) in such case is inappropriate since the principal auditor is assuming full responsibility for the examination and the opinion.

When the auditor decides to make reference to another auditor, the report should indicate clearly the division of responsibility that exists between the auditors. This is accomplished by modifying the auditor's standard report as follows:

- In the scope paragraph, the magnitude of the portion of the financial statements examined by the other auditor should be indicated.
- In the opinion paragraph, reference should be made to the other auditor.

These modifications do not result in either a three-paragraph report or a qualified opinion. Reference to the other auditor in the opinion paragraph only indicates the divided responsibility among the auditors. This form of reporting should not be regarded as being inferior to a report in which no reference is made to another auditor. An example of a report in which reference is made to another auditor is shown in Figure 16-3.

If the principal auditor concludes that reliance cannot be placed on the other auditor's work and the work done by the other auditor is material to the financial statements taken as a whole, a scope limitation exists. In such cases, the considerations described earlier in this chapter for scope limitations should be followed in modifying the auditor's standard report.

Nonconformity with GAAP

The first standard of reporting requires the auditor to explicitly express an opinion as to whether the financial statements are presented in conformity with GAAP. This standard is limited to the expression of an opinion rather than a statement of fact. For purposes of this standard, GAAP include not only accounting principles, such as the cost principle, but also the methods of applying them, such as the first in, first out (FIFO) and last in, first out (LIFO) methods for inventories and the straight line and sum of the years' digits methods for depreciation.

In reaching a decision as to conformity with GAAP, the auditor must obtain evidence concerning whether

---

Board of Directors and Shareowners Martin Marietta Corporation

We have examined the consolidated balance sheet of Martin Marietta Corporation and consolidated subsidiaries as of December 31, 1981 and 1980, and the related consolidated statements of earnings, shareowners' equity, and changes in financial position for each of the three years in the period ended December 31, 1981. Our examinations were made in accordance with generally accepted auditing standards and, accordingly, included such tests of the accounting records and such other auditing procedures as we considered necessary in the circumstances. We did not examine the financial statements of Martin Marietta Aluminum Inc. and consolidated subsidiaries, which statements reflect total assets constituting 40% in 1981 and 37% in 1980, and total revenues constituting 19% in 1981, 26% in 1980, and 27% in 1979, of the related consolidated totals. These statements were examined by other auditors whose reports thereon have been furnished to us, and our opinion expressed herein, insofar as it relates to the amounts included for Martin Marietta Aluminum Inc. and consolidated subsidiaries, is based solely upon the reports of other auditors.

In our opinion, based upon our examinations and the aforementioned reports of other auditors, the financial statements referred to above present fairly the consolidated financial position of Martin Marietta Corporation and consolidated subsidiaries at December 31, 1981 and 1980, and the consolidated results of their operations and changes in their financial position for each of the three years in the period ended December 31, 1981, in conformity with generally accepted accounting principles applied on a consistent basis.

Washington, D.C.   *Ernst & Whinney*
January 22, 1982

FIGURE 16-3. Auditor's Report Indicating Reliance on Other Auditors

- The accounting principles used have general acceptance.
- The accounting principles are appropriate in the circumstances.
- The financial statements, including the related notes, are informative of matters that may affect their use, understanding, and interpretation.
- The information presented in the financial statements is classified and summarized in a reasonable manner.
- The statements reflect the underlying events and transactions in a manner that presents financial position, results of operations, and changes in financial position within reasonable and practicable limits.[5]

The third and fourth items relate to the adequacy of informative disclosures.

The phrase *generally accepted accounting principles* includes broad guidelines of general applicability as well as specific conventions, rules, and procedures. There is no single compilation of all established accounting principles. Pronouncements of the Financial Accounting Standards Board are considered to be the primary source of GAAP. In the absence of FASB pronouncements, the auditor should look to the following order of authoritative sources in determining whether an accounting principle is generally accepted:

- Pronouncements of other bodies composed of expert accountants that follow a due process procedure, such as the AICPA Accounting Standards Executive Committee. Publications in this category include AICPA Statements of Position and AICPA Industry Audit Guides and Accounting Guides.
- Practices or pronouncements that are widely recognized as being generally accepted because they represent prevalent practice. Publications in this category include FASB Technical Bulletins, AICPA Accounting Interpretations, and prevailing industry practices.
- Other accounting literature. This category includes APB Statements, AICPA Issues Papers, FASB Statements of Financial Accounting Concepts, pronouncements of trade associations or regulatory agencies, and accounting textbooks and articles.[6]

Inadequate Disclosure

The third standard of reporting provides that informative disclosures in the financial statements are to be regarded as reasonably adequate unless otherwise stated in the report.

Informative disclosures involve material matters relating to the form, arrangement, and content of the financial statements and the accompanying notes. Authoritative bodies, such as the FASB and the SEC, frequently include disclosure requirements in their pronouncements. Informative disclosure extends to subsequent events and to reporting segment information.

[5] Auditing Standards Board, *op. cit.,* AU § 411.04.
[6] Auditing Standards Board, *op. cit.,* AU § 411.05-08.

In previous chapters of this book, many specific disclosure requirements have been enumerated under the caption "Statement Presentation and Disclosure," such as the basis and methods of inventory costing, market values of securities, liens on assets, and contingencies.

When the client refuses to make adequate disclosure of data essential to a fair presentation in conformity with GAAP, the auditor is required to

- Provide the necessary information in an explanatory paragraph, if practicable, unless its omission from the auditor's report is recognized as appropriate by a specific Statement on Auditing Standards.
- Express either a qualified opinion or an adverse opinion.

Two omissions have been specifically allowed in Statements on Auditing Standards. The auditor is not required to present (1) a statement of changes in financial position when that statement is omitted by a client, or (2) omitted segment information. In both instances, however, the auditor should identify the omitted data in the explanatory paragraph and appropriately modify his opinion.

Modifications of the auditor's report because of inadequate disclosure occur infrequently. Since the necessary data, in most cases, are going to be disclosed, management ordinarily prefers to make the disclosures that will permit a standard audit report.

Effects on Auditor's Report

When a departure from a GAAP has a material effect on the financial statements, the auditor should explain the basis and effects of the departure in an explanatory paragraph if reasonably determinable and express a qualified or adverse opinion. In deciding whether to express a qualified or adverse opinion, the auditor should consider such factors as the (1) dollar magnitude of the effects, (2) significance of the item to the client, (3) number of statement items affected, and (4) impact of the misstatement on the statements taken as a whole.[7]

Nonconformity with Promulgated Accounting Principles

Rule 203 of the American Institute of Certified Public Accountants (AICPA) Code of Professional Ethics requires the auditor to determine whether the principles used by the client comply with promulgated accounting principles.[8] Acting under the provisions of this rule, the Council of the AICPA designated the Financial Accounting Standards Board (FASB) as the body to establish accounting principles. In addition, Council formally recognized three sets of authoritative pronouncements: (1) statements and interpretations issued by the FASB, (2) Accounting Principles Board (APB) opinions,

---

[7] Auditing Standards Board, *op. cit.,* AU § 509.16.
[8] Rule 203 is fully explained in Chapter 18.

and (3) AICPA accounting research bulletins. Rule 203 specifies that the client's financial statements must comply with these pronouncements, unless due to unusual circumstances compliance with the pronouncements would cause the financial statements to be misleading.[9] The unusual circumstances contemplated by the rule consist primarily of new legislation or the evolution of a new form of business transaction.

Alternative accounting principles, such as different depreciation methods and inventory costing methods, may be applicable in the circumstances. Unless the promulgating body has established criteria for selecting among alternative principles, the auditor may recognize that more than one principle is acceptable.

Effects on Auditor's Report

A departure from a promulgated principle which has a material effect on the financial statements may occur in the absence of unusual circumstances or because of unusual circumstances. The effects on the auditor's standard report depend on the underlying cause of the departure. When unusual circumstances do not exist, the auditor will be required to give all of the substantive reasons in an explanatory paragraph and express either a qualified or an adverse opinion. An appropriate audit report based on assumed data is shown in Figure 16-4.

When there are unusual circumstances, the client may have to depart from a promulgated principle in order to prevent the financial statements from being misleading. Assuming the client uses an established principle from other sources that is applicable to the unusual circumstances, the auditor is permitted under the first reporting standard to issue an unqualified opinion concerning conformity with GAAP. In such case, the report should describe approximate efforts thereof, if practicable, and the reasons why compliance with the promulgated principle would result in a misleading statement.

Inconsistent Application of GAAP

The second standard of reporting requires the auditor to state whether accounting principles have been consistently applied. The objectives of this standard are: (1) to give assurance that the comparability of financial statements between accounting periods has not been materially affected by changes in accounting principles and (2) to require appropriate reporting by the auditor when comparability has been materially affected by such changes. The consistency standard does not extend to the effects on comparability of changed business conditions, such as the acquisition (or disposal) of a subsidiary company or the introduction of a new product line and acts of God such as fire, floods, and similar occurrences.

---

[9] Auditing Standards Board, *op. cit.,* AU § 509.18.

To the Shareholders and Board of Directors of The Advertising Agency:

We have examined the consolidated balance sheets of The Advertising Agency and consolidated subsidiaries as of December 31, 19X2 and December 31, 19X1 and the related consolidated statements of income, shareholders' equity, and changes in financial position for each of the three years in the period ended December 31, 19X2. Our examinations were made in accordance with generally accepted auditing standards and, accordingly, included such tests of the accounting records and such other auditing procedures as we considered necessary in the circumstances.

The Company's treatment of its investment in the common stock of A.D., Inc., a wholly-owned, unconsolidated subsidiary, is at variance with Opinion No. 18 of the Accounting Principles Board of the American Institute of Certified Public Accountants. This Opinion states that an investment in the common stock of an unconsolidated subsidiary should be accounted for by the equity method in consolidated financial statements. The Company carries its investment in the common stock of A.D., Inc., at cost. If the Accounting Principles Board Opinion had been followed, income would have been increased by $200,000 ($2.00 per share) in 19X2 and $125,000 ($1.25 per share) in 19X1 and the amount of retained earnings at December 31, 19X2 would have been increased by $975,000.

In our opinion, except for the investment in common stock of the unconsolidated subsidiary which has not been accounted for in accordance with generally accepted accounting principles as described in the preceding paragraph, the financial statements referred to above present fairly the consolidated financial position of The Advertising Agency and consolidated subsidiaries at December 31, 19X2, and the consolidated results of their operations and changes in their financial position for each of the three years in the period ended December 31, 19X2, in conformity with generally accepted accounting principles applied on a consistent basis.

February 20, 19X3

Reddy & Abel

FIGURE 16–4. Auditor's Report Qualified Because of Departure from Promulgated GAAP

A change in an accounting principle results from adoption of a GAAP different from the one previously used in the preparation of financial statements. As used in the consistency standard, a change in an accounting principle includes:

- A change in the principle itself such as a change from a sales basis to a production basis in recording farm revenue.
- A change in the method of applying a principle, such as a change from the straight line method of depreciation to the sum of the years' digits method.
- A change in the reporting entity such as presenting consolidated statements in place of individual company statements or changes in specific subsidiaries comprising the consolidated group.
- The correction of an error in principle, as, for example, a change from a principle not generally accepted to one that is generally accepted.
- A change in principle inseparable from a change in estimate, such as a change from capitalizing and amortizing a cost to recording it as an expense when incurred because future benefits are now doubtful.

Accounting changes involving accounting estimates, corrections of errors not involving a principle, classifications and reclassifications, variations in the format of the statement of changes in financial position, and substantially different transactions or events are not covered by the consistency standard. Such matters, however, may require disclosure under the third standard of reporting.

Effects on Auditor's Report

When the auditor is reporting only on the current year, the period to which the consistency standard relates is the preceding year. In contrast, when the auditor is reporting on two or more years, this standard relates to the consistency of principles between such years and also to the consistency with the immediately preceding year if it is presented with the financial statements being reported on. The consistency standard does not apply in the first year's examination of a new company.

When a report is qualified because of an inconsistency, the auditor must (1) explicitly express his concurrence by using the expression *with which we concur,* and (2) use "qualifying" language following the consistency wording. The report in Figure 16-5 illustrates both a change in accounting principle that requires restatement of prior year statements and a change reported as a cumulative effect in the current year's income statement. Lack of consistency in the application of generally accepted accounting principles is the primary cause of qualified opinions.

The auditor is required to comply with the second standard of reporting

---

To the Board of Directors and Stockholders of AMF Incorporated

We have examined the accompanying consolidated balance sheet of AMF Incorporated at December 31, 1981 and 1980, and the consolidated statements of income, stockholders' equity, and changes in financial position for each of the three years in the period ended December 31, 1981. Our examinations were made in accordance with generally accepted auditing standards and, accordingly, included such tests of the accounting records and such other auditing procedures as we considered necessary in the circumstances.

In our opinion, the statements mentioned above present fairly the consolidated financial position of AMF Incorporated at December 31, 1981 and 1980, and the consolidated results of operations and the consolidated changes in financial position for each of the three years in the period ended December 31, 1981, in conformity with generally accepted accounting principles applied on a consistent basis during the period after restatement of the consolidated financial statements for 1979 and 1980 to give retroactive effect to the change, with which we concur, in the method of accounting for foreign currency translation as described in Note 1 to the consolidated financial statements and except for the change in 1981, with which we concur, in the method of accounting for investment tax credits as described in Note 11 to the consolidated financial statements.

Arthur Young & Company

February 16, 1982

FIGURE 16–5. Auditor's Report Qualified for Inconsistent Application of GAAP

in his first examination of an established client. Where adequate accounting records are kept by the client, it ordinarily is possible for the auditor to obtain satisfaction as to the consistency of the application of accounting principles between the current and the preceding year. However, when the auditor is not able to do so and the amounts involved are material, he would be unable to express an unqualified opinion on the results of operations and changes in financial position for the current period but could give an unqualified opinion on the balance sheet without reference to consistency. In such case, the circumstance would be explained in an explanatory paragraph.

Uncertainties

The term *uncertainties* applies to the outcome of any statement items or disclosures that are not susceptible of reasonable estimation prior to issuance of the statements. Uncertainties differ from accounting estimates in that the latter are capable of reasonable determination by the client in the preparation of financial statements. Uncertainties may range from a single event where the effect on the financial statements can be isolated and understood to multiple events whose possible effects on the financial statements are complex and difficult to assess. The former include the outcome of a lawsuit or an IRS audit of a tax return; the latter include recurring operating losses and major financial problems that affect the ability of the company to continue in existence.

Uncertainties present a special problem for the auditor because evidence of their resolution does not exist prior to completing the examination. On the basis of evidence that is available, the auditor has the responsibility of determining whether the uncertainties are properly accounted for and disclosed. The auditor is not expected to predict the outcome of the uncertainties.

In a typical audit, the auditor assumes the entity will continue as a going concern. However, when his normal auditing procedures reveal information contrary to that assumption, the auditor should consider and evaluate such data. Contrary information may pertain to

- Solvency problems such as working capital shortages and defaults on loan agreements.
- Internal matters such as the loss of key management personnel and work stoppages.
- External matters such as legal proceedings and the loss of important customers.[10]

In evaluating the significance of the contrary information, the auditor should (1) weigh any mitigating factors, (2) consider management plans for dealing with the problems, and (3) perform such substantive tests as are reasonable and practicable.

---

[10] Auditing Standards Board, *op. cit.*, AU § 340.04.

Effects on Auditor's Report

The effects of uncertainties on the auditor's report depend on the auditor's professional judgment. When the auditor concludes that the resolution of an uncertainty will not have a material effect on the financial statements, a standard report may be issued. However, when the auditor believes the uncertainty may have a material effect on the financial statements, his report must be appropriately modified. As shown in Figure 16-6, the uncertainty should be described in the explanatory paragraph and a qualified (subject to) opinion should be expressed.

Emphasis of a Matter

In some situations, the auditor may wish to emphasize in his report a matter which is properly accounted for and adequately disclosed while still expressing an unqualified opinion. To do so, the auditor should (1) use standard wording in the scope and opinion paragraph, (2) describe the matter being emphasized in an explanatory paragraph, and (3) make no reference to the explanatory material in the opinion paragraph. Reference in the opinion paragraph to the matter being emphasized is prohibited because a phrase "with the foregoing explanation" could be misconstrued as a qualification of the auditor's opinion. Items that may merit emphasis in a given case include related party transactions, a change in an accounting estimate, and changes in operating conditions.

Summary of Departures from Auditor's Standard Report

The effects of the circumstances discussed in this chapter on the auditor's standard report are tabulated in Figure 16-7. It may be observed that the effects do not always result in a three-paragraph report or a change from an unqualified opinion.

OTHER CONSIDERATIONS

Reporting on Comparative Statements

As indicated earlier in this chapter, the fourth standard of reporting applies not only to the financial statements of the current period but also to statements of any prior periods presented on a comparative basis with those of the current period. During his examination for the current year, the auditor should be alert for circumstances and events relating to prior-period financial statements.

The auditor's current examination may produce evidence that the opinion on the prior year's statements should be different than the opinion originally expressed. This could result from such events as (1) subsequent resolution of an uncertainty that existed in the prior year, (2) discovery of an uncertainty applicable to the prior year that was not known when the opinion

Shareholders and Board of Directors, Chrysler Corporation

We have examined the accompanying consolidated balance sheet of Chrysler Corporation and consolidated subsidiaries at December 31, 1981 and 1980, and the related consolidated statements of operations and changes in financial position for each of the three years in the period ended December 31, 1981. Our examinations were made in accordance with generally accepted auditing standards and, accordingly, included such tests of the accounting records and such other auditing procedures as we considered necessary in the circumstances.

The financial statements referred to above have been prepared using generally accepted accounting principles applicable to a going concern which contemplate the realization of assets and the satisfaction of liabilities in the normal course of business. The Corporation incurred substantial losses in 1979, 1980 and 1981. The continuation of the Corporation as a going concern is dependent upon a return to sustained profitable operations and, if needed, availability of additional financing. The Corporation has been able to fund its losses primarily through federally guaranteed loans, concessions from its lenders, employees and suppliers, and the sale of assets. Through restructuring of its operations, the Corporation has reduced fixed costs significantly, but its ability to achieve sustained profitability will be affected by many factors (Note 2) some of which are beyond its control. The deterioration in the Corporation's financial condition has diminished its ability to absorb future losses which, if incurred, could adversely affect its ability to continue as a going concern. Additionally, the Corporation is continuing negotiations for an industrial cooperation agreement with Peugeot S.A. (see Note 6), and accordingly continues to value its 14% ownership in Peugeot as a long-term investment. However, the carrying value of the Peugeot stock may require adjustment if the nature of this investment changes.

In our report dated February 27, 1981, we did not express an opinion as to whether the 1979 and 1980 financial statements of the Corporation were presented fairly because in view of the uncertainties and the ongoing restructuring described therein, we were unable to determine whether or not the use in those statements of generally accepted accounting principles applicable to a going concern was appropriate. Although there continues to be uncertainty regarding the Corporation's going concern status, the business and financial progress made by the Corporation in 1981 has reduced the need for ongoing restructuring. Consequently, we are now in a position to render an opinion on the 1979 and 1980 financial statements subject to the going concern uncertainties described above.

In our opinion, subject to the effects of such adjustments, if any, which might have been required had the outcome of the uncertainties regarding the Corporation's going concern status and its investment in Peugeot been known, the accompanying financial statements present fairly the financial position of Chrysler Corporation and consolidated subsidiaries at December 31, 1981 and 1980 and the results of their operations and changes in their financial position for each of the three years in the period ended December 31, 1981 in conformity with generally accepted accounting principles applied on a consistent basis, except for the changes, with which we concur, in the capitalization of interest in 1980 and in depreciation methods in 1981.

Touche Ross & Co.

Touche Ross & Co.
Certified Public Accountants

February 24, 1982
Detroit, Michigan

FIGURE 16–6. Auditor's Report Qualified Because of an Uncertainty (*Authors' Note:* Paragraph 3 refers to a change in the auditor's opinion issued in the preceding year. This topic is explained on pages 550 and 552. This report also includes a consistency exception.)

Circumstance	Scope Paragraph Modification	Explanatory Paragraph	Opinion Paragraph Modification	Type of Opinion
Scope limitation	Yes	Yes	Yes	Qualified or disclaimer
Other auditors:				
• Make reference	Yes	No	Yes	Unqualified
• Do not make reference	No	No	No	Unqualified
Departure from GAAP	No	Yes	Yes	Qualified or adverse
Departure from promulgated principle:				
• Justified	No	Yes	No	Unqualified
• Not justified	No	Yes	Yes	Qualified or adverse
Inconsistency	No	No	Yes	Qualified
Uncertainties	No	Yes	Yes	Qualified (subject to) or disclaimer
Emphasis of a matter	No	Yes	No	Unqualified

FIGURE 16–7. Summary of Effects of Circumstances on Auditor's Standard Report

on the prior year's statements was rendered, and (3) restatement of prior-period statements to bring them into conformity with GAAP. In such cases, the auditor should indicate in the explanatory paragraph of his current year's report that a different opinion is being expressed on the prior year's financial statements and explain the substantive reasons therefor, as illustrated in Figure 16-6.

When there has been a change in auditors during the periods covered by the comparative statements, the predecessor auditor should perform any procedures considered appropriate before agreeing to reissue his report or consenting to the reuse of the report.

Reporting on Segment Information

FASB Statement No. 14, "Financial Reporting for Segments of a Business Enterprise," requires certain companies to include specified information about an entity's operations in different industries, its foreign operations and export sales, and its major customers in annual financial statements prepared for stockholders. Such information is referred to as segment information, and it is considered to be an integral part of the financial statements.

The objective of applying auditing procedures to segment information is to provide the auditor with a reasonable basis for concluding whether the information is presented in conformity with *FASB Statement No. 14.* From an auditing point of view, segment information is considered to be a matter of informative disclosure under generally accepted accounting principles (GAAP). The auditor should inquire of management, test the entity's application of the percentages specified in *FASB Statement No. 14,* and apply analytical review procedures in examining segment information.

The auditor's standard report should not make any reference to segment information when the data have been presented in conformity with GAAP. Modification of the report is required for (1) inadequate disclosure when the segment information is either misstated or omitted or (2) a scope limitation when the auditor is unable to apply the procedures considered necessary in the circumstances.[11] As explained earlier, the auditor is not required to present the omitted information in his report.

Reporting on Information Accompanying Audited Financial Statements

Information accompanying audited financial statements consists of: (1) supplementary information required by the FASB, (2) voluntary information provided by management, and (3) additional information provided by the auditor. The auditor is not required by GAAS to examine any of the information because the data are outside the basic financial statements. However, the auditor has some responsibilities concerning the information as explained below.

Required Supplementary Information

The FASB has determined that certain supplementary information is an essential part of a company's financial reporting. As a result of FASB pronouncements, the presentation of supplementary information is currently required on (1) the effects of changing prices, (2) oil and gas reserves, and (3) mineral reserves. The Auditing Standards Board (ASB) has issued an SAS on the auditor's basic responsibilities for such information and separate SASs on the information that is currently required.

The auditor is required to apply certain limited procedures to the information and to report any deficiencies in or omissions of such information. The limited procedures involve inquiry of management regarding the methods of preparing the information, and comparison of the information for consistency with other available data. The auditor's reporting responsibility is referred to as *exception reporting.* Since the information is not audited and is not a required part of the basic financial statements, a standard audit report should be issued except in the following circumstances:

- The supplementary information required in the circumstances is omitted.
- The auditor has concluded that the measurement or presentation of the

---

[11] Auditing Standards Board *op. cit.,* AU § 435.08.

supplementary information departs materially from guidelines prescribed by the FASB.
- The auditor is unable to complete the prescribed procedures.[12]

These circumstances should be described in one or more explanatory paragraphs of the auditor's report. The auditor need not present the supplementary information when it is omitted by the entity. The foregoing circumstances have no effect on either the scope or opinion paragraphs of the auditor's report.

Voluntary Information Provided by Management

The audited financial statements of a client are usually presented in a document called an *annual report*. This document includes such information as financial highlights, a letter from the president and/or chairman of the board, comparative financial statistics, schedules, and graphic presentations of financial data that is voluntarily provided by management. The auditor is required to read this information to determine whether the data, or the manner of presentation, is materially inconsistent with the financial statements on which an opinion is being expressed.

For example, in referring to per-share earnings in the president's letter, a client may only state earnings per share before an extraordinary loss when the income statement shows earnings per share data in accordance with *APB Opinion No. 15*. When a material inconsistency appears to exist, the auditor should determine whether the statements, the audit report, or the other information should be revised. If it is the latter, and if the client refuses to make the necessary changes, the auditor may elect to (1) include an explanatory paragraph in the audit report on the matter, (2) withhold his audit report, or (3) withdraw from the engagement.[13]

In reading the voluntary information, the auditor may also believe there is a material misstatement of fact. If the matter is not resolved to the auditor's satisfaction, the auditor should notify the client in writing and consult with his legal counsel on the matter.

Additional Information Provided by the Auditor

This information refers to auditor prepared documents that are presented to the client with the auditor's standard report. Such data include details of statement items, historical summaries of the statements, and statistical data. This information is presented for analysis and is not necessary for a fair presentation of the financial statements.

When additional information is submitted, the auditor is required by the fourth standard of reporting to indicate the degree of responsibility he is

---

[12] Auditing Standards Board, *op. cit.,* AU § 553.08.
[13] Auditing Standards Board, *op. cit.,* AU § 550.04.

taking. Thus, he must either express an opinion as to the fairness of the data in relation to the financial statements or disclaim an opinion. The wording of the report and the expression of an opinion are shown in Figure 16-8. The auditor's report may be added as a separate paragraph of the standard report or be attached to the additional information.

Reporting on Condensed Financial Statements and Selected Financial Data

The auditor may be engaged to report on condensed financial statements and selected financial data (e.g. a five year financial summary) derived from financial statements that he has audited. Because such information does not constitute a fair presentation of financial position, results of operations, and changes in financial position in conformity with GAAP, the auditor's report should differ from his report on the complete financial statements. The report should indicate

- That the auditor has examined and expressed an opinion on the complete financial statements
- The date of the auditor's report and type of opinion expressed on the complete financial statements
- Whether, in the auditor's opinion, the information set forth in the condensed financial statements (or in the selected financial data) is fairly stated in all material respects in relation to the complete financial statements from which it has been derived.[14]

Condensed financial statements are usually presented separately from the complete financial statements whereas selected financial data are presented in a document (e.g. an annual report) that includes the complete financial statements. Thus, the auditor's report on condensed financial statements ordinarily is a separate report whereas his report on selected financial data is generally presented as an additional paragraph in his report on the complete financial statements.

Our examination was made for the purpose of forming an opinion on the basic financial statements taken as a whole. The (identify accompanying information) is presented for purposes of additional analysis and is not a required part of the basic financial statements. Such information has been subjected to the auditing procedures applied in the examination of the basic financial statements and, in our opinion, is fairly stated in all material respects in relation to the basic financial statements taken as a whole.

FIGURE 16–8. Auditor's Report on Additional Information Submitted with Audit Report (SOURCE: Auditing Standards Board, *op. cit.*, AU § 551.12.)

[14] Auditing Standards Board, *op. cit.*, AU § 552.05 and 552.09.

CONCLUDING COMMENTS

This chapter completes the coverage of the auditing process when the auditor is engaged to make an examination of financial statements prepared in conformity with GAAP. Each of the four reporting standards plays a vital role in reporting on audited financial statements. When circumstances occur that prevent the issuance of a standard report, the auditor must modify his report and express the type of opinion that is justified by the findings.

REVIEW QUESTIONS

16–1.　　a. What aspects of a company's financial statements are covered in the first three reporting standards?
　　　　　b. What is the objective of the fourth standard of reporting?

16–2.　　Explain the reference in the fourth standard of reporting to (a) financial statements, (b) character of the examination, and (c) the degree of responsibility the auditor is taking.

16–3.　　Identify and explain the four types of opinions an auditor may render.

16–4.　　What conditions must be met to warrant the expression of an unqualified opinion?

16–5.　　Identify the circumstances that may warrant the expression of (a) a qualified opinion, (b) an adverse opinion, and (c) a disclaimer of opinion.

16–6.　　What are the effects on the form of the auditor's report of (a) a qualified opinion and (b) a disclaimer of opinion?

16–7.　　Indicate the changes in language in the opinion paragraph for each opinion that is other than unqualified.

16–8.　　What circumstances may cause substantive changes in the auditor's standard report?

16–9.　　a. What factors may cause a scope limitation?
　　　　　b. What report modifications result from a scope limitation?

16–10.　　What factors should be considered by an auditor in determining (a) whether he can serve as the principal auditor, and (b) whether, as principal auditor, he should make reference to the work of another auditor?

16–11.　　What are the effects on the auditor's standard report of the decision to (a) make reference and (b) not make reference to another auditor?

16–12.　　When are financial statements presumed to be in conformity with GAAP?

16–13.　　What effect does inadequate disclosure have on the auditor's report?

16–14.　　a. What body is authorized by the AICPA to issue pronouncements on GAAP?
　　　　　b. Which pronouncements are recognized as being authoritative under Rule 203?

16–15.　　Indicate the possible effects on the auditor's report of a departure from (a) a promulgated principle and (b) a GAAP.

16–16.　　Enumerate the types of changes that are covered by the consistency standard.

16–17.　　a. What is meant by the term *uncertainties?*
　　　　　b. Indicate the effects on the auditor's report of an uncertainty when the resolution of the matter may have a material effect on the financial statements.

16–18.　　What reporting requirements apply when the auditor wishes to emphasize a matter in his report?

16–19.　　What are the responsibilities of (a) the continuing auditor and (b) a predecessor auditor concerning comparative statements?

16–20.　　a. Identify the three types of information that may accompany audited financial statements.
　　　　　b. Describe the nature of the auditor's reporting responsibility for required supplementary information.

COMPREHENSIVE QUESTIONS

16–21.　　On completion of the examination of his client's financial statements the CPA, in his report, must either express an opinion or disclaim an opinion on the statements taken as a whole. His opinion may be unqualified, qualified, or adverse.

Required
a. Under what general conditions may a CPA express an unqualified opinion on his client's financial statements?
b. Define and distinguish among (1) a qualified opinion, (2) an adverse opinion, and (3) a disclaimer of opinion on the statements taken as a whole.
c. Indicate the effect of the opinions in (b) above on the form of the auditor's report.
d. Indicate the proper qualifying language for the opinions in (b) above.

16–22. Assume that the following separate circumstances are sufficiently material to cause a departure from the auditor's standard report.

1. Change from LIFO to FIFO, necessitating a restatement of prior years' statements.
2. Other auditors, Jones and Jones, audited a subsidiary company that accounts for 5 percent of the consolidation's total assets and 10 percent of total revenues.
3. The client is the defendant in major litigation that has not been settled at the statement date.
4. Replacement cost is used in the basic financial statements for inventories, cost of sales, plant assets, and depreciation.
5. The continuation of the company as a going concern is in doubt.
6. Pensions are properly recorded, but the total pension expense of $532,000 and the company's policy to fund accrued pension costs are not disclosed in the notes as required by *APB Opinion No. 8*.
7. The fact that 25 percent of the company's inventories result from related party transactions is disclosed in the notes to the statements but the auditor decides to emphasize this fact in the audit report.
8. Finished goods stored in a foreign country were not observed or test counted. The items constitute 10 percent of ending inventory.
9. The lease provisions of *FASB Statement No. 13* were not properly followed in accounting for leases.
10. Note X of the financial statements indicates that the company changed from the straight line to the sum of the years' digits method in computing depreciation.

Required
a. Indicate the type of circumstance and its effects on the auditor's standard report using the format illustrated on page 552 of this chapter.
b. Prepare the parts of the auditor's standard report that are changed by each circumstance.

16–23. You are newly engaged by the James Company, a New England manufacturer with a sales office and warehouse located in a western state. The James Company audit must be made at the peak of your busy season when you will not have a senior auditor available for travel to the western outlet. Furthermore, the James Company is reluctant to bear the travel expenses of an out-of-town auditor.

Required
a. Under what conditions would you, the principal auditor, be willing to accept full responsibility for the work of another auditor?
b. What would be your requirements with respect to the integrity of the other auditor? To whom would you direct inquiries about the other auditor?
c. What reference, if any, would you make to the other auditor in your report if you were
1. Assuming full responsibility for his work?
2. Not assuming responsibility for his work?

AICPA

16–24. Presented below is an independent auditor's report that contains deficiencies. The corporation being reported on is profit oriented and publishes general-purpose financial statements for distribution to owners, creditors, potential investors, and the general public.

We have examined the consolidated balance sheet of Belleno Corporation and subsidiaries as of December 31, 19X0, and the related consolidated statements of income and retained earnings and changes in financial position for the year then ended. Our examination was made in accordance with generally accepted auditing standards and accordingly included such tests of the accounting records and such other auditing procedures as we considered necessary in the circumstances.

We did not examine the financial statements of Seidel Company, a major consolidated subsidiary. These statements were examined by other auditors whose report thereon has been furnished to us, and our opinion expressed herein, insofar as it relates to Seidel Company, is based solely upon the report of the other auditors.

In our opinion, except for the report of the other auditors, the accompanying consolidated balance sheet and consolidated statements of income and retained earnings and changes in financial position present fairly the financial position of Belleno Corporation and subsidiaries at December 31, 19X0, and the results of its operations and the changes in its financial position for the year then ended, in conformity with generally accepted accounting principles applied on a basis consistent with that of the preceding year.

Required
Describe the reporting deficiencies, explain the reasons therefor, and briefly discuss how the report should be corrected. Do not discuss the addressee, signature, and date. Also, do not write the foregoing auditor's report. Organize your answer sheet as follows:

Deficiency	Reason	Correction

AICPA (adapted)

16–25. Sturdy Corporation owns and operates a large office building in a desirable section of New York City's financial center. For many years the management of Sturdy Corporation has modified the presentation of their financial statements by:
1. Reflecting a write-up to appraisal values in the building accounts.
2. Accounting for depreciation expense on the basis of such valuations.

Wyley, a successor CPA, was asked to examined the financial statements of Sturdy Corporation, for the year ended December 31, 19X0. After completing the examination Wyley concluded that, consistent with prior years, an adverse opinion would have to be expressed because of the materiality of the apparent deviation from the historical-cost principle.

Required
a. Describe in detail the form of presentation of the middle paragraph of the auditor's report on the financial statements of Sturdy Corporation for the year ended December 31, 19X0, clearly identifying the information contained in the paragraph. Do not discuss deferred taxes.
b. Write a draft of the opinion paragraph of the auditor's report on the financial statements of Sturdy Corporation for the year ended December 31, 19X0.

AICPA

16–26. Lancaster Electronics produces electronic components for sale to manufacturers of radios, television sets, and phonographic systems. In connection with his examination of Lancaster's financial statements for the year ended December 31, 19X1, Don Olds, CPA, completed field work two weeks ago. Olds now is evaluating the significance of the following items prior to preparing his auditor's report. Except as noted none of these items has been disclosed in the financial statements or footnotes.

Item 1
Recently Lancaster interrupted its policy of paying cash dividends quarterly to its stockholders. Dividends were paid regularly through 19X0, discontinued for all of 19X1 in order to finance equipment for the company's new plant and resumed in the first quarter of 19X2. In the annual report, dividend policy is to be discussed in the president's letter.

Item 2
A ten-year loan agreement, which the company entered into three years ago, provides that dividend payments may not exceed net income earned after taxes subsequent to the date of the agreement. The balance of retained earnings at the date of the loan agreement was $298,000. From that date through December 31, 19X1 net income after taxes has totaled $360,000 and cash dividends have totaled $130,000. Based upon these data the staff auditor assigned to this review concluded that there was no retained earnings restriction at December 31, 19X1.

Item 3
The company's new manufacturing plant building, which cost $600,000 and has an estimated life of 25 years, is leased from the Sixth National Bank at an annual rental of $100,000. The company is obligated to pay property taxes, insurance, and maintenance. At the conclusion of its ten-year noncancelable lease, the company has the option of purchasing the property for $1. In Lancaster's income statement the rental payment is reported on a separate line.

Item 4
A major electronics firm has introduced a line of products that will compete directly with Lancaster's primary line, now being produced in the specially designed new plant. Because of manufacturing innovations, the competitor's line will be of comparable quality but priced 50 percent below Lancaster's line. The competitor announced its new line during the week following completion of field work. Olds read the announcement in the newspaper and discussed the situation by telephone with Lancaster executives. Lancaster will meet the lower prices which are high enough to cover variable manufacturing and selling expenses but will permit recovery of only a portion of fixed costs.

Required
For each item 1 to 4 above, discuss the following:
a. Any additional disclosure in the financial statements and footnotes that the CPA should recommend to his client.
b. The effect of this situation on the CPA's report upon Lancaster's financial statements. For this requirement assume that the client did not make the additional disclosure recommended in a above.

Complete your discussion of each item (both a and b above) before beginning discussion of the next item. The effects of each item on the financial statements and the CPA's report should be evaluated independently of the other items. The cumulative effects of the four items should not be considered.

AICPA

16–27. The CPA must comply with the GAAS of reporting when he prepares his opinion on the client's financial statements. One of the reporting standards relates to consistency.

Required
a. Discuss the statement regarding consistency that the CPA is required to include in his opinion. What is the objective of requiring the CPA to make this statement about consistency?
b. Discuss what mention of consistency, if any, the CPA must make in his opinion relating to his first audit of the financial statements of the following companies:
   1. A newly organized company ending its first accounting period.
   2. A company established for a number of years.
c. Discuss whether the changes described in each of the cases below would require recognition in the CPA's opinion as to consistency. (Assume the amounts are material.)
   1. The company disposed of one of its subsidiaries that had been included in its consolidated statements for prior years.
   2. After two years of computing depreciation under the declining balance method for income tax purposes and under the staight line method for reporting purposes, the declining balance method was adopted for reporting purposes.
   3. The estimated remaining useful life of plant property was reduced because of obsolescence.

AICPA

16–28. Various types of "accounting changes" can affect the second reporting standard of the generally accepted auditing standards. This standard reads, "The report shall state whether such principles have been consistently observed in the current period in relation to the preceding period."

Assume that the following list describes changes which have a material effect on a client's financial statements for the current year.

1. A change from the completed-contract method to the percentage-of-completion method of accounting for long-term construction contracts.
2. A change in the estimated useful life of previously recorded fixed assets based on newly acquired information.
3. Correction of a mathematical error in inventory pricing made in a prior period.
4. A change from prime costing to full absorption costing for inventory valuation.
5. A change from presentation of statements of individual companies to presentation of consolidated statements.
6. A change from deferring and amortizing preproduction costs to recording such costs as an expense when incurred because future benefits of the costs have become doubtful. The new accounting method was adopted in recognition of the change in estimated future benefits.
7. A change to including the employer share of FICA taxes as "retirement benefits" on the income statement from including it with "other taxes."
8. A change from the FIFO method of inventory pricing to the LIFO method of inventory pricing.

Required
Identify the type of change which is described in each item above, state whether any modification is required in the auditor's report as it relates to the second standard of reporting, and state whether the prior year's financial statements should be restated when presented in comparative form with the current year's statements. Organize your answer sheet as shown on next page.

For example, a change from the LIFO method of inventory pricing to the FIFO method of inventory pricing would appear as shown below:

Item No.	Type of Change	Should Auditor's Report Be Modified?	Should Prior Year's Statements Be Restated?
Example	An accounting change from one generally accepted accounting principle to another generally accepted accounting principle.	Yes	Yes

AICPA

16–29.   Nancy Miller, CPA, has completed field work for her examination of the financial statements of Nickles Manufacturers, Inc. for the year ended March 31, 19X1, and now is preparing her auditor's report. Presented below are three independent, unrelated assumptions concerning this examination:

Assumption 1

The CPA was engaged on April 15, 19X1, to examine the financial statements for the year ended March 31, 19X1 and was not present to observe the taking of the physical inventory on March 31, 19X1. Her alternative procedures included examination of shipping and receiving documents with regard to transactions during the year under review as well as transactions since the year end, extensive review of the inventory count sheets, and discussion of the physical inventory procedures with responsible Company personnel. She has also satisfied herself as to inventory valuation and consistency in valuation method. Inventory quantities are determined solely by means of physical count. (*Note:* Assume that the CPA is properly relying upon the examination of another auditor with respect to the beginning inventory.)

Assumption 2

As of April 1, 19X1, Nickles has an unused balance of $1,378,000 of federal income tax net operating loss carryover that will expire at the end of the Company's fiscal years as follows: $432,000 in 19X2, $870,000 in 19X3, and $76,000 in 19X4. Nickles' management expects that the Company will have enough taxable income to use the loss carryover before it expires.

Assumption 3

On February 28, 19X1, Nickles paid cash for all of the outstanding stock of Ashworth, Inc., a small manufacturer. The combination was consummated as of that date and has been appropriately accounted for as a purchase.

Required

For each assumption described above, discuss the following:
a. In detail, the appropriate disclosures, if any, in the financial statements and accompanying footnotes.
b. The effect, if any, on the auditor's standard report. For this requirement assume that Nickles makes the appropriate disclosures.

Note: Complete your discussion of each assumption (both a and b above) before beginning discussion of the next assumption. In considering each independent assumption, assume that the other two situations did not occur. Organize your answer sheet as follows:

Assumption Number	*(a) Financial Statements and Footnotes*	*(b) Auditor's Report*

AICPA (adapted)

16–30. Charles Burke, CPA, has completed field work for his examination of the Willingham Corporation for the year ended December 31, 19X0, and now is in the process of determining whether to modify his report. Presented below are two independent, unrelated situations which have arisen.

Situation I

In September 19X0, a lawsuit was filed against Willingham to have the court order it to install pollution-control equipment in one of its older plants. Willingham's legal counsel has informed Burke that it is not possible to forecast the outcome of this litigation; however, Willingham's management has informed Burke that the cost of the pollution-control equipment is not economically feasible and that the plant will be closed if the case is lost. In addition, Burke has been told by management that the plant and its production equipment would have only minimal resale values and that the production that would be lost could not be recovered at other plants.

Situation II

During 19X0, Willingham purchased a franchise amounting to 20 percent of its assets for the exclusive right to produce and sell a newly patented product in the northeastern United States. There has been no production in marketable quantities of the product anywhere to date. Neither the franchisor nor any franchisee has conducted any market research with respect to the product.

Required

In deciding the type of report modification, if any, Burke should take into account such considerations as follows:

a. Relative magnitude.
b. Uncertainty of outcome.
c. Likelihood of error.
d. Expertise of the auditor.
e. Pervasive impact on the financial statements.
f. Inherent importance of the item.

Discuss Burke's type of report decision for each situation in terms of the above and other appropriate considerations. Assume each situation is adequately disclosed in the notes to the financial statements. Each situation should be considered independently. In discussing each situation, ignore the other. It is not necessary for you to decide the type of report which should be issued.

AICPA

16–31. The following tentative auditor's report was drafted by a staff accountant and submitted to a partner in the accounting firm of Better & Best, CPAs:

To the Audit Committee of
American Widgets, Inc.

    We have examined the consolidated balance sheets of American Widgets, Inc., and subsidiaries as of December 31, 19X2 and 19X1, and the related consolidated statements of income, retained earnings, and changes in financial position, for the years then ended. Our examinations were made in accordance with generally accepted auditing standards as we considered necessary in the circumstances. Other auditors examined the financial statements of certain subsidiaries and have furnished us with reports thereon containing no exceptions. Our opinion expressed herein, insofar as it relates to the amounts included for those subsidiaries, is based solely upon the reports of the other auditors.

As discussed in Note 4 to the financial statements, on January 8, 19X3, the company halted the production of certain medical equipment as a result of inquiries by the Food and Drug Administration, which raised questions as to the adequacy of some of the company's sterilization equipment and related procedures. Management is not in a position to evaluate the effect of this production halt and the ensuing litigation, which may have an adverse effect on the financial position of American Widgets, Inc.

As fully discussed in Note 7 to the financial statements, in 19X2 the company extended the use of the last-in, first out (LIFO) method of accounting to include all inventories. In examining inventories, we engaged Dr. Irwin Same (Nobel Prize winner 19X0) to test check the technical requirements and specifications of certain items of equipment manufactured by the company.

In our opinion, except for the effects, if any, on the financial statements of the ultimate resolution of the matter discussed in the second preceding paragraph, the financial statements referred to above present fairly the financial position of American Widgets, Inc., as of December 31, 19X2, and the results of operations for the years then ended, in conformity with generally accepted accounting principles applied on a basis consistent with that of the preceding year.

To be signed by
Better & Best, CPAs

March 1, 19X3, except
for Note 4 as to which
the date is January 8, 19X3

Required
Identify deficiencies in the staff accountant's tentative report which constitute departures from the generally accepted standards of reporting. Do not consider any AICPA exposure drafts that are currently outstanding.

AICPA

16–32. The annual reports of three major United States corporations contained departures from the auditor's standard report because of the following notes to financial statements:

R.J. Reynolds Industries, Inc.

Notes to Financial Statements
Note C—Commitments and Contingencies
In July 19X2, two civil actions purporting to be class actions were brought against the six major United States cigarette manufacturers, including the Company, and others, by certain tobacco farmers alleging violations of the antitrust laws and seeking damages aggregating approximately $2.5 billion plus attorneys' fees and costs. Both actions are in their early stages and investigation of the facts is not complete. Counsel has advised the Company, based on its investigation and the formal discovery to date, that in its opinion these cases are not proper class actions and the Company has substantial factual and legal defenses to the charges made. Accordingly, the Company has made no provision for this matter in its financial statements.

DOW CHEMICAL COMPANY

Notes to Financial Statements
B. Inventories—In 19X2, the Company abandoned its historical worldwide practice of valuing inventories on the first-in, first-out basis in favor of the last-in, first-out basis in order to more effectively match current costs and revenues. If the LIFO method had not been adopted, inventories at December 31, 19X2 would have been $993 million, or $271 million greater than the carrying value at that date. The effect of the change was to reduce earnings per share by $1.53.

THE GOODYEAR TIRE AND RUBBER COMPANY

Accounting Change
In accordance with a recent ruling of the Financial Accounting Standards Board, research and development expenses were excluded as an element of cost used for pricing inventory. This has been done on a retroactive basis and consequently prior years have been restated. Inventories and taxes have been decreased by $20,853,000 and $9,692,000, respectively at December 31, 19X2 and 19X1. The effect of this change on 19X2, 19X1, and 19X0 income was not significant.

Required
a. Write the explanatory and opinion paragraphs of the auditor's report for each company. Cover the balance sheets at December 31, 19X2 and 19X1, and the statements of income, retained earnings, and changes in financial position for each of the three years ended December 31, 19X2.
b. Write the explanatory paragraph of the audit report for R. J. Reynolds in the succeeding year. Assume the lawsuits were settled in 19X3 in favor of the company.

16–33. Roscoe, CPA, has completed the examination of the financial statements of Excelsior Corporation as of and for the year ended December 31, 19X1. Roscoe also examined and reported on the Excelsior financial statements for the prior year. Roscoe drafted the following report for 19X1.

March 15, 19X2

We have examined the balance sheet and statements of income and retained earnings of Excelsior Corporation as of December 31, 19X1. Our examination was made in accordance with generally accepted accounting standards and accordingly included such tests of the accounting records as we considered necessary in the circumstances.

In our opinion, the above mentioned financial statements are accurately and fairly presented in accordance with generally accepted accounting principles in effect at December 31, 19X1.

Roscoe, CPA
(Signed)

Other information:

1. Excelsior is presenting comparative financial statements for 19X1 and 19X0.
2. Excelsior does not wish to present a statement of changes in financial position for either year.
3. During 19X1, Excelsior changed its method of accounting for long-term construction contracts and properly reflected the effect of the change in the current year's financial statements and restated the prior-year's statements. Roscoe is satisfied with Excelsior's justification for making the change. The change is discussed in footnote number 12.
4. Roscoe was unable to perform normal accounts receivable confirmation procedures but alternate procedures were used to satisfy Roscoe as to the validity of the receivables.

5. Excelsior Corporation is the defendant in a litigation, the outcome of which is highly uncertain. If the case is settled in favor of the plaintiff, Excelsior will be required to pay a substantial amount of cash which might require the sale of certain fixed assets. The litigation and the possible effects have been properly disclosed in footnote number 11.

6. Excelsior issued debentures on January 31, 19X0, in the amount of $10 million. The funds obtained from the issuance were used to finance the expansion of plant facilities. The debenture agreement restricts the payment of future cash dividends to earnings after December 31, 19X6. Excelsior declined to disclose this essential data in the footnotes to the financial statements.

Required

Consider all facts given and rewrite the auditor's report in acceptable and complete format incorporating any necessary departures from the standard report.

Do not discuss the draft of Roscoe's report but identify and explain any items included in "*Other Information*" that need not be part of the auditor's report.

AICPA

CASE STUDY

16-34.* You recently completed the December 31, 19X0, examination of a new client, Staid, Inc., and the senior accountant has asked your advice in preparing the auditor's report. Staid, Inc. had not previously been audited.

Staid, Inc. is a manufacturing company with accounts receivable of $100,000, inventories of $140,000, net worth of $800,000, and an annual sales volume of $1.6 million. The company refused to permit circularization of customer receivables because it was having warranty problems and did not want to give the customers an opportunity to further crystallize their complaints by reducing them to writing. Also, the company would not permit observation of the taking of the year-end physical inventory because the procedure was so costly (*every* count checked two times) and the company felt we would add cost without adding accuracy. The company takes its inventory once a year and maintains no perpetual inventory records.

The business is a one-plant operation. All manufacturing, sales, and accounting activities are conducted on the premises. The management is composed primarily of officer-stockholders. In general you have evaluated internal control as weak in the area of accounts payable and adequate in all other areas.

You prepared an aging of the accounts receivable and examined collections from the balance sheet date to a date near the end of your field work. The accounts were otherwise tested and the billing procedures reviewed and you were satisfied as to the validity and collectibility of the accounts and the reasonableness of the amounts in relationship to the volume of business.

You inquired into the inventory-taking, purchase, and sales cutoff procedures. You tested some quantities of inventory items against their physical existence, and reviewed inventory turnover and gross profit ratios, the results of which revealed no unusual items. You feel reasonably sure not only that the company has inventories and receivables, but also that it has them in approximately the amounts stated. You have also satisfied yourself that accounting principles have been applied on a consistent basis from the preceding year.

The senior proposes to include the following auditor's report:

> We have examined the balance sheet of Staid, Inc., as of December 31, 19X0, and the related statements of income, stockholders' equity and changes in financial position for the year then ended. Except that we were

not authorized to confirm customers' accounts receivable, as to which amounts we reasonably satisfied ourselves by other auditing procedures, or to verify inventory quantities by physical tests or observation thereof, our examination was made in accordance with generally accepted auditing standards and, accordingly, included such tests of the accounting records and such other auditing procedures as we considered necessary in the circumstances.

In the opinion paragraph the senior states:

In our opinion, subject to the exceptions stated above relating to the verification of accounts receivable, the financial statements referred to above present fairly the financial position of Staid, Inc., at December 31, 19X0, and the results of its operations and the changes in its financial position for the year then ended, in conformity with generally accepted accounting principles applied on a basis consistent with that of the preceding year.

Required
a. Could an unqualified opinion be given in this case? Explain.
b. What would you advise the senior with respect to the report wording?
c. What questions are raised in your mind because of the company's reasons for not allowing you to confirm receivables and observe the physical inventory?

Other Reports
and Services

STUDY OBJECTIVES

The study objectives of this chapter are to acquire an understanding of additional reports that may be issued in an audit engagement and the nature of other services that a CPA may perform for clients. To achieve these objectives, it is necessary for the reader to

- Identify and distinguish among the three types of services that a CPA may render to a client.
- Know the nature and forms of additional reports that may be issued in audit engagements.
- Become knowledgeable of the objectives, procedures, and reports relating to review services.
- Comprehend the nature of accounting services and the reports applicable thereto.

As an auditor and accountant in a firm, a certified public accountant (CPA) may render three types of services to a client: audit, review, or accounting. This chapter has two primary objectives: to describe and illustrate additional types of reports pertaining to audit engagements and to explain the objectives, procedures, and reports relating to performing review and accounting services for a client.

AUDITING SERVICES

The audit or attest function has been and continues to be the central purpose of this book. In rendering audit services, the auditor is expected to make the examination and report his findings in accordance with generally accepted auditing standards (GAAS). In Chapter 16, reporting is directed solely on the auditor's standard report. Now it is appropriate to consider other reports that may result from audit engagements. These consist of special reports, reports on personal financial statements, and reports on internal accounting control.

Special Reports

Reports issued in connection with the following criteria constitute special reports:

- Financial statements prepared in accordance with a comprehensive basis of accounting other than generally accepted accounting principles (GAAP).
- Specific elements, accounts, or items of a financial statement.
- Compliance with aspects of contractual agreements or regulatory requirements related to audited financial statements.
- Financial information presented in prescribed forms or schedules that require a prescribed form of auditor's report.[1]

The responsibilities of the auditor for the first three types of special reports are explained below.

Comprehensive Basis Other than GAAP

The basis of accounting used by the client is considered to be comprehensive when it is (1) a basis prescribed by a regulatory body, (2) a basis used in filing its income tax return, (3) the cash or modified cash basis, or (4) a basis having substantial support, such as the price level or replacement cost basis.

The use of these alternative bases is common. Many companies subject

---

[1] Auditing Standards Board, *Codification of Statements on Auditing Standards* (New York: American Institute of Certified Public Accountants, 1983), Auditing Section 621.01 (Hereinafter referred to and cited as AU §).

to regulatory bodies keep their accounts solely on the basis prescribed by the agency. For example, railroads conform with the requirements of the Interstate Commerce Commission (ICC), public utilities use the basis set forth by the Federal Energy Regulatory Commission, and insurance companies follow state insurance commission accounting requirements. In addition, many small companies and individual practitioners, such as doctors, lawyers, and CPAs, use the income tax, cash, or modified cash basis of accounting. When an entity uses a basis other than GAAP, the notes to the financial statements should indicate the basis and how it differs from GAAP.

All of the GAAS are applicable whenever the auditor examines and reports on any financial statement regardless of the basis of accounting used in preparing the statement. The major difference in this case is that the statements are not intended to present fairly financial position, etc., in conformity with GAAP. However, the first standard of reporting is satisfied by indicating whether the statements are presented fairly in conformity with the basis of accounting used.[2]

In reporting on statements prepared on a comprehensive basis other than GAAP, the auditor should issue a three-paragraph report which contains

- A *scope paragraph* that may be standard except that more distinctive titles should be used for each statement, such as statement of assets and liabilities (cash basis) for the balance sheet and statement of revenue collected and expenses paid for the income statement.
- An *explanatory paragraph* that should (1) refer to the note to the financial statements that describes the basis of accounting and how it differs from GAAP and (2) indicate that the statements are not intended to be in conformity with GAAP.
- An *opinion paragraph* that indicates whether (1) the financial statements are fairly presented on the basis described and (2) the disclosed basis has been applied on a consistent basis.

When the auditor concludes that the financial statements are not presented fairly, a qualified or adverse opinion should be expressed as explained in the preceding chapter. A special report for financial statements prepared on a cash basis is illustrated in Figure 17-1.

Specified Elements, Accounts, or Items of a Financial Statement

This category of special reports includes the expression of an opinion on rentals, royalties, profit participation plans, or provisions for income taxes. An engagement to express an opinion on one or more of these items may be made in conjunction with an examination of financial statements or it may be done in a separate engagement. In such an engagement, all of the GAAS apply except the first and second standards of reporting. The first standard of reporting is not applicable because the specified items do not constitute a

[2] *Ibid.*

We have examined the statement of assets and liabilities arising from cash transactions of *XYZ* Company as of December 31, 19*XX*, and the related statement of revenue collected and expenses paid for the year then ended. Our examination was made in accordance with generally accepted auditing standards and, accordingly, included such tests of the accounting records and such other auditing procedures as we considered necessary in the circumstances.

As described in Note *X*, the Company's policy is to prepare its financial statements on the basis of cash receipts and disbursements; consequently, certain revenue and the related assets are recognized when received rather than when earned, and certain expenses are recognized when paid rather than when the obligation is incurred. Accordingly, the accompanying financial statements are not intended to present financial position and results of operations in conformity with generally accepted accounting principles.

In our opinion, the financial statements referred to above present fairly the assets and liabilities arising from cash transactions of *XYZ* Company as of December 31, 19*XX*, and the revenue collected and expenses paid during the year then ended, on the basis of accounting described in Note *X*, which basis has been applied in a manner consistent with that of the preceding year.

FIGURE 17–1. Auditor's Report on Financial Statements Prepared on Cash Basis (SOURCE: Auditing Standards Board, *op. cit.*, AU § 621.08.)

financial statement. The consistency standard applies only if the items have, in fact, been stated in conformity with GAAP.

In reporting, the auditor may use either a two- or a three-paragraph report. In the scope paragraph, the specific elements, accounts, or items should be identified and the character of the examination should be indicated. The latter is done by reference to GAAS. In addition, the report should indicate (1) the basis on which the items are presented, (2) whether they are presented fairly on that basis, and if applicable, (3) whether the basis was applied in a manner consistent with the preceding period. An example of a three-paragraph report is illustrated in Figure 17-2. Generally, a special report on specific items should not be issued if the auditor has expressed an adverse opinion or disclaimed an opinion on the financial statements taken as a whole.

An accountant may accept an engagement to apply agreed-upon procedures to specified elements, accounts, or items of a financial statement. For example, in a proposed acquisition the prospective purchaser may only ask the accountant to reconcile the bank balances and confirm the accounts receivable of the entity that may be acquired. This type of engagement is permitted provided (1) the parties involved have a clear understanding of the procedures to be performed and (2) distribution of the report is restricted to named parties involved.

An engagement to perform agreed-upon procedures does not constitute an examination in accordance with GAAS. Only the three general standards and the first standard of field work are applicable. The accountant's report on the results of agreed-upon procedures should

- Indicate the elements, accounts, or items to which the procedures were applied.

Board of Directors
XYZ Corporation

We have examined the schedule of royalties applicable to engine production of the Q Division of XYZ Corporation for the year ended December 31, 19XX, under the terms of a license agreement dated May 14, 19XX, between ABC Company and XYZ Corporation. Our examination was made in accordance with generally accepted auditing standards and, accordingly, included such tests of the accounting records and such other auditing procedures as we considered necessary in the circumstances.

We have been informed that, under XYZ Corporation's interpretation of the agreement referred to above, royalties were based on the number of engines produced after giving effect to a reduction for production retirements that were scrapped, but without a reduction for field returns that were scrapped, even though the field returns were replaced with new engines without charge to customers. This treatment is consistent with that followed in prior years.

In our opinion, the schedule of royalties referred to above presents fairly the number of engines produced by the Q Division of XYZ Corporation during the year ended December 31, 19XX, and the amount of royalties applicable thereto under the license agreement referred to above, on the basis indicated in the preceding paragraph.

FIGURE 17–2. Auditor's Report on Royalties (SOURCE: Auditing Standards Board, *op. cit.,* AU § 621.14.)

- State the intended distribution of the report.
- Enumerate the procedures performed.
- State the findings.
- Disclaim an opinion with respect to the elements, accounts, or items.
- State that the report relates only to the specified items and does not extend to the entry's financial statements taken as a whole.[3]

Compliance Reports Related to Audited Financial Statements

This type of special report pertains to contractual agreements, such as bond indentures, and regulatory requirements of such agencies as the Federal Home Loan Mortgage Corporation. The auditor's involvement with such reports arises from the desire by the lender or agency to obtain assurance from an independent party concerning compliance. In such circumstances, the auditor is not required to audit the data for compliance. However, if the auditor has audited the related financial statements, it is permissible for the auditor to give *negative assurance* on compliance. This type of assurance is expressed as "nothing came to our attention which would indicate that these amounts [or items] are not fairly presented [stated]."

Compliance reports may be issued as a separate report, or they may be included as an "add on" to the auditor's report on the accompanying financial statements. In the latter, an explanatory third paragraph is often added after the opinion paragraph. Such positioning serves to keep intact the two-paragraph standard auditor's report. A separate report on compliance is illustrated in Figure 17-3.

[3] Auditing Standards Board, *op. cit.,* AU § 622.04.

Board of Directors
XYZ Company

We have examined the balance sheet of XYZ Company as of December 31, 19X1, and the related statements of income, retained earnings, and changes in financial position for the year then ended, and have issued our report thereon dated March 5, 19X2. Our examination was made in accordance with generally accepted auditing standards and, accordingly, included such tests of the accounting records and such other auditing procedures as we considered necessary in the circumstances.

In connection with our examination, nothing came to our attention that caused us to believe that the Company had failed to comply with the limitation and increased investment requirement in section 993(d)(2) and (3) of the Internal Revenue Code of 1954. However, it should be noted that our examination was not directed primarily toward obtaining knowledge of noncompliance with such requirements.

FIGURE 17–3. Auditor's Report on Compliance with Regulatory Requirements (Source: Auditing Standards Board, *op. cit.*, AU § 621.19.)

Reports on Personal Financial Statements

Personal financial statements present the assets and liabilites of an individual or a group of individuals (a family) and, if appropriate, a statement of changes in net assets. Such statements may be prepared for personal use or for the use of others such as those interested in the financial affairs of public officials and candidates for public office.

The basic personal financial statement is the "statement of assets and liabilities" as of a specified date. The general guidelines for this statement are as follows:

- Assets and liabilities should be stated at current values.
- GAAP and the accrual basis of accounting should be used.
- The statements should include adequate disclosures.

In addition, a statement of changes in net assets may be prepared. This statement shows revenues, expenses, and changes in the estimated values of assets and liabilities for a given period of time.

Personal financial statements are no different from any other financial statements concerning the applicability of GAAS. The auditor is required, for example, to have a reasonable basis for expressing an opinion on the statements. In achieving this objective, the auditor may have to rely primarily, if not exclusively, on substantive tests, because internal controls may be nonexistent or known, on the basis of a preliminary review, to be ineffective. In examining personal financial statements, the auditor should obtain corroborating evidence of current value and perform the procedures necessary to determine that all assets and liabilities have been recorded.

Special wording is required in the auditor's report on personal financial statements. The standard report is illustrated in Figure 17-4. The auditor may, when circumstances warrant, issue a qualified or adverse opinion or

We have examined the statements of assets and liabilities of Mr. and Mrs. Person as of December 31, 19X1 and 19X0, and the related statements of changes in net assets for the years then ended. Our examinations were made in accordance with generally accepted auditing standards and, accordingly, included such tests of the accounting records and such other auditing procedures as we considered necessary in the circumstances.

In our opinion, the financial statements referred to above present fairly the financial position of Mr. and Mrs. Person as of December 31, 19X1 and 19X0, and the changes in net assets for the years then ended, in conformity with generally accepted accounting principles applied on a consistent basis.

FIGURE 17–4. Auditor's Report on Personal Financial Statements

disclaim an opinion on personal financial statements in the same manner as described for other financial statements.

Reports on Internal Accounting Control

An independent accountant issues a report on internal accounting control (IAC) when he is engaged to

- Express an opinion on the entity's system of IAC in effect as of a specified date.
- Report on the entity's system based solely on the study and evaluation of IAC made as part of an audit of the entity's financial statements in accordance with GAAS.
- Report on all or part of an entity's system based on pre-established criteria of regulatory agencies.
- Issue other special-purpose reports on all or part of an entity's system.[4]

Consideration will be given below to the first three circumstances.

Engagement to Express an Opinion

The study and evaluation of IAC for the purpose of expressing an opinion may be made separately from or in conjunction with an audit of the entity's financial statements. In the latter case, it generally will be necessary for the accountant to expand the scope of his study in order to have a reasonable basis for an opinion of the internal accounting control system as a whole. For example, all control procedures should be reviewed and tested for compliance, not just the controls that are to be relied upon to determine the extent to which other auditing procedures are to be restricted.

In making a study for the purpose of expressing an opinion, the accountant should (1) plan the scope of the engagement, (2) review the design of the system, (3) test compliance with prescribed procedures, and (4) evaluate the results of his review and tests. These steps are analogous to those described

---

[4] Auditing Standards Board, *op. cit.*, AU § 642.02.

in Chapter 4 when the study and evaluation of IAC was made as part of a financial statement audit. In addition, the CPA should obtain a written representation from management that acknowledges management's responsibility for establishing and maintaining the system of internal control and states that management has disclosed to the CPA all material weaknesses in the system of which it is aware. When the study is made as part of a financial statement audit, the auditor is not required to duplicate any procedures that may be performed in the audit.

The accountant's report in this type of engagement should include:

- A description of the scope of the engagement.
- The date to which the opinion relates.
- A statement that the establishment and maintenance of the system is the responsibility of management.
- A brief explanation of the broad objectives and inherent limitations of IAC.
- The accountant's opinion on whether the system taken as a whole was sufficient to meet the broad objectives of IAC insofar as those objectives pertain to the prevention or detection of errors or irregularities in amounts that would be material in relation to the financial statements.[5]

An illustrative report containing an unqualified opinion is shown in Figure 17-5. There are no restrictions on the distribution of the accountant's report in this type of engagement. An unqualified opinion does not indicate whether a company is in compliance with the IAC provisions of the Foreign Corrupt Practices Act. However, it may be useful to management's own evaluation of compliance.

Modifications of the standard report are required when material weaknesses exist or when a scope limitation has occurred. Material weaknesses should be described in the report and either a qualified or an adverse opinion should be expressed on the system as a whole. The treatment of a scope limitation is the same as in a report on audited financial statements.

Engagement Based Solely on Financial Statement Audit

A study and evaluation of IAC made as part of a financial statement audit is not sufficient for an expression of an opinion on the system taken as a whole. The auditor may report on the system provided the report

- Indicates that it is intended solely for management, a specified regulatory agency, or other specified third party.
- Describes the limited purpose of the study and evaluation.
- Disclaims an opinion on the system taken as a whole.[6]

---

[5] Auditing Standards Board, *op. cit.*, AU § 642.38.
[6] Auditing Standards Board, *op. cit.*, AU § 642.48.

To the Board of Directors and Shareholders of XYZ Company

We have made a study and evaluation of the system of internal accounting control of *XYZ* Company and subsidiaries in effect at December 31, 19XX. Our study and evaluation was conducted in accordance with standards established by the American Institute of Certified Public Accountants.

The management of *XYZ* Company is responsible for establishing and maintaining a system of internal accounting control. In fulfilling this responsibility, estimates and judgments by management are required to assess the expected benefits and related costs of control procedures. The objectives of a system are to provide management with reasonable, but not absolute, assurance that assets are safeguarded against loss from unauthorized use or disposition, and that transactions are executed in accordance with management's authorization and recorded properly to permit the preparation of financial statements in accordance with generally accepted accounting principles.

Because of inherent limitations in any system of internal accounting control, errors or irregularities may nevertheless occur and not be detected. Also, projection of any evaluation of the system to future periods is subject to the risk that procedures may become inadequate because of changes in conditions, or that the degree of compliance with the procedures may deteriorate.

In our opinion, the system of internal accounting control of *XYZ* Company and subsidiaries in effect at December 31, 19XX, taken as a whole, was sufficient to meet the objectives stated above insofar as those objectives pertain to the prevention or detection of errors or irregularities in amounts that would be material in relation to the consolidated financial statements.

FIGURE 17–5. Report on Internal Control Based on Engagement to Express an Opinion (SOURCE: Auditing Standards Board, *op. cit.*, AU § 642.39.)

The standard report contains a scope paragraph, two middle paragraphs that are identical with the corresponding paragraphs of the report illustrated in Figure 17-5, a conclusions paragraph, and a paragraph restricting the distribution of the report. The wording of the standard report is illustrated in Figure 17-6.

Observe that the conclusions paragraph contains

- A statement that the examination (of the financial statements) would not necessarily disclose all material weaknesses in the system.
- A disclaimer of opinion on the system taken as a whole.
- A statement that the examination disclosed no material weaknesses.

As indicated previously, the auditor is required to communicate material weaknesses in internal control to senior management and the board of directors. When the communication is in writing, the fourth paragraph of the report in Figure 17-6 should (1) contain a description of the material weaknesses that have come to the auditor's attention and (2) state that the weaknesses were considered in determining the substantive tests to be applied in the examination of the financial statements.

To the Board of Directors of XYZ Company

We have examined the financial statements of XYZ Company for the year ended December 31, 19X1, and have issued our report thereon dated February 23, 19X2. As part of our examination we made a study and evaluation of the Company's system of internal accounting control to the extent we considered necessary to evaluate the system as required by generally accepted auditing standards. The purpose of our study and evaluation was to determine the nature, timing, and extent of the auditing procedures necessary for expressing an opinion on the Company's financial statements. Our study and evaluation was more limited than would be necessary to express an opinion on the system of internal accounting control taken as a whole.

The management of XYZ Company is responsible for establishing and maintaining a system of internal accounting control. In fulfilling this responsibility, estimates and judgments by management are required to assess the expected benefits and related costs of control procedures. The objectives of a system are to provide management with reasonable, but not absolute, assurance that assets are safeguarded against loss from unauthorized use or disposition, and that transactions are executed in accordance with management's authorization and recorded properly to permit the preparation of financial statements in accordance with generally accepted accounting principles.

Because of inherent limitations in any system of internal accounting control, errors or irregularities may nevertheless occur and not be detected. Also, projection of any evaluation of the system to future periods is subject to the risk that procedures may become inadequate because of changes in conditions, or that the degree of compliance with the procedures may deteriorate.

Our study and evaluation made for the limited purpose described in the first paragraph would not necessarily disclose all material weaknesses in the system. Accordingly, we do not express an opinion on the system of internal accounting control of XYZ Company taken as a whole. However, our study and evaluation disclosed no condition that we believed to be a material weakness.

This report is intended solely for the information of management (or specified regulatory agency or other specified third party) and should not be used for any other purpose.

FIGURE 17–6. Report on Internal Control Based Solely on Audit Engagement. (Source: Auditing Standards Board, *op. cit.,* AU § 642.49.)

Engagement Based on Pre-established Criteria

Some governmental and regulatory agencies require reports on IAC of entities under their jurisdiction. In such case, specific criteria may be provided for evaluating the adequacy of the controls. When the criteria are set forth in reasonable detail and in terms susceptible to objective application, an accountant may accept an engagement to review and report on the entity's system.

The accountant's report should (1) clearly identify the matters covered by his study (2) indicate whether the study included tests of compliance with the procedures covered by his study, (3) describe the objectives and limitations of IAC and of accountants' evaluations of it, (4) state the accountant's conclusion based on the agency's criteria, concerning the adequacy of the procedures studied, with an exception as to any material weaknesses, and (5) state it is intended for use in connection with the grant or other purpose to which the report refers and that it should not be used for any other purpose.[7]

REVIEW SERVICES

Review services are a relatively new development in the public accounting profession. This activity resulted from the profession's efforts to be responsive to the needs of clients, regulatory agencies, and the investing public for a service that would provide some form of limited assurance as to the reliability of financial data without requiring an examination in accordance with GAAS.

A review differs significantly from an audit as to procedures and objectives. For example, a review generally is limited to two types of procedures: inquiry and analytical review; and a review does not result in the expression of an opinion. In addition, the individual making the review should not be referred to as an auditor. It is possible, however, for a CPA to render both auditing and review services to the same client. The major types of review engagements and the AICPA group authorized to establish guidelines for the service are as follows:

TYPE OF REVIEW	AICPA GROUP
Interim financial information of a public entity[8]	Auditing Standards Board
Financial statements of a nonpublic entity[8]	Accounting and Review Services Committee
Financial forecasts	Financial Forecasts and Projections Task Force.

The guidelines for each type of review service are described below.

Reviewing Interim Financial Information for Public Entities

Interim financial information (IFI) includes current data during a fiscal year on financial position, results of operations, and changes in financial position. Such information may be issued on a monthly or quarterly basis or at other intervals. IFI may take the form of either complete financial statements, summarized financial statements, or summarized financial data.[9] IFI may be presented alone or in a note to audited financial statements.

In this type of a review, the accountant is expected to (1) possess (or acquire) a level of knowledge of the accounting principles and practices of the industry in which the entity operates and (2) have (or obtain) an under-

---

[7] Auditing Standards Board, *op. cit.,* para. 56.

[8] The distinction between the types of entities is based primarily on whether the entity's securities are traded either on a stock exchange or in the over-the-counter market.

[9] *APB Opinion No. 28, Interim Financial Reporting* (New York: American Institute of Certified Public Accountants, 1973).

standing of the entity's business and accounting practices. The knowledge and understanding are ordinarily obtained through prior experience with the entity or its industry and from inquiry of entity personnel.

Objective and Procedures

The objective of the review of IFI is to provide the accountant with a basis for reporting whether material modifications should be made for such information to conform with GAAP.[10] This objective differs significantly from the objective of an audit which is to have a basis for expressing an opinion on the fairness of the financial statements. The review program for IFI should include:

- Inquiry concerning (1) the accounting system, to obtain an understanding of the manner in which transactions are recorded, classified, and summarized in the preparation of interim financial information and (2) any significant changes in the system of internal accounting control, to ascertain their potential effect on the preparation of interim financial information.
- Application of analytical review procedures to interim financial information to identify and provide a basis for inquiry about relationships and individual items that appear to be unusual.
- Reading the minutes of meetings of stockholders, board of directors, and committees of the board of directors to identify actions that may affect the interim financial information.
- Reading the interim financial information to consider, on the basis of information coming to the accountant's attention, whether the information to be reported conforms with GAAP.
- Obtaining reports from other accountants, if any, who have been engaged to make a review of the interim financial information of significant segments of the reporting entity, its subsidiaries, or other investees.
- Inquiry of officers and other executives having responsibility for financial and accounting matters concerning (1) whether the interim financial information has been prepared in conformity with GAAP consistently applied, (2) changes in the entity's business activities or accounting practices, (3) matters as to which questions have arisen in the course of applying the foregoing procedures, and (4) events subsequent to the date of the IFI that would have a material effect on the presentation of such information.
- Obtain written representations from management concerning its responsibility for the information, completeness of the minutes, subsequent events and other matters.[11]

Note that the accountant is not required to make a study and evaluation of internal control or obtain corroborating evidence needed in an audit. The

[10] Auditing Standards Board, *op. cit.,* AU § 722.03.
[11] Auditing Standards Board, *op. cit.,* AU § 722.06.

extent of these procedures will be influenced by the accountant's knowledge of (1) the client's accounting and reporting practices, (2) weaknesses in internal accounting control, (3) changes in nature or volume of the client's business activities, and (4) the effects of new accounting pronouncements on the client.

Accountant's Report

The report on IFI should contain the following elements:

- A statement that the review was made in accordance with the standards for such reviews.
- An identification of the IFI reviewed.
- A description of the procedures for a review of IFI.
- A statement that a review is significantly less in scope than an examination in accordance with GAAS and, accordingly, no opinion is expressed.
- A statement as to whether the accountant is aware of any material modifications that should be made to the information to make it conform with GAAP.[12]

The report should be addressed and dated in the same manner as the auditor's standard report. In addition, each page of the interim financial information should be clearly marked "unaudited." An illustrative report is presented in Figure 17-7.

Reviewing Financial Statements of a Nonpublic Entity

A CPA may be engaged to review interim and/or annual financial statements of a nonpublic entity. The objective, procedures, and reporting for this type

---

We have made a review of [describe the information or statements reviewed] of *ABC Company* and consolidated subsidiaries as of September 30, 19X1, and for the three-month and nine-month periods then ended, in accordance with standards established by the American Institute of Certified Public Accountants.

A review of interim financial information consists principally of obtaining an understanding of the system for the preparation of interim financial information, applying analytical review procedures to financial data, and making inquiries of persons responsible for financial and accounting matters. It is substantially less in scope than an examination in accordance with generally accepted auditing standards, the objective of which is the expression of an opinion regarding the financial statements taken as a whole. Accordingly, we do not express such an opinion.

Based on our review, we are not aware of any material modification that should be made to the accompanying financial (information or statements) for them to be in conformity with generally accepted accounting principles.

FIGURE 17–7. Accountant's Report on Review of Interim Financial Information for a Public Entity (SOURCE: Auditing Standards Board, *op. cit.*, AU § 722.18.)

---

12 Auditing Standards Board, *op. cit.*, AU § 722.17.

of review service for a nonpublic entity are similar to those described above for a public entity, but they are not identical. The objective of a review for a nonpublic entity includes *other comprehensive bases of accounting* as well as GAAP.[13] This addition recognizes that smaller companies may use a cash or income tax basis of accounting.

The principal changes in review procedure are: (1) inquiry should be made concerning the entity's accounting principles and practices, and (2) it is not necessary to inquire about changes in internal accounting control or to obtain a representation letter from management.

There is one substantive change in reporting: the report should state that all information in the financial statements is the representation of the management (owners) of the entity.[14] In addition, each page of the financial statements reviewed by the accountant should include a reference such as "See Accountant's Review Report." A review report is illustrated in Figure 17-8.

If the accountant is unable to perform the review considered necessary in the circumstances, a review report should not be issued.

Reviewing Financial Forecasts

A financial forecast for an entity is an estimate of the most probable financial position, results of operations, and changes in financial position for one or more future periods of time. Financial forecasts have been an important tool of management in internal planning and decision making for many years. They have also been used externally by companies in obtaining loans and in the private and public placement of debt and equity securities.

I [we] have reviewed the accompanying balance sheet of *XYZ* Company as of December 31, 19*XX*, and the related statements of income, retained earnings, and changes in financial position for the year then ended, in accordance with standards established by the American Institute of Certified Public Accountants. All information included in these financial statements is the representation of the management [owners] of *XYZ* Company.

A review consists of inquiries of company personnel and analytical procedures applied to financial data. It is substantially less in scope than an examination in accordance with generally accepted auditing standards, the objective of which is the expression of an opinion regarding the financial statements taken as a whole. Accordingly, I [we] do not express such an opinion.

Based on my [our] review, I am [we are] not aware of any material modifications that should be made to the accompanying financial statements in order for them to be in conformity with generally accepted accounting principles.

FIGURE 17–8. Accountant's Report on Review of Financial Statements for a Nonpublic Entity. (SOURCE: *SSARS No. 1, op. cit.,* para. 35.)

---

[13] Accounting and Review Services Committee, *Statement on Standards for Accounting and Review Services No. 1, Compilation and Review of Financial Statements* (New York: American Institute of Certified Public Accountants, 1978), para. 4 (Hereinafter referred to and cited as *SSARS No. 1*).

[14] *SSARS No. 1., op. cit.,* para. 32.

In recent years, some companies have started to include financial forecasts in their annual reports, and the inclusion of sales and earnings forecasts in filings with the SEC is now permissible.

In an effort to add credibility to forecasts, some companies have CPAs review and report on them. Standards for such engagements have been established by the AICPA through a Financial Forecasts and Projections Task Force. The recommendations of this group were reviewed by the Auditing Standards Board prior to issuance. The guidelines of the task force are authoritative, but they do not have the same status as an SAS.

Objective and Guidelines

The objective of the accountant's review of a forecast is to provide a basis for reporting whether

- The forecast is properly prepared on the basis of management's stated assumptions.
- The forecast is properly prepared on a basis consistent with the accounting principles expected to be used in the historical financial statements covering the forecast period.
- The underlying assumptions provide a reasonable basis for the forecast.

Ten guidelines are given for the preparation of a financial forecast. These guidelines are presented in Appendix 17A.

Procedures

As in other review engagements, the accountant relies primarily on inquiry and analytical review procedures in making the review. The accountant's working papers should include written representations from management acknowledging its responsibility for both the forecast and the underlying assumptions. The scope of the accountant's review is influenced by (1) the accountant's knowledge of the business, (2) management's record in previous forecasts, (3) the length of the forecast period, and (4) the complexity of the forecasting process.

Accountant's Report

The accountant's standard report on a review of a financial forecast should include

- An identification of the forecast information presented by management and a description of what it is intended to represent.
- A statement that the review was made in accordance with applicable AICPA guidelines for a review of a financial forecast and a brief description of the nature of such a review.
- A statement that the accountant assumes no responsibility to update the

report for events and circumstances occurring after the date of the report.
- A statement regarding whether the accountant believes that the financial forecast is presented in conformity with applicable AICPA guidelines for presentation of a financial forecast and whether the underlying assumptions provide a reasonable basis for management's forecast.
- A caveat regarding the ultimate attainment of the forecast results.[15]

The standard report is illustrated in Figure 17-9. When the accountant concludes that a qualification of his report is required, an adverse opinion generally should be issued in order to minimize possible misinterpretations of the qualification.

ACCOUNTING SERVICES

Attention in this section is directed at two types of accounting services: services pertaining to unaudited financial statements of a public entity and compilation services (i.e., preparation of financial statements) for a nonpublic entity. Accounting services may also include (1) preparing a working trial balance, (2) assisting in adjusting the books of account, (3) consulting on accounting, tax, and similar matters, (4) preparing tax returns, (5) providing various manual or automated bookkeeping or data processing services unless the output is in the form of financial statements, and (6) processing financial data for clients of other accounting firms.[16]

The accompanying forecast balance sheet, statements of income, retained earnings, and changes in financial position, and summary of significant forecast assumptions of XYZ Company as of December 31, 19XX, and for the year then ending, is management's estimate of the most probable financial position, results of operations, and changes in financial position for the forecast period. Accordingly, the forecast reflects management's judgment, based on present circumstances, of the most likely set of conditions and its most likely course of action.

We have made a review of the financial forecast in accordance with applicable guidelines for a review of a financial forecast established by the American Institute of Certified Public Accountants. Our review included procedures to evaluate both the assumptions used by management and the preparation and presentation of the forecast. We have no responsibility to update this report for events and circumstances occurring after the date of this report.

Based on our review, we believe that the accompanying financial forecast is presented in conformity with applicable guidelines for presentation of a financial forecast established by the American Institute of Certified Public Accountants. We believe that the underlying assumptions provide a reasonable basis for management's forecast. However, some assumptions inevitably will not materialize and unanticipated events and circumstances may occur; therefore, the actual results achieved during the forecast period will vary from the forecast, and the variations may be material.

FIGURE 17–9. Standard Report on Review of A Financial Forecast (SOURCE: *Forecast Guide, op. cit.,* p. 22.)

[15] Financial Forecasts and Projections Task Force, *Guide for a Review of a Financial Forecast,* AICPA, 1980, p. 21 (Hereinafter referred to as *Forecast Guide*).

[16] *SSARS No. 1, op. cit.,* para. 2.

The responsibility for setting standards for accounting services is shared by two AICPA groups: the Auditing Standards Board for public entities and the Accounting and Review Services Committee for nonpublic entities.

Unaudited Financial Statements

An accountant is associated with financial statements when he (1) has consented to the use of his name in a report, document, or written communication containing the statements, or (2) submits to clients or others financial statements that he has prepared or assisted in preparing even though his name is not appended to the statements.[17]

When accountants are associated with unaudited financial statements of public entities, but have not audited or reviewed them, they are required to

- Include a disclaimer of opinion.
- State that an audit was not made.
- Mark each page of the statements as unaudited.

The first two requirements are illustrated in Figure 17-10.

The accountant is not required to perform any auditing procedures in an accounting service engagement. If any procedures are performed, they should not be described in the accountant's report. When a CPA knows, from knowledge about the client or the work done, that the unaudited statements are not in conformity with generally accepted accounting principles, the client should be requested to make the necessary revisions in the statements. If the client refuses, the accountant should clearly state his reservations on the statements along with a disclaimer of opinion. If, in such case, the client will not accept the accountant's report, the CPA should refuse to be associated with the statements and, if necessary, withdraw from the engagement.

The accompanying balance sheet of X Company as of December 31, 19X1, and the related statements of income, retained earnings, and changes in financial position for the year then ended were not audited by us and, accordingly, we do not express an opinion on them.

_____
Signature

Date: _____

FIGURE 17–10. Accountant's Report on Unaudited Statements (SOURCE: Auditing Standards Board, _op. cit.,_ AU § 504.05.)

[17] Auditing Standards Board, _op. cit.,_ AU § 504.03.

Compilation of Financial Statements

A CPA may be engaged to compile the financial statements of a nonpublic entity. In a compilation engagement, as in other engagements, the accountant should establish a clear understanding with the entity regarding the services to be performed. The understanding should be set forth in an engagement letter describing (1) the nature of the service, (2) the limitations of the service (i.e., cannot be relied upon to disclose errors and irregularities), and (3) the nature of the compilation report.[18] Lack of a clear understanding as to the nature of the engagement resulted in significant damages against a local CPA firm for failing to discover fraud in the *1136 Tenants' Corporation* case. For a discussion of this case, see Appendix 17B.

Objective and Nature

The objective of this type of accounting service is to present in the form of financial statements information supplied by an entity without giving any assurance as to the conformity of the statements with generally accepted accounting principles or another comprehensive basis of accounting. In completing a compilation engagement, the CPA is expected to be knowledgeable of the client and the accounting principles and practices of the industry in which the client operates. He should also have a general understanding of its accounting records, the qualifications of its accounting personnel, and the form and content of its financial statements. Such knowledge is ordinarily obtained from experience with the client and inquiry of client personnel.

The CPA is not required to verify information furnished by the client. However, he may deem it necessary to perform other accounting services during the compilation engagement. Before issuing his report, the accountant should read the compiled statements to determine that they are appropriate in form and free from obvious material errors.

Accountant's Report

The CPA should issue a report stating that

- A compilation has been performed in accordance with standards established by the AICPA.
- A compilation is limited to presenting in the form of financial statements information that is the representation of management (owners).
- The statements have not been audited or reviewed and, accordingly, the accountant does not express an opinion or any other form of assurance on them.[19]

[18] *SSARS No. 1, op. cit.*, para. 8.

[19] Accounting and Review Services Committee, Statement on Standards for Accounting and Review Services, No. 5 Reporting on Compiled Financial Statements, (New York: American Institute of Certified Public Accountants, July 1982) para. 1 (Hereinafter referred to and cited as SSARS No. 5).

I (we) have compiled the accompanying balance sheet of XYZ Company as of December 31, 19XX, and the related statements of income, retained earnings, and changes in financial position for the year then ended, in accordance with standards established by the American Institute of Certified Public Accountants.

A compilation is limited to presenting in the form of financial statements information that is the representation of management [owners]. I [we] have not audited or reviewed the accompanying financial statements and, accordingly, do not express an opinion or any other form of assurance on them.

FIGURE 17–11. Accountant's Report on Compilation of Financial Statements. (SOURCE: SSARS No. 5 op. cit., para 2.)

In addition, each page of the financial statements should include a reference to the accountant's compilation report. If management elects to omit disclosures or to only include selected disclosures, the report should so state. The standard report for a compilation service is illustrated in Figure 17-11.

Change of Engagements

In the course of rendering professional services, a CPA may be asked to change from one type of service to another. The change may involve the acceptance of a greater or lesser degree of responsibility. For example, a CPA may be asked to change from an audit to a review or from a compilation to a review. A change in service is permissible if the CPA believes it is justified in the circumstances. When a change of engagement occurs, the accountant should follow the standards for the service performed.

CONCLUDING COMMENTS

A CPA should tailor his communication to the type of service that has been performed. For audit services, the auditor may issue (1) special reports, (2) reports on personal financial statements, and (3) reports on internal accounting controls. For review services, the accountant may issue reports on (1) interim financial information for public entities, (2) financial statements of nonpublic entities, and (3) financial forecasts. For accounting services, the accountant may issue reports on (1) unaudited financial statements of public entities and (2) the compilation of financial statements of nonpublic companies.

In issuing these reports, it is imperative that the CPA clearly indicate in the report the nature of the work done and express the findings in a manner that is appropriate to the service rendered.

APPENDIX 17A

AICPA Guidelines
Preparation of Financial Forecasts[20]

1. *Single most probable result.* A financial forecasting system should provide a means for management to determine what it considers to be the single most probable forecast

---

[20] Forecast Guide, *op. cit.*, p. 47.

result. In addition, determination of the single most probable result generally should be supplemented by the development of ranges or probabilistic statements.

2. *Accounting principles used.* The financial forecasting system should provide management with the means to prepare financial forecasts using the accounting principles that are expected to be used when the events and transactions envisioned in the forecast occur.

3. *Appropriate care and qualified personnel.* Financial forecasts should be prepared with appropriate care by qualified personnel.

4. *Best information available.* A financial forecasting system should provide for seeking out the best information, from whatever source, reasonably available at the time.

5. *Reflection of plans.* The information used in preparing a financial forecast should reflect the plans of the enterprise.

6. *Reasonable assumptions suitably supported.* The assumptions utilized in preparing a financial forecast should be reasonable and appropriate and should be suitably supported.

7. *Relative effect of variations.* The financial forecasting system should provide the means to determine the relative effect of variations in the major underlying assumptions.

8. *Adequate documentation.* A financial forecasting system should provide adequate documentation of both the forecast and the forecasting process.

9. *Regular comparison with attained results.* A financial forecasting system should include the regular comparison of the forecast with attained results.

10. *Adequate review and approval.* The preparation of a financial forecast should include adequate review and approval by management at the appropriate levels.

APPENDIX 17B

1136 Tenants' Corp. v. Max Rothenberg & Co.[21]

The plaintiff, a corporation owning a cooperative apartment house, sued the defendant, a CPA firm, for damages resulting from the failure of the defendant to discover the embezzlement of over $110,000 by the plaintiff's managing agent, Riker. Riker had orally engaged Rothenberg at an annual fee of $600.

The plaintiff maintained that Rothenberg had been engaged to perform all necessary accounting and auditing services. The defendant claimed he was only engaged to do write up work and prepare financial statements and related tax returns. As evidence of their respective contentions, the plaintiff booked the accountant's fee as auditing expenses and the defendant marked each page of the financial statements as unaudited. In addition, the accountant in a letter of transmittal to the financial statements stated that the statements were (1) prepared from the books and records of the corporation and (2) no independent verifications were undertaken thereon. However, the accountant did not issue a report with a disclaimer of an opinion. The trial court found that the defendant was engaged to perform an audit because Rothenberg admitted that he had performed some limited auditing procedures such as examining bank statements, invoices, and bills. In fact, the CPA's working papers included one entitled "Missing Invoices," which showed over $40,000 of disbursements that did not have supporting documentation. The CPA did not inform the plaintiff of these invoices and no effort was made to find them. The trial court also found the CPA negligent in the performance of the service and awarded damages totaling $237,000. The appellate court affirmed saying

---

[21] *1136 Tenants' Corp. v. Max Rothenberg & Co.*, 36 Ad 30 NY2d 804, 319 NYS2d 1007 (1971).

- Regardless of whether the CPA was making an audit or performing write-up work, there was a duty to inform the client of known wrongdoing or other suspicious actions by the client's employees.
- Defendant's work sheets indicate that defendant did perform some audit procedures.
- The record shows that the defendant was engaged to audit the books and records and the procedures performed by the defendant were "incomplete, inadequate, and improperly performed."

REVIEW QUESTIONS

17–1. What criteria are necessary for a report to be considered a "special report"?

17–2. What bases of accounting other than GAAP qualify as comprehensive bases?

17–3. a. Indicate the applicability of generally accepted auditing standards to an examination of financial statements prepared on a comprehensive basis other than GAAP.
 b. Explain the primary requirements in reporting on such statements.

17–4. In reporting on specific elements, accounts, or items of a financial statement, what are (a) the applicability of GAAS and (b) the primary reporting requirements?

17–5. a. What type of assurance is an auditor permitted to give in a compliance report?
 b. Identify the alternative ways in which this type of special report may be issued.

17–6. a. Describe the essential characteristics of personal financial statements.
 b. How does the auditor's standard report on personal financial statements differ from the report on other financial statements?

17–7. Identify the four circumstances in which the CPA may report on internal accounting control.

17–8. What steps are required in an engagement to express an opinion on internal accounting control?

17–9. Enumerate the content of an opinion report on internal accounting control.

17–10. a. What conditions must be met to issue a report on internal accounting control as a by-product of an audit engagement?
 b. Indicate the essential points to be covered in reporting to a governmental agency on the basis of pre-established criteria.

17–11. What two types of procedures are generally involved in the performance of a review service?

17–12. Identify the types of review services and the corresponding AICPA group responsible for setting guidelines.

17–13. Indicate the steps to be performed in the review of interim financial information (IFI) for a public entity.

17–14. Enumerate the elements that should be included in a report on IFI for a public entity.

17–15. Identify the major differences in objectives, procedures, and reporting between a review of a nonpublic entity and a public entity.

17–16. a. What is the objective of the accountant's review of a forecast?
 b. What types of evaluations can an accountant make about the underlying assumptions of a forecast?

17–17. List the essential elements of the accountant's report on a forecast.

17–18. a. What types of services may be rendered when an accountant performs accounting services for a client?
 b. Who has the authority to set standards for accounting services?

17–19. What are the accountant's reporting requirements when he is associated with unaudited financial statements for a public entity?

17–20. a. What is a CPA expected to do in completing a compilation engagement for a nonpublic entity?
 b. Enumerate the essential aspects of the accountant's report on a compilation service.

COMPREHENSIVE QUESTIONS

17–21. Jiffy Clerical Services is a corporation which furnishes temporary office help to its customers. Billings are rendered monthly based on predetermined hourly rates. You have examined the company's financial statements for several years. Following is an abbreviated statement of assets and liabilities on the modified cash basis as of December 31, 19X0:

Assets:

Cash	$20,000
Advances to employees	1,000
Equipment and autos, less accumulated depreciation	25,000
Total assets	$46,000

Liabilities:

Employees' payroll taxes withheld	$ 8,000
Bank loan payable	10,000
Estimated income taxes on cash basis profits	10,000
Total liabilities	$28,000
Net assets	$18,000

Represented by:

Common stock	$ 3,000
Cash profits retained in the business	15,000
	$18,000

Unrecorded receivables were $55,000 and payables were $30,000.

Required

a. Prepare the report you would issue covering the statement of assets and liabilities as of December 31, 19X0, as summarized above, and the related statement of cash revenue and expenses for the year ended that date.

b. Briefly discuss and justify your modifications of the conventional report on accrual basis statements.

AICPA

17–22. The following cases involve other comprehensive bases of accounting:

1. The financial statements of the *XYZ* Market, a retail grocery operated as an individual proprietorship, are prepared on the basis of cash receipts and disbursements. These statements do not purport to present the financial position and results of operation of the company.

2. The financial statements of the Raintree County Hospital, a private nonprofit organization, are prepared in accordance with the principles and practices of uniform accounting prescribed by a national hospital.

Required

a. What are the limitations in applying the GAAS of an opinion as to conformity of financial statements with GAAP?

b. Indicate the general effects of its application on the wording of the opinion in the auditor's *special report* in each of the above cases.

AICPA (adapted)

17–23. Rose & Co., CPAs, have satisfactorily completed the examination of the financial statements of Bale & Booster, a partnership, for the year ended December 31, 19X0. The financial statements which were prepared on the entity's income tax (cash) basis include footnotes which indicate that the partnership was involved in continuing litigation of material amounts relating to alleged infringement of a competitor's patent. The amount of damages, if any, resulting from this litigation could not be determined at the time of completion of the engagement. The prior years' financial statements were not presented.

Required
Based upon the information presented, prepare an auditor's report which includes appropriate explanatory disclosure of significant facts.

AICPA

17-24. In addition to examining the financial statements of the *ABC* Company at December 31, 19*X*0, the auditor agrees to review the loan agreement dated July 1, 19*X*0 with the Main Street Bank to determine whether the borrower is complying with the terms, provisions, and requirements of sections 14 to 30 inclusive. The auditor finds that the *ABC* Company is in full compliance with the loan agreement.

Required
a. Prepare a report on compliance with contractual provisions assuming it is to be a separate report.
b. Indicate how the report on compliance would differ if it were included as part of the auditor's report on the financial statements.

17-25. In order to obtain information that is necessary to make informed decisions, management often calls upon the independent auditor for assistance. This may involve a request that the independent auditor apply certain audit procedures to specific accounts of a company which is a candidate for acquisition and report upon the results. In such an engagement, the agreed-upon procedures may constitute a scope limitation.

At the completion of an engagement performed at the request of Uclean Corporation which was limited in scope as explained above, the following report was prepared by an audit assistant and was submitted to the auditor for review:

To the Board of Directors of Ajax Corporation:

We have applied certain agreed-upon procedures, as discussed below, to accounting records of Ajax Corporation, as of December 31, 19*X*1, solely to assist Uclean Corporation in connection with the proposed acquisition of Ajax Corporation.

We have examined the cash in banks and accounts receivable of Ajax Corporation as of December 31, 19*X*1, in accordance with generally accepted auditing standards and, accordingly, included such tests of the accounting records and such other auditing procedures as we considered necessary in the circumstances.

In our opinion, the cash and receivables referred to above are fairly presented as of December 31, 19*X*1, in conformity with generally accepted accounting principles applied on a basis consistent with that of the preceding year. We therefore recommend that Uclean Corporation acquire Ajax Corporation pursuant to the proposed agreement.

[signature]

Required
Comment on the proposed report describing those assertions that are:
a. Incorrect or should otherwise be deleted.
b. Missing and should be inserted.

AICPA

17-26. As part of your annual audit of Fall Camper Company, you have the responsibility for preparing a report on internal control. Your workpapers include a completed internal control questionnaire and documentation of other tests of the internal control system which you have reviewed. This review identified a number of material weaknesses; for some of these corrective action by management is not practicable in the circumstances.

Required
a. Discuss the form and content of the report on internal control based on your annual audit.
b. Write the first, fourth, and fifth paragraphs of your report.
c. Discuss the differences in the form and content of the report if it were based on pre-established criteria of a regulatory agency.

17-27. The financial statements of the Liber Company have never been audited by an independent CPA. Recently, Liber's management asked John Burns, CPA, to conduct a special study of Liber's internal accounting controls for the purpose of expressing an opinion on the system. The study will not include an examination of Liber's financial statements. Following completion of his special study, Burns plans to prepare a report that is consistent with the requirements of the engagement.

Required
a. Describe the responsibility of management for internal control and the broad objectives, and inherent limitations of internal accounting control as set forth in a report on internal accounting control.
b. Explain and contrast the study of internal control that Burns might make as part of an examination of financial statements with his engagement to express an opinion as to (1) objectives of review or study, (2) scope of review or study, and (3) nature and content of reports. Organize your answer for b as follows:

Examination of Financial Statements	*Special Study to Express Opinion*
1. Objective	1. Objective
2. Scope	2. Scope
3. Report	3. Report

c. Write the first and fourth paragraphs of the report based (1) on a special study to express an opinion, and (2) solely on a financial statement audit.

AICPA (adapted)

17-28. NorBor Solar Systems is a privately owned manufacturer of passive solar heating systems. There has been increased consumer demand for NorBor's products due to expanded public awareness of energy self-sufficiency and attractive federal tax energy credits. NorBor needs a major expansion of production facilities in order to meet this increased demand. However, management cannot finance this expansion program from internally generated funds. Furthermore, the continued high interest rates have discouraged management from incurring additional debt. Therefore, NorBor is reviewing the option of a public offering of its securities.

NorBor's financial statements have been audited by the external audit firm of Jones & Mattengly since NorBor's creation seven years ago. Each year the firm has issued NorBor an unqualified opinion on its financial statements.

The managing partner of Jones & Mattengly has reminded NorBor's management that a public offering of NorBor's stock would make the company subject to the internal accounting control provisions of the Foreign Corrupt Practices Act of 1977. NorBor's management has decided to engage its external audit firm to conduct an examination of NorBor's internal accounting control system. The external auditor is expected to issue a report which should assist NorBor's management in determining whether it is in compliance with the federal law. Jones & Mattengly's examination will follow the procedures expressed in AU § 642, ''Reporting on Internal Accounting Control.''

Required
a. What role should the management of NorBor Solar Systems play in the examination of the internal accounting control system by the external auditor? Explain your answer.
b. Describe the general content of the report which will be issued by Jones & Mattengly assuming that the standard form of report is used.
c. Identify the types of opinions Jones & Mattengly could render on NorBor's internal accounting control system as well as the underlying conditions that would make each type of opinion appropriate. Use the following format in preparing your answer.

Type of Opinion	*Underlying Conditions*

CMA

17–29. Your staff assistant has prepared a draft of a report on quarterly information of the Royal Company, a public entity. You determine that the first paragraph of the report is correct but that a number of errors exist in the following two paragraphs of the report.

A review of interim financial data consists principally of obtaining evidential matter about the system, determining the accuracy of the data, applying ratio analysis to financial data, and performing substantive tests of transactions. This review does not approximate an examination made in conformity with GAAS. Accordingly, we disclaim an opinion on the data.

Based on our comprehensive review, we believe no material modifications are necessary to make the accompanying financial data be in conformity with generally accepted accounting principles.

Required
a. Identify the words, phrases, and sentences that are incorrect or missing. For each item indicate the proper wording.
b. Draft the first and last paragraphs of the report on interim financial information.

17–30. Loman, CPA, who has examined the financial statements of the Broadwall Corporation, a publicly held company, for the year ended December 31, 19X0 was asked to perform a limited review of the financial statements of Broadwall Corporation for the period ending March 31, 19X0. The engagement letter stated that a limited review does not provide a basis for the expression of an opinion.

Required
a. Explain why Loman's limited review will not provide a basis for the expression of an opinion.

b. What are the review procedures which Loman should perform, and what is the purpose of each procedure? Structure your response as follows:

Procedure	*Purpose of Procedure*

AICPA

17–31. You have been engaged to perform a review service for the partnership of Reed and Wright. Your review does not uncover any material errors of omission or commission in the company's financial statements.

Required

a. Indicate the nature of the review that was performed.
b. Explain the references to standards and to management in the first paragraph of the accountant's standard report on a review.
c. Write the second and third paragraphs of the accountant's report that would be applicable for Reed and Wright.

17–32. An inexperienced staff assistant issues a four-paragraph report on a financial forecast. The first and last paragraphs of the report are shown below.

We have examined the accompanying financial forecast of *XYZ* Company, which includes a forecast balance sheet as of December 31, 19*X*1, forecast statements of income, retained earnings, and changes in financial position for the year then ending. Our study was made in accordance with established guidelines of the American Institute of Certified Public Accountants and, accordingly, included procedures to evaluate the accuracy of the assumptions used by management as a basis for the financial forecast and the presentation of the financial forecast.

In our opinion, the accompanying financial forecast has been prepared using assumptions which form a valid basis for management's forecast and has been presented in conformity with applicable standards established by the American Institute of Certified Public Accountants.

Required

a. List the parts of the report that are in error. Opposite each error indicate the proper report language.
b. Explain the nature and purpose of the two middle paragraphs of the report. (Do not write the middle paragraphs.)

17–33. A CPA was engaged by the Alba Nursing Home to prepare, on the CPA's stationery and without audit, financial statements for 19*X*0 and its 19*X*0 income tax return. From the accounting and other records he learned the following information about the Nursing Home:

1. The Alba Nursing Home is a partnership that was formed early in 19*X*0. The Nursing Home occupies a large old mansion that stands on a sizable piece of ground beside a busy highway. The property was purchased by the partnership from an estate that out-of-state heirs wanted to settle. The heirs were unfamiliar with the local real estate market and sold the property at the bargain price of $10,000 for the house and $5,000 for the land.
2. A few weeks after the purchase the partnership employed a competent independent appraisal firm that appraised the house at $100,000 and the land at $50,000.

3. The property was then written up on the partnership books to its appraisal value, and the partners' capital accounts were credited with the amount of the write-up.
4. Additional funds were invested to convert the mansion to a nursing home, to purchase the necessary equipment and supplies, and to provide working capital.

Required
a. Assume that the CPA prepared the financial statements of the Alba Nursing Home from the accounting records, placed them on his stationery, and labeled each page "Prepared Without Audit." In accordance with the client's preference, the assets were reported only at appraisal values. Under the circumstances presented, what is the CPA's responsibility, if any, to disclose the method of valuation of the assets? Discuss.
b. In this situation, how does the CPA's responsibility for disclosure of the valuation basis of the assets differ, if at all, from the responsibility he would have had if he had made a typical examination of the financial statements?

AICPA (adapted)

17–34. The limitations on the CPA's professional responsibilities when he is associated with unaudited financial statements are often misunderstood. These misunderstandings can be substantially reduced by carefully following professional pronouncements in the course of his work, and taking other appropriate measures.

Required
The following list describes seven situations the CPA may encounter, or contentions he may have to deal with in his association with and preparation of unaudited financial statements. Briefly discuss the extent of the CPA's responsibilities and, if appropriate, the actions he should take to minimize any misunderstandings. Number your answers to correspond with the numbering in the following list.

1. The CPA was engaged by telephone to perform write-up work including the preparation of financial statements. His client believes that the CPA has been engaged to audit the financial statements and examine the records accordingly.
2. A group of businessmen who own a farm which is managed by an independent agent engage a CPA to prepare quarterly unaudited financial statements for them. The CPA prepares the financial statements from information given to him by the independent agent. Subsequently, the businessmen find the statements were inaccurate because their independent agent was embezzling funds. The businessmen refuse to pay the CPA's fee and blame him for allowing the situation to go undetected, contending that he should not have relied on representations from the independent agent.
3. In comparing the trial balance with the general ledger the CPA finds an account labeled "audit fees" in which the client has accumulated the CPA's quarterly billings for accounting services including the preparation of quarterly unaudited financial statements.
4. Unaudited financial statements were accompanied by the following letter of transmittal from the CPA.

> We are enclosing your company's balance sheet as of June 30, 19X0, and the related statements of income and retained earnings and changes in financial position for the six months then ended which we have reviewed.

5. To determine appropriate account classification, the CPA reviewed a number of the client's invoices. He noted in his working papers that some invoices were missing but did nothing further because he felt they did not affect the unaudited financial statements he was preparing. When the client subsequently discovered that invoices were missing he contended that the CPA should not have ignored the missing invoices when preparing the financial statements and had a responsibility to at least inform him that they were missing.

6. The CPA has prepared a draft of unaudited financial statements from the client's records. While reviewing this draft with his client, the CPA learns that the land and building were recorded at appraisal value.
7. The CPA is engaged to review without audit the financial statements prepared by the client's controller. During this review, the CPA learns of several items which by generally accepted accounting principles would require adjustment of the statements and footnote disclosure. The controller agrees to make the recommended adjustments to the statements but says that he is not going to add the footnotes because the statements are unaudited.

AICPA

17–35. Ann Martin, CPA, has been asked by Harry Adams, owner of Adams Cleaners, to prepare the company's annual financial statements from the company's records. Adams, who is unfamiliar with the services of a CPA, also requests Ms. Martin to add as much prestige to the statements as possible in the form of an opinion or some type of assurance.

Required
a. Explain the nature and limitations of an engagement to compile financial statements.
b. Write the accountant's report on a compilation of financial statements.
c. Explain the type of assurance that may be given if Martin is engaged to review Adams's financial statements.
d. Explain why an opinion cannot be expressed.

CASE STUDY

17–36. Brown, CPA, received a telephone call from Calhoun, the sole owner and manager of a small corporation. Calhoun asked Brown to prepare the financial statements for the corporation and told Brown that the statements were needed in two weeks for external financing purposes. Calhoun was vague when Brown inquired about the intended use of the statements. Brown was convinced that Calhoun thought Brown's work would constitute an audit. To avoid confusion Brown decided not to explain to Calhoun that the engagement would only be to prepare the financial statements. Brown, with the understanding that a substantial fee would be paid if the work were completed in two weeks, accepted the engagement and started the work at once.

During the course of the work, Brown discovered an accrued expense account labelel "professional fees" and learned that the balance in the account represented an accrual for the cost of Brown's services. Brown suggested to Calhoun's bookkeeper that the account name be changed to "fees for limited audit engagement." Brown also reviewed several invoices to determine whether accounts were being properly classified. Some of the invoices were missing. Brown listed the missing invoice numbers in the working papers with a note indicating that there should be a follow-up on the next engagement. Brown also discovered that the available records included the fixed asset values at estimated current replacement costs. Based on the records available, Brown prepared a balance sheet, income statement, and statement of stockholders' equity. In addition, Brown drafted the footnotes but decided that any mention of the replacement costs would only mislead the readers. Brown suggested to Calhoun that readers of the financial statements would be better informed if they received a separate letter from Calhoun explaining the meaning and effect of the estimated replacement costs of the fixed assets. Brown mailed the financial statements and footnotes to Calhoun with the following note included on each page:

The accompanying financial statements are submitted to you without complete audit verification.

Required

Identify the inappropriate actions of Brown and indicate what Brown should have done to avoid each inappropriate action. Organize your answer sheet as follows:

Inappropriate Action	_What Brown Should Have Done to Avoid Inappropriate Action_

AICPA

18 | Professional Ethics

STUDY OBJECTIVES

The study objectives of this chapter are to acquire an understanding of professional ethics and the Rules of Conduct that exist within the public accounting profession. To achieve these objectives, it is necessary for the reader to

- Know the importance and composition of the Code of Professional Ethics.
- Comprehend the applicability and enforcement of the Rules of Conduct.
- Realize the Ethical Principles toward which a CPA should strive.
- Understand the specific Rules of Conduct that must be met.

One of the hallmarks of any occupation seeking recognition as a profession is the establishment of a code of ethics. The origin of an ethical code in the public accounting profession has been traced to the turn of the century. The purpose of this chapter is to explain the meaning and importance of professional ethics for individual certified public accountants (CPAs), accounting firms, and those who rely on the services of CPAs. Consideration is given in the chapter to the AICPA Code of Professional Ethics and to the ethical concepts, Rules of Conduct, and Interpretations of Rules of Conduct contained therein. The code of ethics of the Institute of Internal Auditors is presented in Appendix 18A.

BASIC CONSIDERATIONS

Nature and Importance of Professional Ethics

Ethics consist of moral principles and standards of conduct. In general usage, the word *ethics* relates to the philosophy of human conduct and principles of human morality and duty. *Morality,* in turn, focuses on the "right" and "wrong" of human behavior.

Professional ethics extend beyond moral principles. They include standards of behavior for a professional person that are designed for both practical and idealistic purposes. While ethics may be designed in part to encourage ideal behavior, they must be both practical and enforceable. To be meaningful, ethics should be above the law but below the ideal. In summary, professional ethics may be regarded as

> a mixture of moral and practical concepts, with a sprinkling of exhortation to ideal conduct designed to invoke "right action" on the part of members of the profession concerned—all reduced to rules which are intended to be enforceable, to some extent at least, by disciplinary action.[1]

Professional ethics are imposed by a profession on its members, who voluntarily accept standards of professional behavior more rigorous than those required by law. A code of ethics significantly affects the reputation of a profession and the confidence in which it is held. Professional ethics have evolved over time and continue to be in the process of change as the practice of public accounting changes.

The following excerpts from the AICPA's Code of Professional Ethics emphasize the importance of ethical standards for CPAs:

> A distinguishing mark of a professional is his acceptance of responsibility to the public. All true professions have therefore deemed it essential to promulgate codes of ethics and to establish means for ensuring their observance.

> The reliance of the public, the government and the business community on sound

---

[1] John L. Carey and William O. Doherty, *Ethical Standards of the Accounting Profession* (New York: American Institute of Certified Public Accountants, 1966), p. 6.

financial reporting and advice on business affairs, and the importance of these matters to the economic and social aspects of life impose particular obligations on certified public accountants.

Ordinarily those who depend upon a certified public accountant find it difficult to assess the quality of his services; they have a right to expect, however, that he is a person of competence and integrity. A man or woman who enters the profession of accountancy is assumed to accept an obligation to uphold its principles, to work for the increase of knowledge in the art and for the improvement of methods, and to abide by the profession's ethical and technical standards.

The ethical Code of the American Institute emphasizes the profession's responsibility to the public, a responsibility that has grown as the number of investors has grown, as the relationship between corporate managers and stockholders has become more impersonal and as government increasingly relies on accounting information.

The Code also stresses the CPA's responsibility to clients and colleagues, since his behavior in these relationships cannot fail to affect the responsibilities of the profession as a whole to the public.

The Institute's Rules of Conduct set forth minimum levels of acceptable conduct and are mandatory and enforceable. However, it is in the best interests of the profession that CPAs strive for conduct beyond that indicated merely by prohibitions. Ethical conduct, in the true sense, is more than merely abiding by the letter of explicit prohibitions. Rather it requires unswerving commitment to honorable behavior, even at the sacrifice of personal advantage.

Codes of Professional Ethics

Codes of professional ethics for CPAs have been established by organizations of CPAs, such as the American Institute of Certified Public Accountants (AICPA) and state societies of CPAs, and by licensing agencies such as state boards of accountancy. The AICPA Code, which was updated and substantially revised in 1973 and significantly modified in 1978 and 1979, is generally the most comprehensive of the codes, and it frequently serves as the model for the others. Accordingly, attention will be directed primarily on the AICPA Code in this chapter.

AICPA Professional Ethics Division

The AICPA bylaws provide that there shall be a Professional Ethics Division. This division is headed by a director, who is responsible to the vice president of regulation and review of the AICPA. The division consists of a relatively small full-time staff, active volunteer members, and ad hoc investigatory volunteers, as needed. The division functions through an executive committee, which also serves as the ethics committee of the AICPA, and three subcommittees. The executive committee is responsible for

- Planning the programs of the division's subcommittees and supervising their implementation.
- Issuing formal policy statements and pronouncements of the division.

- Establishing prima facie[2] violations of the code or bylaws for possible disciplinary action, including hearings before joint trial boards.
- Proposing changes in the code.

Composition of the Code of Professional Ethics

The AICPA Code of Professional Ethics consists of four parts: (1) Concepts of Professional Ethics, (2) Rules of Conduct, (3) Interpretations of Rules of Conduct, and (4) Ethics Rulings.

The *Concepts* represent positive assertions of the standards of conduct to which every CPA should strive. There are five broad concepts, each of which is stated as an affirmative Ethical Principle. They are intended as broad guidelines rather than as enforceable rules. The concepts constitute the philosophical foundation on which the Rules of Conduct are based.

The *Rules of Conduct* set forth minimum levels of proper conduct. Currently, there are 13 rules. Changes in the rules require a two-thirds vote of the membership. *Interpretations of the Rules of Conduct* provide guidelines as to the scope and applicability of the rules. Over 20 interpretations have been issued. *Ethics Rulings* are issued in response to questions about the rules. They explain the applicability of the rules and interpretations of the rules to specific cases or situations. Over 175 rulings have been issued. Each component of the code of ethics is illustrated later in the chapter.

The rules and interpretations are written in technical language. The following definitions are applicable whenever such terms are used:

Client. The person(s) or entity which retains a member or his firm, engaged in the practice of public accounting, for the performance of professional services.

Council. The Council of the American Institute of Certified Public Accountants.

Enterprise. Any person(s) or entity, whether organized for profit or not, for which a CPA provides services.

Firm. A proprietorship, partnership or professional corporation or association engaged in the practice of public accounting, including individual partners or shareholders thereof.

Institute. The American Institute of Certified Public Accountants.

Member. A member, associate member or international associate of the American Institute of Certified Public Accountants.

Practice of public accounting. Holding out to be a CPA or public accountant and at the same time performing for a client one or more types of services rendered by public accountants. The term shall not be limited by a more restrictive definition which might be found in the accountancy law under which a member practices.

Professional services. One or more types of services performed in the practice of public accounting.

---

[2] *Prima facie* means true or valid at first impression. Legally, such evidence is sufficient to establish a fact or a case unless disproved.

Applicability of Rules of Conduct

The following excerpts from the Code of Professional Ethics indicate the applicability of the Rules of Conduct:

> The Rules of Conduct apply to all services performed in the practice of public accounting, including tax and management advisory services, except (a) where the wording of the rule indicates otherwise and (b) that a member who is practicing outside the United States will not be subject to discipline for departing from any of the rules stated herein so long as his conduct is in accord with the rules of the organized accounting profession in the country in which he is practicing. However, where a member's name is associated with financial statements in such a manner as to imply that he is acting as an independent public accountant and under circumstances that would entitle the reader of the statements to assume that United States practices were followed, he must comply with Rules 202 and 203.[3]

> A member may be held responsible for compliance with the Rules of Conduct by all persons associated with him in the practice of public accounting who either are under his supervision or are his partners or shareholders in the practice.

> A member engaged in the practice of public accounting must observe all the Rules of Conduct. A member not engaged in the practice of public accounting must observe only Rules 102 and 501, since all other Rules of Conduct relate solely to the practice of public accounting.[4]

> A member shall not permit others to carry out on his behalf, either with or without compensation, acts which, if carried out by the member, would place him in violation of the Rules of Conduct.

Where applicable, a member is also expected to observe the ethical standards of state CPA societies, state boards of accountancy, and other governmental agencies.

ENFORCEMENT OF RULES OF CONDUCT

A member can only be charged with a violation of the Rules of Conduct. Ethics interpretations and ethics rulings are not themselves enforceable. However, in the event of an alleged violation of a rule, a member may have to justify any departures from applicable ethics interpretations and rulings.

Instances of alleged violations of the Rules of Conduct result from complaints from members and nonmembers; review of newspapers and publications, such as the *SEC Docket* and the *IRS Bulletin,* by personnel in the Professional Ethics Division; and transmittal of possible violations to the AICPA by certain federal agencies.

Enforcement Groups

Enforcement of the Rules of Conduct rests with three groups: the AICPA, state societies of CPAs, and state boards of accountancy. Each group has the authority to make investigations of complaints, conduct disciplinary

---

[3] Rules 202 and 203 are explained on page 609.

[4] Rules 102 and 501 are explained on pages 607 and 612.

hearings, and impose sanctions and penalties on members who have violated the rules.

The AICPA's enforcement machinery resides in its Ethics Division and Joint Trial Board Division. The former operates through subcommittees; the latter functions through a system of regional trial boards and a national review board. All members of the subcommittees and boards are CPAs. State society enforcement is achieved through state society ethics committees and the joint trial board structure. State boards of accountancy enforcement is accomplished through their own administrative and investigative staffs. The maximum penalty issued by the AICPA and state societies is expulsion from membership. In contrast, state boards of accountancy can suspend or permanently revoke the individual's license to practice as a CPA. Thus, state boards are the most powerful enforcement group since they can terminate a CPA's public accounting career.

Joint Ethics Enforcement Procedures

In an effort to make enforcement of the code more effective, the AICPA has developed a joint ethics enforcement program (JEEP). Slightly over 80 percent of the state societies have signed enabling agreements to participate in joint enforcement. Under the plan, complaints against a member may be filed with either the state society or the AICPA. The complaints are then channeled to either the AICPA ethics division subcommittee or the state society ethics committee. As shown in Figure 18-1, the AICPA has jurisdiction over cases involving more than one state, litigation, and issues of broad national concern. The jurisdictional groups may act independently or jointly. Acting within its authority, a group may

- Issue a constructive letter of comment.
- Close the inquiry.
- Determine on the basis of prima facie evidence (1) to issue an administrative reprimand or (2) to refer the case to the Joint Trial Board.

In a reprimand, the member is requested to terminate the unethical practice, and he may also be asked to meet specific continuing professional education requirements. Referral of a prima facie case to the trial board is reserved for serious cases in which the jurisdictional group believes there should be public disclosure of the misconduct if the member is found guilty.

In a recent year 423 cases were closed and 614 were in process at the end of the year. The disposition of the closed cases resulted in the following:[5]

Administrative reprimands issued	36
Constructive comment letters issued	76
No violation findings	273
Prima facie cases in preparation	2
Referred to Joint Trial Board Division	
Prima facie cases	16
For action under automatic provisions	20

[5] *The CPA Letter,* April 13, 1982, p. 4.

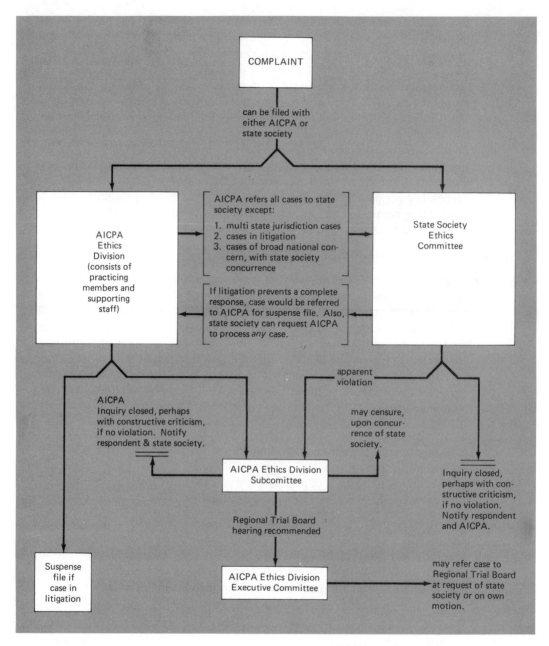

FIGURE 18–1. Joint Ethics Enforcement Procedure (Source: *Joint Effects Enforcement Operations Manual,* AICPA Ethics Division, 1982.)

For the cases in process, 133 were being held pending the outcome of litigation, and the remainder were under investigation by either state societies or the AICPA.

On completion of the disciplinary hearing(s), the Joint Trial Board may decide to either acquit, censure, suspend, or expel a member. The board is required to publish the names of all members found guilty of ethics violations.

Automatic Disciplinary Provisions

The bylaws of the AICPA contain several provisions that result in automatic suspension or termination of membership without a hearing. Suspension results from a judgment or conviction imposed upon any member for

- A crime defined as a felony under the law.
- Willful failure to file any income tax return which he, as an individual taxpayer, is required by law to file.
- The filing of a false or fraudulent income tax return on his or a client's behalf.
- Willful aiding in the preparation and presentation of a false and fraudulent income tax return of a client.

Termination of membership occurs when the member has exhausted all legal appeals on the judgment or conviction.

Under the automatic disciplinary provisions of the bylaws, membership in the AICPA shall be terminated without a hearing should a member's certificate as a CPA be revoked, withdrawn, or canceled as a disciplinary measure by any governmental agency. This provision also applies when a member's last or only certificate is revoked by a state board of accountancy for failing to meet continuing professional education requirements, unless the member is retired or disabled.

Framework for Discussion of Rules of Conduct

Now that the composition of the Code, the applicability of the Rules of Conduct, and the enforcement procedures have been explained, consideration can be given to the Concepts of Professional Ethics, the Rules of Conduct, and interpretations of the rules. The discussion of each concept is in the following format:

- A statement and explanation of the ethical principle (or concept).
- Statement of the Rule(s) of Conduct pertaining thereto.
- Commentary on the rules based in part on published interpretations.

INDEPENDENCE, INTEGRITY, AND OBJECTIVITY

Ethical Principle

A certified public accountant should maintain his integrity and objectivity and, when engaged in the practice of public accounting, be independent of those he serves.

Independence can be defined as the ability to act with integrity and objectivity. This principle recognizes that the public expects CPAs to apply the character traits of integrity and objectivity to their work. *Integrity* is fundamental to reliance on a CPA. A CPA must be honest and trustworthy. *Objectivity* refers to the ability of a CPA to maintain an impartial attitude on all matters that pertain to a professional engagement.

Neither integrity nor objectivity is precisely measurable. In establishing rules on independence, the profession uses the criterion of whether reasonable persons having knowledge of all the facts and, taking into consideration normal strength of character and normal behavior under the circumstances, would conclude that a specified relationship between a CPA and a client poses an unacceptable threat to the CPA's integrity and objectivity.[6]

Rules of Conduct

Two rules of conduct have been issued on this aspect of the code.

RULE 101. Independence

A member or a firm of which he is a partner or shareholder shall not express an opinion on financial statments of an enterprise unless he and his firm are independent with respect to such enterprise. Independence will be considered to be impaired if, for example:

- A. During the period of his professional engagement, or at the time of expressing his opinion, he or his firm
  1. a. Had or was committed to acquire any direct or material indirect financial interest in the enterprise; or
     b. Was a trustee of any trust or executor or administrator of any estate if such trust or estate had or was committed to acquire any direct or material indirect financial interest in the enterprise; or
  2. Had any joint closely held business investment with the enterprise or any officer, director or principal stockholder thereof which was material in relation to his or his firm's net worth; or
  3. Had any loan to or from the enterprise or any officer, director or principal stockholder thereof. This latter proscription does not apply to the following loans from a financial institution when made under normal lending procedures, terms, and requirements:
     a. Loans obtained by a member or his firm which are not material in relation to the net worth of such borrower.
     b. Home mortgages.
     c. Other secured loans, except loans guaranteed by a member's firm which are otherwise unsecured.
- B. During the period covered by the financial statements, during the period of the professional engagement or at the time of expressing an opinion, he or his firm
  1. Was connected with the enterprise as a promoter, underwriter or voting trustee, a director or officer or in any capacity equivalent to that of a member of management or of an employee; or
  2. Was a trustee for any pension or profit-sharing trust of the enterprise.

The above examples are not intended to be all-inclusive.

---

[6] *AICPA Professional Standards* (New York: American Institute of Certified Public Accountants, 1982), Ethics (ET) Section 52.09.

Rule 101 requires the member to be independent in fact and to avoid circumstances that may appear to impair his independence. This rule is ordinarily applied to (1) partners, (2) shareholders in a professional corporation, and (3) professionals participating or located in an office that is responsible for the engagement. However, in many firms, the rule is applied to all partners and shareholders. Three aspects of Rule 101 merit comment.

Time Periods

Three time periods are identified in Rule 101:

- The period of the auditor's professional engagement, which includes both interim and year-end audit work.
- The period covered by the financial statements, which is the client's fiscal year.
- The time of expressing the auditor's opinion which is the date of the auditor's report.

The prohibitions pertaining to financial interest relate to the period of the engagement and the time of expressing an opinion since the member's holdings would seem to a reasonable observer to adversely affect his objectivity. In contrast, the prohibitions relating to business relationships extend from the beginning of the client's fiscal year to the time of expressing the auditor's opinion because the member would be examining and reporting on decisions he participated in while serving in the business association.

Financial Interest

The prohibitions on financial interest are very explicit:

First, the CPA (or his firm) cannot have or be committed to have any direct financial interest or any material indirect financial interest in the client. Thus, a member may not directly own or have an option to buy even one share of stock in a client. *Direct financial interest* includes shares held and commitments by the member's spouse, dependent children, or other relatives living with or supported by the member. *Indirect financial interest* exists when (1) a member owns stock in a mutual fund, for example, which in turn owns stock in a client audited by the member or (2) a member's close kin such as siblings, parents, grandparents, and parents-in-law own or are committed to own shares of stock in a client. Holdings by other kin who do not live with the member, such as uncles and cousins, are generally permitted under this rule. The restriction against an indirect interest is based on materiality. Independence is impaired only if the indirect financial interest is material either to the mutual fund's holdings or to the member's net assets (worth).

Second, a member is not allowed to have a joint closely held business investment with a client company or officers or principal stockholders of such enterprise which is material to either the member's or the firm's net assets. Such a situation would exist when the CPA and an officer of the client each contributed a third of the capital needed to finance (and organize) a tennis and/or swimming club, if the amounts were material.

Third, a member is not permitted to have any loan to or from a client, or its officers or principal stockholders, which is not made under normal lending procedures, terms, and requirements. Any evidence of favoritism in such a transaction could be regarded by a reasonably informed individual as impairing the auditor's independence.

Business Relationships

The purpose of the prohibitions against business relationships is to avoid circumstances where it might appear that the member or his firm is closely aligned with the client's management or is an employee of the client. A member who participates in board of directors decisions on material transactions, for example, would appear to be in an incompatible position in subsequently auditing the financial statements that result from these decisions. Similarly, serving in a fiduciary capacity for a bond sinking fund or funded pension plan of an audit client would suggest a possible conflict of interest. The restrictions against business relations apply to a member's spouse, dependent children, and close kin in the same manner as described above for financial interest.

A CPA who performs manual or automated bookkeeping services for an audit client must meet the following requirements to retain the appearance that he is not an employee and therefore lacking in independence in the eyes of a reasonable observer:

- He must not have any other relationships, such as a financial interest, which would impair his integrity and objectivity.
- The client must accept full responsibility for his financial statements.
- The CPA must not assume the role either of an employee or of management in the client's operations.

Litigation involving CPAs and their clients raises questions about a member's independence. In general, independence is impaired whenever the existence or expressed threat of litigation has significantly altered or is expected to materially change the normal relationship between a client and a CPA. For example, litigation that results in an adversary position between a client and a CPA or which links management and the CPA as co-conspirators in withholding information from stockholders would impair the CPA's independence. In contrast, litigation brought by stockholders against a CPA would not necessarily affect independence.

A CPA is permitted, however, to be a member of the board of directors of charitable, religious, civic, or similar nonprofit organizations which are audited by him or his firm when (1) the board is large and representative of the community's leadership and (2) when the member does not perform or give advice on management functions. In contrast, a CPA would not be independent in serving an audit client when he is a director of a bank that has made a material loan to the audit client.

Over the years, there have been eight interpretations and approximately 60 rulings on Rule 101. The initial publication in each category is as follows:

Interpretation 101-1: Honorary Directorships and Trusteeships

Members are often asked to lend the prestige of their names to not-for-profit organizations that limit their activities to those of a charitable, religious, civic or similar nature by being named a director or a trustee. A member who permits his name to be used in this manner and who is associated with the financial statements of the organization would not be considered lacking in independence under Rule 101 so long as (1) his position is purely honorary, (2) it is identified as honorary in all letterheads and externally circulated materials in which he is named as a director or trustee, (3) he restricts his participation to the use of his name, and (4) he does not vote or otherwise participate in management functions.

It is presumed that organizations to which members lend only the prestige of their names will have sufficiently large boards of directors or trustees to clearly permit the member to limit his participation consistent with the foregoing restriction.

Ruling 1: Acceptance of a Gift

Question: Would the independence of a member's firm be considered to be impaired if an employee or partner accepts a gift or other unusual consideration from a client?

Answer: If an employee or partner accepts more than a token gift from a client, even with the knowledge of the member's firm, the appearance of independence may be lacking.

RULE 102. Integrity and Objectivity

A member shall not knowingly misrepresent facts, and when engaged in the practice of public accounting, including the rendering of tax and management advisory services, shall not subordinate his judgment to others. In tax practice, a member may resolve doubt in favor of his client as long as there is reasonable support for his position.

Whereas Rule 101 applies only to auditing engagements, Rule 102 is applicable to all aspects of the practice of public accounting, including tax and management advisory services. Standards of professional practice in these areas are presented in Appendices 18B and 18C.

GENERAL AND TECHNICAL STANDARDS

Ethical Principle

A certified public accountant should observe the profession's technical standards and strive continually to improve his competence and the quality of his services.

Because of the importance of verifiable accounting data to all segments of the public, CPAs should perform their work at a high level of professionalism. CPAs must constantly strive to improve their competence in the areas of professional practice in which they engage. It is also imperative that CPAs comply with the applicable technical standards of the profession such as generally accepted auditing standards in an audit engagement.

Rules of Conduct

There are four rules on general and technical standards:

RULE 201. General Standards

A member shall comply with the following general standards as interpreted by bodies designated by Council, and must justify any departures therefrom.
a. Professional competence. A member shall undertake only those engagements which he or his firm can reasonably expect to complete with professional competence.
b. Due professional care. A member shall exercise due professional care in the performance of an engagement.
c. Planning and supervision. A member shall adequately plan and supervise an engagement.
d. Sufficient relevant data. A member shall obtain sufficient relevant data to afford a reasonable basis for conclusions or recommendations in relation to an engagement.
e. Forecasts. A member shall not permit his name to be used in conjunction with any forecast of future transactions in a manner which may lead to the belief that the member vouches for the achievability of the forecast.

Rule 201 contains five general standards that are meant to be applicable to all types of services performed in professional engagements. Thus, these standards are not identical with or limited to the category of general standards that are applicable to generally accepted auditing standards in an audit engagement. *Professional competence* involves not only the technical qualifications of the member and the member's staff but also the CPA's ability to supervise and evaluate the quality of the work performed by others. This part of Rule 201 is specifically directed at the member's decision-making process when the CPA is deciding whether to accept or to decline an engagement. If, on the basis of facts known at the time, the CPA believes he has the capability to complete the assignment in accordance with professional standards, it is ethically permissible to accept the engagement. However, if the member knows, for example, that neither he nor the firm has the computer expertise required to audit a client with a sophisticated electronic data processing (EDP) system, it is not ethically proper to accept the engagement.

Due professional care, planning and supervision, and sufficient relevant data codify practices followed by most members. Adherence to these requirements contributes to the quality of performance of professional engagements for the benefit of the public and the profession.

Rule 201e, *forecasts,* does not prohibit a CPA from being associated with a financial forecast. It only prescribes the manner of the association. A CPA cannot be associated with a forecast in a way that would lead a reader to assume that the CPA is attesting, vouching, or guaranteeing the achievability of the forecast. In order to eliminate any uncertainty as to the responsibility that is being taken in connection with a forecast, a CPA should, in describing the association, clearly state that he does not express an opinion on the achievability of the forecast, as is explained and illustrated in Chapter 17.

RULE 202. Auditing Standards

A member shall not permit his name to be associated with financial statements in such a manner as to imply that he is acting as an independent public accountant unless he has complied with the applicable generally accepted auditing standards promulgated by the Institute. Statements on Auditing Standards issued by the Institute's Auditing Standards Board are, for purposes of this rule, considered to be interpretations of the generally accepted auditing standards, and departures from such statements must be justified by those who do not follow them.

Rule 202 officially incorporates the Statements on Auditing Standards (SASs) into the Rules of Conduct. This rule enhances the prestige and influence of the Auditing Standards Board and strengthens the authority of the AICPA over its members who provide auditing services for clients. Each member should take seriously the need to justify any departures from these statements since they represent the views of the members of the AICPA's senior technical committee in this area of practice. Rule 202 does not preclude a member being associated with unaudited financial statements.

RULE 203. Accounting Principles

A member shall not express an opinion that financial statements are presented in conformity with generally accepted accounting principles if such statements contain any departure from an accounting principle promulgated by the body designated by Council to establish such principles which has a material effect on the statements taken as a whole, unless the member can demonstrate that due to unusual circumstances the financial statements would otherwise have been misleading. In such cases his report must describe the departure, the approximate effects thereof, if practicable, and the reasons why compliance with the principle would result in a misleading statement.

Rule 203 is discussed in some detail in Chapter 16. It will be recalled that the Financial Accounting Standards Board (FASB) has been designated by the Council of the AICPA as the promulgating body for purposes of this rule. This rule contributes to greater uniformity in the application of generally accepted accounting principles and significantly strengthens the authority of the FASB.

RULE 204. Other Technical Standards

A member shall comply with other technical standards promulgated by bodies designated by Council to establish such standards, and departures therefrom must be justified by those who depart from them.

At the present time, there are three types of other technical standards:

- The FASB is recognized as the body to promulgate standards of disclosure for financial information outside the basic financial statements in published financial reports containing financial statements.

- The Accounting and Review Services Committee is designated as the body to promulgate standards with respect to unaudited financial statements or other unaudited financial information of nonpublic entities.
- The Management Advisory Services Executive Committee is recognized as the group that promulgates standards for management advisory services.[7]

RESPONSIBILITIES TO CLIENTS

Ethical Principle

A certified public accountant should be fair and candid with his clients and serve them to the best of his ability, with professional concern for their best interests, consistent with his responsibilities to the public.

A CPA is concerned with the welfare of his clients. However, the member must temper this interest with a responsibility to the public. The relationship between a CPA and a client should be based on mutual respect that permits a frank and straightforward discussion of honest differences of opinion. A viable client relationship also requires mutual trust. A CPA therefore should hold in strict confidence client information that is not required to be disclosed by the third standard of reporting.

Rules of Conduct

Two Rules of Conduct apply to the member's responsibilities to clients.

RULE 301. Confidential Client Information

A member shall not disclose any confidential information obtained in the course of a professional engagement except with the consent of the client.

This rule shall not be construed (a) to relieve a member of his obligation under Rules 202 and 203, (b) to affect in any way his compliance with a validly issued subpoena or summons enforceable by order of a court, (c) to prohibit review of a member's professional practices as a part of voluntary quality review under Institute authorization or (d) to preclude a member from responding to any inquiry made by the ethics division or Trial Board of the Institute, by a duly constituted investigative or disciplinary body of a state CPA society, or under state statutes.

Members of the ethics division and Trial Boards of the Institute and professional practice reviewers under Institute authorization shall not disclose any confidential client information which comes to their attention from members in disciplinary proceedings or otherwise in carrying out their official responsibilities. However, this prohibition shall not restrict the exchange of information with an aforementioned duly constituted investigative or disciplinary body.

Compliance with Rule 301 is imperative if the auditor is to make an examination in accordance with generally accepted auditing standards

---

[7] *AICPA Professional Standards, op. cit.,* ET Appendix D.

(GAAS). During an audit, the auditor may require access to a client's confidential and personal business and financial affairs. Disclosure of such information to outsiders, including fellow practitioners, without the client's permission would be a violation of this rule. Moreover, such a breach of confidence would likely prevent the auditor from having access to such data in future engagements.

Some states grant privileged communication to auditors which gives the CPA the right to withhold confidential information in a court of law. However, this privilege should not be used by a CPA as an excuse to remain silent when a client has participated or is participating in an illegal or deceitful act. This rule does not apply to disclosure of any confidential information required to properly discharge the member's responsibility under the profession's own standards.

Rule 301 prohibits a predecessor auditor from allowing a successor auditor access to working papers without the client's permission. Similarly, a CPA who sells his practice to another CPA cannot transfer the working papers to the new owner without the express permission of each client.

RULE 302. Contingent Fees

Professional services shall not be offered or rendered under an arrangement whereby no fee will be charged unless a specified finding or result is attained, or where the fee is otherwise contingent upon the findings or results of such services. However, a member's fees may vary depending, for example, on the complexity of the service rendered.

Fees are not regarded as being contingent if fixed by courts or other public authorities or, in tax matters, if determined based on the results of judicial proceedings or the findings of governmental agencies.

Rule 302 allows the auditor to charge a fee that is based upon the complexity and extent of the work done. Thus, a fee based on the number of days required to do the job is permissible. A member may also elect to lower per diem billing rates for a financially troubled client or perform services without charge for a charitable organization.

However, it is not permissible, by prearrangement, for the member to receive an exceptional financial return that is conditioned on the results of the work. For example, an audit fee should not be based on a percentage of net income or the amount of the loan obtained from a lender's reliance on audited financial statements. Such a contractual arrangement could impair the CPA's objectivity since the member would have a direct financial interest in the outcome of the audit. It is also unethical for a member to indicate that professional services will be performed for a stated fee, estimated fee, or fee range when at the time of the representation the member believes such fees will likely be substantially increased and the prospective client is not advised of this likelihood.

The rule against contingent fees is not applicable when the member bases the fee on the findings or results fixed (or determined) by a court or governmental agency such as the Internal Revenue Service (IRS). In such case, there are recognized constraints against possible bias by the member. However, a member cannot base his fee in preparing a tax return on the amount of taxes he can save his client because the member's duty is to determine the proper tax liability. Thus, there is no basis for computing a saving.

RESPONSIBILITIES TO COLLEAGUES

Ethical Principle

A certified public accountant should conduct himself in a manner that will promote cooperation and good relations among members of the profession.

The development and growth of a profession depend in large measure on the ability of individual members to work together for the common good. It is important therefore that a CPA support the efforts of the AICPA and state societies of CPAs and seek to have and to maintain good relations with fellow practitioners. It is understandable that a CPA may wish to expand his practice. In doing so, however, the member should not seek to displace another CPA in a client relationship or act in a manner that would impinge on the integrity, objectivity, or competency of another CPA. Currently, there are no rules on this subject in the code.

OTHER RESPONSIBILITIES AND PRACTICES

Ethical Principle

A certified public accountant should conduct himself in a manner which will enhance the stature of the profession and its ability to serve the public.

A CPA is a representative of his profession. Accordingly, the member should avoid personal and professional actions and conduct that might reduce public respect and confidence. A CPA is expected to have a professional attitude that places public service above financial reward.

Rules of Conduct

There are five Rules of Conduct pertaining to this aspect of the code.

RULE 501. Acts Discreditable

A member shall not commit an act discreditable to the profession.

Rule 501 is an "open ended" provision covering acts by a member that may damage or otherwise impinge on the reputation and integrity of the profession. This rule enables disciplinary action to be taken against a member for unethical acts not specifically covered by other rules. Discreditable acts include the actions discussed earlier that result in automatic disciplinary provisions, and they also include failing to comply with continuing professional education requirements.

In separate ethics interpretations, the following acts have been designated as discreditable: (1) retention of client records and auditor working papers, such as adjusting entries, necessary to complete the client's records; (2) discrimination in employment; and (3) failure to follow standards and/or other procedures or other requirements in governmental audits. A member who commits a discreditable act usually is suspended or expelled from the AICPA.

RULE 502. Advertising and Other Forms of Solicitation

A member shall not seek to obtain clients by advertising or other forms of solicitation in a manner that is false, misleading, or deceptive.

Rule 502 was adopted by the membership in 1978. Prior to that time, advertising was strictly prohibited as being unprofessional. However, when the U.S. Supreme Court ruled in 1977 against a similar prohibition imposed on lawyers by the American Bar Association, the AICPA moved quickly to permit some forms of advertising by its members. False, misleading, and deceptive advertising includes statements that

- Create unjustified expectations of favorable results.
- Imply an ability to have a persuasive influence on courts and regulatory agencies.
- Consist of self-acclaim not based on verifiable fact.
- Make incomplete comparisons with other CPAs or firms except when based on verifiable fact.
- Contain testimonials or endorsements from clients or others.

The thrust of Rule 502 is that advertising should be informative and objective, be in good taste, and be professionally dignified. It is permissible, for example, to disclose factual information about the number of partners and offices in the firm and the professional services offered.

Other forms of solicitation include requests for professional engagements made by letter, telephone, or in person. Members are expected to use common sense and restraint in obtaining clients. Solicitation by coercive, overreaching, and harassing conduct is prohibited.

RULE 503. Commissions

A member shall not pay a commission to obtain a client, nor shall he accept a commission for a referral to a client of products or services of others. This rule shall not prohibit payments for the purchase of an accounting practice or retirement payments to individuals formerly engaged in the practice of public accounting or payments to their heirs or estates.

Rule 503 on commissions is designed to prevent (1) the client from paying a fee for which commensurate service was not received and (2) the member from becoming involved in conflict of interest situations that may impair his independence.

The first situation pertains to the payment of a commission (or fee) by a member to another party to obtain a client. In such case, it is presumed that the member will pass the commission on to the client and thus the client will be paying for a service that was not received. The second condition involves the receipt of a commission by a CPA from vendors and others in making recommendations to a client. For example, a computer manufacturer may offer the member a commission for equipment purchased by a client on the CPA's recommendation. The acceptance of a commission under such circumstances would cause the client to doubt whether the equipment was the best or whether it was recommended on the basis of the member's personal financial reward. The conflict of interest is not reduced, in the eyes of a reasonable observer, even if the client should approve the acceptance of the commission. This rule does not prevent the member from charging the client a fee for services rendered in making such recommendations.

RULE 504. Incompatible Occupations

A member who is engaged in the practice of public accounting shall not concurrently engage in any business or occupation which would create a conflict of interest in rendering professional services.

Rule 504 prohibits the member from concurrently engaging in an occupation that would create a conflict of interest in completing a professional engagement. The thrust of this rule is to discourage a member from engaging in secondary occupations that pertain to the financial affairs of clients or prospective clients. Such positions as tax assessor, or a broker in insurance, real estate, or securities, are examples of potentially incompatible occupations that could create a conflict of interest for a member in the practice of public accounting.

RULE 505. Form of Practice and Name

A member may practice public accounting, whether as an owner or employee, only in the form of a proprietorship, a partnership or a professional corporation whose characteristics conform to resolutions of Council.

A member shall not practice under a firm name which includes any fictitious name, indicates specialization or is misleading as to the type of organization (proprietorship, partnership or corporation). However, names of one or more past partners or shareholders may be included in the firm name of a successor partnership or corporation. Also, a partner surviving the death or withdrawal of all other partners may continue to practice under the partnership name for up to two years after becoming a sole practitioner.

A firm may not designate itself as "Members of the American Institute of Certified Public Accountants" unless all of its partners or shareholders are members of the Institute.

Rule 505 permits the member to practice as an individual, a partnership, or a corporation. The firm name cannot be fictitious or indicate a specialization. In a professional corporation, all shareholders and the principal executive officer should be persons engaged in the practice of public accounting.

Very few firms are incorporated and those that have elected to use this form of business organization are limited primarily to local firms.

CONCLUDING COMMENTS

It is not enough for a member of a profession to only live within the law. The professional person must also adhere to both the letter and spirit of a code of professional ethics. The ethical standards of the accounting profession extend to independence, general and technical standards, and the CPA's responsibilities to clients, colleagues, and particularly the public.

The Code of Professional Ethics, established and enforced by the AICPA, state associations of CPAs, and state boards of accountancy has contributed significantly to the stature and reputation of the accounting profession. It will continue to do so as long as it is responsive to the changing needs of the profession and individual CPAs rigorously adhere to it.

APPENDIX 18A

Certified Internal Auditor Code of Ethics[8]

The Certified Internal Auditor has an obligation to the profession, management, and stockholders and to the general public to maintain high standards of professional conduct. In recognition of this obligation, The Institute of Internal Auditors, Inc., adopted this Code of Ethics for Certified Internal Auditors.

Adherence to this Code, which is based on the Code of Ethics for members of The Institute, is a prerequisite to maintaining the designation Certified Internal Auditor. A Certified Internal Auditor who is judged by the Board of Directors of The Institute to be in violation of the provisions of the Code shall forfeit the Certified Internal Auditor designation.

Preamble

The provisions of this Code of Ethics cover basic principles in the various disciplines of internal auditing practice. Certified Internal Auditors shall realize that their individual judgment is required in the application of these principles. They have a responsibility to conduct themselves in a manner so that their good faith and integrity should not be open to question. Furthermore, they shall use the "Certified Internal Auditor" designation with discretion and in a dignified manner, fully aware of what the designation denotes and in a manner consistent with all statutory requirements. While having due regard for the limit of their technical skills, they will promote the highest possible internal auditing standards to the end of advancing the interest of their company or organization.

Articles

I. Certified Internal Auditors shall have an obligation to exercise honesty, objectivity and diligence in the performance of their duties and responsibilities.

II. Certified Internal Auditors, in holding the trust of their employer, shall exhibit loyalty in all matters pertaining to the affairs of the employer or to whomever they may be rendering a service. However, a Certified Internal Auditor shall not knowingly be a party to any illegal or improper activity.

---

[8] *Certified Internal Auditor Code of Ethics,* The Institute of Internal Auditors Inc., Altamonte Springs, Florida.

III. Certified Internal Auditors shall refrain from entering into any activity which may be in conflict with the interest of their employer or which would prejudice their ability to carry out objectively their duties and responsibilities.

IV. Certified Internal Auditors shall not accept a fee or a gift from an employee, a client, a customer or a business associate of their employer without the knowledge and consent of senior management.

V. Certified Internal Auditors shall be prudent in their use of information acquired in the course of their duties. They shall not use confidential information for any personal gain or in a manner which would be detrimental to the welfare of their employer.

VI. Certified Internal Auditors, in expressing an opinion, shall use all reasonable care to obtain sufficient factual evidence to warrant such expression. In reporting, Certified Internal Auditors shall reveal such material facts known to them which, if not revealed, could either distort the report of the results of operations under review or conceal unlawful practice.

VII. Certified Internal Auditors shall continually strive for improvements in the proficiency and effectiveness of their service.

APPENDIX 18B

Standards for Management Advisory Services Practice[9]

1. The following general standards apply to both MAS engagements and MAS consultations. They are contained in rule 201 of the AICPA Rules of Conduct, and apply to all services performed in the practice of public accounting[10]

   - *Professional competence.* A member shall undertake only those engagements which he or his firm can reasonably expect to complete with professional competence.
   - *Due professional care.* A member shall exercise due professional care in the performance of an engagement.
   - *Planning and supervision.* A member shall adequately plan and supervise an engagement.
   - *Sufficient relevant data.* A member shall obtain sufficient relevant data to afford a reasonable basis for conclusions or recommendations in relation to an engagement.
   - *Forecasts.* A member shall not permit his name to be used in conjunction with any forecast of future transactions in a manner that may lead to the belief that the member vouches for the achievability of the forecast.

2. The following technical standards apply to MAS engagements. . . . They are established under rule 204 of the AICPA Rules of Conduct. Technical standards for MAS consultations . . . may be established in future statements.

   - *Role of MAS practitioner.* In performing an MAS engagement, an MAS practitioner should not assume the role of management or take any positions that might impair the MAS practitioner's objectivity.

---

[9] Management Advisory Services Executive Committee, *Statement on Standards for Management Advisory Services No. 1, Definitions and Standards for MAS Practice* (New York: American Institute of Certified Public Accountants, 1981).

[10] The use of the terms "MAS engagement" and "MAS consultation" to differentiate the two recognized forms of MAS is not intended to exclude MAS consultations from the meaning of the term "engagement" as it is used in Rule 201.

- *Understanding with client.* An oral or written understanding should be reached with the client concerning the nature, scope, and limitations of the MAS engagement to be performed.
- *Client benefit.* Since the potential benefits to be derived by the client are a major consideration in MAS engagements, such potential benefits should be viewed objectively and the client should be notified of reservations regarding them. In offering and providing MAS engagements, results should not be explicitly or implicitly guaranteed. When estimates of quantifiable results are presented, they should be clearly identified as estimates and the support for such estimates should be disclosed.
- *Communication of results.* Significant information pertinent to the results of an MAS engagement, together with any limitations, qualifications, or reservations needed to assist the client in making its decision, should be communicated to the client orally or in writing.

APPENDIX 18C

Statements on Responsibilities in Tax Practice[11]

1. *Answers to questions on returns*

    A CPA should sign the preparer's declaration on a federal tax return only if he is satisfied that reasonable effort has been made to provide appropriate answers to the questions on the return which are applicable to the taxpayer. Where such a question is left unanswered the reason for such omission should be stated. The possibility that an answer to a question might prove disadvantageous to the taxpayer does not justify omitting an answer or a statement of the reason for such omission.

2. *Recognition of administrative proceeding of a prior year*

    The selection of the treatment of an item in the course of the preparation of a tax return should be based upon the facts and the rules as they are evaluated at the time the return is prepared. Unless the taxpayer is bound as to treatment in the later year, such as by a closing agreement, the disposition of an item as a part of concluding an administrative proceeding by the execution of a waiver for a prior year does not govern the taxpayer in selecting the treatment of a similar item in a later year's return.

3. *Use of estimates*

    A certified public accountant may prepare tax returns involving the use of estimates if such use is generally acceptable or, under the circumstances, it is impracticable to obtain exact data. When estimates are used, the CPA should be satisfied that estimated accounts are not unreasonable under the circumstances.

4. *Knowledge of error: return preparation*

    a. A CPA shall advise his client promptly upon learning of an error in a previously filed return, or upon learning of a client's failure to file a required return. His advice should include a recommendation of the measures to be taken.

    b. If the CPA is requested to prepare the current year's return and the client has not taken appropriate action to rectify an error in a prior year's return that has resulted or may result in a material understatement of tax liability, the CPA should consider whether to proceed with the preparation of the current year's return.

5. *Knowledge of error: administrative proceedings*

    When the CPA is representing a client in an administrative proceeding in respect of a

---

[11] The statements are issued by the AICPA's Division of Federal Taxation. The eight statements currently in effect are presented in summary form rather than in complete detail.

return in which there is an error known to the CPA that has resulted or may result in a material understatement of tax liability, he should request the client's agreement to disclose the error to the Internal Revenue Service. Lacking such agreement, the CPA may be under a duty to withdraw from the engagement.

6. *Advice to clients*

In providing tax advice to his client, the CPA must use judgment to assure that his advice reflects professional competence and appropriately serves the client's needs.

7. *Certain procedural aspects of preparing returns*

In preparing a return, the CPA ordinarily may rely on information furnished by his client. He is not required to examine or review documents or other evidence supporting the client's information in order to sign the preparer's declaration. Although the examination of supporting data is not required, the CPA should encourage his client to provide him with supporting data where appropriate.

8. *Positions contrary to Treasury Department or Internal Revenue Service interpretations of the Code*

In preparing a tax return a CPA may take a position contrary to Treasury Department or Internal Revenue Service interpretations of the Code without disclosure, if there is reasonable support for the position.

In preparing a tax return a CPA may take a position contrary to a specific section of the Internal Revenue Code where there is reasonable support for the position. In such a rare situation, the CPA should disclose the treatment in the tax return.

In no event may a CPA take a position that lacks reasonable support, even when this position is disclosed in a return.

REVIEW QUESTIONS

18–1. Explain the essence of the term *professional ethics*.
18–2. What are the responsibilities of the executive committee of the AICPA Ethics Division?
18–3. Identify and describe the four parts of the Code of Professional Ethics.
18–4. What is the applicability of the Rules of Conduct to the practice of public accounting in (a) the United States and (b) a foreign country?
18–5. a. What groups are responsible for enforcement of the Rules of Conduct?
  b. Indicate the penalties that may be imposed by each group.
18–6. a. Identify the two groups that may receive complaints under the joint ethics enforcement program.
  b. How is jurisdiction decided between the groups?
  c. What actions may each group take?
18–7. a. What criterion is used in determining whether to refer a case to the joint trial board?
  b. Indicate the types of decisions the trial board may render.
  c. Identify the circumstances when automatic disciplinary provisions may be invoked.
18–8. a. In Rule 101—Independence, identify the time periods that are applicable to financial interests.
  b. Distinguish between direct and indirect financial interest as it pertains to a member and his family.
  c. In Rule 101—Independence, identify the time periods that are applicable to business relationships.
  d. Indicate the types of business relationships that are prohibited by Rule 101.
18–9. How may a CPA retain the appearance of independence when he performs bookkeeping services for an audit client?

18–10. Enumerate the five subcategories of Rule 201—General Standards.

18–11. What is the impact of Rule 202—Auditing Standards on the auditor?

18–12. a. What groups are authorized to promulgate technical standards under Rule 204—Other Technical Standards?
 b. Indicate the types of standards each group may issue.

18–13. a. What is the essence of Rule 301—Confidential Client Information?
 b. Indicate three exceptions to this rule.

18–14. a. What is the objective of Rule 302—Contingent Fees?
 b. What exceptions are permitted under this rule?

18–15. What acts are prohibited under Rule 501—Acts Discreditable?

18–16. Briefly explain what is permissible and what is prohibited under Rule 502—Advertising and Other Forms of Solicitation.

18–17. a. What is prohibited by Rule 503—Commissions?
 b. Explain the rationale of this rule.

18–18. a. Why is a member required to avoid incompatible occupations?
 b. Give examples of occupations that potentially are incompatible.

18–19. What forms of business organization are permitted under Rule 505—Form of Practice and Firm Name?

COMPREHENSIVE QUESTIONS

18–20. An auditor must not only appear to be independent; he must also be independent in fact.

Required
 a. Explain the concept of an "auditor's independence" as it applies to third party reliance upon financial statements.
 b. 1. What determines whether or not an auditor is independent in fact?
  2. What determines whether or not an auditor appears to be independent?
 c. Explain how an auditor may be independent in fact but not appear to be independent.
 d. Would a CPA be considered independent for an examination of the financial statements of a
  1. Church for which he is serving as treasurer without compensation? Explain.
  2. Women's club for which his wife is serving as treasurer-bookkeeper if he is not to receive a fee for the examination? Explain.

AICPA (adapted)

18–21. An auditor's report was appended to the financial statements of Worthmore, Inc. The statements consisted of a balance sheet as of November 30, 19X0 and statements of income and retained earnings for the year then ending. The first two paragraphs of the report contained the wording of the standard unqualified report, and a third paragraph read as follows:

The wives of two partners of our firm owned a material investment in the outstanding common stock of Worthmore, Inc. during the fiscal year ending November 30, 19X0. The aforementioned individuals disposed of their holdings of Worthmore, Inc. on December 3, 19X0 in a transaction that did not result in a profit or a loss. This information is included in our report in order to comply with certain disclosure requirements of the Code of Professional Ethics of the American Institute of Certified Public Accountants.

BELL & DAVIS
Certified Public Accountants

Required

a. Was the CPA firm of Bell & Davis independent with respect to the fiscal 19X0 examination of Worthmore, Inc.'s financial statements? Explain.

b. Do you find Bell & Davis' auditor's report satisfactory? Explain.

c. Assume that no members of Bell & Davis or any members of their families held any financial interests in Worthmore, Inc. during 19X0. For each of the following cases, indicate if independence would be lacking on behalf of Bell & Davis, assuming that Worthmore, Inc. is a profit-seeking enterprise. In each case, explain why independence would or would not be lacking.

   1. Two directors of Worthmore, Inc. became partners in the CPA firm of Bell & Davis on July 1, 19X0, resigning their directorships on that date.

   2. During 19X0, the former controller of Worthmore, now a Bell & Davis partner, was frequently called on for assistance by Worthmore. He made decisions for Worthmore's management regarding fixed asset acquisitions and the company's product marketing mix. In addition, he conducted a computer feasibility study for Worthmore.

AICPA

18–22. The attribute of independence has been traditionally associated with the CPA's function of auditing and expressing opinions on financial statements.

Required

a. What is meant by "independence" as applied to the CPA's function of auditing and expressing opinions on financial statements? Discuss.

b. CPAs have imposed upon themselves certain rules of professional conduct that induce their members to remain independent and to strengthen public confidence in their independence. Which of the rules of professional conduct are concerned with the CPA's independence? Discuss.

c. The Wallydrug Company is indebted to a CPA for unpaid fees and has offered to issue to him unsecured interest-bearing notes. Would the CPA's acceptance of these notes have any bearing upon his independence in his relations with the Wallydrug Company? Discuss.

d. The Rocky Hill Corporation was formed on October 1, 19X0 and its fiscal year will end on September 30, 19X1. You audited the corporation's opening balance sheet and rendered an unqualified opinion on it. A month after rendering your report you are offered the position of secretary of the Company because of the need for a complete set of officers and for convenience in signing various documents. You will have no financial interest in the company through stock ownership or otherwise, will receive no salary, will not keep the books, and will not have any influence on its financial matters other than occasional advice on income tax matters and similar advice normally given a client by a CPA.

   1. Assume that you accept the offer but plan to resign the position prior to conducting your annual audit with the intention of again assuming the office after rendering an opinion on the statements. Can you render an independent opinion on the financial statements? Discuss.

   2. Assume that you accept the offer on a temporary basis until the corporation has gotten under way and can employ a secretary. In any event you would permanently resign the position before conducting your annual audit. Can you render an independent opinion on the financial statements? Discuss.

AICPA

18–23. Lakeview Development Corporation was formed on January 2, 19X0, to develop a vacation-recreation area upon land purchased the same day by the corporation for $100,000. The corporation also purchased for $40,000 an adjacent tract of land which the corporation plans to subdivide into fifty building lots. When the area is developed, the lots are expected to sell for $10,000 each.

The corporation borrowed a substantial portion of its funds from a bank and gave a mortgage on the land. A mortgage covenant requires that the corporation furnish quarterly financial statements.

The quarterly financial statements prepared at March 31 and June 30 by the corporation's bookkeeper were unacceptable to the bank officials. The corporation's president now offers you the engagement of preparing unaudited quarterly financial statements. Because of limited funds, your fee would be paid in Lakeview Development Corporation common stock rather than in cash. The stock would be repurchased by the corporation when funds become available. You would not receive enough stock to be a major stockholder.

Required
a. Discuss the ethical implications of your accepting the engagement and the reporting requirements which are applicable if you should accept the engagement.
b. Assume that you accept the engagement to prepare the September 30 statements. What disclosures, if any, would you make of your prospective ownership of Corporation stock in the quarterly financial statements?
c. The president insists that you present the fifty building lots at their expected sales price of $500,000 in the September 30 unaudited statements as was done in prior statements. The write-up was credited to Contributed Capital. How would you respond to the president's request?
d. After accepting your unaudited September 30 financial statements, the bank notified the corporation that the December 31 financial statements must be accompanied by a CPA's opinion. You were asked to conduct the audit and told that your fee would be paid in cash. Discuss the ethical implications of you accepting the engagement.

AICPA (adapted)

18–24. **Part I:** During 19X0 your client, Nuesel Corporation, requested that you conduct a feasibility study to advise management of the best way the corporation can utilize electronic data processing equipment and which computer, if any, best meets the corporation's requirements. You are technically competent in this area and accept the engagement. On completion of your study the corporation accepts your suggestions and installs the computer and related equipment that you recommended.

Required
a. Discuss the effect of the acceptance of this management services engagement would have upon your independence in expressing an opinion on the financial statements of the Nuesel Corporation.
b. A local printer of data processing forms customarily offers a commission for recommending him as supplier. The client is aware of the commission offer and suggests that Mackey accept it. Would it be proper for Mackey to accept the commission with the client's approval? Discuss.

Part II: Alex Pratt, a retired partner of your CPA firm, has just been appointed to the board of directors of Palmer Corporation, your firm's client. Pratt is also a member of your firm's income tax committee which meets monthly to discuss income tax problems of the partnership's clients. The partnership pays Pratt $100 for each committee meeting he attends and a monthly retirement benefit of $1,000.

Required
Discuss the effect of Pratt's appointment to the board of directors of Palmer Corporation on your partnership's independence in expressing an opinion on the Palmer Corporation's financial statements.

AICPA (adapted)

18–25. There currently are thirteen Rules of Conduct. Listed below are circumstances pertaining to some of these rules:

1. A member shall exercise due professional care in the performance of an engagement.
2. In rendering tax services, a member shall not subordinate his judgment to others.
3. A member shall not engage in any business that would create a conflict of interest in rendering professional service.
4. A member shall not accept a commission for a referral to a client of products or services of others.
5. A member's fees may vary depending on the complexity of the service rendered.
6. A member is not precluded from responding to an inquiry by a Trial Board of the AICPA.
7. A member may not serve as a trustee for any pension trust of the client during the period covered by the financial statements.
8. A member shall adequately plan and supervise an engagement.
9. A member may not have or be committed to having any direct financial interest in the client.
10. A member shall not practice under a fictitious firm name.

Required

a. Identify the rule to which each circumstance relates.
b. Indicate one other circumstance that pertains to each rule mentioned in a above.

18–26. In the practice of public accounting an auditor is expected to comply with the Rules of Conduct set forth in the Code of Ethics. Listed below are circumstances that raise a question about an auditor's ethical conduct:

1. The auditor has a bank loan with a bank that is an audit client.
2. An unqualified opinion is expressed when financial statements are prepared according to existing AICPA *Accounting Research Bulletins* without any attendant unusual circumstances.
3. An auditor retains client's records as a means of enforcing payment of an overdue audit fee.
4. A CPA vouches for the achievability of a forecast.
5. An auditor sells her shares of stock in a client company in April prior to beginning work on the audit for the year ending December 31.
6. An auditor accepts an engagement knowing that he does not have the expertise to do the audit.
7. A CPA quotes a client a fee but also states that the actual fee will be contingent on the amount of work done.
8. A CPA firm states in a newspaper ad that it has had fewer lawsuits than its principal competitors.
9. A CPA resigns his position as secretary-treasurer of the client on May 1, prior to beginning audit for year ending December 31.
10. A CPA discloses confidential information about a client to a successor auditor.

Required

a. Indicate for each circumstance whether the effect on the Rule of Conduct is (1) a violation, (2) not a violation, or (3) indeterminate.
b. Identify the rule that is at issue in each case and the reason(s) for your answer.

18–27. The following circumstances may involve violations of the Rules of Conduct:

1. A CPA bases his fee on the findings determined by the IRS.
2. A CPA discloses confidential information in a peer review of the firm's practice.
3. A CPA issues an unqualified opinion when a client departs from GAAP because of a conceptual disagreement with the FASB.

4. Henson, a CPA who is a resident of West Orange, Wyoming, is a stockholder and treasurer of the WOW Public Accounting Firm.
5. Benson seeks to enlarge his CPA practice by preparing a small brochure showing testimonials from existing clients.
6. Abel, CPA, retains client records pending payment of audit fee.
7. Reddy, CPA, is also an insurance broker.
8. A CPA examines the financial statements of a local bank and also serves on the bank's committee that approves loans.
9. Leon, CPA, pays a commission to an attorney to obtain a client.
10. Jenson, CPA, examines the financial statements of a local bank which holds a mortgage on his home.

Required
a. Indicate for each circumstance whether the effect on the Rule of Conduct is (1) a violation, (2) not a violation, or (3) indeterminate.
b. Identify the rule that is at issue in each case and the reason(s) for your answer.

18–28. The following actions by a CPA may involve violations of the Rules of Conduct:

1. Agrees to be the committee chairperson for a local fund-raising activity.
2. Serves as an executor and trustee of the estate of an individual who owned the majority stock of a closely held client corporation.
3. Accepts a gift from a client.
4. Fails to follow standards required in a governmental audit.
5. Bases his fee on the amount of taxes that will be saved in preparing the tax return.
6. Discloses confidential client information requested by a disciplinary body of a state CPA society.
7. Assists a client in preparing a financial forecast.
8. Prepares cost projections for submission to a governmental agency as an application for a rate increase, and the fee will be paid if the agency receives a rate increase.
9. Is convicted of falsifying his income tax return.
10. Accepts a commission from a vendor, with the approval of the client, for recommending the vendor's equipment.
11. Issues an unqualified opinion on the basis that the financial statements are in conformity with FASB exposure drafts.
12. Adopts the name of Test and Check for his incorporated firm.

Required
a. Indicate for each circumstance whether the effect on the applicable Rule of Conduct is: (1) a violation, (2) not a violation, or (3) indeterminate.
b. Identify the rule that is applicable in each case and the reason(s) for your answer.

18–29. Gilbert and Bradley formed a corporation called Financial Services, Inc., each man taking 50 percent of the authorized common stock. Gilbert is a CPA and a member of the American Institute of CPAs. Bradley is a CPCU (Chartered Property Casualty Underwriter). The corporation performs auditing and tax services under Gilbert's direction and insurance services under Bradley's supervision. The opening of the corporation's office was announced by a three-inch, two-column "card" in the local newspaper.

One of the corporation's first audit clients was the Grandtime Company. Grandtime had total assets of $600,000 and total liabilities of $270,000. In the course of his examination, Gilbert found that Grandtime's building with a book value of $240,000 was pledged as security for a ten-year-term note in the amount of $200,000. The client's statements did not mention that the building was pledged as security for the ten-year-term note. However, as the failure to disclose the lien did not affect either the value of the assets or the amount of the liabilities and his examination was satisfactory in all other respects, Gilbert rendered an unqualified opinion on Grandtime's financial statements. About two months after the date of his opinion, Gilbert learned that an insurance company was planning a loan to Grandtime of $150,000 in the form of a first-mortgage note on the building. Realizing that the insurance company was unaware of the existing lien on the building, Gilbert had Bradley notify the insurance company of the fact that Grandtime's building was pledged as security for the term note.

Shortly after the events described above, Gilbert was charged with a violation of professional ethics.

Required
Identify and discuss the ethical implication of those acts by Gilbert that were in violation of the AICPA Code of Professional Ethics.

AICPA

18–30.† The Institute of Internal Auditors has adopted a Code of Ethics for its members.

Required
a. What requirements are imposed on Certified Internal Auditors by the preamble to the Code of Ethics?
b. Indicate the essence of each of the seven articles in the Code of Ethics.
c. For each of the seven articles, indicate the comparable Rule of Conduct, if any, in the AICPA Code of Professional Ethics.
d. What sanction(s) may be imposed on an internal auditor for violating the Code of Ethics?

18–31.† The Management Advisory Committee has promulgated practice standards for MAS.

Required
a. Indicate the two categories of practice standards established for MAS.
b. Identify and briefly describe the four types of technical standards.
c. For each of the following, indicate (1) the specific practice standard that is applicable, and (2) whether the specified standard has been violated.
  1. At the request of the client, the MAS practitioner makes the business decision.
  2. The MAS service is completed in June and the report of the findings is communicated to the client in December.
  3. A new MAS practitioner is not supervised on her initial MAS engagement.
  4. An MAS practitioner with proficiency and training in computers accepts an engagement to redesign the client's EDP system.
  5. An MAS practitioner acquires a reasonable basis for his recommendations to the client.
  6. An MAS practitioner implicitly guarantees the results of his engagement.

18–32.† The senior tax committee of the AICPA issues statements defining a CPA's responsibilities in federal tax practice.

Required
a. Identify and briefly describe the responsibilities a CPA has in rendering federal tax service to a client.
b. What specific responsibilities does the CPA have when:

† Questions 18-30 to 18-32 relate to material contained in the appendices to this chapter.

1. An error is discovered in a previously filed tax return?
2. She takes a position contrary to an IRS interpretation of the Revenue Code?
3. A taxpayer does not answer all applicable questions on a tax return?
4. A taxpayer uses an unreasonable estimate on the tax return?
5. A taxpayer refuses to permit the CPA to disclose an error in an administrative proceeding?

CASE STUDY

18–33.* The following situations involve Herb Standard, staff accountant with the regional CPA firm of Cash & Green:

1. The bookkeeper of Ethical Manufacturing Company resigned two months ago and has not yet been replaced. As a result, Ethical's transactions have not been recorded and the books are not up to date. To comply with terms of a loan agreement, Ethical needs to prepare interim financial statements but cannot do so until the books are posted. Ethical looks to Cash & Green, their independent auditors, for help and wants to borrow Herb Standard to perform the work. They want Herb because he did their audit last year.
2. Herb Standard discovered that his client, Ethical Manufacturing Company, materially understated net income on last year's tax return. Herb informs his supervisor about this and the client is asked to prepare an amended return. The client is unwilling to take corrective measurbs. Herb informs the Internal Revenue Service.
3. While observing the year-end inventory of Ethical Manufacturing Company, the plant manager offers Herb Standard a fishing rod, which Ethical manufactures, in appreciation for a job well done.
4. Herb Standard's acquaintance, Joe Lender, is chief loan officer at Local Bank, an audit client of Cash & Green. Herb approaches Joe for an unsecured loan from Local Bank and Joe approves the loan.
5. Herb Standard is a member of a local investment club composed of college fraternity brothers. The club invests in listed stocks and is fairly active in trading. Last week the club purchased the stock of Leverage Corp., a client of another Cash & Green office. Herb has no contact with the members of this office.

Required

For each situation (a) identify the ethical issues that are involved, (b) discuss whether there has or has not been any violation of ethical conduct. Support your answers by reference to the Rules of Conduct.

19 | Legal Liability

STUDY OBJECTIVES

The study objectives of this chapter are to acquire an understanding of the legal environment that currently exists in the practice of public accounting and the auditor's responsibilities for discovering errors, irregularities, and illegal acts committed by clients. To achieve these objectives, it is necessary for the reader to

- Know the extent of a CPA's legal liability under common law.
- Comprehend the extent of a CPA's legal liability under the 1933 and 1934 federal securities laws.
- Be knowledgeable about major legal cases pertaining to the auditor's legal liability.
- Recognize precautions that a CPA may take to avoid litigation.
- Know the requirements under GAAS for the discovery of errors, irregularities, and illegal acts by clients.

$\mathbf{I}$n the past two decades, many lawsuits have been brought against professionals, including certified public accountants (CPAs). Despite the sharp increase in the number of suits involving accountants, they still represent isolated occurrences when viewed in the light of the growth of the profession and the hundreds of thousands of satisfactory audits performed each year.

Nevertheless, litigation and the threat thereof are an important part of the practice of public accounting. Consideration will be given in this chapter to the auditor's legal liability under both common and statutory law. In addition, the auditor's responsibility for the discovery of client errors, irregularities, and illegal acts will be discussed.

Liability Under Common Law

Common law is frequently referred to as unwritten law. It is based on judicial precedent rather than legislative enactment. Common law is derived from principles based on justice, reason, and common sense rather than absolute, fixed, or inflexible rules. The principles of common law are determined by the social needs of the community. Hence, common law changes in response to society's needs. Under common law, a CPA's legal liability extends principally to two classes of parties: clients and third parties.

Liability to Clients

A CPA is in a direct contractual relationship with clients. In agreeing to perform services for clients, the CPA assumes the role of an independent contractor. This means that the CPA, rather than the client, controls the work done. The specific service(s) to be rendered should preferably be set forth in an engagement letter, as described in Chapter 2. The term *privity of contract* refers to the contractual relationship that exists between two or more contracting parties. In the typical auditing engagement, it is assumed that the audit is to be made in accordance with professional standards (i.e., generally accepted auditing standards) unless the contract contains specific wording to the contrary.

An auditor may be liable to a client for breach of contract. This may occur when the auditor

- Issues a standard audit report when he has not made an examination in accordance with GAAS.
- Does not deliver the audit report by the agreed-on date.
- Violates the client's confidential relationship (Ethics Rule of Conduct 301)

A CPA's liability for breach of contract extends to subrogees. A *subrogee* is a party who has acquired the rights of another by substitution. In Part II of this book, the bonding of employees was considered to be an important part of a company's internal accounting control environment.

When an embezzlement occurs, the bonding company reimburses the insured for its losses. Then, under the right of subrogation to the insured's contractual claim, it can bring suit against the CPA for failing to discover the defalcation.

A CPA may also be liable to a client under tort law. A *tort* is a wrongful act that injures another person's property, body, or reputation. A tort action may be based on any one of the following causes:

- *Ordinary negligence,* which is failure to exercise that degree of care which a person of ordinary prudence (a reasonable man) would exercise under the same circumstances.
- *Gross negligence,* which is the failure to use even slight care in the circumstances.
- *Fraud,* which is intentional deception, such as the misrepresentation, concealment, or nondisclosure of a material fact, that results in injury to another.

The best course of action in a given case involves a consideration of legal technicalities that are beyond the scope of this book. Relief to the injured party in both breach of contract and tort suits is ordinarily awarded in monetary terms. The auditor's working papers are vital in refuting charges for breach of contract and for breach of duty in a tort action.

Liability to Third Parties

The common law liability of the auditor to third parties is of paramount importance in any discussion of the auditor's legal liability. A *third party* may be defined as an individual who is not in privity with the parties to a contract. From a legal standpoint, there are two classes of third parties: (1) a primary beneficiary and (2) other beneficiaries. The former is anyone identified to the auditor by name prior to the audit who is to be the primary recipient of the auditor's report. For example, if at the time the engagement letter is signed the client informs the auditor that his report is to be used to obtain a loan at the City National Bank, the bank becomes a primary beneficiary. In contrast, other beneficiaries are unnamed third parties, such as creditors, stockholders, and potential investors.

The auditor has always been held liable to third parties for fraud. During the past six decades, however, there has been a marked change in the auditor's common law liability to third parties for negligence as seen in the following chronological listing of major legal decisions:

Landell v. Lybrand (1919) held that there was no intent to deceive and, in absence of contract, auditor is not liable for negligence.

Ultramares Corp. v. Touche (1931) held that auditors are not liable for ordinary negligence to unforeseen third parties but may be liable to named third parties for ordinary negligence and to all third parties when negligence is so gross as to constitute fraud.

Rusch Factors, Inc. v. Levin (1968) concluded that auditors should be liable for ordinary negligence to actually foreseen and limited classes of persons, even if not named or identified. The foreseen and limited class of persons includes individuals entitled to receive an audit report in fulfillment of a business transaction (acquisition agreement or loan), but not shareholders and bondholders.

Rhode Island Hospital Trust National Bank v. Swartz (1972) held auditors liable for ordinary negligence to a foreseen (but unnamed) user, a bank, even though a disclaimer of opinion was expressed on the audited financial statements. In this case, the auditor did not give all substantive reasons for the disclaimer. The explanation given actually was misleading in that it represented that certain leasehold improvements existed when in fact the client had made no such improvements.[1]

From these cases, it can be seen that the auditor's common law liability to third parties for negligence has expanded considerably since the first major suit. The present trend in the courts appears to be away from the *Ultramares* rule and toward increasing responsibility as expressed in *Rusch Factors*.

Liability Under Statutory Law

Statutory law is established by state and federal legislative bodies. Most states have "blue sky laws" for the purpose of regulating the issuing and trading of securities within a state. Usually these statutes require that audited financial statements be filed with a designated regulatory agency. Federal statutes are enacted by Congress. The two most important federal statutes affecting auditors are the Securities Act of 1933 and the Securities Exchange Act of 1934, which are administered by the Securities and Exchange Commission (SEC). The 1933 Act requires audited statements in registration statements and the 1934 Act requires annual statements audited by independent public accountants.

The liability of an auditor is more extensive under statutory law than under common law. Two factors are responsible for this condition: (1) Some statutory laws grant unnamed third-party beneficiaries rights against auditors for ordinary negligence, and (2) criminal indictments may be brought against auditors. In-depth consideration is given below to the auditor's legal liability under federal securities laws.

The Securities Act of 1933

The 1933 Act is known as the *Truth in Securities Act*. It is designed to regulate security offerings to the public through the mails or in interstate commerce. Suits against auditors under this Act are usually based on Section 11, Civil Liabilities on Account of False Registration Statement, which states, in part:

---

[1] Additional information about these and other legal cases is presented in Appendix 19A at the end of this chapter.

> In case any part of the registration statement, when such part became effective, contained an untrue statement of a material fact or omitted to state a material fact required to be stated therein or necessary to make the statements therein not misleading, any person acquiring such security (unless it is proved that at the time of such acquisition he knew of such untruth or omission) may . . . sue. . . .

It should be noted that "any person" purchasing or otherwise acquiring the securities may sue. This includes unnamed third-party beneficiaries. The Act makes the auditor liable for losses to third parties resulting from ordinary negligence, as well as from fraud and gross negligence, to the effective date of the registration statement, which may be twenty working days after the statement is filed with the agency.

Section 11 includes two key terms: a *material* fact and *misleading* financial statement. *Materiality* is defined by the SEC as follows:

> The term "material," when used to qualify a requirement for the furnishing of information as to any subject, limits the information required to those matters about which an average prudent investor ought reasonably to be informed.[2]

Financial statements filed with the SEC are presumed to be misleading or inaccurate when a material matter is presented in a financial statement in accordance with an accounting principle that has no authoritative support, or has authoritative support but where the SEC has ruled against its use.[3]

A qualification of the auditor's report and/or disclosure of the circumstances will not overcome the presumption that the statements are misleading.[4] However, disclosure will be accepted in lieu of correction when there is disagreement between the SEC and the registrant as to the proper principle of accounting to be followed, providing the principle has substantial authoritative support and the Commission has not previously expressed its position through SEC pronouncements. The SEC has ruled that the pronouncements of the Financial Accounting Standards Board (FASB) constitute substantial authoritative support.[5] Where the FASB has not issued a pronouncement on the matter, the SEC accepts the other sources of authoritative support for GAAP that are enumerated in Chapter 16.

Under the civil provisions of the 1933 Act, the monetary damages are limited to the difference between (1) the amount the investor paid for the security and (2) the market or sales price at the time of the suit. However, if the security has been sold, the amount recoverable is the difference between the amount paid and the sales price. Criminal penalties provide for penalties on conviction of no more than $10,000 in fines or imprisonment of no more than five years, or both, for *willfully* making an untrue statement or omitting a material fact in a registration statement.

---

[2] Rule 1-02. Regulation S-X.
[3] Financial Reporting Release No. 1 Section 101 (1982).
[4] *Ibid.*
[5] *Ibid.*

Bringing Suit Under the 1933 Act

The principal effects of this Act on the parties involved in a suit may be summarized as follows:

Plaintiff
- May be any person acquiring securities described in the registration statement, whether or not he is a client of the auditor.
- Must base his claim on an alleged material false or misleading financial statement contained in the registration statement.
- Does not have to prove that he relied on the false or misleading statement or that the loss which he suffered was the proximate result of the statement if purchase was made before the issuance of an income statement covering a period of at least twelve months following the effective date of the registration statement.
- Does not have to prove that the auditors were negligent or fraudulent in certifying the financial statements involved.

Defendant
- Has the burden of establishing his freedom from negligence by proving that he had made a reasonable investigation and accordingly had reasonable ground to believe, and did believe, that the statements which he certified were true at the date of the statements and as of the time the registration statement became effective.
- Must establish, by way of defense, that the plaintiff's loss resulted in whole or in part from causes other than the false or misleading statements.

The reasonable investigation concept is often referred to as the *due diligence defense*. Section 11(c) states that the standard of reasonableness is the care required of a prudent person in the management of his own property. For an auditor, the basis for a reasonable investigation of audited financial statements is GAAS.

The Securities Exchange Act of 1934

This Act was passed by Congress to regulate the public trading of securities. The 1934 Act requires companies included under the Act to (1) file a registration statement when the securities are publicly traded for the first time and (2) keep the registration statement current through the filing of annual reports, quarterly reports, and other information with the SEC. Certain financial information, including the financial statements, must be audited by independent public accountants. Because of the recurring reporting requirements with the SEC, the Act is often referred to as the *Continuous Disclosure Act*. The principal liability provisions of the 1934 Act are set forth in Sections 18 and 10:

Section 18 liability. Under Section 18(a),

> any person who shall make or cause to be made any statement in any application, report, or document filed pursuant to this title . . . which . . . was made false or misleading with respect to any material fact, shall be liable to any person (not knowing that such statement was false or misleading) who, in reliance upon such statement, shall have purchased or sold a security at a price which was affected by such statement, for damages caused by such reliance, unless the person sued shall prove that he acted in good faith and had no knowledge that such statement was false or misleading.

Section 18 liability is relatively narrow in scope, since it relates only to a false or misleading statement in documents "filed" with the SEC under the act. Annual reports to shareholders are not deemed to be filed with the SEC.

Section 10 liability. 10(b) provides that

> it shall be unlawful for any person, directly or indirectly, by the use of any means or instrumentality of interstate commerce or of the mails, or of any facility of any national securities exchange to use or employ, in connection with the purchase or sale of any security registered on a national securities exchange or any security not so registered, any manipulative or deceptive device or contrivances in contravention of such rules and regulations as the Commission may prescribe as necessary or appropriate in the public interest or for the protection of investors.

Under this section, the SEC promulgated Rule 10b-5, which states that it is unlawful to

- Employ any device, scheme, or artifice to *defraud*.
- Make *any untrue statement* of a material fact or *omit* to state a material fact necessary in order to make the statements made, in the light of the circumstances under which they were made, not misleading.
- Engage in any act, practice, or course of business which operates, or would operate, as a *fraud* or *deceit* upon any person in connection with the purchase or sale of any security.

Section 10b and Rule 10b-5 are often referred to as the antifraud provisions of the 1934 Act. Section 10 is broad in scope because it applies both to registered and unregistered securities and to the private trading of securities.

Bringing Suit Under the 1934 Act

There are similarities and differences in the effects of Sections 10 and 18 on the parties involved.

Under both sections, the plaintiff (1) may be any person buying or selling the securities, (2) must prove the existence of a material false or misleading statement, and (3) must prove reliance on such statement and damage resulting from such reliance. However, the responsibility of the plaintiff differs under the two sections as to proof of auditor fraud. Under Section 18, the plaintiff does not have to prove that the auditor acted fraudulently, but in a Section 10, Rule 10b-5 action, such proof is required.

The defendant in a Section 18 suit must prove that he (1) acted in good faith and (2) had no knowledge of the false or misleading statement. This means that the minimum basis for liability is gross negligence. Accordingly, the auditor's position under Section 18 is the same as under common law where he may also be held liable to third parties for gross negligence, as explained earlier in the chapter.

An injured plaintiff is allowed to recover his "out of pocket" losses, which are determined by the difference between the contract price and the real or actual value on the transaction date. The latter is generally established by the market price when the misrepresentation or omission occurred. Section 32 of the Act provides for criminal penalties consisting of fines of not more than $10,000 or imprisonment for not more than five years, or both.

Differences Between the 1933 and 1934 Securities Acts

The securities acts apply to different situations. The 1933 Act applies to the initial distribution of securities (capital stock and bonds) for sale to the public by the issuing corporation, whereas the 1934 Act applies to the public and private trading of securities. Differences between Section 11 of the 1933 Act and Sections 10 and 18 of the 1934 Act exist as to (1) the plaintiff, (2) proof of reliance on the false or misleading statement, and (3) the accountant's liability for negligence. The plaintiff in a 1933 Act suit is any person acquiring the security, whereas the plaintiff under the 1934 Act may be either the buyer or seller of the security. In a Section 11 suit, the plaintiff does not have to prove reliance on the financial statements, but in a Section 10 or Section 18 suit, proof of reliance on the audited statements is necessary. Under the provisions of the 1933 Act, the auditor clearly is liable for ordinary negligence, whereas a 1976 U.S. Supreme Court decision appears to effectively preclude ordinary negligence as a basis for sustaining a claim against an accountant under Section 10 of the 1934 Act. This important case and a recent U.S. Court of Appeals ruling are explained below.

The *Hochfelder* Case *(Ernst & Ernst v. Hochfelder)*

Lawsuits against accountants under the 1934 Act are usually based on Section 10(b) and Rule 10b-5. During the decade of the mid-1960s to the mid-1970s, plaintiffs were able to obtain a number of judgments against CPA firms for ordinary negligence under these provisions. A 1976 decision by the United States Supreme Court in *Ernst & Ernst* (now Ernst & Whinney) *v. Hochfelder* may have marked the end of the accountant's liability for ordinary negligence under Section 10 of the 1934 Act.

This case developed from the audit of a small brokerage firm registered with the SEC as a broker-dealer. The president of the securities company had induced customers to invest in an "escrow" account during a five-year period that would yield a high rate of return. The escrow account was not included in the brokerage firm's accounts and was concealed from the auditors by the president's mail rule. This rule specified that mail addressed directly to the president or to his attention could not be opened by any employee. All investors in the escrow account were instructed to make their investments directly through the president. The embezzlement was discovered in the president's suicide note.

The plaintiffs in the case, who were investors in the fictitious escrow account, sued the accounting firm under Rule 10b-5 of the 1934 Act, claiming that the auditor's inexcusable negligence had aided and abetted the president's fraudulent actions. In their suit, the plaintiffs acknowledged that they did not rely on reports prepared by the auditors, and they specifically disclaimed the existence of fraud or intentional misconduct on the part of the auditors. The charge of negligence, however, was based on the plaintiffs' contention that if the auditors had made a proper study and evaluation of internal control, they would have discovered the mail rule. The existence of the rule would then have been disclosed to the Securities and Exchange Commission as an irregular procedure that prevented an effective audit (i.e., a scope limitation). The Commission, in turn, would have ordered an investigation of the rule, and the fraudulent scheme would have been discovered.

The key issue in the case was whether auditors could be liable under Rule 10b-5 for misrepresentations that resulted from ordinary negligence. The first and third prohibitions of Rule 10b-5 expressly refer to fraud, but the second prohibition does not explicitly contain such a reference. The U.S. Supreme Court, in ruling for the accounting firm, stated in part:

> When a statute speaks so specifically in terms of manipulation and deception, and of implementing devices and contrivances—the commonly understood terminology of intentional wrongdoing—and when its history reflects no more expansive intent, we are quite unwilling to extend the scope of the statute to negligent conduct.

Based on this decision, an auditor is no longer liable to third parties under Section 10(b) and Rule 10b-5 of the 1934 Act for ordinary negligence. That is, the auditor has no liability in the absence of any intent to deceive or defraud (legally called scienter). The *Hochfelder* decision, however, was based on a relatively narrow circumstance.

Cenco Incorporated v. Seidman & Seidman

This 1982 case involved a $25 million inventory fraud perpetrated by the top management of Cenco Inc. against corporate suppliers and other outsiders. The fraud was not discovered by the auditors, Seidman & Seidman, in their annual audit. In the suit, which was brought by Cenco's new management team, the defendants were charged with violating Section 10(b) and Rule 10b-5 of the 1934 Act and various federal securities laws. In its ruling, the U.S. Court of Appeals found the auditors not negligent for failing to discover the fraud. The ruling is considered to be the first to distinguish between *management fraud on behalf of a corporation* and *employee fraud against a corporation*. The verdict in the case is consistent with the findings of the U.S. Supreme Court in *Hochfelder*.

Professional Standards and Legal Decisions

A difference of opinion exists among the American Institute of Certified Public Accountants (AICPA), the SEC, and the courts as to the relative importance of professional standards in legal decisions. An awareness of these differences may be useful in understanding the present legal climate.

The AICPA has made the following statements concerning the importance of professional standards and the conclusiveness of expert testimony concerning the standards:

- The standard of communication required is measured by specific generally accepted accounting principles (GAAP) and GAAS and, in the absence of specific rules or customs, by the views of experts (professional CPAs).
- The jury (or court in a case of trial without jury) is never authorized to question the wisdom of the professional standard.[6]

In contrast, the SEC has taken the following positions on professional standards and expert testimony of auditors:

- The auditor has an obligation that goes beyond specific GAAP and GAAS or professional custom to effectively communicate material information.
- If GAAP and GAAS are found lacking, the SEC will not hesitate to invoke its authority to establish meaningful standards of performance regardless of expert testimony as to professional standards.[7]

The SEC position requires *effective* communication of material information so as to fairly and meaningfully inform the layperson investor.

An indication of the courts' position on these two matters is as follows:

- Where the profession has established specific GAAS for reasonably dealing with a perceived problem, the professional duty will be limited to conformance with the standard if resulting financial statements fairly and meaningfully inform the investor. Even if the auditor fails to follow professional standards, liability is imposed only when the resulting financials actually cause damage to plaintiffs. However, when misleading financials cause losses, the courts will not hesitate to penalize the auditor despite strong evidence of conformity with GAAP and GAAS.
- Where application of auditing standards requires expertise in evaluating

---

[6] "AICPA Amicus Brief, *Continental Vending* Case," *Journal of Accountancy*, May 1970, pp. 69-73.

[7] Denzil Y. Causey, Jr., *Duties and Liabilities of the CPA*, rev. ed. (Austin: University of Texas, Bureau of Business Research, 1976), p. 15.

and testing internal controls, statistical sampling of transactions, and obtaining competent evidential matter, expert testimony will be conclusive. However, where communication of findings is involved, expert testimony as to compliance with GAAP will be persuasive but not conclusive.[8]

The foregoing issues were critical in the following two major cases involving auditors.

Continental Vending Case (United States v. Simon)

The SEC used the criminal section of the 1934 Act to refer this case to the U.S. Department of Justice for prosecution. The case involved loans made by Continental Vending to its affiliated company, Valley Commercial Corporation, which subsequently lent the money to the president of Continental (Roth). The loans to Roth were secured primarily by the pledging of Continental common stock owned by Roth. Valley, in turn, pledged this stock as collateral against the loans from Continental. The auditor for Continental did not audit Valley. The defendants (a senior partner, a junior partner, and an audit senior of an international accounting firm) approved the following note:

> The amount receivable from Valley Commercial Corp. (an affiliated company of which Mr. Harold Roth is an officer, director and stockholder) bears interest at 12% a year. Such amount, less the balance of the notes payable to that company, is secured by the assignment to the Company of Valley's equity in certain marketable securities. As of February 15, 1963, the amount of such equity at current market quotations exceeded the net amount receivable.

The government argued that the note should have said:

> The amount receivable from Valley Commercial Corp. (an affiliated company of which Mr. Harold Roth is an officer, director and stockholder), which bears interest at 12% a year, was uncollectible at September 30, 1962, since Valley had loaned approximately the same amount to Mr. Roth who was unable to pay. Since that date Mr. Roth and others have pledged as security for the repayment of his obligation to Valley and its obligation to Continental (now $3,900,000 against which Continental's liability to Valley cannot be offset) securities which, as of February 14, 1963, had a market value of $2,978,000. Approximately 80% of such securities are stock and convertible debentures of the Company.

Specifically, the government charged that the defendant's note was false and misleading because

- Continental's footnote did not show that Roth got the money.
- The nature of the collateral was not disclosed even though 80 percent of it consisted of unregistered securities issued by Continental.
- The net amount of the Valley receivables was improper because the Valley

---

[8] Causey, *op. cit.*, pp. 16-19.

payable which had been offset represented notes discounted with outsiders.

- Reference to the secured position in February did not disclose the significant increase in the Valley receivables at that date.

The defendants, supported by the testimony of eight leaders in the accounting profession, contended that their note was in conformity with GAAP and that such compliance was a conclusive defense against criminal charges of misrepresentation. However, the trial judge rejected this argument and instructed the jury that the "critical test" was whether the balance sheet fairly presented financial position without reference to generally accepted accounting principles. The jury concluded that the balance sheet did not present fairly, and the three defendants were convicted of the criminal charges. The U.S. court of appeals refused to reverse the decision and held that

> we do not think the jury was . . . required to accept the accountants' evaluation whether a given fact was material to overall fair presentation, at least not when the accountants' testimony was not based on specific rules or prohibitions to which they could point, but only on the need for the auditor to make an honest judgment and their conclusion that nothing in the financial statements themselves negated the conclusion that an honest judgment had been made. Such evidence may be highly persuasive, but it is not conclusive, and so the trial judge correctly charged.

The defendants were fined, and their licenses to practice as CPAs were revoked. They eventually received a presidential pardon.

As a result of this case, a Statement on Auditing Standards was issued on the meaning of "present fairly." A major conclusion of this Statement on Auditing Standards was that the auditor's judgment on fairness should be applied within the framework of GAAP, as is explained in Chapter 16.[9]

BarChris (Escott v. BarChris Construction Corp.)

In this case, purchasers of subordinated debentures brought suit charging that the registration statement on the debenture issue contained materially false statements and that significant facts were omitted. The major auditing issue in the case, which did not involve a jury trial, was whether the auditors had exercised due diligence in the performance of a subsequent events review, technically referred to by the SEC as an S-1 review. The court acknowledged that such a review was not a complete audit and that the accounting firm's written program for the review was acceptable. However, the court found the execution of the program by the auditor, who had not yet

[9] Auditing Standards Board, *Codification of Statements on Auditing Standards* (New York: American Institute of Certified Public Accountants, 1983), Auditing Section 411.03 (hereinafter referred to and cited as AU §).

received his CPA certificate and was on his first S-1 review, was unacceptable. In his ruling, the judge held:

> Accountants should not be held to a standard higher than that recognized in their profession. I do not do so here. [The senior's] review did not come up to the standard. . . . Most important of all, he was too easily satisfied with glib answers to his inquiries.

As a result of this case, a Statement on Auditing Standards was issued on subsequent events which includes specific review procedures, as is explained in Chapter 15.[10]

Avoidance of Litigation

CPAs, like other professionals such as doctors and lawyers, are currently practicing in a climate where national public policy is emphasizing protection for the consumer (general public) from substandard work by professionals. An analysis of court cases reveals the following precautions which a CPA may take to help avoid becoming involved in litigation.

Use engagement letters for all professional services. Such letters provide the basis for the contractual arrangements and minimize the risk of misunderstanding as to the services that have been agreed on.

Make a thorough investigation of prospective clients. As indicated in Chapter 2, investigation is necessary to minimize the likelihood that the CPA will be associated with a client whose management lacks integrity.

Emphasize quality of service rather than growth. The ability of a firm to properly staff an engagement is vital to the quality of the work that will result. Acceptance of new business that will likely lead to excessive overtime, abnormally heavy work loads, and limited supervision by experienced professionals should be resisted.

Comply fully with professional pronouncements. Strict adherence to GAAS and Statements on Auditing Standards is essential. An auditor must be able to justify any material departures from established guidelines.

Recognize the limitations of professional pronouncements. Professional guidelines are not all-encompassing. In addition, it should be recognized that subjective tests of reasonableness and fairness will be used by judges, juries, and regulatory agencies in judging the auditor's work. The auditor must use sound professional judgment during the examination in the issuance of the audit report.

---

[10] Auditing Standards Board, *op. cit.,* AU § 560.

Establish and maintain high standards of quality control. As suggested in Chapter 2, both the CPA firm and individual auditors have clearly established responsibilities for quality control. Outside peer reviews provide important independent assurance of both the quality and the continued effectiveness of prescribed procedures.

Exercise caution in engagements involving clients in financial difficulty. The impending threat of insolvency or bankruptcy may lead to intentional misrepresentations in the financial statements. Many lawsuits against auditors have resulted from subsequent bankruptcies of companies. The auditor should carefully weigh the sufficiency and competency of the evidence he has obtained in his examination of such companies.

ERRORS AND IRREGULARITIES

Much has been written about the auditor's responsibility for discovering errors and irregularities in an audit engagement. Many users of audit reports, in fact, believe that such discovery either is or should be the primary purpose of an audit. The basic meaning of these two terms is explained in Chapter 4.

- The term *errors* refers to unintentional mistakes, including (1) mathematical or clerical mistakes in underlying accounting data from which financial statements are prepared, (2) mistakes in the application of accounting principles, and (3) oversights or misinterpretation of facts in preparing financial statements.
- The term *irregularities* refers to intentional distortions of financial statements resulting from deliberate misrepresentations (fraud) by management, or misappropriation (defalcations) of assets. Irregularities may result from such acts as the falsification or omission of transactions and/or the related accounting records, intentional misapplication of accounting principles, and improper diversion of assets.[11]

The two terms differ significantly in relation to underlying motive and effect. An error is accidental and the individual responsible for the error neither expects nor realizes any personal gain. In contrast, an irregularity is premeditated and the perpetrator usually hopes to achieve personal gain or some other specific objective.

Auditor's Responsibility

The auditor's responsibility for the detection of errors and irregularities should be considered in relationship to GAAS. An examination made in accordance with these standards is designed to enable the auditor to express an opinion on the client's financial statements. Since errors or irregularities could materially affect the fairness of these statements, the auditor has a

---

[11] Auditing Standards Board, *op. cit.,* AU § 327.02–03.

responsibility under GAAS to plan his examination *to search* for material errors or irregularities. This responsibility is not the same as a responsibility *to discover* all material errors or irregularities. It means that in the planning and execution of an audit program, the auditor should be aware of the possibility of errors or irregularities. If, in the performance of the work, the auditor obtains evidence that material errors or irregularities may exist, he also has the responsibility, if practicable, to extend his auditing procedures to determine whether in fact they do exist.

An examination made in accordance with GAAS cannot guarantee the discovery of all material errors or irregularities. The examination involves selective testing procedures which include the inherent risk that these items will not be detected. Furthermore, there is the risk that collusion and overt management actions will circumvent prescribed internal control procedures and preclude detection by the auditor.

Effects on the Examination

The auditor's efforts to discover material errors or irregularities are not discharged through a specially designed fraud detection program, nor are they concentrated in a series of procedures performed at or near the end of the engagement. Rather, the auditor should plan and perform the entire examination with an awareness that errors or irregularities may exist. For example, the auditor's evaluation of internal accounting control involves a determination of weaknesses in the system that might permit errors or irregularities to occur. Similarly, the objective of performing substantive tests may be stated in terms of obtaining evidence of the possible existence of any material errors or irregularities in the accounting treatment of transactions and balances. Such evidence may be found in differences disclosed by confirmations, reconciliations, etc.

When the audit examination provides evidence that material errors or irregularities may exist, the auditor should discuss the matter and the extent of any further investigation with an appropriate level of management. If the discussion does not eliminate the auditor's suspicions, the circumstances should be communicated to the board of directors or its audit committee. If practicable, the auditor should extend audit procedures to obtain evidential matter as to whether material errors or irregularities do in fact exist. If the auditor is unable to obtain such evidence, because of the circumstances or a management restriction, the auditor should consider withdrawing from the engagement, indicating his reasons and findings in writing to the board of directors.[12]

Effects on Auditor's Report

The auditor's standard report implicitly indicates the auditor's belief that the financial statements are not materially misstated as a result of errors or irregularities. When there is evidence to the contrary, the auditor's opinion

---

[12] Auditing Standards Board, *op. cit.,* AU § 327.14.

should be appropriately modified. If the auditor remains uncertain of the existence of material errors or irregularities in the statements, a qualified opinion or disclaimer of opinion should be rendered.

ILLEGAL CLIENT ACTS

The term *illegal act* refers to the payment of bribes, the making of illegal political contributions, and the violation of other specific laws and regulations. All U.S. companies are subject to the illegal payments provisions of the Foreign Corrupt Practices Act, which prohibits payments to foreign government officials for the purpose of obtaining or retaining business in a foreign country. Many laypersons believe that an audit will surely detect all illegal acts committed by a client. An audit may result in the detection of illegal acts, but it cannot be relied on to do so for the following reasons:

- The determination of whether an act is illegal involves matters of law which may be beyond the auditor's competence.
- Illegal acts may pertain to aspects of the company's operations, such as the Equal Opportunity Employment Act, that are generally unrelated to the financial statements.[13]

It should also be recognized that management may be able to effectively conceal the occurrence of illegal acts. Moreover, there are limitations in the auditing process that may permit illegal acts to remain undiscovered.

Effects on Examination

The auditor does not have a responsibility to search for illegal acts. However, in making an examination in accordance with GAAS, the auditor should be aware that illegal acts may have a material effect on the financial statements. Procedures performed for the purpose of expressing an opinion on the client's financial statements may provide evidence of possible illegal acts. When the auditor believes illegal acts may have occurred, he should (1) inquire of management, (2) consult with the client's legal counsel, and (3) consider performing additional procedures to obtain an understanding of the acts and their possible effects on the financial statements. In evaluating the possible effects, the auditor should consider related fines, penalties, damages, and possible loss contingencies such as expropriation of property and forced discontinuance of operations.

Effects on Auditor's Report

The effects of material illegal acts on the auditor's report are as follows:

---

[13] Auditing Standards Board, *op. cit.*, AU § 328.03.

CIRCUMSTANCE	TYPE OF OPINION
Properly accounted for and disclosed	Unqualified
Unable to obtain sufficient competent evidential matter	Qualified or disclaimer because of scope limitation
Improper accounting or inadequate disclosure	Qualified or adverse because of lack of conformity with GAAP
Not capable of reasonable estimation	Qualified or disclaimer because of uncertainty

Other Considerations

When the auditor determines that an illegal act has occurred, the findings should be reported at a level of authority high enough for appropriate action. This may be the audit committee or board of directors in some cases. If such action is not forthcoming, the auditor should consider severing any further business relationships with the client. The auditor has no obligation to notify other parties concerning illegal acts. Such notification is the responsibility of management.

CONCLUDING COMMENTS

Litigation has had a significant impact on the public accounting profession in the past two decades and it seems reasonable to expect that it will continue to do so in the foreseeable future. Litigation has been costly to the auditor and has caused an increased awareness of the need for improved quality control (see Chapter 2) in audit engagements. It also seems clear that society will continue to ask auditors to assume greater responsibilities in financial reporting and in discovering management improprieties. It is essential that auditors be responsive to legitimate requests for extending their service to the public. At the same time, however, there must be adequate recognition by the public of the added legal risks that this additional service may entail.

APPENDIX 19A

Chronological Summary of Legal Cases under Common and Statutory Law[14]

A wealth of valuable case information documents and defines auditors' continually evolving legal responsibilities. By the end of 1974, approximately 200 decisions involving auditors had been rendered in the United States. The following paragraphs briefly describe cases that appear to be significant in identifying legal trends. The purpose of the analysis is to identify significant findings and ideas related to auditing that have been expressed by the courts and SEC.

Many of these findings and ideas represent court "dicta," which are expressions of opinion by a judge. Although dicta do not have the force of rule of law, they appear to be very useful in gaining insight into trends in the legal environment.

Cases Prior to 1940

Prior to 1940, litigation against auditors focused on the auditors' common law liability for failure to perform adequate auditing procedures rather than questions of accounting principles, securities law violations, or criminal liability. The most common complaint against auditors was a breach of contract based upon their alleged failure to detect embezzlement. This type of complaint is illustrated by the following cases.

Smith v. London Assurance Corp. (1905)

Auditors were found liable to their client for breach of contract for failure to discover an embezzlement of a large sum of money by one of the client's employees. The court noted that

- Public accountants constitute a skilled professional class and are therefore subject to the same risks of liability for negligence in the practice of their profession as are members of other skilled professions. The degree of skill implied by one who holds himself out as a professional is that commonly possessed by others in the same employment.
- The contract expressly called for certain auditing procedures that were not actually carried out with reasonable care and diligence.

Ultramares Corp. v. Touche (1931)

Auditors failed to discover an overstatement of capital and surplus that had been accomplished by management through recording of fictitious accounts receivable and other assets. The court noted that

- Auditors are not liable to a third party for ordinary negligence, except possibly to a third party who is identified at the time of the audit to be a primary beneficiary of the audited information.
- Auditors are liable to third parties for fraud, and fraud may be inferred from gross negligence.

State Street Trust Co. v. Ernst (1938)

Auditors examined accounts receivable but failed to discover the fact that the receivables were overstated because many of the accounts were uncollectible. The court noted that

---

[14] The commentary and analysis of all cases through the early 1970s are based on data prepared by Peat, Marwick, Mitchell & Co. and published in *Research Opportunities in Auditing* (New York: Peat, Marwick, Mitchell & Co., 1976), pp. 85-91.

- An auditor may be liable to third parties for fraud even where there is no deliberate or active fraud on his part. The court indicated that fraud on the part of the auditor may be inferred from any or all of the following:

  - Certifying as true to the knowledge of the auditor when he possessed insufficient knowledge as a basis for the certification.
  - Reckless misstatement.
  - Flimsy grounds for an opinion.
  - A failure to investigate doubtful facts or circumstances.
  - Heedlessness and reckless disregard of consequences.

National Surety Corp. v. Lybrand (1939)

The auditors failed to discover embezzlements of cash that were concealed through lapping and kiting practices. The court indicated that

- The contract for services explicitly required a determination of the client's cash position and therefore implied that certain auditing procedures should be undertaken.
- Expert testimony established that ordinary professional care and the use of proper auditing methods would have identified well-known danger signals and that follow-up inquiries would have led to discovery of the embezzlement.

Cases in the 1940s and 1950s

Litigation against auditors occurred infrequently during the 1940s and 1950s. However, the following three cases are of significance because they shed light on auditors' criminal liability with respect to securities law violations. In addition, they indicate the courts' and SEC's willingness to challenge the adequacy of the profession's standards.

McKesson & Robbins (SEC Accounting Series Release No. 19 (1940))

The SEC found that the auditors failed to employ a necessary degree of diligence and inquisitiveness which resulted in their failure to discover an overstatement of assets that management had created through recording and manipulation of fictitious inventories. The SEC noted that

- Numerous auditing procedures required strengthening (e.g., inventory, accounts receivable, accounts payable, investigation of new clients, audit committee review).
- Auditors should be responsible for detecting gross misstatements whether resulting from collusion or otherwise.
- Auditors must recognize their responsibility to the public investor by including management activities in their review.

United States v. White (1941)

The auditor was convicted of criminal fraud under Section 17 of the Securities Act of 1933 for his failure to disclose several instances of questionable accounting practices in connection with a registration statement. The court expressed the following thought with respect to the sufficiency of evidence in a criminal case:

- Items of questionable accounting, which taken individually do not demonstrate knowledge of falsity, may acquire greater significance as proof when considered together.

Speed v. Transamerica Corp. **(1951)**

This case did not involve auditors. Nevertheless, it is of significance because of the standard that the court used to evaluate the usefulness of financial information. The case involved an offer by majority shareholders to buy out the minority interest. Although the adequacy of generally accepted accounting principles was not a major issue in this case, the court's treatment of a specific GAAP related to inventory valuation is significant. The court found that

- Majority shareholders had violated Section 10, Rule 10b-5 of the 1934 Act by failing to disclose that the current value of inventory was significantly higher than historical cost, which was reported in the financial statements in accordance with generally accepted accounting principles.

Cases in the 1960s

A barrage of litigation has been brought against auditors commencing in the late 1960s. According to a *Wall Street Journal* article (November 15, 1966), nearly 100 lawsuits were pending against auditors in late 1966. Compared to previous legal activity, this number represented explosive growth. In June 1968, *Fortune* estimated that as many suits were filed against auditors in the previous twelve months as in the previous twelve years.

This period is not only distinguished by the growth in the volume of litigation against auditors. As the following cases demonstrate, the courts also continued to extend the concepts of auditors' criminal liability and liability for negligence to third parties. They also defined more precisely auditors' obligations under the securities acts and made more frequent judgments regarding the adequacy of measurement and reporting standards.

United States v. Benjamin **(1964)**

The auditor was convicted in a criminal action under Section 24 of the 1933 Act for his failure to exercise due diligence that would have revealed misrepresentations in pro forma financial statements used in conjunction with sales of unregistered securities. The court stated:

- In our complex society the accountant's certificate and the lawyer's opinion can be instruments for inflicting pecuniary loss more potent than the chisel or the crowbar. Of course, Congress did not mean that any mistake of law or misstatement of fact should subject an attorney or an accountant to criminal liability simply because more skilled practitioners would not have made them. But Congress equally could not have intended that men holding themselves out as members of these ancient professions should be able to escape criminal liability on a plea of ignorance when they have shut their eyes to what was plainly to be seen or have represented a knowledge they knew they did not possess.

Fischer v. Kletz **(1967)**

In this case, commonly known as *Yale Express,* the auditor did not disclose errors in a previously issued audit report which were discovered three months later during a management services engagement. In ruling on the case which involved actions under common law and Section 10(b), Rule 10b-5, and Section 18 of the 1934 Act, the court noted that

- An auditor has a duty to anyone still relying on his report to disclose subsequently discovered errors in the report. This duty exists regardless of the auditor's lack of financial interest in any transactions to which the information relates. The obligation arises because of the auditor's special relationship that provides access to the information.

Rusch Factors, Inc. v. Levin **(1968)**

The auditor was held liable to a third party for his certification of financial statements that showed a corporation to be solvent when in fact it was insolvent. This case is of interest because it extended the auditor's third-party liability for ordinary negligence to "foreseen and limited classes," which is an extension beyond the *Ultramares* rule. Additionally, the court argued:

- Why should an innocent reliant party be forced to carry the weighty burden of an accountant's professional malpractice? Isn't the risk of loss more easily distributed and fairly spread by imposing it on the accounting profession, which can pass the cost onto the entire consuming public? Finally, wouldn't a rule of foreseeability elevate the cautionary techniques of the accounting profession? For these reasons it appears to this Court that the decision in *Ultramares* constitutes an unwarranted inroad upon the principle "the risk reasonably to be perceived defines the duty to be obeyed."

Escott v. BarChris Construction Corp. **(1968)**

In this case, the auditors were found liable to third-party investors under Section 11 of the 1933 Act for failure to make a reasonable investigation in an audit and for failure to perform an S-1 review with due diligence. The court noted that

- The reporting of an entire gain on a sale and leaseback at the time of the sale is false and misleading.
- An error in earnings per share of 15 percent ($.75 vs. $.65 true value) is immaterial in a growth-oriented company, but an error in the current ratio of 19 percent (1.9 vs. 1.6 true value) is material.
- Accountants should not be held to a standard higher than that recognized in their profession.

United States v. Simon **(1969)**

In this case, commonly referred to as *Continental Vending,* auditors were convicted of criminal liability under Section 32 of the 1934 Act for failure to disclose adequately certain significant transactions that had occurred between the audited corporation and one of its officers. The court noted that

- Proof that certified information is in compliance with generally accepted accounting principles is evidence which may be very persuasive but not necessarily conclusive that an auditor acted in good faith.
- The critical test for financial statements is: do they fairly present?
- Independent accountants have a duty to reveal known dishonesty by a high corporate officer.
- Sufficient evidence of criminal intent need "not show that defendants were wicked men with designs on anyone's purse, . . . but rather that they had certified a statement knowing it to be false."

Cases in the 1970s

There was a significant decline in the number of legal suits brought against accountants during this period. In addition, a landmark Supreme Court decision may have ended any further extension of the accountant's liability for ordinary negligence under statutory law.

Herzfeld v. Laventhol, Kreckstein, Horwath & Horwath **(1974)**

This case involved a private placement of securities by a corporation engaged in real estate syndication. The auditors were found liable under Section 10(b), Rule 10b-5 of the 1934 Act for failure to fully disclose the facts and circumstances underlying their qualified opinion. The court noted that

- The accountant's professional duty to investors cannot be fulfilled by merely following generally accepted accounting principles.
- The financial reports must fairly present the true financial position to the "untutored eye of an ordinary investor."
- An auditor's qualified opinion should disclose the reasoning and facts which prompted it.

United States v. Natelli **(1975)**

In this case, commonly known as the *National Student Marketing Corporation* case, two auditors were convicted of criminal liability under Section 32 of the 1934 Act for failing to properly disclose the write off of uncollectible accounts. In the financial statements of the current year (1969), uncollectible accounts pertaining to 1968 regular sales on advertising contracts, which had only been verified by telephone, were reported in part as a retroactive adjustment against sales acquired by pooling in 1968. The accompanying footnote failed to state either that regular sales for 1968 were overstated 20 percent or that actual net earnings were only 46 percent of reported earnings. The court concluded that

- The treatment of the retroactive adjustment was done intentionally to conceal the errors in the 1968 statements.

Hochfelder v. Ernst **(1976)**

Auditors were not liable under Section 10, Rule 10b-5 of the 1934 Act for failure to discover a fraudulent scheme perpetrated by the president of a brokerage firm. In this landmark decision, the Supreme Court held that

- A private cause of action for damages will not lie under Section 10, and Rule 10b-5 of the Securities Exchange Act of 1934 in the absence of any allegation of "scienter"—intent to deceive, manipulate, or defraud.

McLean v. Alexander **(1979)**

The plaintiff was a sophisticated investor who sat on the board of directors of several large corporations. Plaintiff purchased stock in a company whose audited financial statements showed receivables "Considered Fully Collectible." The receivables were consignment sales that were never realized. The auditors failed to obtain positive confirmations from the three or four accounts that comprised 90% of the balance and failed to document or make inquiry of management as to the financial status of these new accounts. The auditors were held liable under Section 10(b), Rule 10b-5 of the 1934 Act for more than mere negligence but short of a preconceived actual intent to defraud by a U.S. District Court in 1976.

    This decision was reversed by the U.S. Court of Appeals for the Third Circuit in 1979. The court conceded that the auditor might have been guilty of negligence but held that the auditor's conduct did not meet the minimum threshold for liability as adopted from a Seventh Circuit opinion:

- Reckless conduct may be defined as highly unreasonable conduct, involving not merely simple, or even inexcusable negligence, but an extreme departure from the standards of ordinary care, and which presents a danger of misleading buyers or sellers that is either known to the defendant or is so obvious that the actor must have been aware of it.

Cases in the Early 1980s

Two jury trials involving the auditor's failure to discover management fraud occurred. The verdicts, which found the auditors not guilty of negligence, may be indicative of a change in the public perception of the auditor's liability for detecting this type of fraud.

Cenco Incorporated v. Seidman & Seidman (1982)

In this case the U.S. Court of Appeals for the Seventh Circuit in Chicago, Illinois, in a three-judge decision, upheld an earlier jury verdict in favor of the auditors, Seidman & Seidman. The defendants were charged with violating various federal securities laws and SEC rules, notably Rule 10b-5. The case pertained to the auditor's failure to detect a $25 million inventory fraud perpetrated by top management in its annual audit. In the decision, the judges said:

- Auditors aren't detectives hired to ferret out fraud.
- Auditors must investigate if they suspect fraud; but in this case, the former management made fraud difficult to detect since top executives turned the company "into an engine of theft against outsiders."

The court also gave the auditors permission to sue Cenco for the amount paid ($3.5 million) as damages to Cenco stockholders in a 1980 class action suit settlement pertaining to the fraud.

Cedars of Lebanon Hospital Corp. v. Touche Ross & Co. (1982)

In this Florida circuit court case, a jury found the auditors, Touche Ross & Co., not guilty of negligence for failing to detect in their annual audit an embezzlement scheme by the administrator of the Cedars of Lebanon Hospital Corp. The suit was brought by the hospital and its board of directors. The case involved collusive fraud by the administrator. In commenting on the decision, counsel for the defendant said that the jury's ability to grasp the technical issues in the case was impressive.[15]

REVIEW QUESTIONS

19–1. What is meant by *common law?*

19–2. Under common law, a CPA may be liable to a client.
   a. Explain the meaning and importance of the term *privity of contract.*
   b. How may an auditor breach a contract?
   c. What cause ordinarily underlies a tort action?

19–3. a. Who are the two classes of third parties that may sustain suits against auditors under common law?
   b. Under what circumstances may an auditor be held liable to third parties?

19–4. Indicate the significance of *Ultramares, Rusch Factors,* and the *Rhode Island Hospital Trust* cases on the auditor's liability for negligence.

---

[15] *Journal of Accountancy,* May 1982, p. 12.

19–5. Why is the auditor's liability more extensive under statutory law than under common law?

19–6. a. Who may bring suit under the 1933 Securities Act?
b. What is the basis for such action?

19–7. Under what circumstances will a statement be presumed to be misleading?

19–8. What are the responsibilities of the plaintiff and the defendant in a 1933 Act suit?

19–9. a. Who may bring suit under the 1934 Securities Exchange Act?
b. Is the basis for action the same as in a 1933 Act suit? Explain.

19–10. What are the conditions associated with liability under Rule 10b-5 of the 1934 Act?

19–11. What are the responsibilities of the plaintiff and the defendant in a 1934 Act suit?

19–12. Enumerate the principal differences in legal liability between the two securities acts.

19–13. a. What was the basis for the *Hochfelder* case?
b. What is the significance of the decision in the case?

19–14. Contrast the essence of the relative importance of professional standards in legal cases between the AICPA, the SEC, and the courts.

19–15. a. What were the critical issues in (a) the *Continental Vending* case and (b) the *Bar-Chris* case?
b. What action was taken by the profession as a result of each case?

19–16. Identify actions which the auditor may take to avoid litigation.

19–17. a. Distinguish between errors and irregularities.
b. What is the auditor's basic responsibility for errors or irregularities?

19–18. a. What responsibility does the auditor have when he believes material errors or irregularities may exist?
b. What are the possible effects of the foregoing on the auditor's standard report?

19–19. a. Define *illegal acts*.
b. What is the auditor's basic responsibility for such acts?

19–20. a. Can an examination made in accordance with generally accepted auditing standards be relied upon to detect illegal acts? Why or why not?
b. What are the possible effects of illegal acts on the auditor's report?

COMPREHENSIVE QUESTIONS

19–21. Watts and Williams, a firm of certified public accountants, audited the accounts of Sampson Skins, Inc., a corporation that imports and deals in fine furs. Upon completion of the examination the auditors supplied Sampson Skins with 20 copies of the certified balance sheet. The firm knew that Sampson Skins wanted that number of copies of the auditor's report to furnish to banks and other potential lenders.

The balance sheet in question was in error by approximately $800,000. Instead of having a $600,000 net worth, the corporation was insolvent. The management of Sampson Skins had "doctored" the books to avoid bankruptcy. The assets had been overstated by $500,000 of fictitious and nonexisting accounts receivable and $300,000 of nonexisting skins listed as inventory when in fact Sampson Skins had only empty boxes. The audit failed to detect these fraudulent entries. Martinson, relying on the certified balance sheet, loaned $200,000 to Sampson Skins. He seeks to recover his loss from Watts and Williams.

1. If Martinson alleges and proves negligence on the part of Watts and Williams, he would be able to recover his loss.
2. If Martinson alleges and proves constructive fraud, i.e., gross negligence on the part of Watts and Williams, he would be able to recover his loss.
3. Martinson is not in privity of contract with Watts and Williams.
4. Unless actual fraud on the part of Watts and Williams could be shown, Martinson could not recover.
5. Martinson is a third-party beneficiary of the contract Watts and Williams made with Sampson Skins.

Required
Indicate whether each of the foregoing statements is true or false under common law. Give the reason(s) for each answer.

AICPA (adapted)

19–22.   a. Jackson was a junior staff member of an accounting firm. He began the audit of the Bosco Corporation, which manufactured and sold expensive watches. In the middle of the audit, he quit. The accounting firm hired another person to continue the audit of Bosco. Due to the changeover and the time pressure to finish the audit, the firm violated certain generally accepted auditing standards when it did not follow adequate procedures with respect to the physical inventory. Had the proper procedures been used during the examination the firm would have discovered that watches worth more than $20,000 were missing. The employee who was stealing the watches was able to steal an additional $30,000 worth before the thefts were discovered six months after the completion of the audit.

Required
Discuss the legal problems of the accounting firm as a result of the above facts.

   b. Walter Young, doing business as Walter Young Fashions, engaged the CPA partnership of Small & Brown to examine his financial statements. During the examination, Small & Brown discovered certain irregularities which would have indicated to a reasonably prudent accountant that James Smith, the head bookkeeper, might be engaged in a fraud. More specifically, it appeared to Small & Brown that serious defalcations were taking place. However, Small & Brown, not having been engaged to discover defalcations, submitted an unqualified opinion in the report and did not mention the potential defalcation problem.

Required
What are the legal implications of the above facts as they relate to the relationship between Small & Brown and Walter Young? Explain

AICPA (adapted)

19–23.   Donald Sharpe recently joined the CPA firm of Spark, Watts, and Wilcox. He quickly established a reputation for thoroughness and a steadfast dedication to following prescribed auditing procedures to the letter. On his third audit for the firm, Sharpe examined the underlying documentation of two hundred disbursements as a test of purchasing, receiving, vouchers-payable, and cash disbursement procedures. In the process he found twelve disbursements for the purchase of materials with no receiving reports in the documentation. He noted the exceptions in his working papers and called them to the attention of the in-charge accountant. Relying on prior experience with the client, the in-charge accountant disregarded Sharpe's comments, and nothing further was done about the exceptions.

Subsequently it was learned that one of the client's purchasing agents and a member of its accounting department were engaged in a fraudulent scheme whereby they diverted the receipt of materials to a public warehouse while sending the invoices to the client. When the client discovered the fraud, the conspirators had obtained approximately $70,000, $50,000 of which was after the completion of the audit.

Required
Discuss the legal implications and liabilities to Spark, Watts, and Wilcox as a result of the above facts.

AICPA

19–24.   Keen, a CPA and sole practitioner, was retained by Arthur & Son, a partnership, to audit the company books and prepare a report on the financial statements for submission to several prospective partners as part of a planned expansion of the firm. Keen's fee was fixed on a per-diem basis. After a period of intensive work, Keen had completed about half of the necessary field work when he suffered a paralyzing stroke. He was forced to abandon all his work and in fact retired from the profession. The planned expansion of the firm failed to materialize because the prospective partners would act only upon the basis of the report which Keen was to have submitted and lost interest when the report was not available.

Required
a. Arthur & Son sues Keen for breach of his contract. Will it recover? Explain.
b. Keen sues Arthur & Son for his fee for the work he was able to complete or, in the alternative, for the reasonable value of the services performed. Will he recover? Explain.
c. Arthur & Son demands from Keen all of the working papers relative to the engagement including several canceled checks, the articles of copartnership, and some other records of the firm. Will the firm succeed in its demand? Explain.

AICPA

19–25. Barney & Company, CPAs, has been engaged to perform an examination of the financial statements of Waldo, Inc., for several years. The terms of the engagement have been set out in an annual engagement letter signed by both parties. The terms of each engagement included the following:

> This being an ordinary examination, it is not primarily or specifically designed, and cannot be relied upon, to disclose defalcations and other similar irregularities, although their discovery may result.

Three years ago Harold Zamp, head cashier of Waldo and an expert in computer operations, devised a previously unheard-of method of embezzling funds from his employer. At first, Zamp's thefts were small but increased as time went on. During the current year, before Barney began working on the engagement, the thefts became so large that serious variances in certain accounts came to the attention of the controller. When questioned about the variances, Zamp confessed and explained his unique embezzlement scheme. Investigation revealed that Zamp had stolen $257,550. Zamp has no assets with which to repay the thefts.

Waldo submitted its claim for $257,550 to Multi-State Surety Company in accordance with the terms of the fidelity bond covering Zamp. Fulfilling its surety obligation, Multi-State paid the claim and now seeks to recover its losses from Barney.

In defense, Barney asserts, in the alternative, the following defenses:

1. Multi-State has no standing in court to sue because it was not a party to the contract (i.e., lacking in privity) between Barney and its client, Waldo.
2. Even if Multi-State had the standing to sue, its claim should be dismissed because Barney's engagements with Waldo did not specifically include the discovery of defalcations other than those which might arise in the process of an ordinary examination.
3. Even if Barney's contract had made it responsible for discoverable defalcations, it could not have discovered Zamp's defalcations with the exercise of reasonable care. Zamp's technique was so new and novel that no accounting firm could have discovered the defalcations in any event.

Required
In separately numbered paragraphs, discuss the validity of each of Barney's defenses.

AICPA

19–26. The CPA firm of Martinson, Brinks & Sutherland, a partnership, was the auditor for Masco Corporation, a medium-sized wholesaler. Masco leased warehouse facilities and sought financing for leasehold improvements to these facilities. Masco assured its bank that the leasehold improvements would result in a more efficient and profitable operation. Based on these assurances, the bank granted Masco a line of credit.

The loan agreement required annual audited financial statements. Masco submitted to the bank its 19X0 audited financial statements which showed an operating profit of $75,000, leasehold improvements of $250,000, and net worth of $350,000. In reliance thereon, the bank loaned Masco $200,000. The audit report which accompanied the financial statements disclaimed an opinion because the cost of the leasehold improvements could not be determined from the company's records. The part of the audit report dealing with leasehold improvements reads as follows:

> Additions to fixed assets in 19X0 were found to include principally warehouse improvements. Practically all of this work was done by company employees and the cost of materials and overhead were paid by Masco. Unfortunately, fully complete detailed cost records were not kept of these leasehold improvements and no exact determination could be made as to the actual cost of said improvements. The total amount capitalized is set forth in note 4.

In late 19X1, Masco went out of business, at which time it was learned that the claimed leasehold improvements were totally fictitious. The labor expenses charged as leasehold improvements proved to be operating expenses. No item of building material cost had been recorded. No independent investigation of the existence of the leasehold improvements was made by the auditors.

If the $250,000 had not been capitalized, the income statement would have reflected a substantial loss from operations and the net worth would have been correspondingly decreased.

The bank has sustained a loss on its loan to Masco of $200,000 and now seeks to recover damages from the CPA firm, alleging that the accountants negligently audited the financial statements.

Required
Answer the following, setting forth reasons for any conclusions stated:

a. Will the disclaimer of opinion absolve the CPA firm from liability?
b. Are the individual partners of Martinson, Brinks & Sutherland, who did not take part in the audit, liable?
c. Briefly discuss the development of the common law regarding the liability of CPAs to third parties.

19–27. Risk Capital Limited, a Delaware corporation, was considering the purchase of a substantial amount of the treasury stock held by Florida Sunshine Corporation, a closely held corporation. Initial discussions with the Florida Sunshine Corporation began late in 19X0.

Wilson and Wyatt, Florida Sunshine's accountants, regularly prepared quarterly and annual unaudited financial statements. The most recently prepared financial statements were for the year ended September 30, 19X1.

On November 15, 19X1, after protracted negotiations, Risk Capital agreed to purchase 100,000 shares of no par, class A capital stock of Florida Sunshine at $12.50 per share. However, Risk Capital insisted on audited statements for calendar year 19X1. The contract specifically provided:

> Risk Capital shall have the right to rescind the purchase of said stock if the au-

dited financial statements of Florida Sunshine for calendar year 19X1 show a material adverse change in the financial condition of the Corporation.

The audited financial statements furnished to Florida Sunshine by Wilson and Wyatt showed no such material adverse change. Risk Capital relied upon the audited statements and purchased the treasury stock of Florida Sunshine. It was subsequently discovered that, as of the balance sheet date, the audited statements were incorrect and that in fact there had been a material adverse change in the financial condition of the Corporation. Florida Sunshine is insolvent and Risk Capital will lose virtually its entire investment.

Risk Capital seeks recovery against Wilson and Wyatt.

Required
a. Discuss each of the theories of liability that Risk Capital will probably assert as its basis for recovery.
b. Assuming that only ordinary negligence is proven, will Risk Capital prevail? State "yes" or "no" and explain.

AICPA

19-28. Pelham & James, CPAs, were retained by Tom Stone, sole proprietor of Stone Housebuilders, to compile Stone's financial statements. Stone advised Pelham & James that the financial statements would be used in connection with a possible incorporation of the business and sale of stock to friends. Prior to undertaking the engagement, Pelham & James were also advised to pay particular attention to the trade accounts payable. They agreed to use every reasonable means to determine the correct amount.

At the time Pelham & James were engaged, the books and records were in total disarray. Pelham & James proceeded with the engagement applying all applicable procedures for compiling financial statements. They failed however, to detect and disclose in the financial statements Stone's liability for certain unpaid bills. Documentation concerning those bills was available for Pelham & James' inspection had they looked. This omission led to a material understatement ($60,000) of the trade accounts payable.

Pelham & James delivered the compiled financial statements to Tom Stone with their compilation report which indicated that they did not express an opinion or any other assurance regarding the financial statements. Tom Stone met with two prospective investors, Dickerson and Nichols. At the meeting, Pelham & James stated that they were confident that the trade accounts payable balance was accurate to within $8,000.

Stone Housebuilders was incorporated. Dickerson and Nichols, relying on the financial statements, became stockholders along with Tom Stone. Shortly thereafter, the understatement of trade accounts payable was detected. As a result, Dickerson and Nichols discovered that they had paid substantially more for the stock than it was worth at the time of purchase.

Required
Answer the following, setting forth reasons for any conclusions stated.

   Will Pelham & James be found liable to Dickerson and Nichols in a common law action for their damages?

AICPA

19-29.* A number of situations that pertain to the auditor's liability under statutory law are described below. At the end of each case, a statement is made concerning one or more of the parties in the suit.

1. In connection with a filing with the SEC, Elite Corporation engaged the public accounting firm of Turner and Miles to examine the financial statements in the registration statement. Two months after the registration statement became effective, it was discovered that a material fact was omitted from Elite's financial statements. One of the investors who acquired securities covered by the registration statement sued Turner and Miles. To win his lawsuit, the investor must prove Turner and Miles was negligent or fraudulent in reporting on the financial statements.

2. Assume it was established that the accountants in question 1 were negligent in certifying Elite's financial statements. They could avoid or reduce their liability by showing that the investor's loss was not due to the omission of the material fact.

3. Assume that:
   a. An auditor issued an unqualified opinion on a set of financial statements containing a material misstatement.
   b. The auditor did not know of the misstatement but failed to observe generally accepted auditing standards in performing his examination.
   c. The owner of another company purchased the firm, although he was aware of the misstatement before doing so. He never apprised the auditor of the misstatement.
   d. After the purchase was completed, the purchaser sued the auditor for damages, asserting the auditor had violated the Federal Securities Laws (Paragraph 10(b) of the Securities Exchange Act of 1934, etc.) and accusing him of common law fraud and negligence. The purchaser would be successful in his suit against the auditor.

4. The *BarChris* decision affirms the proposition, among others, that a court can impose its judgment, *in place of the judgment of the auditor,* on matters of accounting and auditing practices.

Required

Indicate whether you believe the statements made above are true or false. Give reasons in support of your answer.

19–30. The Dandy Container Corporation engaged the accounting firm of Adams and Adams to examine financial statements to be used in connection with a public offering of securities. The audit was completed and an unqualified opinion was expressed on the financial statements which were submitted to the Securities and Exchange Commission along with the registration statement. Two hundred thousand shares of Dandy Container common stock were offered to the public at $11 a share. Eight months later the stock fell to $2 a share when it was disclosed that several large loans to two "paper" corporations owned by one of the directors were worthless. The loans were secured by the stock of the borrowing corporation which was owned by the director. These facts were not disclosed in the financial report. The director involved and the two corporations are insolvent.

1. The Securities Act of 1933 applies to the above described public offering of securities in interstate commerce.
2. The accounting firm has potential liability to any person who acquired the stock in reliance upon the registration statement.
3. An investor who bought shares in Dandy Container would make a prima facie case if he alleges that the failure to explain the nature of the loans in question constituted a false statement or misleading omission in the financial statements.
4. The accountants could avoid liability if they could show they were neither negligent nor fraudulent.
5. The accountants could avoid or reduce the damages asserted against them if they could establish that the drop in price was due in whole or in part to other causes.
6. The Dandy investors would have to institute suit within one year after discovery of the alleged untrue statements or omissions.

7. The SEC would defend any action brought against the accountants in that the SEC examined and approved the registration statement.

Required

Indicate whether each of the above statements is true or false under statutory law. Give the reason(s) for your answer.

19–31. Gordon & Groton, CPAs, were the auditors of Bank & Company, a brokerage firm and member of a national stock exchange. Gordon & Groton examined and reported on the financial statements of Bank which were filed with the SEC.

Several of Bank's customers were swindled by a fraudulent scheme perpetrated by Bank's president, who owned 90 percent of the voting stock of the company. The facts establish that Gordon & Groton were negligent but not reckless or grossly negligent in the conduct of the audit and neither participated in the fraudulent scheme nor knew of its existence.

The customers are suing Gordon & Groton under the antifraud provisions of Section 10(b) and Rule 10b-5 of the Securities Exchange Act of 1934 for aiding and abetting the fraudulent scheme of the president. The customers' suit for fraud is predicated exclusively on the negligence of the auditors in failing to conduct a proper audit, thereby failing to discover the fraudulent scheme.

Required

Answer the following, setting forth reasons for any conclusions stated.

a. What is the probable oucome of the lawsuit?
b. What other theory of liability might the customers have asserted?

AICPA

19–32. Herbert McCoy is the chief executive officer of McCoy Forging Corporation, a small but rapidly growing manufacturing company. For the past several years, Donovan & Company, CPAs, had been engaged to do compilation work, a systems improvement study, and to prepare the company's federal and state income tax returns. In 1980, McCoy decided that due to the growth of the company and requests from bankers, it would be desirable to have an audit. Moreover, McCoy had recently received a disturbing anonymous letter which stated: "Beware you have a viper in your nest. The money is literally disappearing before your very eyes! Signed: A friend."

McCoy believed that the audit was entirely necessary and easily justifiable on the basis of the growth and credit factors mentioned above. He decided he would keep the anonymous letter to himself.

Therefore, McCoy on behalf of McCoy Forging engaged Donovan & Company, CPAs, to render an opinion on the financial statements for the year ended June 30, 19X1. He told Donovan he wanted to verify that the financial statements were "accurate and proper." He did not mention the anonymous letter. The usual engagement letter providing for an audit in accordance with generally accepted auditing standards (GAAS) was drafted by Donovan & Company and signed by both parties.

The audit was performed in accordance with GAAS. The audit did not reveal a clever defalcation plan by which Harper, the assistant treasurer, was siphoning off substantiated amounts of McCoy Forging's money. The defalcations occurred both before and after the audit. Harper's embezzlement was discovered in October 19X1. Although the scheme was fairly sophisticated, it could have been detected had additional checks and procedures been performed by Donovan & Company. McCoy Forging demands reimbursement from Donovan for the entire amount of the embezzlement, some $20,000 of which occurred before the audit and $25,000 after. Donovan has denied any liability and refuses to pay.

Required

Answer the following, setting forth reasons for any conclusions stated.

a. In the event McCoy Forging sues Donovan & Company, will it prevail in whole or in part?
b. Might there be any liability to McCoy Forging on McCoy's part and if so, under what theory?

AICPA

19–33. a. Whitlow & Company is a brokerage firm registered under the Securities Exchange Act of 1934. The Act requires such a brokerage firm to file audited financial statements with the SEC annually. Mitchell & Moss, Whitlow's CPAs, performed the annual audit for the year ended December 31, 19X9, and rendered an unqualified opinion, which was filed with the SEC along with Whitlow's financial statements. During 19X9 Charles, the president of Whitlow & Company, engaged in a huge embezzlement scheme that eventually bankrupted the firm. As a result substantial losses were suffered by customers and shareholders of Whitlow & Company, including Thaxton who had recently purchased several shares of stock of Whitlow & Company after reviewing the company's 19X9 audit report. Mitchell & Moss's audit was deficient; if they had complied with generally accepted auditing standards, the embezzlement would have been discovered. However, Mitchell & Moss had no knowledge of the embezzlement nor could their conduct be categorized as reckless.

Required

Answer the following, setting forth reasons for any conclusions stated.

1. What liability to Thaxton, if any, does Mitchell & Moss have under the Securities Exchange Act of 1934?
2. What theory or theories of liability, if any, are available to Whitlow & Company's customers and shareholders under the common law?

b. Jackson is a sophisticated investor. As such, she was initially a member of a small group who was going to participate in a private placement of $1 million of common stock of Clarion Corporation. Numerous meetings were held among management and the investor group. Detailed financial and other information was supplied to the participants. Upon the eve of completion of the placement, it was aborted when one major investor withdrew. Clarion then decided to offer $2.5 million of Clarion common stock to the public pursuant to the registration requirements of the Securities Act of 1933. Jackson subscribed to $300,000 of the Clarion public stock offering. Nine months later, Clarion's earnings dropped significantly and as a result the stock dropped 20% beneath the offering price. In addition, the Dow Jones Industrial Average was down 10% from the time of the offering.

Jackson has sold her shares at a loss of $60,000 and seeks to hold all parties liable who participated in the public offering including Allen, Dunn, and Rose, Clarion's CPA firm. Although the audit was performed in conformity with generally accepted auditing standards, there were some relatively minor irregularities. The financial statements of Clarion Corporation, which were part of the registration statement, contained minor misleading facts. It is believed by Clarion and by Allen, Dunn, and Rose that Jackson's asserted claim is without merit.

Required

Answer the following, setting forth reasons for any conclusions stated.

1. Assuming Jackson sues under the Securities Act of 1933, what will be the basis of her claim?
2. What are the probable defenses which might be asserted by Allen, Dunn, and Rose in light of these facts?

19–34. In the audit of different clients, you encounter the following pertaining to illegal acts:

1. You are unable to determine the amounts associated with certain events or if, in fact, an act is illegal.
2. You conclude that an illegal act is material in amount and that is has been buried in miscellaneous deferred charges on the balance sheet.
3. You decide that an illegal act has occurred but you are unable to assess the potential consequences of the act.
4. The client's legal counsel is unable or unwilling to commit itself as to whether an act is illegal.
5. Top management refuses to take appropriate action concerning an illegal act that is not disclosed in the financial statement.

Required
a. Indicate the modification that should be made in the auditor's report for each circumstance.
b. Explain the steps that can or should be taken by the auditor when he believes an illegal act has occurred.
c. Indicate the extent of public disclosure, if any, that should be made by the auditor for illegal acts.

CASE STUDY

19–35.* Several years ago, Dale Holden organized Holden Family Restaurants. Holden started with one restaurant that catered to the family trade. Holden's first restaurant became very popular because the quality of the food and service was excellent, the restaurant was attractive yet modest, and the prices were reasonable.

The success with his first restaurant encouraged Dale Holden to expand by opening additional Holden Family Restaurants in other metropolitan locations throughout the state. Holden has opened at least one new restaurant each year for the last five years, and there are now a total of eight restaurants. All of the restaurants are successful because Holden has been able to maintain the same high standards that were achieved with the original restaurant.

With the rapid expansion of the business, Holden has hired a controller and supporting staff. The financial operations of the restaurants are managed by the controller and his department. This allows Holden to focus his attention on the restaurant operations and to plan for future locations.

Holden has applied to the bank for additional financing to open another restaurant this year. For the first time ever the bank asked him to provide financial statements audited by a CPA. The bank assured Holden that the certified statements were not being required because it doubted his integrity or thought him to be a poor credit risk. The loan officer explained that bank policy required all businesses over a certain size to supply audited statements with loan applications, and Holden's business had reached that size.

Holden was not surprised by the bank's requirement. He had ruled out an audit previously because he has great respect for his controller's ability, and he wanted to avoid the fee associated with the first audit as long as possible. However, the growth of his business and the increased number of restaurant locations make an audit a sound business requirement. He also believes that an additional benefit of the independent audit will be the probable detection of any fraud which may be occurring at his restaurants.

To fulfill the bank request for audited statements, Dale Holden has hired Hill & Associates, CPAs.

Required
a. Hill & Associates has been hired to perform an audit leading to the expression of an opinion on Holden Family Restaurants' financial statements. Discuss Hill & Associates' responsibilities for the review of internal control and the detection of fraud in a general-purpose audit.
b. What effect, if any, would the detection of fraud during the audit of Holden Family Restaurants by Hill & Associates have on their expression of an opinion on the financial statements? Give the reasons for your answer.

CMA

20

The Independent Accountant and the Securities and Exchange Commission

STUDY OBJECTIVES

The study objectives of this chapter are to acquire an understanding of the impact of the Securities and Exchange Commission and its impact on the independent accountant under the 1933 and 1934 Federal Securities Acts. In order to achieve these objectives, it is necessary for the reader to:

- Know the organizational structure of the SEC and the divisions and office that most directly affect the independent accountant (auditor).
- Be aware of the major types of SEC accounting related pronouncements.
- Be cognizant of the SEC's requirements pertaining to the qualifications of the independent accountant and his reports.
- Comprehend the auditor's responsibilities in the filing of registration statements under the Securities Act of 1933 and the Securities Exchange Act of 1934.
- Be familiar with the auditor's periodic and special reporting responsibilities under the Securities Exchange Act of 1934.
- Realize the enforcement proceedings that may be conducted by the SEC.

In the preceding chapter, the liability of the certified public accountant (CPA) under the securities acts is explained. It is the purpose of this chapter to describe the organization of the Securities and Exchange Commission (SEC), the impact it has on the day-to-day activities of independent CPAs who have clients that are subject to SEC regulations, and the principal financial reporting requirements of the Securities Act of 1933 (the 1933 Act) and the Securities Exchange Act of 1934 (the 1934 Act).

The discussion of the responsibilities of the CPA concerning filings under the federal securities acts is limited to accounting and auditing matters and is not intended to offer legal interpretations of the acts.

In the acts, the term *independent public accountant* is used to describe the individual who is required to perform the audit function. Technically, the individual need not be certified (he may be either a CPA or a public accountant), but, in practically all cases, the individual is a CPA. Throughout this chapter, the terms *independent public accountant* and *independent accountant* are considered to be synonymous with the term *auditor* used in previous chapters of this book.

Background of the SEC

The SEC was established by the 1934 Act as an independent federal regulatory agency to administer the federal securities acts. Both the SEC and the 1933 and 1934 Acts, which it administers, resulted from efforts by Congress to restore investor confidence in the securities markets which had been severely shaken during the depression. In the words of the SEC:

> Congress, in enacting the Federal Securities laws, created a continuous disclosure system designed to protect investors and to assure the maintenance of fair and honest securities markets. The Commission, in administering and implementing these laws, has sought to coordinate and integrate this disclosure system. . . . The legislative history of the Securities Act of 1933 indicates that the main concern of Congress was to provide full and fair disclosure in connection with the offer and sale of securities.[1]

The authority of the SEC extends to the offer and initial sale of the securities to the public and to the subsequent trading of such securities in national securities and over-the-counter markets. Thus, virtually all companies offering securities for sale to the public and all companies that have securities publicly traded are subject to the jurisdiction of the SEC. Currently, approximately 10,000 companies are registered with the SEC.

In administering the securities acts, the SEC does not pass upon the merit of a security, and federal laws do not prohibit the sale or trading of highly speculative securities provided their speculative characteristics or risks are disclosed in the filing with the Commission.

Information filed with the SEC generally is a matter of public record. In

---

[1] Securities and Exchange Commission, *SEC Docket* (Vol. 4, No. 5, May 7, 1974), p. 155.

addition, information previously considered to be confidential is now available to the general public under the Freedom of Information Act, commonly referred to as the Sunshine Act.

Organization of the SEC

The SEC is headed by a five-person commission appointed by the President of the United States with the approval of the U.S. Senate. Each commissioner serves for a five-year term with one member's term expiring each year. No more than three commissioners may be from the same political party. Traditionally, most appointees have been from the legal profession. One member of the Commission is designated as chairman by the President. The Commission directs a staff of about 2,000 that includes accountants, lawyers, securities analysts, engineers, examiners, and administrative and clerical personnel. The professional staff is organized into five divisions and numerous offices as illustrated in Figure 20-1. The independent accountant's involvement with the SEC is usually made through the Division of Corporation Finance and the Office of the Chief Accountant.

Division of Corporation Finance

The principal responsibility of this Division is to prevent (1) fraudulent offerings of securities to the public and (2) the distribution of incomplete, false, or misleading information pertaining to security offerings. In discharging its responsibility, this Division

- Assists the Commission in the establishment of standards of economic and financial information to be included in documents filed with the SEC.
- Enforces adherence to such standards by issuers, underwriters, and others with respect to securities offered for sale to the public or listed for trading on securities exchanges or in over-the-counter markets by reviewing and processing registration statements and periodic reports under the applicable securities acts.
- Prescribes and enforces the information to be included in proxy solicitations.
- Administers the disclosure requirements of the federal securities laws.
- Prepares Staff Accounting Bulletins (SABs) (see page 665) in conjunction with the Office of the Chief Accountant.

This Division also (1) drafts the rules, regulations, and forms to be used in filings with the SEC and (2) gives advice and answers inquiries pertaining to the application and interpretation of the statutes, and registration and reporting procedures.

Office of the Chief Accountant

The chief accountant is the SEC's principal expert adviser on all matters relating to accounting and auditing. The chief accountant

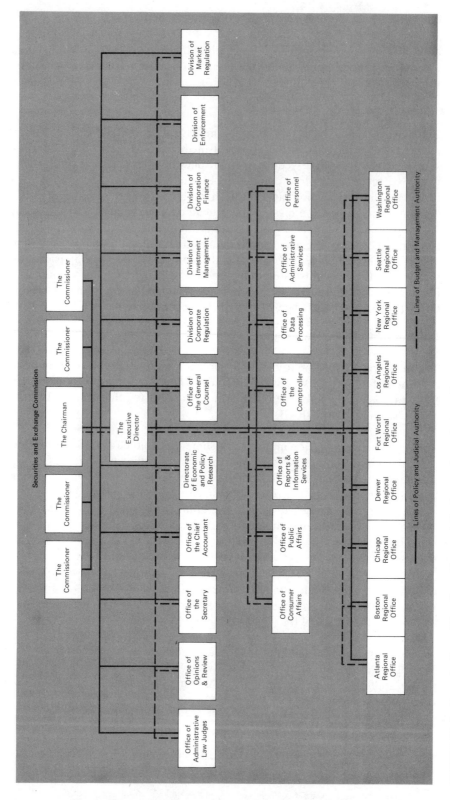

FIGURE 20–1. Organization of the Securities and Exchange Commission (SOURCE: Securities and Exchange Commission, *The Work of the Securities and Exchange Commission,* Washington, D.C.: U.S. Government Printing Office, 1978, p. iv.)

- Carries out SEC policy on accounting principles and the form and content of financial statements filed with it.
- Consults and rules on accounting questions from registrants and independent accountants.
- Directs administrative policy pertaining to accounting and auditing matters.
- Maintains liaison with accounting authorities, professional organizations, independent public accountants, and government officials.
- Participates in administrative and court proceedings involving accounting and auditing matters.
- Recommends to the Commission the taking of disciplinary action against accountants under the SEC's Rules of Practice.
- Considers cases on the independence and qualifications of independent accountants who practice before the SEC.
- Prepares Financial Reporting Releases (FRRs).
- Issues Accounting and Auditing Enforcement Releases (AAERs).
- Issues SABs in conjunction with the Division of Corporation Finance.

The chief accountant is in a position to exert substantial influence on the development of generally accepted accounting principles (GAAP) and generally accepted auditing standards (GAAS). There is no fixed term of office for the chief accountant.

Overview of the SEC's Reporting System

The SEC has the authority to prescribe the accounting and reporting requirements for companies under its jurisdiction. Throughout its history, however, the SEC has cooperated with the private sector in the development of GAAP and it has indicated that it

> intends to continue its policy of looking to the private sector for leadership in establishing and improving accounting principles and standards through the [Financial Accounting Standards Board] with the expectation that the body's conclusions will promote the interests of investors.[2]

The SEC's authority also generally extends to annual reports to shareholders that are issued by corporations, as well as to the periodic reports required under the 1934 Act and registration statements filed under the 1933 Act.

The SEC has identified a basic package of financial and other business information that is required to be disclosed by companies under its jurisdiction. Accordingly, many of the disclosures required for annual reports to shareholders and for filings under the 1933 or 1934 Acts are the same. Information included in a filing that has been made with the SEC usually may

---

[2] Financial Reporting Release No. 1, Section 101 (1982).

be incorporated by reference into a later filing if the same information is required again.

The SEC's reporting system is intended to serve both the average and the sophisticated investor. Certain of the disclosures required are intended to meet the needs of the average investor. In addition to being filed with the SEC, these disclosures must also be furnished to all present security holders or to any potential purchasers of the securities, as appropriate. Other disclosures are intended primarily for institutional investors, security analysts, or the sophisticated individual investor. This information is contained in the filing made by a company with the SEC. Generally, all information in filings made with the SEC is considered public information. Copies of any reported data may be obtained from the SEC at nominal cost.

For companies required to report to the SEC, the first step is to select the proper form for filing. Although the instructions for each form contain the rule or eligibility requirements for its use, it often is necessary for legal counsel to be consulted in making this determination. Once the form has been selected, additional instructions on the form identify the item number in the accounting pronouncements of the SEC that specify the business disclosures and financial reporting requirements that are to accompany the filing.

Types of Accounting Pronouncements

The SEC issues four major types of accounting-related pronouncements to be used by companies required to make filings and by their independent accountants. These are Regulation S-X, Regulation S-K, FRRs, and SABs. In addition, administrative rulings may affect the filing of financial statements. Nearly all the disclosure requirements under the 1933 and 1934 Acts are contained in these pronouncements.

Regulation S-X

Regulation S-X is the principal accounting regulation of the SEC. It covers the requirements for financial statements to be filed with the SEC. The instructions specify the required time periods and the form and content of financial statements, including the classification, presentation, and disclosure of material financial statement items. Regulation S-X is subject to amendments in response to changing conditions and the need for additional or less information by investors. Amendments are made by issuing FRRs.

In accordance with the SEC's policy of cooperating with the private sector, Regulation S-X contains an explicit requirement that the financial statements are to be prepared in accordance with generally accepted accounting principles. In a few instances, the financial statement disclosure requirements of the Regulation exceed the disclosure requirements under GAAP. These additional regulatory requirements are referred to as "compliance notes."

Regulation S-K

Regulation S-K is referred to as the uniform disclosure regulation. It covers the disclosure requirements for nonfinancial statement or text information required under the Act in the same manner that Regulation S-X prescribes the requirements for financial statements.

The Regulation has nine major sections. Some of the sections include instructions regarding disclosures about the company's business, securities, management, and financial information other than the financial statements. Another section covers the information to be provided about the securities being sold. The final section lists the SEC-prepared industry guides to be used by companies operating in specialized areas, such as those with oil and gas operations, bank holding companies, and real estate limited partnerships.

The particular items that are to be included in filings under Regulation S-K are indicated by the instructions accompanying the form to be filed. Inclusion of an item of information as prescribed under Regulation S-K is required only to the extent that the form governing a particular document specifically directs the inclusion of such information.

Financial Reporting Releases (FRRs)

The Commission has the authority to amend existing rules and regulations of the securities acts and to issue new ones. Notice of changes in accounting-related matters is made by publishing FRRs. These releases include:

- New disclosure requirements or specified accounting treatment for certain types of transactions.
- Opinions of the Commission on major accounting issues.
- Amendments to the financial statement requirements of various reporting forms.
- Clarification of existing rules and regulations, such as the rule on independence.

Releases on accounting and auditing matters are usually issued initially as proposals, and copies are distributed to various professional and other interested groups for their criticism and suggestions. Others also are invited to submit their views regarding a proposal. Experience demonstrates that the SEC carefully considers comments on the proposals before adopting any changes.

Staff Accounting Bulletins (SABs)

The Division of Corporation Finance and the Office of the Chief Accountant have the authority to issue SABs.[3] They are issued to provide guidance for handling events and transactions with similar accounting implications.

---

[3] In 1981 the SEC codified all relevant SABs in *Staff Accounting Bulletin No. 40.*

SABs are not rules or interpretations of the Commission, and they are not published as bearing the Commission's official approval. However, they are generally regarded as "interpretations" of Regulation S-X and GAAP. When a registrant and its independent accountant believe that due to its peculiar circumstances, the appropriate accounting should be different than would result from following the practice expressed in an SAB, the registrant is encouraged to discuss the specifics with the staff.

Administrative Rulings

Some of the SEC's accounting requirements are informal and are adopted administratively. Although such items may have general applicability to all registrants, they are not always publicized. In such case, the independent accountant may only learn of the Commission's position as a result of the SEC's review and related comments on a client's registration statement. There have been few administrative rulings since SABs were first issued.

Qualifications of Independent Accountants

Regulation S-X prescribes the qualifications of accountants as follows:

> (a) The Commission will not recognize any person as a certified public accountant who is not duly registered and in good standing as such under the laws of the place of his residence or principal office. The Commission will not recognize any person as a public accountant who is not in good standing and entitled to practice as such under the laws of the place of his residence or principal office.
> (b) The Commission will not recognize any certified public accountant or public accountant as independent who is not in fact independent.
> (c) In determining whether an accountant may in fact be not independent with respect to a particular person, the Commission will give appropriate consideration to all relevant circumstances, including evidence bearing on all relationships between the accountant and that person or any affiliate thereof, and will not confine itself to the relationships existing in connection with the filing of reports with the Commission.[4]

The SEC rules on independence closely parallel the AICPA's Rules of Conduct on independence (Rule 101), but there are exceptions. For example, the SEC will not consider the accountant independent if he provides any accounting services to an audit client. The SEC believes that such services automatically impair the accountant's independence, whereas the American Institute of Certified Public Accountants (AICPA) permits the rendering of accounting services to an audit client.

Requirements for Accountant's Reports

Regulation S-X also sets forth the standards of reporting for accountant's reports. The requirements are as follows

[4] SEC Regulation S-X, Rule 2-01.

(a) Technical requirements.—The accountant's report (1) shall be dated; (2) shall be signed manually; (3) shall indicate the city and state where issued; and (4) shall identify without detailed enumeration the financial statements covered by the report.

(b) Representations as to the audit.—The accountant's report (1) shall state whether the audit was made in accordance with generally accepted auditing standards; and (2) shall designate any auditing procedures deemed necessary by the accountant under the circumstances of the particular case, which have been omitted, and the reasons for their omission.
Nothing in this rule shall be construed to imply authority for the omission of any procedure which independent accountants would ordinarily employ in the course of an audit made for the purpose of expressing the opinions required by paragraph (c) of this rule.

(c) Opinion to be expressed.—The accountant's report shall state clearly: (1) the opinion of the accountant in respect of the financial statements covered by the report and the accounting principles and practices reflected therein; and (2) the opinion of the accountant as to the consistency of the application of the accounting principles, or as to any changes in such principles which have a material effect on the financial statements.

(d) Exceptions.—Any matters to which the accountant takes exception shall be clearly identified, the exception thereto specifically and clearly stated, and, to the extent practicable, the effect of each such exception on the related financial statements given. (See FRR No. 1 Section 101.)[5]

From the foregoing, it can be seen that the responsibility of the independent accountant resulting from the inclusion of his report on financial statements in a filing under the securities acts is in substance essentially the same as that involved in reporting on audited financial statements in Chapter 16 of this text.

Pursuant to Rule 2-02, the SEC will not accept (1) an adverse opinion or (2) a qualified opinion on audited financial statements except when the qualification pertains to an inconsistency or an uncertainty.

As in the case of financial statements used for other purposes, management has the responsibility for the assertions made in financial statements filed under the federal securities statutes.

Registration of Securities

Registration is a major part of all the acts administered by the SEC. The primary purpose of registration is to provide prospective investors with financial and other information concerning the company and its securities being offered for public sale. The reporting standard in a registration statement is disclosure of all material facts needed by investors to appraise the merits of the securities.

---

[5] SEC Regulation S-X, Rule 2-02.

Registration does not insure investors against loss in their purchase nor does it guarantee the accuracy of all the information presented. Moreover, the SEC does not pass on the merits of the securities or have the authority to disapprove a registration because securities lack merit. The Commission has the power to deny registration when disclosures are incomplete, inaccurate, and/or misleading. In addition, the federal securities acts prohibit false and misleading information under penalty of fine, or imprisonment, or both.

All data contained in a registration are kept by the SEC and are available to the general public. Securities cannot be sold until the registration is accepted by the SEC and the registration becomes effective.

Registration is a time-consuming, complex, and expensive undertaking. This is especially true the first time a privately owned company decides to "go public" with its equity securities. In a recent year, approximately 4,300 registration statements for securities valued at $144 billion were filed with the SEC.[6]

Review of Registration Statements

The SEC's review process is designed to ascertain compliance with the securities laws or, conversely, to detect materially untrue, incomplete, or misleading information in the filing of registration statements. Reviews are made by the Division of Corporation Finance.

A review may be complete or limited, based on an initial evaluation of the registration by the staff. The SEC's practice is to do a complete review of only certain filings, including:

- Initial public offerings under the Securities Act of 1933.
- Initial registration statements under the Securities Exchange Act of 1934.

Other filings may be reviewed only on a sample basis. In some instances, registration statements of established companies may be allowed to become effective with no staff review.

In the case of a complete review, the examination of the registration statement is made by a team consisting of a financial analyst, an attorney, and an accountant. Memoranda are submitted by each reviewer, which culminate in a "letter of comments" (generally known as a *deficiency letter*) that is sent to the registrant for required amendments to the registration statement and other appropriate action.

If the prospective registrant is unwilling or unable to eliminate the deficiencies in its original filing, the SEC has three courses of action:

- *Allow the statement to become effective in a deficient manner.* This is rarely done because it is contrary to the SEC's objective of protecting the investor, and its exposes the issuing company to possible lawsuits.
- *Issue a refusal order.* This action has been used sparingly because the

[6] Securities and Exchange Commission, *Annual Report 1981,* p. 140.

order must be issued within ten days of the filing and a hearing must be held during the next ten days to allow for correction.

- *Issue a stop order.* This action halts further consideration of the registration statement if issued before the effective date. Alternatively, it halts further trading of the security if it is issued after the effective date.

These actions ordinarily are not needed since most companies act promptly to correct any deficiencies in the filing.

The Registration Process

The registration process involves a number of participants including the board of directors, representatives of management (usually the president and/or vice president of finance), legal counsel, a lead underwriter (i.e., an investment brokerage firm that assumes responsibility for selling the securities), the independent accountant, and company accountants. An illustrative timetable and specific steps in the registration process are presented in Figure 20-2. The example assumes an issue of common stock by a company that has a fiscal year ending December 31.

The foregoing are specifically applicable to the 1933 Act but also have general applicability to registrations under other acts.

The Securities Act of 1933

The 1933 Act pertains to the initial offer and distribution of securities to the public. Often referred to as the *truth in securities* law, the Act has two basic objectives:

- To provide investors with material financial and other information concerning securities offered for public sale.
- To prohibit misrepresentation, deceit, and other fraudulent acts and practices in the sale of securities generally (whether or not required to be registered).[7]

Registration Under the 1933 Act

Registration under the 1933 Act consists of preparing and filing a registration statement with the SEC. The registration statement consists of two parts: a prospectus and other detailed information.

A *prospectus* is a separate booklet or pamphlet, given to prospective purchasers of the security, that describes the company and the securities offered. The prospectus includes all information to be presented to prospective investors. Part II of the registration statement contains ancillary information, including expenses of issuance and distribution, indemnification of directors and officers, and certain exhibits and financial statement schedules. Part II is

---

[7] Securities and Exchange Commission, *The Work of the Securities and Exchange Commission* (Washington, D.C.: U.S. Government Printing Office, 1974), p. 1.

June 1	Board of directors authorizes filing of registration statement and notifies independent auditors, lawyers, and under-writer(s) of the pending filing
June 5	Management meets with underwriters and tentative agreement is reached concerning sale of securities
June 15	Management, independent accountant, and legal counsel have prefiling conference with SEC staff in Washington, D.C.
June 20	Management and legal counsel select appropriate registration form
June 25-July 25	Data for registration are collected by company accountants, reviewed by lawyers, and reviewed and/or audited by independent accountants
July 28	Management prepares draft of registration statement and obtains board of directors approval
August 1	Management finalizes registration statement, which is filed with SEC by legal counsel
August 15	Management receives letter of comment from SEC concerning deficiencies and necessary adjustments
September 5	Management prepares amendments which are responsive to SEC's comments—these are filed with SEC by legal counsel
September 7	Due diligence meeting is held to review registration statement and other matters affecting sale of issue—this meeting is primarily for the benefit of the underwriter(s) and is attended by management, legal counsel, the independent accountant, and underwriter(s)
September 10	SEC notifies management by phone of acceptance of registration statement
September 11	Management approves offering price of securities and the agreement with underwriter(s) for sale of the stock is finalized
September 12	Legal counsel files amendment to registration statement for offering price—registration statement becomes effective 5:00 P.M.
September 17	Underwriter transfers net proceeds of issue to issuer

FIGURE 20-2. Registration Process Timetable

required to be filed only with the SEC, although the information is available to interested investors upon request.

There are three primary forms used by most companies in filings under the 1933 Act. The choice of form depends on the size of the company and the period of time it has been subject to the SEC's periodic reporting requirements.

- *Form S-3* is an abbreviated filing that incorporates by reference information that is available in previous reports filed with the SEC. It is intended for use by large companies that are widely followed by financial analysts.
- *Form S-2* is designed for use by companies that have been subject to the

periodic reporting requirements of the SEC for at least three years, but are not as widely followed by analysts. An S-2 filing may include only the information required for an S-3 filing, provided the company delivers its latest annual report to all potential investors. If the annual report is not included, then this information must be in the filing. Financial information for the most recent quarter also must be provided.

- *Form S-1* is used by companies that do not fit other categories.

Form S-1 is the most widely used under this Act, and it is the most comprehensive. The principal financial information requirements under this form are explained below.

Business Disclosures

Form S-1 requires disclosure of a considerable amount of information about the company and its business. These disclosures, which are described in Regulation S-K, include items such as the following:

- History and description of the business (including industry segments and foreign operations).
- Description of properties.
- Background information about directors and executive officers, including their security holdings, remuneration, and material pending legal proceedings to which management is a party.
- Description of the securities being registered, including details of any underwriting arrangements, an estimate of the net proceeds, and the uses to which such proceeds will be put.

Financial Statements

Financial statements must be presented for the issuing company in one of the following forms:

- Financial statements for the company itself, if it has no subsidiaries which must be consolidated.
- Consolidated financial statements only, unless it is necessary to include "separate parent company" statements on a supplemental schedule.

In addition, under some circumstances, the issuer may have to present financial statements for (1) unconsolidated subsidiaries and 50 percent or less owned companies accounted for under the equity method, and (2) affiliated companies whose securities are pledged as collateral for debt securities that are being registered.

Balance sheets. Audited balance sheets must be filed as of the end of each of the two preceding fiscal years. In addition, the general rule is that the filing must include a balance sheet as of an interim date within 135 days of the date of the filing if the most recent audited balance sheet does not fall within this period. The interim balance sheet may be in condensed form and need not be audited.

Other statements. An income statement must be filed for each of the three fiscal years preceding the date of the latest fiscal year-end balance sheet filed, and for the period, if any, between the close of the latest fiscal year and the date of the latest balance sheet filed. The statements of retained earnings, changes in financial position, and changes in stockholders' equity must be filed for the same periods as the income statement. All statements relating to the three fiscal years must be audited; comparative statements covering the period from the latest fiscal year to the date of the latest balance sheet may be in condensed form and need not be audited.

Selected Financial Data

Form S-1 requires a five-year summary of selected financial data. This requirement is intended to present significant trend data relating both to an enterprise's financial condition and to its results of operations. Elements from the company's balance sheet and income statement that must be presented include the following:

- Net sales or operating revenues.
- Income (loss) from continuing operations.
- Income (loss) from continuing operations per common share.
- Total assets.
- Long-term obligations (including capital leases) and redeemable preferred stock.
- Cash dividends declared per common share.

If the company is required by the Financial Accounting Standards Board to present a five-year summary of the effects of inflation and changing prices, this information may be presented under this caption. Alternatively, it may be presented as supplementary financial information. Figure 20-3 shows a five-year summary of selected financial data. A discussion of the factors that materially affect the comparability of the selected financial data also should be included.

Management's Discussion and Analysis of Financial Condition and Results of Operations

This section is intended to provide a meaningful analysis of significant changes in financial condition and results of operations. The discussion must cover the three years presented in the audited financial statements and the statements for any interim period. When trends are discussed, reference has to be made to the five years of selected financial data, as appropriate. The discussion must include at least the following aspects of the business:

Chris-Craft Industries, Inc. and Subsidiaries
Five Year Summary of Selected Financial Data
(In Thousands of Dollars Except per Share Data)

As of and for the years ended August 31,

	1981	1980	1979	1978	1977
Operating revenues	$ 64,982	$ 55,009	$ 49,731	$ 42,831	$ 37,646
Operating income	$ 10,311	$ 10,509	$ 11,655	$ 9,536	$ 8,769
Equity income	1,640	3,324	2,116	1,451	494
Other expense, net	(4,607)	(7,562)	(3,163)	(526)	(1,993)
Income taxes	(2,525)	(1,825)	(4,350)	(4,375)	(3,660)
Income from continu- ing operations	$ 4,819	$ 4,446	$ 6,258	$ 6,086	$ 3,610
Income from continuing operations per share—					
Primary	$ 1.25	$ 1.15	$ 1.49	$ 1.08	$ .52
Fully diluted	1.07	.99	1.22	.94	*
Cash and marketable sec- urities	$109,062	$ 12,502	$ 15,582	$ 20,982	$ 7,364
Total assets	214,557	161,443	145,743	122,391	125,053
Working Capital	99,326	24,482	25,474	30,835	48,400
Long-term debt	68,442	72,386	48,291	23,525	20,357

* Amount not presented as it is antidilutive.

FIGURE 20–3. Five-year Summary of Selected Financial Data

- The company's liquidity, capital resources, and results of operations.
- Favorable or unfavorable trends, significant uncertainties, and unusual or infrequent events and their possible effects.
- Causes of material changes in the financial statements.
- Narrative discussion of the effects of inflation and changing prices.

The discussion of liquidity and capital resources should deal with available sources of funds and the company's expected short- and long-term requirements. Trend information on cash flow from operations may be included, together with plans to deal with any insufficiency of funds from internal sources or changed circumstances.

At its option, the company also may include forward-looking information. This may be in the form of formal financial forecasts or simply information that may be useful to those who wish to work out a forecast of future operating results.

Independent Accountant's Involvement in Registrations Under 1933 Act

The independent accountant is an active participant in the registration process. His major responsibilities are to:

- Make an examination of the financial statements in accordance with GAAS.
- Read any unaudited condensed financial statements included therein for matters that might require disclosure in the audited financial statements.
- Read the entire registration statement for data that may be materially inconsistent with the financial statements or be a material misstatement of fact.
- Perform a subsequent events review up to the effective date of the registration statement.
- Issue a comfort letter to underwriters.

Audited Financial Statements

The audit of the financial statements included in a registration is the same as the examination of any financial statements prepared in conformity with GAAP. Accordingly, the ten GAAS and the audit procedures described in previous chapters of this book are applicable.

Unaudited Financial Statements

When unaudited financial statements for an interim period are included with audited financial statements, the independent accountant who made the examination is associated with the unaudited statements. The independent accountant's responsibilities for the interim statements are basically the same as described in Chapter 17 for other unaudited financial statements. However, in an SEC registration, the accountant should consider withholding consent to the use of his report on audited financial statements, if the client is unwilling to revise the unaudited statements to conform with GAAP.[8]

Other Data

The independent accountant is required to read the nonfinancial data in the prospectus and the other detailed information in the registration statement. The independent accountant is not expected to perform any auditing procedures on the data. The primary objective is to determine whether there are any material inconsistencies or statements in the text that contradict data relied on in preparing the financial statements included in the registration. When such instances are found, the independent accountant should see that appropriate revision is made.

---

[8] Auditing Standards Board, *Codification of Statements on Auditing Standards* (New York: American Institute of Certified Public Accountants, 1983), Auditing Section 711.13 (Hereinafter referred to and cited as AU §).

Subsequent Events Review

The independent accountant's statutory liability under the 1933 Act extends to the circumstances existing as of the effective date of the registration statement. Specifically, the accountant is required to make a "reasonable investigation" and have "reasonable grounds" as to the fairness of the financial statements included in a registration up to the effective date of the filing.[9] To provide proof of a "reasonable investigation," the accountant should extend the subsequent events procedures described in Chapter 15 up to the effective date or as close thereto as possible.

In addition, the accountant should

- Read the entire prospectus and other pertinent parts of the registration statement.
- Inquire of and obtain written confirmation from officers and other executives having responsibility for financial and accounting matters (limited where appropriate to major locations) as to whether there have occurred any events other than those reflected or disclosed in the registration statement which, in the officers' or other executives' opinion, have a material effect on the audited financial statements included therein or which should be disclosed in order to keep those statements from being misleading.[10]

The performance of these procedures is facilitated when the client keeps the accountant informed during the progress of the registration proceedings. The subsequent events review described above is referred to as an S-1 review. This is not an accurate description, as the same review applies to other registration forms under the 1933 Act. This review was one of the key issues in the *BarChris* case discussed in Chapter 19. In the registration schedule shown in Figure 20-2, the S-1 review would extend from the date of the audit report through September 12, the effective date of the registration statement.

Letters for Underwriters

As indicated earlier in the chapter, an underwriting agreement is common in the issuance of securities under the securities acts. This agreement is a contract between the underwriter(s) and the issuer of the securities. Typically, the provisions of an underwriting agreement provide for a comfort letter from the independent accountant. The letter is so named because it is designed to give comfort (assurance) to underwriters that the financial and accounting data not covered by the independent accountant's opinion on the audited financial statements included in a prospectus are (1) in compliance with the Securities Act of 1933 and (2) in conformity with GAAP, consistently applied. Underwriters seek this comfort in the form of negative

---

[9] Securities Act of 1933 § 11(b).
[10] Auditing Standards Board, *op. cit.,* AU § 711.10.

assurance as a due diligence (or reasonable investigation) defense against possible legal claims under the Act. Comfort letters are not required under the 1933 Act, and copies of such letters are not filed with the SEC. The rendering of this type of letter should be based on an agreement between the underwriter and the independent accountant. A comfort letter involves a limited review by the independent accountant of data requested by the underwriter rather than an audit. The review permits the expression of negative assurance, but not an opinion.

In a comfort letter engagement, the underwriter specifies the limited review procedures and takes responsibility for the adequacy of the procedures to be performed by the accountant. Normally, these procedures include

- Reading the minutes of stockholder and board of directors meetings since the date of his report on the audited statements.
- Inquiring of company officials.
- Reading unaudited financial statements.

A comfort letter generally will refer to one or more of the following:

- The independence of the accountants.
- Compliance as to form in all material respects of the audited financial statements and schedules with the applicable accounting requirements of the Act and the published rules and regulations thereunder.
- Unaudited financial statements or condensed financial statements included in the registration statement.
- Changes in selected financial statement items during a period subsequent to the date and period of the latest financial statements in the registration statement.
- Tables, statistics, and other financial information in the registration statements.[11]

Based on his audit, the accountant should be able to express an opinion on compliance with SEC requirements. However, the CPA's comments on unaudited financial statements and other data should be in the form of negative assurance (i.e., nothing came to the accountant's attention that caused him to believe the specified data does not meet a specified standard). The review procedures should be enumerated together with a statement that they do not constitute an examination made in accordance with GAAS and would not necessarily reveal matters of significance on items on which negative assurance has been given.

The comfort letter should conclude with the caveat that the letter is solely for the use of the underwriter in connection with the specified security issue under the Act, and that it is not to be used, circulated, quoted, or otherwise referred to, for any other purpose.[12]

[11] Auditing Standards Board, *op. cit.,* AU § 631.06.
[12] Illustrative comfort letters are presented in Auditing Standards Board, *op. cit.,* AU § 631.49-.56.

Accountant's Report Under 1933 Act Registrations

The Securities Act imposes a variety of reporting requirements on the independent accountant when he is associated with a registration statement. The major circumstances are explained below.

Reports on Financial Statements

The accountant's report on the audited financial statements included in a registration statement is, for all practical purposes, identical with the auditor's standard report described in Chapter 16. The report must cover the two years of balance sheets and the three years of statements of income and changes in financial position that are included. In addition, the accountant reports on certain supporting schedules.

Accountant's Consent

The 1933 Act provides that "if any accountant is named as having prepared or certified any part of the registration . . . the written consent of such person shall be filed with the registration."[13] In addition, the Act requires consent to the use of the accountant's name as an expert.[14] These requirements are met by issuing a letter of consent, as illustrated in Figure 20-4. The letter of consent should be made only when a "reasonable investigation" has been made of the data to which the consent refers. The accountant's reasonable investigation must be premised upon an audit; it cannot be accomplished short of an audit.[15] Thus, the expertizing declaration should be limited to the financial presentations covered by the accountant's certificate.

If the accountant has reported on unaudited financial information included in a registration statement, a second letter, known as a *letter of acknowledgement*, must be included. Although the accountant does not have a responsibility for a report on unaudited information within the meaning of Section 11 of the 1933 Act, the SEC nevertheless requests that the

---

To the Board of Directors of Illustrative Company:

We consent to the reference to our firm under the caption "Selected Financial Data" and "Experts" and to the use of our reports dated _____ in the Registration Statement (Form S-1) and related Prospectus of the Illustrative Company in the registration of 1,000,000 shares of its common stock.

_____
CPA's Signature

FIGURE 20-4. Accountant's Consent

[13] Securities Act of 1933 § 7.
[14] Securities Act of 1933 § 11(b)(3)(B).
[15] Auditing Standards Board, *op. cit.,* AU § 631.02.

accountant acknowledge awareness of the use of such a report in a separate letter included in the filing.[16]

Certain kinds of securities offerings are exempt from the requirement for registration under the 1933 Act. These include offerings of governmental units, offerings sold intrastate, and "private placements." An abbreviated registration statement, Regulation A, is available for certain offerings not exceeding $1,500,000. Further, certain other offerings are governed by special provisions.

The Securities Exchange Act of 1934

The 1934 Act is known as the *continuous disclosure act*. It provides for both the registration of securities and the filing of annual and other periodic reports to keep current the data in the original filing. This Act originally applied to the public trading of securities on national securities exchanges. Through the enactment of a subsequent amendment to the securities acts, the provisions of the 1934 Act also apply to equity securities of companies traded over-the-counter when company assets exceed $3 million and shareholders number 500 or more. In general, transactions in securities which are consummated other than on a national exchange are said to be traded over the counter.

The scope of the Securities Exchange Act extends to (1) proxy solicitations, (2) tender offer solicitations, (3) insider trading, (4) margin trading, (5) market surveillance, and (6) registration of exchanges and broker dealers. These aspects of the 1934 Act are beyond the scope of this book.

Registration Under the 1934 Act

Before trading can occur on a national securities exchange, companies must file a registration application with both the exchange and the SEC. A similar registration form must be filed with the SEC for over-the-counter trading when the foregoing size test is met. The financial and other data prescribed under a 1934 Act registration generally are identical with that required in a 1933 Act registration. However, there is no provision for the dissemination of the registration statement to investors through a prospectus or similar medium. Instead, the information is available for public inspection at the offices of the SEC and the exchanges.

Under the 1934 Act, an entire class of securities can be registered for trading at one time with no amount specified. Thus, the number of registrations is significantly fewer under this Act than under the 1933 Act. A variety of registration forms are prescribed under the Act. Form 10 (not to be confused with annual reporting Form 10-K, which is discussed later) is the most commonly used form. It is required when no other form applies.

Information to be filed in a listing application with an exchange may differ from SEC requirements. The New York Stock Exchange (NYSE), for

---

[16] Auditing Standards Board, *op. cit.*, AU § 711.09.

example, requires a 10-year earnings summary. The requirements of an exchange are not a substitute for the SEC requirements or vice versa.

The involvement of the independent accountant in the registration process under the 1934 Act is similar to the involvement in 1933 Act registrations.

Annual Reporting Under the 1934 Act

The 1934 Act provides for continuous reporting by the registrant of "adequate and accurate disclosure of material facts" to investors because the securities may be actively traded for many years.[17] Such disclosure does not guarantee the worth or establish the value of any security. The foregoing disclosure requirement is met through annual, quarterly, and special reports.

Form 10-K is the general report form to be used by companies when no other report form is authorized or prescribed. The purpose of a Form 10-K filing is to provide an annual update of the data included in the registration statement. The information in Form 10-K is organized in four parts:

Part I. Description of the business, properties, legal proceedings, and matters voted on by security holders during the fourth quarter.
Part II. Financial statements, selected financial data, management's discussion and analysis, and certain information about the market for the company's stock.
Part III. Information about the directors and officers of the company, compensation, any transactions with the company, and security ownership of certain beneficial owners and management.
Part IV. Exhibits, financial statement schedules, and other data.

The requirements for audited financial statements, selected financial data, and management's discussion and analysis are the same as those described under 1933 Act filings.

The SEC's regulations further prescribe that certain of the information in Form 10-K must be included in the annual report issued by the corporation to its shareholders. This requirement applies to a portion of the information about the business in Part I and all the information in Part II. The information in Part III may be provided separately to shareholders in a proxy or information statement. The remaining information in Part IV is required only in the filing with the SEC.

By requiring that only certain information on Form 10-K be provided directly to stockholders, the SEC is recognizing that not all financial statement users are interested in the detailed information that is provided. Some corporations voluntarily include all Form 10-K information in their annual reports. When this is not done, there must be a statement in the annual report that a copy of Form 10-K is available, without charge, to any shareholder on request. Conversely, all information in an annual report may not

[17] Securities Exchange Act of 1934 Rule 12b-23.

be included in a Form 10-K report. The president's letter, financial high-lights, and graphic analysis of financial data are among the excluded items. The SEC regulations assure that owners of the company's securities receive at least basic financial information about the company.

The time constraints on the filing of Form 10-K often are demanding on both the company and the independent accountant. Parts I and II and a portion of Part IV of Form 10-K must be filed with the SEC within 90 days of the company's year-end. The remaining information may be filed separately and is due within 120 days. Few extensions of time are granted.

Quarterly Reporting Under the 1934 Act

A registrant under the 1934 Act is required to keep investors and other interested parties informed of interim changes in its operations and financial position by submitting quarterly reports to the SEC. In making its report, the registrant uses Form 10-Q, which must be filed within 45 days after the end of each of the first three quarters of each fiscal year. The annual report covers the entire year's operations. Form 10-Q contains two major accounting requirements: (1) interim financial information (IFI) and (2) an accountant's letter on the preferability of changes in accounting principles.

Interim Financial Information

Form 10-Q requires condensed financial statements, management's analysis of financial conditions and results of operations, and certain other information. The IFI is to be prepared in accordance with GAAP applied on a consistent basis.

The SEC does not require that IFI be either audited or reviewed by an independent accountant. However, companies that meet certain trading and size tests must show quarterly revenues, gross profit, net income, and earnings per share data as supplemental information in the annual financial statements. The supplemental information must be reviewed by the independent accountant. For these companies, the question is whether to have quarterly reviews or to have only an annual review of interim financial information. Many companies elect the former to avoid year-end embarrassment or potentially more serious consequences if changes in quarterly data are needed.

When a review has been made of IFI, the accountant's report should be included as an exhibit to the filing.

Changes in Accounting Principles

Registrants must report any change in accounting principles or practices or change in the method of applying them that will materially affect the financial statements filed or to be filed in the current year. This requirement must be met in the first Form 10-Q filed subsequent to the date of the accounting change.

Regardless of whether the independent accountant has reviewed interim financial information in a Form 10-Q filing, Regulation S-X requires:

. . .

[I]n the first Form 10-Q filed subsequent to the date of an accounting change, a letter from the registrant's independent accountants indicating whether any change . . . is to an alternative principle that in his judgment is preferable in the circumstances. Except that no letter from the accountant needs to be filed when the change is made in response to a standard adopted by the Financial Accounting Standards Board . . .

Thus, a preferability letter must be sent to the client to file as an exhibit to Form 10-Q. The wording of the accountant's letter should state:

In our opinion, the change in accounting principle described in Note X is preferable in your circumstances.

SAB 40 contains guidance to assist the independent accountant in meeting this requirement.

Special Reporting Under the 1934 Act

The SEC requires companies under the jurisdiction of this statute to file special reports when certain material corporate events have occurred. The reporting is done on Form 8-K and the report must be filed within 15 days after the occurrence of a material corporate event. The following are illustrative of events that should be considered for inclusion in a Form 8-K filing:

- Changes in control of the company.
- Major acquisitions and disposals of assets.
- Bankruptcy or receivership.
- Changes in the company's independent accountant.
- Resignation of the company directors.

A company is also expected to report any other significant events, such as losses from fire, flood, and so on, within a reasonable time after their occurrence. Form 8-K does not have a specific format but is a narrative report that gives the registrant considerable flexibility in reporting.

Form 8-K requires the registrant to submit written statements on any auditor changes. Auditor changes must be reported when the principal accountant resigns, declines to stand for reelection, or is dismissed, as well as when a new auditor is engaged. In addition, any changes in other auditors of significant subsidiaries or divisions relied on by the principal auditor must be reported. The report must state whether there were any disagreements with the former auditor during the audits of the last two fiscal years and subsequent interim period on any matter of (1) accounting principles, (2) financial statement disclosure, or (3) auditing scope or procedure, which would have caused the auditors to make reference in expressing their opinion to the subject matter of the disagreement regardless of whether the disagreement was resolved to the auditors' satisfaction.

The former auditor must also furnish the registrant with a letter, addressed to the SEC, stating whether he agrees with the statements made by the registrant, and if not, the reasons therefor. The general form of the auditor's letter is illustrated in Figure 20-5. During the first four and one-half years of this requirement, there were 1,667 auditor changes.[18]

Enforcement of the Securities Acts

As indicated in Chapter 19, the SEC has the authority to initiate legal actions against independent accountants for violations of the securities acts. Through its Division of Enforcement, the SEC also has the authority to impose sanctions against independent accountants through administrative proceedings.

Injunctive Proceedings

The SEC has the authority under both the 1933 and the 1934 Acts to initiate injunctive proceedings in the courts to restrain future violations of the provisions of these Acts. In addition to stopping the unacceptable practice, an injunction seeks assurances that future actions will be in compliance with the securities acts. The effect of an injunction may be damaging to a defen-

---

June 25, 19X1

Securities and Exchange Commission
Washington, D.C. 20549

To the Commissioners of the SEC:

We were previously principal accountants for Illustrative Company and, under date of March 15, 19X1, we reported on the consolidated financial statements of the Company and consolidated subsidiaries as of and for the two years ended December 31, 19X0. On June 10, 19X1, we resigned [or we declined to stand for reelection—or our appointment as principal accountants was terminated]. We have read Illustrative Company's statements included under Item 4 of its Form 8-K dated June 25, 19X1 and we agree with such statements.

Yours truly,

Reddy & Abel
Reddy & Abel

FIGURE 20-5. Letter of Agreement Concerning Change of Auditors

[18] *The CPA Letter* (New York: American Institute of Certified Public Accountants, November 21, 1976).

dant in subsequent civil suits for damages, and it may expose the person(s) enjoined to criminal action.

The conditions under which the SEC will bring injunctive proceedings were generalized by an SEC chairman as follows:

> Put very simply, when the Commission discerns that the auditor has not been alert to his duty, that he has gone through an exercise by rote or that he has not been true to the duty of fair presentation, then in my estimation, the Commission should properly authorize an action to enjoin the accountant from a repetition of those faults.[19]

An injunction must be issued by a court of law. The SEC has consistently maintained that ordinary negligence is sufficient to support an injunctive action.

Administrative Proceedings

Sanctions against auditors may be brought under the SEC's Administrative Rule 2(e), which states that

> *the Commission may disqualify and deny, temporarily or permanently, the privilege of appearing or practicing before it* to any accountant who is found by the Commission . . . (1) not to possess the requisite qualifications to represent others, (2) to be lacking in character or integrity, (3) to have engaged in unethical or improper professional conduct, (4) to have willfully violated, or willfully aided and abetted the violation of any provision of the federal securities laws.[20]

In addition, the Commission may suspend from appearing or practicing before it an auditor who has been (1) "convicted of a felony, or a misdemeanor involving moral turpitude," (2) the subject of a revocation or suspension of his license to practice, (3) "permanently enjoined . . . from violation . . . of any provision of the federal securities laws," or (4) "found by any court . . . or found by this Commission in any administrative proceeding . . . to have violated . . . any provision of the federal securities laws . . . (unless the violation was found not to have been willful)."

The SEC has imposed the following innovative sanctions against auditors under Rule 2(e):

- Peer reviews and inspections of accounting firms to determine the extent of compliance with professional and firm auditing standards and procedures.
- Restrictions for specified periods against mergers with other firms.
- Prohibitions for specified periods against undertaking new engagements likely to result in filings with the SEC.

---

[19] A. A. Sommer, Jr., "Accountants: A Flexible Standard," *Litigation* (Winter 1975), pp. 35-39.

[20] *Ibid.*

- Requirements to develop and implement auditing procedures for certain types of transactions.
- Imposition of continuing education programs.

These sanctions are viewed by one commissioner as being neither punitive nor retributive but rather as providing assurance that the possibility of recurrence of specific problems caused by pervasive control deficiencies will be reduced.[21]

Rule 2(e) proceedings are public unless the SEC, on its own motion or at the request of a party, should direct otherwise. All known Rule 2(e) proceedings have involved consent decrees. Consent decrees are negotiated settlements in which the SEC publishes only the settlement and the CPA firm neither denies nor admits guilt.

CONCLUDING COMMENTS

The SEC has had a profound influence on the public accounting profession, accounting firms, and individual CPAs. In the exercise of its regulatory powers, the SEC has maintained direct interaction with such groups as the Financial Accounting Standards Board and the AICPA's Auditing Standards Board in the development of GAAP and GAAS. A number of the Statements on Auditing Standards, for example, were initiated by new disclosure requirements of the SEC.

The provisions of the federal securities acts administered by the SEC have significantly affected the day-to-day practice of accounting firms and independent public accountants. Moreover, these statutes establish the basis for both civil and criminal actions against independent accountants.

Based upon its record to date and its ongoing responsibility to provide investors with reliable financial data, it appears likely that the SEC will continue to have a significant influence on the accounting profession and independent accountants.

REVIEW QUESTIONS

20–1.   How extensive is the SEC's authority over the public sale of securities?
20–2.   Describe the responsibilities and primary functions of the Division of Corporation Finance.
20–3.   Enumerate the principal duties of the Chief Accountant.
20–4.   Identify and briefly describe the types of authoritative pronouncements issued by the SEC.
20–5.   List the specific types of information included in Regulation S-K and Financial Reporting Releases.
20–6.   Briefly describe the SEC's rules concerning (a) qualifications of independent accountants and (b) accountant's reports.
20–7.   The registration of securities is designed to insure investors against loss. Do you agree or disagree? Why?

[21] Sommer, *op. cit.,* p. 37.

20–8.   a. Describe the complete review that is made of a registration statement.
      b. Indicate the courses of action the SEC may take when an original filing is deficient.
20–9.   Identify the steps in the registration process that occur after the registration statement is filed with the Commission.
20–10.   a. What are the two basic objectives of the Securities Act of 1933?
      b. Distinguish between a registration statement and a prospectus.
20–11.   Enumerate the basic information that is common to registrations under the 1933 Act.
20–12.   Describe the basic types of financial data required under the 1933 Act, including the time period covered and whether the data must be audited.
20–13.   Identify the major responsibilities of the accountant in a 1933 Act registration.
20–14.   a. What is an S-1 Review?
      b. What specific steps are required in making an S-1 Review?
20–15.   a. What procedures are generally required in a comfort letter engagement?
      b. What is included in a comfort letter?
20–16.   Identify the four categories of data required in a Form 10-K filing and what data, if any, must be audited.
20–17.   Briefly explain the two major accounting requirements in filing quarterly reports under the 1934 Act.
20–18.   a. What data are required in a Form 8-K filing?
      b. What information must be submitted in regard to auditor changes?
20–19.   Distinguish between injunctive and administrative proceedings in enforcement of the securities acts.
20–20.   a. What sanctions may be imposed under Rule 2(e)?
      b. What sanctions have been used under this rule?

COMPREHENSIVE QUESTIONS

20–21.   Four types of accounting-related pronouncements are issued by the SEC: (1) Regulation S-X, Regulation S-K, *Financial Reporting Releases* (FRRs), and *Staff Accounting Bulletins* (SABs). Listed below are statements that relate to one of the four pronouncements.

1. Contains accounting provisions that closely parallel GAAP.
2. Includes opinions of the Commission on major accounting issues.
3. Contains guidance for handling events and transactions with similar accounting interpretations.
4. Pertains to disclosure of management remuneration.
5. Contains disclosure requirements that may exceed GAAP.
6. Sets forth the results of disciplinary proceedings against accountants.
7. Requires disclosure of material pending legal proceedings to which management is a party.
8. Provides clarification of existing rules and regulations.
9. Requires disclosure of securities holdings of management.
10. Includes amendments to financial statements requirements of various forms.

Required
a. Describe briefly the nature of the four pronouncements and identify who is authorized to issue each pronouncement.
b. List the number of the foregoing statements and indicate the pronouncement to which it pertains.

20–22.   A number of steps are involved in the registration process under the 1933 Securities Act. Ten of these steps are listed below in random order:

1. Data for registration are collected by company accountants, reviewed by lawyers, and reviewed and audited by independent accountants.

2. Management and legal counsel select appropriate registration form.
3. Management prepares amendments which are responsive to SEC's comments. These are filed with SEC by legal counsel.
4. Management prepares draft of registration statement and obtains board of directors approval.
5. Management receives letter of comment from SEC concerning deficiencies and necessary adjustments.
6. SEC notifies management by phone of acceptance of registration statement.
7. Due diligence meeting is held to review registration statement and other matters affecting sale of issue.
8. Management finalizes registration statement, which is filed with SEC by legal counsel.
9. Legal counsel files amendment to registration statement for offering price. Registration statement becomes effective 5:00 P.M.
10. Management, independent accountant, and legal counsel have prefiling conference with SEC staff in Washington, D.C.

Required
Arrange the steps in proper sequence.

20–23. Ensign Corporation is a manufacturing firm with ten domestic plants. Increased demand for the company's products and a near full capacity production have caused management to decide to build a new plant. The plant expansion is to be financed by a public issue of $10,000,000 of long-term bonds. Before the issue can be sold to the public, a registration statement will have to be filed with the Securities and Exchange Commission using a Form S-1. Ensign Corporation's financial statements have been certified by the corporation's independent accountants for many years.

Required
a. Several parties are involved in the preparation, filing, and approval of the registration statement. Briefly indicate the responsibility of (1) Ensign Corporation management, (2) Ensign's independent accountants, and (3) the Securities and Exchange Commission in this procedure.
b. Indicate the general types of financial information and statistical data that would be disclosed in the schedules and reports included in the registration statement and the time period(s) to which this information and data must refer.

CMA

20–24. Below are events pertaining to a public client subject to SEC jurisdiction:

1. There is a change in independent auditors that is not related to a disagreement over accounting principles.
2. There is a change in an accounting principle which the auditor believes is preferable.
3. Interim financial information is filed following review by the independent accountant.
4. A comfort letter is issued by the accountant to an underwriter.
5. Selected financial data for five years is filed.
6. There was a major acquisition during the year.
7. Unaudited financial statements for a "stub" period are included.

Required
a. Indicate the SEC reporting form(s), if any, on which each of the foregoing would appear.
b. Explain the auditor's specific responsibilities under 1 to 3 above.

20–25. The Jerford Company is a well-known manufacturing company with several wholly owned subsidiaries. The company's stock is traded on the New York Stock Exchange, and the company files all appropriate reports with the Securities and Exchange Commission. Jerford Company's financial statements are audited by a public accounting firm.

Part I: Jerford Company's Annual Report to Stockholders for the year ended December 31, 19*X*1, contained the following phrase in boldface type: The company's 10-K is available on written request.

Required
a. What is Form 10-K, who requires that the form be completed, and why is the phrase "The company's 10-K is available on written request" shown in the annual report?
b. What information not normally included in the company's annual report could be ascertained from the 10-K?
c. Indicate three items of financial information that are often included in annual reports that are not required for the 10-K.

Part II: Jerford Company changed independent auditors during 19*X*1. Consequently, the financial statements were certified by a different public accounting firm in 19*X*1 than in 19*X*0.

Required
What information is Jerford Company responsible for filing with the SEC with respect to this change in auditors? Explain your answer completely.

CMA

20–26. The most common annual report required by the SEC is Form 10-K. Form 10, another SEC report, is often used to register under the Securities Exchange Act of 1934. Both Form 10-K and Form 10 call for "Selected Financial Data." Form S-1, used in the registration of securities for public sale under the Securities Act of 1933, also requires this information. Thus, this summary is an important disclosure requirement in meeting annual reporting and initial filing requirements with the SEC.

Required
a. Identify the basic information that must be disclosed in the "Selected Financial Data," including the period covered and any explanatory notes needed.
b. Is the "Selected Financial Data" required to be audited?

CMA adapted

20–27. The Securities and Exchange Commission (SEC) has encouraged managements of public companies to disclose more information in the shareholders' annual report. As a consequence, a significant amount of the information required in the SEC's Form 10-K now appears in published annual reports.

At the same time, the SEC has attempted to make the annual financial reporting process simpler and more efficient. During 1980 the SEC approved a new integrated disclosure system.

Required
a. Identify the major classes of information that must be included in both the annual report to shareholders and Form 10-K filed with the SEC.
b. The integrated disclosure system is intended to simplify the annual reporting process with the SEC by expanding the ability to incorporate by reference.
   1. Define what is meant by *incorporating by reference* and identify the documents that are involved when incorporating by reference.
   2. Explain how the integrated disclosure system should reduce managements' efforts in filing annual reports with the SEC.

3. Explain the SEC's principal reasons for making the changes in the annual reporting process.
4. Identify and explain potential problems the integrated disclosure system could have on the annual reporting process from the aspect of users of financial information.

CMA

Content Specification Outline for the Auditing Section of the Uniform Certified Public Accountant Examination (Effective November 1983) *

T he Auditing section tests the candidate's knowledge of generally accepted auditing standards and auditing procedures. The scope of the Auditing section includes professional responsibilities, internal control, audit evidence and procedures, and reporting.

In preparing for this section, candidates should study publications such as:

- AICPA Code of Professional Ethics
- Statements on Auditing Standards
- Statements on Standards for Accounting and Review Services
- Statements on Quality Control Standards
- Statements on Management Advisory Services
- Statements on Responsibilities in Tax Practice
- AICPA Audit Guides
- Auditing textbooks
- Leading accounting journals

Auditing—Content Specification Outline

    I.   Professional Responsibilities (15%)
        A. General Standards and Rules of Conduct
            1. Proficiency
            2. Independence
            3. Due Care
            4. Rules of Conduct

* Board of Examiners, *Content Specification Outlines for the Uniform Certified Public Accountant Examination,* (New York: American Institute of Certified Public Accountants, 1981), p. 22-23 (Effective November 1983).

B. Control of the Audit
1. Planning and Supervision
2. Quality Control
C. Other Responsibilities
1. Detection of Errors or Irregularities
2. Illegal Acts by Clients
3. Responsibilities in Management Advisory Services
4. Responsibilities in Tax Practice
5. Continuing Professional Education and Familiarity with Topics of Current Concern to the Profession

II. Internal Control (30%)
A. Definitions and Basic Concepts
1. Purpose of Auditor's Study and Evaluation
2. Definitions and Basic Concepts
B. Study and Evaluation of the System
1. Review of the System
2. Tests of Compliance
3. Evaluation of Weaknesses
C. Cycles
1. Sales, Receivables, and Cash Receipts
2. Purchases, Payables, and Cash Disbursements
3. Inventories and Production
4. Personnel and Payroll
5. Property, Plant, and Equipment
D. Other Considerations
1. Required Communication of Material Weaknesses
2. Reports on Internal Control
3. Sampling
4. Effects of EDP
5. Flowcharting
6. Effects of an Internal Audit Function

III. Audit Evidence and Procedures (30%)
A. Audit Evidence
1. Nature, Competence, and Sufficiency of Evidential Matter
2. Analytical Review Procedures
3. Evidential Matter for Receivables and Inventory
4. Evidential Matter for Long-term Investments
5. Client Representations
6. Using the Work of a Specialist
7. Inquiry of a Client's Lawyer
8. Related Party Transactions
B. Specific Audit Objectives and Procedures
1. Tests of Details of Transactions and Balances
2. Documentation
C. Other Specific Topics
1. Use of the Computer in Performing the Audit
2. Use of Statistical Sampling in Performing the Audit
3. Subsequent Events
4. Operational Auditing

    IV. Reporting (25%)
        A. Reporting Standards and Types of Reports
            1. Scope of Examination
            2. Generally Accepted Accounting Principles
            3. Consistency
            4. Disclosure
            5. Reporting Responsibilities
            6. Unqualified
            7. Qualified
            8. Adverse
            9. Comparative
            10. Disclaimer
            11. Compilation and Review
            12. Review of Interim Financial Information
            13. Special Reports
            14. Negative Assurance

        B. Other Reporting Considerations
            1. Subsequent Discovery of Facts Existing at the Date of the Auditor's Report
            2. Dating of the Auditor's Report
            3. Part of Examination Made by Other Independent Auditors
            4. Letters for Underwriters
            5. Filing Under Federal Securities Statutes
            6. Segment Information
            7. Other Information in Documents Containing Audited Financial Statements
            8. Supplementary Information Required by the FASB
            9. Information Accompanying the Basic Financial Statements

Index